AMBROSIASTER'S COMMENTARY ON THE PAULINE EPISTLES: ROMANS

WRITINGS FROM THE GRECO-ROMAN WORLD

General Editors
John T. Fitzgerald

Editorial Board
Christopher A. Baron
Andrew Cain
Margaret M. Mitchell
Teresa Morgan
Ilaria L. E. Ramelli
Clare K. Rothschild
Karin Schlapbach
James C. VanderKam
L. Michael White

Number 41
Volume Editor
Andrew Cain

AMBROSIASTER'S COMMENTARY ON THE PAULINE EPISTLES: ROMANS

Translated with Notes by Theodore S. de Bruyn,
with an Introduction by Theodore S. de Bruyn,
Stephen A. Cooper, and David G. Hunter

Atlanta

Copyright © 2017 by SBL Press

All rights reserved. No part of this work may be reproduced or transmitted in any form or by any means, electronic or mechanical, including photocopying and recording, or by means of any information storage or retrieval system, except as may be expressly permitted by the 1976 Copyright Act or in writing from the publisher. Requests for permission should be addressed in writing to the Rights and Permissions Office, SBL Press, 825 Houston Mill Road, Atlanta, GA 30329 USA.

Cataloging-in-Publication Data is on file with the Library of Congress

Printed on acid-free paper.

Contents

Acknowledgments vii
Abbreviations ix

Part 1: Introduction

1. The Author, Date, and Provenance (*David G. Hunter*) xxiii
2. The Transmission and Editions of the Commentary
   (*Theodore S. de Bruyn*) xxxi
3. Ambrosiaster's Biblical Text (*Theodore S. de Bruyn*) lvii
4. Ambrosiaster's Exegesis of the Pauline Epistles
   (*Stephen A. Cooper*) lxi
5. Ambrosiaster's Theology (*Stephen A. Cooper*) lxxvii
6. Polemical Aspects of the Commentary (*Theodore S. de Bruyn,
   Stephen A. Cooper, and David G. Hunter*) xcvii
7. Ambrosiaster and Christian Life at Rome (*David G. Hunter*) cxv
8. A Note on the Translation cxxix

Part 2: Ambrosiaster's Commentary on Romans
Theodore S. de Bruyn

Synopsis 3
Romans 1 7
Romans 2 37
Romans 3 55
Romans 4 75
Romans 5 89
Romans 6 111
Romans 7 123
Romans 8 143
Romans 9 171

Romans 10 193
Romans 11 203
Romans 12 219
Romans 13 233
Romans 14 241
Romans 15 253
Romans 16 265

Bibliography 275
Index of Biblical Citations 295
Index of Ancient Works 304
Index of Manuscripts 313
Index of Modern Authors 315
Index of Subjects 316

Acknowledgments

We are grateful to John T. Fitzgerald, general editor of the series Writings from the Greco-Roman World, not only for engaging us to prepare a translation of Ambrosiaster's Commentary on the Pauline Epistles some time back but also for seeing this volume into print now. We also thank Ronald Hock, general editor of the series when the manuscript was submitted, for moving this volume closer to publication. We are especially grateful to Andrew Cain for agreeing to be the general editor of this volume and for his meticulous review of the manuscript. Daniel Persigehl assisted in the preparation of the bibliography. We are each indebted to our institutions for support over the many years of this project. Theodore S. de Bruyn wishes to thank the Faculty of Arts of the University of Ottawa for a half-year academic leave in 2008 and a yearlong academic leave in 2013–2104, portions of which were spent on the translation and the introductory essays. Stephen A. Cooper expresses his gratitude to Franklin and Marshall College for sabbatical leaves during the academic years 2007–2008 and 2014–2015, portions of which were spent on the translation and the introductory essays. David G. Hunter wishes to acknowledge the American Academy of Religion for a Collaborative Research Grant (2003) and the National Endowment for the Humanities for a Summer Stipend (2003) that facilitated some of the initial work on this project.

Theodore de Bruyn
Stephen Cooper
David Hunter

Abbreviations

Ambrosiaster's Works

In 1 Cor.	Commentarius in Epistulam ad Corinthios primam
In 1 Thess.	Commentarius in Epistulam ad Thessalonicenses primam
In 1 Tim.	Commentarius in Epistulam ad Timotheum primam
In 2 Cor.	Commentarius in Epistulam ad Corinthios secundam
In 2 Thess.	Commentarius in Epistulam ad Thessalonicenses secundam
In 2 Tim.	Commentarius in Epistulam ad Timotheum secundam
In Col.	Commentarius in Epistulam ad Colossenses
In Eph.	Commentarius in Epistulam ad Ephesios
In Gal.	Commentarius in Epistulam ad Galatas
In Phil.	Commentarius in Epistulam ad Philippenses
In Philem.	Commentarius in Epistulam ad Philemonem
In Rom.	Commentarius in Epistulam ad Romanos
In Titus	Commentarius in Epistulam ad Titum
Quaest.	*Quaestiones veteris et novi testamenti*

Additional Ancient Sources

Ab. urbe cond.	Livy, *Ab urbe condita*
Acts Pet.	Acts of Peter
An.	Tertullian, *De anima*
Ap. John	Apocyrphon of John
Ar.	Marius Victorinus, *Adversus Arium*
Bar	Baruch

Basil. reg.	Rufinus, *Regula Basilii*
C. du. ep. Pelag.	Augustine, *Contra duas epistulas Pelagianorum ad Bonifatium*
Cat.	Cicero, *In Catalinam*
Cod. Justin.	Codex justinianus
Comm. Os.	Jerome, *Commentariorum in Osee libri III*
Comm. Rom.	Origen-Rufinus, *Commentarii in Romanos*
Comm. Tit.	Jerome, *Commentariorum in Epistulam ad Titum liber*
Conf.	Augustine, *Confessionum libri XIII*
Did. Spir.	Jerome, *Liber Didymi de Spiritu Sancto*
Div. quaest. Simpl.	Augustine, *De diversis quaestionibus ad Simplicianum*
Enarrat. Ps.	Ambrose, *Enarrationes in XII Psalmos Davidicos*; Augustine, *Enarrationes in Psalmos*
Ep.	Augustine, *Epistulae*; Cyprian, *Epistulae*; Innocent I, *Epistulae*; Jerome, *Epistulae*; Leo I, *Epistulae*; Siricius, *Epistulae*
Exp. Ps. 118	Ambrose, *Expositio Psalmi CXVIII*
Faust.	Augustine, *Contra Faustum Manichaeum*
Gos. Jud.	Gospel of Judas
Haer.	Augustine, *De haeresibus*
Hist.	Tacitus, *Historiae*
Hist. eccl.	Eusebius, *Historia ecclesiastica*; Theodoret, *Historia ecclesiastica*
Idol.	Tertullian, *De idolatria*
In Phil.	Pelagius, Commentarius in Epistulam ad Philippenses
In Rom.	Pelagius, Commentarius in Epistulam ad Romanos
Inv.	Cicero, *De inventione rhetorica*
Inst.	Cassiodorus, *Institutiones divinarum et saecularium litterarum*; Lactantius, *Divinarum institutionem libri VII*; Quintilian, *Institutio oratoria*
Jov.	Jerome, *Adversus Jovinianum libri II*
Marc.	Tertullian, *Adversus Marcionem*
Med.	Celsus, *De medicina*
m. Qidd.	Mishnah Qiddushin
m. Yevam.	Mishnah Yevamot
Off.	Ambrose, *De officiis ministrorum*

Orat. paneg.	Gregory of Nazianzus, *Oratio panegyrica in Origenem*
Pan.	Epiphanius, *Panarion (Adversus haereses)*
Prax.	Tertullian, *Adversus Praxean*
Qu. hebr. Gen.	Jerome, *Quaestionum hebraicum liber in Genesim*
Quaest. hom. Odd.	Porphyry, *Quaestionum homericarum ad Odysseam pertinentium reliquae*
Rec.	Pseudo-Clementines, Recognitions
Res.	Tertullian, *De resurrectione carnis*
Retract.	Augustine, *Retractionum libri II*
Rhet. Her.	Rhetorica ad Herennium
Serm.	Augustine, *Sermones*
Sifre Deut.	Sifre Deuteronomy
Test.	Cyprian, *Ad Quirinium testimonia adversus Judaeos*
Tract. ep. Jo.	Augustine, *In epistulam Johannis ad Parthos tractatus*
Trin.	Hilary of Poitiers, *De Trinitate*; Novatian, *De Trinitate*

Sigla

α	*recensio* α
β	*recensio* β
γ	*recensio* γ
§	section in introduction
⌈ ⌉	indicates passage where text is attested only by "mixed" manuscripts
f.	folio
MS(S)	manuscript(s)

Manuscripts

Amiens 87	Manuscript Amiens 87. Amiens, France, Bibliothèque municipale
Ashburnham 60	Manuscript Ashburnham 60. Florence, Italy, Biblioteca Medicea Laurenziana
Augiensis 108	Manuscript Augiensis CVIII. Karlsruhe, Germany, Badische Landesbibliothek

Brussels 971	Manuscript Brussels 971. Brussels, Belgium, Bibliothèque royale de Belgique
Brussels 972	Manuscript Brussels 972. Brussels, Belgium, Bibliothèque royale de Belgique
Budapest 1	Codex latinus medii aevi 1. Budapest, Hungary, Magyar Nemzeti Múzeum
Clm 6265	Manuscript Clm 6265. Munich, Germany, Bayerische Staats Bibliothek
Cologne 34	Manuscript Cologne 34. Cologne, Germany, Erzbischöfliche Diözesan- und Dombibliothek
Cologne 39	Manuscript Cologne 39. Cologne, Germany, Erzbischöfliche Diözesan- und Dombibliothek
Dublin 52	Manuscript Dublin 52. Dublin, Ireland, Trinity College
Fulda Aa 18	Manuscript Fulda Aa 18. Fulda, Germany, Hessische Landesbibliothek Fulda
Göttweig 42	Manuscript Göttweig 42. Göttweig, Austria, Stiftsbibliothek
Graz 369	Manuscript Graz 369. Graz, Austria, Universitätsbibliothek
Guelf. 64 Weiss	Manuscript Guelferbytano 64 Weiss. Wolfenbüttel, Germany, Herzog-August-Bibliothek
Laon 107	Manuscript Laon 107. Laon, France, Bibliothèque municipale
Laud. Misc. 106	Manuscript Miscellaneos Laudianos complectens 106. Oxford, England, Bodleian Library
Lyell 9	Manuscript Lyell 9. Oxford, England, Bodleian Library
Monte Cassino 150	Manuscript Monte Cassino 150. Monte Cassino, Italy, Biblioteca del Monumento Nazionale di Monte Cassino
Monza C 2	Manuscript Monza C 2. Monza, Italy, Biblioteca Capitolare della Basilica di San Giovanni Battista
Oxford 157	Manuscript Oxford 157. Oxford, England, Balliol College
Oxford 756	Manuscript Oxford 756. Oxford, England, Bodleian Library
Padua 94	Manuscript Padua 94. Padua, Italy, Biblioteca Antoniana

Paris lat. 1759	Manuscript Paris lat. 1759. Paris, France, Bibliothèque nationale de France
Paris lat. 1761	Manuscript Paris lat. 1761. Paris, France, Bibliothèque nationale de France
Paris lat. 1763	Manuscript Paris lat. 1763. Paris, France, Bibliothèque nationale de France
Paris lat. 13339	Manuscript Paris lat. 13339. Paris, France, Bibliothèque nationale de France
Salzburg a IX 25	Manuscript Salzburg a IX 25. Salzburg, Austria, Benediktiner-Erzabtei Sankt Peter
St. Gall 100	Manuscript St. Gall 100. Saint-Gall, Switzerland, Stiftsbibliothek
St. Gall 101	Manuscript St. Gall 101. Saint-Gall, Switzerland, Stiftsbibliothek
St. Gall 330	Manuscript St. Gall 330. Saint-Gall, Switzerland, Stiftsbibliothek
St. Mihiel 16	Manuscript St. Mihiel 16. Saint-Mihiel, France, Bibliothèque municipale
Trier 122	Manuscript Trier 122. Trier, Germany, Stadtbibliothek
Troyes 128	Manuscript Troyes 128. Troyes, France, Bibliothèque municipale
Troyes 432	Manuscript Troyes 432. Troyes, France, Bibliothèque municipale
Vat. lat. 4919	Manuscript Vatican lat. 4919. Vatican, Biblioteca Apostolica Vaticana
Verona 75	Manuscript Verona 75. Verona, Italy, Biblioteca Capitolare
Vienna 743	Manuscript Vienna 743. Vienna, Austria, Österreichische Nationalbibliothek
Vienna 4600	Manuscript Vienna 4600. Vienna, Austria, Österreichische Nationalbibliothek
Zwettl 33	Manuscript Zwettl 33. Zwettl, Austria, Bibliothek des Zisterzienserstifts

Modern Journals and Series

AARRT	American Academy of Religion Religion in Translation Series

AB	Anchor Bible
AChrT	Ancient Christian Texts
AGLB	*Aus der Geschichte der lateinischen Bibel* (= *Vetus Latina: Die Reste der altlateinischen Bibel: Aus der Geschichte der lateinischen Bibel*). Freiburg: Herder, 1957–
AJSUFS	Arbeiten aus dem Juristischen Seminar der Universität Freiburg (Switzerland)
AmJT	*American Journal of Theology*
AnCl	*Antiquité classique*
AnNic	Analecta Nicolaiana
ANRW	Temporini, Hildegard, and Wolfgang Haase, eds. *Aufstieg und Niedergang der römischen Welt: Geschichte und Kultur Roms im Spiegel der neueren Forschung*. Part 2, *Principat*. Berlin: de Gruyter, 1972–
APB	*Acta Patristica et Byzantina*
ASEs	*Annali di storia dell'esegesi*
Aug	*Augustinianum*
AugStud	*Augustinian Studies*
AUS	American University Studies
BAug	Bibliothèque augustinienne
BAC	Bible in Ancient Christianity
BBB	Bonner biblische Beiträge
BETL	Bibliotheca Ephemeridum Theologicarum Lovaniensium
BGBE	Beiträge zur Geschichte der biblischen Exegese
BJHS	*British Journal for the History of Science*
BLE	*Bulletin de littérature ecclésiastique*
BNP A	Cancik, Hubert. *Brill's New Pauly: Encyclopaedia of the Ancient World. Antiquity*. 15 vols. Leiden: Brill, 2002–2010.
BPat	Biblioteca patristica
BZNW	Beihefte zur Zeitschrift für die neutestamentliche Wissenschaft
CBET	Contributions to Biblical Exegesis and Theology
CBiPa	Cahiers de Biblia Patristica
CCAM	Clavis Commentariorum Antiquitatis et Medii Aevi
CClCr	*Civiltà classica e cristiana*

CCSL	Corpus Christianorum: Series Latina. Turnhout: Brepols, 1953–
CCT	Corpus Christianorum in Translation
ClM	Clio Medica
ClR	Classical Review
CNS	Cristianesimo nella storia
CRINT	Compendia Rerum Iudaicarum ad Novum Testamentum
CSEL	Corpus Scriptorum Ecclesiasticorum Latinorum
CSLMA	Clavis Scriptorum Latinorum Medii Aevi
CSPC	Cambridge Studies in Palaeography and Codicology
CTePa	Collana di testi patristici
CTSt	Collana di testi storici
DA	Deutsches Archiv für Erforschung des Mittelalters
DBSup	Pirot, Lous, and André Robert, eds. *Dictionnaire de la Bible: Supplément*. Paris: Letouzey & Ané, 1928–
DNP	Cancik, Hubert, and Helmuth Schneider, eds. *Der neue Pauly: Enzyklopädie der Antike*. Stuttgart: Metzler, 1996–
ECC	Eerdmans Critical Commentary
EDST	Excerpta e Dissertationibus in Sacra Theologia
EE	Estudios Eclesiásticos
EHS	Europäische Hochschulschriften
EO	Ecclesia orans
EPRO	Etudes préliminaires aux religions orientales dans l'empire romain
ErasSt	Erasmus Studies
ET	English translation
ETJ	Eastern Theological Journal
ExpTim	Expository Times
FC	Fathers of the Church
FG	Filologia Germanica
FGJ	Forschungen zur Geschichte der Juden
FZPhTh	Freiburger Zeitschrift für Philosophie und Theologie
GCS	Die griechischen christlichen Schriftsteller der ersten [drei] Jahrhunderte
GIF	Giornale Italiano di Filologia
Greg	Gregorianum

HCS	Hellenistic Culture and Society
HeyJ	*Heythrop Journal*
HOB	Handschriftenverzeichnisse Österreichischer Bibliotheken
HOSt	Handbook of Oriental Studies
HTh	*Ho Theològos*
HTR	*Harvard Theological Review*
IDS	*In die Skriflig*
IJOT	*International Journal of Orthodox Theology*
IPM	Instrumenta Patristica et Mediaevalia
JAC	*Jahrbuch für Antike und Christentum*
JAC.E	*Jahrbuch für Antike und Christentum*—Ergänzungsband
JBL	*Journal of Biblical Literature*
JECS	*Journal of Early Christian Studies*
JEH	*Journal of Ecclesiastical History*
JR	*Journal of Religion*
JSJ	*Journal for the Study of Judaism in the Persian, Hellenistic, and Roman Periods*
JTS	*Journal of Theological Studies*
Laur	*Laurentianum*
LCC	Library of Christian Classics
LCL	Loeb Classical Library
LNTS	The Library of New Testament Studies
LWQF	Liturgiewissenschaftliche Quellen und Forschungen
LXX	Septuagint
MH	*Museum Helveticum*
MilS	*Milltown Studies*
NA^{28}	Aland, Barbara, Kurt Aland, et al., eds. *Novum Testamentum Graece*. 28th ed. 2nd corr. printing. Stuttgart: Deutsche Bibelgesellschaft, 2013
NAWG	*Nachrichten (von) der Akademie der Wissenschaften in Göttingen*
NHMS	Nag Hammadi and Manichaean Studies
NovTSup	Supplements to Novum Testamentum
NRTh	*La nouvelle revue théologique*
NTAbh	Neutestamentliche Abhandlungen
NTL	New Testament Library
NTS	*New Testament Studies*

Abbreviations xvii

OECS	Oxford Early Christian Studies
PAB	Potsdamer Altertumswissenschaftliche Beiträge
PG	Patrologia Graeca [= Patrologiae Cursus Completus: Series Graeca]. Edited by Jacques-Paul Migne. 162 vols. Paris, 1857–1886
PhA	Philosophia Antiqua
PL	Patrologia Latina [= Patrologiae Cursus Completus: Series Latina]. Edited by Jacques-Paul Migne. 217 vols. Paris, 1844–1864
PLS	Patrologia Latina supplementum [= Patrologiae Cursus Completes: Series Latina. *Supplementum*]. Edited by Adalbert Hamman. 5 vols. in 6. Paris: Garnier, 1958–1974
PPSD	Pauline and Patristic Scholars in Debate
PPSer	Popular Patristics Series
ProOr	Pro Oriente
PW	*Paulys Real-Encyclopädie der classischen Altertumswissenschaft*. New edition by Georg Wissowa and Wilhelm Kroll. 50 vols. in 84 parts. Stuttgart: Metzler and Druckenmüller, 1894–1980
RAC	Klauser, Theodor, et al. *Reallexikon für Antike und Christentum*. Stuttgart: Hiersemann, 1950–
RBén	*Revue bénédictine*
RBPH	*Revue belge de philologie et d'histoire*
RCT	*Revista catalana de teologia*
REAug	*Revue des études augustiniennes*
RechAug	*Recherches Augustiniennes*
Rec.LLTC	Recentiores: Later Latin Texts and Contexts
RGRW	Religions in the Graeco-Roman World
RHLR	*Revue d'histoire et de littérature religieuses*
RHR	*Revue de l'histoire des religions*
RicRel	*Ricerche religiose*
RicSRel	*Ricerche di storia religiosa*
RQ	*Römische Quartalschrift für christliche Altertumskunde und Kirchengeschichte*
RSPT	*Revue des sciences philosophiques et théologiques*
RSR	*Recherches de science religieuse*
RSV	Revised Standard Version
RTAM	*Recherches de théologie ancienne et médiévale*

RThom	*Revue thomiste*
RTSFR	*Rivista trimestrale di studi filosofici e religiosi*
SacEr	*Sacris erudiri: Jaarboek voor Godsdienstwetenschappen*
SAChr	*Studia Antiquitatis Christianae*
SBS	Stuttgarter Bibelstudien
SC	Sources chrétiennes
S&C	*Scrittura e Civiltà*
Schol	*Scholastik*
SEAug	Studia Ephemeridis Augustinianum
SFAM	Studi di filologia antica e moderna
SGLG	Studia Graeca et Latina Gothoburgensia
SO	*Symbolae Osloenses*
SPAA	Spicilegium Pontificii Athenaei Antoniani
SPAW.PH	*Sitzungsberichte der Preußischen Akademie der Wissenschaften: Philosophisch-Historische Klasse*
SSRel	*Studi storico-religiosi*
ST	*Studia Theologica*
STAC	Studien und Texte zu Antike und Christentum
StMed	*Studi Medievali*
StOr	Studia Orientalia
StPatr	Studia Patristica
STPIMS	Studies and Texts, Pontifical Institute of Medieval Studies
StT	Studi e Testi, Biblioteca apostolica vaticana
TK	Texte und Kommentare
TRE	Krause, Gerhard, and Gerhard Müller, eds. *Theologische Realenzyklopädie*. Berlin: de Gruyter, 1977–
TS	Texts and Studies
TS	*Theological Studies*
TTH	Translated Texts for Historians
VC	*Vigiliae Christianae*
VCSup	Supplements to Vigiliae Christianae
VetChr	*Vetera Christianorum*
VL	Vetus Latina
VLB	Vetus Latina, Beuron
VoxPat	*Vox Patrum*
WGRW	Writings from the Greco-Roman World
WiWei	*Wissenschaft und Weisheit*

WolfMS	Wolfenbütteler Mittelalter-Studien
WS	*Wörter und Sachen*
WSA	The Works of Saint Augustine
WSt	*Wiener Studien*
WTJ	*Wesleyan Theological Journal*
WUNT	Wissenschaftliche Untersuchungen zum Neuen Testament
ZKG	*Zeitschrift für Kirchengeschichte*
ZKT	*Zeitschrift für katholische Theologie*
ZNW	*Zeitschrift für die neutestamentliche Wissenschaft und die Kunde der älteren Kirche*
ZTK	*Zeitschrift für Theologie und Kirche*
ZWT	*Zeitschift für wissenschaftliche Theologie*

Part 1
Introduction

1. The Author, Date, and Provenance

"Ambrosiaster" is the name coined in the early modern period to refer to the author of the first complete Latin commentary on the Pauline epistles (hereafter, the Commentary).[1] The word is derived from the pejorative suffix *-aster* attached to "Ambrosius," the name of the famous bishop of Milan to whom the Commentary was attributed in most of the manuscript tradition.[2] Some scholars have claimed that Erasmus or the Maurists first coined the term Ambrosiaster, but the recent study of Jan Krans has shown that Erasmus did not use the word and that its use predates the Maurist edition of Ambrose's works, which was published in 1686–1690.[3] According to Krans the name goes back at least to the *Notationes in sacra biblia* of Lucas Brugensis, a collection of text-critical notes on the Vulgate that appeared in 1580.[4]

Several other works have been attributed, with greater or lesser confidence, to Ambrosiaster. In 1905 Alexander Souter definitively demonstrated that the same author was responsible for the *Questions on the Old and New Testaments* (*Quaestiones veteris et novi testamenti*), a collection of questions and answers on biblical topics (as well as treatises on other matters) that circulated in the Middle Ages under the name of Augustine.[5] Like the Commentary, the *Quaestiones* exist in multiple versions or recen-

---

1. The critical edition is Heinrich J. Vogels, ed., *Ambrosiastri qui dicitur commentarius in epistulas paulinas*, CSEL 81.1–3 (Vienna: Hoelder-Pichler-Tempsky, 1966–1969).

2. The commentary on Romans circulated in at least one branch under the name of Hilary of Poitiers. See below §2.

3. Jan Krans, "Who Coined the Name 'Ambrosiaster'?," in *Paul, John, and Apocalyptic Eschatology: Studies in Honour of Martinus C. de Boer*, ed. Jan Krans et al., NovTSup 149 (Leiden: Brill, 2013), 274–81.

4. Ibid., 279–80.

5. Alexander Souter, *A Study of Ambrosiaster*, TS 7.4 (Cambridge: Cambridge University Press, 1905). Souter's work confirmed the earlier work of Josef Langen, "De

sions: one with 151 questions, another with 127.⁶ Fragments of several other works have been attributed to Ambrosiaster: a discussion of the parable of the three measures of flour into which the woman poured the yeast (Matt 13:33; Luke 13:21), a commentary on Matt 24, and a treatment of the arrest of Jesus in Gethsemane and Peter's denial.⁷ It has been suggested that Ambrosiaster was also the compiler of the curious collection of legal materials known as the *Mosaicarum et Romanarum legum collatio*, but this attribution has not received the unanimous support of scholars.⁸

One peculiar feature of the Commentary and the *Quaestiones* is that both works seem to have been issued anonymously in all of the recensions. This apparently deliberate anonymity has naturally led scholars to attempt to discern the true identity of Ambrosiaster. Educated guesses were attempted as early as the seventeenth century and have continued

---

commentariorum in epistulas Paulinas qui Ambrosii et quaestionum biblicarum quae Augustini nomine feruntur scriptore dissertation" (PhD diss., Bonn, 1880).

6. Souter published the critical edition: *Pseudo-Augustini Quaestiones Veteris et Novi Testamenti CXXVII*, CSEL 50 (Vienna: Tempsky; Leipzig: Freytag, 1908). Unfortunately, he did not fully present both versions of the *Quaestiones*. A full critical addition of the *Quaestiones* is presently being prepared by Marie-Pierre Bussières for the CCSL series.

7. These fragments were edited by Giovanni Mercati, "Anonymi chiliastae in Matthaeum c. XXIV fragmenta," in Giovanni Mercati, *Varia Sacra* I, StT 11 (Rome: Tipografia Vaticana, 1903), 3–49. The texts are reprinted in A. Hamman, PLS 1:655–70. The most thorough arguments for the attribution of these fragments to Ambrosiaster can be found in Coelestinus Martini, *Ambrosiaster: De auctore, operibus, theologia*, SPAA 4 (Rome: Pontificium Athenaeum Antonianum, 1944), 50–73. Most recently Emanuele Di Santo has affirmed this attribution: *L'Apologetica dell'Ambrosiaster: Cristiani, pagani et giudi nella Roma tardoantica*, SEAug 112 (Rome: Institutum Patristicum Augustinianum, 2008), 21–22.

8. For positive attribution of *Mosaicarum et Romanarum legum collatio*, see now the edition and translation by Robert M. Frakes, *Compiling the "Collatio Legum Mosaicarum et Romanarum" in Late Antiquity* (Oxford: Oxford University Press, 2011). For debate about this attribution, see Alexander Souter, "Prolegomena," in CSEL 50:xxiii: *fortasse ipse quoque est auctor illius Mosaicarum et Romanarum legum collationis*. Both the *Collatio* and Ambrosiaster refer to a lost rescript of Diocletian against the Manichaeans. Di Santo, *L'Apologetica*, 22, seems doubtful, but see Andrew Jacobs, "'Papinian Commands One Thing, Our Paul Another': Roman Christians and Jewish Law in the *Collatio legum Mosaicarum et Romanarum*," in *Religion and Law in Classical and Christian Rome*, ed. Clifford Ando and Jörg Rüpke, PAB 15 (Stuttgart: Steiner, 2006), 85–99.

to the present day.⁹ Distinguished patristic scholar Dom Germain Morin offered no less than five different suggestions over the course of nearly thirty years.¹⁰ The most recent (and unsuccessful) candidates to have been proposed are Maximus of Turin and Simplicianus of Milan.¹¹ Given the inconclusiveness of all these attempts, it seems best to maintain agnosticism on the question.¹²

Despite our ignorance of Ambrosiaster's real name, it is possible to discern some salient facts about the date and place of his literary activity. It is certain that the anonymous author composed some of his work in Rome during the pontificate of Damasus, that is, between October 366

---

9. E.g., Richard Simon, *Histoire critique des principaux commentateurs du Nouveau Testament, depuis le commencement du Christianisme jusques à nôtre tems: Avec une dissertation critique sur les principaux actes manuscrits qui ont été citez dans les trois parties de cet ouvrage* (Rotterdam: Leers, 1693), 133–34. Simon thought the most probable guess to be the Roman deacon named Hilary, who had been associated with the Luciferian party against which Jerome polemicized in his *Altercatio Luciferiani et orthodoxi seu dialogus contra Luciferiano*. Further discussion of Ambrosiaster's identity can be found in Marie-Pierre Bussières, ed., *Ambrosiaster: Contre les païens (Question sur l'Ancien et le Nouveau Testament 114) et Sur le destin (Question sur l'Ancien et le Nouveau Testament 115)*, SC 512 (Paris: Cerf, 2007), 30–38; also Di Santo, *L'Apologetica*, 21–25.

10. Dom Germain Morin, "L'Ambrosiaster et le Juif converti Isaac, contemporain du pape Damase," *RHLR* 4 (1899): 97–121 (Isaac, a converted Jew); "Hilarius l'Ambrosiaster," *RBén* 20 (1903): 113–31 (Decimius Hilarianus Hilarius); "Qui est l'Ambrosiaster? Solution nouvelle," *RBén* 31 (1914–1919): 1–34 (Evagrius of Antioch); "Una nuova possibilità a proposito dell'Ambrosiastro," *Athenaeum* 6 (1918): 62–71 (Cl. Callistius); "La critique dans une impasse: À propos du cas de l'Ambrosiaster," *RBén* 40 (1928): 251–59 (Nummius Aemilianus Dexter, son of Bishop Pacian of Barcelona).

11. Maximus of Turin: Othmar Heggelbacher, "Beziehungen zwischen Ambrosiaster und Maximus von Turin? Eine Gegenüberstellung," *FZPhTh* 41 (1994): 5–44. The suggestion of Maximus has been subjected to decisive critique by Andreas Merkt, "Wer war der Ambrosiaster? Zum Autor einer Quelle des Augustinus—Fragen auf ein neue Antwort," *WiWei* 59 (1996): 19–33. Simplicianus of Milan: Maciej Bielawski, "Simpliciano e Ambrosiaster: potrebbero essere la stessa persona?," in *Le "Confessioni" di Agostino: Bilancio e prospettive, 402–2002* (Rome: Institutum Patristicum Augustinianum, 2003), 533–39. The suggestion of Simplicianus is highly unlikely; if he were the author of the commentary, Augustine's *Ep.* 37 to him and the *Div. quaest. Simpl.* would surely contain some reference to the work.

12. See Bussières, *Ambrosiaster*, 38: "En effet, si son identité devait rester inconnue de ses contemporains, quelle chance aurions-nous de pouvoir le démasquer plus d'un millénaire de demi plus tard?"

and December 384. In his commentary on 1 Tim 3:15, he refers to the church "whose rector at present is Damasus."[13] In *Quaest.* 115, "On Fate," Ambrosiaster speaks of being "here in the city of Rome and its environs," and in one of the recensions of his comment on Rom 16:3–5 he mentions being "here, that is, in Rome."[14] Ambrosiaster also gave attention to issues specific to the church at Rome. For example, one of the *Quaestiones* is a treatise attacking deacons at Rome who claimed to be the equal of presbyters.[15] There can be little doubt that the bulk of the Commentary and *Quaestiones* was produced at Rome at some point during the reign of Damasus, although it is possible that individual questions were composed and circulated after this date.

But even greater precision can be reached regarding the date of Ambrosiaster's floruit. There are numerous indications that portions of the Commentary and the *Quaestiones*—at least in their later recensions—were composed in the early to mid-380s. In 1956 Heinrich Vogels published an article that demonstrated connections between a letter of Jerome, written in 384, and the commentary on Romans by Ambrosiaster.[16] In *Ep.* 27, addressed to Marcella, Jerome complains of certain "two-legged asses" who are criticizing his revision of the New Testament gospels based on Greek codices. Jerome cites a handful of disputed readings, and Vogels showed that these were taken from Ambrosiaster's commentary on Romans. Moreover, Vogels also demonstrated that one of the later recensions of Ambrosiaster's Romans commentary contains a more elaborate defense of his preference for the Old Latin versions (VL) and an explicit defense of the readings that Jerome had criticized. Vogels concluded that Ambrosiaster had first criticized Jerome in the first edition of his Romans commentary, then Jerome had responded in *Ep.* 27, and then Ambrosiaster had revised and reissued the Romans commentary to respond to Jerome.

---

13. In 1 Tim. 3:15 (CSEL 81.3:270): *ecclesia … cuius hodie rector est Damasus.*

14. *Quaest.* 115.16 (SC 512:168): *Hic enim in urbe Roma et in finibus…*; In Rom. 16:3–5 (CSEL 81.1:479): *Hic, id est Romae* (in the *gamma* recension). On the recensions of the Commentary, which Vogels identified as *alpha* (α), *beta* (β), and *gamma* (γ), see below §2.1. See also below §2.2 n. 89.

15. *Quaest.* 101, "The Boasting of the Roman Deacons" (CSEL 50:193–98). It is worth noting that *Quaest.* 101 is followed by *Quaest.* 102, "Against Novatian." Novatianists were a persistent problem at Rome, even in the fourth century.

16. Heinrich Vogels, "Ambrosiaster und Hieronymus," *RBén* 66 (1956): 14–19.

Vogels's thesis has garnered widespread support from scholars.[17] Although he did not draw out all of the implications for dating, his arguments show that Ambrosiaster was active in Rome during the years of Jerome's sojourn there, that is, between 382 and 385. More recent studies have confirmed this. In her Sources Chrétiennes edition of *Quaest.* 114 and *Quaest.* 115, Marie-Pierre Bussières has dated the composition of these texts to shortly after 386.[18] Likewise, in her monograph on Ambrosiaster's political theology, Sophie Lunn-Rockliffe has suggested a date of circa 384 for *Quaest.* 115 and a date of no later than the mid-380s for the rest of his work.[19] A collection of articles examining Ambrosiaster's revisions of his own writings by Bussières, Theodore S. de Bruyn, Stephen A. Cooper, and David G. Hunter has presented evidence that suggests the influence of the Council of Constantinople I (381) and a Roman synod of 382 on Ambrosiaster's theology of the Holy Spirit.[20] Cooper and Hunter have also argued for further literary encounters between Ambrosiaster and Jerome. The emerging consensus is that the later revisions of the Commentary and the *Quaestiones* date from the mid-380s. The earlier versions would have been written in the early 380s, or perhaps sometime in the later 370s.

In addition to these chronological indications, there is internal evidence in the *Quaestiones* and the Commentary that contributes to a biographical sketch of our author. It seems virtually certain, for example, that he was a member of the Roman clergy. Although Souter thought that Ambrosiaster was a layman, he admitted that his arguments were not

---

17. E.g., Henry Chadwick, *The Church in Ancient Society: From Galilee to Gregory the Great*, Oxford History of the Early Church (Oxford: Oxford University Press, 2001), 380; and Andrew Cain, "In Ambrosiaster's Shadow: A Critical Re-evaluation of the Last Surviving Letter Exchange between Pope Damasus and Jerome," *REAug* 51 (2005): 257–77, esp. 268–72.

18. Bussières, *Ambrosiaster*, 40–41.

19. Sophie Lunn-Rockliffe, *Ambrosiaster's Political Theology*, OECS (Oxford: Oxford University Press, 2007), 12–17. As Lunn-Rockliffe, 15, observes, the existence of multiple versions of both the *Quaestiones* and the Commentary complicates the question of dating. We cannot be sure how much time elapsed between the recensions, and some *quaestiones* may have circulated independently.

20. "L'Ambrosiaster révise l'Ambrosiaster/Ambrosiaster Revising Ambrosiaster," *REAug* 56 (2010): 21–91. The importance of the councils of 381 and 382 for the development of Ambrosiaster's pneumatology had already been noted in regards to the *Quaestiones* by Marie-Pierre Bussières, "L'influence du synode tenu à Rome en 382 sur l'exégèse de l'Ambrosiaster," *SacEr* 45 (2006): 107–24.

conclusive, and most scholars have not followed him.[21] There are many good reasons to think that Ambrosiaster was a presbyter. First, his writings show extensive knowledge of ecclesiastical customs, especially those pertaining to church office.[22] For example, he had a special interest in the origins of the office of bishop and provides a historically nuanced account of the distinction between presbyters and bishops.[23] In several places Ambrosiaster refers to liturgical practices such as the singing of hymns, fasting, and the bestowal of nuptial blessings at marriages of Christians.[24] His writings offer early evidence for the requirement of permanent sexual continence for the higher clergy, a practice he defended enthusiastically.[25] As noted above, his *Quaest*. 101, "The Boasting of the Roman Deacons," contains a vigorous defense of the authority of presbyters, their (nearly equal) status with bishops, and their superior status over deacons. It is difficult to imagine anyone but a Roman presbyter investing himself so deeply in these issues.

Perhaps the most compelling argument for Ambrosiaster's status as presbyter is that several of his *quaestiones* appear to be sermons directed to an audience of "beloved brethren," and in one he even refers to the speaker (almost certainly himself) as a *sacerdos* ("priest").[26] Lunn-Rockliffe has proposed that Ambrosiaster may have been a presbyter attached to one of

---

21. Alfred Stuiber, "Ambrosiaster," *TRE* 2:357, says that Ambrosiaster's clerical status cannot be determined for certain. Peter Brown refers to him without discussion as an "anonymous Roman priest": *The Body and Society: Men, Women, and Sexual Renunciation in Early Christianity* (New York: Columbia University Press, 1988), 377. Lydia Speller suggests that Ambrosiaster was "a presbyter who once hoped to be bishop": "Ambrosiaster and the Jews," StPatr 17 (1982): 75.

22. See the extensive discussion in Lunn-Rockliffe, *Ambrosiaster's Political Theology*, 106–26, and the discussion below in §7.1.

23. See In Eph. 4:11–12 (§§2–5) and the discussion in Maurice Bévenot, "Ambrosiaster's Thoughts on Christian Priesthood," *HeyJ* 18 (1977): 152–64; and David G. Hunter, "The Significance of Ambrosiaster," *JECS* 17 (2009): 1–26.

24. In 1 Cor. 14:14: on Latin Christians singing hymns in Greek; *Quaest*. 120 (CSEL 50:361–63): on fasting; *Quaest*. 127.3 (CSEL 50:400), In 1 Cor. 7:40, and In 1 Tim. 3:12 (§1): on nuptial blessings.

25. *Quaest*. 127.35–36 (CSEL 50.414–16); see In 1 Cor. 7:5 (§§1–2).

26. See the opening words of *Quaest*. 120 (CSEL 50:361): *Congruum est, fratres carissimi, devotissime dei sacerdotem et praepositum plebes Christi exortari populum suum sub cura sua positum in doctrina sana, sicut mandat apostolus*. Lunn-Rockliffe, *Ambrosiaster's Political Theology*, 74–75, provides an extensive list of the sermonic elements in Ambrosiaster's *Quaestiones*.

the great cemetery churches at Rome outside the city walls. These Roman presbyters, unlike those within the city proper, had the right to preside, preach, and consecrate the eucharistic elements.[27] This suggestion is very convincing, and it helps to explain what seems to be Ambrosiaster's status as simultaneously an insider and an outsider to clerical culture at Rome. He was deeply involved in pastoral and liturgical activities, and yet he sometimes cast a critical eye at the behavior of his confrères in church office. Nevertheless, he offers strong arguments for the authority of clerical office and, in particular, for the prerogatives of presbyters. While none of these arguments in itself is conclusive, the cumulative import of the evidence strongly suggests that Ambrosiaster was a Roman presbyter, most likely at one of the suburban churches.

---

27. Lunn-Rockliffe, *Ambrosiaster's Political Theology*, 80–86. Lunn-Rockliffe, 84, acknowledges the contribution of an unpublished paper by Janet Fairweather, which had previously pointed to the Church of St. Paul-outside-the-Walls as a possible location for Ambrosiaster's pastoral activity.

2. The Transmission and Editions of the Commentary

Ambrosiaster's Commentary was well known to later patristic and medieval writers, but it was conveyed to them anonymously or pseudonymously.[1] Pelagius made extensive use of it, without naming its author, when he wrote his own commentary on the Pauline epistles in Rome between 405 and 410.[2] Augustine, as is well known, quotes several sentences from Ambrosiaster's comment on Rom 5:12 in *Against Two Letters of the Pelagians* (4.4.7 [CSEL 60:528]), which he composed in 420–421. Augustine attributes the statements to Hilary, presumably meaning the bishop of Poitiers. Augustine's wording varies slightly from Ambrosiaster's.[3] He appears not to have had a complete manuscript of the commentary before him at the time; it may be that he was citing from a collection of excerpts available in his library.[4] In the sixth century Cassiodorus had heard of but

---

1. Parts of the following discussion will appear in a more condensed form as Theodore S. de Bruyn, "Ambrosiaster: *Commentarius in xiii epistulas Paulinas*," in *Traditio Patrum: The Transmission of the Latin Fathers in the Middle Ages*, ed. Emanuela Colombi et al. (Turnhout: Brepols, forthcoming). I am grateful to Brepols for permission to reproduce the substance of that text.

2. See Alfred J. Smith, "The Latin Sources of the Commentary of Pelagius on the Epistle of St Paul to the Romans," *JTS* 19 (1917–18): 167–230; and Theodore S. de Bruyn, *Pelagius's Commentary on St Paul's Epistle to the Romans*, OECS (Oxford: Oxford University Press, 1993), passim. For the date of Pelagius's commentary, see ibid., 11. Since Pelagius does not name the authors of any of the commentaries he consulted, his silence about attribution does not necessarily imply that the Commentary was already circulating anonymously in Rome at the beginning of the fifth century. But in all likelihood it was, since Ambrosiaster's *Quaestiones* appears also to have circulated without attribution.

3. See A. C. de Veer, "Saint Augustin et l'Ambrosiaster," in *Premières polémiques contre Julien*, ed. F.-J. Thonnard, E. Bleuzen, and A. C. de Veer, BAug 23 (Paris: Desclée de Brouwer, 1974), 817. The wording of Augustine's quotation corresponds to the version of the comment in *recensio* β, not, as de Veer states, *recensio* γ; see n. 57 below.

4. Ibid., 817–24. For differing views about Augustine's possible debt to Ambro-

not seen the Commentary, which he understood to be a copy of the Pauline epistles annotated by Ambrose.[5] His remark indicates that the Commentary was circulating at that time. Several ninth-century writers who used the Commentary also believed it to be by Ambrose: Claudius of Turin, Hatto of Vercelli, Amalarius of Metz, Haymo of Halberstadt, Sedulius Scottus, Hrabanus Maurus, Prudentius of Troyes, and Hincmar of Reims.[6]

In a few early manuscripts the text was conveyed anonymously. MS Monte Cassino 150, a seventh-century manuscript whose text of the Commentary dates from before 570, when a reader added a note at the end of Romans, transmitted the text without attribution; though the initial and final pages of this manuscript are lost, the explicits to the individual commentaries do not name an author.[7] (MS Guelf. 64 Weiss., an eighth-century palimpsest that preserves portions of a sixth-century manuscript of the commentary on Romans,[8] yields no information about attribution.) In Munich, MS Clm 6265, a ninth-century manuscript from the Freising scriptorium, the incipits also do not name an author; an attribution

---

siaster during his intensive study of Paul's Letters in the 390s, see, in addition to de Veer, Bernard Leeming, "Augustine, Ambrosiaster and the *massa perditionis*," *Greg* 11 (1930): 58–91; and A. Bastiaensen, "Augustine's Pauline Exegesis and Ambrosiaster," in *Augustine: Biblical Exegete*, ed. Frederick Van Fleteren and Joseph C. Schnaubelt (New York: Lang, 2001), 33–54.

5. Cassiodorus, *Inst.* 1.8.10 (*Cassiodori Senatoris Institutiones*, ed. Roger A. B. Mynors [Oxford: Clarendon, 1963], 30): *dicitur enim et beatum Ambrosium subnotatum codicem epistularum omnium sancti Pauli reliquisse suavissima expositione completum; quem tamen adhuc invenire non potui, sed diligenti cura perquiro*; ET: *Cassiodorus: "Institutions of Divine and Secular Learning" and "On the Soul,"* trans. James W. Halporn with an introduction by Mark Vessey, TTH 42 (Liverpool : Liverpool University Press, 2004), 129: "It is reported also that blessed Ambrose left an annotated version of all the epistles of St Paul filled with his own satisfying commentary; up to now, however, I have not been able to find this work but I am looking for it assiduously."

6. Heinrich J. Vogels, "Die Überlieferung des Ambrosiasterkommentars zu den paulinischen Briefen," *NAWG* 7 (1959): 108; Heinrich J. Vogels, "Prolegomena," CSEL 81.1:xi.

7. Francis Newton, *The Scriptorium and Library at Monte Cassino, 1058–1105*, CSPC 7 (Cambridge: Cambridge University Press, 1999), 251, 362, and pl. 116; Vogels, "Überlieferung," 108–9, 132; Vogels, "Prolegomena," xi, xxxiv–xxxv.

8. Carla Falluomini, *Der sogenannte Codex Carolinus von Wolfenbüttel (Codex Guelferbytanus 64 Weissenburgensis) mit besonderer Berücksichtigung der gotischlateinischen Blätter (255, 256, 277, 280)*, WolfMS 13 (Wiesbaden: Harrassowitz, 1999), 37–39.

to Ambrose is added in a later hand. The same is true of MS Salzburg a IX 25, a contemporary and rather slavish copy of MS Clm 6265, from the same scriptorium.⁹ Several eighth- and ninth-century manuscripts in the Irish-Latin tradition mention or cite Ambrosiaster's commentary on Romans under the name of Hilary,¹⁰ probably following Augustine. The majority of manuscripts of the Commentary, seventy-two of which were known to Heinrich J. Vogels when he prepared his edition,¹¹ attribute it to Ambrose.

On the strength of the medieval manuscript tradition, the Commentary was included in early printed editions of Ambrose's works.¹² Erasmus did not question the attribution when he published his edition of Ambrose's works in 1527,¹³ a lightly amended version of the *editio princeps* printed by Johann Amerbach in 1492. The Roman edition of Ambrose's works, prepared by Cardinal Felice di Montalto and published between 1580 and 1587, also maintained that the Commentary was by Ambrose. In fact, it substituted a biblical text from Ambrose for the one in manuscripts of the Commentary.¹⁴ The Maurists Denis-Nicolas le Nourry and Jacques du Frische definitively rejected Ambrosian authorship in their 1686–1690 edition of Ambrose's works. They did so for stylistic, doctrinal, and linguistic reasons.¹⁵ Their edition of the Commentary, based on

---

9. Vogels, "Überlieferung," 125, 127–28; Vogels, "Prolegomena," xxvi–xxvii, xxx.

10. Alexander Souter, *A Study of Ambrosiaster*, TS 7.4 (Cambridge: Cambridge University Press, 1905), 162–63; Vogels, "Überlieferung," 108; Vogels, "Prolegomena," x–xi.

11. Vogels, "Überlieferung," 115–18.

12. For details of the editions and reprintings, see Vogels, "Überlieferung," 113; Vogels, "Prolegomena," xviii–xx. On early printed editions of Ambrose's works, see Gérard Nauroy, introduction to *Ambroise de Milan: Jacob et la vie heureuse*, ed. Gérard Nauroy, SC 534 (Paris: Cerf, 2010), 210–14.

13. As Jan Krans, "Who Coined the Name 'Ambrosiaster'?," in *Paul, John, and Apocalyptic Eschatology: Studies in Honour of Martinus C. de Boer*, ed. Jan Krans, Bert Jan Lietaert Peerbolte, Peter-Ben Smit, and Arie Zwiep, NovTSup 149 (Leiden: Brill, 2013), 278–79, has pointed out, Erasmus questioned only the attribution of the synopses that prefaced the individual commentaries.

14. On the failings of the Roman edition, see Heinrich J. Vogels, *Das Corpus Paulinum des Ambrosiaster*, BBB 13 (Bonn: Hanstein, 1957), 16–18; see also Alexander Souter, *The Earliest Latin Commentaries on the Epistles of St. Paul* (Oxford: Clarendon, 1927), 53–54.

15. *Sancti Ambrosii Mediolanensis episcopi opera, ad manuscriptos codices Vaticanos, Gallicanos, Belgicos, &c. necnon ad editiones veteres emendata, studio et labore*

thirteen French manuscripts, was a considerable advance on the Roman edition.[16] The Maurists observed that in previous printed editions the comments from 1 Cor 15:42 to 2 Cor 1:6 were not by Ambrosiaster but by Pseudo-Jerome (i.e., Pelagius), and they did not include a commentary on Hebrews, as had the Roman edition.[17] The Maurists' edition is the basis of the text in Jacques-Paul Migne's Patrologia Latina, whose republication is, however, marred by many errors.[18] A subsequent edition by Paulo Angelo Ballerini, published in Milan from 1875 to 1883, did not improve on the Maurists' edition.[19]

Work on a critical edition of the Commentary for the series Corpus Scriptorum Ecclesiasticorum Latinorum (the CSEL edition) was begun by M. Ihm.[20] Upon his death, H. Brewer took up the project, and when Brewer died in 1922, A. Grimm carried on.[21] Because their work was lost during the Second World War,[22] Vogels, the next editor, began collating the text from the manuscripts afresh. When the papers of Brewer and Grimm were found in the monastery of St. Blasien and conveyed to Vogels in 1957, his collation of the commentary on Romans was almost complete.[23] Nevertheless, he was able to benefit from Brewer's collation of the commentary on Romans and Grimm's collation of the commentaries on Galatians to Philemon.[24] Vogels died before his edition of the entire Commentary was published. It fell to Vincent Bulhart, with the assistance of Leopoldina Swoboda and Michaela Zelzer, to complete the task.[25]

---

monachorum Ordinis S. Benedicti, è Congregatione S. Mauri (Paris: Coignard, 1686–1690), 2: appendix, 21–22. The introduction is reprinted in Ambrose, *Opera omnia*, PL 17:39–42.

16. Vogels, "Überlieferung," 114; Vogels, "Prolegomena," xx.

17. See *Sancti Ambrosii Mediolanensis episcopi opera*, 2: appendix, 23–26. The commentary was in fact by Alcuin; see Marie-Hélène Jullien and Françoise Perelman, eds., *Clavis des auteurs latins du Moyen Âge, Territoire français 735–987, Tomus II: Alcuin*, CSLMA 2 (Turnhout: Brepols, 1999), 375–77.

18. PL 14–17; the Commentary is found in PL 17:45–508. See Vogels, "Überlieferung," 114; Vogels, "Prolegomena," xx.

19. Vogels, "Überlieferung," 114–15; Vogels, "Prolegomena," xx–xxi.

20. Vogels, *Das Corpus*, 16.

21. Ibid.; Heinrich J. Vogels, "Praefatio," CSEL 81.1:vii.

22. Vogels, "Praefatio," vii.

23. Vogels, "Überlieferung," 122; Vogels, "Praefatio," vii.

24. Vogels, "Praefatio," viii.

25. Rudolf Hanslik, "Ad lectorem," CSEL 81.1:1; 81.2:vii; 81.3:vii.

2.1. The Recensions

The CSEL edition is now the standard text of the Commentary, but the complexities it dealt with are formidable. The Maurists had observed major differences among the manuscripts of the Commentary, particularly in the commentaries on Romans and 1 and 2 Corinthians. They took the shortest version of the text to be the original version and attributed the modifications or additions found in longer versions to medieval glossators and copyists.[26] Brewer was the first to argue that the several versions of the Commentary found in the medieval manuscripts in fact go back to the author.[27] His hypothesis was accepted with corrections and refinements by Vogels,[28] who concluded that Ambrosiaster had revised his commentary on Romans twice, the commentaries on 1 and 2 Corinthians at least once and possibly twice, and the remaining commentaries once.

The argument that the several versions of the Commentary all go back to a single author is based on a number of grounds. First, manuscripts of the Commentary fall into several important groups.[29] The shortest version of the Commentary, which Vogels named *recensio α*, is attested by a group of manuscripts that derive from a common archetype:[30] MS Cologne 34 (ninth century), MS Göttweig 42 (ninth–tenth century), MS Clm 6265 (ninth century), MS Salzburg a IX 25 (ninth century), and MS Zwettl 33 (twelfth century).[31] These manuscripts present the commentaries in the sequence Romans, 1 and 2 Corinthians, Philippians, 1 and 2 Thessalonians, Colossians, Titus, 1 and 2 Timothy, and Philemon;[32] they do not have the commentaries on Galatians and Ephesians; and their commentaries on Romans and 2 Corinthians break off at Rom 16:19 and 2 Cor

---

26. *Sancti Ambrosii mediolanensis episcopi opera*, 2: appendix, 21–22.
27. Souter, *Earliest Latin Commentaries*, 49–54.
28. Vogels, "Überlieferung," 119–22.
29. I discuss only the major groupings. For a complete list of the ways in which manuscripts are related, see Vogels, "Überlieferung," 124.
30. Since the CSEL edition sometimes uses the same letter of the alphabet as a siglum for different manuscripts in the list of codices at the beginning of each of the volumes, I do not refer to the sigla here.
31. Vogels, "Überlieferung," 125–26; Vogels, "Prolegomena," xxvi–xxviii.
32. Vogels, "Überlieferung," 124; Vogels, "Prolegomena," xxix incorrectly places In Titus before In Col.; cf., e.g., Günter Glauche, *Katalog der lateinischen Handschriften der Bayerischen Staatsbibliothek München: Clm 6201–6316*, Catalogus codicum manu scriptorum Bibliothecae Monacensis 3, n.s. 2.1 (Wiesbaden: Harrassowitz, 2000), 118.

13:3. Four of the manuscripts form a subgroup whose text is derived one from the other in the following sequence: MS Clm 6265, MS Salzburg a IX 25, MS Göttweig 42, and MS Zwettl 33.[33] (Two additional manuscripts have since been found to belong to this group. One was overlooked by Vogels: MS Graz 369.[34] Its text is closest to MS Göttweig 42, whose corrections it incorporates.[35] The other, a ninth-century witness to the commentaries on Romans and 1 Corinthians, has been identified recently: MS Laud. Misc. 106. The commentary in this manuscript had previously been attributed to Raban Maur.[36]) The text in the ninth-century Munich manuscript (MS Clm 6525) is related by common readings and omissions to the text in the tenth-century Cologne manuscript, although the latter appears to be more influenced by *recensio* β (see below). The version of the commentary on Romans in these two manuscripts corresponds to that in two other early but incomplete ninth-century witnesses: the prologue to Romans in the Book of Armagh (MS Dublin 52, f. 106r, ca. 807) and a fragment of the commentary on Rom 9:17–10:11, MS Verona 75 (ninth century).[37] The archetype of MS Clm 6525, MS Cologne 39, and MS Verona 75 was probably an early ninth-century Italian manuscript, since the version found in it was used by Claudius of Turin, who died in 827.[38] For the commentaries on 1 and 2 Corinthians, Vogels supplemented the witness of MS Clm 6525 and MS Cologne 39 with another manuscript deriving from the same archetype, MS Vat. lat. 4919, an eleventh/twelfth-century manuscript with 1 and 2 Corinthians only, breaking off at 2 Cor

---

33. Vogels, "Überlieferung," 127–28; Vogels, "Prolegomena," xxx.

34. Anton Kern, *Die Handschriften der Universitätsbibliothek Graz*, HOB 2 (Leipzig: Harrassowitz, 1942), 222. Kern provides only the total number of folios and the explicit *nisi in solo Christo* at In Philem. 1:22 (CSEL 81.3:341). The University Library in Graz kindly provided a digital reproduction of the manuscript to the editors of *Traditio Patrum*, allowing for a more precise identification of the contents and the recension.

35. A comparison of readings is possible only for In Rom., since the CSEL edition does not list variants from the Göttweig manuscript in the apparatus for the remaining commentaries.

36. Nicolas De Maeyer and Gert Partoens, "A New Identification of the Pauline Commentary in Manuscript *Oxford Bodleian Library Laud. Misc. 106*," SacEr 53 (2014): 12 n. 27.

37. Vogels, "Überlieferung," 129; Vogels, "Prolegomena," xxviii–xxx.

38. Vogels, "Überlieferung," 129; Vogels, "Prolegomena," xxx.

12:20.³⁹ For the remaining commentaries Vogels relied primarily on MS Ashburnham 60 (eighth century), noting variants in MS Clm 6265 and MS Cologne 34 (which, however, do not have commentaries on Galatians and Ephesians) in the apparatus.⁴⁰

A longer version of the Commentary, which Vogels named *recensio* γ, is attested by a group of manuscripts that also derive from a common archetype: MSS Brussels 971 (eleventh-twelfth century) and 972 (twelfth century); MS Fulda Aa 18 (ninth century); MS Monza C 2 (ninth-tenth century); MS Oxford 756 (eleventh century); MSS Paris lat. 1761 (eighth-ninth century) and 1763 (thirteenth century); MSS St. Gall 100 and 101 (ninth century); MS Troyes 128 (twelfth century); and MS Vienna 4600 (fifteenth century).⁴¹ They present the commentaries in the sequence Romans, 1 and 2 Corinthians, Galatians, Ephesians, Philippians, Titus, Colossians, 1 and 2 Thessalonians, 1 and 2 Timothy, and Philemon; the explicit to the commentary on Romans is followed by text taken from the end of the commentary on 1 Corinthians;⁴² and the comments from 1 Cor 15:44 to 2 Cor 1:5 are taken from Pelagius.⁴³ In addition to these "pure" witnesses to *recensio* γ, Vogels identified several important "mixed" witnesses that, while they attest *recensio* γ, also have readings found in *recensio* β.⁴⁴ One of these is MS Monte Cassino 150, the oldest manuscript of the Commentary. It shares with the manuscripts already listed certain omissions in the biblical text as well as the substitution of the material from Pelagius. It therefore derives from the same archetype as they do. But its text of the Commentary has readings in common with *recensio* β as well as *recensio* γ. Two manuscripts containing only the commentaries on Romans and 1 and 2 Corinthians—MS Amiens 87 (eighth-ninth century) and MS Paris

---

39. Vogels, "Prolegomena," xlv–xlvi. For the date of this manuscript, see now Mariapia Branchi, *Lo scriptorium e la biblioteca di Nonantola* (Nonantola: Edizioni Artestampa, 2011), 247–48.

40. Vogels, "Prolegomena," lii–lvi. See the lists of codices at CSEL 81.3:x, 70, 128, 166, 210, 250, 322, 336.

41. Vogels, "Überlieferung," 130–31; Vogels, "Prolegomena," xxxi–xxxiv.

42. Vogels, "Prolegomena," xxxv–xxxvi; see Ambrosiaster, In 1 Cor. 16:21–24 (CSEL 81.2:193–94).

43. Vogels, "Überlieferung," 124. This anomaly, present already in MS Monte Cassino 150, is found in a large number of manuscripts; see Vogels, "Prolegomena," xlv.

44. Vogels, "Überlieferung," 134–35; Vogels, "Prolegomena," xxxiv–xxxv, xxxviii–xxxxix.

lat. 1759 (eighth–ninth century[45])—also attest readings found in *recensio* β, though they rarely agree with one another in so doing. MS Amiens 87 shares with another manuscript, MS Vienna 743 (eighth century[46]), a biblical text taken from Rufinus of Aquileia's translation of Origen's *Commentary on Romans*. But the text of the commentary in the Vienna manuscript, which has Romans only, is more consistent with *recensio* γ, though it too has readings found in *recensio* β. For *recensio* γ of the commentaries on 1 and 2 Corinthians, Vogels selected several of the older manuscripts he used for the commentary on Romans, with the addition of MS Paris lat. 13339 (eleventh century),[47] a manuscript with only these three commentaries but whose version of the commentary on Romans corresponds to *recensio* β. For *recensio* γ of the remaining commentaries Vogels similarly supplemented a selection of the older above witnesses with the following manuscripts: MS Augiensis 108 (ninth century); MS Monza C 2; MS Lyell 9 (fifteenth century[48]); MS Padua 94 (scaffale V) (ninth century); MS St. Gall 330 (ninth century); and MS Verona 75 (with only Gal 1:23 to Eph 6:20).[49]

Finally, there are manuscripts with a text that falls between *recensio* α and *recensio* γ. This phenomenon is most clearly seen in the commentary on Romans, but is also present in the commentaries on 1 and 2 Corinthians. Vogels named this version *recensio* β. Most manuscripts assigned to *recensio* β have the commentary on Romans alone or in conjunction with commentaries by other authors. Vogels observed that while these manuscripts all agreed in including material found in *recensio* γ, they nevertheless formed three subgroups based on variances with one another. Vogels used the first subgroup to establish *recensio* β of the commentary on Romans: MS Trier 122 (eighth–ninth century), the oldest witness of *recensio* β; MS Cologne 39 (ninth century); MS Augiensis 108; MS Laon 107 (ninth century); MS Lyell 9; and MS St. Mihiel 16 (tenth century).[50] When

---

45. Donatella Nebbiai-Dalla Guarda, *La bibliothèque de l'Abbaye de Saint-Denis en France du IXe au XVIIIe siècle* (Paris: Éditions du Centre national de la recherche scientifique, 1985), 208.

46. Elias A. Lowe, ed., *Codices latini antiquiores* (Oxford: Clarendon, 1934–1971), 10:15 (no. 1488).

47. Vogels, "Prolegomena," xlv–xlvi.

48. Albinia de la Mare, *Catalogue of the Collection of Medieval Manuscripts Bequeathed to the Bodleian Library Oxford by James P. R. Lyell* (Oxford: Clarendon, 1971), 293–95.

49. Vogels, "Prolegomena," lii–liv.

50. Vogels, "Überlieferung," 136–37; Vogels, "Prolegomena," xl–xlii.

Vogels turned to the commentaries on 1 and 2 Corinthians, he observed that several manuscripts—MS Augiensis 108, MS Lyell 9, and MS Troyes 432 (ninth–tenth century)—both agreed with *recensio* α and filled in lacunae in *recensio* α with text from *recensio* γ. He thought it probable that there was a version between *recensio* α and *recensio* γ for these commentaries as well, but at the same time he acknowledged that borrowings between versions in the course of transmission made it difficult to be certain.[51] (MS Amiens 87, which agrees with each of the versions at different points in the commentaries on Romans and 1 and 2 Corinthians, illustrates the problems that a mixed text, albeit an extreme example, can pose.[52]) The CSEL edition presents only *recensio* α and *recensio* γ for 1 and 2 Corinthians but notes the position of the above three manuscripts between these two versions.[53] For the remaining commentaries Vogels did not believe that the variances among the manuscripts attesting *recensio* γ were sufficient to posit an intermediate version.[54]

A second element of the argument for single authorship is the antiquity of all the versions of the Commentary. As already noted, the text of the commentary on Romans in the Monte Cassino manuscript can be dated to a period before 570 because of a reader's note at the end of the commentary. Since this manuscript preserves material assigned to *recensiones* β and γ, these versions were evidently already in circulation by the beginning of the sixth century. MS Guelf. 64 Weiss, the eighth-century palimpsest, corroborates the existence of *recensio* γ at that time.[55] On several pages one can read portions of a sixth-century manuscript of *recensio* γ of the commentary on Romans, erased to make way for later writing.[56] When Augustine quotes part of the comment on Rom 5:12 in *Two Letters against the Pelagians*, his wording is closest to that found in *recensio* β and MS Monte Cassino 150.[57] Thus *recensio* β was already in circulation in the early fifth

---

51. Vogels, "Prolegomena," xlvi.
52. See ibid., xxxvi–xxxviii, xlvii–li.
53. Heinrich J. Vogels, "Conspectus codicum," CSEL 81.2:viii.
54. Vogels, "Prolegomena," liv.
55. See above n. 8.
56. The manuscript does not, however, follow *recensio* β at points where MS Monte Cassino 150 does; see the transcription by S. Gehrke, Digitale Edition der Handschrift Cod. Guelf. 64 Weiss, at http://tinyurl.com/SBL1645a.
57. Augustine, *C. du. ep. Pelag.* 4.4.7 (CSEL 60:528): *in quo, id est Adam, omnes peccaverunt ... manifestum in Adam omnes peccasse quasi in massi*; Ambrosiaster, In Rom. 5:12 (§§2a–3) (CSEL 81.1:164–65), *recensio* β: *in quo—id est in Adam—omnes*

century. To this external evidence one can add internal clues. The reference in the comment on 1 Tim 3:14–15 (§1) to Damasus being the "rector" of the church in Rome—important for dating the commentary[58]—occurs in manuscripts of *recensio* α, as does the reference in the comment on 2 Thess 2:7 to recent persecution under the emperor Julian.[59] Ambrosiaster's response to Jerome's withering remarks in *Ep.* 27 (384)[60] appears in *recensio* β of his comment on Rom 5:14 (§§4e, 5, 5a) and 12:11 (§1b). The additions at Gal 1:19 and 1 Cor 7:33–34 that suggest that Ambrosiaster had read Jerome's *Against Helvidius* (383 or early 384) appear in *recensio* γ.[61] In a comment on 1 Cor 1:13 (§1) in *recensio* γ, Donatists are among those who "create many churches under their own name." This would appear to reflect tensions between Catholics and Donatists in Rome at the end of the 370s, when a Roman synod convened by Damasus petitioned the emperors Gratian and Valentinian to expel the Donatist bishop Claudian.[62] A long comment added in *recensio* γ at 1 Thess 3:9–10 (§2), insisting on the unity of divine substance while distinguishing between the persons of Trinity, was almost certainly occasioned by deliberations about the status of the Holy Spirit in the years immediately before and after the Council of Constantinople in 381.[63]

It is always possible, of course, that these allusions to contemporary events were retained while material was either introduced or altered by scribes who copied the text. Thus, a final aspect of the argument concerning the authorship of the versions turns on the probable sequence and evolution of the versions. For the commentary on Romans, the differences

---

peccaverunt … manifestum itaque est in Adam omnes peccasse quasi in massa; *recensio* γ: *in quo—id est in Adam* [MS Monte Cassino 150: *id est Adam*]*—omnes peccaverunt … manifestum itaque est omnes in Adam* [MS Monte Cassino 150: *in Adam omnes*] *peccasse quasi in massa*.

58. See above §1.

59. See, however, Ambrosiaster's comment on Rom 12:11 (§2), where an allusion to a time of peace is not present in *recensio* α; it is introduced in *recensio* β.

60. See above §1.

61. Stephen A. Cooper and David G. Hunter, "Ambrosiaster *redactor sui*: The Commentaries on the Pauline Epistles (Excluding Romans)," *REAug* 56 (2010): 72–78. On the problems this raises for the dating of *recensio* γ of Romans, see Theodore S. de Bruyn, "Ambrosiaster's Revisions of His *Commentary on Romans* and Roman Synodal Statements about the Holy Spirit," *REAug* 56 (2010): 65–68.

62. Cooper and Hunter, "Ambrosiaster *redactor sui*," 79–84.

63. Ibid., 84–86; de Bruyn, "Ambrosiaster's Revisions," 63–65.

between *recensiones* α and β are greater than those between *recensiones* β and γ. The variances between the *recensiones* α and β are both substantive and stylistic. *Recensio* β has a great deal of additional material that expands on or supports a point made in *recensio* α.[64] Much of the additional material in *recensio* β is also found in *recensio* γ, with occasional stylistic changes in vocabulary, word order, case endings, and verb tenses. Elsewhere the text in *recensio* β agrees with *recensio* α rather than *recensio* γ in wording and length. Vogels therefore concluded that *recensio* β was an expansion of *recensio* α rather than that *recensio* α was a reduction of *recensio* β, and that *recensio* β stood between *recensiones* α and γ, at times preserving the shorter length and word order of comments in *recensio* α, at times adding material that is also found with minor variations in *recensio* γ.[65] All three versions, according to Vogels, originate from the same author. Vogels found similar evidence that changes in *recensio* γ to the commentary on 1 Corinthians were authorial corrections and additions to the text in *recensio* α.[66] Vogels came to the conclusion that Ambrosiaster first composed a commentary on Romans alone (*recensio* α). He then wrote commentaries on the remaining epistles (*recensio* α) and at that time revised the commentary on Romans (*recensio* β) in light of his greater knowledge of the Pauline epistles and of relevant biblical passages. Finally, he revised the entire set of commentaries (*recensio* γ).[67]

2.2. Lingering Questions and Complexities

Although the CSEL edition has met with general acceptance, the attribution of all the material in the three recensions to Ambrosiaster has recently been called into question. In a unpublished paper presented in 1998, Janet Fairweather, who at the time had translated the commentaries on 1 and 2 Corinthians into English and was translating the commentary on Romans, discussed some passages in light of what we know about the workings of medieval scholiasts, who would drop or add portions to the text being summarized.[68] Fairweather had come to the conclusion that it makes better sense to assume that all the manuscripts of the Commentary derive

---

64. Vogels, *Das Corpus*, 27–29.
65. Vogels, "Überlieferung," 122; Vogels, "Prolegomena," xxiii–xxiv.
66. Vogels, "Überlieferung," 139–40; Vogels, "Prolegomena," xlii–xliii.
67. Vogels, *Das Corpus*, 13–14.
68. Janet Fairweather, "Ambrosiaster: A Fourth-Century Commentator on Paul"

from a common archetype and that alterations to this common text in all the manuscripts are the work of later hands—corruptions, abbreviations, interpolations, and the like. An English translation of the Commentary has since been published by Gerald Bray,[69] who made use of Fairweather's unpublished draft translations of the commentaries on 1 and 2 Corinthians. In general Bray preferred the shorter recension of the comments on the assumption that it is the oldest version, while at the same time including later material that rounds out the meaning of the earliest text and omitting material that bears no relation to it or that contradicts it.[70]

In view of this recent discussion we deemed it prudent to examine the relations among the recensions more closely. Theodore S. de Bruyn undertook a close analysis of all the variants in the first five chapters of the commentary on Romans. All three collaborators examined substantive (as distinguished from stylistic) variants as they arose in the course of translation. We have concluded, with Vogels, that the most likely explanation is that the several versions of the Commentary were the work of Ambrosiaster. But we have also noted, with Bray, occasional interpolations.

Our reasons for attributing all the recensions to Ambrosiaster are the following. First, the frequency and nature of the variants in the commentary on Romans are such that it is difficult to suppose that they are mostly the work of later copyists. The revisions to the text are thoroughgoing rather than occasional. They consist in changes in word order, substitutions of vocabulary, grammatical changes (often in the mood or the tense of a verb or the case of a noun), additions to a comment (a word, a phrase, a few sentences, a paragraph), replacement or modification of a comment,

---

(unpublished paper, 1998). I am grateful to Dr. Fairweather for providing me with a copy of her paper.

69. Gerald L. Bray, trans., *Ambrosiaster: Commentaries on Romans and 1–2 Corinthians*, AChrT (Downers Grove, IL: InterVarsity Press, 2009); Gerald L. Bray, trans., *Ambrosiaster: Commentaries on Galatians–Philemon*, AChrT (Downers Grove, IL: InterVarsity Press, 2009).

70. Bray, *Ambrosiaster: Commentaries on Romans and 1–2 Corinthians*, xvii: "For this translation, editorial additions which round out the text and are uncontested by rival alternatives are included without further comment. Where a second possibility exists, it is put in a footnote. As a general rule the shorter version has been preferred for the main text and the longer one has been consigned to a footnote, on the assumption that the shorter text is more likely to be the older one. Interpolations which bear no relation to the rest of the text or which clearly contradict it have been omitted, though it should be said that there are very few of these."

Table 2.1. Frequency of Types of Variants in the Commentary on Romans 1–5

Types of Variants									
word order	vocabulary	grammar	additional word	additional phrase	additional sentence(s)	additional paragraph	modified comment	deletion	γ follows α rather than β
α to β (n= 694; see note)									
70	158	170	147	101	47	20	34	62	—
10.1%	22.8%	24.5%	21.2%	14.6%	6.8%	2.9%	4.9%	8.9%	—
α/β to γ (n = 706; see note)									
173	246	241	83	32	9	2	19	61	55
24.5%	34.8%	34.1%	11.8%	4.5%	1.3%	0.3%	2.7%	8.6%	7.8%

Note: α to β: 694 entries, 593 with one type of variant, 101 with two or more types of variants; α/β to γ: 706 entries, 507 with one type of variant, 199 with two or more types of variants.

and deletions. While one gets a sense of this when reading through the CSEL edition, it is instructive to consider a more precise analysis of the variants. Table 2.1 summarizes the frequency of different types of variants in the first five chapters of the commentary on Romans. The revisions in both *recensiones* β and γ are extensive: 694 instances in moving from *recensio* α to *recensio* β, and 706 instances in moving from *recensio* β to *recensio* γ. A portion of these revisions entail more than one type of variant: 101 instances in moving from *recensio* α to *recensio* β, and 199 instances in moving from *recensio* β to *recensio* γ. While both versions incorporate stylistic changes (word order, vocabulary, grammar) and substantive changes (additions, modifications, and deletions), on balance a greater percentage of the changes in *recensio* β are substantive, whereas a greater percentage of the changes in *recensio* γ are stylistic. Even if one allows for imprecision or error in the coding of the variants (although the data have been checked several times), the prevailing pattern suggests the work of a thoroughgoing reviser rather than an occasional glossator. This is particularly the case with changes in word order and vocabulary or minor grammatical adjustments. The scenario of an author making such changes while dictating a revised version of the text is more plausible than the scenario of a scribe making such changes while copying the text.

Second, from comments where *recensio* γ incorporates yet also modifies material added or altered in *recensio* β, it is clear that *recensio* β stands between *recensiones* α and γ. Examples of this are numerous; the following are instances in the first chapter on Romans: 1:1 (§3); 1:3 (§2); 1:4 (§3);

1:5 (§2); 1:8 (§4); 1:9–10 (§1); 1:9–10 (§7); 1:11 (§3); 1:13 (§2); 1:13 (§4); 1:14 (§1) (but with *natura* from α); 1:16 (§2) (but with *evangelio* from α); 1:16 (§4); 1:17 (§1); 1:17 (§4); 1:20 (§1) (but with *recipere* from α); 1:20 (§2); 1:23 (§2); 1:24 (§2); 1:25 (§2); 1:26; 1:27 (§1a); 1:28.[71] The comment at Rom 1:20 (§2) illustrates the pattern as well as the complexity (single underline for changes in *recensio* β relative to *recensio* α; double underline for changes in *recensio* γ relative to *recensio* β):

α: sempiterna quoque virtus eius et divinitas, ut sint inexcusabiles. ut excusari impietas non possit, adiecit etiam virtutem dei in divinitatem sempiternam cognitam esse ab hominibus et stupore quodam hebetasse ad honorandum deum, quem et esse et operari non negarent; ea enim quae humanis usibus evoluto anno gignuntur ipsum decrevisse nulli in dubium venit. aeterna ergo virtus eius est, qua instituit quae non erant et in eo manent; divinitas vero, qua in opere sibi decreto perseverant elementa rerum.[72]

β: sempiterna quoque virtus eius ac divinitas, ut sint inexcusabiles. ut omnino excusari impietas non possit, adiecit etiam virtutem dei in divinitatem sempiternam cognitam esse ab hominibus et stupore quodam hebetasse ad honorandum deum, quem et esse et operari ad utilitatem suam non ignorarent; ea enim quae humanis usibus evoluto anno gignuntur ipsum decrevisse nulli in dubium venit. aeterna ergo virtus eius Christus est, qua instituit quae non erant et in eo manent, cuius si dudum persona agnita non est, opera tamen manifestata sunt; divinitas vero, qua in opere sibi decreto perseverant elementa rerum.[73]

---

71. One must consult the Latin text in the CSEL edition, since in our English translation we note only substantive changes.

72. "*Even his eternal power and divinity—so that they are without excuse.* In order that ungodliness may not be excused, he added that God's power and eternal divinity were recognized by humankind, but that the impulse to honor God, whom they did not deny both to exist and to work, was dulled by a kind of stupor. For no one doubts that he directed the things that grow in the course of a year for use by humankind. *His* eternal *power*, therefore, is that by which he brought into being things that did not exist, and in him they abide. [His] *divinity*, on the other hand, is what keeps the material elements in the operation assigned to them."

73. "*Even his eternal power and divinity—so that they are without excuse.* In order that ungodliness may not in any way be excused, he added that God's power and eternal divinity were recognized by humankind, but that the impulse to honor God, whom they knew both to exist and to work for their benefit, was dulled by a kind of stupor. For no one doubts that he directed the things that grow in the course of a year for use

γ: sempiterna quoque virtus eius <u>ac</u> divinitas, ut sint inexcusabiles. ut <u>omnino</u> excusari impietas non possit, adiecit etiam virtutem dei in <u>sempiternam divinitatem</u> cognitam esse ab hominibus et stupore quodam hebetasse ad honorandum deum, quem et esse et <u>providere utilitati suae non ignorarent</u>; ea enim quae <u>evoluto anno humanis gignuntur usibus</u> ipsum decrevisse nulli <u>venit in dubium</u>. aeterna ergo virtus <u>dei</u> <u>Christus</u> est, <u>per quem</u> instituit quae non erant et in eo manent, <u>cuius si dudum persona agnita non est, opera tamen</u> <u>manifesta</u> <u>sunt</u>; divinitas vero, qua in opere sibi decreto <u>perdurant</u> elementa rerum.[74] (In Rom. 1:20 [§2] [CSEL 81.1:40.16–26, 41.17–26])

One can observe the middle position of *recensio* β between *recensiones* α and γ. The minor changes in word order and vocabulary in *recensio* γ—*sempiternam divinitatem*; *evoluto anno humanis gignuntur usibus*; *perdurant*—render it unlikely that *recensio* γ stands between *recensiones* α and β. One would have to explain why changes introduced in a second version were reversed in a third version. There are instances where *recensio* γ follows *recensio* α rather than *recensio* β—discussed further below—but they are relatively rare compared to the prevailing pattern described above. Assuming, then, that *recensio* β stands between *recensiones* α and γ, one can see how the sentence *aeterna ergo virtus eius est, qua instituit quae non erant et in eo manent* ("*His* eternal *power*, therefore, is that by which he brought into being things that did not exist, and in him they abide") might first evolve to *aeterna ergo virtus* <u>Christus</u> *est, qua instituit quae non erant et in eo manent* ("*His* eternal *power*, therefore, is Christ, by which he brought into being things that did not exist, and in him they abide") and then to *aeterna ergo virtus* <u>dei</u> <u>Christus</u> *est,* <u>per quem</u> *instituit quae non erant et in*

---

by humankind. *His* eternal *power*, therefore, is Christ, by which he brought into being things that did not exist, and in him they abide. If his person is not yet known, his works nevertheless have been made plain. [His] *divinity*, on the other hand, is what keeps the material elements in the operation assigned to them."

74. "*Even his eternal power and divinity—so that they are without excuse.* In order that ungodliness may not in any way be excused, he added that God's power and eternal divinity were recognized by humankind, but that the impulse to honor God, whom they knew both to exist and to provide for their benefit, was dulled by a kind of stupor. For no one doubts that he directed the things that grow in the course of a year for use by humankind. The eternal *power* of God, therefore, is Christ, through whom he brought into being things that did not exist, and in him they abide. If his person is not yet known, his works nevertheless are plain. His *divinity*, on the other hand, is what keeps the material elements in the operation assigned to them."

eo manent ("The eternal *power* of God, therefore, is Christ, through whom he brought into being things that did not exist, and in him they abide"). *Recensio* α echoes the lemma *sempiterna virtus eius*. *Recensio* β explains that Christ is this eternal power but retains the relative pronoun *qua*, referring back to *virtus*, from *recensio* α. *Recensio* γ adjusts the relative pronoun to *quem*, referring now to Christ as God's agent of creation.

Third, the three recensions are similar in style and language. On the basis of such similarities Souter argued that the Commentary and the *Quaestiones* were by the same author.[75] The same argument can be made with regard to the recensions.[76] For example, among the particles discussed by Souter, in the Romans commentary *ac per hoc* occurs in all recensions at 1:12, 1:16 (§2); 2:11; 3:5 (§1), 3:19 (§2); 4:15 (§1), 4:16 (§1); and 5:13 (§2), and in *recensiones* β and γ at 1:28; 2:8 (§1), 2:16 (§2b); 3:4 (§4a); and 5:14 (§3a); *etenim* occurs in all recensions at 11:8–10 (§2) and 12:8 (§6), and in *recensiones* β and γ at 2:16 (§2c) and 5:14 (§1) (instead of *enim*); *numquid* occurs in all recensions at 2:6 (§2), 2:22 (§2), and in *recensiones* β and γ at 1:22 (§1a); 4:9 (§1); and 5:14 (§4b); *per id quod* occurs in all recensions at 2:3 (§3) and 3:4 (§1), and in *recensiones* β and γ at 8:10 (§1a); *propter quod* occurs in all recensions at 1:1 (§4) and 3:27, in *recensiones* β and γ at *argumentum* §2 (instead of *propterea*), 5:14 (§4a), and 5:15 (§1a), and in *recensio* γ at Rom 1:13 (§5) (instead of *per quod*); *quanto magis* occurs in all recensions at 1:10 (§3), 1:22 (§1); 4:16 (§2); 5:6–7 (§1), 5:10 (twice), 5:13 (§3), and 5:17 (§2), and in *recensiones* β and γ at 1:32 (§3a) and 5:14 (§3a); *quippe cum* occurs in all recensions at 1:11 (§3); 2:3 (§3); and 5:13 (§3), and in *recensiones* β and γ at 3:8 (§1) and 3:21 (§1); *quomodo ergo* occurs in all recensions at 4:5 (§2) and 5:13 (§2), and in *recensiones* β and γ at 1:32 (§4a) and 3:20 (§3) (instead of *ergo*). Among the more common expressions discussed by Souter, in the commentary on Romans *apertum est* occurs in all recensions at 3:21 (§1), and in *recensio* γ at 3:14 (instead of *hoc dicit* in α and *manifestum est* in β, also common expressions in Ambrosiaster); *manifestum est* occurs with *quia* very frequently, unchanged from one recension to the next, with the exception of 13:4 (§1a), a lemma and comment missing from *recensio* α almost certainly

---

75. Souter, *Study of Ambrosiaster*, 63–148; see also Souter, *Earliest Latin Commentaries*, 84–95.

76. The following examples are taken from chapters 1 to 5 of the commentary on Romans; if there are no instances in those chapters, examples from the remaining chapters of the commentary are adduced.

because of a scribal error; *proficere ad* or *proficere in* occurs in all recensions at 3:12; 5:21 (§1); and 7:10 (§2), and in *recensiones* β and γ at 5:20 (§2b); *quantum ad* with *pertinet* occurs in all recensions at 7:25 (§2), and in *recensiones* β and γ at 5:7 (§3a); *subiecit*, to indicate what follows in a biblical text, occurs in all recensions at 1:29; 3:5 (§1 second instance); and 5:14 (§7), in *recensiones* β and γ at 1:27 (§1a), 1:32 (§1a); 2:16 (§2a); and 3:8 (§1) (instead of *subiunxit*), and in *recensio* γ at 3:5 (§1 first instance) (instead of *dicit*) and 3:18 (§1) (instead of *sequitur*). No doubt, one could undertake a more detailed and subtle analysis of the style and language of the recensions. But the above soundings suffice to reinforce the sense that the recensions all come from the same author.

Furthermore, in a few comments *recensio* γ supplies an additional quotation from Scripture. The version quoted is the Vetus Latina used by Ambrosiaster. For example, at Rom 1:1 (§5a) *recensio* γ quotes John 17:3: "This is eternal life, that they may know you, the only and true God, and Jesus Christ whom you have sent."[77] In the Vulgate the verse reads "the only true God" (*solum verum deum*). In Ambrosiaster's writings the verse always reads "the only and true God" (*solum et verum deum*).[78] Similarly, at Rom 2:4 (§1) *recensio* γ adds a quotation from Isaiah: "[God's judgment] is coming in the future, so that in the life to come he may repent that he did not believe that God is a judge who, to display the terror of his future judgment and to show that his patience should not be scorned, says: *I have kept silent. Will I always keep silent? [tacui. numquid semper tacebo?]*."[79] This version of Isa 42:14 is found elsewhere in Ambrosiaster's writings, as well as other Latin patristic texts up to the early fifth century.[80] The Vulgate, however, has "I have always held my peace, I have kept silence, I have been patient" (*tacui semper, silui, patiens fui*).

---

77. In Rom. 1:1 (§5a) (CSEL 81.1:13.10–12): *haec est vita aeterna, ut cognoscant te solum et verum deum et quem misisti Iesum Christum.*

78. In 1 Cor. 15:24–26 (CSEL 81.2:173); In 1 Tim. 2:1–4 (CSEL 81.3:260); *Quaest.* 3.4, 113.1, app. 78.1 (CSEL 50:24, 299, 472).

79. In Rom. 2:4 (§1) (CSEL 81.1:65.13–16): *futurum est, ut in ventura vita paeniteat illum iudicem deum non credidisse, qui ut terrorem futuri iudicii sui ostenderet et paenitentiam non contemnendam, ait: tacui. numquid semper tacebo.* The first part of the sentence, up to *credidisse*, is found in *recensio* β, which in turn has modified *recensio* α.

80. Ambrosiaster, *Quaest.* 1.2, 68.2 (CSEL 50:14, 118). For other early Latin witnesses, consult the Library of Latin Texts-Series A (Brepols Publishers Online).

Finally, as we have already discussed, one can see allusions to contemporary events in comments introduced into *recensio* β or *recensio* γ. Moreover, in one telling alteration there is a clue as to why Ambrosiaster may have revised his work. In the commentary on Romans he refers to Rome as "the city" in *recensio* α (and sometimes *recensio* β), but as "Rome" in *recensio* γ.[81] Vogels, who first noted this variant, raised the possibility that the work was composed in Rome and then revised in another location, necessitating the change.[82] But given allusions to events in Rome in the Commentary, it is more likely, as Lunn-Rockliffe has argued, that the work was initially composed for personal use or a local circle and then revised for a wider audience.[83]

Complexities remain, however. The great majority of variants fit the pattern of a sequential evolution from *recensio* α to *recensio* β to *recensio* γ. However, at times *recensio* γ follows *recensio* α rather than *recensio* β. Table 2.2 lists instances from the first five chapters of the commentary on Romans. Most of these anomalies consist only in a word or a phrase and do not alter the meaning of the comment. Nevertheless, they are intriguing because they occur in sentences or comments where otherwise *recensio* γ follows *recensio* β. Some of the instances may be explained as scribal errors, omissions, or alterations that entered into *recensio* β early in the course of its transmission. For example, the switch from *deum/dei* to *dominum/domini* at Rom 2:14 and 3:20 (§2) may have resulted from a scribal substitution in the archetype of *recensio* β. The switch from *ipsi* to *illi* in the quotation from Matt 4:10 (see Deut 6:13) at Rom 5:12 (§2) probably reflects the influence of the Vulgate on *recensio* β, since *ipsi* is attested elsewhere in Ambrosiaster's writings.[84] Thus, the apparent reversion to *recensio* α in *recensio* γ may at times be an artifact of changes introduced by scribes into *recensio* β.

Sometimes, however, the passages in question are longer, and the reasons for the reversion harder to explain. For instance, at Rom 1:1 (§1) *recensio* γ agrees with *recensio* α in offering a short explanation as to why Saul changed his name to Paul. *Recensio* β adds further remarks that,

---

81. In classical and patristic Latin, *urbs*, as in "the City," was understood to refer to Rome. For the relevant passages, see the translation at Rom 1:9–10 (§4) n. 59.

82. Vogels, "Prolegomena," xv.

83. Sophie Lunn-Rockliffe, *Ambrosiaster's Political Theology*, OECS (Oxford: Oxford University Press, 2007), 15–16.

84. In Rom. 9:5 (§4) (CSEL 81.1:306–7); *Quaest.* 91.6 (CSEL 50:156).

frankly, are hard to reconcile with what has already been said in *recensio* α. At Rom 3:4 (§3) *recensio* γ agrees with *recensio* α in a short comment on the quotation of Ps 50:6, whereas *recensio* β has instead a much longer comment.[85] But one sentence from *recensio* β appears at the end of the comment in *recensio* γ, where it is seemingly out of context. At Rom 3:5 and 3:8 the comment in *recensio* γ has elements from both *recensiones* α and β. The comment at Rom 3:8 (§1) serves as an illustration (single underline for changes in *recensiones* β or γ relative to *recensio* α; double underline for changes in *recensio* γ relative to *recensio* β):

> α: hoc est unde sibi quaestionem fecit apostolus. a perversis hoc opponebatur, quasi hic esset sensus praedicantium remissionem peccatorum, ut facerent mala et venirent bona, hoc est, peccarent, ut remittendo illis deus videretur bonus. quod blasfemium appellat et abicit a sensu divinae doctrinae. nec enim peccari debere fides suadet, sed delinquentibus dat medelam, ut recuperata sanitate iam non peccent.[86]

> β: <u>nunc aperit, quorum causa haec sollicite et cum reverentia disputat</u>. a perversis <u>enim</u> hoc opponebatur, quasi hic esset sensus praedicantium remissionem peccatorum, ut facerent mala et venirent bona, hoc est, peccarent, ut remittendo illis deus videretur bonus. <u>secundum quae supra dicta sunt</u>. quod blasfemium appellat et abicit a sensu divinae doctrinae. nec enim peccari debere fides <u>tradit, quippe cum deum iudicaturum praedicet</u>, sed delinquentibus <u>consulit</u>, ut recuperata <u>salute sub dei lege viventes</u> iam non peccent.[87]

---

85. As already noted by Vogels, "Überlieferung," 137–38.

86. "The reason the apostle has put this question to himself is this: wrong-headed people countered with the view—as though this were the meaning of the proclamation of forgiveness of sins—that they did evil and good resulted. In other words, they held that they sinned so that God might seem good in forgiving them. The apostle calls this slander and distances it from the meaning of the divine teaching. For the faith does not encourage one to sin. Rather, it offers a remedy for transgressors, so that, having recovered their health, they may sin no longer."

87. "Now it becomes clear on whose account he discusses this matter carefully and thoughtfully. Wrong-headed people countered with the view—as though this were the meaning of the proclamation of forgiveness of sins—that they did evil and good resulted. In other words, they held that they sinned so that God might seem good in forgiving them, as was said above. The apostle calls this slander and distances it from the meaning of the divine teaching. For the faith does not teach one to sin, especially since it proclaims that God will come in judgment. Rather, it counsels transgressors,

Table 2.2. Instances Where γ Follows α Rather Than β in the Commentary on Romans 1–5

Verse	Page.line	α	β	Page.line	γ
1:1	8.9–12	—	apud veteres nostros … postquam autem credidit	9.9	—
1:1	8.13–14	—	secundum supra dictum sensum	9.10	—
1:1	8.16	—	quasi ex temptatore factum	9.12	—
1:1	8.16–17	—	humilemque vel parvulum	9.12	—
1:7	20.11	—	dicit	21.12	—
1:11	26.28	non sensum fidei	non fidem	29.4	non sensum fidei
1:12	28.20	acceperant	accipiebant	29.23–24	acceperant
1:14	32.17	natura	natione	33.17	natura
1:16	34.18–19	de evangelio	de evangelium	35.20	de evangelio
1:20	40.13	recipere	percipere	41.14	recipere
1:25	48.20	deo vero benedicto	deus vero benedictus	49.24	deo vero benedicto
2:5	66.2–3	habet	habens	67.5	habet
2:5	66.4	in diem	in die	67.6	in diem
2:5	66.9	sentient	sentiunt	67.10	sentient
2:7	66.22	declaravit	declarat	67.22–23	declaravit
2:7	68.1	his	eis	67.27	his
2:13	74.9	dicatur	dicitur	75.10	dicatur
2:14	74.19	deum	dominum	75.22	deum
2:14	74.24	in sese	in se	75.27	in sese
2:16	76:24	si credere noluerint	si credere noluerunt	77.18–19	si noluerint credere
2:21	84.10	quod praedicas non fieri, facis	—	85.11	quod praedicat non fieri, facit
2:24	86.14	quasi qui	quasi	87.16	qui quasi
2:24	86.21	blasfemia	blasfemium	87.23	blasfemia
2:24	86.23	sit profecta	sit profectum	87.24	sit profecta
2:25	88.14	esse Abrahae	Abrahae esse	89.13	esse Abrahae
3:4	96.3	est enim	autem est	97.3	est enim
3:4	96.19–28	deum iustum in promissis et verbis suis profeticus sermo testatur … mendax.	—	97.14–22	deum iustum in promissis et verbis suis profeticus sermo testatur … mendax.
3:5	100.5	et cetera	et reliqua	101.5	et cetera
3:5	100.6	id	hoc	101.6	id

Verse	Page.line	α	β	Page.line	γ
3:5	100.9–12	absit, secundum hominem dico. hoc est: hic sensus homini convenit, non deo, quia non cadit in deum, ut iniquus sit, sed in hominem	—	101.11–14	sed absit, secundum hominem dico. hoc est: sensus hic homini convenit, non deo, quia non cadit in deum, ut iniquus sit, sed in hominem
3:5	100.16	cum dicit	dum dicit	101.18	cum dicit
3:5	100.18	cum iudicaris	dum iudicaris	101.20	cum iudicaris
3:5	100.20	dei iustificationi	ad dei iustificationem	101.22	dei iustificationi
3:5	100.24–25	vindicet	vindicaret	103.1	vindicet
3:5	100.26–102.10	non enim vult nos peccare. ideoque iustus est, si infert iram.	quia non est iniquus … quae fecit.	103.2	non enim vult nos peccare. ideo quia iustus est infert iram.
3:8	102.27–29	hoc est unde sibi quaestionem fecit apostolus.	nunc aperit, quorum causa haec sollicite et cum reverentia disputat.	103.18	hoc est unde sibi quaestionem fecit apostolus.
3:8	104.3	suadet	tradit	105.3	suadet
3:8	104.4–5	dat medelam	consulit	105.4	dat medelam
3:19	112.16	pertinere	pervenire	113.15	pertinere
3:20	114.15–16	dei	domini	115.9	dei
3:25	120.3	credant	credat	121.7	credant
3:26	120.23	—	in	121.24	—
3:31	124.25	legis	legi	125.23	legis
3:31	126.13	illorum	eorum	127.14	illorum
3:31	126.16	iam	tantum	127.17	iam
4:6	130.22	etiam	—	131.23	etiam
5:3	152.20–21	magnum meritum	magni meriti	153.19	magnum meritum
5:5	154.16	… diversis linguis …	—	155.13–14	… diversis linguis …
5:6–7	156.5	deo	dei	157.5	deo
5:6–7	156.25–26	pro uno bono	pro bono uno	157.22–23	pro uno bono
5:12	162.29	ipsi	illi	165.1	ipsi
5:14	178.16–17	apostoli	apostolus	179.8	apostoli
5:18	182.21	unius delicto	per unius delictum	183.21	unius delicto
5:19	184.2–3	per fidem Christi	—	185.4	per fidem Christi
5:20	186.23	sicut dixi	—	187.12	sicut dixi

γ: <u>hoc est unde sibi quaestionem fecit apostolus</u>. a perversis <u>enim</u> hoc opponebatur, quasi hic esset sensus praedicantium remissionem peccatorum, ut facerent mala et venirent bona, hoc est, peccarent, ut remittendo illis deus videretur bonus.[88] quod blasfemium appellat et abicit a sensu divinae doctrinae. nec enim peccari debere fides <u>suadet</u>, <u>quippe cum dominum iudicaturum praedicet</u>,[89] sed delinquentibus <u>dat medelam</u>,[90] ut recuperata salute[91] iam non peccent.[92] (In Rom. 3:8 [§1] [CSEL 81.1:102.27–103.6; 103.18–105.6])

In this instance it is difficult to decide whether the changes in *recensio* β were made by Ambrosiaster or a later writer. In fact, no general rule can be applied to these types of anomalies. Each one must be assessed in turn.

The "mixed" manuscripts—especially MSS Amiens 87 and Paris lat. 1759, but also MS Monte Cassino 150 and the second hand in MS St. Gall 101—introduce further complications, as can be seen from the notes to the above example. These manuscripts combine material from *recensio* β with material from *recensio* γ, particularly in the initial chapters of the commentary on Romans. At times they singly or together are the sole witnesses for the reiteration in *recensio* γ of material found in *recensio* β. Should one accept their version of the text of *recensio* γ at such points, or should one reject their witness as influenced by *recensio* β? The CSEL edition relegates their witness to the apparatus when the other manuscripts of *recensio* γ propose an alternative to the text in *recensio* β and (usually but not always) includes their witness in the text, set apart by the sigla ⌜ ⌝, when the other

---

so that, having recovered their health and living under the law of God, they may sin no longer."

88. MSS Amiens 87 and Paris lat. 1759 add *secundum quae supra dicta sunt*.

89. Only MSS Amiens 87 and Paris lat. 1759 have *iudicaturum*; MS Amiens 87 has *deum* instead of *dominum*.

90. MS Amiens 87 has *consulit* instead of *dat medelam*.

91. MSS Amiens 87, Oxford 756, Paris lat. 1759, and, in a second hand, St. Gall 101 add *salute sub dei lege viventes*.

92. "The reason the apostle has put this question to himself is this: wrong-headed people countered with the view—as though this were the meaning of the proclamation of forgiveness of sins—that they did evil and good resulted. In other words, they held that they sinned so that God might seem good in forgiving them. The apostle calls this slander and distances it from the meaning of the divine teaching. For the faith does not encourage one to sin, especially since it proclaims that the Lord will come in judgment. Rather, it offers a remedy for transgressors, so that, having recovered their health and living under the law of God, they may sin no longer."

manuscripts are silent. It would be more consistent always to relegate material attested only by MSS Amiens 87 and Paris lat. 1759 to the apparatus, as Rudolf Hanslik opined at Rom 1:1 (§5).[93] But there are instances where their witness is necessary to make sense of the text, as at Rom 1:7 (§1) and 1:16 (§2). The lack of a consistent pattern makes it difficult to establish a general rule.

The variants in the manuscripts of *recensio* γ at Rom 3:4–9 are illustrative.[94] At Rom 3:4 the majority of manuscripts (including MS Monte Cassino 150, itself a "mixed" manuscript, but important as the oldest extant witness to *recensio* γ) agree with *recensio* β for sections 1 and 2, but agree with *recensio* α for section 3, except that they add a sentence found only in *recensio* β near the end of section 5a (In Rom. 3:4 [CSEL 81.1:97.22–4, 98.18–21]). MSS Amiens 87 and Paris lat. 1759, on the other hand, agree with *recensio* β in replacing section 3 with sections 3a to 5a. At Rom 3:5 the majority at times follow *recensio* α rather than *recensio* β, at times follow *recensio* β rather than *recensio* α, and at times introduce changes not found in *recensiones* α and β, all at variance with the Amiens manuscript or the Paris manuscript or both.[95] At Rom 3:6 all the manuscripts—both the majority and the "mixed"—retain an addition introduced in *recensio* β, with the exception of one variant from *recensio* β preserved in the Amiens manuscript (In Rom. 3:6 [CSEL 81.1:103.8]).[96] At Rom 3:7, however, the majority differ with the Amiens and Paris manuscripts in following *recensio* α rather than *recensio* β.[97] At Rom 3:8 (§1) the majority combine elements of both versions, though less so than the "mixed" manuscripts.[98] At Rom 3:8 (§2) the majority attest the first element from *recensio* β but not the second, which is found only in the Amiens and Paris manuscripts.[99] At

---

93. In Rom. 1:1 (§5) (CSEL 81.1:11, lines 25–29 apparatus).

94. For what follows, compare the text on the facing pages of CSEL 81.1:96–105, focusing on changes introduced into *recensio* β, indicated by parentheses ( ) or braces { }, and the corresponding witness of the "mixed" manuscripts of *recensio* γ, indicated by the sigla ⌈ ⌉, but bearing in mind as well the variants in individual "mixed" manuscripts in the apparatus to *recensio* γ.

95. For the witness of MS Amiens 87 and the Paris manuscripts, consult the apparatus at CSEL 81.1:99.29, 101.7, and 103.1.

96. MS Amiens 87 retains *remittat non erit* from *recensio* β but nevertheless attests *sed absit* in *recensio* γ.

97. In Rom. 3:7 (CSEL 81.1:103.13–14): *quia non voluntate sed*.

98. See nn. 87–90 above.

99. In Rom. 3:8 (§2) (CSEL 81.1:105.7, 9): *id est hominum; quod supra dictum est*.

Rom 3:8 (§2a) the majority follow *recensio* β, but with minor modifications that are not attested by the Amiens and Paris manuscripts.[100] Finally, at Rom 3:9—where, importantly, the witness of MS Monte Cassino 150 begins[101]—MS Amiens 87 and MS Monte Cassino 150 preserve three readings from *recensio* β against the majority, and the MS Amiens 87 and MS Vienna 743 preserve one reading from *recensio* β.[102]

Should one follow the majority or the "mixed" manuscripts in these instances? When more than one version of the Commentary was held by a library, readers could compare the versions and make marginal notes. The cathedral library in Cologne has two manuscripts of the Commentary. One, MS Cologne 34, has the text of *recensio* α; the other, MS Cologne 39, the text of *recensio* β. Comments from the latter can be found written in the margins of the former. Similarly, MS St. Gall 101, which presents the text of *recensio* γ, was revised by a second hand in light of *recensio* β, indicating that at one point a reader had access to two manuscripts of the Commentary.[103] When such manuscripts were copied later, their marginal notes could be incorporated into the body of the text. This is a possible explanation for the text at Rom 3:4 in the majority of manuscripts for *recensio* γ: section 3 from *recensio* α was substituted for sections 3a to 5a from *recensio* β, with the exception of the last sentence in section 3, which was retained from section 5a. But one cannot be certain, and there is no single explanation for all variants discussed above. Furthermore, the divided testimony of the "mixed" manuscripts makes it difficult to decide when to accept their witness. Thus, the decision of the CSEL editors not to accept the witness of the "mixed" manuscripts when they individually vary with the majority, and to note substantial points where singly or together they are the sole witnesses for material found in *recensio* β, seems justified.

To make matters even more complicated, one cannot rule out the possibility of interpolation. For example, the comment at Rom 1:17 (§1a) is almost certainly an interpolation. It is attested only by MS Amiens 87 and differs from what precedes and what follows in its interpretation of *in eo*.[104] The double set of comments on Rom 1:29–32 also points toward interpola-

---

100. In Rom. 3:8 (§2a) (CSEL 81.1:105.9–10): *praedicet*; *praebeat*.
101. Vogels, *Das Corpus*, 19; Vogels, "Überlieferung," 116.
102. In Rom. 3:9 (CSEL 81.1:105.18–19, 22, 23, and 25): *id est gentiles*; *est*; *viderentur*; *dei gratiam*.
103. Vogels, "Überlieferung," 123.
104. See the translation of the commentary, p. 23 n. 90.

tion. The first set of comments presented in the CSEL edition is found in *recensiones* β and γ.[105] The second set of comments is found in *recensiones* α and β, as well as MS Paris lat. 1759.[106] The latter set would appear to be an interpolation. The text it explains is from the Vulgate, and it refers to a prior discussion of the sin of Sodom and Gomorrah, which cannot be found in the preceding comments on the chapter.[107] Similarly, the supplementary comment introduced into *recensiones* β and γ at Rom 12:13 (§1a) also appears to be an interpolation, since it explains the verse as found in the Greek witnesses and the Vulgate: "Contribute to the needs of the saints." But if one admits of interpolation here, then one must admit the possibility of interpolations elsewhere. This obviously presents major challenges when dealing with a text that was as extensively revised as the commentary on Romans. However, unless there are strong reasons to suspect an interpolation, it is best to proceed conservatively and begin by assuming that additional comments introduced into a later version are from Ambrosiaster. It is to be expected that the process of revision would not be seamless, particularly if Ambrosiaster is emphasizing a difficult or disputed point or if he is reacting to the views of others.

---

105. CSEL 81.1:52.23–56.13, 53.26–57.17.
106. CSEL 81.1:56.14–60.15, 57.18–61.12. It is puzzling that *recensio* β presents both sets of comments. Here the absence of a full apparatus for *recensio* β in the CSEL edition is a considerable handicap.
107. See the translation of the commentary, p. 34 n. 159 and p. 35 n. 166.

3. Ambrosiaster's Biblical Text

Ambrosiaster read the Bible in Latin translation rather than in the original Hebrew or Greek. The particular translation he used was one of several regional Latin versions circulating in the West prior to the appearance of Jerome's Vulgate in the early fifth century. Today these non-Vulgate versions are designated as "Old Latin" or "Vetus Latina" (VL). Ambrosiaster's version was the one used in Rome and its environs in the fourth century.[1] Through the painstaking work of the Vetus Latina Institute, the principal regional versions have been reconstructed from manuscripts of the Latin Bible and from quotations and allusions in Latin Christian writings.[2] The Institute has published critical editions of the Vetus Latina of all the Pauline Epistles except Romans, 1 and 2 Corinthians, and Galatians.[3] Preliminary materials for the editions of Romans and 1 Corinthians were published,[4] but a complete edition was not realized. A new research team has since taken up the task.[5]

Ambrosiaster commented on the Pauline epistles by first quoting and then explaining a portion of the text.[6] The quoted portion (lemma;

---

1. For a description of this text, referred to as I-type, see Hermann J. Frede, ed., *Epistula ad Ephesios*, VLB 24.1 (Freiburg: Herder, 1962–1964), 33*–35*; Uwe Fröhlich, ed., *Epistula ad Corinthios I*, VLB 22 (Freiburg: Herder, 1995–1998), 197–99.

2. See the Institute's webpage at http://tinyurl.com/SBL1645b.

3. Frede, *Epistula ad Ephesios*; Hermann J. Frede, ed., *Epistulae ad Philippenses et ad Colossenses*, VLB 24.2 (Freiburg: Herder, 1966–1969); Hermann J. Frede, ed., *Epistulae ad Thessalonicenses, Timotheum, Titum, Philemonem, Hebraeos*, VLB 25 (Freiburg: Herder, 1975–1982).

4. Hugo S. Eymann, ed., *Epistula ad Romanos*, VLB 21 (Freiburg: Herder, 1996), and Fröhlich, *Epistula ad Corinthios I*.

5. The Pauline Commentaries Project, based in the Institute for Textual Scholarship and Electronic Editing at Birmingham University and led by Dr. Hugh Houghton (http://tinyurl.com/SBL1645c).

6. See below §4.

plural: lemmata) may range in length from a part of a verse to a block of several verses. The lemma is usually grammatically separate from the ensuing explanation. In the earliest manuscripts of Ambrosiaster's Commentary (up to the eighth or ninth century), each lemma is written out in full and set off by various scribal techniques (indentation, projection into the margin, rubrication, or marginal quotation marks).[7] Because the lemmata were visually demarcated and grammatically discrete, it would have been possible to substitute the Pauline text used by Ambrosiaster with another version known to the scribe. This in fact appears to have occurred already in the early transmission of the Commentary. In some instances, the wording of the comment was altered to correspond to the new wording of the lemma.[8] This evidently complicates the effort to ascertain, in such instances, the wording of Ambrosiaster's text on the basis of the wording of his comment. The practice of abbreviating lemmata by writing only the first and last words of a lemma could also have led to the substitution of Ambrosiaster's Pauline text, since later scribes would quote the Pauline text known to them if they expanded the lemmata when copying the Commentary. Consequently, manuscripts of Ambrosiaster's Commentary sometimes present a Pauline text that has been influenced or replaced by versions not known to Ambrosiaster, particularly the Vulgate. Prior to the publication of the first volume of the CSEL edition of the Commentary, Heinrich J. Vogels prepared a critical edition of Ambrosiaster's Pauline text free of such later influences.[9] The text in this earlier publication is more reliable than the text in the CSEL edition, since regrettably errors crept into the latter during its final preparation.[10] It should be consulted along with the Vetus Latina editions for Ephesians, Philippians, Colossians, 1 and 2 Thessalonians, 1 and 2 Timothy, Titus, and Philemon.

The Latin version used by Ambrosiaster differed at points from the text of the epistles in Greek manuscripts circulating in the fourth century.

---

7. See Hugh A. G. Houghton, "The Layout of Early Latin Commentaries on the Pauline Epistles and Their Oldest Manuscripts," StPatr, forthcoming. I am grateful to Dr. Houghton for making a manuscript of his paper available prior to its publication.

8. Ibid. To the example given at n. 54 one may add, e.g., the correspondence at In Gal. 5:12 (CSEL 81.3:57–58) between *abscidantur* in the lemma in *recensio* γ and *abscidantur* and *absciderentur* in the comment (the latter instance only in *recensio* γ).

9. Heinrich J. Vogels, *Das Corpus Paulinum des Ambrosiaster*, BBB 13 (Bonn: Hanstein, 1957).

10. See Frede, *Epistula ad Thessalonicenses*, 136–40; Fröhlich, *Epistula ad Corinthios I*, 199–202.

Ambrosiaster was aware of this, but he preferred—and defended—his Latin version because of its antiquity.[11] This was a source of tension between Jerome and him, as we have already noted.[12] Ironically, Ambrosiaster's tenacity in this regard has been a boon for biblical scholars, as his Commentary is an important witness to the so-called Western text of the Pauline epistles. Sometimes readings attested by him in conjunction with other biblical witnesses (Greek, Coptic, Syriac, and Latin) are preferred to alternate readings. For this reason, in our translation we note passages where Ambrosiaster's Pauline text differs significantly from the Greek text in the current critical edition of the New Testament (NA[28]).

---

11. See Ambrosiaster's comments at In Rom. 5:14 (§§4e, 5, 5a); 12:11 (§1b).
12. See above §1.

4. Ambrosiaster's Exegesis of the Pauline Epistles

4.1. A Developing Latin Tradition

An efflorescence of Latin exegesis on Paul spanning a half-century and involving six different commentators has been characterized as "the rediscovery of Paul in the Latin theology of the fourth century."[1] While the idea of Paul needing to be "rediscovered" in the early church has been rendered problematic by recent scholarship,[2] it is nonetheless true that Latins lagged behind Greeks in the production of scriptural commentaries, as in theological writing generally. Indeed, more than a century of exegetical works on Paul by Origen and other Greek commentators preceded the engagement of Latin exegetes with the Pauline corpus.[3] The Latin tradition of Pauline

---

1. Thus the title of the important article by Bernhard Lohse, "Beobachtungen zum Paulus-Kommentar des Marius Victorinus und zur Wiederentdeckung des Paulus in der lateinischen Theologie des vierten Jahrhunderts," in *Keryma und Logos*, ed. A. M. Ritter (Göttingen: Vandenhoeck & Ruprecht, 1979), 351–66. More properly one should refer to it as a "discovery of Paul for systematic commenting," according to Joachim Stüben, "Erasmus von Rotterdam und der Ambrosiaster: Zur Identifikationsgeschichte einer wichtigen Quelle Augustins," *WiWei* 60 (1997): 3.

2. In addition to the arguments of Benjamin L. White, *Remembering Paul: Ancient and Modern Contests over the Image of the Apostle* (New York: Oxford University Press, 2014), see David L. Eastman, *Paul the Martyr: The Cult of the Apostle in the Latin West* (Atlanta: Society of Biblical Literature, 2011), 20–24, 71–84, who shows that by 258 celebratory banquets in honor of Peter and Paul were held at the catacombs on the Via Appia.

3. For a good overview of both Greek and Latin commentators, see Maria Grazia Mara, *Paolo di Tarso e il suo epistolario*, CTSt 16 (L'Aquila: Japadre, 1983), 6–64. For the fragments of Greek commentators between Origen and Chrysostom, see Karl Staab, *Pauluskommentare aus der griechischen Kirche*, 2nd ed. (Münster: Aschendorff, 1984). Origen's commentary on Romans, in an abridged translation by Rufinus (*Der Römerbriefkommentar des Origenes: Kritische Ausgabe der Übersetzung Rufins*, ed. Caroline P. Hammond Bammel, AGLB 16, 33, 34 [Freiburg: Herder, 1990–1998]), is the only

exegesis began in the early 360s, independent of the Greek tradition, with an incomplete series on the epistles by the celebrated rhetor and convert to Christianity Marius Victorinus.[4] A little over a decade after Victorinus had produced these works, Ambrosiaster began writing his commentaries, also in Rome; his revisions of all the commentaries appear to have been completed by the end of 384. Some two years later Jerome composed lengthy treatments of Galatians, Ephesians, Titus, and Philemon during his stay in Bethlehem, works heavily dependent on Greek commentators, especially Origen.[5] Proclaiming his status as a pioneer in Latin commentary in the

---

one of Origen's works on Paul that survives in more than fragments; see Origen, *Commentary on the Epistle to the Romans*, trans. Thomas P. Scheck, 2 vols., FC 103–104 (Washington: Catholic University Press of America, 2001–2002), 1:53–59.

4. Belonging to the prehistory of Latin engagement with the Pauline corpus is Tertullian's extensive review of Marcion's Pauline canon in book 5 of *Adversus Marcionem*, which is dominated by polemical rather than exegetical purposes. See Stephen A. Cooper, "*Communis magister Paulus*: Altercation over the Gospel in Tertullian's *Against Marcion*," in *Tertullian and Paul*, ed. Todd D. Still and David Wilhite, PPSD (London: T&T Clark, 2013), 224–46. On the independence of the Greek tradition, see Stephen A. Cooper, "Philosophical Exegesis in Marius Victorinus' Commentaries on Paul," in *Interpreting the Bible and Aristotle in Late Antiquity: The Alexandrian Commentary Tradition between Rome and Baghdad*, ed. Josef Lössl and John W. Watt (Farnham, Surrey, UK: Ashgate, 2011), 67–89. Victorinus's commentaries on Galatians, Ephesians, and Philippians are extant; and internal references make it clear that he wrote on Romans and the Corinthians correspondence as well. See Franco Gori, ed., *Marii Victorini opera pars II: Opera exegetica*, CSEL 83.2 (Vienna: Hoelder-Pichler-Tempsky, 1986). For Victorinus as a commentator, see Stephen A. Cooper, *Marius Victorinus' Commentary on Galatians: Introduction, Translation, and Notes*, OECS (Oxford: Oxford University Press, 2005), and Stephen A. Cooper, *Metaphysics and Morals in Marius Victorinus' Commentary on the Letter to the Ephesians*, AUS 5.155 (New York: Lang, 1995). See also the unsurpassed monograph of Pierre Hadot, *Marius Victorinus, recherches sur sa vie et ses œuvres* (Paris: Études Augustiniennes, 1971).

5. St. Jerome, *Commentary on Galatians*, trans. Andrew Cain, FC 121 (Washington, DC: Catholic University Press of America, 2010), 12. Jerome's commentaries on Paul have not been fully reedited since Migne's edition (PL 26:307–468). There is a new critical edition of his work on Galatians by Giacomo Raspanti, ed., *Commentarii in epistulam Pauli apostoli ad Galatas*, CCSL 77A (Turnhout: Brepols, 2006); likewise on Titus and Philemon by Federica Bucchi, ed., *Commentarii in epistulas Pauli apostoli ad Titum et ad Philemonem*, CCSL 77C (Turnhout: Brepols, 2003). Besides the translation of the Galatians commentary by Andrew Cain mentioned in the preceding note, see also St. Jerome, *Commentaries on Galatians, Titus, and Philemon*, trans. Thomas Scheck (Notre Dame, IN: University of Notre Dame Press, 2010). On the extent of Jerome's dependence on Greek commentators, see Ronald E. Heine, *The Commentaries*

prologue to his work on Galatians, Jerome scorned the work of Victorinus as that of a secular academic "completely ignorant of scripture"[6] and made no mention whatever of Ambrosiaster's commentaries. Likewise, in his *De viris illustribus* Jerome passed over Ambrosiaster in silence, despite that fact that Damasus had drawn to his attention some excerpts from the *Quaestiones*.[7] In 394 Augustine composed three works on Paul, one on Galatians and two on Romans, none of which are complete continuous commentaries.[8] The final years of the fourth century (or the beginning of the fifth) saw the production of another anonymous explanation of all the Pauline letters—also not a verse-by-verse continuous commentary—that of the so-called Budapest Anonymous.[9] Late in the first decade of the fifth century, Pelagius composed his concise running commentaries on all the epistles, Hebrews included.[10] The work of these earliest Latin commenta-

---

of Origen and Jerome on St. Paul's Epistles to the Ephesians (Oxford: Oxford University Press, 2002).

6. Andrew Cain, introduction to St. Jerome, *Commentary on Galatians*, 57 (see 32–33 for Cain's critical discussion of Jerome's dismissal of the work of his Latin predecessors on Paul).

7. On Jerome's attitude to Ambrosiaster, see Andrew Cain, "In Ambrosiaster's Shadow: A Critical Re-evaluation of the Last Surviving Letter Exchange between Pope Damasus and Jerome," *REAug* 51 (2005): 257–77.

8. Johannes Divjak, ed., *Augustini opera*, sect. IV, pars I: *Expositio quarundam propositionum ex Epistola ad Romanos; Epistolae ad Galatas expositionis liber unus; Epistolae ad Romanos inchoata expositio*, CSEL 84 (Vienna: Hoelder-Pichler-Tempsky, 1971). The works on Romans have been reedited and translated by Paula Fredriksen Landes, with facing Latin, as *Augustine on Romans* (Chico, CA: Scholars Press, 1982). The commentary on Galatians has been translated, with Divjak's text facing, by Eric Plumer, *Augustine's Commentary on Galatians*, OECS (Oxford: Oxford University Press, 2002).

9. H. J. Frede, *Ein neuer Paulustext und Kommentar*, 2 vols., vols. 7–8 of *AGLB* (Freiburg: Herder, 1973–1974). This anonymous author appears to have read Greek and been influenced by both Origen and the methods (and forms) of Antiochene exegetes (ibid., 1:205–15, 247–49). As regards the relation of the Budapest Anonymous to Latin commentators on Paul, Frede states that "there are, moreover, occasional points of contact with Ambrosaister and likely also to the early writings of Augustine, but they are not the sort that allow one to speak of dependency" (215).

10. Alexander Souter, ed., *Pelagius's Expositions of Thirteen Epistles of St Paul*, 2 vols., TS 9.1–2 (Cambridge: Cambridge University Press, 1922; repr., Eugene, OR: Wipf & Stock, 2004). Of these, only the work on Romans has been completely translated: Theodore S. de Bruyn, *Pelagius's Commentary on St Paul's Epistle to the Romans*, OECS (Oxford: Oxford University Press, 1993).

tors on Paul represents a distinct phase in the history of Latin exegesis, since no further commentary on Paul was produced by Latins until the mid-sixth century—properly the Byzantine period of the Latin church—when Cassiodorus and his school took it up.[11] Further Latin engagement with the Pauline corpus came during the Carolingian revival of the ninth century, when a number of important authors produced works on Paul drawing heavily on Ambrosiaster's Commentary as part of the opus of the sainted bishop of Milan.[12]

4.2. Ambrosiaster's Exegetical Methodology

As Alexander Souter aptly stated over a century ago, the approach of Ambrosiaster in his Commentary "springs from a desire, first, to interpret the Apostle's meaning plainly and naturally, and, secondly, to enforce the lessons he sought to teach."[13] This basic approach to the text is shared by five of the six other early Latin authors—Jerome the noted exception. Their preference for "a literal style, beginning and often remaining with the historical and grammatical meaning of the biblical text,"[14] represents the Latin Christian adaptation of the literary-critical tools of the grammarian to the biblical text. Accordingly, the preference of the Latin commentators for precisely this approach to Paul can be best explained as a methodological decision taken in light of the nature of the writings to be commented. The Pauline epistles, representing a record of the pastoral activity of the apostle Paul (and his fellow ministers), contain directly didactic material spanning important teachings about God and Christ as well as the Christian life in its moral and liturgical dimensions. Hence the appropriateness of the grammarian's approach to Paul's epistles.[15] The

---

11. For the anti-Pelagian adaptation of Pelagius's work falsely attributed to Primasius, the bishop of Hadramentum (d. 565), but composed by Cassiodorus and his school (PL 68:416–794), see Kevin L. Hughes, *Constructing Antichrist: Paul, Biblical Commentary, and the Development of Doctrine in the Early Middle Ages* (Washington, DC: Catholic University Press of America, 2005), 117–21.

12. See the thorough work of Johannes Heil, *Kompilation oder Konstruktion? Die Juden in den Pauluskommentaren des 9: Jahrhunderts*, FGJ, Abteilung A: Abhandlungen 6 (Hannover: Hahn, 1998).

13. Alexander Souter, *A Study of Ambrosiaster*, TS 7.4 (Cambridge: Cambridge University Press, 1905), 7.

14. De Bruyn, *Pelagius's Commentary*, 2.

15. Ambrose's perspective in *Ep.* 7.1 (= *Ep.* 37 in PL 16:1084) is revealing: *Proxime*

largely literal treatment of this material made it applicable to the various theological controversies of the fourth century, as we discuss in the following section of this introduction.

Ambrosiaster's basic exegetical method consists of giving an explanatory paraphrase of the epistolary texts, which he treats as historical documents dominated by the aims of pastoral admonition and theological clarification. This has led modern scholars to see Ambrosiaster's "literal" and "historical-literal" approach as a significant anticipation of aspects of modern historical-critical exegesis.[16] Indeed, on one of the few occasions when Ambrosiaster makes any methodological remarks, he explicitly acknowledges the role of both history (*historia*) and text (*litterae*) in making exegetical decisions.[17] One can also characterize the immediate aim of Ambrosiaster's exegesis of Paul as the search for the epistles' "narrative meaning," to employ the term of Rowan Greer in his discussion of Theodore of Mopsuestia's com-

---

cum veteris amoris usu familiaris inter nos sermo caderetur, delectari te insinuisti mihi, cum aliquid de Pauli apostoli scriptis coram populo ad disputandum adsumerem, quod eius profundum in consiliis vix conpraehendatur, sublime in sententiis audientem erigat, disputantem accendat, tum quia in plerisque ita se ipse suis exponat sermonibus, ut is, qui tractat, nihil inveniat, quod adiciat suum, ac si velit aliquid dicere, grammatici magis quam disputatoris fungatur munere (CSEL 82:43–44); ET: *St. Ambrose of Milan: Letters* (Oxford: Parker, 1881), 235: "When we were lately conversing together, in the intimacy of an old-standing affection, you let me see that you were much pleased by my taking a passage from the writings of the Apostle Paul to preach upon to the people. You said further that this was the case, because the depth of his counsels is difficult to grasp, while the loftiness of his sentiment rouses the audience, and stimulates the preacher; and also because his discourses are so fully, for the most part, the interpreters of his meaning, that the expounder of them finds nothing to add of his own, and, if he would say anything, fills the part of a grammarian rather than of a preacher" (slightly modified).

16. For the literal approach, see e.g., Coelestinus Martini, *Ambrosiaster: De auctore, operibus, theologia*, SPAA 4 (Rome: Pontificium Athenaeum Antonianum, 1944), 77; Angelo di Berardino, ed., *The Golden Age of Latin Patristic Literature from the Council of Nicea to the Council of Chalcedon*, vol. 4 of *Patrology* (Westminster, MD: Christian Classics, 1992), 183. For the historical-literal approach, see Maria Grazia Mara, *Paolo di Tarso e il suo epistolario*, CTSt 16 (L'Aquila: Japadre, 1983), 36. For discussion of some of Ambrosiaster's methodological remarks in the *Quaestiones*, see Charles Kannengiesser, *Handbook of Patristic Exegesis* (Leiden: Brill, 2006), 168–75.

17. In this passage, to accept the reading of Gal 2:5 without the negative particle (In Gal. 2:5 [§8] [CSEL 81.3:22]: *litterae enim hoc indicant, quia cessit et historia factum exclamat*). He considers Acts to provide relevant data, namely, the fact that Paul did give way in the case of Timothy's circumcision.

mentaries on Paul.[18] Ambrosiaster sought to render the epistles' narrative meaning by reconstructing from the language of the epistles what he calls an account of "the mystery."[19] From the literary-critical perspective we can say that the Commentary as a whole seeks to provide a master narrative of the relationships between the parties involved, not just those between Paul and his addressees but also those of God and Christ to all concerned, including Ambrosiaster's intended audience.

The method of textual exposition employed by both Greek and Latin Christian commentators was the most basic tool in the grammarian's kit. Scholars associated with the library of Alexandria had formulated the technique in the Hellenistic period, and its legacy was carried on by Greek, Latin, Syriac, and eventually Arabic schools, all of which taught these expository methods for reading both secular and sacred texts.[20] In part, this involved the identification of figures of speech and figures of thought. Thus Ambrosiaster mentions hyperbaton (In Gal. 5:4)[21] and irony (In 2 Cor. 11:19 [§2]),[22] and he also uses the technical term *prooemium* for one of the key parts of a speech (*partes orationis*) (In Gal. 3:1). Ambrosiaster also occasionally uses ornamental figures such as *homoeoteleuton* (In Phil. 1:18–21).[23] A more central feature of the methodology, however, was the principle of interpreting authors primarily in light of their own utterances, a theory later famously formulated by Porphyry as reading "Homer from Homer" (*Quaest. hom. Odd.* 12–14).[24] This latter principle was relevant to

---

18. Thus Rowan Greer, *Theodore of Mopsuestia: The Commentaries on the Minor Epistles of Paul*, WGRW 26 (Atlanta: Society of Biblical Literature, 2010), xiv.

19. See below §4.1.

20. See George Kennedy, ed., *Classical Criticism*, vol. 1 of *The Cambridge History of Literary Criticism* (Cambridge: Cambridge University Press, 1989), 29–35. Further, see Christoph Schäublin, "Zur paganen Prägung der christlichen Exegese," in *Christliche Exegese zwischen Nicaea und Chalcedon*, ed. Jan van Oort and Ulrich Wickert (Kampen: Kok Pharos, 1992), 148–73. See also the editors' introduction in Lössl and Watt, *Interpreting the Bible and Aristotle*.

21. *Recensio* α (CSEL 81.3:55). For a discussion of figures in ancient rhetorical theory, see *Rhet. Her.* 4.1; also Quintilian, *Inst.* 9.3.23–27.

22. See also In 1 Cor. 4:8 (§1). On *ironia* in ancient literary theory, see Quintilian, *Inst.* 9.4.44–53.

23. See also In 2 Cor. 11:11, where Ambrosiaster has a figure of sound (*parechesis*), with similar-sounding words from different roots: *incipientem vera de semetipso narrare insipientem se dicit*.

24. Thus Christoph Schäublin, "Homerum ex Homero," *MH* 34 (1977): 221–27. On the origin of this principle, see Jaap Mansfeld, *Prolegomena: Questions to Be Settled*

rhetorical instruction due to its potential application in legal cases, particularly concerning inheritances disputed because of ambiguous language in a will. Cicero's treatment of this principle in his handbook of rhetoric *De inventione* (2.40.117) ensured that it was widely known throughout the Latin world as a means to ascertain an author's intention through the examination of his own writings or other relevant documents.[25] It is in this milieu of theory and practice that Ambrosiaster read the apostle's epistolary utterances, discerning their literary context and historical setting from the letters themselves or from the limited data provided in Acts of the Apostles.

Commentaries on Paul written by Antiochene exegetes display a similar exegetical method.[26] This fact indicates no dependence of Ambrosiaster on that "school"[27]—he shows no indication of knowing Greek[28]—but

---

before the Study of an Author, or a Text, PhA 61 (Leiden: Brill, 1995), 204–5. Porphyry's *Homeric Questions* is now available in the edition and translation of John A. MacPhail Jr., *Porphyry's Homeric Questions on the Iliad: Text, Translation, Commentary*, TK 36 (Berlin: de Gruyter, 2011).

25. This is apparent from Victorinus's commentary on *De inventione*, which, although it does not treat the key passage in detail, provides an interesting remark that makes this connection: "Next [i.e., in *Inv.* 2.40] he adds a precept directing us to look for the time at which what has been written was written, since from this one understands the intention [*voluntas*] of the writer" (Antonella Ippolito, ed., *Marii Victorini Explanationes in Ciceronis Rhetoricam*, CCSL 132 [Turnhout: Brepols, 2006], 235).

26. See Greer, *Theodore of Mopsuestia*, xiii–xx.

27. As Manlio Simonetti has noted, a lack of allegorizing on the part of commentators on the Pauline Epistles—which do not require allegorizing to be made religiously relevant—is no ground for considering an exegete to be of the "Antiochene tendency" (*Lettera e/o allegoria: Un contributo all storia dell'esegesi patristica*, SEAug 23 [Rome: Institutum Patristicum Augustinianum, 1985], 245). For the integrity of the category "Antiochene exegesis," see Richard J. Perhai, *Antiochene Theōria in the Writings of Theodore of Mopsuestia and Theodoret of Cyrus* (Minneapolis: Augsburg Fortress, 2015), 34–43.

28. Pace Michaela Zelzer, "Zur Sprache des Ambrosiaster," WS 83 (1970): 196–213, and E. W. Watson in his review of Souter's CSEL edition of the *Quaestiones*, ClR 23 (1909): 236–37. These two scholars have adduced a number of reasons for thinking Latin was not his first language, but they have not supplied convincing demonstrations that he actually knew Greek. As Mundle has pointed out, the fact that Ambrosiaster refers to textual variants in the Greek as a matter of hearsay (e.g., on Rom 12:11 he says *in Graeco dicitur habere sic*: "It is said that in the Greek one reads…") shows he hardly has independent knowledge of Paul in Greek. Mundle thus concluded that Ambrosiaster "ist ein Römer vom reinsten Wasser gewesen"; see Wilhelm Mundle, *Die Exe-*

rather the independent absorption of secular literary critical techniques by Greek commentators of all sorts as well as by Latin Christian scholars. A further characteristic shared with the Antiochenes is the avoidance of extensive allegorizing, a feature that distinguishes Ambrosiaster's exegesis markedly from that of Ambrose. This difference between the bishop of Milan's exegesis and that of Ambrosiaster was noted by Richard Simon in 1693, in his important *History of the Chief Commentators of the New Testament from the Beginning of Christianity to Our Times*: "their style is so different, one from the other, and their manners of interpreting Scripture resemble each other so little, that one need only cast one's eyes upon them to judge that St. Ambrose is not the author of these commentaries."[29] The paucity of allegorical interpretation in Ambrosiaster's commentaries on Paul, however, should not be taken as a principled reaction against Origen's allegorical approach, or against the Latins who followed this method before Jerome (Victorinus of Pettau, Hilary of Poitiers, and Gregory of Elvira). Some of the treatises of Ambrosiaster's *Quaestiones* contain the sort of typological exegesis to which he had occasional recourse to in the Commentary (in some case following the apostle himself).[30] They also show great readiness to deviate, when necessary, from the program of literal and historical interpretation when necessary to give sense to biblical texts, or when relevant to his pastoral and moral ends.[31] In the Commen-

---

gese der paulinischen Briefe im Kommentar des Ambrosiaster (Marburg: Schaaf, 1919), 12–13, 17. Lack of acquaintance—or very limited acquaintance—with Greek would seem also to be indicated in his comments on Gal 5:2e. There he observes that the word χριστός in Greek means "anointed" (which does not demonstrate knowledge of the language) but then takes the *christi* of the lemma not as a genitive singular (which any consultation of the Greek would show) but as a nominative plural (a syntactically possible but contextually unlikely reading).

29. Richard Simon, *Histoire critique des principaux commentateurs du Nouveau Testament, depuis le commencement du Christianisme jusques à nôtre tems: Avec une dissertation critique sur les principaux actes manuscrits qui ont été citez dans les trois parties de cet ouvrage* (Rotterdam: Leers, 1693), 133.

30. See his comments on Rom 4:10 and 1 Cor 5:7; 11:26. He is also perfectly willing to give additional figurative interpretation to metaphors used in Scripture, as he does in regard to the "coals" of Rom 12:20.

31. E.g., as in *Quaest.* 38 (CSEL 50:65), when dealing with Ps 31:9 LXX (Ps 32:9 English), he opens by observing, "It is not to be understood as the words sound." On Ambrosiaster in relation to the Antiochene method (as well as his deviation from a historical-literal exegesis), see Marie-Pierre Bussières, "Ambrosiaster's Method of Interpretation in the *Questions on the Old and New Testament*," in *Interpreting the Bible*

tary at Gal 4:23–24, where the apostle confesses to allegorizing the story of Sarah, Hagar, Ishmael, and Isaac, Ambrosiaster supplies a school definition of allegory[32] and renders a figurative meaning for the two sons fitting the issue of the epistle. But for the most part the kind of applied, pastoral exegesis Ambrosiaster practiced in his Commentary simply had no need of any extensive application of allegory.

4.3. Formal Features of the Commentary

Ambrosiaster's works on Paul are continuous or running commentaries, one of several options in the genre of commentary.[33] They consist for the most part of an explanatory paraphrase in which the commentator's voice emerges to conduct the inquiry in the presence of an audience, which is then variously implicated.[34] The commentaries open with a preface

---

and Aristotle, ed. Lössl and Watt, 49–65. Simonetti has observed that the *Quaestiones* "give evidence of non-univocal mode of interpretation" and concludes that although "the literal interpretation predominates … it is clear that Ambrosiaster did not intend to be rigidly tied to a single interpretive practice but kept himself open to deciding the matter on the basis of diverse contexts" (*Lettera e/o allegoria*, 245).

32. There he states that allegory means to signify "one thing from another" (*aliud ex alio*), which is close to the definition Quintilian gives in *Inst*. 8.6.44: "Allegory … presents one thing in words and another in meaning" (*aliud verbis aliud sensu ostendit*); *The Institutio Oratoria of Quintilian*, trans. H. E. Butler, LCL (Cambridge, MA: Harvard University Press, 1966), 3:327.

33. The running commentary was first developed by Aristarchus of Samothrace, head of the library of Alexandria in the mid-second century BCE, who wrote commentaries on literary works, from which fragments on Homer survive (Kennedy, *Classical Criticism*, 208). This genre arose from oral instruction, where a portion of a literary or philosophical text would be read aloud and then commented on by the professor. For a superb discussion of this form of commentary in the philosophical schools, see Ilsetraut Hadot, "Der fortlaufende philosophische Kommentare," in *Der Kommentar in Antike und Mittelalter: Beiträge zu seiner Erforschung*, ed. Wilhelm Geerlings and Christian Schulze, CCAM 2 (Leiden: Brill, 2002), 183–99. Jerome classified Origen's commentaries—as he tells us in the prologue to his translation of Origen's commentary on Ezekiel—as *excerpta*, homilies, or *volumina* (thus Wilhelm Geerlings, "Die lateinisch-patristischen Kommentare," in Geerlings and Schulze, *Der Kommentar in Antike*, 3). *Volumina* or τόμοι would include running commentaries of various degrees of comprehensiveness.

34. This fullest account of Ambrosiaster's exegetical method is Giacomo Raspanti, "Aspetti formali dell'esegesi paolina dell'Ambrosiaster," *ASEs* 16 (1999): 507–36. See also Wilhelm Geerlings, "Zur exegetischen Methode des Ambrosiaster," in *Stimuli*:

(*argumentum* is his term of choice), which provides a synopsis of key elements for the interpretation of the epistle. This may include the history and present situation of the church or—as in the case of the Pastorals and Philemon—the persons addressed, as well as the apostle's aims in writing to them. Each of the thirteen commentaries covers the entire text of the epistle, with segments of text (lemmata) followed by a corresponding comment. The lemmata vary in length but for the most part are between one and three verses long. The explanatory remarks often quote words or phrases from the lemma, occasionally referring to other epistles (less frequently other biblical books) for clarification or expansion. The exposition proceeds largely by a summarizing paraphrase (often omitting any discussion of the individual elements of the passage),[35] which Ambrosiaster tends to introduce by a formula: *dicit* or *dixit* ("he says/said"), *exponit* ("he explains"), *manifestum est* ("it is obvious"), *verum est* ("it is true"), *ostendit* ("he shows/has shown"), *monet* ("he admonishes"), *admonet* ("he advises"). Phrases such as *hoc est* and *id est* ("this is/this means" and "that is/that means") abound to explain individual words, phrases, or the fuller content expressed by the language of the text. (Philosophical commentators distinguished between λέξις and θεωρία,[36] the explanation of individual words and the interpretation of the content.) Very frequently Ambrosiaster introduces a paraphrase with *significat* ("he means") or *vult* ("he wants"). The comments to a particular lemma only rarely conclude with any reference to the next section of the lemma.

The Commentary contains other recurrent formal elements, including explanatory glosses that define key elements of the text, as well as cross-references, both to the commentator's previous remarks as well as to other passages in the letter and in other epistles. Ambrosiaster occasionally identifies thematic structures and internal divisions of the epistles, and he often provides explanatory examples of two general kinds: references to

---

Exegese und ihre Hermeneutik in Antike und Christentum; Festschrift für Ernst Dassmann, ed. Georg Schöllgen and Clemens Scholten (Münster: Aschendorff, 1996): 444–49. Mundle, *Die Exegese*, 36–41, contains astute observations of Ambrosiaster's methods as well.

35. As an example see his treatment of Paul's extended "armor of God" metaphor in Eph 6:13–17. While Victorinus treats all the different elements of the armor (Cooper, *Metaphysics and Morals*, 108–11), Ambrosiaster discusses none of them but just explains the general point of the metaphor.

36. Hadot, "Der fortlaufende philosophische Kommentar," 184.

realia and biblical references. Striking and revelatory of the commentator's agenda are the dramatic turns to address the audience (in the second and third person).[37]

A regular formal feature is the prefaces with which Ambrosiaster opens each commentary. As regards the scope of material covered, his prefaces are moderate in comparison with the fuller program developed by literary critics and commentators on secular texts.[38] This program was absorbed and applied in varying degrees for the purposes of Christian commentators among the Greeks by Origen and others and among Latins by Hilary and Marius Victorinus.[39] Jerome provides more extensive prefaces for his biblical commentaries (including the Pauline ones), giving not only traditional expository material (e.g., plot summaries of biblical books) but also his own apologetic interventions.[40] Although Ambrosiaster does not seem to have provided headings for these prefaces, most of the manuscripts of the commentaries label them *argumentum* (less frequently *prologus*).[41] We have translated *argumentum* as "synopsis," for Ambrosiaster's prefaces function similarly to the acrostic-poem plot summaries called *argumenta* that formed the initial part of the prologues Plautus prefixed to his plays.[42]

---

37. This paragraph draws heavily on Raspanti, "Aspetti formali," 515–21.

38. For the fuller program, see Eric W. Scherbenske, *Canonizing Paul: Ancient Editorial Practice and the Corpus Paulinum* (Oxford: Oxford University Press, 2013), 62–65, 130.

39. See the contributions of Alfons Fürst, "Origen: Exegesis and Philosophy in Early Christian Alexandria," and Sophie Lunn-Rockliffe, "Prologue Topics and Translation Problems in Latin Commentaries on Paul," in Lössl and Watt, *Interpreting the Bible and Aristotle*, 13–21 and 33–47 (respectively). Hilary's *Commentary of Matthew* lacks any such prologue, as it was composed before he had traveled to the East and become acquainted with Origen's appropriation of the full range of philological methods. His *Commentary on the Psalms*, however, is heavily dependent on Origen and contains a very lengthy prologue (PL 9:231–47), which represents a far fuller version of the form than anything found in any of the Latin commentators on Paul, with the exception of Jerome.

40. See Andrew Cain, "Apology and Polemic in Jerome's Prefaces to His Biblical Scholarship," in *Hieronymus als Exeget und Theologe: Interdisziplinäre Zugänge zum Koheletkommentar des Hieronymus*, ed. Elisabeth Birnbaum and Ludger Schwienhorst-Schönberger, BETL 268 (Leuven: Peeters, 2014), 107–28.

41. Heinrich J. Vogels, "Die Überlieferung des Ambrosiasterkommentars zu den Paulinischen Briefen," *NAWG* 7 (1959): 113.

42. See the brief discussion of Wolfgang De Melo, ed. and trans., *Plautus* I, LCL (Cambridge: Harvard University Press, 2011), lv. Also see Rudolf Pfeiffer, *History of*

The term *argumentum* is thus a translation of ὑπόθεσις, that is, the prefatory material ancient scholars included in manuscripts of Greek dramas.[43] These *hypotheseis* consist of "highly condensed prefatory notices intended to provide the more scholarly reader with essential information about the play and its background."[44] Ambrosiaster's *argumenta*, by comparison, provide only very basic factual information about each epistle and its context. His most extensive *argumentum* precedes his commentary on Romans, followed in length by those on Galatians and 1 Corinthians. The remainder are rather brief, especially those on Colossians, 2 Thessalonians, 2 Timothy, Titus, and Philemon, which consist of one or two sentences.

These *argumenta* contain some material of a more theoretical nature, concerning, for example, the relationship of Christianity to Judaism (particularly in Galatians) and on Ambrosiaster's general approach to the interpretation of the epistles. The *argumentum* to the commentary on Romans is as close as our exegete ever comes to describing his exegetical method, one central component of which is a historical understanding.[45] "In order to have an understanding of things," thus he opens, "one needs to grasp their origins." He then acknowledges that the evidence of the situation of the Roman church is found in the letter itself: "Only if one is familiar with this book will it be easier to explain the reason for the dispute [*causae ratio*]," concluding that "if we describe the approach and motive [*modum et rationem*] of the letter before us, it can be seen that what we say is true." As Joachim Stüben has observed, "Ambrosiaster lays out here a simple but sound methodology."[46] In

---

Classical Scholarship: From the Beginnings to the Hellenistic Age (Oxford: Clarendon, 1968), 192–96.

43. For a full treatment of ancient literary prefaces and their use in biblical commentaries, see Matthias Skeb, *Exegese und Lebensform: Die Proömien der antiken griechischen Bibelkommentare*, CCAM 5 (Leiden: Brill, 2007).

44. Thus W. S. Barrett, *Euripides: Hippolytos* (Oxford: Clarendon, 1964), 153. For fuller discussion, see Wolfgang Luppe, "ΣΚΟΛΑΙ, ΥΠΟΜΝΗΜΑΤΑ und ΥΠΟΘΕΣΕΙΣ zu griechischen Dramen auf Papyri," in *Der Kommentar in Antike*, ed. Geerlings and Schulze, 55–77.

45. His approach with its concern for not merely events but also causes has been compared to that of Greek historians by Alessandra Pollastri, "Il prologo del commento alla Lettera ai Romani dell'Ambrosiaster," *SSRel* 2 (1978): 99.

46. Stüben, "Erasmus von Rotterdam und der Ambrosiaster," 9–10, has noted how Ambrosiaster's *argumentum* here refers to *ratio* and *causae*, much as did Tacitus, *Hist.* 1.4: "so that not only the events and consequences might be known … but the reason and motives as well [*ratio etiam causaeque*]." (Stüben's reference to Tacitus incorrectly

modern terms, it is the rhetorical situation that functions as the hermeneutical key, as François Tolmie has noted.[47]

The second section of the *argumentum* on Romans proceeds to the historical task and gives a reconstruction of the origin of the church at Rome, which agrees with modern scholarship in supposing that it arose among Christian Jews living in Rome who spread the word to the gentiles there.[48] To Ambrosiaster's regret, these Jewish believers "taught the Romans that those who confess Christ should keep the law."[49] This set the stage for the problems in the church that Paul sought to resolve with his letter. The "mistaken understanding of Christ" with its loyalty to the law was a threat, because it undermined the claim that there was "complete salvation in Christ"—a proposition that for Ambrosiaster was axiomatic. Similar to the Galatians in their error, these Roman believers nonetheless did not elicit the apostle's anger but his praise, since they received the gospel apart from true apostles and their miracles.

Within the body of the commentaries, the running exposition for the most part adheres closely to the text and its epistolary context. References to other biblical books—particularly those outside the Pauline corpus—are infrequent and minimally obstructive to the textual exposition. It is a sign of his focus on context that Ambrosiaster refers often to the Acts of the Apostles, usually for information about Paul and his missions. He cites the Gospels of John and Matthew about as frequently as Acts, usually to confirm or clarify a Pauline doctrine or moral teaching.[50] The Johannine Epistles and Revelation are occasionally referenced. Of the books of the Hebrew Bible, Genesis and the Psalms are those Ambrosiaster most frequently cites, followed by Isaiah.[51] Ambrosiaster cites them not only when Paul himself quotes or alludes to biblical passages and characters

---

cites the *Annals* instead of the *Histories*.) Although in this passage of Ambrosiaster *causa* does not refer to historical cause (as in Tacitus) but has the more primary sense of a legal case or dispute, the terms *modum* and *ratio* express the basic historical orientation of his approach.

47. D. François Tolmie, "Ambrosiaster se uitleg van die Filemonbrief en die retoriese analise van hierdie brief," *IDS* 49, no. 2 (2015), doi:10.4102/ids.v49i2.

48. Joseph Fitzmyer, *Romans*, AB 33 (New York: Doubleday, 1992), 29–30.

49. In Rom. *argumentum* §2.

50. E.g., the gospel citations at In Gal. 1:6 and In Phil. 2:9–11. Quotations from Luke are not uncommon, though references to Mark are far fewer.

51. Souter, *Study of Ambrosiaster*, 196, 201.

but very often to provide prophetic testimony to Christ and the validity of Christianity.[52]

Despite frequent reference to other Pauline epistles or other scriptural books and apocrypha for purposes of clarification and elaboration,[53] Ambrosiaster does not engage in comprehensive citation and/or quotation of parallels or become drawn into discussion of the extraneous passages. Occasionally the consultation of a similar passage in another letter will bring him to admit—as in the case of Eph 5:2, which led him to quote a phrase from Rom 8:32—that "this seems a contradiction, so far as pertains to the language," requiring more inquiry. But for the most part Ambrosiaster, like Marius Victorinus,[54] chose to write a relatively brief but continuous commentary, where the primary aim of expositing of the Pauline text is kept in view even while quoting or referencing other biblical texts.

Yet digressions from the basic task of textual exposition reveal Ambrosiaster's distinctly didactic purposes. The commentator's voice emerges in slight asides, where the reader is invited to share his outrage, scorn, wonder, or gratitude.[55] The lengthier digressions—up to a paragraph long—are stimulated by passages fraught with theological and exegetical difficulties, for example, the Christ-hymn in the second chapter of Philippians. Briefer digressions discuss church practices (and their deficiencies) or explain historical or geographical references in the text (thus his statements about Scythians and Amazons at Col 3:11). Polemical remarks hail errors of Paul's day as precedents of contemporary heresies and schisms. The opposed doctrines are characterized very cursorily, sometimes with moderate hostility or ridicule; often Ambrosiaster omits to name the author of the doctrine in question. These apologetic and polemical elements, however, do not threaten to overshadow the exegesis, for such digressions are mostly brief and create only temporary interruptions of the running paraphrase.

In sum, the formal elements of the Commentary reveal—as Giacomo Raspanti has argued—the relationship of the exegetical and pastoral aspects of Ambrosiaster's work. This is particularly apparent from the

---

52. See, e.g., In Rom. 1:3–4 and in the *argumentum* to Galatians.

53. Noted in Souter, *Study of Ambrosiaster*, 39–40.

54. Victorinus claimed to be writing a *commentatio simplex* and frequently excused himself for both making and not making fuller remarks. The presence of philosophical digressions in Victorinus's commentaries on Paul should not obscure this similarity with Ambrosiaster; see Cooper, *Marius Victorinus' Commentary on Galatians*, 241–46.

55. See, e.g., In Rom. 1:23 (§2); In Eph. 4:26; In Phil. 2:13–14.

alternation between the dominating paraphrase (which lends an objective quality to Paul's claims and statements) and the occasional breaks from this objective and impersonal presentation of Paul's world, in a dramatic turn through a first-person address to the exhortation of the audience.[56] The audience is included in the discourse, and "the text of Paul assumes the value of a living and contemporary *auctoritas*, immediate present and tangible in all it clarity and plainness."[57] This alteration in perspective between the world of Paul, as constructed through the paraphrase, and the contemporary world of the audience enables the "repositioning of the Pauline text to the contemporary needs of believers." The net effect, then, of the formal aspects of the commentaries is "to actualize and transform the exegesis into preaching, paraenesis, or polemics."[58] In his Commentary Ambrosiaster thus engages in "living catechesis,"[59] a task that required both a clear comprehension of what the apostle had written as well as an understanding of how his teachings were applicable as norms in the commentator's day.

---

56. Raspanti, "Aspetti formali," 525–26.
57. Ibid., 530.
58. Ibid., 532–33.
59. Ibid., 536.

5. Ambrosiaster's Theology

5.1. The Context

The Commentary presents itself as transmitting what Paul, the "teacher of the gentiles" (1 Tim 2:7),[1] taught about God, Christ, the gospel, faith, salvation, and the Christian way of life. Nonetheless, Ambrosiaster also interprets the topics of the apostle's discussion in light of the doctrinal and ecclesiastical developments in the three centuries that separated Paul from our anonymous commentator. Of particular import were the Trinitarian debates about the status of Christ in the period between the Council of Nicaea (325) and that of Constantinople in 381, which reauthorized the Nicene Creed in slightly modified form.[2] In the meantime a dispute about Christology broke out because of a suggestion proffered by Apollinaris of Laodicea (a supporter of the Nicene Creed) to account for the God-human union in the incarnation.[3] His "extreme version of the Word-flesh Christology" supposed the Logos to have taken the place of a human mind in Jesus, a view that became controversial after the Council of Alexandria in 362 and was officially condemned at Constantinople.[4] An additional point of dispute was the status of the Holy Spirit. This issue rose to prominence in the late 350s, when Athanasius in his four letters to Serapion denounced

---

1. Ambrosiaster frequently calls Paul *magister gentium* (e.g., In Rom. 1:14; 15:15; In 2 Cor. 10:7; In Gal. 2:8; 5:2.

2. Ambrosiaster wrote a treatise against those who opposed pro-Nicene theology in his *Quaest.* 97 (CSEL 50:171–87). For theological development under Damasus, see Theodore S. de Bruyn, "Ambrosiaster's Revisions of His *Commentary on Romans* and Roman Synodal Statements about the Holy Spirit," *REAug* 56 (2010): 47–56.

3. On Apollinaris, see Silke-Petra Bergjan, Benjamin Gleede, and Martin Heimgartner, eds., *Apollinarius und seine Folgen*, STAC 93 (Tübingen: Mohr Siebeck, 2015).

4. J. N. D. Kelly, *Early Christian Doctrines*, rev. ed. (San Francisco: Harper & Row, 1978), 291.

any who regarded the Spirit as a creature.[5] Opposition to such "Pneumatomachians" (later called "Macedonians"[6]) became "a new norm of orthodoxy" after the Synod of Alexandria in 362.[7] The Roman church's awareness of the various debates was keen in the late 370s (or early 380s), as is evident from a missive of Damasus to Eastern bishops.[8]

As a Roman presbyter, Ambrosiaster probably would have been familiar with these developments through documents connected to the Roman church in the years leading up to its engagement in the Council of Antioch of 379. These discussions prepared the ground for the Council of Constantinople. We are informed about this by synodal letters from Rome dating from the mid-370s, which make up a dossier called the *Exemplum synodi*. The documents of this collection—known as *Confidimus, Ea gratia, Illut sane*, and *Non nobis*[9]—all combat doctrinal deviations related to the Trinitarian controversy, in particular to erroneous views of the Holy Spirit. The second of these Roman letters, *Ea gratia*, states that "we confess even that the Holy Spirit, being uncreated, is of one majesty, of one *ousia*, of one power with God the Father and our Lord Jesus Christ." An even clearer anticipation of Constantinople occurs in the opening salvo of *Ea gratia*: "We all say with one voice that the Trinity is of one power [*unius virtutis*], one majesty, one divinity, one *ousia*, such that it is an indivisible power [*inseparabilem potestatem*]—but we do assert there are three persons."[10] A slightly later text of the Roman church, the *Tome of Damasus* (*Tomus*

---

5. For a translation of these letters with an introduction, see Mark DelCogliano, Andrew Radde-Gallwitz, and Lewis Ayres, *Works on the Spirit: Athanasius the Great and Didymus the Blind*, PPSer 43 (Yonkers, NY: St. Vladimir's Seminary Press, 2011).

6. Named after Macedonius, bishop of Constantinople, who was removed from office in 360 because of this controversy.

7. Wolf-Dieter Hauschild, "Geist/Heiliger Geist/Geistesgaben: IV Dogmengeschichtlich," TRE 12:200.

8. This letter is preserved in Theodoret, *Hist. eccl.* 5.10 (PG 82:1219–22); ET in James T. Shotwell and Louise Roper, eds., *The See of Peter* (New York: Columbia University Press, 1927), 673–74. Shotwell and Roper date this letter to 378, while Giuseppi L. Dossetti, *Il simbolo di Nicea e di Costantinopoli: Edizione critica* (Rome: Herder, 1967), 106, dates it to 379–382.

9. Contained in the late eighth-century Codex Veronensis LX (58). See Lester J. Field, ed., *On the Communion of Damasus and Meletius: Fourth-Century Synodal Formulae in the Codex Veronensis LX*, STPIMS 145 (Toronto: Pontifical Institute of Medieval Studies, 2004). For more recent discussion, see Ursula Reutter, *Damasus, Bischof von Rom (366–384): Leben und Werk* (Tübingen: Mohr Siebeck, 2009).

10. Field, *On the Communion*, 14–16 (lines 63–65 and 48–50, respectively; trans-

Damasi),[11] documents the Roman council of 382, which sought to implement the decisions of the council at Constantinople.[12] Both the creed of Constantinople and its affirmation at the Roman council framed themselves as reaffirmations of the Nicene Creed (hence the *Tome of Damasus* opens with a Latin translation of the Nicene Creed). The *Tome* denounces both older heresies as well as the more recent error, namely, those who "dare to say with sacrilegious mouth that the Holy Spirit was made through the Son."[13] Further anathemas excoriate other failures to recognize or properly articulate the full divinity of the Spirit. In language similar to that of *Ea gratia*, the *Tome* emphasizes the necessity of maintaining the distinctions of one and three: "anyone who will not say that there is one divinity, majesty, power, and dominion of the Father, Son, and Spirit … is a heretic.… If anyone will have said there are not three true persons of Father, Son, and Holy Spirit … he is a heretic."[14]

Ambrosiaster's revisions of his work recently have been shown to bear marks of their context in the doctrinal debates. Marie-Pierre Bussières has demonstrated how the pronouncements of the Roman council about the Holy Spirit influenced Ambrosiaster's revisions of some of the treatises in his *Quaestiones*.[15] We have likewise argued that the conciliar statements about the Spirit left traces in his Romans commentary (in *recensiones* β and

---

lations our own). Field dates *Ea gratia* to "after 374, and received by Meletius and his Antiochene synod by 379" (156).

11. Critical edition as appendix 7 in Cuthbert H. Turner and Eduard Schwartz, eds., *Ecclesiae occidentalis monumenta iuris antiquissima: Canonum et conciliorum Graecorum interpretationes Latinae* (Oxford: Clarendon, 1899), 1:281–96.

12. Discussion of dating in Field, *On the Communion*, 176–77, 185. For an overview of the development of pro-Nicene theology to the Council of Constantinople, see Lewis Ayres, "Articulating Identity," in *The Cambridge History of Early Christian Literature*, ed. Francis Young, Lewis Ayres, and Andrew Louth (Cambridge: Cambridge University Press, 2004), 436–43.

13. Turner and Schwartz, *Ecclesiae occidentalis monumenta*, 1:284–85 (lines 32–34).

14. Ibid., 1:290–91 (lines 111–23).

15. Bussières, "L'influence du synode tenu à Rome en 382 sur l'exégèse de l'Ambrosiaster," *SacEr* 45 (2006): 107–24, shows how the version of *Quaest.* 97 found in the collection of 127 questions was rewritten to accommodate "the valorization of the Spirit in the new symbol of faith proposed" at that Eastern council of 382 (120–21). See also Marie-Pierre Bussières, "L'esprit de Dieu et l'Esprit Saint dans les 'Questions sur l'Ancien et le Nouveau Testament' de l'Ambrosiaster," *REAug* 56 (2010): 25–44.

γ), as well as in the revision of comments on 1 Thess 3:9–10.[16] Yet there are reasons not to overestimate the influence of the contemporary context. As Coelestinus Martini pointed out, the theology of the Commentary reveals elements of more archaic patterns of Christian thought alongside the formulations of current orthodoxy.[17]

An aspect of Ambrosiaster's theology not dependent on the doctrinal controversies for its salience is his systematic recourse to the Pauline concept of "the mystery."[18] The Vetus Latina renders the Greek μυστήριον simply as the loanword *mysterium* (the Vulgate prefers *sacramentum*).[19] In classical and Hellenistic Greek the term referred to secret rites—"mysteries"—and by association, the objects used in connections with them. Paul's recourse to the term depends on apocalyptic use and refers to the revelation of what had been concealed in God (e.g., Dan 2:18).[20] Although Ambrosiaster uses the term in the plural in the *Quaestiones* to refer to pagan rites (*Quaest.* 84.3 [CSEL 50:145]) or the "deep things of God" (*Quaest.* 125.12, 16 [CSEL 50:389, 390]), it elsewhere appears in the singular, following Paul's own practice. Exceptionally, Ambrosiaster employs *mysterium* to refer to the sacraments (*mysterium eucharistiae*; In 1 Cor. 11:23–25), but otherwise his recourse to the term is almost entirely for the revelatory sense established in previous Latin exegesis on Paul. Marius Victorinus employed *mysterium* systematically to frame the entirety of salvation history relative to Christ as a history of the divine self-disclosure;[21] and the term similarly

---

16. De Bruyn, "Ambrosiaster's Revisions"; Stephen A. Cooper and David G. Hunter, "Ambrosiaster *redactor sui*: The Commentaries on the Pauline Epistles (Excluding Romans)," *REAug* 56 (2010): 84–86.

17. Coelestinus Martini (*Ambrosiaster: De auctore, operibus, theologia*, SPAA 4 [Rome: Pontificium Athenaeum Antonianum, 1944], 76, 92–96) notes that while Ambrosiaster is intent on defending the Nicene doctrine of consubstantiality, he lags behind the times in his account of the generation of the Word, remaining stuck at the level of the apologists.

18. The significance of this term for Ambrosiaster is noted by Juan Chapa Prado, "El comentario de Ambrosiaster a las epístolas de San Pablo," *EDST* 10 (1986): 53–62.

19. Ambrosiaster shows awareness that μυστήριον was also translated as *sacramentum*. See In 1 Cor. 2:10 (§1) and In Rom. 1:2 (§3).

20. Benjamin L. Gladd, *Revealing the Mysterion: The Use of Mystery in Daniel and Second Temple Judaism with Its Bearing on First Corinthians*, BZNW 160 (Berlin: de Gruyter, 2008).

21. For discussion, see Stephen A. Cooper, *Marius Victorinus' Commentary on Galatians: Introduction, Translation, and Notes*, OECS (Oxford: Oxford University Press, 2005), 253 n. 14. See also Victorinus's comments in the preface to his commen-

serves Ambrosiaster to signal the key elements of the faith that are revealed objects of knowledge.

5.2. The Mystery of the One God and the Mystery of the Trinity

Using a metaphor drawn from imperial Rome, Ambrosiaster saw the promotion of monotheism as part of Christ's mission:[22] "Just as an emperor asserts power over his kingdom through his soldiers, so too does the savior through us his servants defend the profession and practice of the one God" (In 2 Cor. 10:4). Unlike the philosophical elucidation of the nature of God in the opening treatise of Ambrosiaster's *Quaestiones* (a work titled "What Is God?"; *Quaest.* 1 [CSEL 50:13–17]),[23] his exegesis of the epistles makes only occasional use of the commonplaces of philosophical theology, which had long been melded with the God of the Bible by both Jews and Christians. The Commentary betrays an author disinclined to discuss the divine reality abstractly but ready to show how God is knowable in human experience even apart from Scripture or revelation. "The rigors of bodily existence" in the world of transient things, which are all in themselves "futile," can lead to understanding of "the mystery of the creator," in whose light the goodness of created things can be rightly used (In Rom. 8:20 [§1a]). Ambrosiaster explicitly grounds the authority of Scripture in its character as witness to the revelation of the mystery: "The scriptures are holy because they condemn faults and because in them is contained the mystery of the one God and the incarnation of the Son of God for the salvation of humankind, attested by miraculous signs" (In Rom. 1:2 [§3]). Paul's role in transmitting the mystery that has been revealed makes him "singular" (*singularis*) among the apostles and therefore "dubbed *a chosen vessel* (Acts 9:15) by divine judgment" (In 1 Cor. 2:10 [§1]).

---

tary on Ephesians, his remarks on Eph 1:4 and 6:19–21; ET: Cooper, *Metaphysics and Morals in Marius Victorinus' Commentary on the Letter to the Ephesians: A Contribution to the History of Neoplatonism and Christianity*, AUS 5.155 (New York: Lang, 1995), 43, 47–50, 112–13.

22. On Ambrosiaster's use of imperial imagery, see Sophie Lunn-Rockliffe, *Ambrosiaster's Political Theology*, OECS (Oxford: Oxford University Press, 2007), 44–49.

23. The title of the treatise in the collection of 127 questions is "What Is God?," but the version of the *Quaestiones* with 151 questions has the same treatise under the title "Concerning God and Free Will." Apart from §§1–2 (which treat the nature of God), the remainder of the treatise is devoted to the question of evil and free will.

The existence of God had always been an object of possible human knowledge through the evidence of creation, the natural law, and then the books of Moses.[24] As the growth of sin rendered humankind under collective condemnation, the inadequacy of these provisions became evident. From all eternity God had a more effective intervention in mind. The statement in Titus that "the saving grace of our God has shone upon all" elicits a telling comment: "The truth of the one God has been revealed in Christ, so that in a godly profession we may proclaim the creator in the unity of the Trinity" (In Titus 2:11 [§1]). Likewise Ambrosiaster refers to "the mystery of the one God … in Christ" (In Eph. 3:10 [§1]). Paul was sent to teach the gentiles this mystery "with a dual focus": to teach that Christ "is always in God" and that through him God made salvation available to gentiles "without circumcision and other commands of the law."[25]

Ambrosiaster speaks more generally of "the mystery of the Trinity" in pointing out how Paul's doxological greeting of Romans includes all three divine persons, even when the text does not do so explicitly. "In saying *Son of God*, he meant *of God the Father*, and with the addition of *the Spirit of sanctification* he displayed the mystery of the Trinity" (In Rom. 1:4 [§1]). The gospel is thus the revealing of "the mystery of God," which is Christ (In Rom. 1:1 [§5a]). The appropriate response to this revelation, as Ambrosiaster observes, is faith, which "removes the cloud of error and bestows perfect knowledge of God in the mystery of the Trinity, which had not been known by the ages" (In Rom. 2:28 [§2]). When the error of "the supposition of many gods" has been removed through the revelation of the divinity of Christ, humanity will be able to "adore the one God in Trinity" (In 2 Cor. 5:17). This revelation of Christ, Ambrosiaster is careful to specify, brings about a renewed proclamation of "the creator in the unity of the Trinity" (In Titus 2:11 [§1]).

More explicit traces of the fourth-century doctrinal controversies are the unmarked phrases from the Nicene Creed found throughout the Commentary. Ambrosiaster explains how Christ was "born, not made" (*non factus sed natus est*) (In Rom. 8:29 [§3]); he states that Christ is "God

---

24. Ambrosiaster gives an account of "natural law" as tripartite; see In Rom. 5:13 (§4). For the books of Moses, see Ambrosiaster's elucidations at In Rom. 1:18–19. Not just the Torah but the whole Hebrew Bible is, of course, regarded as prophetic by Ambrosiaster, even to the point of revealing the mystery of Christ, though this was only knowable after the fact; see his comments at In Rom. 1:2 (§3).

25. See his full discussion at In Eph. 3:9–11.

from God" (In Rom. 14:11).²⁶ The latter creedal phrase recurs in revised comments (In Eph. 1:17 [§2]).²⁷ Ambrosiaster also employs a number of formulations to express the ὁμοούσιον, which was translated variously in Latin. Marius Victorinus had suggested *consubstantialis* or *eiusdem substantiae*;²⁸ and the *Tome of Damasus* renders the term with *unius substantiae*.²⁹ Explaining how all things are "from him (i.e., God) and through him and in him" (Rom 11:36), Ambrosiaster invokes the controversial phrase: "Because they are from him, they began to exist through his Son, who is in truth of the same substance [*qui eiusdem utique substantiae est*] and whose work is the Father's work" (In Rom. 11:36 [§1]). He uses *substantia* as the functional equivalent to οὐσία to signal the common nature of the persons, as he states, "the Father and Son are one power and one divinity and substance" (In 2 Thess. 2:16–17).

Paul's references to the Father and the Son are the most frequent occasions for Ambrosiaster's Trinitarian elucidations. At the opening thanksgiving in 2 Cor 1:3 ("Blessed be the God and Father of our Lord Jesus Christ"), he remarks on the apostle's manner of writing: "In every letter he always transmits the order of the mystery as he comes to speak about God the Father, about his gift, and about his son, the Lord Jesus Christ.… Just as two things are mentioned, two would also be understood to exist, such that each would be considered a subsistent reality [*subsistens*], although they exist as a single substance." Parallel to the efforts of Greek theologians, Ambrosiaster sought coherent language to distinguish the individual reality of the persons through the term *subsistens* (= ὑπόστασις, in the later technical sense)³⁰ from that which is one (the divine *substantia* or οὐσία). Discussing the "one God" and "one mediator" of 1 Tim 2,

---

26. The language corresponds to the Latin translation of the Nicene Creed found in the *Tome of Damasus*: *natum non factum*.

27. *Recensio* γ.

28. See Marius Victorinus's Trinitarian treatises for this usage: *On the Homoousion* 2: *Recte dicitur eiusdem esse substantiae, hoc est ὁμοούσιον* (CSEL 83.1:280). In *Ar.* 4.14 (CSEL 83.1:245), Victorinus observes how *homoousion* can be expressed by *consubstantialis* or *eiusdem substantiae*.

29. Turner and Schwartz, *Ecclesiae occidentalis monumenta*, 1:283.

30. For the conscious shift made by Greek theologians away from the usage of *hypostasis* as synonymous with *ousia*, see Khaled Anatolios, "Discourse on the Trinity," in *Constantine to c. 600*, ed. Augustine Casiday and Frederick W. Norris, vol. 2 of *The Cambridge History of Christianity* (Cambridge: Cambridge University Press, 2007), 439–41.

he distinguishes the person while referring to the divine substance as a single nature: "Father and Son are one not in respect of their person but in respect of their indistinguishable nature [sed indifferenti natura]" (In 1 Tim. 2:5 [§1]). Likewise his comments on 2 Cor 5:18b–21 ("It is God who through Christ reconciled us to himself etc.") draw on both substance and relation language for the Trinity:

> Because their substance is one [una substantia], the Father is understood to be in the Son. For where there is no differentiating factor [nulla est differentia], there exists unity. And that is why they are mutually related [ac per hoc invicem sunt], since there is one image and one likeness of them, such that one who sees the Son would be said to have seen the Father, just as the Lord himself states: *One who has seen me has also seen the Father* (John 14:9). (In 2 Cor. 5:18–21 [§2])

A similar discussion of the Father-Son relation recurs in Ambrosiaster's comments on Col 1, which also incorporate language of seeing from the Fourth Gospel. Apropos of the statement that Christ is "the image of the invisible God," he clarifies that the "seeing" by which one sees the Father through the Son is not "with their fleshly eyes" but "by their understanding [intellectu] of his divine works" (In Col. 1:15 [§3]). The coordination of Pauline and Johannine utterances in a number of such doctrinally oriented passages is a significant element of Ambrosiaster's attempt to create a solid scriptural foundation for pro-Nicene theology. The Commentary, however, does not replicate the thoroughness of Ambrosiaster's *Quaestiones* in treating these issues.[31]

Ambrosiaster emphasizes the Holy Spirit as a fully divine member of the Trinity at numerous passages, although the Commentary's latest recension (*recensio* γ) contains many more such references than the earlier version(s). As noted above, Ambrosiaster's comments on 1 Thess 3:9–10 (§2) in *recensio* α make no mention of the Holy Spirit, but the later recension shows an expansion on these remarks with an additional comment on

---

31. See particularly the treatise *Quaest.* 122, "De principio," where he engages with the creedal phrase *deus de deo* in light of the first two verses of the Johannine Prologue and a number of Pauline passages (1 Cor 1:24 and Col 1:15–16). "The gospels of the apostles John and Paul agree," he states, "for they are saying the same things: that the Son God was begotten before any creation in order to create the spiritual powers and the world and the things that are visible in it" (CSEL 50:369).

the Trinity aimed at clarifying the equal rank of the Spirit.[32] In this comment Ambrosiaster is most explicit about the need for appropriate Trinitarian distinctions:

> There is one way to discuss the nature of the Father and the Son, and there is another way to discuss the persons. The Father is Unbegotten, but the Son is Begotten. In respect to the persons, there is distinction, although the unity of nature is undivided. For the unity exists not in person, but in substance. But the Holy Spirit is not considered as inferior because he is ranked third.

Although it has become clear to Ambrosiaster that language about the nature of God is different from that required for discussions of the persons, he struggles to articulate abstractly what in the persons—that is, in the distinct *persona* of each—is the basis of their differentiation. At Eph 2:3 he gives some thought to the problem as it emerges in his reflections about "God" as a name or term (*nomen*): "Nonetheless, there is this distinction between the Father and the Son: that the Father receives this name from no-one; the Son, however, receives all things from the Father through his being begotten [*per generationem*], so that the Son differs in nothing from the Father in terms of power, substance, and name." Following a path laid down in Latin theology by Tertullian,[33] Ambrosiaster locates the distinction between Father and Son in the divine begetting, which is what ensures the Son's full inheritance of all that God is and does. Ambrosiaster has not achieved the clarity of the Cappadocian solution—where the terms indicating what is particular (ἰδίωμα) to the persons do not designate substance but signify the nature of the relation (σχέσις) between the persons[34]—to the point of articulating the Spirit's peculiar mode of relationship to the other person as that of "processing." Rather, his account of the Holy Spirit simply

---

32. See In 1 Thess. 3:9–10 (§2) and related notes.
33. Lewis Ayres, *Nicaea and Its Legacy: An Approach to Fourth-Century Trinitarian Theology* (Oxford: Oxford University Press, 2004), 74 (citing Tertullian, *Prax.* 8).
34. Sergey A. Chursanov, "'That They May Be One, as We Are': The Significance of the Cappadocian Fathers' Trinitarian Comprehension of Divine Persons for the Theological Understanding of the Constitutive Features of Human Persons," *IJOT* 2 (2011): 42. Chursanov cites Gregory of Nazianzus's classical statement of the distinction in *Orat. paneg.* 29 (= *Third Theological Oration* §16; ET: Edward Hardy, *Christology of the Later Fathers*, LCC 3 [Philadelphia: Westminster, 1954], 171).

insists on the fully divine nature of the Spirit, as in his comment on 2 Cor 5:4, where he states that the Holy Spirit "in substance is Christ."[35]

In line with his arguments grounded in the Fourth Gospel, which present the common action of Father and Son as proof of their unity, Ambrosiaster asserts the same as regards the Holy Spirit. The Spirit's activity is evidence that the Father is "in the Holy Spirt" (In Rom. 11:36 [§2]). The Holy Spirit, moreover, is the Spirit of both Father and Son[36]—the idea of the *filioque* is foreign to him, as Langen noted[37]—and this too is an argument for their identity of substance and nature. His comments at Eph 3:17 ("for Christ to dwell in your hearts through faith") effectively synthesize Pauline and Johannine passages to promulgate a scriptural basis for recent pro-Nicene positions articulating the distinction between the *personae* of the Trinity and the divine *natura* (πρόσωπον and φύσις, in contemporary Greek theology):

> We should have no doubt that Christ dwells in us, through the Spirit, obviously. For the Spirit is *another Advocate* (John 14:26), between whom and Christ there is a difference of persons, not of nature, because the Spirit receives what is of Christ (see John 16:14) and is sent forth from God.[38] Those realities whose unity belongs to their nature are mutually related to each other.[39] That is the sense of the Lord's saying: *All that the Father has is mine, and what is mine is of the Father* (John 16:15). (In Eph. 3:17 [§§2–3])

While Ambrosiaster does not cite in the Commentary any Johannine passages mentioning the Paraclete, that title features in his explication of the closing doxology in Romans. Although it was only at the time of Christ that "the mystery … hidden in God was proclaimed," believers must understand that "both the Word and the Paraclete are with him from eternity" (In Rom. 16:25–27 [§1]).

---

35. See In 1 Cor. 12:6 (§1) and In 2 Cor. 5:4.

36. See his comments at In 1 Cor. 2:11 (§2); In 2 Cor. 1:21 (§2); and In Gal. 4:6.

37. Joseph Langen, "De commentariorum in epistulas Paulinas qui Ambrosii et quaestionum biblicarum quae Augustini nomine feruntur scriptore dissertatio" (PhD diss., Bonn, 1880), 9.

38. Similar formulation in *Quaest.* 125.5 (CSEL 50:386).

39. See In 2 Cor. 5:18–21 (§§1–2) for similar language about the Father and Son. See *Quaest.* 122.12 (CSEL 50:369) for another formulation of this relational understanding of the Trinity.

5.3. The Mystery of Christ

Many passages of the Commmentary contain formulations relating to the debates about the person of Christ in the period leading up to the Council of Constantinople in 381.[40] Martini has maintained that Ambrosiaster (at In Rom. 1:3 and In Phil. 2:10) anticipates the centerpiece of the creed of Chalcedon (451)—the doctrine of hypostatic union—even if Ambrosiaster has not quite formulated its "two natures" stipulation.[41] Concerns about Christ needing to have a full human nature had already been part of the front against Apollinaris's truncation of Jesus's humanity. Yet Ambrosiaster retained some exegetical independence of this context. As Desmond Foley, author of the fullest study in English on Ambrosiaster's Christology, has observed, the anonymous commentator "believes in the unity of Christ and in his divinity and humanity, but he does not seem to feel the need to involve himself in the terminology being worked out by his contemporaries to deal with the problem."[42]

Ambrosiaster's defense of Christ as fully human and fully divine appears first in the commentary on Romans, in his remarks on Paul's opening declaration about himself as a "slave of Jesus Christ" (Rom 1:1). The question concerns what is signified by the names "Jesus" and "Christ," and why they appear sometimes together and sometimes apart. In Paul's epistolary greeting, the apostle "referred to both names of Jesus Christ in order to indicate the person of both God and the human being, since the Lord is present in both." According to Ambrosiaster, this greeting in the twofold name "Jesus Christ," on the one hand, excludes the Christology of Marcion (which denied the reality of Christ's body), and on the other, confounds

---

40. As Wilhelm Mundle, *Die Exegese der paulinischen Briefe im Kommentar des Ambrosiaster* (Marburg: Schaaf, 1919), 36, has observed, Ambrosiaster "does not shy away from digressions, and in the case of difficult christological questions and polemics he allows himself to be led into lengthy elucidations."

41. Martini, *Ambrosiaster: De auctore*, 114. Martini refers to the critical Chalcedonian formulation as *de duobus naturis*. Critical scholarship has subsequently established the better reading to be ἐν δύο φύσεσιν; see Jaroslav Pelikan and Valerie Hotchkiss, eds., *Creeds and Confessions of Faith in the Christian Tradition* (New Haven: Yale University Press, 2003), 1:173.

42. Desmond Foley, "The Christology of Ambrosiaster—I," *MilS* 39 (1997): 28. See also Desmond Foley, "The Christology of Ambrosiaster—II," *MilS* 40 (1997): 31–52. On this topic see also Alessandra Pollastri, *Ambrosiaster, commento alla Lettera ai Romani: Aspetti cristologici*, CTSt (L'Aquila: Japadre, 1977), 64–105.

"the Jews" and Photinus,[43] who deny his divine nature. But what if the double name is lacking in a mention of Christ? Ambrosiaster formulates a rule that allows context to determine each case: "Whenever scripture says either Jesus or Christ, it sometimes means the person of God, sometimes the person of the human being" (In Rom. 1:1 [§§2–3]).

Other Pauline references to the double name "Jesus Christ" find similar explanation. Ambrosiaster comments on the statement in Rom 1:3 that Christ was "from the seed of David according to the flesh" so as to elaborate the explanation offered at Rom 1:1 and also to correlate the epistolary text with the incarnational elements of the Johannine prologue:

> He says that he who was Son of God according to the Holy Spirit—that is, according to God, because God is spirit (see John 4:24) and is undoubtedly holy—was made Son of God according to the flesh from Mary, as in the verse: *And the Word was made flesh* (John 1:14). As a result, there is now one Son of both God and a human being, Christ Jesus, so that just as he is true God, so also was he a true human being. He will not, however, be a true human being unless he is made of flesh and soul, so as to be complete. (In Rom. 1:3 [§2])[44]

Here is a clear rejection of anything resembling the "Word-flesh" Christology of Apollinaris. Christ possessed a complete human nature, although Ambrosiaster carefully insists elsewhere that his being "true God" and "true human being" does not detract from the unity of the person Jesus. Thus, he states that "since the Son of God is the same one [*idem*] as the Son of Man and is said to be both Jesus and Christ, he is called by two names so that he would be signified to be both man and God" (In 2 Tim. 4:22). Other passages similarly emphasize the unity of the person of Jesus.[45]

The question of Christ's birth from Mary, however, is only one facet of the "mystery concerning Christ"—a mystery on account of the fact that "what became incarnate had been hidden from the ages in God" (In 1 Cor. 2:1–2 [§§1–2]). Elsewhere in the Commentary Ambrosiaster also refers to the incarnation as a "mystery" (In 2 Cor. 11:26 [§1]).[46] The Christ-hymn

---

43. See below §6.3.
44. This is one of the passages regarded by Martini as illustrating Ambrosiaster's anticipation of the hypostatic union.
45. See the discussion by Foley, "Christology of Ambrosiaster—I," 36–37.
46. See also In Phil. 1:8.

of Phil 2:5–11, a passage of the greatest interest among patristic exegetes,[47] elicits from Ambrosiaster extensive discussion of many questions surrounding this mystery. His remarks on this pericope involve greater digression than usual from the strict analysis of the text, whether for the sake of pro-Nicene pleas for the full divinity of Christ or to treat issues pertaining more specifically to the relation between the human and divine natures in Christ.[48] Here we attend briefly to the some of the latter.

Ambrosiaster's concern for correct christological teaching is evident in his worry about the potential of some parts of the passage to be misinterpreted, particularly Phil 2:7, with its ambiguous phrasing: "But he emptied himself, taking the form of a slave, made in human likeness and found in the human condition." The expressions "likeness" and "like a human being" could suggest the incarnate Christ did not possess a full human nature. Clearing up this potentially troublesome language requires the right understanding of the opening of the passage. What does it mean that Jesus "was in the form of God" (Phil 2:6)?

> The Son of God born as a man was *in the form of God* in this way: although he appeared a human being, he was doing the works of a god. One thought to be only a human being seemed to be a god in the things he did. His works indicated his form.... What is the form of God, except a concrete instance of God's appearance in raising the dead, giving hearing to the deaf, cleansing lepers, and the rest? Why then is he said to have been made like a human being, if he was just human all along? And what is the reason he was discovered to be *human in condition*, if he were not also God? (In Phil. 2:7–8 [§§4–5])

Only of one who was so clearly like a god in power does it make sense to speak of as being "made like" a human being. Here Ambrosiaster notably has rejected the dominant patristic exegesis that "taking the form of a slave" meant the assumption of human nature by the preexistent Logos. Ambrosiaster and Pelagius were exceptional in arguing that it is precisely

---

47. See Paul Henry, "Kénose," *DBSup* 5:7–161.

48. His exegesis of these six verses takes up seven pages of the CSEL edition; by contrast, the comments on the preceding thirty-four verses of that letter cover fewer than ten pages. See especially his comments at In Phil. 2:9–11, for pro-Nicene pleas for the full divinity of Christ.

the incarnate Christ who was "in the form of God" (Ambrosiaster, In Phil. 2:7–8 [§2]; Pelagius, In Phil. 2:5–8).⁴⁹

Ambrosiaster's way of warding off potential christological errors lurking beneath the words "in the likeness" is also idiosyncratic:

> Paul speaks of him as being like a human being to make this point: that he was also God. He is saying that Christ was a god who was made like human beings in respect of weakness. He expresses this in what follows, saying: *He humbled himself and became obedient to the point of death, even death on a cross.* From here one may deduce the sense of his being discovered to be *human in condition*. Withholding his power so that it would not be apparent in him, the one who knows no death was killed and seemed like a human being. (In Phil. 2:6–7 [§6])

Just as "in the form of God" means one who appeared divine in his works, so too his being found "human in condition" signifies Jesus's apparent subjection to mortality. While Christ was truly human, his death for Ambrosiaster was something he willingly embraced, not a fate he was compelled to share with all humanity. As Foley has noted, the identity of the preexistent Christ with the incarnate one is the central feature of Ambrosiaster's interpretation of the Christ-hymn, for it means that Christ "can act in both capacities, consecutively, as man and as God."⁵⁰ It is in this dual capacity that Christ can save, that is, impart the immortality his own human nature received in virtue of his divinity. It is in this regard, according to Ambrosiaster, that "the whole mystery ... of God's revelation [*omne mysterium sacramenti dei*] lies in Christ. For he is the one in relation to whom all creatures will perish unless they have placed hope in him" (In Col. 2:1–3 [§2]).

---

49. Henry, "Kenose," 124. Pelagius thinks the dominant interpretation is insufficiently anti-Arian; the self-emptying refers not to his divine nature but to his services rendered, such as foot washing. Martini cites Hilary, *Trin.* 10.22, as an exegete whom Ambrosiaster may have had in mind (*Ambrosiaster: De auctore*, 115 n. 3). See also Marius Victorinus on this verse, who suggested a number of interpretive options (CSEL 83.2:188–89).

50. Foley, "Christology of Ambrosiaster—I," 36–37.

5.4. The Mystery of the Cross

The aim of God's work in Christ is to ameliorate the situation of human beings under the reign of sin.[51] This work was necessitated by the fact that most people between Adam and Moses "sinned after the manner of Adam's transgression"—Ambrosiaster's biblical text at Rom 5:14 lacks the negative particle[52]—and because the law given through Moses had only limited success in inhibiting the reign of death, even among Jews. Those who lived before the law were responsible for their sins. As the apostle said to the Romans, the creator can be grasped from creation: "God made a thing that, in being visible, plainly shows its maker" (In Rom. 1:19). Human beings are accordingly accountable for their willful ignorance and its consequences (In Rom. 1:20). Idolatry, Ambrosiaster maintains in accordance with early Christian tradition, is both the result of the first sin and the cause of later sins,[53] for the worship of idols is a sure indication of a lack of hope in the true God, the creator (In 1 Cor. 10:14). This vision of sinful humanity underlies Ambrosiaster's conception of salvation. Christ's death on the cross is redemptive for sinners, who merit not only the common death of the body inherited from Adam's sin but also eternal death after the final judgment.[54]

Ambrosiaster incorporated the connection Paul had forged in Rom 5:12–21 between Adam and Christ into his soteriology and Christology. Although Jesus's human nature is derived from his human birth from the Virgin, it was a special human birth involving the transmission of a complete human nature apart from the normal means of conception.[55] His explanation of Paul's phrase that the Son was "in the likeness of the flesh of sin" (Rom 8:3) elucidates the point: "The likeness of the flesh consists in this: although his flesh is the same as ours, it nevertheless was not formed in the womb and born in the same way our flesh is. It was sanctified in the

---

51. See Juan B. Valero, "Pecar en Adán según Ambrosiaster," *EE* 65 (1990): 147–91.

52. See In Rom. 5:14 (and the accompanying notes) for his lengthy defense of this reading and its meaning.

53. He discusses this in numbers of passage of his commentary on Romans: In Rom. 1:29–32 (§1a); 5:14 (§§2 and 4d); 6:6.

54. In Rom. 1:16 (§2): "those who have been signed with the mystery of the cross cannot be held by the second death."

55. For the components of which, see Pollastri, *Ambrosiaster, commento alla Lettera ai Romani: Aspetti cristologici*, 51–63.

womb and born without sin, and besides, he did not sin in it" (In Rom. 8:3 [§1]). Christ's sinlessness is necessary for the salvation of those who "all sinned in Adam as in a lump" (*quasi in massa*). The word *massa* comes to Ambrosiaster from his text of the Pauline Letters, where it renders φύραμα ("mixture," as of dough). Paul had exploited the metaphorical senses of φύραμα (Rom 9:21; 11:16; 1 Cor 5:6; Gal 5:9), and Ambrosiaster expanded it in a way that caught Augustine's eye.[56]

Ambrosiaster's interpretation of this Pauline image must be understood in the fuller soteriological framework. Romans 5:12 elicits from him the crucial remarks: "All sinned in Adam as in a lump [*quasi in massa*]. Once he was corrupted by sin, those he begat were all born under sin. All sinners, therefore, derive from him, because we are all from him" (In Rom. 5:12 [§3]).[57] Yet, as Ambrosiaster observes, the Bible makes it clear that there were people who pleased God before the law was given, just as there were some who were righteous under the law (In Rom. 5:14 [§§3a and 4a]; see also 5:17 [§1]). These righteous people of the pre-Mosaic period who did not sin like Adam, along with those who adhered to the law faithfully after it was given, will all be held in "house arrest" postmortem in the underworld as they await judgment (In Rom. 5:14 [§3a]). From Adam they inherited death—it was communicated to all *quasi in massa*—but not the "second death" (In Rom. 5:12 [§§1, 4]), the "punishments of the underworld" reserved for those who do not repent and persist in sinning (In Rom. 4:25 [§2]). The "title of inheritance" (In Rom. 8:12 [§1]) of the first death brings corruption of the body, which eventually entails "the separation of the soul from the body" (In Rom. 5:12 [§3]). The punishments of both deaths thus make up an "inheritance of transgression." It is this Christ came to purify people from, so that they may be relieved of their sins and able to "resist the adversary" with God's help (In Rom. 7:24 [§1a]).[58] As Alessandra Pollastri has explained, Ambrosiaster's idea of the transmission

---

56. For discussion, see Pier Franco Beatrice, *The Transmission of Sin: Augustine and the Pre-Augustinian Sources*, trans. Adam Kamesar, American Academy of Religion Religions in Translation (Oxford: Oxford University Press, 2013), and the notes to the translation ad loc.

57. See the notes there.

58. See his treatment of this issue in *Quaest.* 112.8, "On Psalm 50," where Ambrosiaster explains what human beings inherited from Adam's sin, "so that all people born from him through propagation, all people would be liable to sin" (CSEL 50:290). See the full discussion of this in Pollastri, *Ambrosiaster, commento alla Lettera ai Romani: Aspetti cristologici*, 106–45.

of sin does not entail a full "traducianist" notion. What is passed down from Adam to all humanity is simply the tendency of the body to decay, leading inevitably toward physical death. The sin of Adam's soul is not transmitted to posterity "because the soul does not exist *de traduce*,[59] and, moreover, the free choice of the will lies in the human soul."[60] One does not find here a doctrine of original sin such as appears in Augustine and afterwards; what Ambrosiaster wants to affirm with his metaphor of all humanity sinning *quasi in massa* is that "there is a real and universal relation between Adam and the sinful human race."[61]

There also exists in Ambrosiaster's theology a potentially real and universal relation between Christ and humanity. In a brief but seminal article, Vít Hušek has recently shown that the central structure of Ambrosiaster's soteriology involves a *duplex gratia*, both heads of which are deeply anchored in the apostle's own presentations of the matter.[62] The phrase occurs in remarks on Eph 1:7 ("In him we have redemption through his blood, the forgiveness of sins"): "He presses us to understand that the grace is two-fold, since Christ has both redeemed us by his own blood and not imputed our sins to us, that is, has redeemed us and signed our bill of release from slavery [*redemit et manumisit*]" (In Eph. 1:7). Redemption, then, is distinct from nonimputation of sins (see In Eph. 1:9 [§1]); taken together, they make up the *duplex gratia*. Ambrosiaster conceives the dual aspect of grace somewhat differently in commenting on Rom 1:1, where the forgiveness of sins is distinguished from becoming "children of God" (In Rom. 1:1 [§5a]).

The distinction Ambrosiaster draws at Eph 1:7 between redemption and manumission—a "buying back" and a "setting free"—is central to his soteriology and relates to the key Pauline notions of justification and atonement. Ambrosiater's comments at Rom 3:24 illustrate the relation between these distinct ideas. The passage notably contains the phrase *sola fide* ("by

---

59. The phrase *de traduce* could be translated somewhat expansively as "from a continuous line of physical transmission."

60. Pollastri, *Ambrosiaster, commento alla Lettera ai Romani: Aspetti cristologici*, 112. Ambrosiaster's emphasis on "the free choice of the will" as being innate to the mind (*animus*) occurs only in *recensio* γ of his comments at In Rom. 7:22.

61. Thus Valero, "Pecar en Adán," 153.

62. Vít Hušek, "*Duplex gratia*: Ambrosiaster and the Two Aspects of His Soteriology," in *Für uns und für unser Heil: Soteriologie in Ost und West*, ed. Th. Hainthaler et al., ProOr 37 (Innsbruck-Vienna: Tyrolia Verlag, 2014), 51–59.

faith alone") as an explication of justification and also illustrates the exegete's adherence to what in the history of atonement theology has been called the "fish-hook" theory.[63] Ambrosiaster breaks up the verse into two parts to highlight justification and redemption as discrete and sequenced elements. The order of these elements in the verse appears to be contrary to the order in which they transpire:

> *They are justified freely through his grace.* They are justified freely because they are sanctified by faith alone as a gift of God; they do nothing and render nothing in return. *Through the redemption which is in Christ Jesus.* The apostle bears witness that the grace of God is *in Christ* because by the will of God we have been redeemed by Christ so that we, having been set free, might be justified, as the apostle also says to the Galatians: *Christ has redeemed us by offering himself for us* (Gal 3:13). For he surrendered himself to the raging devil, who, however, did not know what was coming. (In Rom. 3:24)

Believers are "justified" after Christ "redeemed us"; redemption is the first aspect of grace by which the devil lost his hold on guilty humanity. Unlike later "satisfaction" theories of atonement that rejected the notion of justice regulating God's dealing with the devil,[64] Ambrosiaster's theory follows from his premise that God does no injustice, not even against the devil. This is clear in his comment on the "powers and principalities" of Col 2:13–15, which Paul says Christ triumphed over on the cross. These powers are not human rulers but the devil's "henchmen" (*satellites*) and lords of the underworld:

---

63. See Dongsun Cho, "Ambrosiaster on Justification by Faith Alone in His Commentaries on the Pauline Epistles," *WTJ* 74 (2012): 277–90; see also Daniel H. Williams, "Justification by Faith: A Patristic Doctrine," *JEH* (2006): 649–67; Robert B. Eno, "Some Patristic Views on the Relationship of Faith and Works in Justification," *RechAug* 19 (1984): 3–27; Gustaf Aulén, *Christus Victor: An Historical Study of the Three Main Types of the Idea of Atonement*, trans. A. G. Hebert (New York: Macmillan, 1969), 52. Gregory of Nyssa coined the metaphor of Christ as the bait on a fishhook taken by the devil (Aulén cites Nyssa's *Great Catechism*, §24; ET: Hardy, *Christology of the Later Fathers*, 301). Augustine preferred the metaphor of the "mouse trap" (*muscipula*) in *Serm.* 130 (PL 38:726).

64. The classical formulation is that of Anselm, *Cur Deus homo* 1.7, which explicitly rejects the patristic "ransom" theory.

> The cross signifies not the death of the Savior but the death of sin. An innocent who is killed in this way renders guilty [*reos*] those by whom he is killed. We should, however, understand "sin" to refer to the princes and powers, through whose effort Adam first sinned. For the term "sin" is to be referred to its authors, whose death the apostle indicates by their despoiling. The death of these princes and powers consists in this: that, having been conquered by the Savior, they are put to death when they are despoiled of the souls which they were holding in captivity. (In Col. 2:13–15 [§6])[65]

Christ's work of redemption is thus objectively accomplished by the divine for humanity and suffices to remove humans from the grip of the devil and death.

Being "justified freely," as his remarks at Rom 3:24 quoted above suggest, seems on the one hand to refer to the entire process of grace: being "sanctified by faith alone ... they do nothing and render nothing in return." On the other hand, the same comments present justification as entailing a second phase subsequent to the redemption: "so that we, having been set free, might be justified." That this latter aspect of grace involves human cooperation is evident from Ambrosiaster's remarks on 2 Cor 5:19, which clarify how people are reconciled to God after having been freed from the devil's clutches:

> Because all the things God had made through Christ had by error become fallen, forgetful of their own creator, God Almighty, the progenitor of Christ, thought it right for Christ our Lord to come from his holy seat to the things of earth; he was made from flesh, in the human manner, so that he might be an example [*forma*] for human beings how they might make God, their own creator, be at peace with them. (In 2 Cor. 5:18–21 [§1])

Human freedom is thus an essential part of the process, as Hušek has elsewhere argued. To believe (*credere*), Ambrosiaster emphatically states, is an act of the will that cannot be compelled but only urged.[66] But it is not only believing that requires human cooperation. The gradual reconstruction of sinners in the wake of this twofold grace is something in which the

---

65. *Recensio* γ. *Recensio* α (§3) contains the same idea but with less elaboration.
66. Vít Hušek, "Human Freedom according to the Earliest Latin Commentaries on Paul's Letters," StPatr 44 (2010): 288–89. Hušek cites In Rom. 4:4 for Ambrosiaster's notion of belief as a free act; see Victorinus on Eph 6:13 (CSEL 83.2:87).

Holy Spirit, given in baptism, plays an essential role.[67] Humans are now empowered by the Spirit to struggle more effectively against the flesh (In Rom. 8:13 [§2]). As debtors grateful for being relieved of the burden of a crushing sin-debt, believers are now obligated to "keep the law of Christ" and so "render service to the redeemer" (In Rom. 8:12).[68] In the "mystery of love," the divine persuasion leads humans to play their part in the restoration of humanity through the "love of Christ surpassing knowledge." This active love, as he says at Eph 3:19 ("that for the sake of humankind, even God would be born as a human being and then die for the sake of human beings"), obligates humans henceforth to serve God. Ambrosiaster does not treat this service as sufficient in itself or outside the mercy of divine grace: "we ... are by no means able to pay our debts, even if we maintain our faith in him until the day of our death" (In Eph. 3:19 [§2]). In maintaining that grace always precedes and makes possible appropriate human responses that contribute to justification, Ambrosiaster's theology is a doctrine of grace.[69] His way of correlating God's grace and human activity, at any rate, falls within the range of models developed by modern scholarship for understanding how Paul himself understood this point of theology.[70]

---

67. Hušek, "*Duplex gratia*," 157.

68. Yet Ambrosiaster can also insist that "as long as one has faith in God and in Christ one is just" (In Rom. 3:26 [§3]). This remark is made in explanation of Hab 2:4.

69. For a critique of the line of scholarship that reads Ambrosiaster anachronistically as a pathway to Pelagius, see Cho, "Ambrosiaster on Justification," 278–81. See also Josef Jäntsch, "Führt der Ambrosiaster zu Augustinus oder Pelagius?," *Schol* 15 (1939): 92–99.

70. John M. G. Barclay and Simon J. Gathercole, eds., *Divine and Human Agency in Paul and His Cultural Environment*, ECC/LNTS 335 (London: T&T Clark, 2006), 6–7.

6. Polemical Aspects of the Commentary

It is unsurprising that in the Commentary Ambrosiaster frequently casts aspersion on the beliefs and practices of pagans, Jews, and heretical Christians, when the Pauline epistles themselves regularly engage on similar fronts. His authorial voice reveals the stance of one fully intent on Paul's program of clarifying the truth of the gospel through the refutation and rebuke of erroneous views and practices. Ambrosiaster's relatively lengthy *argumenta* to the commentaries on Romans and 1 Corinthians present Paul as chiefly preoccupied with problems of diversity internal to the church, despite his concerns about potential opponents *ad extra*, pagans and unbelieving Jews. Ambrosiaster's normative program seems likewise largely internally directed. The Commentary as well as the *Quaestiones*, Emanuele Di Santo has argued, have a chief apologetic aim: "to present the authentic Christian doctrine by distinguishing it from paganism, Judaism, and from contemporary heterodox groups of Christians."[1] Ambrosiaster doubtless would affirm this formulation, but modern scholars also see in the Commentary the attempt—as Andrew Jacobs has argued—"to deploy the apostle in order to construct more careful boundaries against the religious 'others' of his day, particularly 'pagans,' heretics, and Jews."[2] The Commentary itself betrays no sense on the author's part of blurred boundaries in his time between Christians, Jews, and pagans, but Ambrosiaster's "rhetoric of difference"[3] may obscure areas of shared life with those whom he identies as religiously other.

---

1. Emanuele Di Santo, *L'Apologetica dell'Ambrosiaster: Cristiani, pagani e giudei nella Roma tardoantica*, SEAug 112 (Rome: Institutum Patristicum Augustinianum, 2008), 9.

2. Andrew S. Jacobs, "A Jew's Jew: Paul and the Early Christian Problem of Jewish Origins," *JR* 86 (2006): 265.

3. Sophie Lunn-Rockliffe, *Ambrosiaster's Political Theology*, OECS (Oxford: Oxford University Press, 2007), 41.

6.1. Pagans

There have been several recent studies of Ambrosiaster's views of the cults, practices, and beliefs of his pagan contemporaries, a subject of remarks throughout the Commentary and the *Quaestiones* and the focus of two long *quaestiones*, one "Against the Pagans" (*Quaest.* 114 [SC 512:116–52]), the other "On Fate" (*Quaest.* 115 [SC 512:154–232]).[4] "Pagan" (*paganus*)—today a problematic term for many scholars of ancient religion because of its pejorative connotations—is in fact a word Ambrosiaster uses for participants in the traditional cults of his day; he also uses "gentiles" (*gentiles, gentes*) and related terms (e.g., *gentilitas*) derived from language for non-Jews in Pauline discourse.[5] Needless to say, Ambrosiaster's views of pagans are prevailingly negative. Still, it is worth noting what he does—and does not—say, as well as the impetus for his remarks, whether issuing from the Pauline text or elsewhere.

In the Commentary, Ambrosiaster does not dwell at length on contemporary cults in Rome, though he does occasionally mention specific cults. Sometimes he appears to be drawing mainly on literary sources. Commenting on Rom 1:22–23, where Paul says that people "changed the glory of the incorruptible God into the likeness of an image of a corruptible human being and of birds and four-footed animals and serpents," Ambrosiaster observes that people do not simply deify dead heroes but also create images of them to worship (In Rom. 1:23 [§1]), and then he offers a few examples of human and nonhuman gods: Bel and the dragon in Babylonia, the bull Apis and many other animals in Egypt, and the raven (with

---

4. "On Fate" is addressed, in fact, to Christians. For recent studies, see Joachim Stüben, "Das Heidentum im Spiegel von Heilsgeschichte und Gesetz: Ein Versuch über das Bild der Paganitas im Werk des Ambrosiaster" (ThD diss., Universität Hamburg, 1990); Marie-Pierre Bussières, introduction to *Ambrosiaster: Contre les païens (Question sur l'Ancien et le Nouveau Testament 114) et Sur le destin (Question sur l'Ancien et le Nouveau Testament 115)*, ed. Marie-Pierre Bussières, SC 512 (Paris: Cerf, 2007), 50–96; Di Santo, *L'Apologetica*, esp. 112–72. Prior studies include Franz Cumont, "La polémique de l'Ambrosiaster contre les païens," *RHLR* 8 (1903): 417–40, and Pierre Courcelle, "Critiques exégétiques et arguments antichrétiens rapportés par Ambrosiaster," *VC* 13 (1959): 133–69.

5. Stüben, "Das Heidentum," 15–17. For an overview of terms used for non-Christians, see Ilona Opelt, "Griechische und lateinische Bezeichnungen der Nichtchristen: ein terminologischer Versuch," *VC* 19 (1965): 1–22, with discussion of *paganus, gentes*, and *gentilis* at 14–18.

possible reference to its role in Mithraism) (In Rom. 1:23 [§§3-5]).[6] Other remarks appear to reflect current practice in Rome. The tenor can vary. Ambrosiaster's characterizations of the mystery cults of the "Phrygian goddess" (the Great Mother or Cybele), Isis, and Mithras betray greater animus than his references to traditional Greco-Roman cults. For example, when commenting on 1 Cor 8:5 ("There may be those who are called 'gods' and 'lords,' whether in heaven or on earth"), Ambrosiaster explains matter-of-factly that pagans regard the sun, moon, and stars as heavenly gods, and Apollo, Aesculapius,[7] Hercules, and Minerva as earthly gods (In 1 Cor. 8:5). But when revising his explanation of what it means to be "slaves of sin," he singles out the cult of the Great Mother and her devotees (*galli*), castrated men with long hair who wore female garments and jewelry, as the epitome of degradation (In Rom. 6:20-21 [§1a]).[8] Ambrosiaster's disgust for the cult and its effeminate attendees was, in fact, a traditional Roman sentiment.[9] It is not altogether surprising, therefore, that he would make an example of the cult when he wished to illustrate the depths to which misdirected pagan worship could lead.

Ambrosiaster regards all pagan cults as forms of idolatry,[10] which consists in attributing to a creature qualities and worship due only to God (In Rom. 1:25 [§§1-2]; In Col. 3:5 [§2]; In Eph. 5:5 [§1]). It is, in Ambrosiaster's words, "a most serious offense and the source of every error" (In

---

6. With the notes there.

7. Ambrosiaster refers to Aesculapius by the name *Scolapius* (CSEL 81.2:93), a spelling attested in medieval Latin (Charles du Fresne du Cange et al., eds., *Glossarium mediae et infimae latinitatis* [Niort: Favre, 1883-1887], 7.359c). If the spelling is Ambrosiaster's, it is noteworthy, since writers Ambrosiaster would have read (Tertullian, Lactantius, Arnobius) refer to the god as Aesculapius. On sanctuaries and other evidence for the cult Aesculapius in Rome, attested into the fourth century CE, see Paul Roesch, "Le culte d'Asclépios à Rome," in *Mémoires III: Médecins et médecine dans l'antiquité*, ed. Guy Sabbah (Saint-Étienne: Publications de l'Université de Saint-Étienne, 1982), 171-79.

8. See also *Quaest.* 114.7-8, 115.18 (SC 512:122-24, 170). Early on, Cumont drew attention to these passages ("La polémique de l'Ambrosiaster," 422-23). On the origins of the name *galli*, see Eugene N. Lane, "The Name of Cybele's Priests the 'Galloi,'" in *Cybele, Attis, and Related Cults: Essays in Memory of M. J. Vermaseren*, ed. Eugene N. Lane, RGRW 131 (Leiden: Brill, 1996), 117-33. For an overview of the cult in Rome in the imperial period, see Robert Turcan, *The Cults of Roman Empire*, trans. Antonia Nevill (Oxford: Blackwell, 1996), 43-56.

9. Di Santo, *L'Apologetica*, 136 n. 93.

10. Ibid., 161-73.

Rom. 6:6),[11] "the primary and very grave offense" (In Col. 3:5 [§2]), "the greatest sin of all" (In Eph. 5:5 [§1]). (The seriousness Ambrosiaster assigns to idolatry, in keeping with prior tradition,[12] obliges him to explain why Paul likens it to the seemingly lesser sin of greed in In Eph. 5:5 [§§1–2]; In Col. 3:5 [§§2–3].) Even the devil did not arrogate for himself divine status, according to Ambrosiaster (In Rom. 1:30–32 [§§1a–2a]). Rather, the devil fostered the worship of many gods among human beings in order to make them his associates in sin, usurping for himself what belongs only to God.[13] Thus, the worship of idols is, in reality, the worship of the devil (In 1 Cor. 10:19–20).

The worship of heavenly bodies (*elementa*) is not as contemptible as the worship of handcrafted images (In Rom. 1:22 [§1]; 1:30–32 [§2a]; 8:22 [§1]), but it still is a dangerous form of idolatry, according to Ambrosiaster.[14] By *elementa* he usually means the sun, moon, and stars (In Rom. 8:22 [§1]; In Col. 2:18–19 [§2]), though the word also can refer more broadly to the fundamental elements of physical creation (earth, air, water, fire) (*Quaest.* 108.1 [CSEL 50:252]).[15] Ambrosiaster's comments on verses where Paul uses the word (Gal 4:9; Col 2:8, 20) reveal his own preoccupation with contemporary astrological theory and practice.

On a philosophical level, Ambrosiaster cannot accept the basis on which pagans conducted their astrological inquiries, which elicit a derisory attack from him:

> They consider themselves *wise* because they think that they have investigated the physical order, examining the course of the stars and the size of the elements, but spurning the God of these things.… They say that through these things one can come to God, just as one is led to the king by the *comites*. Let this be granted. But is anyone so mad or reckless about his life as to claim the king's honorary title for the *comes*? If people were found out even discussing such an idea, they would be justly condemned for treason. (In Rom. 1:22 [§§1–1a])

---

11. The phrase "and the source of every error" appears only in *recensio* γ.
12. Cf., e.g., Tertullian, *Idol.* 1.1 (CCSL 2:1101), noted at In Col. 3:5 (§2).
13. In Eph. 2:1–2; 3:10 (§2); In Col. 2:11–12 (§2); In 1 Thess. 2:7; see also *Quaest.* 113.5–7 (CSEL 50:301–2). On this theme in Ambrosiaster's thought, see Lunn-Rockliffe, *Ambrosiaster's Political Theology*, 146, 149–52.
14. See Stüben, "Das Heidentum," 140–52; Di Santo, *L'Apologetica*, 151–60.
15. See In Rom. 2:3 (§3); In Col. 2:20 (§2).

Ambrosiaster does not deny that the elements are instrumental in sustaining human life. He simply insists that they are under God's direction (In Rom. 2:3 [§3]; In Eph. 2:3 [§1]), and that God, as their originator and governor, is not limited by the natural order (In Rom. 8:7 [§§1–2]). Hence the animus of Ambrosiaster's comment on Col 2:8–9, where Paul warns the Colossians against "philosophy ... according to the elements of this world." In their splendor and arrangement, heavenly bodies are seductive both as a stimulus to human inquiry—"human calculation tries to compress the power of God within the limits of its own systematic knowledge" (In Col. 2:8–9 [§3])—and as a basis for human prognostication—"they assign every impetus to the heavenly bodies" (In Col. 2:8–9 [§2]). They lead human beings to the seemingly evident conclusion that there are many gods in the heavens, all deserving of worship (In Col. 2:8–9 [§3], 2:20 [§3], 2:21–22). Part of the reason for Ambrosiaster's animus, one suspects, is the evident appeal of this form of theology in aristocratic and learned circles in Rome.[16] But his disdain extends to all forms of higher learning, since they "make people chase all the more after error and lead them away from God," as he says in a remark about the *quadrivium* of astrology, geometry, arithmetic, and music (In Col. 2:1–3 [§3]). One senses a profound association, in Ambrosiaster's mind, between classical *paideia* and pagan culture, perhaps a legacy of the emperor Julian's educational program.[17]

At a more practical level, Ambrosiaster objects to the popular, deeply ingrained belief that the movements of the heavens influence human affairs. In his comment on Gal 4:9–10, where Paul accuses Galatians who observe a Jewish calendar of reverting to their former servitude to "the elements," Ambrosiaster explains each of the words of Paul's charge—"You are observing days, months, times, and years!"—by referring to ways that Romans identify auspicious days and mark seasons or years: "one ought not set out on a journey tomorrow, for after tomorrow one ought not start anything"; "tools ought not to be made on the seventh day of the moon"; "the day after tomorrow are the Vulcanalia"; "the new year comes on the calends of January" (In Gal. 4:10 [§§1–2]). Ambrosiaster does not, however, use the

---

16. Eliciting from Ambrosiaster's *quaestiones* and comments a sense of the critiques to which Ambrosiaster may have been responding, Courcelle, "Critiques exégétiques," 138, 164–69, nicely conveys how Ambrosiaster's pagan contemporaries would have viewed their astrological inquiries and beliefs.

17. Glen W. Bowersock, *Julian the Apostate* (Cambridge, MA: Harvard University Press, 1978), 83–85; see In 2 Thess. 2:7.

occasion to develop a more general argument against the seeming determinism of astrology, as he would in his long treatise "On Fate" (*Quaest.* 115 [SC 512:154–233]). In fact, he does not mention the prognostic practice of "astrology" (*ars matheseos*) or "astrologers" (*mathematici*) in the Commentary, and he only refers to "fate" (*fatum*) in an aside (In Col. 2:13–15 [§7]).

6.2. Jews

Valuable studies have enriched scholarly perspectives about Ambrosiaster's views on Jews and Judaism.[18] At the end of the nineteenth century, Germain Morin drew attention to parallels between Ambrosiaster and a convert from Judaism named Isaac, author of a brief Trinitarian treatise (*Fides Isatis ex Iudaeo* [CCSL 9:336–43]) and a notorious opponent of Damasus.[19] Morin soon abandoned the suggestion in favor of another, as objections were considerable, including passages of the Commentary and *Quaestiones* where Ambrosiaster at least rhetorically self-identifies with a gentile

---

18. Lydia Speller, "Ambrosiaster and the Jews," StPatr 17 (1982): 72–78. Further, see Alessandra Pollastri, "Sul rapporto tra cristiani e guidei secondo il commento dell'Ambrosiaster ad alcuni passi paolini," *SSRel* 4 (1980): 313–27; Shaye J. D. Cohen, "Was Timothy Jewish (Acts 16:1–3)? Patristic Exegesis, Rabbinic Law, and Matrilineal Descent," *JBL* 105 (1986): 251–68; Jeremy Cohen, "The Mystery of Israel's Salvation: Romans 11:25–26 in Patristic and Medieval Exegesis," *HTR* 98 (2005): 247–81; Jacobs, "Jew's Jew," 265–68; Di Santo, *L'Apologetica*, ch. 3; Tim Denecker, "Heber or Habraham? Ambrosiaster and Augustine on Language History," *REAug* 60 (2014): 1–32.

19. Germain Morin, "L'Ambrosiaster et le juif converti Isaac, contemporain du pape Damase," *RHR* 4 (1899): 111. See also Heinrich J. Vogels, "Prolegomena," CSEL 81.1:xiv. For discussion of Ambrosiaster as Isaac, see Coelestinus Martini, *Ambrosiaster: De auctore, operibus, theologia*, SPAA 4 (Rome: Pontificium Athenaeum Antonianum, 1944), 149–60; and Lunn-Rockliffe, *Ambrosiaster's Political Theology*, 33–44. The fullest recent case for Isaac as Ambrosiaster is Ulrich Manthe, "Wurde die Collatio vom Ambrosiaster Isaak geschrieben?," in *Festschrift für Rolf Knütel zum 70. Geburtstag*, ed. Holger Altmeppen (Heidelberg: Müller, 2009), 737–54. Isaac apparently had filed capital charges in 370 with Maximinus, the (pagan) *praefectus annonae urbis Romae*, against Damasus on account of the massacre of his rival Ursinus's supporters in the bid for the see of Rome after the death of Liberius in 366. See Henry Chadwick, *The Church in Ancient Society: From Galilee to Gregory the Great*, Oxford History of the Early Church (Oxford: Oxford University Press, 2001), 315–17. Further, see Lunn-Rockliffe, *Ambrosiaster's Political Theology*, 35–40, and the detailed account of Altay Coşkun, "Der Praefect Maximinus, der Jude Isaak und des Strafprozeß gegen Bischof Damasus von Rom," *JAC* 46 (2003): 17–44.

audience.²⁰ Alexander Souter's 1905 study drew attention to Ambrosiaster's "great interest in Judaism," which coexists with the usual anti-Jewish polemics, as Morin noted.²¹ Ambrosiaster's anonymity leaves open the question of his ethnicity, but at least one scholar has argued that his knowledge of Judaism is not so exceptional as to demand Jewish origins.²² His location in Rome, with its flourishing Jewish community that archaeological evidence shows was "neither assimilated nor isolated," will in any case have provided ample occasion to observe and learn about Jewish life.²³

Ambrosiaster refers occasionally to contemporary Jewish practices as being exemplary.²⁴ Paul in 1 Cor 14:22 wanted that church to follow the "tradition of the synagogue" in having the elders eminently seated and those of lesser status appropriately arrayed on lower seats and mats (In 1 Cor. 14:31; see In 1 Tim. 5:1–2 [§1]).²⁵ He praises the Jewish custom of

---

20. Morin, "Hilarius l'Ambrosiaster," *RBén* 20 (1903): 113: "j'avais soigneusement évité de rien proclamer quant à l'identité même de l'auteur, je m'étais contenté d'appeler l'attention sur le juif Isaac." The passages in question have been examined by Heinrich Brewer, "War Ambrosiaster der bekehrte Jude Isaak?," *ZKT* 37 (1913): 214–16. The other major (and long-noted) problem is the relation to Damasus, whom Isaac despised and Ambrosiaster acknowledged as bishop of Rome.

21. Alexander Souter, *A Study of Ambrosiaster*, TS 7.4 (Cambridge: Cambridge University Press, 1905), 183; Souter, *The Earliest Latin Commentaries on the Epistles of St. Paul* (Oxford: Clarendon, 1927), 72–75; Morin, "L'Ambrosiaster et le Juif converti Isaac," 113, referring to Ambrosiaster's *Quaest.* 44, "Against the Jews," and some "épithètes fort dures" in *Quaest.* 92 (CSEL 50:478). In the treatise "Against the Jews" Ambrosiaster remarks that "a believing Jew is hard to find and so rare" (*Quaest.* 44.12 [CSEL 50:78]).

22. Speller, "Ambrosiaster and the Jews." Some scholars still think Ambrosiaster may well have been a convert from Judaism, e.g., Luigi Fatica, trans., *Ambrosiaster: Commento alla Lettera ai Galati: Traduzione, introduzione e note*, CTePa 61 (Rome: Città Nuova Editrice, 1986), 18–19.

23. Leonard Victor Rutgers, *The Jews in Late Ancient Rome: Evidence of Cultural Interaction in the Roman Diaspora*, RGRW 126 (Leiden: Brill, 1995), 266. Contact with Jews informed both Jerome and Epiphanius, as Josef Lössl has shown in "Hieronymus und Epiphanius von Salamis über das Judentum ihrer Zeit," *JSJ* 33 (2002): 410–36. For Jerome's knowledge of Judaism, see the studies cited by Andrew Cain, *The Letters of Jerome: Asceticism, Biblical Exegesis, and the Construction of Christian Authority in Late Antiquity*, OECS (Oxford: Oxford University Press, 2009), 59 nn. 68–69.

24. See Souter, *Study of Ambrosiaster*, 180–83.

25. For archaeological evidence of the elders' seating in synagogues, see Rachel Hachlili, *Ancient Synagogues—Archaeology and Art: New Discoveries and Current Research*, HOSt 105 (Leiden: Brill, 2013), 508.

providing religious education for children, a provision the church adopted initially but discontinued (In 1 Cor. 12:28; In Eph. 4:11–12 [§2]).[26] In explaining Paul's circumcision of Timothy (Acts 16:3), he betrays knowledge that Jews of the period reckoned descent matrilineally (a ruling unattested in the Second Temple period) (In Gal. 2:4–5 [§§4–5]; In 1 Tim. *argumentum*).[27] Shaye J. D. Cohen points out Ambrosiaster's familiarity with rabbinic law in this regard and notes how unusual this is among Christian commentators.[28] Recent researches by Jeremy Cohen, Jacobs, Di Santo, and Tim Denecker have highlighted how aspects of Ambrosiaster's interest in Judaism relate to issues of Christian theology and identity.[29] His exegesis of Paul's claim to be "a Hebrew born of Hebrews" (Phil 3:5), Jacobs argues, works "to transform the seemingly hyper-Jewish epithet ... from a linguistic and ethnic marker of religious particularity into a claim of universalizing, Christian faith."[30] Denecker also discerns a similar appropriation of Jewish tradition in Ambrosiaster's treatise "On Where Hebrew Got Its Name" (*Quaest.* 108 [CSEL 50:251–56]).[31] The treatise argues for an

---

26. On the synagogue as a site of education, see Lee Levine, *The Ancient Synagogue: The First Thousand Years* (New Haven: Yale University Press), 398–404.

27. See also his *Quaest. app.* 60.2 (CSEL 50:455). Ambrosiaster treats Paul's circumcision of Timothy as one of the occasions that the apostle sought to avoid scandal. Taking on Timothy, an uncircumcised Jew, as an associate in his ministry would be unfeasible in view of the Jewish presence.

28. Cohen, "Was Timothy Jewish," 259–65. This halakah is attested in the Mishnah, in m. Qidd. 3:12 and in m. Yebam 7:5 (the child of a Jewish woman and a gentile is a ממזר but nonetheless a Jew) and not at all in the Second Temple period. See *Quaest.* 81.1 (CSEL 50:137) for Ambrosiaster's recognition of how Jewish identity is constituted by birth into a culture of worship (*devotio creatoris*).

29. Cohen, "Mystery of Israel's Salvation," supports Speller's claim that Ambrosiaster had only minimal interest in Jews as such; the focus of his exegesis "hinges much more on matters of heavenly foreknowledge, human will, and divine justice" (270). Jacobs, "Jew's Jew," 267: "By taking hold of Paul at his most Jewish (*Hebraeus ex Hebraeis*) and making him speak instead in an unequivocally non-Jewish voice, Ambrosiaster maintains a thick barrier between his own Christian apostle and the Jews who (rhetorically) threaten the integrity of his faith and practice." See Di Santo, *L'Apologetica*, 192: "The anti-Jewish polemic in Ambrosiaster seems to us ... instrumental to the construction of a Christian identity that knows how to keep itself equally distant from the errors of paganism and from falsifying Jewish interpretations—or better, judaizing and heretical interpretations—of christological doctrine and Scripture." Denecker, "Heber or Habraham?," 7–12.

30. Jacobs, "Jew's Jew," 266.

31. Denecker, "Heber or Habraham?," 16.

eponymous link between the "Abraham" and "Hebrew," which highlights the patriarch as the father of all believers, not just Jews, the progenitor in whom God's gifts were fully present.[32]

Ambrosiaster's explanatory paraphrase of Paul denounces the Jewish understanding of the law, the Jewish rejection of Jesus, and Judaism, as the epistolary texts give occasion. Much of this replicates familiar anti-Jewish tropes of early Christianity.[33] Thus the Commentary speculates about the Jewish refusal of Christ. Ambrosiaster is sensitive to nuance in Paul's presentation—"he shows affection and love toward his people" (In Rom. 9:1-4 [§2])—and he does not depict Jewish responses to the gospel monolithically.[34] He envisions two main types of Jewish disbelief: one based on ignorance—and therefore potentially remediable—and another so deeply anchored in ill will that he regards it as predestined (In Rom. 9:11-13 [§3]). God foreknew that "ungodly [*impii*] Jews" would be "thrown into a fury out of jealousy [*aemulatione*] for the gentiles" (In Rom. 3:26 [§1a]). The motif of Jewish jealousy recurs often, notably in combination with reflections on the Jews' role in the death of Christ in Ambrosiaster's discussion of "the curse of the law" in Gal 3:11. There Ambrosiaster shows how "the Savior's cross is the Jews' sin and a curse upon them" (In Gal. 3:13 (§2) [CSEL 81.3:35]),[35] and he cites John 19:12 to identify the real motive as jealousy over the popularity of Jesus's teaching (In Gal. 3:13 [§4]).[36] God also can use envy (*invidia*) as "the avenger of unbelief," to which Ambrosia-

---

32. See esp. §§2 and 8. His *Quaest.* 4.4 refers to Abraham as "the father of the Jews" but goes on to insist that "the race of the Christian has existed from the beginning.... Christianity always was" (CSEL 50:28). See Di Santo's discussion, *L'Apologetica*, 222-25.

33. See Heinz Schreckenberg, *Die christlichen Adversus-Judaeos-Texte und ihr literarisches und historisches Umfeld (I.-XI. Jh.)*, rev. ed., EHS, Ser. 23 Theologie, 497 (Bern: Lang, 1990), 30-38, 311-13, for a brief discussion of Ambrosiaster. On the implications of these repeated motifs in the history of Christianity, see Jeremy F. Worthen, *The Internal Foe: Judaism and Anti-Judaism in the Shaping of Christian Theology* (Newcastle-upon-Tyne: Cambridge Scholars Press, 2009).

34. Good treatment of this in Cohen, "Mystery of Israel's Salvation," 266-70.

35. *Crux enim salvatoris peccatum et maledictum est Iudaeorum* (see also §3: *maledictum illorum, a quibus suspensus est*). Adding an additional section (§4) to the comment, he warms again to the topic: "How much of this relates to the Jews!"

36. Further, see his remarks at In Gal. 3:14, as well as In 1 Thess. 2:15-16, where he follows Paul in putting responsibility for Christ's death on Jews and indicates God will take vengeance.

ster remarks that Jews "are always thrown into a rage and tormented when they hear that the law and the prophets belong to us who believe in Christ" (In Rom. 10:19 [§2]).

The Jewish claim to the law was likewise irksome to Ambrosiaster,[37] and he invokes the apostle's postconversion conduct to counter it. A zealous Pharisee, Paul persecuted the church because he was "unaware that the time for the assertion of the law was over." Once corrected, he abandoned it (In Gal. 1:13–14 [§2]). Still, aspects of the law retain validity (In Rom. 3:20 [§4]):[38] the *lex divina*, the first four of the Ten Commandments; and the *lex moralis*, which consists of the remaining six commandments and overlaps with the *lex naturae* known to pagans. The greater part falls under the "law of deeds" (*lex factorum*), contrasted by both apostle and commentator with the *lex fidei* or "law of faith" (Rom 3:27).[39] Ambrosiaster found this analysis of the law as composite in a key passage from Ezekiel that he cites at Titus 1:13. The Jews, "because they had profaned the law of God and his commandments [*iustificationes eius*], received ordinances that were not good and statutes that were not good (see Ezek 20:25), by which they could not be justified" (In Titus 1:13 [§2]). These punitive additions need no longer be observed.[40] Sabbath and circumcision, however, were in the original law and "possessed their own righteousness in their day, because they were given as a type of things to come" (In Rom. 9:32 [§1a]).[41] Reception of the

---

37. As the opening of his "Against the Jews" suggests (CSEL 50:78): "So why do they say 'it is our law', when it is obvious that a gift of God belongs to all who want it? Let this reckless usurpation come to end, since the grace of God is common to all—with what shame do they deny that our Christ was promised in the law?"

38. Wilhelm Geerlings presents Ambrosiaster's tripartite understanding of the law in "Das Verständnis von Gesetz im Galaterbriefkommentar des Ambrosiaster," in *Die Weltlichkeit des Glaubens in der alten Kirche: Festschrift für Ulrich Wickert*, ed. Dietmar Wyrwa (Berlin: de Gruyter, 1997), 101–13.

39. The opening of his commentary on Galatians also invokes the "law of deeds" as productive of error.

40. In Titus 1:13 (§4): "These statutes were given as a punishment, so that at the time when the promised gift of the God arrived, the mercy of God might relax all the prohibitions that had previously been imposed. The Jews, who do not understand this, remain under the yoke and wish to curtail the freedom of others with these chains."

41. The quotation of Ezek 20:25 follows immediately. The same prophetic text features in *Quaest.* 44.9 (CSEL 50:76); in *Quaest. app.* 51 (CSEL 50:429), where he misidentifies the text as from Jeremiah; and in *Quaest. app.* 75.2 (CSEL 50:469), also misidentified as Jeremiah. This misidentification in the *Quaestiones* strongly suggest that the Commentary was composed after at least these *quaestiones*.

"faith of Christ" entails the abandonment by both Jews and gentiles of their former religious practices, although for different reasons.[42]

6.3. Heretics

Ambrosiaster lived in the heyday of early Christian heresiology.[43] The *Panarion* ("Medicine Chest against All Heresies") of Epiphanius, bishop of Salamis, had appeared only a few years earlier (376–378), shortly before Epiphanius visited Rome in 382 in the company of Jerome. Filastrius of Brescia composed his own *Diversarum hereseon liber* sometime between 380 and 390 (CCSL 9:207–324). Other Latin handbooks against heretics include *Adversus omnes haereses* of Pseudo-Tertullian (CSEL 47:213–26), the *Indiculus de haeresibus* of Pseudo-Jerome (PL 81:636–44), and *De haeresibus* of Augustine (CCSL 46:286–345). Ambrosiaster likewise attacked those Christians whom he perceived to be "heretics." But rather than taking the encyclopedic approach of some of his contemporaries, he tended to focus on those who were still influential in his own time and place. Among the *Quaestiones* there are several treatises directed against specific heretics, such as Photinus, Arius, and Novatian.[44] Ambrosiaster refers to other heretics in the course of his discourses on specific topics: for example, in a polemic against heretics who condemned marriage, he explicitly mentions Marcion and Manichaeus.[45] All of them are named in the Commentary as well as in the *Quaestiones*.

---

42. In Eph. 2:17–18: "All would receive the faith of Christ, through which they are made one, their previous rites having been canceled" (*sublato praeterito ritu susciperent fidem Christi per quam efficerentur unum*). Ambrosiaster even likens the church's unbiased reception of all peoples to the Roman empire's extension of citizenship to all nations who come seeking peace and bearing gifts (In Eph. 2:19).

43. Judith McClure, "Handbooks against Heresy in the West, from the Late Fourth to the Late Sixth Centuries," *JTS* n.s. 30 (1979): 186–97, provides a good orientation to the Western antiheretical literature.

44. *Quaest.* 91 (CSEL 50:151–60), "Against Photinus"; *Quaest.* 97 (CSEL 50:171–87), "Against Arius"; and *Quaest.* 102 (CSEL 50:199–224), "Against Novatian."

45. *Quaest.* 127.17 (CSEL 50:406): Marcion; *Quaest.* 127.18 (CSEL 50:406): Manichaeus. Ambrosiaster refers to the prophet Mani as "Manichaeus." According to Augustine, *Haer.* 46.1, Mani's disciples began to call him "Manichaeus" because his name in Greek "Manes" was too close to the word for "mania." See Jürgen Tubach and Mohsen Zakeri, "Mani's Name," in *Augustine and Manichaeism in the Latin West: Pro-*

As Ambrosiaster saw it, the early church had been plagued by heresy since its inception, and the apostolic writers were engaged in a persistent effort to combat erroneous opinions. For example, in the preface to the commentary on 1 Corinthians, he lists the resolution of conflicts caused by heretics as the primary reason for Paul's epistle: "The first reason for his writing is this: people were disagreeing with each other in the manner of heretics, claiming allegiance to human beings. They wished to be called 'followers of Paul' [*Pauliani*], 'followers of Peter' [*Petriani*], and 'followers of Apollos' [*Apolloniaci*], not of Christ" (In 1 Cor. *Argumentum* [§2]; see *Quaest*. 127.34 [CSEL 50:414]). Elsewhere Ambrosiaster suggests that an excess of knowledge and a lack of love could lead to heresy. Commenting on 1 Cor 13:2 ("And if I have prophetic powers, and understand all mysteries and all knowledge, and if I have all faith, so as to remove mountains, but have not love, I am nothing"), he observes: "On account of envy they destroyed their charity and reduced their knowledge to nothing. For both Tertullian and Novatian were persons of no small knowledge, but because they ruined the bonds of charity through their jealousy, they turned towards schism and created heresies to their perdition" (In 1 Cor. 13:2 [§3]). Ambrosiaster does not appear to have had a well-developed definition of "heresy" or its distinction from "schism."[46]

In his *Quaestiones* and Commentary Ambrosiaster gives attention to three distinct groups of heretics. First, there are teachers whose views deviated significantly on fundamental issues of cosmology and salvation, such as Marcion and the Manichaeans. A second group consists of teachers, such as Arius and Photinus, whom Ambrosiaster critiques on Trinitarian or christological grounds. Finally, there are those whose teachings fit more precisely into the category of schismatic, that is, who held views about the nature of the church and church discipline (e.g., penance and rebaptism) that led to separation from the body that Ambrosiaster regarded as the

---

ceedings of the Fribourg-Utrecht International Symposium of the IAMS, ed. Johannes van Oort, Otto Wermelinger, and Gregor Wurst, NHMS 49 (Leiden: Brill, 2001), 272–86.

46. For example, at In Phil. 3:5–6 (§1) Ambrosiaster refers to the *haeresis farisaeorum*. Di Santo, *L'Apologetica*, 64–65, would see in Ambrosiaster's phrase *qui extra ecclesiam vel contra ecclesiam sedes sibi instituerunt* at *Quaest*. 110.7 (CSEL 50:274) a distinction between "schismatics" (*extra ecclesiam*) and "heretics" (*contra ecclesiam*), but Ambrosiaster never made the distinction explicit. As Di Santo, *L'Apologetica*, 70, notes, the formal distinction between heresy and schism was not widely used prior to Augustine.

catholic church. It is necessary to give attention to all three of these types of heresy.

Ambrosiaster often mentions the teachings of Marcion and Manichaeus (or the Manichaeans) as examples of kindred heresies. Both denied the reality of Christ's incarnation (In 1 Tim. 4:2 [§5]); both saw the crucifixion of Jesus as an illusion (In 1 Cor. 1:2 [§2]); both rejected marriage (*Quaest.* 127.17–18 [CSEL 50:406–7]).[47] But Ambrosiaster could also distinguish between the two, a fact that suggests he had some detailed knowledge of their teachings, at least by hearsay. Although he never mentions Marcion's interest in the Gospel of Luke and Paul's epistles, Ambrosiaster contrasts Marcion's teaching on creation with that of the Manichaeans. While Marcion taught that a wicked demon, Saclas, created the world with the assistance of evil angels, Ambrosiaster claims, Manichaeus held that the true God created the world, but the first human being was created by the demon Saclas (*Quaest.* 3.1 [CSEL 50:21]).[48] In general, however, Ambrosiaster was less interested in Marcion than in the Manichaeans, probably because, as he notes in his comment on 1 Tim 4:2, "the Marcionites have almost all died out" (In 1 Tim. 4:2 [§5]).

By contrast, it is clear that the Manichaeans were a lively presence in Rome in Ambrosiaster's day, and he addresses their errors with greater urgency and in greater detail.[49] In one of his *quaestiones* Ambrosiaster shows an awareness of Manichaean books and mythology. After noting that Manichaeans believed that the soul "was poured into the realm of shadows and clings to 'hylic' (i.e., material) things," he observes: "You have it written in your books that the soul is liberated by being born, so that after leaving the body and having been received by the moon, it is passed on to the sun, which you claim is the god of your souls" (*Quaest.* 127.18

---

47. The Manichaean rejection of sex and marriage was not absolute; it pertained only to the Elect, not to the Auditors. See the comments of the Manichaean leader Faustus in Augustine, *Faust.* 30.4 (CSEL 25.1:750–52).

48. On the role of Saclas (more usually Saklas or Sakla) in the Manichaean mythology, see Paul Van Lindt, *The Names of Manichaean Mythological Figures: A Comparative Study of Terminology in the Coptic Sources*, StOr 26 (Wiesbaden: Harrassowitz, 1992), 205–6. In Sethian gnosticism the term was used for the demiurge or creator god. See, e.g., Ap. John 11.15–20 and Gos. Jud. 13.1–7, where he is the creator of Adam and Eve. The word means "fool" in Aramaic.

49. Augustine, *Conf.* 5.10.19, attests to the presence of numerous Manichaeans at Rome in the early 380s. Imperial legislation against the Manichaeans accelerated throughout the later fourth century.

[CSEL 50:406–7]). Elsewhere Ambrosiaster refers to the elaborate myths that were prominent in the Manichaean cosmology. Commenting on the words of 2 Tim 4:4, where the apostle warns against those who would "turn away from listening to the truth and wander into myths," he observes: "This is characteristic above all of the Manichaeans, who have countless fictions which they call by pretentious names, although they are trifling matters and utterly absurd" (In 2 Tim. 4:4 [§3]). In several places Ambrosiaster refers to legal proceedings against the Manichaeans initiated by Roman emperors, and once he even cites from Diocletian's edict against the sect (*Quaest*. 127.18 [CSEL 50:407]; In 2 Tim. 3:6–7 [§2]).[50] Like Augustine, that other great opponent of Manichaeism, Ambrosiaster accused the sect of professing sexual and alimentary asceticism, while practicing indulgence in both.[51]

The second group of heretics that was the subject of Ambrosiaster's attack are those concerned with doctrinal matters, especially the divinity and humanity of Christ. As noted above, Ambrosiaster vigorously defended the Nicene Creed of 325 and its expansion at the Council of Constantinople I in 381.[52] But in addition to attacking Arius and opponents identified as "Arians" (*Arriani*), Ambrosiaster devoted considerable attention to another figure, whose influence in his day seems to have rivaled that of Arius: Bishop Photinus of Sirmium.[53] A disciple of Marcellus of Ancyra, Photinus became bishop of Sirmium in the mid-340s. Following the monarchial tendencies of Marcellus's pro-Nicene theology, Photinus appears to have developed its christological implications: stressing the one substance (*mia hypostasis*) of the Godhead, Photinus denied the personal, eternal subsistence of the divine Word or Son. The result, according to Photinus's opponents, was the view that the Son of God did not truly exist

---

50. The full text of Diocletian's edict against the Manichaeans is found in the *Mosaicarum et Romanarum legum collatio* 15.3 (Robert M. Frakes, *Compiling the "Collatio Legum Mosaicarum et Romanarum" in Late Antiquity* [Oxford: Oxford University Press, 2011], 191–92). The *Collatio* has sometimes been attributed to Ambrosiaster; see above §1.

51. The primary motivation behind Augustine's books *De moribus ecclesiae catholicae* and *De moribus Manichaeorum* was to unmask the contradiction in Manichaean conduct; see his *Retract*. 1.6(7) (CCSL 57:18).

52. See above §4.1–2.

53. A thorough overview of Ambrosiaster's discussion of Photinus can be found in Lydia Speller, "New Light on the Photinians: The Evidence of Ambrosiaster," *JTS* n.s. 34 (1983): 99–113. The name is often spelled "Fotinus."

until his birth from the virgin in Bethlehem. While Photinus did not deny the virginal conception of Jesus, he appears to have applied biblical texts about Christ's divine power and preexistence to his righteous actions and teaching as a human being.[54]

Despite opposition from men such as Hilary of Poitiers, Marius Victorinus, and Ambrose of Milan, the views of Photinus became influential. Writing in the *Confessions* of his own earlier christological views, Augustine notes that he had been influenced by the views of Photinus:

> I took a different view at the time, regarding Christ my Lord as no more than a man, though a man of excellent wisdom and without peer. I was the more firmly persuaded of this because he had been born of a virgin and made plain to us by his own example that disdain for temporal goods is a condition for winning immortality.... I admit that it was later still that I learned how sharply divergent is Catholic truth from the falsehood of Photinus. (Augustine, *Conf.* 7.19.25 [BAug 13:632–34])[55]

Persistent polemics from Ambrosiaster and other late fourth-century authors strongly suggest that the teaching of Photinus remained a potent force in the Latin-speaking world well into the early fifth century.[56]

The third group of heretics to which Ambrosiaster devoted his attention was those whose views touched on matters of church discipline: the Cataphrygians (also known as "Montanists" or adherents of the "New Prophecy"), Donatists, and Novatianists, who are sometimes mentioned in tandem with one another (In Rom. 2.16 [§2b]; In Cor. 1:13 [§1]; 1:14 [§2]). Of these, the Cataphygians seem to be mostly a matter of historical interest: they do not appear in the *Quaestiones* at all and appear only rarely in the Commentary. Ambrosiaster knew, however, that the second-century prophet Montanus and his associates Priscilla and Maximilla had claimed

---

54. As is usually the case with those condemned for heresy, we must rely on the reports of their opponents. For a full discussion of these sources, see Daniel H. Williams, "Monarchianism and Photinus of Sirmium as the Persistent Heretical Face of the Fourth Century," *HTR* 99 (2006): 187–206.

55. ET: *The Confessions*, trans. M. Boulding, WSA I.1 (Hyde Park, NY: New City Press, 1997), 179–80.

56. See Williams, "Monarchianism," 206: "Not only were monarchial systems of theology not as ephemeral in Latin thought as later historiography makes it, but the persistence and influence of another voice of post-Nicene orthodoxy was a critical part in the shaping of early Latin theology."

to utter prophecies and to speak for the Holy Spirit (In 1 Thess. 5:22 [§3]). He also was aware that women held prominent roles in Montanist or Cataphrygian communities and notes disapprovingly in his comment on 1 Tim 3:11 that they ordained women as deacons (In 1 Tim. 3:11).[57]

Of somewhat greater concern to Ambrosiaster was the Donatist community, which dominated church life in North Africa in the fourth century. Ambrosiaster does not explicitly mention Donatists in the *Quaestiones*, although he may have had them in mind in Quaestio 110, where he discussed the *cathedra pestilentiae* of Ps 1:1.[58] Ambrosiaster linked Donatists and Novatianists together explicitly in several places, most notably in his comments on 1 Cor 1:14–16, a passage in which Paul points to the rivalry among Christians at Corinth and indicates that he baptized very few Christians there: "For they were just like the Novatianists and Donatists nowadays, who claim baptism for themselves, rejecting those who have been baptized by us; and those who have been baptized by them boast in the persons of those who have baptized them. Having renounced the name of Christ, they are proud to be called 'Novatianists' and 'Donatists'" (In 1 Cor. 1:14–16 [§2]). Other than this reference to rebaptism, Ambrosiaster betrays no further knowledge of or interest in the Donatists.

The situation is otherwise with Novatian and the Novatianists, who are mentioned frequently in the Pauline commentary and in an extended *quaestio* "Against Novatian" (*Quaest.* 102 [CSEL 50:199–224]). Novatian was a prominent presbyter and theologian at Rome, most notably the author of a distinguished treatise *On the Trinity*.[59] In the spring of 251, in the wake of the persecution by the emperor Decius, Novatian was elected bishop of Rome in opposition to Cornelius. The central issue that divided them was the question of whether or not reconciliation should be offered to those Christians who had denied their faith during the persecution of Decius. Novatian represented the rigorist party that rejected the possibil-

---

57. According to Epiphanius, *Pan.* 49.2.5 (GCS 31:243), Montanists had female bishops and presbyters, as well as deacons.

58. Sophie Lunn-Rockliffe has suggested that Ambrosiaster may have been thinking of Claudian, a Donatist bishop at Rome in the 370s and early 380s: "Bishops on the Chair of Pestilence: Ambrosiaster's Polemical Exegesis of Psalm 1:1," *JECS* 19 (2011): 79–99.

59. For a recent study and English translation of Novatian's theological writings, see *Novatian: On the Trinity, Letters to Cyprian of Carthage, Ethical Treatises*, trans. James L. Papandrea. CCT 22 (Turnhout: Brepols, 2015).

ity of postbaptismal penance for serious sins, such as adultery and apostasy. Eventually the issue of rebaptism entered the picture, with clergy loyal to Novatian rejecting the validity of baptism received in the catholic (i.e., non-Novatianist) communities. While the majority of bishops sided with Cornelius, including prominent bishops Cyprian of Carthage and Dionysius of Alexandria, Novatianist churches persisted into the fourth and fifth centuries in Constantinople as well as in Rome.[60]

Ambrosiaster clearly considered the teachings of Novatian to be a live issue in his day, and he countered Novatianist positions in several passages of his Commentary. In addition to the issue of rebaptism mentioned above, Ambrosiaster rejected Novatian's notion that the Christian church could admit only persons of the highest degree of holiness. Commenting on 2 Tim 2:20 ("In a great house there are not only vessels of gold and silver but also of wood and clay, some for special use, some for ordinary use"), Ambrosiaster argued against the ecclesial elitism of Novatian, who accepted only the "gold" and "silver" into his church: "In this statement [Paul] indicated that there are different kinds of people in the church: some are good and excellent men, whom he desires to be understood as gold. Others are only good, whom he marks out as silver. But others are not good; these he calls utensils *of wood and clay*. I think this statement is clear to everyone" (In 2 Tim. 2:20 [§1]).[61] Ambrosiaster also criticized Novatian's teaching that certain sins cannot be forgiven. He argued strenuously that both Testaments maintain the possibility of repentance for all sins, and he rejects the idea that one person's sin might contaminate the entire church (In 1 Cor. 6:18 [§§1–5]; *Quaest.* 102 passim). Moreover, in Quaestio 102 he anticipated Augustine's anti-Donatist arguments by insisting that the efficacy of a sacrament such as baptism did not depend on the holiness of the clergy who administered it (*Quaest.* 102.28–32 [CSEL 50:221–24]).[62]

---

60. See the legislation of Innocent I, *Ep.* 2.8.11 (PL 20:475); *Ep.* 6.2.6 (PL 20:499); *Ep.* 17.5.10 (PL 20:532); and Leo I, *Ep.* 12.6 (PL 54:653).

61. According to Ambrosiaster, Novatian interpreted the "great house" to refer not to the church but to the world. See *Quaest.* 102.22 (CSEL 50:216–17).

62. No less a luminary than Adolf von Harnack has observed, "In some of the sentences we imagine that we are listening to Augustine"; cited in David G. Hunter, "The Significance of Ambrosiaster," *JECS* 17 (2009): 21 n. 66.

7. Ambrosiaster and Christian Life at Rome

One of the most striking features of Ambrosiaster's Commentary and *Quaestiones* is the perspective he provides on the life of the Christian community at Rome. As a presbyter, Ambrosiaster was deeply knowledgeable about the organization and traditions of the church in Rome, including its hierarchical structure, liturgical practices, and social mores. Just as he was especially concerned with heretical movements that affected the church in Rome, so too he was attuned to developments within the church that influenced daily life and practice there, and he often wrote as a partisan or advocate of particular traditions (e.g., clerical sexual continence). In this section we will explore the unique perspectives that Ambrosiaster offered on the life of the Christian community in Rome.

7.1. Liturgy and Clerical Culture at Rome

One of the strongest arguments for Ambrosiaster's position as a presbyter in the Roman church is the great interest he shows in matters pertaining to liturgy and church office. In addition to referring to baptism and the Eucharist, Ambrosiaster alluded to numerous other liturgical practices. At one point, for example, he noted that it was common practice at Rome to offer the Eucharist twice a week in places of pilgrimage (*peregrinis in locis*) (In 1 Tim. 3:12–13 [§4]). He provides the earliest extant reference to a blessing bestowed on Christian marriages, a tradition he says emerged out of synagogue practice.[1] Ambrosiaster argued that the blessing should be bestowed only on first marriages (In 1 Cor. 7:40; In 1 Tim. 3:12 [§1]).[2] He also gives a glimpse into the persistence of the Greek language in the

---

1. *Quaest.* 127.3 (CSEL 50:400): "The tradition of this thing has remained in the synagogue and now is celebrated in the church."

2. Discussion in Korbinian Ritzer, *Le mariage dans les Églises chrétiennes du Ier au XIe siècle* (Paris: Cerf, 1970), 223.

liturgy at Rome. Commenting on Paul's discussion of speaking in tongues, Ambrosiaster observed that Latin-speaking Christians preferred to recite the creed in Greek (In 1 Cor. 14:19), and he noted with regret that they were accustomed to sing hymns in Greek, "delighted by the sound of the words, but without understanding what they are saying" (In 1 Cor. 14:14).[3] Echoing the apostle Paul, Ambrosiaster expressed reservations about the practice of speaking in unknown tongues because this manner of prayer offered no benefit to the human mind.

Ambrosiaster also provides illuminating information regarding the participation of laypeople in the feasts of the church. At one point he refers to periodic sexual abstinence practiced by the laity during solemn feasts:

> Sometimes a Christian is permitted to have intercourse with his wife, but at other times he is not permitted to do so. For when a solemn procession day occurs [*dies processionis*], one is sometimes not allowed to have intercourse, since one should abstain even from licit activities in order to obtain more easily what one asks for. That is why the apostle says: "One should abstain for a time in order to be free for prayer" (1 Cor 7:5). (*Quaest.* 127.35 [CSEL 50:415])

Ambrosiaster believed that the temporary sexual abstinence of the laity, like the permanent sexual abstinence of the higher clergy, served to make their prayers more effective.[4]

Ambrosiaster offered a similar rationale for liturgical fasting. Commenting on the annual fast that preceded the feast of Pascha or Easter,[5] he argued that periodic abstention from food and drink enabled a person to grow in self-knowledge:

> Just as a person does not see himself as he really is when he looks into a dirty mirror, so, too, if a person is weighed down with food and wine, he perceives himself to be something other than he is. Lust is aroused, anger ignited, pride inflamed, extravagance produced.... But if the body is tempered by the practice of fasting, knowledge of oneself returns and

---

3. Hymns in Latin were still a novelty in the Western church, having been introduced by Marius Victorinus and Ambrose.

4. On clerical sexual abstinence, see *Quaest.* 127.35–36 and the discussion below.

5. Ambrosiaster discusses the meaning of Pascha on several occasions: *Quaest.* 116, "The Meaning of Pascha"; *Quaest.* 121, "Praise and Glory of Pascha."

the soul understands with what devotion it should obey the redeemer. (*Quaest.* 120.3 [CSEL 50:362])

But, beyond increasing self-knowledge, fasting had the benefit of showing that a person truly wished his or her prayers to be answered. Ambrosiaster proposed Cornelius the centurion, who "gave alms generously to the people and prayed constantly to God" (Acts 10:2), as the model to be emulated. His fasting was truly effective because it was accompanied by prayer and almsgiving. When Cornelius fed the poor, Ambrosiaster observed, "it was their fullness [*saturitas*] that made his fasting acceptable" (*Quaest.* 120.5 [CSEL 50:363]).

Ambrosiaster also displayed remarkable interest in the status and roles of the Roman clergy, a fact that points to his own clerical status as well as to the importance of these matters in the world of late fourth-century Rome. The legitimacy of the clergy was a lively topic in his day, stimulated in part by competing claims to the bishopric of Rome and mob violence that emerged during the election of Damasus in 366, as well as during the reign of his predecessor, Liberius.[6] An additional factor was the spread of various forms of ascetic piety, such as the house-based asceticism of women championed by Jerome, who did not hesitate to ridicule the Roman clergy and assert the superior moral stature of his female patrons. The persistent presence of rival ecclesial communities, such as the followers of Novatian, also led Ambrosiaster to examine the basis of clerical authority and sacramental power.[7] In this volatile environment the status of the Roman clergy was under siege, and Ambrosiaster's work can be seen as an effort to articulate a strong rationale for the authority of bishops and presbyters and their relationship to other members of the Christian community.

In his Commentary Ambrosiaster often takes the Pauline text as an occasion to comment on the organization of the church in his day. He informs us that a single bishop governed the church in Rome, assisted by seven deacons; along with these there were numerous presbyters, usually

---

6. See John R. Curran, *Pagan City and Christian Capital: Rome in the Fourth Century* (Oxford: Clarendon, 2000), 129–37 (Liberius versus Felix), 137–42 (Damasus versus Ursinus).

7. See *Quaest.* 102.31 (CSEL 50:223–24), where Ambrosiaster argues that the efficacy of a priest's sacramental actions do not depend on his personal moral state, a point later argued by Augustine against the Donatists.

two of them in each of the local churches (In 1 Tim. 3:12–13 [§3]).[8] He was especially aware of the fact that historical changes had taken place since the days of the first apostles, and he attempted to explain why these developments occurred:

> In order that the members would grow and multiply, therefore, it was granted to everyone in the earliest period to evangelize, baptize, and explain the scriptures in church. But when the church came to encompass all places, congregations were set up and rectors and other offices were ordained for the churches, so that none of the clergy would presume to take over an office that he knew had not been entrusted or granted him. (In Eph. 4:11–12 [§4])

Initially, Ambrosiaster suggests, the bishop was supposed to be succeeded by the presbyter next in seniority. But over time it became clear that not all presbyters were worthy to become bishops; hence there developed the custom of choosing bishops on the basis of merit rather than seniority (In Eph. 4:11–12 [§5]).

Ambrosiaster was also aware that in the first century there did not exist a clear distinction between bishops and presbyters. He noted that Paul had appointed Timothy to be presbyter but also instructed him to appoint other presbyters, a task that could be performed only by a bishop. Ambrosiaster concluded that Timothy must have been both presbyter and bishop: a bishop was simply the "first among the presbyters": "And accordingly he indicates that Timothy was ordained a presbyter, but since he did not have anyone who ranked ahead of him, he was also a bishop" (In 1 Tim. 3:8–10 [§2]).[9] Taking this historical argument one step further, Ambrosiaster argued for an essential identity between bishops and presbyters. Noting that the author of 1 Timothy moves directly from a discussion of the qualifications of bishops to those of deacons, Ambrosiaster observed: "Why did he do this, except because there is one ordination for a bishop and a presbyter. Each of them is a priest [*sacerdos*], but the bishop is the

---

8. In *Quaest.* 101.4 (CSEL 50:196) he mentions the offices of exorcist and lector as well. Already in the middle of the third century, the church in Rome possessed forty-six presbyters, seven deacons, seven subdeacons, and an abundance of lower clergy, according to a letter of Bishop Cornelius to Fabius of Antioch preserved in Eusebius, *Hist. eccl.* 6.43.11–12 (GCS n.s. 6.2:618).

9. Ambrosiaster also refers to Timothy as a "bishop" (*episcopus*) at In Phil. 1:1.

first presbyter, just as every bishop is a presbyter, but not every presbyter is a bishop" (In 1 Tim. 3:8-10 [§1]).

It is important to acknowledge the innovative character of Ambrosiaster's position. Beginning in the third century, Latin Christian writers, such as Cyprian of Carthage, had applied the term "priest" (*sacerdos*) to the Christian clergy, but it had been used almost exclusively for bishops, not presbyters.[10] While *sacerdos* later became a common term for the presbyter, this usage was unusual in Ambrosiaster's day. In fact, Ambrosiaster and Jerome are the only writers in the late fourth century who explicitly identify the priesthood of the presbyter with that of the bishop. Jerome argues for this identity in his *Commentary on the Letter to Titus* and in his *Ep.* 146 to Evangelus, both of which appear to postdate Ambrosiaster's floruit, and it is very likely that Jerome knew and used Ambrosiaster on this point.[11]

There are several reasons that might account for Ambrosiaster's development in this area. Because there were numerous churches in the vicinity of Rome, especially outside the city walls, it was common for their presbyters not only to baptize and receive penitents but also to consecrate the eucharistic elements. According to a letter of Innocent I to Decentius of Gubbio (416), presbyters within the city were to receive the consecrated bread (*fermentum*) from the bishop, but those outside of the walls had the right to consecrate on their own (*Ep.* 25.5.8 [PL 20:556-57]). There are good reasons to believe that such a custom obtained in Ambrosiaster's day.[12] In his comment on 1 Tim 4:14 ("Do not neglect the gift that is in

---

10. Maurice Bévenot, "'Sacerdos' as Understood by Cyprian," *JTS* n.s. 30 (1979): 413-29; Pierre-Marie Gy, "Remarques sur le vocabulaire antique du sacerdoce chrétien," in *Études sur le sacrement de l'ordre* (Paris: Cerf, 1957), 125-45: "De la seconde moitié du IVe siècle jusqu'au VIe, *sacerdos* désigne normalement l'évêque: Sauf indication contraire du contexte, *sacerdos* est synonyme d'*episcopus*; Mais on l'applique aussi occasionnellement au prêtre dans son pouvoir eucharistique et cultuel" (quotation at 144-45).

11. See Jerome, *Comm. Tit.* 1:5b (PL 26:563) and *Ep.* 146 (CSEL 56:308-12), which is evidently dependent on Ambrosiaster, *Quaest.* 101 (CSEL 50:193-98), "The Boasting of the Roman Deacons." On the priority of Ambrosiaster, see Alexander Souter, *A Study of Ambrosiaster*, TS 7.4 (Cambridge: Cambridge University Press, 1905), 170-71. Ferdinand Prat also maintained the priority of Ambrosiaster and the dependence of Jerome: "Les prétentions des diacres romaines au quatrième siècle," *RSR* 3 (1912): 463-75. For the contrary view, see Sophie Lunn-Rockliffe, *Ambrosiaster's Political Theology*, OECS (Oxford: Oxford University Press, 2007), 20-22.

12. According to the *Liber pontificalis* 40, Siricius, successor of Damasus in the

you, which was given to you through prophecy with the laying on of hands by the council of elders"), Ambrosiaster described the result of ecclesial ordination thus: "The words of the laying on of hands are mystical: through them the one chosen for this work is confirmed, receiving authority, as his own conscience testifies, so that he may dare to offer to God the sacrifice in place of the Lord" (In 1 Tim. 4:13–14 [§2]). If Ambrosiaster was a presbyter in one of the extramural churches at Rome, his sense of the priesthood of presbyters would have been shaped by his own work in offering the eucharistic sacrifice.

But there may be another reason for Ambrosiaster's strong insistence on the identity of the presbyter as "priest" (*sacerdos*). Among the *Quaestiones* there is a brief text titled "The Boasting of the Roman Deacons" (*Quaest.* 101). Addressed to an anonymous deacon at Rome who claimed that deacons were equal or even superior to presbyters, this *quaestio* presents a vigorous defense of the superior status of presbyters. Ambrosiaster's argument entails the claim that, unlike deacons, presbyters and bishops were the true "priests" (*sacerdotes*) and "chief priests" (*antestites*) of God. Deacons were merely "servants" (*ministri*) of priests, like the Levites of the Old Testament, whose task had been to carry the tabernacle (1 Chr 23:26), cut wood, and draw water for the altar (Josh 9:27). To equate deacons with presbyters, Ambrosiaster argued, is as outrageous as equating slaves with masters or attendants with prefects (*Quaest.* 101.2 [CSEL 50:191]). Citing Num 3:6 ("Bring the tribe of Levi near, and set them before Aaron the priest, that they may serve him"), Ambrosiaster noted that presbyters continued in the role of Aaron the priest, to be served by the deacons as Levites: "What is more obvious than this example, which even now is preserved in the church?"[13] Ambrosiaster's polemic against the unnamed deacon suggests that intraclerical rivalry partly motivated his insistence on the priestly identity of presbyters.

Another dimension of Ambrosiaster's concern with clerical status and identity is his emphasis on the discipline of complete sexual continence for the higher clergy after ordination. He addressed this topic both in the *Quaestiones* and in the Commentary. His comments are among the earliest

---

see of Rome, "decreed that no presbyter was permitted to consecrate without receiving the consecrated element from the bishop of that place." Text in Louis Duchesne, ed., *Le Liber pontificalis: Texte, introduction et commentaire*, 3 vols. (Paris: Thorin, 1886), 1:87.

13. *Quaest.* 101.3 (CSEL 50:191): *Quid hoc exemplo apertius, quod etiam nunc in ecclesia custoditur?*

pieces of evidence for this requirement, roughly contemporaneous with the letter *Ad Gallos episcopos*, probably to be attributed to Damasus, a text that also presented the continence requirement.[14] Although Ambrosiaster does not state that the practice was an innovation, the fact that he provided an extended explanation of it suggests that he may have been aware that clerical sexual continence was not universally observed. The contemporary witness of *Ad Gallos episcopos*, the *De officiis* of Ambrose, and the decretals of Siricius also show that clerical sexual continence was not always observed and was sometimes even unknown outside Italy.[15]

Ambrosiaster offered two slightly different arguments for the continence discipline. In *Quaest.* 127, "The Sin of Adam and Eve," he engaged in a vigorous defense of the goodness of sexual relations and procreation in the face of critiques by radical ascetics, such as Marcion, the Manichaeans, and, perhaps, Jerome.[16] At the end of this treatise, he raised the following question: "If marriage is something licit and good, why are priests [*sacerdotes*] not allowed to have wives, that is, why are they no longer allowed to have intercourse after they have been ordained?" Ambrosiaster proceeded to answer the question, explaining how sexual relations could be good and yet something from which ordained clergy needed to abstain. Just as temporary abstinence from good and licit behavior is sometimes required of the laity, he argued, so permanent abstinence is required of the higher clergy:

---

14. Though sometimes attributed to Siricius, *Ad Gallos episcopos* more likely was the product of a Roman synod under Damasus, perhaps edited with the assistance of Jerome. For this argument, see Yves-Marie Duval, *La décrétale Ad Gallos Episcopos: Son texte et son auteur*, VCSup 73 (Leiden: Brill, 2005), 125–38; see also Ursula Reutter, *Damasus, Bischof von Rom (366–384): Leben und Werk* (Tübingen: Mohr Siebeck, 2009), 192–233. For a different view, see Christian Hornung, *Directa ad decessorem: Ein kirchenhistorisch-philologischer Kommentar zur ersten Dekretale des Siricius von Rom*, JAC.E, Kleine Reihe 8 (Münster: Aschendorff, 2011), 267–83, who defends authorship by Siricius.

15. In his *De officiis*, composed in 386, Ambrose observes, "In quite a number of out-of-the-way places [*in plerisque abditioribus locis*], men who have been exercising a ministry—even, in some cases, the priesthood itself—have fathered children" (*Off.* 249; text and translation in Ivor Davidson, ed., *Ambrose: De officiis* [Oxford: Oxford University Press, 2001], 1:260–61). Similar conclusions can be drawn from *Ad Gallos episcopos* 1.2 and 2.5 (Duval, *La décrétale Ad Gallos Episcopos*, 26 and 30–32), and from Siricius, *Ep.* 1.7 (PL 13:1138) and *Ep.* 5.3 (PL 13:1160–61).

16. Argued by David G. Hunter, "*On the Sin of Adam and Eve*: A Little-Known Defense of Marriage and Childbearing by Ambrosiaster," HTR 82 (1989): 283–99.

> Is everything that is permitted in the presence of other people also permitted in the presence of the emperor? How much more in matters that concern God! This is why God's chief priest [*antestitem eius*] must be purer than other people, for he has the role [*personam habere*] of God. He is God's representative [*vicarius*], so that what is permissible for others is not permissible for him, because every day he must act in the place of Christ [*Christi vicem*], either by praying for the people, or by offering the sacrifice, or by baptizing. (*Quaest.* 127.36 [CSEL 50:415]).

In *Quaest.* 127 Ambrosiaster's primary argument for clerical sexual abstinence is that the priest is a representative or *vicarius* of God. Like an official who serves and represents the emperor, the bishop or presbyter needs to present himself in a state of purity worthy of his lord.

Ambrosiaster presents a somewhat different argument in his Commentary, where he treats the question in the context of a note on 1 Tim 3:12–13. Here he stresses ritual purity as the primary motivation for the requirement and appeals to the temporary sexual continence observed by Old Testament priests as a precedent for the conduct of Christian priests:

> For the ancient Levites and priests were allowed to have relations with their wives, because they spent much of their time free from the duties of ministry or priesthood. For there were a large number of priests and a great many Levites, and each one served at the divine ceremonies for a fixed period of time, according to the procedures established by David (see 1 Chr 6:31–53).... So during the time when they were not required to serve at the altar, they were looking after their own households. But whenever the time for their ministry approached, they underwent purification for several days before going to the temple to make offering to God. (In 1 Tim. 3:12–13 [§§2–3])

After thus citing the Old Testament precedent, Ambrosiaster turned to the Christian clergy and argued that they, too, are under similar restrictions of ritual purity, but no longer have the opportunity to practice rites of purification because of the daily demands of sacramental practice. He appealed specifically to the organization of the Roman church:

> But now it is necessary that there be seven deacons and a good number of presbyters, so that there might be two of them in each of the churches, and one bishop in the city. And because of this all of them must abstain from intercourse with women, because it is necessary for them to be ready each day in the church; nor do they have any interval during which

they might undergo legitimate purification after intercourse, as was the case with the ancient priests. For the offering must be made in places of pilgrimage every seven days, if not on a daily basis, or even twice a week. (In 1 Tim. 3:12–13 [§§3–4])

As a presbyter in the church at Rome, Ambrosiaster was knowledgeable about the requirement of sexual continence and familiar with its various rationales. In this instance, he presents the discipline as the result of the specific needs of the Roman church in its liturgical ministries. While his extended explanation of the requirement might indicate that the requirement was a relatively recent development at Rome and, therefore, needed explanation, he says nothing to suggest that the matter was seriously disputed, at least not within clerical circles at Rome.

7.2. Roles and Status of Women

One of the most striking—indeed, disconcerting—aspects of Ambrosiaster's work is the attention he gives to the place of women both in society at large and in the church. While "misogynistic" would be too strong and anachronistic a word to use, one could certainly classify his views as patriarchal in the literal and classic sense. He believed strongly in a natural order of creation that included a hierarchy of gender relations both in the church and in Roman society. Ambrosiaster based his understanding of this hierarchy on a reading of the opening chapters of Genesis as viewed through the lens of the Pastoral epistles and other Pauline letters. At the center of this vision was the notion that women were not created according to the image of God. The practical result of Ambrosiaster's theories was his insistence on the subordination of women to men in the domestic sphere, in the church, and in the wider society.[17]

Ambrosiaster's position can be traced to his peculiar notion of the image of God in human beings. Commenting on Gen 1:26, Ambrosiaster portrayed the image of God as signifying a relationship of derivation: "This is what it means for a human being [*hominem*] to be made 'in the image of God': that one made one, so that just as all things are from one God, so too the entire human race is from one human being. But this is the 'likeness': that just as the Son is from the Father, so also is the woman from the man

---

17. A more detailed account can be found in David G. Hunter, "The Paradise of Patriarchy: Ambrosiaster on Woman as (Not) God's Image," *JTS* n.s. 43 (1992): 447–69.

[*de viro mulier*], so that the authority of the one beginning is preserved" (*Quaest.* 21 [CSEL 50:47–48]). Recalling the account of the woman's creation from the side of the man (Gen 2:21–22), Ambrosiaster concluded that only the man (*vir*) could be the image of the one God because he was the one source of the woman: "This is the image of God in the man: that one God made one human being, so that just as all things come from one God, so too all human beings came from one human being" (In 1 Cor. 11:5–7 [§2]). He confirmed this interpretation by invoking 1 Cor 11:7, "The man should not veil his head because he is the image and glory of God," and by appealing to 1 Tim 2:12, "The woman is not permitted to teach or to have authority over a man."

For Ambrosiaster, this theory of woman's subordination to man had direct social consequences. In *Quaest.* 45, "On the Image," he cited restrictions on women's roles in Roman civil law as evidence of their subordinate status: "How can it be said of woman that she is the image of God, when it is clear that she is subject to the dominion of a man and has no authority? For she is not able to teach or to be a witness [*testis*] or to guarantee a legal pledge [*fidem dicere*] or to be a judge [*iudicare*]. All the more so is she unable to give commands [*imperare*]!" (*Quaest.* 45.3 [CSEL 50:83]).

In another of the *Quaestiones* Ambrosiaster argued that the power to rule (*imperium*) itself constitutes the image of God in man, insofar as rulers model the authority of the one God: "This is the image of God in man, that he was made, as it were, one lord from whom all the rest would arise. He holds the *imperium* of God as his representative [*vicarius*], since every king bears the image of God. And that is why woman was not made in the image of God." (*Quaest.* 106.17 [CSEL 50:243]). As several scholars have observed, Ambrosiaster stands at the beginning of a potent tradition in Western political thought that identified the earthly ruler as God's representative (*vicarius Dei*).[18]

Ambrosiaster presented a slightly different viewpoint in his Commentary by focusing on the subjection of women within the church. He takes patriarchal notions that were present in the Pauline text and exaggerates them by inserting new levels of meaning. For example, while commenting on 1 Cor 11:3–16, where Paul stated that women must pray or prophesy with

---

18. See Ernst Kantorowicz, *The King's Two Bodies: A Study in Medieval Political Theology* (Princeton: Princeton University Press, 1957), 88–91 and 161, and Robert A. Markus, "The Latin Fathers," in *The Cambridge History of Medieval Political Thought*, ed. J. H. Burns (Cambridge: Cambridge University Press, 1988), 100–101.

a veil or "power" over their heads "on account of the angels" (1 Cor 11:10), Ambrosiaster offered a novel interpretation of the significance of the veil:

> The veil signifies "power." He says that the "angels" are the bishops, as the Revelation of John teaches.... Therefore the woman ought to veil her head because she is not the image of God, but so that she may be shown to be subordinate. Since the transgression began through her, she ought to have this sign, so that in the church out of reverence for the bishop she should not have her head uncovered, but veiled; nor should she have the power to speak, because the bishop has the role [*personam*] of Christ. Therefore, because guilt originated with her, she ought to appear subordinate in the presence of a bishop, as if she were before a judge, since he is the representative of the Lord. (In 1 Cor. 11:8–10)

Here Ambrosiaster alludes to the teaching of 1 Tim 2:11–14, where the author attributes the subordinate place of women to Eve's role in the first sin. Now, it is not only the order of creation that dictates a woman's submission, in Ambrosiaster's view, but also "because guilt originated with her." This twofold rationale for female subordination is made explicit in his comment on 1 Cor 14:34 ("Let your women be silent in the churches"): "she is ordered to be subordinate for two reasons: because she is from the man and because sin entered through her" (In 1 Cor. 14:34). Ambrosiaster was sensitive to the different rationales for female submission, and he was careful to argue that the gendered hierarchy is not merely a result of the fall but is based in the original order of creation or *lex naturae*.[19] It has been suggested that Ambrosiaster's emphasis in this matter may have been a reaction against exegetes, such as Jerome, who tended to see female celibacy as a way for women to escape their guilt and transcend their subordinate status.[20] In Ambrosiaster's view, female subordination would have been inescapable because it was grounded in the order of creation.

7.3. Marriage, Celibacy, and Asceticism

Consistent with his traditionalist approach to church leadership and women's roles, Ambrosiaster expressed little enthusiasm for the ascetic renun-

---

19. He makes this argument explicitly in *Quaest.* 127.29–30 (CSEL 50:411–12) and In 1 Tim. 2:13–14; for the expression *lex naturae* as grounds for women's submission, see In 1 Cor. 14:34.

20. Hunter, "Paradise of Patriarchy," 458–68.

ciation that was sweeping the Roman world in the late fourth century. Although he was clearly sympathetic to compulsory sexual continence for the higher clergy—and, at one point, even suggested that a clergyman is better off unmarried (see In 1 Tim. 3:3–4)—there is no trace of that zeal for female virginity or monasticism that was so characteristic of some of his contemporaries, such as Ambrose of Milan or Jerome.[21] As Peter Brown once observed, Ambrosiaster "went out of his way to show that it was quite possible to enjoy the dignity of a celibate priesthood without sharing Jerome's undisguised contempt for once-married clergymen.... It was a view more acceptable to the *esprit de corps* of the clergy than was Jerome's invidious exaltation of a purity better left to nuns."[22] In this respect Ambrosiaster's views cohered more closely with those of Siricius, the successor of Damasus in the see of Rome, and (we must believe) with those of the majority of the Roman clergy.[23]

Ambrosiaster's moderation in matters of sexuality can be illustrated in several ways. In *Quaest.* 127, "On the Sin of Adam and Eve," he argued vigorously against the Marcionite and Manichaean repudiation of sexual relations. He insisted that sex is something good and created by God, not merely the result of some fallout from the first sin, as many of his contemporaries taught.[24] Unlike other fourth-century Christians who exalted the life of the Christian virgin, Ambrosiaster appears to be somewhat cautious about female virginity. For example, while commenting on 1 Cor 7:34–35, where Paul notes that the married woman is "anxious about the affairs of the world, how to please her husband," whereas virgins are free to "think about the affairs of the Lord," Ambrosiaster observed that matters are not always so simple: "For we see virgins thinking about the world and those who are joined in matrimony being zealous for the Lord's works. God will not impute sanctity to these virgins and God will grant a reward to these marriages, since though bound by earthly and carnal ties, they put forth

---

21. Curiously, the words *monk* and *monastery* never appear in his oeuvre, perhaps a sign of his reluctance to embrace the new movement.

22. Peter Brown, *The Body and Society: Men, Women, and Sexual Renunciation in Early Christianity* (New York: Columbia University Press, 1988), 377–78.

23. See David G. Hunter, *Marriage, Celibacy, and Heresy in Ancient Christianity: The Jovinianist Controversy*, OECS (Oxford: Oxford University Press, 2007), 159–70, 208–19, 239–42. The moderate attitude of the Roman clergy toward marriage has also been noted by Charles Pietri, "Le mariage chrétien à Rome," in *Histoire vécue du peuple chrétien*, ed. Jean Delumeau (Toulouse: Privat, 1979), 1:105–31.

24. See Hunter, "*On the Sin of Adam and Eve.*"

the effort, so that in the future they would merit something of the eternal prize" (In 1 Cor. 7:35 [§2]).

Ambrosiaster expressed similar sentiments in his commentary on 1 Tim 5, where the apostle recommended that younger widows should remarry and become *matres familias*. As Ambrosiaster saw it, the ascetic life presented the real danger of hypocrisy:

> For it is better to look after one's own home than to be a cringing flatterer in someone else's home. It is much more profitable to get married than to strut ostentatiously under a good and pious profession. It is better modestly to seek sustenance by one's own hands than shamelessly to wait in idleness for handouts from someone else. For Satan finds an occasion to overthrow thoughtless souls when they behave improperly while professing pious things. For nothing is as dangerous as when one's deeds contradict one's profession. (In 1 Tim. 5:14–15)

Ambrosiaster's observations about the possibility of genuine sanctity in the married life and his warning about the pitfalls of pride in the ascetic life were echoed in subsequent decades by men as diverse as Jovinian and Augustine. As a conservative clergyman at Rome, he harbored serious reservations about the new modes of ascetic piety that were beginning to impact the Western church in the late fourth century.

Finally, it is noteworthy that Ambrosiaster's moderate attitude toward ascetic piety is also evident in his discussion of wealth and poverty. This is most apparent in his *Quaest.* 124 (CSEL 50:381–84), "Does the Praise or Blame of an Action Vary According to Persons?" In this brief *quaestio* Ambrosiaster argued that the moral evaluation of human virtues and vices varies according to the wealth or poverty of the person concerned. Displays of charity (*misericordia*), for example, are more praiseworthy in a poor person who lacks resources and thereby demonstrates greater trust in God (*Quaest.* 124.1). Likewise, theft is more damnable in a rich person than in a poor person whose penury compels him to steal, unlike the rich person who is not content with his own property but often seizes what belongs to the poor (*Quaest.* 124.2). Conversely, pride and lust are more to be condemned in a poor person than in a rich person, whose riches and power present more frequent occasions for these vices, whereas for the poor to take pride in their poverty is akin to "madness" (*insania*) (*Quaest.* 124.4, 7). As Sophie Lunn-Rockliffe has observed, Ambrosiaster's discussion "should be located within the context of [the] Christian debate about the relative worth of poverty and riches, which was part of a wider debate between moderates and ascetics in late fourth-century Rome."[25] Unlike many of his ascetic contemporaries who categorically elevated poverty over wealth, Ambrosiaster took a more nuanced approach and argued that neither wealth nor poverty constituted an inherently superior state of life and that both states offered opportunities and pitfalls for the moral life. In this respect Ambrosiaster stood "in a long Christian tradition of 'defending the rich man,'" such as that represented by Clement of Alexandria.[26]

---

25. Sophie Lunn-Rockliffe, "A Pragmatic Approach to Poverty and Riches: Ambrosiaster's *quaestio* 124," in *Poverty in the Roman World*, ed. Margaret Atkins and Robin Osborne (Cambridge: Cambridge University Press, 2009), 117.

26. Ibid., 129. As Lunn-Rockliffe goes on to note, Ambrosiaster's view "identifies him firmly as less icy and more flexible in his attitude to renunciation than his more rigorous ascetic opponents, such as Jerome."

8. A Note on the Translation

It is customary in the series Writings from the Greco-Roman World to present text and translation on facing pages. However, because of the complexity of the text of Ambrosiaster's Commentary, we decided that it would be neither feasible nor wise to do so, particularly for the commentary on Romans. Its text is already presented on facing pages in the CSEL edition, and anyone wishing to consult the Latin should in fact consult all three recensions.

We have translated *recensio* γ and have noted all substantive changes from prior recensions. We also have noted any passage where the text is attested only by "mixed" manuscripts (indicated in the edition by the sigla ⌈ ⌉), as well as any passage where the text is problematic or suspect.[1] We have not noted stylistic changes from prior recensions that do not substantially alter the meaning of a comment: changes in word order, vocabulary, the case of a noun, the mood or tense of a verb, and so on. We have not provided the Latin text for the changes that we note, since anyone wishing to examine these changes more closely should consult the CSEL edition, where they will be able to consider all the changes in a given comment, both substantive and stylistic.

In our translation we have followed the Latin text fairly closely while at the same time aiming for readable English. Ambrosiaster's Latin has a number of stylistic habits that can appear tedious if they are replicated in English. He often uses an initial *et* or a postpostive *enim* to indicate a new sentence or a further thought, and he regularly strings together a number of *ut*-clauses. We have not felt ourselves bound to render such constructions mechanically, and we have broken up longer sentences to make them more understandable in English.

---

1. See above §2.2.

Quotations from Scripture, whether in the lemma or the comment, are italicized. When Ambrosiaster quotes, refers to, or echoes expressions from the lemma in his comment, we have placed these in italics as well, so as to highlight what he is paraphrasing or explaining. Wherever Ambrosiaster's biblical text differs significantly from the standard Greek text,[2] we have identified the relevant readings in a note.

The work of translating the Commentary was a collaborative one. Primary responsibility for the translation of individual commentaries was apportioned as follows: Romans (Theodore S. de Bruyn), 1 Corinthians (David G. Hunter), 2 Corinthians (Stephen A. Cooper), Galatians to Colossians (Cooper), 1 Thessalonians to Philemon (Hunter). In order to achieve a relatively consistent style, each translation was read by one other member of the group.

---

2. See above §3.

Part 2
Ambrosiaster's Commentary on Romans

Synopsis

(1)[1] In order to have an understanding of things, one needs to grasp their origins.[2] In fact, only if one is familiar with this book will it be easier to explain the reason for the dispute.[3] Accordingly, if we describe the approach and motive of the letter before us, it can be seen that what we say is true.

(2) It happened, then, that in the time of the apostle Jews were dwelling in Rome because they were living under Roman rule. Among these Jews, those who had come to believe taught the Romans that those who confess Christ should keep the law, for, when the report of the miracles of Christ was heard, the Romans, being sagacious, had been quick to believe. And this reputation for sagacity was deserved, for they immediately amended their ways and remained in Christ, even though they were improperly instructed. Those believers, then, who came from a Jewish background and had a mistaken understanding of Christ were quick to say that the law should be kept, as if in Christ there was no complete salvation.[4]

---

1. *Recensio* α presents the synopsis in the order 1, 4, 2, 3, and 5. *Recensiones* β and γ present it in the order 1, 2, 3, 4, and 5. The order in *recensiones* β and γ is the correct one, since section 5 flows logically from section 4 rather than from section 3.

2. *Recensio* α has "In order to have a knowledge of things, one needs to grasp the origins of things." *Recensio* β has "In order to have a more complete knowledge of things, one needs first to grasp the origins of things."

3. *Recensiones* α and β have "It is easier to explain the reason for the dispute if one is familiar with its beginning." Ambrosiaster understands the dispute among the Roman Christians to be between believers who continued to observe Jewish customs and those who did not; see section 3 of the synopsis.

4. *Recensiones* α and β have "Those, then, who believed in Christ from a Jewish background did not accept, as one is given to understand, that Christ is God from God, thinking that this is contrary to the one God." The difference between *recensiones* α and β and *recensio* γ here is significant. Whereas in the first two recensions Ambrosiaster argues that the error of the believers from a Jewish background was that they denied the divinity of Christ, in the third recension Ambrosiaster argues that their error was to insist that believers should continue to observe the law. Alessandra Pollastri, "Il pro-

(3) The apostle said, therefore, that these believers[5] had not received the spiritual grace of God.[6] They are the same as those who also undermined the Galatians such that the Galatians abandoned the teaching of the apostle and followed Jewish observances.[7] The apostle was angry with the Galatians because they had been easily misled even though they were well instructed. With the Romans, on the other hand, one should not be angry.[8] One should rather praise their faith because, although they had seen no miraculous signs,[9] they had accepted the faith in Christ, though in a faulty sense. They in fact had not heard of the mystery of the cross of Christ. But with the arrival in Rome of some people from Judea, such as Aquila and Priscilla, who understood the faith rightly, questions arose about whether meat should or should not be eaten.

(4) The apostle therefore addresses the Romans on four topics,[10] accusing the human race from the outset partly on natural grounds, partly by way of the law.[11] (The Romans are, in fact, the head of all the nations, so

---

logo del commento alla Lettera ai Romani dell'Ambrosiaster," *SSRel* 2 (1978): 93–127, explores the development of Ambrosiaster's interpretation of the letter in order to explain this discrepancy. She argues that Ambrosiaster's efforts to explain Gal 3:20 in the *Quaestiones* and the commentary on Galatians led him to revise his interpretation of the position of believers from a Jewish background in Romans.

5. I.e., the believers in Rome from a Jewish background.

6. *Recensio* α adds "and that therefore they are without confirmation."

7. Literally, "Judaized" (*iudaizarent*). *Recensiones* α and β have "such that they [i.e., the Galatians] abandoned the teaching of the apostles."

8. For the remainder of the section, *recensiones* α and β have "One should rather praise their faith because, although they had seen no miraculous signs from any of the apostles, they [α: had] accepted the faith in Christ, [β: though in accordance with Jewish observance], in words rather than in sense. For the mystery had not been explained to them. Therefore with the arrival of those who had believed rightly, questions arose about whether meat should or should not be eaten and whether the hope that is in Christ is sufficient or whether the law should be kept as well."

9. In *recensio* γ "nor any of the apostles" is attested only by MS Amiens 87. This manuscript often combines material from *recensio* β with material from *recensio* γ; see the introduction §2.1.

10. These four topics or lines of argument are woven throughout the ensuing commentary. See Pollastri, "Il prologo," 120–27.

11. *Recensiones* α and β have "accusing the human race from the outset on natural grounds." As Pollastri, "Il prologo," 126, observes, Ambrosiaster regards the Roman Christians as a microcosm of the whole human race because they comprise believers from both Jewish and gentile backgrounds and illustrate the situation of those who adhere to the law of Moses and those who are outside the law of Moses.

that all nations learn from their case.¹²) The first topic is where he presents himself (see Rom 1:1–17): who he is and to whom he belongs and what he did and how, too, he attacks heresies. The second topic is where he charges that they did not submit, in keeping with nature, to the one God, and that they did such indecent and shameful things with one another, for which they were spurned by God. Believers, therefore, should be applauded. The third topic is that the Romans rejected the law that had been given, which is why the apostle placed the Jews ahead of the Greeks. The fourth topic is where he teaches that the Jews had deviated from the law and the prophets with regard to Christ¹³ and became like the gentiles, so that both are in need of the mercy of God and must hope for salvation not through the law but through faith in Christ Jesus.

(5) This is the reason why he devotes all his energies to detaching them from the law—for *the law and the prophets were until John* (Luke 16:16)—and establishing them in faith alone in Christ. He defends the gospel as if he were against the law, though he did not destroy the law but preferred Christianity. He shows that Christ was promised in such a way that with his coming the law came to an end¹⁴—although not entirely, because an abridgement was made of the law which provided for salvation in a shortened form. For the ancients were instructed about many things because of the hardness of their heart, and the result was a heavy burden. God's mercy abridged these things through Christ, granting forgiveness for past actions. A person who wants to live under the law is, therefore, ungrateful for God's mercy. In fact, Moses had said: *Thus you will make the children of Israel afraid* (Lev 15:31), so that wherever they turned they would encounter the law and would never be entirely without anxiety. In order, then, to teach that hope for life and salvation should be placed in Christ without the law and to explain that he is Lord of all, the apostle begins as follows:

---

12. In *recensio* γ MS Amiens 87 has "so that all the other gentiles learn from their case."

13. *Recensio* α has "from the law and the promise of God." *Recensio* β has "from the law and the promise of God with regard to Christ."

14. *Recensiones* α and β have "with his proclamation the law came to an end." The majority of manuscripts of *recensio* γ skip from here to the last sentence of the section. MS Amiens 87 has the intervening material, but it follows *recensiones* α and β for all of the text of section 5.

Romans 1

1:1 *Paul, a slave of Jesus Christ.* (1) He calls himself Paul—that is, "changed"—after having been called Saul.[1] Because Saul means "turmoil" or "tribulation," he calls himself Paul—that is, "tranquil"—after he came to faith in Christ, since our faith is peace now.[2] Although initially he inflicted trials upon the servants of God out of zeal for the law,[3] subsequently he himself suffered trials on account of the hope that earlier he had denied out of love for Judaism. (2) Moreover, by declaring himself to be *a slave of Jesus Christ*, he shows himself to have been freed from the law. He referred to both names of Jesus Christ in order to indicate the person of both God

---

1. In the New Testament "Saul" and "Paul" are mentioned together only at Acts 13:9. Patristic interpreters offered various explanations for the two names; see Michael Compton, "From Saul to Paul: Patristic Interpretation of the Names of the Apostle," in *In Dominico Eloquio/In Lordly Eloquence: Essays on Patristic Exegesis in Honor of Robert Louis Wilken*, ed. Paul M. Blowers et al. (Grand Rapids: Eerdmans, 2002), 50–68. Ambrosiaster is among those who hold that Paul changed his name after his conversion. The etymologies proposed by Ambrosiaster—and it is puzzling that he offers two for "Paul"—are not found elsewhere.

2. *Recensio* β has "Among our ancestors names were devised for a reason, such as Isaac on account of laughter and Jacob on account of his heel. In the same way Paul was called Saul on account of turmoil, but after he believed he calls himself Paul instead of Saul, that is, 'changed.' Because Saul, according to the interpretation just discussed, means 'turmoil' or 'tribulation,' he refers to himself as Paul— that is, as someone who after having been the cause of tribulation has become tranquil and lowly or childlike— after he came to faith in Christ, since our faith is peace now." Augustine frequently associates "Paul" with "lowly" (*humilis*) and "little" (*modicus*); e.g., *Tract. ep. Jo.* 8.2 (SC 75:342), *Enarrat. Ps.* 72.4 (CCSL 39:988), *Serm.* 295.7 (PL 38:1352). The oblique similarity to Augustine and that *recensiones* α and γ agree against *recensio* β suggest that the comment has been altered by a later hand.

3. *Recensiones* α and β have "out of concern for Judaism" rather than "out of zeal for the law."

and the human being,[4] since the Lord is present in both, as the apostle Peter also attests when he says, *He is the Lord of all* (Acts 10:36). Since, then, he is Lord, he is also God, as David says, *The Lord himself is God* (Ps 99:3 LXX = Ps 100:3 ET). The heresies deny this. (3) Thus, to Marcion it seems right out of aversion for the law to deny Christ and his body, and to profess Jesus.[5] But to the Jews and to Photinus it seems right out of zeal for the law[6] to deny that Jesus is God.[7] For whenever scripture says either Jesus or Christ, it sometimes means the person of God, sometimes the person of the human being,[8] as in the gospel, among other passages:[9] *And one Lord Jesus through whom are all things* (1 Cor 8:6),[10] which assuredly refers to the Son of God, in that he is God. Also in the gospel:[11] *For Jesus increased in age and wisdom* (Luke 2:52), which certainly befits a human being.

Called an apostle. (4) Because he acknowledged the Lord and confesses him, having become a capable servant, he indicates that he was promoted when he says *called an apostle*, that is, sent by the Lord to do his work. By this he shows that one who serves Christ, not the law, has merit before God.[12] *For the Son of Man is lord even of the Sabbath* (Matt 12:8).

Set apart for the gospel of God. (5) The gospel of God is the good news by which sinners are called to forgiveness. Because as a Pharisee the apostle held the position of teacher within Judaism, he says that he was *set apart* from the preaching of Judaism *for the gospel of God*, so that, without being

---

4. *Recensiones* α and β do not have "to indicate the person of both God and the human being"; see n. 8 below.

5. *Recensio* α does not have "out of aversion for the law" and "and to profess Jesus." On Marcion, see the introduction §6.3.

6. *Recensio* α does not have "out of zeal for the law."

7. On Photinus, see the introduction §6.3.

8. Where *recensio* γ has "the person of God" and "the person of the human being," *recensiones* α and β have "God" and "human being"; see n. 4 above.

9. The reference in *recensio* γ to the gospel appears to anticipate the second of the quotations that follow. *Recensio* α has only "as in this passage," and *recensio* β has only "as in another passage"; see n. 11 below.

10. Ambrosiaster's Latin text of 1 Cor 8:6, both here and at In 1 Cor. 8:6, reads *one Lord Jesus* (*unus dominus Iesus*). The Greek text of the verse reads *one Lord Jesus Christ* (εἷς κύριος Ἰησοῦς Χριστός). Ambrosiaster alludes to the verse often in his commentary on Romans; see In Rom. 1:10 (§2a); 2:14; 9:30 (§1).

11. *Recensio* α has "Also in another passage."

12. *Recensiones* α and β have "this merit" (*hoc meritum*); *recensio* γ, with *hunc meritum*, either mistakenly takes *meritum* to be masculine rather than neuter or understands *hunc* to refer to the one who has merit.

concerned about the law, he might proclaim Christ, who justifies those who believe in him, something the law was not able to do.[13] (5a)[14] If, then, the law that was given through Moses is from God and the proclamation of the new law is from God, what is the difference? Why does the apostle say that he was transferred from the law which God gave to the gospel of God? This is the difference: it is as if someone advanced from the second rank to the first rank, from something good to something better. The law was given by God to amend conduct, but the gospel of God is the means by which the mystery of God that was hidden for ages in God (see Eph 3:9), namely, Christ, is revealed. All those invited to the gospel get a double gift:[15] they receive forgiveness of sins and become children of God, so that they can no longer die from the second death.[16] This is why the Lord says in the gospel: *This is eternal life, that they may know you, the only and true God, and Jesus Christ whom you have sent* (John 17:3).

1:2 *Which he promised beforehand.* (1) To show that the hope of faith is firm and complete in Christ, he says that the gospel of Christ was already promised by God beforehand so that through it he might teach that Christ is a sufficient guarantor of life. He shows that before Christ came there was witness to him, as the apostle Peter similarly testifies: *For there is given no other name under heaven by which we must be saved* (Acts 4:12).

---

13. *Recensiones* α and β continue: "Yet the gospel is not against the law, but for the law. Indeed, the law itself says that the gospel will come, as the prophet Isaiah says: *There will come from Zion one who will take away and turn away ungodliness* [β: *subjugation*] *from Jacob, and this is my covenant with them, when I have taken away their sins.*" In *recensio* γ MS Amiens 87 alone has the text found in *recensio* β. The sentence attributed to Isaiah combines portions of Isa 59:20 and 27:9. Ambrosiaster also cites these words at In Rom. 9:32 (§3) and 3:22 (§2), and at *Quaest.* 44.3 (CSEL 50:73). There the text reads *avertat impietatem a Iacob* as in *recensio* α, rather than *avertat captivitatem ab Iacob* as in *recensio* β and MS Amiens 87. In fact, *recensio* β and the Amiens manuscript are the only witnesses to this variant in the VL; see Roger Gryson, ed., *Esaias*, VLB 12 (Freiburg: Herder, 1987–1993), 1476–77.

14. Sections whose number is followed by the letter *a* are found only in *recensiones* β and γ or only in *recensio* γ. In this instance, section 5a is found only in *recensio* γ.

15. The term *apophorita* (normally spelled *apophoreta*, from ἀποφορήτα, "things carried away") refers to presents that guests would receive at table to take home with them. Ambrosiaster refers to the practice at *Quaest.* 123.16 (CSEL 50:380).

16. In the Bible the phrase "the second death" is found in Rev 2:11; 20:6, 14; 21:8. According to Ambrosiaster, it refers to confinement in the underworld after the death of the body; see *Quaest.* 47.4 (CSEL 50:93). It is the fate of those who spurn God; see *Quaest.* 33.2 (CSEL 50:62). See the introduction §5.4.

Through his prophets. (2) To indicate more clearly that the coming of Christ was salvific, the apostle even mentioned the individuals through whom God made the promise known, so that from them it would be apparent how true and wonderful the promise is. No one announces something paltry by means of grand forerunners.

In the holy scriptures. (3) He added this to the accumulation of reliable[17] evidence in order to give the believers greater assurance and to commend the law. For the scriptures are holy because they condemn faults and because in them is contained the mystery of the one God and the incarnation of the Son of God for the salvation of humankind, attested by miraculous signs.[18]

1:3 *Concerning his Son.* Because God was promising the world his very own Son, it was fitting that he promised him through eminent men. From them one could know how very mighty the person being foretold was,[19] since God introduced his future coming in the holy scriptures. What is foretold by the saints in the scriptures cannot be regarded as false.[20]

Who was made for him from the seed of David according to the flesh. (2) He says that he who was Son of God according to the Holy Spirit—that is, according to God, because God is spirit (see John 4:24) and is undoubtedly holy[21]—was made Son of God according to the flesh from Mary,[22] as in the verse: *And the Word was made flesh* (John 1:14). As a result, there is now one Son of both God and a human being, Christ Jesus,[23] so that just as he is true God, so also was he a true human being. He will not, however, be

---

17. *Recensio* α does not have "reliable."
18. *Recensio* α has "For the scriptures, which condemn wickedness, are holy, and they contain the mystery both of the one God and of the incarnation of the Son of God for the salvation of humankind."
19. The comment in *recensio* α ends here.
20. The grammatical structure of the concluding clause of the comment in *recensio* β differs from that in *recensio* γ.
21. This parenthetical comment is found only in *recensiones* β and γ. It was probably occasioned by increasing precision in the West about the divinity of the Holy Spirit. See Theodore S. de Bruyn, "Ambrosiaster's Revisions of His *Commentary on Romans* and Roman Synodal Statements about the Holy Spirit," *REAug* 56 (2010): 45–68.
22. *Recensiones* α and β have "from the seed of David" instead of "from Mary."
23. *Recensio* α has "As a result, there is now one Son of God and a human being, the Son of God." *Recensio* β has "As a result, there is now one Son of both God and a human being, the Son of God Christ Jesus." The remainder of the sentence after "Christ Jesus" is found only in *recensio* γ.

a true human being unless he is made of flesh and soul, so as to be complete.²⁴ When God wanted him who was Son of God from eternity but was not known by creation to be revealed for the salvation of humankind, he made him visible and corporeal,²⁵ because he also wanted him to be recognized in power, so that by his passion he might wash people from sins,²⁶ death having been vanquished in the flesh. (3) He was made *from the seed of David* in order that, just he was born of God as king before the ages, so too he would derive his origins *according to the flesh* from a king. He was made by the work of the Holy Spirit from a virgin—in other words, born²⁷—so that, by virtue of the veneration reserved for him on account of this, he might be acknowledged to be more than a human being. For he departed from the human law of birth, as had been foretold by the prophet Isaiah: *Behold a virgin will conceive in the womb* and so on (Isa 7:14), so that when this novel and remarkable event was observed, one might discern that a certain providence of God regarding the visitation of the human race was unfolding.

1:4 *Who was predestined Son of God in power according to the Spirit of sanctification by the resurrection of the dead of Jesus Christ our Lord.*²⁸ (1) In saying *Son of God*, he meant *of God the Father*, and with the addition of *the Spirit of sanctification* he displayed the mystery of the Trinity. Thus, he who was incarnate, who hid what he was, *was predestined according to the Spirit of sanctification* to be revealed *in power* as the *Son of God* when he rose from the dead, as is written in Ps 84: *Truth has sprung from the ground* (Ps 84:12 LXX). (2) All uncertainty and doubt about his resurrection were crushed and suppressed, since even the centurion, seeing the mighty acts, confesses him to be the son of God while he was still on the cross (Matt

---

24. This sentence is found only in *recensio* γ. It is directed against Apollinaris, who held that in Jesus the divine Word or Logos displaced the human soul or mind. See de Bruyn, "Ambrosiaster's Revisions," 60–61.

25. *Recensiones* α and β have "he had to be made visible and corporeal."

26. *Recensiones* α and β have "because he wanted him to be recognized in power and to wash humankind from sins."

27. *Recensio* α has only "He was born of a virgin." On the version of the comment in *recensiones* β and γ, see de Bruyn, "Ambrosiaster's Revisions," 58–59.

28. The VL of Rom 1:4 incorrectly renders ὁρισθέντος, "was designated," as *praedestinatus est*, "was predestined." In his translation of Origen's commentary on Romans, Rufinus notes that the Greek should have been rendered *destinatus*. See Caroline P. Hammond Bammel, *Der Römerbrieftext des Rufin und seine Origenes-Übersetzung*, vol. 10 of *AGLB* (Freiburg: Herder, 1985), 213–14.

27:21–54). For even the disciples had doubts in the face of his death; Cleopas and Ammaus,[29] among others, said: *We supposed that he was the one who was beginning to set Israel free* (Luke 24:21). In fact, the Lord himself says: *When you have lifted up the Son of Man, then you will know that I am he* (John 8:28). Again: *When I am lifted up from the earth, I will draw all things to me* (John 12:32), that is, then I will be recognized to be Lord of all. (3) Moreover, the apostle did not simply say *by the resurrection of Jesus Christ*, but added *of the dead*, because the resurrection of Christ gives rise to the general resurrection.[30] In fact, in Christ one sees this great power and victory: that when he was dead he worked the same power that he had worked when he was alive.[31] From this feat it is clear that he made a fool of death in order to redeem us.[32] This is why the apostle calls him *our Lord*.

1:5 *Through whom we have received grace and apostleship to bring about the obedience of faith among all the nations for his name's sake.* (1) When Jesus was revealed to be Son of God in power after the resurrection, he gave grace by justifying sinners and he established apostles,[33] whose associate Paul here says he is. Apostleship, therefore, came with the grace of God's gift, which is not the case with the apostles from the Jews.[34] (2) The apostles received this power from God the Father through Christ the Lord so that in his place they might render the teaching of the Lord persuasive through powerful signs (see Mark 3:14–15). As a result, when unbelieving Jews saw the same power that they envied in the Savior astonish the

---

29. Relying on a text of Luke 24:13 that takes "Emmaus" to be the name of a disciple rather than a town, Ambrosiaster refers to the two disciples as Cleopas and Ammaus. See Ambrosiaster, *Quaest.* 77.2 (CSEL 50:131–32); Alexander Souter, "'Emmaus' Mistaken for a Person," *ExpTim* 13 (1901–1902): 429–30; and Adolf Jülicher, Walter Matzkow, and Kurt Aland, eds., *Lucas-Evangelium*, vol. 3 of *Itala: Das Neue Testament in altlateinischer Überlieferung*, 2nd ed. (Berlin: de Gruyter, 1976), 272.

30. Ambrosiaster takes the phrase *ex resurrectione mortuorum Iesu Christi* to refer not only to Jesus's own resurrection from death (see §1 above) but also to his raising of others from death. For Ambrosiaster, Jesus's victory over death is manifested immediately after his crucifixion in the release of the righteous dead from the underworld. See the introduction §5.4.

31. This clause is found only in *recensiones* β and γ.

32. *Recensio* α has "By this feat he redeemed us."

33. *Recensiones* α and β have "nominated apostles."

34. The "apostles from the Jews" refers to believers from a Jewish background who had instructed the first Roman believers that they should observe the law. See In Rom. synopsis (§2) and 1:9–10 (§3).

crowds in his servants, they were tormented all the more fiercely.³⁵ Since what is preached is incredible to the world, power bears witness to teaching in order to render the preaching believable through deeds. (3) He calls *apostles* those who were sent to preach the faith to *all the nations* so that they might obey and be saved. It would, therefore, be clear that the gift of God was granted no longer to the Jews alone but in fact to all the nations as well, and that it is God's will to have mercy on all people in Christ and through Christ through the preaching of his representatives, that is, *for his name's sake*, as he says elsewhere: *for whom we discharge the office of ambassador* (2 Cor 5:20).

1:6 *Among whom you also have been called to belong to Jesus Christ.* That is, through the office of ambassador that we discharge among all the nations for the sake of the name of Jesus Christ, among whom *you also have been called*, since God's gift has been sent to everyone.³⁶ The apostle says this so that when the Romans hear that they have been called along with the others, they might understand that they should no longer operate under the law, because the other nations took up faith in Christ without the law of Moses.³⁷

1:7 *To all who at Rome are in the love of God,* ³⁸ *called saints.* (1) Although he writes to the Romans, he nevertheless specifies that he writes to those *who are in the love of God*. Who are they, if not those who have the right understanding about the Son of God? They are *saints*, and they are said to be *called*.³⁹ For someone who understands wrongly is not said to be *called*.⁴⁰ For example, those who operate under the law do not understand Christ in the right way and do God the Father an injustice when they doubt whether there is complete salvation in Christ. They are, therefore, not saints and they are not called *called*.⁴¹

---

35. This sentence is found only in *recensiones* β and γ.
36. In *recensio* γ "since God's gift has been sent to everyone" is attested by only some manuscripts.
37. *Recensiones* α and β have "law of Christ" instead of "faith of Christ."
38. Although Ambrosiaster's biblical text has "in the love of God" (*in caritate dei*), among biblical witnesses there is stronger support for "God's beloved" (ἀγαπητοῖς θεοῦ). See Bruce M. Metzger, *A Textual Commentary on the Greek New Testament*, 2nd ed. (Stuttgart: Deutsche Bibelgesellschaft, 1994), 446; and Robert Jewett with Roy D. Kotansky, *Romans: A Commentary*, Hermeneia (Minneapolis: Fortress, 2007), 95.
39. *Recensio* α has "and they are *called*" instead of "and they are said to be *called*."
40. *Recensiones* α and β do not have this sentence; see In Rom. 1:13 (§§1–2).
41. *Recensiones* α and β have "For those who operate under the law understand

Grace to you and peace from God our Father and the Lord Jesus Christ. (2) He says that grace and peace are with those who believe in the right way. *Grace* is the means by which sinners are cleansed; *peace*, the means by which those who were considered enemies are reconciled to the creator,[42] as the Lord says: *Whatever house you enter and they welcome you, say: "Peace to this house"* (Luke 10:5). (3) Furthermore, to show that there is no peace and no hope without Christ, the apostle added that grace and peace are not only from God the Father but also from Christ Jesus. He says that God is *our Father* because he is our source, since everything comes from him. He says that Christ is *Lord* because, having been redeemed by his blood, we have been made children of God.

1:8 *First, I truly thank my God through Jesus Christ,*[43] *because your faith is proclaimed throughout the world.* (1) Having finished the preface, he first of all declares, in his capacity as apostle to the gentiles, that it gives him joy that the Romans, though they reigned supreme in the world, have submitted themselves to the Christian faith, a faith that appeared base and foolish to the wise of this age. (2)[44] Although there were, in fact, many reasons he rejoiced in the Romans—they were attentive to instruction and enthusiastic in good work and assiduous[45] in doing well rather than speaking well (something that is not far removed from divine religion) —nevertheless he says that he especially rejoices that the report of their

---

Christ in the wrong way and do God the Father an injustice when they doubt whether there is complete hope of salvation in Christ. They are, therefore, not saints." In *recensio* γ this part of the comment is attested only by MS Amiens 87. I have translated the text as printed in the edition because if the text attested by the Amiens manuscript is removed the transition from *vocatus, sicut* to *neque vocati vocantur* is problematic.

42. *Recensiones* α and β have "Grace consists in the fact that they were absolved from their sins; peace, that they were reconciled to the creator from among the ungodly."

43. Ambrosiaster's biblical text omits the phrase "for all of you" (*pro omnibus vobis*), which corresponds to περὶ πάντων ὑμῶν in the Greek text.

44. *Recensiones* α and β have "Although there were, in fact, many reasons he rejoiced in the Romans—they were remarkable in teaching and desirous of good work rather than good speech (something that is not far removed from divine religion)— nevertheless he says that above all he rejoices in the fact that their faith sped everywhere. Although it was not according to the rule of truth handed down from its author, he still gives thanks because they began to worship that which was from the one God as presented under the name of Christ, for he knows that they are able to grow."

45. In *recensio* γ "and assiduous" is attested only by MSS Amiens 87 and Paris lat. 1759.

faith was traveling everywhere. For it was wonderful to behold the rulers of the nations being turned toward the promise of the Jews.[46] Even though they did not have a correct faith, he still gives thanks because with the introduction of the name of Christ they had begun to worship what is from the one God, for he knows that they are able to grow. (3) With this he shows his love toward them as well, when he rejoices with them in their good beginning and encourages them to grow. The reason he says that he gives thanks only to *his* God—since God was not yet entirely their God—is that all fatherhood is from him (see Eph 3:15). (4) Moreover, because the whole arrangement of our salvation is indeed from God but through Christ, not through the law or through any of the prophets, he says that he truly gives thanks *to God*—but does so *through Christ*—that the report of their faith had emanated from many people, so that this too may be attributed to God's providence through Christ.[47] For either the rest of the believers rejoiced to be confirmed in their faith[48] when they saw their rulers become their brothers in the faith,[49] or unbelievers, surely, were able to believe easily as a result of their example.[50] For someone of lower status is quick to do what he sees done by a more important person.[51]

1:9 *For God is my witness, whom I serve in my spirit in the gospel of his Son, that without ceasing I remember you* **1:10** *always in my prayers.* (1) To encourage them to love, he names God as witness, whom he serves and to whom he also prays for them.[52] He serves God not in the law,[53] but *in the gospel of his Son*; that is, not in what Moses the slave handed down, but in what the beloved Son taught. For the gospel is as different from the law as a master is from a slave. This is not because the law is unsatisfactory,[54] but because the gospel is better. (2) He serves God in the gospel of his Son, therefore, to show that it is God's will that God be believed in Christ.

---

46. This sentence is found only in *recensio* γ.
47. *Recensio* α does not have "so that this too may be attributed to God's providence through Christ."
48. *Recensio* α does not have "to be confirmed in their faith."
49. *Recensiones* α and β have "Christians" instead of "their brothers in the faith."
50. *Recensiones* α and β do not have "easily."
51. *Recensiones* α and β have "For a subordinate easily does what he sees done by a superior."
52. *Recensio* α does not have "to whom he also prays for them."
53. I have not translated *serviendo*. It is not found in *recensiones* α or β and is attested only by MS Amiens 87 in *recensio* γ.
54. *Recensiones* α and β have "is bad."

Whom I too serve. How? *In my spirit*, he says; not in circumcision performed by hand or in new moons and the sabbath and the distinction between foods, but in spirit, that is, in the mind. Since God is spirit, he should be served[55] in spirit or with the heart; for someone who is served with the heart is served out of faith. (2a)[56] The Lord also bore witness to this to the Samaritan woman who thought that God wishes to be worshiped on a mountain, when he said: *The hour is coming and is now here, when the true worshipers will worship the Father in spirit and truth. For the Father seeks such as these who worship him. God is spirit; therefore, those who worship must worship in spirit and truth* (John 4:23–24). It is not the place that commends the prayer, but a devout heart. That is, they should in truth worship in spirit God as spirit and Christ, the one from whom are all things and the one through whom are all things (see 1 Cor 8:6).[57] These are the worshipers the Father seeks. (3) He stresses that he remembers them in his prayers in order to sow love in them; it creates longing for him in them. For who does not love the person whom he hears was mindful of him? If they willingly listened to instruction in the name of Christ from those who had not been sent,[58] how much more would they not long to listen to him whom they knew to be an apostle and whose words were accompanied by power.

Asking if somehow I may now at last find the way propitious in the will of God for coming to you. (4) He explains the meaning of his prayer for them. He says that he entreats God that, by the will of God, whose gift he proclaims, he might come to Rome for their benefit.[59] For if an action is

---

55. I have not translated *potius*. It is not found in *recensiones* α or β and is attested only by MS Amiens 87 in *recensio* γ.

56. This section is found only in *recensiones* β and γ.

57. In this compressed remark, which echoes the passage from John, Ambrosiaster appears to add that to worship of God in spirit and truth one must worship both God the Father and Christ.

58. *Recensio* α has "If they willingly accepted instruction in the name of Christ, but with false words, from those who had not been sent." *Recensio* β does not have "but with false words." On the "those who had not been sent," see the synopsis (§2).

59. *Recensiones* α and β have "the city" instead of "Rome." This is also the case at In Rom. 1:13 (§1). However, at In Rom. 1:9–10 (§7); 15:22–24 (§1); and 16:3–5 (§1) only *recensio* α refers to the city without naming it. This suggests that *recensio* α was written in Rome for personal use or a Roman audience, since there was no need to specify that the city to which Paul wished to come was Rome, and that *recensiones* β and γ were revised for a broader audience.

taken by the will of God, it will be beneficial. (5) He prays that for some reason he might now be given an occasion to come to the city, because he had been busy preaching to other people. He deems the way propitious if he comes with God willing it, because God's will is provident. The way is propitious, therefore, when the effort of the journey is not in vain. (6) He asks that God finish calling them to his grace. He speaks with an eager spirit; he longs for them, knowing that it benefits both them and him, as he says elsewhere: *What is our joy and our crown? Is it not you at the coming of the Lord?* (see 1 Thess 2:19). For the apostle's yield is more bountiful if he wins many people.[60] Besides, the rejoicing is greater when the powerful of the earth turn back to God; the worse the enemy, the greater the need to be reconciled and the more bountiful the apostle's yield, if he wins many people.[61] (7) And so, the occasion for his wish was granted,[62] that when he was arrested, he appealed to Caesar, was sent, with God willing it, to Rome,[63] and fulfilled the purpose of his own will. Then, when he was shipwrecked, the Lord stood by him and said: *"Don't be afraid, Paul. For just as you have testified about me in Jerusalem, so too in Rome"* (Acts 23:11).[64]

---

60. In *recensio* γ "as he says elsewhere: *What is our joy and our crown? Is it not you at the coming of the Lord?* For the apostle's yield is more bountiful if he wins many people" is attested only by MSS Amiens 87 and Paris lat. 1759, with the same wording as in *recensio* α. These two manuscripts also do not have the concluding clause of the next sentence, which repeats what has already been said: "and the more bountiful the apostle's yield, if he wins many people."

61. *Recensio* α does not have this sentence.

62. *Recensio* α does not have "his," i.e., Paul's.

63. *Recensio* α has "to the city for another reason"; *recensio* β has "to the city Rome for another reason"; *recensio* γ has simply "to Rome," except for MS Amiens 87, which has the text found in *recensio* β. MS Amiens 87 has "the city" instead of "Rome" at In Rom. 1:9–10 (§4) and 1:13 (§1) as well. See n. 59 above.

64. Ambrosiaster is not exactly correct about the order of the events reported in Acts. The vision of the Lord's encouragement occurs while Paul is being held by the tribune in Jerusalem (see Acts 21:7–23:11). Paul is then sent to Antonius Felix, the procurator of Judea, who resided in Caesarea Maritima (see Acts 23:12–24:25). Felix keeps Paul in prison for two years, hoping for a bribe (see Acts 24:26–27). When Paul is granted a hearing by Felix's successor, the procurator Porcius Festus, he appeals to Caesar by virtue of his Roman citizenship (see Acts 25:10–12). His request is granted, and he is conveyed to Rome by sea; en route the voyagers are shipwrecked on Malta (see Acts 27:1–28:10).

1:11 *For I long to see you, so that I may impart*[65] *a spiritual grace to you to strengthen you.* (1) This strengthening requires three parties: God who helps, the apostle who ministers, and the people who receive. Therefore, he now explains his longed-for wish, what his prayer was concerning them. When he says, *so that I may impart a spiritual grace to you*, he indicates that they followed a fleshly understanding of the faith, because under the name of Christ they had followed not what Christ taught, but what had been handed down by the Jews. (2) Moreover, he explains that he desires to come to them sooner in order to extricate them from this tradition and deliver a spiritual gift to them; to obtain them for God, making them partakers of a spiritual grace, so that they might be perfected in the faith and in their profession. From this we are given to understand that above he praised not their understanding of the faith, but rather their eagerness and dedication toward Christ. Professing themselves to be Christians, they naively operated under the law as it had been conveyed to them. In fact, however, God's mercy was given so that the burdens of the law might end, as I have already said several times. For out of consideration for human weakness God decreed that that the human race should be saved by faith alone, supplemented by natural law. (3) Given that he corrects them in writing and extricates them from a carnal understanding, why does he say that his presence is required to impart a spiritual gift to them, since the things he writes are spiritual? Is not this the reason: his words are regularly misconstrued to mean something different, as is done by heretics? He longs, therefore, to convey also in person the evangelical teaching as it is understood in what he writes, lest error might not be dispelled but rather reinforced by the authority of his letters. He wants to do this especially because whenever he was present in person, things he was unable to convince people of through words he convinced them of by power, so as to be more effective in bringing them into the faith.[66]

1:12 *That is, that we may be mutually encouraged by each other's faith, both yours and mine.* He says that he is encouraged by them if they comprehend spiritual things. For although he rejoices in their faith, he nevertheless

---

65. Ambrosiaster's quotation in the comment that follows supports *ministrem*, attested by many manuscripts of *recensio* γ, rather than *administrem*; see CSEL 81.1:27, l. 19 with apparatus.

66. *Recensio* α has "He longs, therefore, to convey also in person the evangelical teaching as it is understood in what he writes, so as to be more effective in bringing them into the faith."

grieves that they had not received the faith in the right way. The apostle was so sensitive that he grieved for another person's failings as if they were his own. Thus, *we may be encouraged*, he says, by one and the same faith, so that if they were established in the one faith in Christ, their encouragement would then be one, and the imparting of spiritual grace through the evangelizing of the apostle would achieve this result.

1:13 *I do not suppose that you are unaware,*[67] *brothers, that I have often planned to come to you and have thus far been prevented.* (1) He explains his plan and prayer. In fact, he is sure that they know of it from the brothers who came from Jerusalem or its neighboring cities to Rome[68] for some reason—perhaps a religious reason, as we read of Aquila and Priscilla[69]—and made his prayer known among the Romans. Since he often wanted to come but was prevented, it came about that he wrote a letter to avoid a situation where they would not be easily corrected because they had become accustomed over a long period of time to the wrong approach. He calls them *brothers* not only because they had been reborn, but also because there were among them people—if only a few—who understood rightly. (2) This is why he says, *called saints* (Rom 1:7). But what does *called saints* mean? If they are already saints, in what sense are they called to be sanctified? This, however, has to do with the foreknowledge of God,[70] since those whom God knows will be saints are already saints in his sight and continue as called. To return to the verse, he says that up to the time of writing the letter he was prevented from coming—by God, no less, who, knowing that the Romans were not yet ready, directed the apostle to other

---

67. Although Ambrosiaster's biblical text has "I do not suppose that you are unaware" (*non arbitror*), among biblical witnesses there is stronger support for "I do not want you to be unaware" (οὐ θέλω). See Metzger, *Textual Commentary*, 447; and Jewett, *Romans*, 127.

68. *Recensiones* α and β have "the city" instead of "Rome"; see nn. 59 and 63 above.

69. Aquila and Prisca (the diminutive "Priscilla" is also used) were among the Jews expelled from Rome by the emperor Claudius. They settled in Corinth, where they worked as tentmakers. When Paul arrived in Corinth, he stayed with them and worked as a tentmaker while preaching in the synagogue (see Acts 18:1–4). Later, when Paul returned to Jerusalem, they traveled with him as far as Ephesus (see Acts 18:18–19). By the time Paul wrote the Letter to the Romans, they had presumably returned to Rome (see Rom 16:3). Ambrosiaster comments further on the character and contribution of this couple at In Rom. 16:3–5 (§1).

70. *Recensio* α has "He says this, however."

cities[71] that were already able to receive the truth. (3) Although the believers at Rome lived under the name of the Savior, they were nevertheless prevented by their negligence[72] from being worthy at that time of learning more about spiritual things. In fact, when Paul and Silas once wanted to go to Bithynia, they were prevented by the Holy Spirit (Acts 16:7). Why would this happen, unless the Holy Spirit knew that as yet there was no point? Among the Corinthians, on the other hand, the apostle is urged on by the Lord, when he says: *Speak, and do not be silent, for I have many people in this city* (Acts 18:9, 10). (4) Therefore, it is not superfluous for the apostle to say that he was prevented. He wants the reasons for the delays to be understood, and he urges them to prepare themselves, to render themselves worthy to receive, when they hear it, the spiritual grace that is to be imparted to them.[73]

In order that I may enjoy some fruit among you as well as among the rest of the gentiles. (5) He states that he is desirous of coming to them for their mutual advantage: so that they may receive the salvation of spiritual grace when they obtain confirmation of the profession of their faith, and so that he may enjoy the fruit of his service in the sight of God, which is why he rouses them to the right faith by the example of the rest of the gentiles. For someone is readier to accept to what is passed on to him if he sees that many people assent to it.

1:14 *I am under obligation to Greeks and to barbarians, to the wise and to the foolish.* (1) He says that he is *under obligation* to these people he mentions, because he was sent for this reason: to preach to everyone.[74] By this he also indicates that all are under obligation. For to acknowledge God the creator, from whom are all things and through whom are all things (see 1 Cor 8:6), is a duty and an honor that brings salvation to the one who acknowledges. (2) He used the term *Greeks* to refer to gentiles, includ-

---

71. *Recensio* α has "to others."

72. *Recensiones* α and β have "carnal vices"; see n. 73 below.

73. *Recensio* α has "He described the reasons for the delay, and he urged them to prepare themselves, so that, when they hear of the spiritual grace that is to be imparted to them, they render themselves worthy by refraining from carnal vices." *Recensio* β has "He described the reasons for the delay, and he urged them to prepare themselves, so that by refraining from carnal vices they render themselves worthy to receive, when they hear of it, the spiritual grace that is to be imparted to them."

74. *Recensio* α has "He says that he is *under obligation*, because he was sent for this reason."

ing those who are called Romans, whether by birth or by adoption.[75] He used the term *barbarians*, on the other hand, to refer to those who are not Romans, who are hostile to the Romans and are not gentiles. Furthermore, he termed *wise* those who, being learned in the sciences of this world, are called wise in this age, as they observe the stars or measures or numbers, or study the art of grammar or oratory or music.[76] To all these people he shows that these things are of no use and that people are not truly wise unless they believe in Christ.[77] (3) He termed *stupid*, on the other hand, those who, taking the path of artless simplicity, are unacquainted with these matters. He testifies that he has been sent to preach to all these people. He did not mention the Jews, however, because he is the teacher of the gentiles. Accordingly, he declares that he is under obligation, since he received the teaching of the faith to this end: to pass it on, and when passing it on, to gain believers.[78]

1:15 *Accordingly, inasmuch as it lies with me, I am eager to preach the gospel also to you who are in Rome.* Although he says that he has been sent to preach to all the gentiles, he nevertheless declares that he is *eager* to bring the gospel of God's grace to the Romans, among whom the head and seat of Roman rule is located. For if the head is not anxious, it contributes to the benefit or repose of the members of the body. He desires the peace of the Romans so that Satan may not boast much and so that he himself may enjoy more bountiful fruit from his work.[79]

1:16 *For I am not ashamed of the gospel; it is the power of God for salvation to every one who believes.* (1) With these words he alludes to the people from whom the Romans had received an incorrect faith. Power

---

75. *Recensio* β has "by ethnicity" instead of "by birth."

76. Ambrosiaster refers to six of the seven medieval liberal arts, omitting dialectic: grammar, rhetoric, music, geometry, astronomy, and arithmetic. The seven disciplines are described by Martianus Capella in the early fifth century, but exactly when they became a regular feature of Roman education has been a matter of debate; see Mark Vessey, introduction to *Augustine and the Disciplines: From Cassiciacum to Confessions*, ed. Karla Pollmann and Mark Vessey (Oxford: Oxford University Press, 2005), 4–9.

77. *Recensiones* α and β do not have this sentence. In *recensio* γ it is attested only by MSS Amiens 87, Paris lat. 1759, and, in a second hand, St. Gall 101. It appears to be an interpolation, since it interrupts the sequence of remarks about the terms "Greek," "barbarian," "wise," and "stupid."

78. In *recensio* γ this sentence is attested only by MSS Amiens 87 and Paris lat. 1759.

79. In *recensio* γ "and that he himself may enjoy more bountiful fruit from his work" is attested only by MSS Amiens 87 and Paris lat. 1759.

was always commending the teaching of the apostles so that, since what was preached seemed incredible, the signs and wonders performed by the apostles would be evidence that one should not doubt what was being said by them, in whom such power was found. There is no doubt that words are less effective than power. (2) Therefore, because no portents had been seen from those people, their preaching was without the power of God. The apostle says that he is *not ashamed of the gospel* of God, but that they are, because what they had conveyed to the Romans fell into disrepute,[80] was in no way confirmed by evidence, and was at odds with the apostolic teaching.[81] The *power of God*, therefore, is that which invites people to the faith and grants salvation to everyone who believes; it forgives sins and justifies, so that those who have been signed with the mystery of the cross cannot be held by the second death.[82] (3) For the proclamation of the cross of Christ is an indication that death has been vanquished,[83] as the apostle John says: *For the Son of God came for this purpose, to destroy the works of the devil* (1 John 3:8), so that everyone who believes is not held captive by death, because he has the sign that death has been conquered.

To the Jew first and also to the Greek. (4) That is, to the one who is a descendant of Abraham, and to the one who comes from the gentiles. By *Greek* he means a gentile, and by *Jew* he means one who was descended from Abraham.[84] In fact, Abraham's descendants began to be called *Jews* from the time of Judas Maccabaeus,[85] who in a time of great devastation held fast against the sacrilege of the gentiles,[86] brought the populace together in reliance upon God, and defended his people. He was, moreover,

---

80. In *recensio* γ "what they had conveyed to the Romans fell into disrepute" is attested only by MS Amiens 87.

81. *Recensio* α does not have "was in no way confirmed by evidence, and was at odds with the apostolic teaching."

82. In the Christian rite of initiation, believers were signed with the cross after having been immersed in water. On "the second death," see the introduction §5.4.

83. In *recensio* γ the remainder of the comment is attested only by MSS Amiens 87 and Paris lat. 1759.

84. This sentence and the next two, which discuss Judas Maccabaeus, are found only in *recensiones* β and γ.

85. The Maccabee family led the Jewish revolt against the hellenizing regime of the Seleucid King Antiochus IV in 167 BCE. After Matthias, the father of the family, died in 166, the leadership passed to Judas, who defeated the Seleucid armies and eventually achieved a treaty granting the Jews the right to follow their own laws (1 Macc 3–6).

86. Antiochus IV imposed a series of repressive measures on the Jews in 168 and

descended from the sons of Aaron. Although, therefore, the apostle gives precedence to the Jew for his ancestors' sake, he nevertheless says that even the Jew likewise needs the gift of the gospel of Christ. So, if even the Jew is not justified except through faith in Christ Jesus, what need is there to be under the law?

1:17 *For the righteousness of God is revealed in him from faith to faith.*[87] (1) He says this[88] because the righteousness of God is clearly evident in the one who believes,[89] whether Jew or Greek.[90] (2) For the truth and righteousness of God are displayed in him when he believes and professes. The righteousness is *of God* because God has given what he promised. Therefore, one who believes that he has obtained what God had promised through his prophets shows that God is just and is a witness to his righteousness.[91] *From faith to faith.* What else does *from faith to faith* mean, but that the faith of God consists in what he has promised,[92] and the faith of the person consists in believing the one who promises? Thus, the righteousness of God is revealed from the faith of God who promises in the faith of the person who believes. (3) To the believer God appears to be just, but to the unbeliever he seems unjust. For one who does not believe that God has given what he promised denies that God is truthful. The apostle says this against the Jews, who deny this Christ to be the one whom God promised.

As it is written: "The righteous live from faith" (Hab 2:4). (4) He turns to the quotation from the prophet Habakkuk to make it clear that it was

---

167 BCE, prohibiting Jewish practices, profaning Jewish times and places, and erecting an altar of Baal Shamen or the Olympian Zeus in the temple (1 Macc 1:41–64).

87. Ambrosiaster understands *in eo* to refer to the believer.

88. In *recensio* γ "he says this" is attested only by MSS Amiens 87, Paris lat. 1759, and, in a second hand, St. Gall 101.

89. *Recensio* α does not have "who believes."

90. MS Amiens 87 continues with a comment that is not attested by any other manuscript of *recensio* α, β, or γ: "(1a) He says that the righteousness of God—since God freely justifies the ungodly through faith without the works of the law, as he says elsewhere: *In order that I may be found in him, not having a righteousness of my own that comes from the law, but one that comes from faith, the righteousness from God based on faith* (Phil 3:9)—he says that this righteousness was revealed in the gospel, when it gives a person the faith through which he is justified." Unlike section 1, this comment understands *in eo* in Rom 1:17 to refer to the gospel rather than the believer. It is almost certainly an interpolation.

91. I.e., the believer is a witness to God's righteousness.

92. *Recensiones* α and β have "has promised about himself."

shown long ago that the righteous live not from the law but from faith;[93] in other words, that a person is not justified in God's sight by the law, but by faith. The life which comes from faith is not this present life, but is the life to come, because *the righteous live from faith*—true, but in God's sight.[94]

1:18 *For the wrath of God is revealed from heaven against all ungodliness and unrighteousness of people who suppress the truth of God in unrighteousness.*[95] (1) Just as the righteousness of God is revealed in someone who believes (as I noted above), so too *ungodliness and unrighteousness* are revealed in someone who does not believe. (1a)[96] From the very construction of heaven it is apparent that God is angry with them. For he created such beautiful stars precisely so that one might recognize from them how great and how wonderful their creator is, and that he alone is to be worshiped. Hence it is written in Ps 18: *The heavens declare the glory of God, and the firmament proclaims his handiwork* (Ps 18:2 LXX = Ps 19:1 ET). (2) Therefore, by means of natural law God renders the human race guilty. For by means of the law of nature they could have learned what Moses transmitted through the written law, inasmuch as the construction of the world testifies that its maker, God, should alone be loved (see Deut 6:5).[97] But they were rendered ungodly by not worshiping the creator, and unrighteousness is revealed in them when, although they see, they turn away from the truth by not acknowledging the one God.[98]

1:19 *For what is known about God is plain to them.* The knowledge of God has been plainly shown from the construction of the world. In order that God, who is by nature invisible, could still be known from visible things,[99] God made a thing that, in being visible, plainly shows its maker. Thus, what is open to doubt could be known through what is beyond doubt, and the one who made this thing—a work beyond the ability of everyone else[100]—might be believed to be the God of all.

---

93. *Recensio* α does not have "that it was shown long ago."

94. In *recensio* γ "because *the righteous live from faith*—true, but in God's sight" is attested only by MSS Amiens 87 and Paris lat. 1759.

95. Ambrosiaster's biblical text has "the truth of God" (*veritatem dei*), whereas the Greek text has simply "the truth" (τὴν ἀλήθειαν). See Jewett, *Romans*, 148.

96. This section is found only in *recensiones* β and γ.

97. *Recensio* α has "inasmuch as the construction of the world testifies that its maker is God."

98. *Recensio* α does not have "by not acknowledging the one God."

99. *Recensio* α has only "could be known."

100. *Recensiones* α and β have "of others."

For God has shown it to them. God showed himself when he made the thing through which he can be known by faith.

1:20 *For from the creation of the world his invisible qualities have been perceived, understood through the things which were made.* (1) The meaning is the same. He repeated it in order to explain more fully that, although the power and majesty of God cannot be seen in themselves with physical eyes,[101] they are seen when the work of the construction of the world is understood. With this argument he accuses those who lived without the natural law and that of Moses.[102] They overwhelmed the law of nature by the habit of sinning, wiping out any recollection of it. They did not wish to accept the law that had been given to reform them.[103] As a result, they were subject to condemnation on two accounts.

Even his eternal power and divinity—so that they are without excuse. (2) In order that ungodliness may not in any way be excused,[104] he added that God's power and eternal divinity were recognized by humankind, but that the impulse to honor God, whom they knew both to exist and to provide for their benefit,[105] was dulled by a kind of stupor. For no one doubts that he directed the things that grow in the course of a year for use by humankind. The eternal *power* of God, therefore, is Christ,[106] through whom[107] he brought into being things that did not exist, and in him they abide. If his person is not yet known, his works nevertheless are plain.[108] His *divinity*, on the other hand, is what keeps the material elements in the operation assigned to them. *So that they are without excuse.* Someone who is found guilty on many counts cannot be excused.

1:21 *Because although they had known God, they did not honor him as God or give thanks to him.* (1) They were not so unaware as to fail to acknowledge that the origin from which all things—things in heaven and on earth and in the underworld (see Phil 2:10)—received their beginning is one, and that it is this one who determined the natural properties and

---

101. *Recensio* α does not have "physical" (*creaturae*).
102. *Recensiones* α and β have "without the law of nature and of Moses."
103. I.e., the law of Moses.
104. *Recensio* α does not have "in any way."
105. *Recensio* α has "whom they did not deny both to exist and to work." *Recensio* β has "whom they knew both to exist and to work for their benefit."
106. See In Rom. 8:39 (§3) with n. 151.
107. *Recensio* α has "His eternal power, therefore, is that by which." *Recensio* β has "His eternal power, therefore, is Christ, by which."
108. This sentence is found only in *recensiones* β and γ.

functions for all things. Even though they knew this, they did not give thanks. He is speaking of people in the past, in order to correct those living in the present and the future.[109]

But they became futile in their thinking. (2) Truly, futility consists in this, that, while they recognized the truth, they thought that something else should be worshiped, something they did not know to be true. Thus, turning away from God, they worshiped idols.[110]

And their foolish heart was darkened. (3) A cloud of error has covered their heart because,[111] although properly they ought to honor the creator all the more on account of the things he made, they became dull-minded. Having abandoned God, they said that for them it was sufficient to worship only these things they see.[112]

1:22 *Claiming to be wise, they became stupid.* (1) They consider themselves *wise* because they think that they have investigated the physical order, examining the course of the stars and the size of the elements,[113] but spurning the God of these things.[114] Therefore, they are *stupid*, for if these things are praiseworthy,[115] how much more is their creator! (1a)[116] Nevertheless, when they are ashamed for having disregarded God, they usually have some poor excuse. They say that through these things one can come to God, just as one is led to the king by the *comites*.[117] Let this be granted.[118] But is anyone so mad or reckless about his life as to claim the king's honorary title for the *comes*? If people were found out even discussing such an

---

109. This sentence is found only in *recensiones* β and γ.

110. *Recensiones* α and β have "Seeing the world fitted in marvelous array, they turned from the one they had acknowledged to be its maker."

111. *Recensio* α does not have "of error."

112. *Recensiones* α and β have "they said that these things alone sufficed them for salvation."

113. *Recensiones* α and β have "the qualities of the elements" instead of "the size of the elements."

114. See Ambrosiaster's comment at In Col. 2:8–9 (§§1–3).

115. *Recensiones* α and β have "if these things are to be praised."

116. Sections 1a and 1b are found only in *recensiones* β and γ.

117. The emperor Constantine created the order of *comites*, or imperial companions, who held office at the pleasure of the emperor and performed a variety of services at his behest. See A. H. M. Jones, *The Later Roman Empire 284-602: A Social, Economic, and Administrative Survey* (Oxford: Blackwell, 1964; repr., Baltimore: Johns Hopkins University Press, 1992), 1:104–6.

118. *Recensio* β has "Go ahead."

idea, they would be justly condemned for treason. Yet these people who consider themselves wise do not think that they are guilty when they claim the honor of God's name for the creation and, having abandoned the master, worship their fellow servants, as if there were something else reserved for God above and beyond this. (1b) In fact, the reason one approaches the king through the tribunes or *comites* is that the king is only human and does not know to whom he should entrust public office.[119] But to gain the favor of God, from whom nothing whatsoever is hid (he knows everyone's merits), one does not need a *suffragator*,[120] but only a devout mind. Wherever a devout person speaks to him, he will answer him.

1:23 *And they changed the glory of the incorruptible God into the likeness of an image of a corruptible human being.* (1) Their heart was so blinded that they transformed the majesty of the invisible God, whom they had recognized from these works, not into human beings but—what is worse and an unpardonable offense—into the *likeness* of human beings. Thus, the form of a *corruptible human being*—that is, a figure of a human being—is called *God* by these people; they admit images of the dead, whom they would not dare give this name while they are living, into the glory of God. (2) What stupidity,[121] what foolishness, that these people, for whom an image avails more than the truth and the dead are mightier than the living, call themselves wise to their own damnation![122] Falling away from the living God, they prefer the dead, in whose company they belong, as it is written in the Wisdom of Solomon:[123] *The dead fashions the dead with wicked hands* (Wis 15:17). This is said in the Wisdom of Solomon about such people.

And of birds and four-footed animals and serpents. (3) By referring to these as well, the apostle added to the penalty for stupidity, so that such people are beyond foolishness and futility. They reduced the grandeur and glory of God to the point that they gave the title *God* to the likeness of these

---

119. The comment describes the imperial system of preferment, where candidates for public office depended on the recommendation of a member of the emperor's entourage. The system takes its name—*suffragium*—from the term for the person making the recommendation: *suffragator*. For a discussion of the system (with reference also to Ambrosiaster's comment), see Jones, *Later Roman Empire*, 1:391–96.

120. See n. 119 above.

121. *Recensiones* α and β have "what sickness."

122. *Recensio* α has "for whom the dead avail more than the living." *Recensio* β has "for whom the dead avail more than the living and the dead are mightier than the living."

123. *Recensio* α does not have this clause. *Recensio* β has "as it is written."

things, which are so small and puny. In fact, the early Babylonians called the figure of Bel *God*; he was a mortal at one time,[124] and is said to have established an empire among them.[125] (4) They also worshiped a serpent, the dragon that Daniel, the man of God, killed (see Dan 14:22–30); they still have its likeness. The Egyptians, too, worshiped a four-footed animal in the likeness of a cow, which they called Apis. Imitating this evil practice, Jeroboam set up cows in Samaria, to whom the Jews offered sacrifices (see 1 Kgs 12:25–33),[126] as well as birds, because the pagans have sacred ravens.[127] (5) Indeed, the Egyptian worships likenesses of all the things that I have mentioned, as well as others that I need not discuss at this time.[128] These likenesses were made by those who considered themselves to be wise in the world. Because they did not honor God, whom they knew to be invisible,[129] when they made these likenesses, they also were unable to be discerning about things that are visible. For it is hard for someone who is injudicious in minor matters to be astute in greater ones.

1:24 *Therefore God also*[130] *gave them up in the desires of their heart to impurity, to degrade their bodies among themselves.* (1) Because, he says, they deified figures and likenesses of things, thereby offending God the

---

124. *Recensio* α does not have "at one time."

125. The idea that Bel was promoted from human to divine status among the Babylonians can be found in Lactantius, *Inst.* 1.23.2 (CSEL 19:93); Jerome, *Comm. Os.* 1.2.16–17 (CCSL 76:28).

126. Christian writers associated Egyptian worship of the bull Apis with Israelite worship of the golden calf and, less frequently, the cult that Jeroboam introduced into the northern kingdom of Israel. See K. A. D. Smelik and E. M. Hemelrijk, "'Who Knows Not What Monsters Demented Egypt Worships?' Opinions on Egyptian Animal Worship in Antiquity as Part of the Ancient Conception of Egypt," *ANRW* 17.4:1995–96.

127. In his account of the cult of Mithras at *Quaest.* 114.11 (CSEL 50:308), Ambrosiaster describes how initiates imitate the raven. See Emanuele Di Santo, *L'Apologetica dell'Ambrosiaster: Cristiani, pagani e giudei nella Roma tardoantica*, SEAug 112 (Rome: Institutum Patristicum Augustinianum, 2008), 135 n. 88; Marie-Pierre Bussières, ed., *Ambrosiaster: Contre les païens (Question sur l'Ancien et le Nouveau Testament 114) et Sur le destin (Question sur l'Ancien et le Nouveau Testament 115)*, SC 512 (Paris: Cerf, 2007), 130–31 n. 3.

128. Negative stereotypes about the Egyptian worship of animals were common in the Greco-Roman world. These stereotypes were taken up by Christian writers in arguments against Jews and pagans. See Smelik and Hemelrijk, "'Who Knows,'" 1981–96.

129. *Recensiones* α and β have "Because they did not honor the invisible God when they made these likenesses."

130. *Recensio* α does not have "also."

creator, they were given up to ruinous amusements. They were given up, not so that they carried out things they did not want to do, but so that they accomplished what they desired. Herein lies the goodness of God. For although it would have been fitting for them to be forced to do what they did not want to do and to be tortured—for though a thing may be good, it is bitter and evil if it is done against one's will—instead they, in turning away from God, were given up to the devil. (2) To give up, however, is to allow, not to incite or to instigate,[131] so that with the help of the devil[132] they achieved in deeds what they had conceived in desires. For such people cannot have a good thought.[133] Therefore, they were given up *to impurity*, to degrade their bodies among themselves. Although he recounts past events, he is also referring to the present time, because up until now[134] they are given up to degrade their bodies. (3) For up until now there are people of such origins, who are said to dishonor their bodies one with another. When the thoughts of the soul are reprehensible, the body is said to be dishonored. Why so, unless the stain of the body is a sign of the sin of the soul? For when the body is polluted, there can be no doubt that there is sin in the soul.

1:25 *They exchanged the truth of God for a lie and worshiped and served the creature rather than the creator, who is blessed forever. Amen.* (1) *They exchanged the truth of God for a lie* when they gave the name of God who is the true God to those who are false gods.[135] For, divesting stones and wood and various metals of what they are, they attribute to them something they are not. Consequently, when a stone is called *God, the truth of God* is a *lie*.[136] When this happens, it defames the God who is true, so that, because false and true are contemplated by a common name, the true God is likewise believed to be false. This is to change what is true into what is false. (2) For a thing is no longer called *stone* or *wood*, but *God*. This is *to serve the creature rather than the creator*.[137] They do not, in fact, deny God; rather, they serve the creature.[138] They have applied the honor

---

131. In *recensio* γ "not to incite or to instigate" is attested only by MS Amiens 87.
132. *Recensio* α does not have "with the help of the devil."
133. *Recensio* α does not have "good."
134. *Recensio* α does not have "up until now."
135. *Recensiones* α and β have "to those who are not gods."
136. *Recensio* α does not have this sentence and the next one.
137. *Recensio* α does not have this sentence.
138. From this sentence on *recensiones* α and β have "For they do not deny God;

of God to these things so that it seems right that they worship them. Consequently, the worship of these things is an injustice to God. They increase their punishment because, while they know God, they dishonor him, *who is blessed forever. Amen,* that is, truly. (3) To God indeed, he says, be blessing forever, because God endures, whereas ungodliness renders honor to idols[139] for a time. For that reason it is not true honor; in God, however, truth abides. Elsewhere he applies this benediction to the Son of God, saying, among other things: *And from them comes Christ according to the flesh, who is God over all, blessed forever. Amen* (Rom 9:5). Either each of the passages refers to Christ,[140] or he said the same thing about the Son as he did about the Father.[141]

1:26 *On account of this God gave them up to disgraceful passions. For their females exchanged natural intercourse for that intercourse which is contrary to nature.* He bears witness that these things befell the human race because God was angered by idolatry: a female would seek to have intercourse with a female out of base lust.[142] Some explain this differently

---

rather, they serve the creature. They are not excused by this, but rather are accused, because, while they know him [β: God], they do not honor God, *who is blessed forever. Amen,* that is, truly."

139. *Recensiones* α and β have "the gods of the nations" instead of "idols."

140. I.e., both Rom 1:25 and 9:5.

141. I.e., Rom 1:25 applies to God the Father, and Rom 9:5 applies to God the Son. In *recensio* γ this sentence is attested only by MSS Amiens 87 and St. Gall 101, in a second hand.

142. *Recensio* α has "He bears witness that because God was angered by idolatry it befell the human race that females offered themselves to men in ways other than nature prescribed. He explains the nature of their impure behavior, regarding which he now states." *Recensio* β has "He bears witness that because God was angered by idolatry it befell the human race that a woman would seek to have intercourse with a woman out of base lust. Some explain this differently because they do not perceive clearly the import of the words. For what does it mean to exchange natural intercourse for intercourse that is contrary to nature, if not to engage in another form of intercourse after having submitted to the permissible form of intercourse, so that one and the same part of the body offers itself to a form of intercourse other than the permissible form? For if that part of the body is meant, how did they exchange the intercourse of nature, since that part of the body does not have such a use given by nature? He had already stated above that they were given up to impurity (Rom 1:24), but he had not explained the nature of their impure behavior, regarding which he now states." Thus, Ambrosiaster initially took Rom 1:26 to refer to "unnatural" sexual relations between women and men, and subsequently interpreted it as referring to "unnatural" sexual relations between women. On the significance of this revision and

because they do not perceive clearly the import of the words. What in fact does it mean to exchange *natural intercourse for that intercourse which is contrary to nature*, if not to engage in another form of intercourse once the permissible form of intercourse has been done away with, so that one and the same part of the body[143] offers itself to a form of intercourse other than the permissible form? If, then, that part of the body is meant,[144] how did they exchange natural intercourse, since that part of the body does not have such a use given by nature?[145] He had, therefore, already stated above that they were given up to impurity (Rom 1:24), but he had not explained the character of the impurity of their behavior, which he now states.

1:27 *And likewise the males, too, having forsaken natural intercourse with females, were consumed with desire for one another, males committing shameful acts with males.* (1a)[146] He has now made plain how what he said above about the women should be understood. When he added: *And likewise the males, too, were consumed with desire for one another*,[147] he clearly showed the sin of the women. In short, he did not say that the men exchanged natural intercourse with one another, because such intercourse is not permitted for this part.[148] When even today one may come upon such women, is it surprising that just as that intercourse is devised by men, so too this intercourse is devised by women? For he charges the women with each other, and the men likewise. (1) It is clear, therefore, that, because they exchanged the truth of God for a lie, they also exchanged natural intercourse for a form of intercourse by which they were shamefully

---

on its location within patristic interpretations of Rom 1:26–27, see Theodore S. de Bruyn, "Ambrosiaster's Interpretations of Romans 1:26–27," *VC* 65 (2011): 463–83.

143. In *recensio* γ a second hand in MS St. Gall 101 adds "of each sex with each other together." The phrase is otherwise not attested by manuscripts of *recensio* β or γ.

144. MSS Amiens 87 and Paris lat. 1759 of *recensio* γ add "as they think." The phrase is otherwise not attested by manuscripts of *recensio* β or γ.

145. Ambrosiaster refers here to the anus. He argues that since the anus is not intended for sexual relations, whereas the vagina is, women who have vaginal sexual relations with women can be said to have exchanged natural intercourse for unnatural intercourse, whereas men who have anal intercourse with men are described as having abandoned natural intercourse (Rom 1:27). See de Bruyn, "Ambrosiaster's Interpretations," 470–71.

146. *Recensio* α does not have section 1a.

147. *Recensio* β does not have "with one another."

148. *Recensio* β does not have this sentence or the next one.

disgraced, and were condemned to the second death.¹⁴⁹ For because Satan cannot give another law—since he has nothing acceptable or lawful at his disposal—he took another approach, so that when they behaved otherwise than was permitted, they became sin.¹⁵⁰

And receiving in themselves the recompense their error deserves. He says that this is the recompense from God when he has been scorned, namely, lewdness and obscenity.¹⁵¹ This is in fact the first cause of sin.¹⁵² What is worse, what is baser, than this sin, which both beguiled the devil and subjected human beings to death?¹⁵³ Just as idolatry is a most godless and serious transgression, so too is its recompense a dreadful and disgusting passion.¹⁵⁴

1:28 *And since they thought that God took no notice of these things,*¹⁵⁵ *God gave them up to a debased mind, so that they do things that are unseemly.* For having wrongly worshiped images, they were given up to performing shameful acts with each other, as has already been said. Moreover, because they thought that they could do these things with impunity, reckoning that God was indifferent and could therefore be disregarded, there was a further consequence. As their conscience became increasingly dulled, they

---

149. *Recensio* α has "death" instead of "second death." On the "second death," see the introduction §5.4.

150. In *recensio* γ this sentence is attested only by MSS Amiens 87 and, in a second hand, St. Gall 101.

151. *Recensiones* α and β have "pollution" instead of "obscenity."

152. Ambrosiaster holds that lewdness and obscenity are a result of rebellion against God as the creator and as alone worthy of worship. At *Quaest.* 110.2 (CSEL 50:269–70) he explains that this rebellion began among the angels in heaven and then spread to humankind on earth. It appears, therefore, that Ambrosiaster was familiar with the account of fallen angels in 1 Enoch and the book of Jubilees. On the early Christian reception of the Enochic myth of the descent of angels, see James C. VanderKam, "1 Enoch, Enochic Motifs, and Enoch in Early Christian Literature," in *The Jewish Apocalyptic Heritage in Early Christianity*, ed. James C. VanderKam and William Adler, CRINT 3.4 (Assen: Van Gorcum; Minneapolis: Fortress, 1996), 33–101; Annette Yoshiko Reed, *Fallen Angels and the History of Judaism and Christianity* (Cambridge: Cambridge University Press, 2005), 147–55, 160–89.

153. *Recensiones* α and β do not have "which both beguiled the devil and subjected human beings to death."

154. In *recensio* γ this sentence is attested only by MS Paris lat. 1759.

155. Ambrosiaster's biblical text takes τὸν θεόν in the Greek text to be the subject rather than the object of ἔχειν ἐν ἐπιγνώσει. The latter is the preferred reading: "And since they did not see fit to acknowledge God."

became more inclined to permit every kind of evil, believing that God does not punish deeds that they certainly knew offended people. The apostle now lists all the evils that additionally accrued to them, so that, if they thereby returned to a natural understanding, they might recognize that these things befell them because God was angered.

1:29 *They were filled*, he says, *with every manner of wickedness*. He stated this as a summary,[156] and followed with the individual types of wickedness: *malice*, he says, *shamelessness, covetousness, villainy; full of envy, murders, strife, deceit, spite. They are gossips,* **1:30** *slanderers, despicable to God, insolent, haughty, boastful, inventors of evil, disobedient to parents,* **1:31** *foolish, disorderly, without feeling, without mercy.* **1:32** *Although they had known the righteousness of God, they did not realize that those who do such things deserve to die, not only those who do them but also those who agree with those who do them.*[157] (1a) [158] The principal source of wickedness he termed *malice*. *Lewdness* and *covetousness* he listed as the work of malice. Then he added *villainy*, whose disposition begets *envy* and *murders, strife* and *deceit*. After these he added *spite*, which gives birth to *gossips* and *slanderers*. Because these things displease God, he says *despicable to God*. Since these things do not please people either, he says *insolent, haughty, boastful, inventors of evil*, that is, authors of evil. Evil evidently has not existed forever. In fact, these authors of evil, having become imitators of their father the devil, came up with the evil of idolatry, through which all the vices and the greatest ruin were brought into the world. (2a) Now although the devil, whom the scripture testifies sinned from the beginning (see 1 John 3:8), aspires to tyrannical audacity, he nevertheless has not dared to declare, to say: *I am God* (see 2 Thess 2:4). Thus, among other things he says to God: *All these have been given over to me* (see Luke 4:6);

---

156. I.e., "every kind of wickedness" is a summary of the various forms of wickedness that are subsequently listed.

157. Ambrosiaster's biblical text of 1:32 differs from the Greek text at several points; see the text and apparatus in NA[28] and Jewett, *Romans*, 164. In English the text reads: "Although they know God's decree that those who do such things deserve to die, they not only do them but approve those who practice them."

158. There are two sets of comments on Rom 1:29–32. The sections translated here, 1a to 4a, are found in *recensiones* β and γ (CSEL 81.1:52, 54, 56 and 55, 57). *Recensio* α has a different set of comments, which are also found, with some modifications and additions, in *recensio* β (CSEL 81.1:56, 58, 60) and in MS Paris lat. 1759 of *recensio* γ (CSEL 81.1:57, 59, 61). There are several reasons to not attribute the second set of comments to Ambrosiaster; see the appendix to this chapter.

he does not say: *They are from me*, or: *They are mine*. In the book of Job he asks that power be given to him (see Job 2:6), and in the prophet Zechariah he presumes to oppose the high priest (see Zech 3:1); he does not arrogate power to himself. For this reason those who claim divinity not only for the elements but even for images are worse. (3a) *Disobedient to parents.* They are seized with so much arrogance that they do not even recognize that they should honor their parents! He therefore said that they were *foolish* and *disorderly*, without feeling for either God or people. As a result, they were also merciless. For if one is cruel toward one's own, how much more toward others! Once, then, they had become obdurate in all these evils, though they were aware of God's righteousness, they were unwilling to take to heart that these things are deserving of death and that those who *agree with those who do these things*, even if they did not do these things themselves, are not immune from such death. (4a) When the consenters neither recoil nor reprimand, the perpetrators go on to do worse. For when someone sees that he is honored by those who are not so bad, he grows more evil and possibly prides himself on being so bad. For this reason it is fitting that they should all be punished with one and the same penalty. Moreover, every conscience knows that God's righteousness has been bestowed on the world, because things that deserve to be punished are done in secret. How then do they imagine that the things they dare not do openly will go unpunished?

Appendix: Alternate Comments on Romans 1:29–32[159]

1:29 *Malice, fornication.*[160] Fornication here also includes adultery. If the apostle had said *adultery*, he would have seemed to have excused fornica-

---

159. This set of comments is found in *recensio* α (which does not have the first set of comments), *recensio* β, and MS Paris lat. 1759 of *recensio* γ (see n. 158 above). There are several inconsistencies that are problematic. The lemma and accompanying comment follow the Vulgate rather than the VL at one point (see n. 160 below); the comment on Rom 1:31 in fact applies to Rom 1:32 (see n. 164); and the comment after Rom 1:32 refers to a prior discussion that is in fact missing (see n. 166). All of this suggests that this set of comments was reworked or interpolated after Ambrosiaster.

160. This lemma and its accompanying comment have the Vulgate *fornicatio*, whereas the lemma and its accompanying comment in the first set of comments have the VL *inpudicitia*, "shamelessness." Since Ambrosiaster did not have the Vulgate, it would appear that this comment is not by him. Neither variant is accepted in NA[28]; see Metzger, *Textual Commentary*, 447; and Jewett, *Romans*, 164.

tion, as Roman law does.¹⁶¹ He therefore listed the lesser offense so that the greater offense could not be considered to be unpunishable. He then lists the rest, which are self-evident: *covetousness, villainy; full of envy, murders, strife, deceit, spite. They are gossips,* **1:30** *slanderers, hateful to God, insolent, haughty, boastful, inventors of evil, disobedient to parents.* They are seized with so much arrogance¹⁶² that they do not even acknowledge their own parents, who were their progenitors in giving birth! Although they rejoiced at their own birth, they showed contempt for those through whom they came into being. This is to be without understanding, without love—the love, that is, of God. For love of the flesh was in fact present among them.

1:31 *Foolish, disorderly, without feeling, without mercy.* Because they were aware of the righteousness of God through the law of nature, they knew that in fact these things displeased God. But they were unwilling to take to heart the fact *that those who do* these things *deserve to die,*¹⁶³ *and not only those who do them, but also those who agree with those who do them*; assent is, in fact, participation.¹⁶⁴

1:32¹⁶⁵ *Although they had known the righteousness of God, they did not realize that those who do such things deserve to die, not only those who do them but also those who agree with those who do them.* (1) All these evils constitute the body of sins. Those who have been given up to it are controlled by its power so that they do things deserving of punishment. This occasion for evil began with the offense toward God committed by the people of Sodom, as was discussed above.¹⁶⁶ Its branches spread into almost

---

161. Roman law did not punish extramarital sexual relations that citizens from the upper classes had with persons of lower social status, prostitutes, or slaves. See Elke Hartmann, "Sexuality," *BNP* A13:375.

162. The first part of this sentence is also found in section 3a in the prior set of comments.

163. Instead of these two sentences, *recensio* α has "They were aware of the righteousness of God to the point that they did not deny that all these things they do are deserving of punishment and death."

164. This sentence pertains to Rom 1:32, which follows, rather than to Rom 1:31.

165. This lemma is attested only by *recensiones* α and β; it is not found in MS Paris lat. 1759.

166. Although Ambrosiaster explains at In Rom. 1:27 (§2) that rebellion against God is the source of all other sins, he does not refer there to Sodom and Gomorrah. There is in fact no prior mention of Sodom and Gomorrah in Ambrosiaster's comments on Rom 1.

every part of the world, making known the wrath of God toward idolatry, which is the initial aspect of error and ungodliness. The apostle condemns this aspect first so that when it has been corrected the customary vices may be easily rectified as well. If the seed of malice is suppressed, the fruit of villainy withers; a tree whose branches have been cut off does not bear fruit. (2) In fact, this is why Moses, too, recorded the events of Sodom and Gomorrah and did not keep quiet about their end (see Gen 19:24–25),[167] in order to instill fear of the thing that must be avoided. Therefore, this vice, and the pollution of a shameful life, are not allowed in by one who thinks about God in his heart. There are some people who think that they are not guilty if they do not do wicked things, even though they *agree with those who do them*. One agrees if one is silent when one could reprove or if, upon hearing stories of escapades, one cheers the teller on. (3) When a foul and depraved person knows that people are aware of what he does, and that he will not be in the least bit shunned, but will in fact be honored, he may boast of the fact that he is such a person and be unable to be distressed by his actions, seeing that he is applauded and followed by those who are not like him. So it is right that those who provide an incentive for the crimes of such people are accordingly found guilty of an equal offense. There are others, on the other hand, who not only *do* wicked things but also *agree with those who do* them, so that they not only do them but also agree with those who do them. (4) The iniquity of these people is therefore twofold. Those who do these things and at the same time object to those who do them are not as bad; knowing that such actions are wicked, they do not defend them. But the others, who both *do* these things and *agree with those who do* them, are the worst, as they do not fear God and seek to give rise to more wickedness. In order to persuade others that these actions do not have to be avoided, they do not reprove them.

---

167. In his comment at In Rom. 5:13 (§3) Ambrosiaster remarks that the destruction of Sodom and Gomorrah would have been completely forgotten if it had not been recorded by Moses.

Romans 2

2:1 *Therefore you are without excuse, every one of you who passes judgment. Inasmuch as you pass judgment on another, you condemn yourself. For you do the very same things that you judge.* Because he explained that one who does wicked things and agrees with those who do them is deserving of death (see Rom 1:32)—lest perhaps a person who does these things and presents himself as not agreeing with people who do them might think that he is excused since he temporarily hides his true disposition, when he pretends outwardly to be shocked at the deed and condemns it, but inwardly does the same things—the apostle teaches that such a person will be *without excuse*. It is not right that he get away with it just because he appears, hypocritically, not to be such an evildoer, though he is found out to be even worse. For it is deceptive that he appears worthy of honor when he should be punished.[1]

2:2 *Now we know that the judgment of God upon those who do such things is in accordance with the truth.* In other words, we are not ignorant of the fact that God will judge these people in truth, when we ourselves judge them. For if something displeases us, how much more does

---

1. *Recensio* α has "Because he explained that one who does wicked things and agrees with those who do them is deserving of death—lest perhaps a person who does these things and appears not to agree with the people who do them might think that he can be excused—the apostle teaches that such a person is *without excuse*. Because he does not agree with people who do these things, but judges them instead, he passes judgment on himself along with them, since he does the very things that he condemns in them." *Recensio* β has "Because he explained that one who does wicked things and agrees with those who do them is deserving of death—lest perhaps a person who does these thing and appears not to agree with the people who do them might think that he is excused—he teaches that such a person will be *without excuse*. It is not right that he get away with it just because he appears, hypocritically, not to be such an evildoer, though he is found out to be even worse. For it is deceptive that he appears worthy of honor when he should be punished."

it displease God, who is truly just and deeply concerned about his own work.² Therefore, when the apostle says *in truth*, he means that God will most certainly judge these people. He instills terror, as the very one whom the faithless say is indifferent indicates that he will certainly judge the wicked;³ that is, he will harshly pay each one back as he deserves, and will not forbear.

2:3 *Do you then suppose, every one of you who judges those who do such things and do the same things, that you will escape the judgment of God?* (1) He does not want them to expect to get away with this crime, since it is not right for them to be granted power to try a case and pass judgment on these sorts of evil deeds or sexual violations, although they are the same kind of people.⁴ Because even if there is no one, he says, to pass judgment on you at present, you still will not be able to escape the judgment of God in the future.⁵ For God, with whom flattery and favoritism no longer figure, will pass judgment over him. (2) Otherwise, if it really seems right to someone that such a person should be immune from punishment, he should say so. Because if it is just that such a person not escape, let him believe that God will judge. Then the fact that he judges God to be just turns out to be true;⁶ at the same time he confesses that God, the creator of the world, will providentially and solicitously inquire into the merits of his creation. (3) For if God made it and then ignored it, one would say he was a bad creator, since by neglecting it he shows that the things he made, he did not make well. But because one cannot deny that he has made good things⁷—for it

---

2. *Recensiones* α and β have "more just" instead of "truly just."

3. *Recensiones* α and β have "Therefore, when he says that God will pass judgment on these people in truth, he instills terror, as the very one whom these people say is indifferent says that he will judge the wicked in accordance with the truth; that is, he will harshly pay each one back as he deserves, and will not forbear."

4. I have translated the sentence without incorporating the word *effugere*, which is attested in *recensio* γ only by MS Amiens 87, in a second hand.

5. In place of the first two sentences of this section, *recensiones* α and β have "That is: Because the power of trying a case and judging evil deeds [β: and sexual violations] is granted to you, will you escape the judgment of God when you do the same things and there is no one to judge you at present? Certainly not, because if you have eluded the judgment of God in this world, you will not elude it in the future, since all this power and judgment is from God."

6. *Recensio* α has "both turns out to be true and is fulfilled."

7. *Recensio* α does not have "good," although the word (*bona*) can be inferred from both the preceding and following clauses.

is unbecoming and impossible[8] for him, being good, to have made bad things—he must be said to take care of them. It is an insult to him, and an accusation, if he is presented as ignoring the good things made by him, especially since through his will and providence life itself is governed by the ministering elements,[9] as the Lord himself says: *Who commands his sun to rise on the good and the evil, and sends rain on the righteous and the unrighteous* (Matt 5:45). Therefore, does not he who furnishes these elements take care to preserve what he has made, in order to reward those who love him and condemn those who reject him?

2:4 *Or do you scorn the riches of his goodness and patience?*[10] *Do you not know that God's goodness leads you to repentance?* (1) He says these things so that one does not think that he has already escaped if God's *goodness* bears with him while he sins for a long time, or so that one does not think that God's *patience* may be scorned as if it is unconcerned about human affairs.[11] Rather, one should understand that his conduct is being overlooked because the promise was that God's judgment would not come in this life. It is coming in the future, so that in the life to come he may repent that he did not believe that God is a judge who, to display the terror of his future judgment and to show that his patience should not be scorned, says: *I have kept silent. Will I always keep silent?* (Isa 42:14).[12] (2)[13] Therefore, once such a person is in fact placed under punishment,

---

8. *Recensiones* α and β have "unlikely" instead of "impossible."

9. *Recensiones* α and β have "life itself was sustained by the ministry of the elements" instead of "life itself is governed by the ministering elements."

10. Many manuscripts in *recensio* α and MS Paris lat. 1759 in *recensio* γ have "his goodness and patience and forbearance" (*bonitatis eius et patientiae et longanimitatis*), which agrees with the Greek witnesses (τῆς χρηστότητος αὐτοῦ καὶ τῆς ἀνοχῆς καὶ τῆς μακροθυμίας). The addition of *longanimitatis* is supported by the comment at In Rom. 2:4 (§2).

11. Instead of the following two sentences, *recensio* α has "human affairs, but so that he knows that he has been preserved for so long in order that here he may repent that he did not believe that God is judge."

12. *Recensio* β does not have "who, to display the terror of his future judgment and to show that his patience should not be scorned, says: *I have kept silent. Will I always keep silent?*"

13. In *recensiones* α and β this section reads as follows: "Once he is in fact placed under punishment, he will repent, but without the benefit of repentance, because he did not believe in the judgment of God, which he sees is real. For it is inevitable that one whom the forbearance of patience did not amend should be amended in a more painful way and, indeed, should be tortured with unending punishments. This very

he will repent, but to no avail, when he beholds the judgment of God, the judgment he denied would come. For one who thought that the *forbearance* of God's goodness was a joke also does not have the sense of shame to beseech God.[14]

2:5 *But by your hardness and your unrepentant heart you are storing up wrath for yourself on the day of wrath and of the revelation of God's righteous judgment,* **2:6** *who will repay each one according to his deeds.* (1) One who expects to sin with impunity not only becomes hardened, remaining unalterable and intractable, but sins even more brazenly, confident that there will be no future retribution.[15] He has an *unrepentant heart*, not realizing that wrath is building up for him *on the day of wrath*. For it is inevitable that someone who over a long period of deferral not only was unwilling to change his ways but, adding further to his offense, heaped up sins, should be punished with a harsher penalty and, indeed, should be tortured with unending flames.[16] The day of wrath is for sinners, the day when they will be punished.[17] The wrath is thus for those who will experience punishment *on the day of the revelation of God's righteous judgment*. (2) What is now denied to be coming will be made plain, that is, will be acknowledged. When what is believed not to exist is displayed, it is revealed. It is displayed to those who deny—since it is plain to believers—so that they may confess, albeit unwillingly, God's righteous judgment when they see that *each one* is repaid *according to his deeds*. Will they not even acknowledge that this is justly done, when they see evil deeds avenged in their turn?

2:7 *To those who by patience of good work seek glory and honor and incorruption, eternal life.* (1) Because he is proclaiming God's righteous judgment, he has explained what it will be like for those who are good. They are those who realize that God's patience has been prolonged partly for the purpose of admonition and partly for the greater punishment of those who do not correct their ways. The good repent of their earlier works

---

harsh statement is made, knowing that a wicked mind cannot [β: easily] be called back from vice [β: vices] except by fear."

14. See n. 10 above.

15. *Recensio* α has "One who expects to sin with impunity becomes hardened, remaining unalterable and intractable, confident that the retribution will be in the future."

16. This sentence is found only in *recensiones* β and γ. *Recensio* β has "during the lengthy patience of God" instead of "over a long period of deferral." There is a similar remark at In Rom. 2:4 (§2) in *recensiones* α and β.

17. *Recensio* α has "The day of wrath is the day when sinners will be punished."

and are occupied with doing good, confident because of their trust in God's faithfulness that, though they have been placed here for a long time, they will not incur the loss of the promised life.[18] He will therefore give them *glory and honor*. In case this might not seem especially great in comparison with the present life (because here too people appear glorious and honorable), the apostle has added *and incorruption*, so that by this a different glory and a different honor might be understood, accompanied at the same time by incorruption. (2) For at the present time honor or glory is often lost, because the person who gives, what he bestows, and the person who receives are corruptible. In the day of God's judgment, however, honor and glory will be given to those who are already incorruptible, so that they are altogether eternal. For the substance itself will be glorified by a certain unchangeability of its qualities. Therefore, those who have not only a good profession but also a good life are *seeking eternal life*.[19]

2:8 *But to those who are factious and do not believe the truth, but obey wickedness,* **2:9** *wrath and indignation and tribulations.*[20] (1) That is, repeated tribulation.[21] When they do not believe the judgment of God that will happen through Christ,[22] and as a result also spurn his patience, they strive to nullify it,[23] although it is true and sure. They trust in *wickedness*.[24] It is wickedness to deny what God has foretold will happen. The apostle then listed three other things that rightly befit unbelief: *wrath and indignation and tribulations*. (2) *Wrath* does not belong to the one who judges but to the one who is judged, when he is found guilty. For God is

---

18. *Recensio* α has "Because he is proclaiming that God's judgment is just, he has explained how it will be good. He describes those who, knowing that God's lengthy patience has been prolonged for the impunity of those who do not correct themselves, are occupied with doing good, shining brightly with divine works, so that though they have been placed here for a long time they may not be found in their number" (i.e., among the condemned). *Recensio* β is similar to *recensio* γ, with a few variants.

19. Ambrosiaster has already explained that the Christian both believes and professes the faith; see In Rom. 1:11 (§2) and 1:17 (§2). Here he adds a third aspect of authentic Christianity, a good life.

20. Ambrosiaster's biblical text has "tribulations" (*angustiae*), but the Greek text has "tribulation and distress" (θλῖψις καὶ στενοχωρία); see NA[28].

21. In *recensio* γ this sentence is attested only by MS Paris lat. 1759.

22. See Rom 2:16.

23. I.e., the coming judgment.

24. *Recensio* α has "Because they do not believe the judgment of God that will happen through Christ and strive to nullify it, although it is true, they trust in *wickedness*."

said to be angered so that he may be believed to be one who will avenge;[25] God's nature, however, is free of these passions. Furthermore, so that he may be believed not only to be angered but also to avenge, the apostle has added *and indignation*. By adding this on top of anger,[26] he indicates that he[27] will avenge the wrong done to him. *Tribulations*, moreover, are the means by which one who has been sentenced and bound will be tormented in punishment.

Upon every human soul that does evil. (3) By this action he means not only deeds, but also professions of faithlessness. He is speaking about the unbeliever, and therefore he said *upon the soul*, because he does not mean bodily punishment, but rather spiritual punishment. For the soul will be oppressed by invisible punishments.

The Jew first and also the Greek. (4) He always puts the Jew first on account of ancestral prerogative, so that he may be either crowned first or condemned first. Just as when he believes he is worthy of greater honor on account of Abraham, so when he does not believe he must be treated worse, since he rejected the gift promised to his fathers.

2:10 *But glory and honor and peace for all who do good, the Jew first and also the Greek.* Just as he has listed three dolorous things for unbelievers, so too he has listed three magnificent things for believers: that they may receive real *honor* as children of God; that *glory* may occur in the transformation; and *peace* for the reason that those who live well will be tranquil in the future, troubled by no disturbance, and because everyone who guards himself from wrongs has a peaceable judge.[28]

---

25. Recensiones α and β have "will come in judgment" instead of "will avenge."

26. *Recensiones* α and β and a second hand in MS St. Gall 101 have "Indignation is that which, by adding etc."

27. MSS Paris lat. 1759 and, in a second hand, St. Gall 101 have "God" instead of the implied subject "he."

28. The concluding series of clauses in this comment, which varies slightly in all three recensions, is difficult to translate. *Recensio* α has "Just as he has listed three punishments for unbelievers, so he has listed three great things for believers: that they may possess true *honor* as children of God; that *glory* may come about in the transformation; and *peace* for the reason that those who live well will be tranquil in the future, troubled by no disturbance." *Recensio* β has: "Just as he has listed three punishments for unbelievers, so too he has listed three magnificent things for believers: that they may receive real *honor* as children of God; that *glory* may occur in the transformation; and *peace* for the reason that those who live well will be tranquil in the future, troubled by no disturbance, especially because everyone who keeps himself from wrongs has peace in the presence of the judge."

2:11 *For there is no partiality in God's sight.* The apostle has explained that neither Jew nor Greek is shunned by God (provided that each believes in Christ), but that the righteousness of faith is credited to them both. Furthermore, he has explained that they are equally condemned when they do not believe, for circumcision will be injurious without faith and uncircumcision will be beneficial through faith. He thereby teaches that God shows no partiality. For God does not accede to the prerogative of ancestry, so as to accept someone who does not believe for the sake of his fathers and cast away from himself someone who believes on account of the unworthiness of his parents. Rather, he either rewards or condemns each one according to his own merit.

2:12 *Whoever sinned without the law will perish without the law.* (1) How is it possible to sin *without the law*, when it is evident that all are subject to natural law? But he is speaking of the law of Moses, to which the Jews are accountable as long as they do not believe,[29] and likewise the gentiles, but a long time ago,[30] because they did not want to yoke themselves to the law of Moses.[31] Therefore, unbelieving gentiles are found guilty on two counts, because they neither acquiesced to the law given through Moses nor accepted the grace of Christ.[32] For that reason it is fitting that they perish. (1a)[33] Therefore, just as one who sins without the law will perish, so too one who without the law has kept the law will be justified. For one who naturally preserves righteousness is a keeper of the law. If *the law was laid down not for the righteous but for the unrighteous* (1 Tim 1:9), one who does not sin is a friend of the law. For this person faith alone is required, by which he is made perfect, because it will not benefit him in

---

29. *Recensio* α does not have "as long as they do not believe"; see In Rom. 2:12 (§2).

30. *Recensio* α has "a short time ago" instead of "a long time ago."

31. Ambrosiaster suggests that there was a time in the past when the gentiles could have submitted to the law of Moses along with the Jews but chose not to do so; they are answerable for this choice. The offer of the law to the gentiles is discussed in halakic midrashim on Exodus and Deuteronomy, Mekilta of Rabbi Ishmael, Bahodesh 5, and Sifre Deut. 343; for a comparative analysis, see Steven D. Fraade, *From Tradition to Commentary: Torah and Its Interpretation in the Midrash Sifre to Deuteronomy* (Albany: State University of New York Press, 1991), 32–37. It is mentioned also in a fragment from Origen's *Homilies on Deuteronomy* (PG 12:816D13–817A2).

32. *Recensio* α has "Consequently, unbelievers are found guilty on two counts, because they did not acquiesce to the law given through Moses and did not accept Christ who was promised by the law."

33. This section is found only in *recensiones* β and γ.

God's sight to refrain from wrong unless he accepts faith in God, so that he is righteous on both accounts. The former righteousness is temporal; the latter is for eternity.

And whoever has sinned under the law will be judged by the law. (2)[34] Just as the gentiles, even if they keep the law of nature, will nevertheless perish unless they accept the faith of Christ—for it is more important to confess the only Lord, because God is one, than to refrain from other sins: the latter is for God's sake; the former, for ours[35]—so too the Jews, who are operating under the law and are accused by the law, will be judged because they did not accept Christ as promised in the law. If you ask, the sorrow of the Jews is greater than that of the gentiles; it is worse to have lost a promise than not to have received what one did not hope for. For the latter did not enter the kingdom, whereas the former was cast outside.[36]

2:13 *For it is not the hearers of the law who are righteous before God, but the doers of the law who will be justified.* He says this because those who hear the law are not righteous unless they believe in Christ, whom that same law promised; this is what it means to do the law.[37] In fact, how can someone who does not believe the law do the law, as long as he does not accept him to whom the law bears witness?[38] Rather, the person who appears not to be under the law, because he is uncircumcised in the flesh, but believes in Christ, is said to have done the law, whereas the person who says that he is under the law, namely the Jew, is not a *doer of the law,* but

---

34. *Recensiones* α and β have "Because the Jews have the law in which they were promised salvation, they will be judged since they do not believe or do not accept him who was promised by the law under which they lived. For since the law itself accuses them, they suffer punishment. In fact, among those who are judged the case of the Jews is far more serious than that of the gentiles; just as they are given preference when they believe, so too they are found to be worse when they do not believe. It is indeed more disagreeable for one to lose what one had than to not have been able to obtain what one did not hope for."

35. Ambrosiaster's argument is that to confess that Christ alone is Lord is of greater import, since it avails for salvation, whereas to refrain from transgressions of the law, while it shows respect for God, will not so avail.

36. This sentence is also found, with a small variant, in *recensio* β.

37. Here, echoing the lemma, Ambrosiaster speaks of "doing the law" (*facere legem*). In his comment on the next verse, he speaks more idiomatically of "keeping the law" (*legem servare*).

38. *Recensiones* α and β have "But everyone who does not believe the law does not do the law, as long as he does not accept him to whom the law bears witness." There are additional minor variants in the remainder of the comment.

a *hearer*, because he does not transfer what is said in the law to his mind.[39] For he does not believe in Christ who was written about in the law, as Philip said to Nathaniel: *We have found him about whom Moses wrote in the law, and also the prophets, Jesus* (John 1:45).

2:14 *When gentiles, who do not have the law, do by nature what pertains to the law.* With the term *gentiles*—for he is the teacher of the gentiles, as he says elsewhere: *For I am speaking to you gentiles* (Rom 11:13)[40]—he refers to Christians who are uncircumcised and do not keep the new moons and the sabbath and the dietary laws (see Col 2:16), yet with nature as a guide believe in God and Christ, that is, in the Father and in the Son. For this is what it means to keep the law: to acknowledge the God of the law.[41] For the first part of wisdom is this (see Sir 1:16): to fear God the Father, from whom are all things, and the Lord Jesus his Son, through whom are all things (see 1 Cor 8:6). Therefore, nature itself by its own discernment acknowledges its creator, not through the law, but by reason of nature.[42] A thing that is made perceives its maker within itself.[43]

They are a law unto themselves, even though they do not have the law. **2:15**[44] *They show that the work of the law is written on their hearts.* (1) The meaning is the same, since when with nature as a guide they believe, they show *the work of the law* not in writing but in their conscience. The work of the law is faith. When someone displays faith in God's pronouncements,[45] he shows by a natural discernment that he is a law unto himself, because he does on his own what the law commands: to believe in Christ.

While their conscience bears witness. (2) With their conscience as an internal witness, they believe. For they are conscious that it is fitting for them to believe—it is not incongruous for a creature to believe and revere its maker—and that it is not absurd that a slave acknowledge a master.[46]

---

39. *Recensiones* α and β do not have this clause.
40. *Recensiones* α and β do not have this clause.
41. *Recensio* β has "the Lord of the law."
42. *Recensio* α has "by reason of being created."
43. See Ambrosiaster, *Quaest.* 115.82 (CSEL 50:349).
44. The beginning of verse 15 is placed here, as in modern texts of Romans, rather than at the beginning of the lemma (verse 14b), as in the CSEL edition.
45. *Recensiones* α and β have "When someone displays faith in the pronouncements to God."
46. *Recensio* α has "With their conscience as a witness, they believe. It is fitting for a creature to believe and revere its creator. Nor is it absurd that a servant acknowledge his master."

And their thoughts, debating with each other, accuse or even defend them **2:16** *on the day when God will judge the secrets of humankind according to my gospel through Jesus Christ our Lord.*[47] (1) The apostle has said that the Jews who do not believe will be judged by the law (see Rom 2:12–13)—for the law, which promised them the Christ, will accuse those who were unwilling to receive him when he came—whereas the gentiles, who clearly do not have the law, will be judged by their conscience, if they are unwilling to believe. First, in fact, believing gentiles will accuse unbelieving gentiles[48] in the same way that the Lord, when speaking of his disciples, said to unbelieving Jews: *They will be your judges* (Matt 12:27); the faithlessness of the Jews[49] will be judged by the faith of the apostles, who, although they were from the Jews, believed while other Jews did not. (2) Then the gentiles will be accused by their own thoughts, if they were unwilling to believe despite having been spurred by the faithfulness and power of the creator. Alternatively, if someone out of some kind of dullness does not think to believe the Lord's words and deeds, his conscience will defend him on the day of judgment because he did not realize that he ought to believe; he is judged not as someone who is malevolent but as someone who is unaware. All the same, he will not go unpunished, because it is not permissible to be unaware.[50] (2a)[51] He refers to gentiles in two senses, as believers and

---

47. Although Ambrosiaster's biblical text has "Jesus Christ our Lord" (*Iesum Christum dominum nostrum*), among the biblical witnesses the preferred reading is simply "Christ Jesus" (Χριστοῦ Ἰησοῦ). See Bruce M. Metzger, *A Textual Commentary on the Greek New Testament*, 2nd ed. (Stuttgart: Deutsche Bibelgesellschaft, 1994), 448; and Robert Jewett with Roy D. Kotansky, *Romans: A Commentary*, Hermeneia (Minneapolis: Fortress, 2007), 193. The addition "our Lord" (*dominum nostrum*), widely attested in the VL, is echoed in section 3 of Ambrosiaster's comment.

48. *Recensio* α has "First, in fact, believers accuse unbelievers."

49. In *recensio* γ "of the Jews" is attested only by MSS Amiens 87 and Paris lat. 1759.

50. *Recensio* α has "Or if out of some kind of dullness they are not moved to repent, someone will defend himself with the Lord's words in his conscience, because he did not realize that he ought to believe, and he is judged not as someone who is malicious but as someone who is unaware. All the same, he will not go unpunished, will he, because it is not permissible to be unaware?" *Recensio* β is similar to *recensio* γ but still begins the sentence in the third-person plural and punctuates it as a question, as does *recensio* α. In Roman law, ignorance of the law did not excuse one of responsibility; see Reinhard Zimmermann, *The Law of Obligations: Roman Foundations of the Civilian Tradition* (Oxford: Oxford University Press, 1996), 604–6.

51. Sections 2a to 2c are found only in *recensiones* β and γ; in *recensio* γ sections 2b and 2c are attested only by MS Paris lat. 1759.

as unbelievers. Above he speaks of believing gentiles (see Rom 2:15), but later he also added this about those gentiles who do not believe: just as gentiles are extolled by their conscience when they believe, so too are they accused by their conscience when they do not believe. Although a person who has not believed may hardly seem guilty to himself because he has not been able to think the matter through for himself, nevertheless he is convicted for the reason that he did not persuade himself that what he saw confirmed by the evidence of miracles and what he saw many people follow was true. (2b)[52] I suppose that the text can also be interpreted as if the whole passage is deemed to have dealt with believing gentiles, in that the scripture says: *For what have I to do with judging those who are outside?* (1 Cor 5:12). And: *One who does not believe,* it says, *is already judged* (John 3:18). And: *Because the wicked will not arise in the judgment* (Ps 1:5). Those who sin without the law will also perish without the law. They will not be able to stand before the judgment-seat of Christ and make a defense, because when they arise they will be led to gehenna. Those whom Paul says are in turn accused or defended by their thoughts on the day of judgment, are Christians. Those who disagree with the catholic church—who hold different views about Christ or about the meaning of the law according to the tradition of the church, whether Cataphrygians,[53] Novatianists, Donatists, or other heretics[54]—their thoughts will in turn accuse them on the day of judgment. If a person understood that the catholic church is the true church and was unwilling to follow it because he did not wish to appear to have been corrected, being ashamed to abandon a view he has held for a long time, on the day of judgment he will be accused by his thinking. (2c)[55] In fact, two ways of thinking in a person will accuse each other, good and bad. The good way of thinking accuses the bad because it has contradicted the truth. The bad way of thinking in turn accuses the good, which did not follow along as it—the bad way of thinking—thought it should.[56] For this

---

52. See n. 51.

53. I.e., Montanists; see the introduction §6.3.

54. There were Novatianist and Donatist churches in Rome in the fourth century. Ambrosiaster's reference to them here, added in *recensio* β and retained in *recensio* γ, is an indication of their continuing vigor. See Stephen A. Cooper and David G. Hunter, "Ambrosiaster *redactor sui*: The Commentaries on the Pauline Epistles (Excluding Romans)," *REAug* 56 (2010): 79–84, and the introduction §6.3.

55. See n. 51.

56. As Ambrosiaster explains in what follows, someone espousing a misguided

reason, a person who knowingly thought that the catholic church was good and true but persevered in heresy or schism, will be found guilty. But with a person who always thought this way,[57] supposing that what he followed was right, his thoughts will in turn excuse him. For it will be said, "When I thought about it, I always supposed that what I followed was right. This was my faith." Although this person must be corrected, his is a less serious case, because he will not be accused by his conscience on the day of judgment. (3) In this manner will *the secrets of humankind* be judged on the day of God's judgment *by Jesus Christ our Lord*.

2:17 *But if you call yourself a Jew.* (1) The cognomen is that of a Jew because it is on account of the father's line that they are called Israelites.[58] (1b)[59] However, if we wish to understand everything about this subject, we should point out that for the Jews the cognomen is significant in three ways. First, because they are children of Abraham, who on account of his faith was made the father of all the nations (see Gen 17:4). Second, because of Jacob, who for the sake of a faith that would increase was called "Israel" (see Gen 32:28); the greatness that began with the fathers gains renown with the children. Third, they are called Jews not so much because of Judah but because of Christ, because he is descended from Judah according to the flesh. For what was to come in Christ was signified in Judah. For it is said: *Judah will be your leader* (Judg 20:18) and *Judah, your brothers extol you* (Gen 49:8). This praise was given, evidently, not for Judah but for Christ, whom all those he has been so gracious as to call his brothers daily praise. He himself said to the women: *Go and tell my brothers that I go before you to Galilee* (see Matt 28:7; Mark 16:7). Who indeed will not praise the one by whose favor he lives? The apostle therefore wished that the whole meaning be comprehended in this sense, which is later in order but more complete in significance.[60] Jews who do not understand this defend the name of the fleshly Judah for themselves.

---

way of thinking can be convinced that other ways of thinking are wrong even when those other ways of thinking are right.

57. E.g., a person raised as a Montanist, Novatianist, or Donatist.

58. In the Roman naming system, the hereditary cognomen served as a personal family name, distinguishing between branches of a family; see Helmut Rix, "Cognomen," *BNP* A3:510–11.

59. This section is found in *recensio* β and in MS Paris lat. 1759 of *recensio* γ.

60. I.e., the third sense of the name, referring to Christ, is the most important.

And rely upon the law and boast in God **2:18**[61] *and know his will and approve what is better, having been instructed by the law.* Paul does not want it to seem so momentous if a Jew believes, since he has been taught by the law. Indeed, it would be perilous if a Jew does not believe, for he has the law as a guide. But a Jew who believes makes much of the importance of his fathers in order to be given preference, for although someone may feel fine with regards to himself he can nevertheless feel ashamed of his relatives.[62]

2:19 *And are sure that you are a guide to the blind, a light for those who are in darkness,* **2:20** *a corrector of the foolish, a teacher of children, having the model of knowledge and truth in the law.* These things are true, because this is the lesson of the law: to instruct the ignorant and to subject the irreligious to God, or to call forth those who are godless in their worship of idols to the assurance of a better hope[63] through the promise which is made in the law. The teacher of the law therefore rightly boasts in these things, because he is conveying the standard of truth. But if he does not accept him whom the law promised, he boasts in the law in vain. He does the law an injury when he rejects Christ who was promised in the law, and he will no longer be *a corrector of the foolish* or *a teacher of children* or *a light for those who are in darkness*, but rather a guide for all of these to damnation.

2:21 *You, then, who teach another, do you not teach yourself?* (1) This means: You who denounce the gentiles because they are without the law and without God—you accuse yourself.[64] For by not believing in Christ who was promised in the law, you find yourself in the same errors that you denounce.

You who preach that one should not steal, do you steal? (2)[65] You do what you preach should not be done.[66] As long as he undermines the faith

---

61. The beginning of 2:18 is placed here, as in modern texts of Romans, rather than at the beginning of the lemma (v. 17b), as in the CSEL edition.

62. Ambrosiaster appears to be saying that believing Jews sought prerogatives in the church on the basis of their ancestry in order to compensate for a discomfort or sense of shame they experienced in the wider community of Jews who did not believe.

63. I translate *ad melioris spei fiduciam* (*recensiones* α and β) instead of *ad meliores spei fiduciam* (*recensio* γ). The latter reading appears to derive from a copyist's error.

64. *Recensiones* α and β have "do you not denounce yourself?" instead of "you accuse yourself."

65. *Recensiones* α and β, and MSS Amiens 87 and Paris lat. 1759 of *recensio* γ, cast the comments on Rom 2:21b–23 in the second person singular rather than the third person singular. The individual variants are not noted except in connection with other substantive variants.

66. In *recensio* γ this sentence is attested only by MSS Amiens 87 and Paris lat.

of Christ through a wrong interpretation, by denying that our Christ was promised in the law, he does what he preached should not be done.[67]

2:22 *You who say that one should not commit adultery, do you commit adultery?* (1)[68] In fact he adulterates the law when he makes off with the truth of Christ and substitutes a lie. For this reason in another letter the apostle says: *Adulterators of the word of God* (2 Cor 2:17).[69]

You who abhor idols, do you commit sacrilege? (2)[70] It is sacrilegious when he denies Christ, whom the law and the word of the prophet refer to as God.[71] For Isaiah says: *Because God is in you and there is no God beside you. You are indeed God and we did not know it. God is the savior of Israel* (Isa 45:14–15).[72] Did the Jews ever say, regarding God the Father: *You are indeed God and we did not know it?*, seeing as the entire law proclaims the authority of God the Father, from whom are all things (see 1 Cor 8:6). Since, however, the Son of God was indeed always visible, but concealed what he was, when he is recognized after the resurrection it is said to him, by way of confession:[73] *You are indeed God and we did not know it.* For in the law he was believed to be one of the angels and the commander of the army of the Lord (see Gen 18; Josh 5:13–15),[74] but when he is understood to be the Son of God, it is said to him, with thanksgiving: *You are indeed God and we did not know it.* By this he means that he is the one who in fact

---

1759. It is not consistent with the third-person comments that follow in *recensio* γ; see n. 65 above.

67. *Recensio* α has "You do what you preach should not be done. As long as you undermine the faith of Christ through a wrong interpretation, you deny that our Christ was promised in the law. What you preach should not be done, you do." The last sentence is omitted in *recensio* β. This version of the comment is also found in MSS Paris lat. 1759 and Amiens 87 of *recensio* γ.

68. See n. 65 above.

69. At In 2 Cor. 2:17 (CSEL 81.2:212) the text of this verse reads *sicut plurimi adulterantes verbum dei*.

70. See n. 65 above.

71. *Recensio* α has "whom the law proclaims as God." *Recensio* β and three manuscripts of *recensio* γ have "whom the law and the word of the prophet refer to as God"; the singular number of the verb does not accord with the plural subject (*quem lex et profeticus sermo deum significat*). The remaining manuscripts of *recensio* γ have "whom the word of the prophet refers to as God."

72. *Recensio* α adds "which means 'Jesus.'"

73. *Recensio* α has "when he is recognized, it is said."

74. *Recensio* α has "For he who in the law was believed to be merely an angel and a commander, when he is understood etc."

appeared to the patriarchs as God, then afterward was incarnate, but had not been understood by everyone.[75]

2:23 *You who boast in the law, do you dishonor God through transgression of the law?*[76] He is[77] a transgressor of the law when he disregards the meaning of the law, which has to do with the incarnation and divinity of Christ.[78] He dishonors God as long as he does not accept the testimony he gave concerning his Son. For he said: *This is my beloved Son* (Matt 3:17; see Ps 2:7).

2:24 *For "the name of God is blasphemed by you among the gentiles," as it is written* (see Isa 52:5). The prophet Isaiah said this because[79] *the name of God is blasphemed among the gentiles* when they did not pay attention to the Jews who were handed over to them because of their trespasses.[80] Instead, they gave glory to their idols who seemingly had conquered the God of the Jews along with the Jews. So too, in the time of the apostles the name of God was blasphemed with regard to Christ, because by denying that Christ is God, the Jews blasphemed the Father as well, as the Lord says: *Whoever receives me, receives not me, but him who sent me* (Luke 9:48). He was blasphemed among the gentiles because the Jews tried to persuade believing gentiles that Christ should not be called *God*, with the result that the blasphemies of the gentiles were propagated by the Jews and the supporters of Photinus.[81]

2:25 *Circumcision is indeed beneficial if you keep the law.*[82] (1) It can be objected: if *circumcision is beneficial*, why is it now passed over? It is

---

75. *Recensio* α has "By this, then, he means that he was the one who had in fact appeared but had not been understood." *Recensio* β has "By this, then, he means that he was the one who had in fact appeared to the patriarchs as God and afterward was incarnate, but had not been understood by all."

76. The CSEL edition does not punctuate this verse as a question.

77. See n. 65 above.

78. *Recensio* α does not have "and divinity."

79. *Recensio* α has "because by you."

80. I.e., the trespasses of the Jews (*noxiis suis*).

81. *Recensio* α has "[He says] *among the gentiles*, because they tried to persuade believing gentiles that Christ should not be believed, with the result that the blasphemies of the gentiles were propagated by Jewish writers." *Recensio* β has the comment as found in *recensio* γ but has *credendum* instead of *dicendum* and *blasphemium* instead of *blasphemia*. On the connection in Ambrosiaster's mind between the error of the Jews and the error of Photinus, see In Rom. 1:1 (§3).

82. Although Ambrosiaster's biblical text has "keep" (*observes*), among the bibli-

beneficial only if you keep the law. Therefore, circumcision ought to be preserved and, so that it may be beneficial, the law should be kept. Why then did the apostle prohibit something that he explained is beneficial if the law is kept? For it seems wrong that something that is not unsatisfactory in itself, but is declared to be fruitless through the neglect of something else, is prohibited.[83]

But if you are a transgressor of the law, your circumcision becomes uncircumcision.[84] (2) This is what he is saying: if the law is not kept, a Jew is turned into a gentile; he used the word *circumcision* instead of *the descendants of Abraham* because circumcision comes from Abraham.[85] For the apostle could not build up what he had taken down (see Gal 2:18).[86] He says this to explain that it is beneficial to be one of the descendants of Abraham only if the law is kept—that is, if one trusts in Christ, who was promised to Abraham—because such descendants possess their own merit in being justified through faith and are granted higher status because of the honor of their fathers. All that is saving in the law is from Christ. Therefore, a person who believes in Christ keeps the law. (3) But if he does not believe, he is a transgressor of the law, because he does not accept Christ whom the law prophesied would come for his justification, something the law itself could not grant.[87] It will be benefit him nothing to be called a child of Abraham, because that person is deservedly a child of Abraham who follows the faith by which Abraham stood out as worthy before God.[88] This is why the apostle says: *Your circumcision becomes uncircumcision*; that is, you become like a gentile when you do not believe in him who was promised in the form of circumcision to Abraham.[89]

---

cal witnesses there is much stronger support for "do" (πράσσῃς). See further Jewett, *Romans*, 219.

83. *Recensio* α does not have this sentence.

84. Literally, "your circumcision becomes foreskin"; see Ambrosiaster's quotation of Jer 4:4 at In Rom. 2:28–29 (§1).

85. See Ambrosiaster, *Quaest.* 81.1 (CSEL 50:137–38).

86. I.e., in his criticism of the Jews in Rom 2:17–24.

87. *Recensio* α has "because he has not accepted Christ, whom the law promised."

88. *Recensio* α has "It will benefit him to be called a child of Abraham if he follows the faith by which Abraham stood out as worthy before God."

89. *Recensiones* α and β have "who was promised as a child of the circumcision to Abraham" (*qui circumcisionis filius promissus est Abrahae*). The text of *recensio* γ is problematic. Most manuscripts have *qui circumcisionis promissus est Abrahae*. MS

2:26 *So, if the uncircumcision keeps the commandments of the law,*[90] *will not their uncircumcision be reckoned as circumcision?* The justice of the law is the Christian faith,[91] as he says elsewhere: *The end of the law is Christ, for the justice of all who believe* (Rom 10:4).[92] From this it is clear that if a gentile believes in Christ, he is a child of Abraham, who is the father of faith.

2:27 *And that which by nature is uncircumcision but fulfills the law will judge you who through the written law and circumcision are a transgressor of the law.* The gentile who,[93] with nature as a guide, believes in Christ condemns the Jew, to whom Christ had been promised through the law and who was unwilling to believe in him when he came.[94] Therefore, as much as the gentile who through nature alone has recognized his author is worthy of honor—as the apostle Peter says, *But you killed the author of life* (Acts 3:15)—so much the more should the Jew who neither through nature nor through the law[95] has acknowledged Christ as his author be punished.

2:28 *For he is not a Jew who is one outwardly, nor is circumcision something plainly visible in the flesh.* **2:29** *But he is a Jew who is one secretly through circumcision of the heart, who is one in spirit not in letter, whose praise is not from people but from God.*[96] (1) It is not hard to see that the apostle denies that *circumcision of the flesh* merits any praise in God's sight. Abraham was justified not because he was circumcised, but because he believed; he was circumcised afterward. *Circumcision of the heart*, however,

---

Paris lat. 1759 has *qui in signo circumcisionis promissus est Abrahae*. MS Amiens 87 has *qui in signo circumcisionis filius promissus est Abrahae*.

90. The lemma has a plural form of *iustitia*, meaning "commandments" or "ordinances." The comment uses a singular form of the word twice, meaning "justice" or "righteousness."

91. *Recensio* α has "faith in Christ" instead of "the Christian faith."

92. See n. 90 above.

93. *Recensio* α has "The believer who."

94. *Recensio* α has "the Jew to whom the law promised Christ and who did not accept him." *Recensio* β has "the Jew to whom the law had promised Christ."

95. *Recensio* α has "neither through nature nor through the written law," with "law" being understood.

96. The RSV, in keeping with the prevailing interpretation of the Greek text, reads περιτομή as a nominative: "and … circumcision is a matter of the heart, spiritual and not literal" (καὶ περιτομὴ καρδίας ἐν πνεύματι οὐ γράμματι). But in the absence of diacritical marks, not used in early witnesses, περιτομή could be read as a dative, here rendered in Latin with the ablative *circumcisione*; see Caroline P. Hammond Bammel, *Römerbrieftext des Rufin und seine Origenes Übersetzung*, vol. 10 of *AGLB* (Freiburg: Herder, 1985), 301–2.

is praiseworthy in God's sight; to circumcise the heart is to acknowledge the creator once error has been cut away.[97] Because circumcision of the heart was to come in the future, first Moses says: *You will circumcise the hardness of your heart* (Deut 10:16), and likewise Jeremiah: *Circumcise the foreskin of your heart* (Jer 4:4). (He said this to Jews who followed idols.)[98] (2) There is a veil around the heart that one who has turned toward God will cut away (see 2 Cor 3:16),[99] because faith removes the cloud of error and bestows perfect knowledge of God in the mystery of the Trinity, which had not been known by the ages.[100] Therefore, for such circumcision there is praise *from God*, hidden from people; what God sees is the merit of the heart, not the flesh. Now, the praise of the Jews is *from people*; they boast of the circumcision of the flesh, which is from their fathers. For this reason in another letter the apostle says, among other things: *their boasting is about things to be ashamed of—they being people whose wisdom is of earthly things* (Phil 3:19)[101]—that is, people who think that the circumcision of the flesh is something to boast about. For the wisdom of one who boasts in the flesh is of earthly things, but one who boasts in the spirit, his praise is from God. He believes *in spirit*, not in the flesh.

---

97. *Recensio* α has "To circumcise the heart is to recognize [one's] author once a cloud has been removed."

98. *Recensio* α does not have this sentence.

99. Ambrosiaster plays on the meaning of *cirumcidere*, which literally means "cut around."

100. See Ambrosiaster's comments at In Rom. 16:25–27 (§1) and In Col. 1:25–26.

101. See Ambrosiaster's comment at In Phil. 3:19, where he understands Paul to criticize Judaizing Christians for boasting about, among other things, their circumcised penises (*gloriantes in pudendis circumcisis*).

Romans 3

3:1 *Then what advantage does the Jew have? Or what is the use of circumcision?* **3:2** *Much in every way. To begin with, the utterances of God were entrusted to them.* (1) Although the apostle refers to many things that pertain to the honor and merit of the offspring of Abraham,[1] he explicitly mentions only this one: that it is greatly to their credit that they were deemed worthy to receive the law by which they might learn to distinguish right from wrong. From this first quality the others can be understood. Moreover, because he showed that the argument from ancestry does not advantage fleshly—that is, unbelieving—Jews (see Rom 2:17–29), he explains that it is very useful for believing Jews to be children of Abraham, in order to avoid seeming to have treated all Jews badly, including believing Jews. (2) For *the utterances of God were entrusted to them* when through the merit of their fathers they received the law—which had fallen into disuse through the sins of humankind (as if one can sin with impunity before God!)—in a restored form and were called the people of God.[2] Furthermore,[3] Egypt is struck with various plagues because of its wrongdoing toward them (see Exod 7:8–13:16). They are fed with bread from heaven (see Exod 16:4). They inspire dread in all the nations, as Rahab, the former prostitute, testifies (see Josh 2:9). Finally, to them Christ the savior was promised for their sanctification. Therefore, he says it is of *much* use

---

1. After this point *recensio* α has "the apostle nevertheless includes everything here when he says: *To begin with, the utterances of God were entrusted to them*, so that after this first point the rest may be understood as implied."

2. Ambrosiaster appears to refer to the second giving of the law, whereby God restores the covenant with the Israelites and reaffirms their status as his people; see Exod 19:3–6; 32:7–14; 34:1–35.

3. Ambrosiaster enumerates further evidence of the meritorious status of the Jews, in addition to their reception of the law, which he has already singled out.

to the Jews *in every way* that they are children of Abraham; for they are granted precedence over the gentiles, provided that they believe.[4]

3:3 *What then if some of them have not believed? Will their unbelief nullify the faithfulness of God? By no means.*[5] (1) He says this because there will be no bias against believing Jews on account of the rest of the Jews who do not believe, such that they would be declared unworthy to receive what God promised, since the promise was made in such a way that the gift of God's grace would benefit those who believe it.[6] (1a)[7] Therefore, since God was not angry on account of their unbelief—that is, the unbelief of the Jews—he will give the believing remnant eternal life, which he promised would come through faith in Christ, because those who have not believed have rendered themselves unworthy without prejudice to the rest. With these words he commends the believing Jews, because it is no disadvantage to them that many of the Jews refused to believe.

3:4 *For God is true, though every human being is a liar,*[8] *as it is written.* (1) Because *God is true*, he therefore grants what he has promised. It is human to deceive; duration of time and weakness of nature[9] render a human being changeable by virtue of the fact that a human being does not have foreknowledge. But God, for whom there is no future,[10] abides unchangeable, as he says: *I am and I do not change*[11] (Mal 3:6). (2) He therefore calls *every human being a liar*, and it is true. For a nature that is

---

4. *Recensio* α does not have "provided that they believe."
5. In English translations of Romans, 3:4 begins at *By no means!*
6. *Recensio* α has "Because some of the Jews have refused to believe what God has promised the children of Abraham, there will not for that reason be a bias against the rest of the Jews who believe, such that they would be declared unworthy to receive what God has promised to those who believe. *By no means*, especially since the promise was made to benefit those who believe." *Recensio* β has "The apostle says that because some of the Jews have refused to believe what God has promised the children of Abraham, there will not for that reason be a bias against the rest of the Jews, such that they would be declared unworthy to receive what God has promised to the faithful, especially since the promise was made in such a way as to benefit those who believe."
7. *Recensio* α does not have this section.
8. Usually I translate *homo* and *homines* as "person" and "people." However, because Rom 3:4 contrasts the truthfulness of God with the mendacity of humankind, I use "human being(s)" here and in the comments that follow on Rom 3:4–6.
9. *Recensio* α has "times and conditions" instead of "duration of time and weakness of nature."
10. *Recensio* α has "with whom what is in the future has already happened."
11. *Recensio* α has "I will not change."

deceived is rightly called a liar. Sometimes one is a liar deliberately; other times, by mistake. But the same should not be expected of God, who is both perfect and kind,[12] so that he fulfills what he has promised.[13] The apostle corroborates this with the prophetic oracle, saying: *It is written, "So that you may be justified by your words and may prevail when you are judged"* (Ps 50:6 LXX = Ps 51:4 ET). (3)[14] The prophetic saying bears witness that God is just in his promises and his words, and that his faithfulness is not diminished by the unbelief of some people but rather prevails by granting what he says. Unbelievers, by not believing, deny that he will grant what he says. He will grant, therefore, what he is deemed not to grant so that he may prevail by doing what it was denied he would do. Then will godlessness, which as long as it does not believe denies that what God has promised is true, be overcome. For it will see the resurrection, which it denied, accomplished as a fact, and it will know that unbelief is overcome by the promise and the truth of God. This is what it means that *God is true, though every human being is a liar.*[15] Having been unjustly killed, Christ rendered the devil, whom he had already overcome by not sinning, to be guilty, with the result that the devil, having been overcome a second time, released those he held captive.[16] (3a)[17] To support what he said above—that God is faithful to his promise and that every human being is a liar—he added the prophetic quotation from Ps 50,[18] where the psalmist indicated both that God is justified by his words and that human beings are liars on account of unbelief. Each of these statements is found in the book of Psalms, both that God is just and true and that every human being is a liar.

---

12. I.e., God cannot lie by mistake or deliberately.

13. *Recensio* α has "so that what he has promised is not a lie."

14. The manuscript tradition for the rest of the comment on Rom 3:4 is complicated. Section 3 is found only in *recensio* α and in all the manuscripts of *recensio* γ except MSS Amiens 87 and Paris lat. 1759. Sections 3a, 4a, and 5a are found only in *recensio* β and in MSS Amiens 87 and Paris lat. 1759 of *recensio* γ. If *recensio* γ is the final version of the commentary, revised by Ambrosiaster himself, it is unlikely to have included section 3 as well as sections 3a, 4a, and 5a, since the latter reiterate what is stated in the former. In all likelihood sections 3a–5a replaced section 3 in *recensiones* β and γ. See n. 16 below.

15. *Recensio* α has "though *every human being* who denies what will be is *a liar.*"

16. *Recensio* α does not have this sentence. It appears here in *recensio* γ and again at the end of section 5a in *recensiones* β and γ. It is more in context in the latter position.

17. See n. 14 above.

18. Ambrosiaster follows the enumeration of the Psalms in the LXX.

He calls a person *a liar* when he does not believe what God has promised; someone who denies that God will grant what he has promised is a liar. (4a) While such a person may be a liar for many reasons, he declares God to be a liar when he does not believe God's promises. The apostle therefore calls every one who does not believe the promises of God a liar.[19] However, this pertains above all to the Jews, on whose account the apostle discusses the point here. Although they saw Christ, they denied that he was the one God promised, and for this reason they are pronounced liars. God, on the other hand, is *true*, because he sent Christ as he promised. So God prevails, when he is judged,[20] because he will grant what it was denied he would grant. (5a) As long as God is not believed, he is judged a liar. But when he grants what he is judged not to grant, he prevails by showing that he is true and that the person who does believe his words is a liar. Such a person will see the Son of God, whom he denied, in majesty. He will also see the resurrection of the flesh, so that he will know that unbelief has been overcome by the promise and the truth of God. In fact, Christ also prevailed when he was judged. For he was unjustly killed and rendered the devil guilty, whom he had already overcome by not sinning, with the result that the devil, having been overcome a second time, released those he held captive in the underworld.[21] This is what it means that *every human being is a liar*, whereas *God* alone is *true*.

3:5 *But if our wickedness commends God's righteousness, what shall we say? That God who inflicts wrath is unjust? I speak in a human way. By no means!*[22] (1) The apostle has added this in keeping with the meaning of the prophet David. Because David had sinned in the affair of Uriah the Hittite (see 2 Sam 11:1–12:25) and knew that the promise cannot be granted to sinners, he prays that the justification of God's words may prevail over judgment—judgment that denies the promise to those who sin[23]—and

---

19. Ambrosiaster's argument is as follows: A person who does not believe God's promises in effect claims that God is not true to his word, i.e., that God is a liar. But since God cannot be a liar, such a person is de facto a liar, i.e., claiming something that is not true.

20. What Ambrosiaster means here becomes clearer in the next section, where he explains that God is judged a liar when he is not believed but prevails nevertheless in doing what he promised.

21. On Ambrosiaster's understanding of the vanquishing of the devil and the release of souls from the underworld, see the introduction §5.4.

22. In English translations of Romans, 3:6 begins at *By no means!*

23. *Recensio* α has "judgment by which those who sin are judged."

may transform the penitent, sanctifying him so that God may grant him what he promised he would grant the righteous. For this reason he added: *But if our wickedness commends God's righteousness*, and so on; in other words, if God is justified because we are sinners, he will be wicked if he punishes. (1a)[24] This is true, provided that our wickedness benefits him. But because it is perilous to say this, God is in fact not wicked if he judges. For our wickedness does not benefit him such that when we sin he is justified; in other words, such that he rejoices at our sins, by which he alone comes out looking just. (2) But the apostle says, *By no means! I speak in a human way.* That is: this reasoning is appropriate for a human being but not for God, because it is not fitting for God to be wicked, but it is fitting for humankind.[25] Nor does our unrighteousness make God just,[26] were he to give to us sinners what he promised to those who are holy. For although we are sinners, we nevertheless are restored through repentance, so that, no longer sinners but as those who have been washed,[27] we are deemed worthy to receive the promise. (3) This, then, is not the meaning of the words of the prophet David when he says, *Against you alone have I sinned and done what is evil in your sight, so that you may be justified by your words and may prevail when you are judged* (Ps 50:6 LXX = Ps 51:4 ET). According to the depraved interpretation of ill-disposed people, David is held to say that human sins and evil actions advance God's justice, that through our wickedness God comes out looking just, and that our unrighteousness shows him to be just. Consequently, since God is not wicked when he inflicts wrath, he is no longer justified by our sins, because if he is justified by our sins, he would be wicked if he punishes. But *by no means!*[28] He does not want us to sin. Therefore, because he is just, he inflicts wrath.

---

24. *Recensio* α does not have section 1a. *Recensio* β has only the following sentence: "For if our wickedness benefited him, he would certainly be wicked if he condemned sinners."

25. *Recensio* α does not have the first two sentences in section 2.

26. *Recensiones* α and β have "that our unrighteousness makes God just" instead of "nor does our unrighteousness make God just." They appear to assume a preceding statement such as "By no means is it the case etc."

27. I.e., those who have been baptized.

28. *Recensio* α has "But *by no means!* He does not want us to sin. Therefore, he is just if he inflicts wrath." *Recensio* β and MS Paris lat. 1759 of *recensio* γ have: "But *by no means!* because he is not wicked when he punishes. It is clear that our wickedness does not commend God's righteousness. If it were to commend it, he would not punish, because he is just. For this reason the apostle added: *I speak in a human way.*"

3:6 *Otherwise, how will God judge this world?* It is true that it would not be just for God to judge the world if the world's sins benefited him, so that God looks good when people who sin with his permission obtain forgiveness; if they did not sin, he would not seem just.[29] For if they do not sin, he would not be good, since he does not have someone to forgive. But *by no means!*

3:7 *For if through my falsehood the truth of God has abounded to his glory, why am I still judged as a sinner?* It is clear that if human falsehood promotes God's glory, such that God alone appears to be true, those who sin should not be called sinners, because they will seem to sin not voluntarily but at his instigation.[30] This is by no means the case.

3:8 *And—as we are slandered and as some people claim we say—why not do evil so that good may come?* (1) The reason the apostle has put this question to himself is this:[31] wrong-headed people countered with the view—as though this were the meaning of the proclamation of forgiveness of sins—that they did evil and good resulted. In other words, they held that they sinned so that God might seem good in forgiving them.[32] The apostle calls this slander and distances it from the meaning of the divine teaching. For the faith does not encourage one to sin, especially since it proclaims that the Lord will come in judgment.[33] Rather, it offers a remedy for transgressors,[34] so that, having recovered their health and living under the law of God,[35] they may sin no longer. The apostle therefore has added: *Their*

By no means! That is, *by no means*, lest God should be called wicked. This applies to humankind, who is known to err and to be deceived and to deceive. God, on the other hand, abides unchangeable and cannot not love what he does."

29. *Recensio* α does not have "if they did not sin, he would not seem just."

30. *Recensio* α and most manuscripts of *recensio* γ have "for they will seem to sin at his instigation." The text translated above is found in *recensio* β and MSS Amiens 87 and Paris lat. 1759 of *recensio* γ.

31. *Recensio* β has "Now it becomes clear on whose account he discusses this matter carefully and thoughtfully."

32. *Recensio* β and MSS Amiens 87 and Paris lat. 1759 of *recensio* γ add "as was said above."

33. *Recensio* α does not have "especially since it proclaims that the Lord will come in judgment." *Recensio* β has "God" instead of "the Lord."

34. *Recensio* β has "counsels transgressors" instead of "offers a remedy for transgressors."

35. *Recensio* α and many manuscripts of *recensio* γ do not have "and living under the law of God." The phrase is found in *recensio* β and MSS Amiens 87, Oxford 756, Paris lat. 1759, and St. Gall 101, in a second hand, of *recensio* γ.

condemnation is just. (2) That is, the condemnation of these people is just,[36] who out of spiteful jealousy attribute to us what was said above.[37] (2a)[38] For the Jews put forward this interpretation in order to incriminate the apostolic teaching. They said that when he proclaims forgiveness of sins he provides kindling for sinning,[39] leading people to sin easily, seemingly without any concern, because of forgiveness, though it is well known that it is perilous to sin after one has accepted the faith and that believers are told as much.

3:9 *What more, then, do we hold?*[40] *For we have argued that Jews and Greeks are all under sin.* In other words, why do we still dwell on this point and discuss it at greater length?[41] For, to repeat the argument, we have shown that all are guilty, Jews as well as Greeks (that is, gentiles), and that therefore the law is kept in vain. First the apostle showed that the Greeks are guilty according to the law of nature and that they also did not receive the law of Moses. Therefore, their situation is dire and grave. Then the apostle showed that the Jews are guilty as well—the Jews who seem[42] to live under the law of God and who insisted on their status on account of their fathers—because[43] they have rejected the promise of their fathers, reducing the grace of God to nothing. In order to strengthen the point, the apostle has supplied a prophetic quotation from Ps 13,[44] saying:

3:10 *As it is written: "For no one whosoever is righteous"* (Ps 13:1 LXX = Ps 14:1 ET). Starting with unrighteousness, he has begun to list their evil deeds, mentioning some of the more wicked ones in order to demon-

---

36. *Recensio* α has "Their condemnation is just."

37. *Recensio* α does not have "what was said above." The phrase is found in *recensio* β and MSS Amiens 87 and Paris lat. 1759 of *recensio* γ.

38. *Recensio* α does not have section 2a.

39. *Recensio* β and MSS Amiens 87 and Paris lat. 1759 of *recensio* γ have "they preach" and "they provide"—that is, the apostles as a group—instead of "he preaches" and "he provides"—that is, the apostle Paul.

40. On the variant readings among the biblical witnesses for the first part of verse 9, see NA[28] and Robert Jewett with Roy D. Kotansky, *Romans: A Commentary*, Hermeneia (Minneapolis: Fortress, 2007), 253. The preferred reading is "What then? Are we better off? No, not at all" (τί οὖν; προεχόμεθα; οὐ πάντως).

41. *Recensio* α has "Why do we still discuss this at greater length?"

42. *Recensiones* α and β have "seemed" instead of "seem."

43. *Recensio* α has "especially because."

44. Ambrosiaster attributes all the verses quoted by Paul at Rom 3:10–18 to Ps 13 LXX = Ps 14 ET. In fact, the quotations at Rom 3:13–18 were drawn from other sources, as noted parenthetically below. These verses were, however, added to Ps 13:3 in certain manuscripts of the Septuagint and the Vulgate on the strength of Paul's quotation.

strate that there will be no hope for them unless they beseech the mercy of Christ, who forgives sins. Then he has added:

3:11 *"No one understands"* (Ps 13:2 LXX = Ps 14:2 ET). This is true, because if one took the trouble to understand, one would not be unrighteous.

"There is no one who seeks God" (Ps 13:2 LXX = Ps 14:2 ET). Nor is it hard to see that if one understood what would help, one would seek God. One would not be like Asa the king of Judah, who despite many blessings from God was so depraved that when he suffered from a disease of the feet he did not seek God even though a prophet was available (see 2 Chr 16:7–10, 12).[45]

3:12 *"All have fallen away, they have all become useless"* (Ps 13:3 LXX = Ps 14:3 ET). No one doubts that all who do not seek God fall away, so that they seek help from what is futile. What is futile is an idol. Therefore, they *become useless*.[46]

"There is no one who does good, not even one" (Ps 13:3 LXX = Ps 14:3 ET). Because they paid no attention to God and became useless, they certainly are unable to do good. Having already become depraved, they develop into something worse.

3:13 *"Their throat is an open grave"* (Ps 5:11 LXX = Ps 5:9 ET). (1) Already given over to evil deeds, they wanted to devour—if that were possible—good people, so that just as a grave opens to receive cadavers so too their throats open against good people.

"They worked deceitfully with their tongues" (Ps 9:28 LXX = Ps 10:7 ET). (2) Since they were so much in the habit of evil deeds, whatever they said was treacherous.

"The venom of asps is under their lips" (Ps 139:4 LXX = Ps 140:3 ET) (3) He says this because the words of such people are a trap.[47] For they speak in order to deceive, so that just as venom is spewed through the lips of a snake so too deception and fraud[48] are spewed through their lips.

3:14 *"Their mouth is full of cursing and bitterness"* (Ps 9:28 LXX = Ps 10:7 ET). It is clear and obvious that the wicked always spread[49] scurrilous

---

45. *Recensio* α does not have this sentence.
46. *Recensio* α does not have this sentence.
47. *Recensio* α has "This means: their words are a trap."
48. *Recensio* α has only "fraud" (*circumventiones*). *Recensiones* β and γ vary slightly in wording.
49. *Recensio* α has "He says this because they always spread etc." *Recensio* β has "It is obvious that the wicked always spread etc."

and acrimonious rumors against good people, breaking out in abuse and slander[50] about them.

3:15 *"Their feet are swift to shed blood"* (Isa 59:7; Prov 1:16). He said this with regard to the slaughter of the prophets, whom they killed with alacrity, being slow to do good, *swift* to commit murder.

3:16 *"Sorrow and misery are in their paths"* (Isa 59:7). Since they were always quick to do evil, he declares their way or progress to be cruel and desolate.

3:17 *"And the path of peace they have not known"* (Isa 59:8). When they chose the path of enmity which goes to the second death, they rejected the way which leads to eternal life. That life is called *peace* because it will experience no disturbance, enjoying the favor of God. They refused to recognize that people of good will will find rest with God.[51]

3:18 *"There is no fear of God before their eyes"* (Ps 35:2 LXX = Ps 36:1 ET). (1) Since people of this sort are without understanding, they have no fear of God. For *the beginning of wisdom is the fear of the Lord*, says Solomon (Prov 1:7).[52] The apostle, moreover, did not say that these people have no fear of God; rather, he says, *there is no fear of God before their eyes*. Because they view their deeds, which are so evil,[53] and do not shudder, they are said to have no fear of God before their eyes. The prophet Jeremiah also referred to all such people when he said, among other things:[54] *Then all rose up against the prophet of the Lord, desiring to kill him* (see Jer 26:8), and added: *But all the people did not allow it* (see Jer 26:16).[55] (2) He therefore said *all* when referring to the former group of people, but meant the wicked, and *all* when referring to the latter group of people, but meant the good. So too, in saying, *All have fallen away* (Rom 3:12), the apostle does not mean the entire people as a whole, but only, as does the prophet mentioned above,[56] that part of the people in which all the wicked had

---

50. *Recensio* α does not have "and slander."
51. *Recensio* α has "The path of peace is a calm mind. For every good life is tranquil, and temperate actions are themselves peaceful." *Recensio* β has "The path of peace is gentle and calm. For every good life is tranquil, and temperate actions are themselves peaceful. Moreover, by these one goes to God. Since, then, they refused to recognize this path, they chose the path of torment which goes to gehenna."
52. *Recensio* α does not have "says Solomon."
53. *Recensio* α does not have "so."
54. *Recensio* α does not have "among other things."
55. Ambrosiaster paraphrases Jer 26:8 and 26:16.
56. *Recensio* α does not have "as does the prophet mentioned above."

congregated. There are always two groups of people in a population.[57] This group, then, is the people whom the Lord upbraided under the name of Jerusalem, when he says: *Jerusalem, Jerusalem, you who kill the prophets* (Matt 23:37), and in another passage he says: *An evil and adulterous generation* (Matt 12:39), and: *Brood of vipers* (Matt 3:7). (3) The prophet Isaiah also bemoaned such people when he said: *Woe, sinful nation, wicked offspring* (Isa 1:4). As long as they produce evil fruit, they are wicked offspring through an evil will. Since they could be changed if they wanted to, the voice of the apostle commends them in another epistle,[58] when he says: *We too were once by nature children of wrath, just like others* (Eph 2:3).[59]

3:19 *Now we know that whatever the law says it speaks to those who are within the law.* (1) It is obvious that the law rebukes those who even at the outset do not believe their leader Moses; nor the prophets, their ancestors, whom they also persecuted and killed; nor the apostles, their relatives according to the flesh, whose blood they shed. They have always been ungodly and rebellious against God. Therefore, they are condemned by the law whose authority, they thought, was to be despised.[60] For just as with the term *evil* a single name applies to all evil people, so too for all good people. In these people, therefore, the evil of all those who are like them is censured.[61] This was a source of consternation for the Jews, who were accustomed to appealing to evidence from the law in support of themselves and their ancestors.

So that every mouth may be stopped, and the whole world may be subject to God. (2) He says this because, with the Jews held fast in sin, *the whole world* was *subject to God*. There is no doubt that the pagans were sunk in transgressions and ungodliness. Thus, the entire world was prostrate before God in order to be able to partake of forgiveness; the whole world comprises Jews and gentiles, from whom the faithful have been set apart.[62]

---

57. *Recensio* α does not have this sentence.

58. *Recensio* α does not have "in another epistle."

59. Ambrosiaster's citation of Eph 2:3 varies slightly from the text on which he comments at In Eph. 2:3 (CSEL 81.3:79).

60. *Recensiones* α and β do not have "whose authority, they thought, was to be despised."

61. *Recensio* α has "of those" instead of "of all those."

62. *Recensio* α has "But with regard to the gentiles, there is no doubt that they were sunk in transgressions. Thus, the entire world was prostrate before God in order to be able to partake of forgiveness, because the whole world consists of Jews and gentiles." *Recensio* β has "There is no doubt that the pagans were sunk in transgressions

When, therefore, the apostle demonstrated that the Jews, who had received the law from God and to whom the promise was made, were guilty of sin, it is beyond doubt that all the Greeks were liable unto death. For this reason the apostle says, *Every mouth may be stopped and the whole world may be subject to God*, because, having been shown to be guilty, they all need God's mercy, the Jews as much as even the Greeks. [63]

3:20 *Because indeed all flesh will not be justified before God on the basis of works of the law.* (1) The reason he maintains that people are in no way justified before God is not that they did not keep the law of righteousness according to its commandments, but that they refused to believe the revelation of the mystery of God,[64] which is in Christ. For through this revelation God decreed that people are not justified through the law, which justifies for the time being but not before God. Those who keep the law are justified in the temporal world, but not before God,[65] because faith, through which people are justified before God, is not present in them. (1a)[66] Faith is in fact greater than the law, because the law pertains to us, while faith pertains to God. Accordingly, the law renders one just for a time, but faith renders one just for eternity. (2) Now, when the apostle said *all flesh*, he meant all people,[67] just as also the prophet Isaiah says that *all flesh will see the salvation of God* (Isa 40:5); that is, all flesh will see the Christ of God,[68] in whom is contained the salvation of all. (2a)[69] They are denoted, moreover, by the word *flesh* because they are subject to sin. For just as righteousness makes people spiritual, so too sins make them carnal, so that a person takes his name from his acts.

For through the law comes recognition of sin. (3) But the abolition of sin comes through faith. Therefore, one should seek after faith. Which law

---

and ungodliness. Thus, the entire world was prostrate before God in order to be able to arrive at forgiveness, because the whole world comprises Jews and gentiles, from whom the faithful have been set apart."

63. After the quotation *recensio* α has "as long as all need God's mercy, the Jews as much as the gentiles."
64. The Latin expression is *sacramentum mysterii dei*.
65. *Recensio* α has "Those who keep the law are called righteous in the temporal world, but unrighteous before God."
66. *Recensio* α does not have section 1a.
67. *Recensio* α has "The apostle calls all people *all flesh*."
68. *Recensio* α has "every person will see the Christ of God." *Recensio* β has "every person will see Christ the Lord."
69. *Recensio* α does not have section 2a.

is the law through which the apostle says sin is recognized? And how is it recognized? We see that the ancients were not unaware of sin, because even Joseph was put in prison—though through false accusation (see Gen 39:7–20)—on account of sin, as well as the butler and the baker of Pharaoh (see Gen 40:1–3). How then were sins concealed?[70] (4) In fact, the law is threefold,[71] inasmuch as the first part has to do with the revelation of the divinity of God,[72] while the second, which corresponds to natural law, is what prohibits sin, and the third concerns the law of deeds, namely, sabbaths, new moons, circumcision, and the rest. The law to which the apostle refers here is,[73] therefore, natural law, which, having been partly improved by Moses and partly strengthened by his authority,[74] made sin known in order to restrain vice. It did this not because sin was hidden, as I have said; rather, it showed that the sins which they commit would not go unpunished before God. (4a)[75] It showed[76] that God's judgment would come, so that no sinner is free from punishment, lest perhaps someone who eluded punishment for a time be thought to have made a mockery of the law. (5) This is what the law showed, that sin was imputed before God.[77]

3:21 *But now the righteousness of God has been revealed without the law, having the benefit of testimony from the law and the prophets.*[78] It is

---

70. *Recensio* α has "Did everyone, then, conceal sins?"

71. *Recensio* α has "twofold." Nevertheless, like the other recensions, it itemizes three parts of the law.

72. The Latin expression is *sacramento divinitatis dei*.

73. Literally, "This law is" (*haec est*).

74. *Recensio* α varies slightly here.

75. *Recensio* α does not have section 4a.

76. All the manuscripts of *recensio* γ except MS Monte Cassino 150 omit the words "that the sins which they commit would not remain unpunished before God. It showed." It appears that at some point in the transmission of *recensio* γ a scribe jumped from the first instance of "it showed" to the second instance of the phrase, omitting the material in between. The omission indicates that these manuscripts, despite their diversity, have a common ancestor.

77. *Recensiones* α and β do not have "that sin was imputed before God."

78. Ambrosiaster's comments on Rom 3:21–22—especially at In Rom. 3:21 (§2), where he feels it necessary to explain that mercy can be called "righteousness"—suggest that he understood *iustitia dei* as God's justice in dealing with humankind; see also Ambrosiaster's use of *iustitia* at In Rom. 11:33 (§§1–2). However, I have translated *iustitia dei* with "the righteousness of God" rather than "the justice of God" because the narrower connotations of the latter phrase in English do not suit all the occasions

clear that the righteousness of God has appeared *without the law*[79]—without, that is, the law of the sabbath and of circumcision and of the new moon and of vengeance, but not without the revelation of the divinity of God, especially since the righteousness of God is part of the revelation of God. Now, when the righteousness of God pardoned those whom the law held fast as guilty, it assuredly[80] did this without the law, because it forgave the sins of those whom the law was going to punish. Lest this action perhaps be thought to be contrary to the law, the apostle added that the righteousness of God had *the benefit of testimony* from *the law and the prophets*; that is, that the law itself, in another section,[81] had long ago said that this would happen, that the one who would save humankind was going to come.[82] For the law was not permitted to forgive sins. (2) What appears to be mercy is called *the righteousness of God* because it originates from a promise, and when a promise of God is fulfilled, it is called *the righteousness of God*. For righteousness consists in the fact that what was promised has been discharged.[83] When one welcomes those who flee to him for refuge, it is called *righteousness*,[84] because not to welcome[85] is wickedness.

3:22 *The righteousness of God, however, through faith in Jesus Christ.* (1a)[86] What else is meant by *through faith in Jesus Christ* but that this righteousness of God consists in the manifestation of Christ? For through faith the gift of the manifestation[87] of Christ, promised by God long ago, is recognized or accepted.

In all and upon all who believe.[88] (2) That is, upon all the Jews and Greeks who believed that the righteousness of God was revealed.

---

where *iustitia dei* arises in Ambrosiaster's biblical text or comments, e.g., Rom 1:17; 6:13; and 10:3.

79. *Recensio* α does not have the remainder of this sentence.
80. *Recensio* α does not have "assuredly."
81. *Recensio* α does not have "in another section."
82. *Recensio* α has "that the one who did what the law could not do was going to come to save humankind."
83. See Ambrosiaster's comment at In Rom. 1:17 (§2).
84. *Recensio* α has "the righteousness of God."
85. *Recensio* α has "not to welcome the one who seeks refuge."
86. *Recensio* α does not have section 1a.
87. *Recensio* β has "the proclamation" instead of "the manifestation."
88. Among the biblical witnesses there is stronger support for "in all" (εἰς πάντας) than for "upon all" (ἐπὶ πάντας) or "in all and upon all" (εἰς πάντας καὶ ἐπὶ πάντας); see Bruce M. Metzger, *A Textual Commentary on the Greek New Testament*, 2nd ed. (Stutt-

3:23 *For there is no distinction. All have sinned and lack the glory of God.* (1) Because the apostle had said that the righteousness—that is, the grace[89]—of God was upon all Jews and Greeks,[90] he has added *For all have sinned* to prove it. This should be understood as applying to everyone, which is why he says: *There is no distinction. All*, he says, *have sinned*, Jews as well as Greeks.[91] (2) *All*. This includes even those who are holy,[92] to show that the law was of no benefit without faith. For the law was given in such a way that faith, which hoped for salvation to come, would also be part of the law. This is why the death of Christ benefits everyone, since it has taught what should be believed and observed here in this age and has set everyone free from the underworld.[93]

3:24 *They are justified freely through his grace.* (1) *They are justified freely* because they are sanctified by faith alone as a gift of God;[94] they do nothing and render nothing in return.

Through the redemption which is in Christ Jesus. (2) The apostle bears witness that the grace of God is *in Christ* because by the will of God we have been redeemed by Christ so that we, having been set free, might be

---

gart: Deutsche Bibelgesellschaft, 1994), 449; and Jewett, *Romans*, 268. *Recensio* α has "upon all" (*super omnes*), the Vulgate reading, which, however, is also found in some pre-Vulgate witnesses, such as Pelagius; see Theodore S. de Bruyn, *Pelagius's Commentary on St Paul's Epistle to the Romans*, OECS (Oxford: Oxford University Press, 1993), 172. *Recensiones* β and γ have "in all and upon all" (*in omnes et super omnes*), which is widely attested in the VL. Since the comment that follows and the comment at In Rom. 3:23 (§1) refer only to *super omnes*, Ambrosiaster's text probably read "upon all."

89. *Recensiones* α and β do not have this phrase.

90. *Recensio* α does not have "Jews and Greeks" (*Iudaeos et Graecos*).

91. *Recensiones* α and β do not have this sentence.

92. *Recensio* α does not have the remainder of this sentence and the following sentence, "to show … part of the law." Instead it has "For no one is without sin."

93. Ambrosiaster's construction emphasizes that the death of Christ is beneficial for people both while they are living (*et hic in saeculo*) and after they have died (*et de inferno*).

94. When Protestant reformers, most notably Martin Luther, appealed to Ambrose as an authority for their understanding of justification by faith alone, they were in fact referring to Ambrosiaster and, among other passages, this comment. The extent to which the Protestant understanding of *sola fide* was anticipated by patristic writers has been studied by, e.g., Adolf von Harnack, "Geschichte der Lehre von der Seligkeit allein durch den Glauben in der alten Kirche," *ZTK* 1 (1891): 82–178; Reimer Roukema, "Salvation *sola fide* and *sola gratia* in Early Christianity," in *Passion of Protestants*, ed. P. N. Holtrop, Frederik de Lange, and Reimer Roukema (Kampen: Kok, 2004), 27–48.

justified,[95] as the apostle also says to the Galatians: *Christ has redeemed us by offering himself for us* (Gal 3:13).[96] For he surrendered himself to the raging devil, who, however, did not know what was coming. Believing that he could hold Christ captive, the devil received him, seemingly, but because the devil could not bear Christ's power, he let go all whom he held captive at the same time he let Christ go.[97]

3:25 *Whom God proposed as the propitiator for faith.*[98] (1) The apostle says this because in Christ *God proposed*—that is, resolved[99]—that he would be propitious to the human race, if they believed.

In his blood. (2) The reason the apostle says *in his blood* is that we have been set free by his death, so that he might both reveal himself and condemn death through his passion.

To show God's righteousness. (3) That is, so that he might make his promise plain, by which we were set free from sin, as he had promised beforehand. When he fulfilled this promise, he showed that he is righteous.[100]

3:26 *On account of the plan*[101] *regarding the prior transgressions in the patience of God.*[102] (1) Since God knew the plan of his good favor,[103] by which he determined to come to the aid of sinners—of those who were among the living as well as of those who were held in the underworld—he waited for each of these groups for the longest time, nullifying[104] the sentence by which it seemed just that all be condemned. He did this to show us that he had decided long ago to set the human race free through Christ,

---

95. *Recensio* α does not have "so that we, having been set free, might be justified."

96. Ambrosiaster appears to be quoting from memory. He paraphrases the substance of Gal 3:13 after quoting the first few words of the verse.

97. See In Rom. 3:4 (§5a).

98. The Greek text of 3:25 is capable of various interpretations. For an overview of patristic interpretations, see Alfons Pluta, *Gottes Bundestreue: Ein Schlüsselbegriff in Röm 3,25a*, SBS 34 (Stuttgart: Katholisches Bibelwerk, 1969), 17–28.

99. Ambrosiaster's explanation (*disposuit*) plays on the word it explains (*proposuit*) by employing the same root verb (*pono*) but altering the prefix—an instance of the rhetorical figure of paronomasia.

100. See In Rom. 3:21 (§2).

101. The Greek text of Romans has πάρεσιν, which refers to forbearing to punish a transgression or extract a debt. The word in Ambrosiaster's biblical text, *propositum*, can mean "intention" or "proposal."

102. In English translations of Romans, 3:26 begins at *in the patience of God*.

103. *Recensio* α has "will" instead of "good favor."

104. *Recensio* α has "overthrowing" instead of "nullifying."

as he promised through the prophet Jeremiah, when he said: *I will be propitious toward their iniquities, and their transgressions I will not remember* (Jer 31:34). Lest perhaps he should seem to have promised this gift to the Jews alone, he says through Isaiah:[105] *My house will be called a house of prayer for all the nations* (Isa 56:7). (1a)[106] For although the promise was made to Judaism, nevertheless because God foreknew that ungodly Jews were going to reject his gift, he promised to let the gentiles receive his grace. Ungodly Jews were thrown into a fury out of jealousy for the gentiles.[107]

At this time.[108] (2) That is, in our time, when God has given what long ago he had promised[109] would be given at the time he has given it.

So that he may be just in justifying the person who by faith is of Jesus Christ.[110] (3) The apostle rightly says that *so that he may be just* God has given what he promised. Moreover, he promised this: to justify those who believe in Christ. In fact, he says in Habakkuk: *The just, however, shall live by my faith* (Hab 2:4), so that as long as one has faith in God and in Christ one is just.

3:27 *Where then is your boasting?*[111] *It is excluded. Through which law? The law of deeds? No, but through the law of faith.* In repeating the argument, the apostle addresses those who operate under the law. He says that they boast without grounds when they flatter themselves about the law and on account of the fact that they are the people of Abraham,[112] since they now see that a person is not justified before God except through faith.

---

105. *Recensio* α has "he says elsewhere." *Recensio* β has "it is said through Isaiah."

106. *Recensio* α does not have section 1a.

107. *Recensio* β has "Having been thrown into a fury out of jealousy for the gentiles, ungodly Jews were tormented."

108. *Recensio* α has the complete lemma, which corresponds to the Greek text: "To demonstrate his righteousness at the present time" (*ad demonstrationem iustitiae eius in hoc tempore*).

109. *Recensio* α has "had proposed" instead of "had promised."

110. Among biblical witnesses there is stronger support for "so that he is just and justifies" (εἰς τὸ εἶναι αὐτὸν δίκαιον καὶ δικαιοῦντα) and "Jesus" (Ἰησοῦ) than for Ambrosiaster's biblical text; see Jewett, *Romans*, 268–69. The last part of Ambrosiaster's biblical text, *qui ex fide est Iesu Christi*, is a literal rendering of the Greek, as is usually the case with the VL. I have chosen to render it literally into English. It could mean the person who by faith belongs to Jesus Christ or the person who has faith in Jesus Christ.

111. The reading "your" (*tua*) in Ambrosiaster's biblical text is not found in the majority of the biblical witnesses. See NA[28] and Jewett, *Romans*, 294.

112. *Recensio* α has "when they flatter themselves about the law on account of the

3:28 *For we hold that a person is justified through faith without the works of the law.* He says that it can be taken as a certainty that a person from the gentiles is justified when he believes, even though he does not do any works of the law; that is, he is justified without circumcision or new moons or observance of the sabbath.[113]

3:29 *Or is God the God of the Jews only? Is he not the God of the gentiles also? Yes, of the gentiles also.* Without doubt, the God of everyone is one God. The Jews cannot on their own claim for themselves that their God is not the God of the gentiles as well, since they read repeatedly that everyone originates from the one Adam and that no one who wishes to join the law is to be prohibited.[114] Indeed, many people left with the Jews for the wilderness of Egypt,[115] and the Jews were commanded to accept them on condition that they be circumcised and eat unleavened bread and the Passover lamb along with the Jews (see Exod 12:48–49; Num 9:14).[116] So too, it was demonstrated by a divine oracle that Cornelius, a non-judaizing gentile,[117] had received the gift of God and that he was justified (see Acts 10).

3:30 *Because in fact God is one, who has justified the circumcision on the basis of faith and the uncircumcision through faith.* By the term *circumcision* the apostle means the Jews, because when they believe that he is the Christ whom God had promised in the law, they are justified *on the basis of faith* in the promise. By the term *uncircumcision* he means the gentiles who have been justified before God *through faith* in Christ. For God has justified the gentiles as well as the Jews in no other way than as believers.[118]

---

fact that they are the people of Abraham or that they received God's commandments through Moses."

113. *Recensio* α does not have "that is, he is justified without circumcision or new moons or observance of the sabbath."

114. *Recensio* α has "since they saw that no one who approached was prohibited from doing so by the law."

115. *Recensio* α has "from Egypt." *Recensio* β has "for the wilderness from the Egyptians."

116. *Recensiones* α and β have "so that they might eat" instead of "and eat."

117. I.e., a gentile who did not observe Jewish dietary laws and similar customs. On the meaning of "to Judaize" in Christian discourse, see Shaye J. D. Cohen, *The Beginnings of Jewishness: Boundaries, Varieties, Uncertainties*, HCS 31 (Berkeley: University of California Press, 1999), 185–92.

118. The phrase "in no other way than as believers," which is found in *recensiones* α and β, is attested in *recensio* γ only by MSS Monte Cassino 150 and, in a second hand, St. Gall 101.

Since one God is the God of everyone, he has justified everyone on one basis.[119] What, then, is the advantage of circumcision of the flesh? Or what is the disadvantage of uncircumcision, when nothing but faith grants status and merit?

3:31 *Do we therefore nullify the law through faith? By no means! Rather, we establish the law.* The apostle says that the law is assuredly not rendered void through faith, but is fulfilled.[120] For its position is reinforced when faith bears witness that what the law said would happen has come about. The apostle said this on account of the Jews, who, not understanding the meaning of the law,[121] suppose that faith in Christ is inimical to the law. The apostle therefore does not *nullify the law* when he teaches that the law should now come to an end, because he rightly states that the law was given in its time but should operate no longer. For in the law itself it is said that the law should come to an end at the time when the promise was fulfilled. (2) Indeed, the angel Gabriel showed the prophet Daniel, who had a longing to understand this matter (see Dan 9:21–23), when he said, among other things, that with the coming of Christ anointing—that is royal unction, which is understood to mean power[122]—would come to end (see Dan 9:26). *And judgment*, he says, *will be no more* (Dan 9:26)—which is the law—*and my sacrifice will be removed* (Dan 9:27). He said *my* so that it might be understood that the ancient form of offering would come to an end. The Savior revealed the meaning of this: *The law*, he says, *and the prophets were until John* (Luke 16:16). (3) Moreover, since God would give better commandments when the law[123] came to an end, the prophet Jeremiah prophesied, saying: *Behold the days will come,*[124] *says the Lord, and I will accomplish a new covenant with the house of Israel and the house of Judah, not like the one I gave to their fathers* (Jer 31:31–32)—with those, clearly, who received Christ when he came as a result of the promise. The Savior therefore says, *I have not come to abolish the law or the prophets, but to fulfill them* (Matt 5:17). Furthermore, since the house of God would

---

119. *Recensio* α does not have this sentence.

120. *Recensiones* α and β have "The law is assuredly not rendered void through faith, but is rather fulfilled."

121. This clause, which is found in *recensiones* α and β, is attested in *recensio* γ only by MS Paris lat. 1759.

122. Recensio α adds "since the kings have already ceased to exist."

123. *Recensiones* α and β have "the law of Moses."

124. *Recensio* α has "Behold, I myself will come."

no longer be in Jerusalem alone but also in other places,[125] the prophet Zechariah says:[126] *I will place Jerusalem in all the nations* (Zech 12:3). This Jerusalem is the church.

---

125. *Recensio* α does not have "but also in other places."
126. *Recensio* α does not have "Zechariah."

Romans 4

4:1 *What then do we say that Abraham, our father according to the flesh, found?*[1] After the apostle showed that no one can be justified before God through works of the law, he makes the point that not even Abraham could merit anything according to the flesh. When he said *the flesh*, he meant circumcision, because Abraham acquired nothing through circumcision; he was justified before he was circumcised.

4:2 *For if Abraham was justified by works of the law,*[2] *he has glory, but not before God.* This is said for the sake of the argument. In fact, Abraham does indeed have glory before God, but by faith, through which he was justified, since by works of the law no one is justified so as to have glory before God. Because those who keep the law are justified at the time, the apostle says: *If Abraham was justified by works of the law, he has glory, but not before God*, but rather before the world, so that Abraham might not appear to be guilty under the law at the time.[3] The faithful, however, have glory before God.[4]

---

1. Although Ambrosiaster's biblical text has "father" (*patrem*), among biblical witnesses there is stronger support for "forefather" (προπάτορα). The position of the verb "found" in Ambrosiaster's biblical text is the one that is preferred among the biblical witnesses. See Bruce M. Metzger, *A Textual Commentary on the Greek New Testament*, 2nd ed. (Stuttgart: Deutsche Bibelgesellschaft, 1994), 450; and Robert Jewett with Roy D. Kotansky, *Romans: A Commentary*, Hermeneia (Minneapolis: Fortress, 2007), 304.
2. The Greek text has simply "by works" (ἐξ ἔργων); see NA^{28}.
3. See In Rom. 3:20 (§§1, 1a).
4. *Recensio* α has "He made this point to himself. In fact, Abraham was justified by faith; no one doubts this. But because those who keep the law—whether the law of Moses or the law of nature—are justified at the time, so as not to be found guilty in a judgment at the time, the apostle says: *If Abraham was justified by works of the law,* he does not have glory before God. For the scripture says, *One who keeps the law shall live by it* (Lev 18:5; Rom 10:5; Gal 3:12), that is, he will not die guilty. Nevertheless, he will not have merit before God on this account, but because of faith." *Recensio* β has "This

4:3 *What then do the scriptures say? Abraham believed God and it was reckoned to him as righteousness.* The apostle has made it clear that Abraham has glory before God not because he was circumcised or because he kept himself from wickedness, but because he *believed God*. This also is why he was justified and will attain the reward of his praise in future.[5]

4:4 *Now to one who works wages are not reckoned as a gift but as due.* What is paid out to one who is subject to the law of deeds—that is, of Moses—or to natural law is not reckoned as credit toward a reward, to the effect that one has glory before God. For such a person is obliged to keep the law, because the requirement to keep the law, whether one wishes to or not, so that one may not be found guilty,[6] is imposed by the law. As the apostle says elsewhere: *Now those who refuse bring condemnation upon themselves* (Rom 13:2),[7] because they are found guilty even now at this time.[8] Moreover, to believe and not to believe is a matter of the will. Nor can any one be forced to accept what is not evident; rather, one is invited to accept,[9] since one is not compelled but is persuaded.[10] That is why it accrues to one's credit. For one believes what one does not see, but rather hopes for.[11]

---

is said for the sake of argument. In fact, Abraham was justified by faith; no one doubts this. He therefore has glory before God. But because those who keep the law—whether the law of Moses or natural law—are justified at the time, so as not to be found guilty by a judgment at the time, the apostle says: *If Abraham was justified by works of the law,* he does not have glory before God. For the scripture says, *One who keeps the law shall live by it* (Lev 18:5; Rom 10:5; Gal 3:12), that is, he will not die guilty. Nevertheless, he will not have merit before God on this account, but because of faith."

5. *Recensio* α has "This also is why he was justified not with a justice belonging to the present time, but with a heavenly, future justice."

6. *Recensiones* α and β have "condemned" instead of "found guilty."

7. Ambrosiaster is citing the verse from memory. His biblical text at In Rom. 13:2b has "resist" (*resistunt*) instead of "refuse" (*contemnunt*).

8. *Recensio* α does not have this clause. In *recensio* γ it is attested only by MSS Monte Cassino 150 and Paris lat. 1759.

9. In *recensio* γ this portion of the sentence is attested only by MSS Monte Cassino 150 and Paris lat. 1759.

10. *Recensio* α does not have this clause.

11. *Recensiones* α and β do not have the last two sentences of this section. Instead they have "For this reason one who consents should be granted rewards, just as Abraham [β: too] believed what he did not see."

4:5 *But to one who does not work.* (1) That is, to one who is guilty of sins because he does not do[12] what the law commands.[13]

But believes in him who justifies the ungodly, his faith is reckoned as righteousness. (2) The apostle says this because for the ungodly person who believes without works of the law—that is, a gentile—*his faith* in Christ *is reckoned as righteousness,* as was Abraham's faith. How then do the Jews believe themselves to be justified through works of the law in accordance with Abraham's justification, when they see that Abraham was justified not by works of the law but by faith alone? Accordingly, there is no need for the law when an ungodly person is justified by faith alone before God.

According to the plan of God's grace.[14] (3) The apostle says it was determined by God that when the law came to an end God's grace would require faith alone for salvation.

4:6 *As also David declares.* The apostle reinforces this point with a quotation from the prophet.

The blessedness of the one to whom God reckons righteousness without works. David declares those people to be blessed whom God decreed would be justified before God by faith alone without toil and any observance. David thus foretells the blessedness of the time when Christ was born, as the Lord himself also says: *Many righteous people and prophets longed to see what you see and to hear what you hear, and they did not hear it* (Matt 13:17).

4:7 *Blessed are those whose iniquities are forgiven and whose sins are covered.* **4:8** *Blessed is the man against whom the Lord has not reckoned sin* (Ps 31:1–2 LXX = Ps 32:1–2 ET). (1) Clearly, those *whose iniquities are forgiven and whose sins*[15] *are covered* without toil or any work are *blessed,* since no works of repentance are demanded of them except that they believe. *Blessed* too is this *man against whom the Lord has not reckoned sin.* The words *to forgive* and *to cover* and *not to reckon* have a single explanation and a single meaning. They all are obtained and granted in one way. (2) However, to some people it seems that these words have a threefold explanation,[16]

---

12. Ambrosiaster echoes the lemma here (*operatur*), but the echo is not easily conveyed in English.
13. *Recensio* α does not have "because he does not do what the law commands."
14. This clause is not found in the Greek text of Romans; see NA²⁸.
15. *Recensio* α has "punishments" instead of "sins."
16. The view that sins are forgiven in baptism, covered through penitence, and not imputed through martyrdom is attested in other late fourth- and early fifth-century

because the prophet used different words and because he proceeds from the plural to the singular.[17] For since the prophet wishes to relay the words of God[18] about the abundance of grace by using several terms for transgressions—since there are various names for *sins*—he has spoken rather expansively. Nevertheless, the words have a single meaning, because when God covers he forgives, and when he forgives he does not reckon. The prophet is talking in a rather prolix way in praise of the grace of God in order to magnify the gift of God.[19] (2a)[20] He created three levels on account of the diversity of transgressions. The first of these levels is wickedness or ungodliness, when the creator is not recognized; the second level consists in committing more serious sins; the third level consists in lighter sins. Nevertheless, he says that these are all wiped out in baptism. With these three levels he has designated the entire body of sin. (3) Moreover, when the prophet says: *Blessed are those whose sins are covered*, how can this statement relate to someone who is penitent, since it is well known that penitents obtain forgiveness of sins by toil and sighing? How does what he says—*Blessed is the man against whom the Lord has not reckoned sin*—fit the martyr, since we know that the glory of the martyrs is obtained through suffering and anguish? Because the prophet foresaw the happy time of the Savior's coming, he called those people whose sins are forgiven and covered and not reckoned without toil or any work through baptism blessed.[21] (4) Nevertheless, on account of the fullness of time and because more grace inhered in the apostles than in the prophets, the apostle proclaims that what we receive from the gift of bap-

---

Latin discussions of this passage (Ps 31:1–2 // Rom 4:7–8): Origen-Rufinus, *Comm. Rom.* 2.1 (*AGLB* 16:99; ET: Origen, *Commentary on the Epistle to the Romans*, trans. Thomas P. Scheck, FC 103 [Washington: Catholic University Press of America, 2001], 102); Anonymous, Commentarius in Epistulam ad Romanos 37A (*AGLB* 8.2:35); Pelagius, In Rom. 4:8 (TS 9.2:37; ET: Theodore S. de Bruyn, *Pelagius's Commentary on St Paul's Epistle to the Romans*, OECS [Oxford: Oxford University Press, 1993], 85); Anonymous, *Consultationes Zacchei christiani et Apollonii philosophi* 2.18.9–10 (SC 402:140). (See the introduction §4.1 on these commentaries on Romans.) Ambrosiaster rebuts this interpretation in section 3 below, referring explicitly to penitents and martyrs; he holds that all sins are forgiven in baptism.

17. *Recensio* α does not have "and because he proceeds from the plural to the singular."
18. *Recensio* α has "the gift of God" instead of "the words of God."
19. *Recensiones* α and β have "grace" instead of "the gift of God."
20. *Recensio* α does not have section 2a.
21. See n. 16 above.

tism is greater. He declares not only that we receive forgiveness of sins, but also that we are justified and made children of God, so that this blessedness possesses perfect glory and security.

4:9 *Does this blessedness abide only among the circumcised or also among the uncircumcised?*[22] (1) That is: Was this blessedness[23] granted only to the children of Abraham, or also to those who are from the gentiles? (1a)[24] For if at that time the gentiles were not barred from coming to the law and to the promise of Abraham,[25] how could it be that at the time of Christ they would be barred from coming to grace, when God has invited them as a whole?

In fact we say—(2) that is, in accordance with the meaning of the law— *that faith was reckoned to Abraham as righteousness.*[26] The apostle starts at the beginning in order to rule out every specious sophistry, because someone who is ruled out at the outset does not have grounds to start to raise questions.

4:10 *How then was it reckoned? While he was circumcised or uncircumcised? Not circumcised but uncircumcised.* **4:11** *And he received the sign of circumcision as the seal of the righteousness of faith which is among the uncircumcised,* **4:12**[27] *so that he might be the father of all believers through uncircumcision, in order that it may be reckoned to them for righteousness.*[28] (1) Although Abraham was uncircumcised, he believed God. What did he believe? That he would have offspring—that is, a son—in whom all the gentiles might be justified through faith while uncircumcised, just as Abraham too was justified. In fact, he received circumcision as a sign of the righteousness of faith. Believing that he would have a son, he received a sign of the thing he believed, so that one might discern that he was justified when he believed. (2) Therefore, circumcision does not have any status,

---

22. The word "only" (*tantum*) in Ambrosiaster's biblical text is considered to be a secondary addition. See Jewett, *Romans*, 304.
23. *Recensio* α has "Was it etc." instead of "Was this blessedness etc."
24. *Recensio* α does not have section 1a.
25. Ambrosiaster holds that the law was available to the gentiles throughout the period of the biblical patriarchs; see In Rom. 2:12 (§1).
26. Among the biblical witnesses the addition of "that" (ὅτι), *quia* in Ambrosiaster's biblical text, appears to be a secondary addition. See Jewett, *Romans*, 304.
27. In English translations of Romans, 4:12 begins at the next lemma.
28. Ambrosiaster's biblical text has "for righteousness" (*ad iustitiam*), but among the biblical witness there is stronger support for the omission of the preposition: "so that righteousness may be reputed to them" (εἰς τὸ λογισθῆναι αὐτοῖς [τὴν] δικαιοσύνην). See Jewett, *Romans*, 305.

but is only a sign. The sons of Abraham[29] received this sign so that they might be recognized to be sons of the one who received this sign when he believed God, and so that they might emulate their father's faith and believe in Jesus, who was promised to Abraham and whom Isaac, when he was born, prefigured. For all the nations are blessed not in Isaac but in Christ, because *there is no other name given under heaven by which one must be saved* (Acts 4:12), says the apostle Peter.[30]

So that he might be the father of the circumcised, of those who are not merely from the circumcised but who also follow the footsteps of faith which belonged to our father Abraham when he was uncircumcised. (3) The apostle says this because Abraham, as the first to believe, was made *the father of the circumcised*—of the circumcised in heart: not only of those who descend from him by birth, but also of those among the gentiles who believe as he did. (3a)[31] For according to the flesh he is the father of the Jews, but according to the faith he is the father of all believers.

4:13 *For not through the law did the promise come to Abraham and his offspring—that he would be heir of the world—but through the righteousness of faith.* It is obvious that the law had not yet been given and that circumcision did not exist at the time when the promise was made *to Abraham* the believer *and his offspring*, namely, Christ, who washed away the sins of everyone. This is why John the Baptist says:[32] *Behold the lamb of God, behold the one who takes away the sins of the world* (John 1:29). Abraham therefore was made *heir of the world* not on account of having kept the law, but on account of faith. Now, the *heir of the world* is the heir of the land which he acquired through his children.[33] Christ, in fact, is heir of the nations, as David prophesies: *And I will give to you the nations as your inheritance, and the ends of the earth as your possession* (Ps 2:8 LXX and ET).[34] *For we ourselves will die, and we live with him.*[35]

---

29. *Recensio* α has "sons of Israel" instead of "sons of Abraham." Whereas elsewhere I render *filii* as "children," here I render it as "sons" since only males were circumcised.

30. *Recensio* α does not have "says the apostle Peter."

31. *Recensio* α does not have section 3a.

32. *Recensio* α has "This is why it says in the Gospel of John."

33. *Recensio* α has "He was made heir of the land which he acquired through his children."

34. *Recensio* α does not have the reference to David and the quotation from Ps 2:8. Ambrosiaster's argument is that Abraham inherited the world through Christ, his offspring, who inherited the nations.

35. *Recensio* α has only "For we ourselves die."

4:14 *If those who are based on the law are the heirs.* That is, if those who are based on the law or under the law are heirs on the basis of the law.[36]

Faith is voided, the promise is annulled. It is obvious that if the inheritance is based on the law, the promise which was made to Abraham based on faith has become worthless. In fact, the promise was made not through the law, but through the righteousness of faith.[37] The apostle shows why it is wrong to hope for the inheritance on the basis of the law.[38]

4:15 *For the law brings wrath.* (1) In order to demonstrate conclusively that a person cannot be justified before God through the law and that the promise could not have been made through the law, the apostle says *the law brings wrath.*[39] It was given specifically for this purpose: to render sinners guilty. Faith, however, is a gift of God's mercy, so that those who are rendered guilty through the law may be pardoned. Hence, faith brings joy. The apostle is not speaking against the law, but he gives faith precedence over the law because those who could not be saved through the law are saved by the grace of God through faith. Thus, the law is not wrath, but it brings wrath—that is, punishment—for the sinner when it punishes rather than pardons. Punishment is produced through wrath, and wrath is born of sin. That is why the apostle wants the law to be relinquished: so that one may take refuge in faith, which pardons sins in order to save.

For where there is no law,[40] *there is no transgression.* (2) The apostle says this because there is no more transgression once the guilty are removed from the power of the law and pardon has been granted. Those who had been sinners through transgression of the law have now been justified. The law of deeds has come to an end, that is, the observance of sabbaths, new moons, circumcision, the differentiation among foods, the need to purge a dead animal or weasel of its blood.[41]

---

36. In *recensio* γ "or under the law" is attested only by MSS Monte Cassino 150 and Paris lat. 1759.

37. *Recensiones* α and β and MS Paris lat. 1759 of *recensio* γ have "But [α: while] the promise was not made through the law, and the inheritance is through the righteousness of faith."

38. *Recensio* α does not have this sentence.

39. *Recensio* α does not have the next three sentences. Instead it has "Faith, on the other hand, brings mercy and joy."

40. Although Ambrosiaster's biblical text has "for" (*enim*), among biblical witnesses there is stronger support for "but" (δέ). See Metzger, *Textual Commentary*, 451; and Jewett, *Romans*, 322.

41. *Recensio* α has "the care given to a dead animal or weasel." At In Titus 1:14 (§2)

4:16 *That is why it is based on faith, so that by grace the promise is assured for all his offspring.* (1) It is not possible for the promise to be assured *for all his offspring*[42]—that is, for every person from every nation—unless it is *based on faith*. The basis of the promise is derived from faith, not from the law, since those who are under the law are guilty;[43] a promise cannot be made with the guilty. They should be purified through faith first, so that they may be made worthy to be called children of God and so that the promise may be assured. (2) Even if they call themselves children of God, as long as they are guilty—that is, as long as they are under the law—the promise is not assured, because the children of God have been freed from sin. If then those who are under the law must be rescued out from under the law in order to be worthy to receive the promise, this is even more true for someone who is without the law.[44] Thus, there is no advantage in placing oneself under the law in order to be able to find the remedy for one's injury in a shorter way.[45]

Not only for offspring that is from the law, but also for someone who is of the faith of Abraham.[46] (3) This means, as the apostle has said above, *for*

---

and 3:9 (§2) Ambrosiaster also mentions care taken by Jews to purge the weasel of its blood. He appears to conflate the command not to eat the blood of an animal (see Gen 9:4; Lev 3:17; 7:26–27; 17:10–14; Deut 12:16, 23) with the command not to eat weasels, mice, lizards, crocodiles, and chameleons (Lev 11:29–30).

42. *Recensio* α does not have this opening clause.

43. *Recensio* α has "from the law" instead of "under the law."

44. *Recensiones* α and β have "not under the law" instead of "without the law."

45. Ambrosiaster is referring to the practice of Christians who observe Jewish regulations. It is unclear whether he is referring to Christians in Rome in Paul's time—see In Rom. 1:11 (§2) and elsewhere—or his own time. He may have both in view.

46. The VL *non ei quod ex lege est tantum, sed et ei quod ex fide est Abrahae* ("not only for offspring that is from the law, but also for offspring that is from the faith of Abraham") follows the Greek text literally in understanding οὐ τῷ ἐκ τοῦ νόμου μόνον ἀλλὰ καὶ τῷ ἐκ πίστεως Ἀβραάμ to refer to τῷ σπέρματι or *omni semini*. The Vulgate *non ei qui ex lege est solum, sed et ei qui ex fide est Abrahae* ("not only for one who is from the law, but also for one who is from the faith of Abraham") renders the clause independently of this antecedent. The lemma as presented in the CSEL edition combines the VL rendering of the first clause with the Vulgate rendering of the second clause. Several manuscripts of *recensio* γ preserve the rendering found in the VL. Ambrosiaster's comment suggests that he took the clause to refer to *omni semini* ("for all his offspring"). It is unlikely that his biblical text conflated the two renderings. Such a conflation is not attested elsewhere. Both renderings are found in Rufinus's translation of Origen's *Commentary on Romans* but are not conflated; see Caroline P. Hammond

all his offspring, those from the Jews, who clearly came from the law, as well as those from the gentiles, who followed the faith of Abraham—the faith which he had as a gentile so that he might be just.[47] Abraham believed without the law. Therefore, Abraham is more closely associated with the gentiles, so that the promise may be assured for those who believe in the one in whom Abraham believed.[48]

4:17 *Who is the father of us all, as it is written: "For I have appointed you the father of many nations"* (Gen 17:4). (1) With this quotation from the law the apostle has confirmed that Abraham is *the father of all*—of all those, that is, who believe—and that accordingly the promise is assured in the event that one withdraw from the law for the sake of faith, because the promise of the kingdom of heaven has been allotted to the righteous, not to sinners. Furthermore, those who are under the law are under sin, because everyone sins, and no one can be under the law and at the same time receive grace, as the apostle says to the Galatians: *You have been separated from Christ, you who are justified by the law; you have fallen away from grace* (Gal 5:4).

In the presence of God, in whom he believed. (2) In order to teach that there is one God of all, the apostle instructs the gentiles that Abraham himself believed God and was justified *in the presence of God*, in whom the gentiles also believe in order to be justified. As a result, there is no difference between Jew and Greek in the context of faith, since, now that circumcision and uncircumcision have been done away with, they are made one in Christ. For even Abraham believed while he was uncircumcised, and was justified.[49]

Who gives life to the dead and calls things which do not exist as things which exist. (3) In saying this, the apostle invites the gentiles to the faith of Abraham, because although he was uncircumcised he believed the God whose faith is now proclaimed in Christ, and was brought to life with his wife. For when they were elderly and worn in years,[50] they recovered their

---

Bammel, *Römerbrieftext des Rufin und seine Origenes Übersetzung*, vol. 10 of *AGLB* (Freiburg: Herder, 1985), 321–22.

47. *Recensio* α does not have "so that he might be just."

48. *Recensio* α has something like "in that the promise is assured on the basis of his faith" instead of "so that the promise may be assured for those who believe in the one in whom Abraham believed"; the infinitive construction—*firmam esse promissionem ex fide Abrahae*—is awkward.

49. This sentence, found in *recensiones* α and β, is attested in *recensio* γ only by MS Paris lat. 1759.

50. *Recensio* α has "for when they were old."

youthly vigor. As a result, Abraham did not doubt that he would have a son by Sarah, whom he knew to be sterile and in whom the menstrual flow belonging to the female nature had already ceased.[51] For this reason the gentiles should not be preoccupied about either uncircumcision or circumcision, and should be eager with regard to the faith, confident because they believe in him *who gives life to the dead* and because there is no one else who has the power to bring things into existence all at once by his will, when he wishes things that do not exist to exist. (4) Therefore, although Abraham was not yet a father, he was called the father of many nations (see Gen 17:4),[52] and he believed, confident in the power of God. (4a)[53] Moreover, in order that people would believe that the father of Christ is the same God in whom Abraham believed, when the promise was fulfilled and Christ was about to come into the world, the same sign was given in the case of Zachariah and Elizabeth as had been given with regard to Abraham and Sarah: the promise was sealed that in old age and with decrepit bodies they would give birth to saint John in a way similar to that in which Isaac had been born (see Luke 1:8–23).

4:18 *Against hope he believed in hope.* (1) It is clear that although he had no hope of giving birth, Abraham believed God, having faith *against hope*[54] that he would give birth, knowing that God can do all things.

That he would become the father of many nations, as it was said: "So shall your offspring be" (Gen 15:5). (1a) This is stated in the book of Genesis.[55] (2) When God showed Abraham the stars of heaven, he said: *So shall your offspring be*, and, believing this, Abraham was justified. Indeed, he believed what seems impossible from an earthly point of view, since in the natural world it does not happen that old people are able to give birth and come to see their offspring multiplied so abundantly that they cannot be numbered. This is why faith is so valuable: contrary to what it sees and knows, it believes something will come to pass. For one is encouraged by this hope: that it is God who promises, (2a)[56] about whom it is right to conceive more than human weakness can grasp.

---

51. *Recensio* α has "in whom the course of nature had already ceased."
52. *Recensio* α does not have "of many nations."
53. *Recensio* α does not have section 4a.
54. *Recensio* α has "hoping *against hope*" instead of "having faith beyond hope."
55. *Recensio* α does not have this sentence. *Recensio* β has "This is in Genesis."
56. *Recensio* α does not have section 2a.

4:19 *And not being weak in faith, he did not consider his decrepit body,*[57] *although he was already about a hundred years old, and the decrepit womb of Sarah.* **4:20** *In face of the promise of God he did not hesitate doubtingly, but was strengthened in faith by giving glory to God,* **4:21** *holding it to be sure that the one who promised is able also to do.* **4:22** *And that is why it was reckoned to him as righteousness.* (1) The apostle declares that Abraham is deserving of this praise because, although he knew that he did not have the capability, he strengthened his weakness with faith, so that he believed that through God he would be able to do what he knew was impossible according to the laws of the world. He thus possesses great merit before God, as he believed God against his own understanding and did not doubt that he—namely, God[58]—was able to do what he knew was impossible according to the reasoning of the world. (1a)[59] In fact, he takes it as certain that God is beyond the reasoning of the world; for no one can be said to exist within the thing he has created.[60] Therefore, Abraham should be rewarded by God in this way, because he attributed more to his creator than he himself understands. This, to be sure, would be of no value if everyone thought likewise, but the faith of believers is singled out for praise before God through the doubting of many. (2) The apostle thus urges the gentiles to have this sureness of faith, such that they receive the promise and grace of God without any ambivalence, according to the unwavering example of Abraham. This, in fact, is why the believer receives more and more praise if he believes what is unbelievable and what seems foolish to the world. For the more what is believed is considered foolish, the more will the believer be worthy of honor. Still, it truly would be foolish to believe this if it were

---

57. Although Ambrosiaster's biblical text has "he did not consider" (*non consideravit*), among the biblical witnesses there is stronger support for the positive formulation: "He did not weaken in faith when he considered his own decrepit body" (καὶ μὴ ἀσθενήσας τῇ πίστει κατενόησεν τὸ ἑαυτοῦ σῶμα [ἤδη] νενεκρωμένον). See Metzger, *Textual Commentary*, 451; and Jewett, *Romans*, 322. Contrary to what Jewett says about the presence of "already" (ἤδη), the word (*iam*) does not occur in this clause in Ambrosiaster's biblical text; it occurs in the next clause, "although he was already about a hundred years old" (*cum iam fere centum annorum esset*).

58. *Recensio* α does not have "namely, God."

59. *Recensio* α does not have section 1a.

60. This sentence, which is found in *recensio* β, is attested in *recensio* γ only by MS Monte Cassino 150.

said to come about without God.⁶¹ (3)⁶² Moreover, the reason that the faith of Abraham is so much more praiseworthy than the faith of other believers is that it was elicited without any miraculous signs. The world, in fact, is governed by a fixed law and power and is directed in a precise way by God, but the learned, with a carnal love for reason, disregarded God, the maker of this world. Therefore, to dispel error and to demonstrate that he is God of all, God wished it to be proclaimed that he was able to do—and that he had done—what is impossible according to the world, so that people who believed this would be singled out and saved, having been delivered to the rule of God,⁶³ while those who disregarded God, being puffed up with the reasoning of the world, would be condemned.⁶⁴

4:23 *But it was written that is was reckoned to him* (see Rom 4:3) *not just for his sake alone,* **4:24** *but also for our sake. It will be reckoned to us who believe in him who has raised Jesus Christ our Lord from the dead,*⁶⁵ **4:25** *who was handed over for our sins and raised for our justification.* (1) The apostle says that in Abraham a model was given for Jews and gentiles so that by his example we may believe in God, Christ, and the Holy Spirit, and it may be reckoned to us as righteousness. Although what is believed now is different, faith nevertheless conveys one common gift. We obtain it because we believe. When we believe that Christ is the Son of God, we are adopted by God as children;⁶⁶ indeed, God could give nothing more to believers than that they be called children of God after having renounced the company of unbelievers. We are called children of God, while they are not worthy to be called slaves. (2) On account of his boundless generosity, God gave this gift to those who love him, a gift worthy of his majesty, not a gift that people deserve. Indeed, in the case of a gift, the munificence of the giver is noticed much more than that of the receiver. For this reason, when a great gift is bestowed upon the lowly through Christ, it garners more

---

61. *Recensio* α does not have this sentence.

62. This section, which is found in *recensiones* α and β, is attested in *recensio* γ only by MS Paris lat. 1759.

63. *Recensio* α has "having been assigned" instead of "having been delivered."

64. In his discussion of Abraham at *Quaest.* 117.3–5 (CSEL 50:352–53), Ambrosiaster similarly contrasts the faith of Abraham with the expertise of worldly knowledge; see Emanuele Di Santo, *L'Apologetica dell'Ambrosiaster: Cristiani, pagani e giudei nella Roma tardoantica*, SEAug 112 (Rome: Institutum Patristicum Augustinianum, 2008), 208–11.

65. The Greek text of Romans does not have "Christ"; see NA²⁸.

66. *Recensio* α does not have "by God."

praise. He allowed himself to be killed for our sake, in order to rescue us through a grant of pardon[67] from the second death (that is, from the punishments of the underworld).[68] Then he arose from the dead (2a) in order to grant us the grace of righteousness by virtue of an exultant triumph over death now conquered, so that we might be worthy of being called children of God. Those who were baptized before his passion received only the forgiveness of sins; Satan killed the Savior out of jealousy over these people.[69] But after his resurrection those who were baptized before, as well as those who were baptized afterward, were all justified through the accepted formula of the Trinitarian faith (see Matt 28:19), after the Holy Spirit, who is the sign for believers that they are children of God, had also been received.[70] To complete our justification, (3)[71] when the Savior arose, he invested his commandments with authority (see Matt 28:20) so that by following them we might grow in the qualities through which we, having attained glory, may shine radiantly in the kingdom of God, based on the pledge that we who have been justified cannot be held by death. Now that it has been conquered by the passion of the Savior, death, which previously held dominion because of sin, does not dare detain those who have been justified by him.[72]

---

67. *Recensio* α does not have "through a grant of pardon."
68. *Recensio* α does not have section 2a and continues with section 3; see n. 71 below.
69. On Christ's conquest of death and Satan, see the introduction §5.4.
70. At *Quaest. app.* 18 (CSEL 50:435), Ambrosiaster discusses how baptism in the Trinitarian formula, unlike the baptism of John the Baptist, bestows the status of children of God.
71. *Recensio* α, which does not have section 2a, begins section 3 as follows: "Then he arose from the dead so that, investing his commandments with authority, he might make us follow them on account of the pledge by which we are justified. Moreover, having been justified, we cannot be held by death, because now that it has been conquered by the death of the Savior, death, which previously held dominion because of sin, does not dare detain those who have been justified by him." *Recensio* β, continuing from section 2a, has "when he arose, so that, investing his commandments with authority, he might make us follow them on account of the pledge by which we are justified, and we might grow in the merits through which we, having attained glory, may shine radiantly in the kingdom of God. For, having been justified, we cannot be held by death; now that it has been conquered by the passion of the Savior, death, which previously held dominion because of sin, does not dare detain those who have been justified by him."
72. I.e., by the Savior.

Romans 5

5:1 *Therefore, since we have been justified by faith, let us have peace with God through our Lord Jesus Christ.*[1] Faith, not the law, makes it possible to have peace with God. For it reconciles us to God, once the sins that had made us enemies of God have been taken away. Because the Lord Jesus is the agent of this grace, we are reconciled to God through him. Indeed, faith is greater than the law.[2] For the law exists on account of us, while faith exists on account of God. Moreover, the law has to do with instruction at the present time, whereas faith has to do with everlasting salvation. Someone, however, who does not have the proper understanding about Christ will not be able to attain the reward of faith, because such a person does not grasp the truth of faith.

5:2 *Through whom we also gain access to this grace in which we stand,*[3] *and we glory in the hope of the glory of God.* It is evident that through Christ we gain admittance to the grace of God. Indeed, he is the arbitrator between God and human beings (see 1 Tim 2:5).[4] By means of his teaching,[5] he

---

1. Ambrosiaster's biblical text has the subjunctive "let us have" (*habeamus*) rather than the indicative "we have" (*habemus*). Both modes are attested among the biblical witnesses. The former has greater external support, but the latter is preferred by NA[28]; see Bruce M. Metzger, *A Textual Commentary on the Greek New Testament*, 2nd ed. (Stuttgart: Deutsche Bibelgesellschaft, 1994), 452. This editorial decision is disputed; see Robert Jewett with Roy D. Kotansky, *Romans: A Commentary*, Hermeneia (Minneapolis: Fortress, 2007), 344.

2. *Recensio* α does not have this sentence and the next two sentences, "Indeed ... everlasting salvation."

3. Among biblical witnesses there is strong support for the presence of "in faith" (τῇ πίστει), omitted in Ambrosiaster's biblical text, before "to this grace." See Metzger, *Textual Commentary*, 452; and Jewett, *Romans*, 344–45.

4. At In 1 Tim. 2:5 Ambrosiaster explains further how Christ is the arbitrator between God and human beings.

5. I.e., Christ's teaching (*doctrina sua*).

made us to hope in the gift of God's grace and to stand in the faith of God. I say *to stand*, because previously we had fallen prostrate, but when we believed we were raised upright, glorying in the hope of the splendor which he promised us.[6]

5:3 *Not only this, we also glory in our tribulations.* (1) Since it is necessary that we enter the kingdom of God by way of tribulations (Acts 14:22), the apostle teaches that we should glory in them as well. For tribulation combined with hope makes the reward greater. Indeed, tribulation, which bears witness to the crown, is a sign of an immovable hope.[7] This is why the Lord says: *Blessed are you when they persecute you and say all manner of evil against you on account of the righteousness of God. Rejoice and be glad, for behold, great is your reward in heaven* (Matt 5:11–12). For to disregard things present and things pleasurable,[8] and not to give in to torment out of hope for things to come, has great merit before God. Therefore, one should glory in tribulation, because the more one perceives oneself to be courageous in tribulation, the more one believes oneself to be worthy of acceptance.

Knowing that tribulation produces patience. (2) That is, tribulation produces patience if the tribulation itself does not experience a feeling of weakness or doubt.

5:4 *And patience, steadfastness.* (1) It is clear that if patience is as we have described it to be, it will appear as unwavering steadfastness.

And steadfastness, hope. (2) One justifiably speaks of hope in a person who appears steadfast. Indeed, such a person is understood to be worthy to receive a recompense[9] in the kingdom of God.

5:5 *And hope does not delude, because the love of God has been poured out in our hearts through the Holy Spirit, who has been given to us.* (1) *Hope does not delude*, even though we are judged to be stupid and doltish by unbelievers, we who believe things that are impossible according to the world.[10] For we have the pledge of the love of God in us through the Holy Spirit who has been given to us. The Holy Spirit, who was given to the

---

6. *Recensio* α has "in the hope of his promise" instead of "in the hope of the splendor which he promised us."
7. *Recensio* α does not have this sentence.
8. *Recensio* α does not have "things present and."
9. *Recensio* α adds "from God."
10. *Recensio* α has "things which worldly reasoning denies." *Recensio* β has "things do not occur according to worldly reasoning."

apostles as well as to us, proves that the promise of God is reliable.¹¹ He performed in various languages¹² so that unlearned apostles might speak in intelligible speech to strengthen hope (see Acts 2:4–11), and in order to commend the love of God to us. The Holy Spirit did this to make us confident of the promise, since it is impossible for those who are beloved to be deceived,¹³ for it is God who made the promise and he made the promise to those whom he wishes to have as his beloved ones. (1a)¹⁴ In fact, human words are incapable of conveying the sense of our faith unless a reasonable person is convinced through the testimony of miracles, which *proclaim without speaking*,¹⁵ to the destruction of the wise of this world. Presumptuous in speech, they fight with earthly weapons against heavenly things and with carnal forces against spiritual things, and do not blush to say that they are wise! Now, just as it is difficult to ascertain the place of origin of a traveler in a foreign land, so too the truth of our faith is a stranger on this earth. Since its nature cannot be explained in words, it is commended through the testimony of power, which is a greater thing.

5:6 *For why did Christ, while we were still sinners, at the time die for the ungodly.*¹⁶ **5:7** *For one hardly dies for a righteous person; on the other hand, for a good person perhaps one may dare to die.* (1) If for the sake

---

11. *Recensio* α has "proves that the promise of God is for believers."
12. *Recensio* β does not have "in various languages" and alters the wording of the remainder of the clause slightly.
13. Instead of the previous two sentences, *recensio* α has "The unlearned apostles spoke in various languages through the Holy Spirit precisely in order to strengthen hope, commending the love of God to us. Because the Holy Spirit calls those who are beloved, we can be confident of the promise, for etc."
14. *Recensio* α does not have section 1a. The wording of the section varies slightly in *recensio* β.
15. Ambrosiaster echoes a well-known phrase from Cicero's *First Oration against Catiline* (*Cat.* 1.21). After he has explicitly commanded Catiline to leave Rome, Cicero observes that the senators do not protest; their silence proclaims their assent (*cum tacent clamant*). Latin rhetorical education entailed intensive study of Cicero's orations against Catiline, and their influence can be observed in Christian oratory; see Harald Hagendahl, *Von Tertullian zu Cassiodor: die profane literarische Tradition in dem lateinischen christlichen Schrifttum*, SGLG 44 (Goteborg: Acta Universitatis Gothoburgensis, 1983), 79–80. This is the only allusion to a classical author noted by the editors of the Commentary. Allusions to several other classical authors have been noted in the *Quaestiones* (CSEL 50:501–20).
16. On the variants in the Greek and Latin witnesses to this verse, including Ambrosiaster, see Jewett, *Romans*, 345.

of unbelievers and enemies of God Christ gave himself to death for the time being—he was dead for the time being, because he arose on the third day—how much more will he protect us with his forces when we believe in him. Indeed, he died for us for this purpose: to obtain both life and glory for us. So, if he died for his enemies, it should be obvious how much he undertakes for his friends. Among humankind—that is, *at the time*—he appeared, therefore, to be dead;[17] in fact, he was among the inhabitants of the underworld, judging the irreverent and vile spirits for the sake of the salvation of the souls there.[18] (1a)[19] Periods of time derive from the world, where the sun rises and sets and the moon waxes and wanes and day and night do not last in their position. A thing that is subject to time and age is always changeable. With regard to this time, therefore, Christ was dead when he departed from his body. But where there is no time or age, there he was found not only alive but also victorious. (2) When the apostle said: *One hardly dies for a righteous person*, he wanted to commend the Savior's feeling toward us. But Christ *died for the ungodly*. If someone hardly dies for a righteous person, how can it be that anyone will die for the ungodly? If for a single good person someone may perhaps dare to die or may perhaps not dare to die—for the apostle indicates that both of these options are hard—how can it come to pass that someone dares to die for the ungodly actions of many?[20] (2a)[21] Even though someone may perhaps dare to die for a righteous person or a good person, being drawn in by a certain pity or by an esteem for his good works, nevertheless in the case of the ungodly not only is the reason that would persuade one to die absent, but also the feeling that would draw forth tears. (3) But Christ died for the ungodly actions even of a people that did not yet belong to him, as when someone undertakes to pledge his word at a late date for some hardened debtors. (3a)[22] The apostle thus creates two categories: the righteous and

---

17. For the remainder of the sentence *recensio* α has "while he was alive among the inhabitants of the underworld, he was breaking down the gates of the underworld by the power of his might."

18. On Christ's stay in the underworld, see the introduction §5.4.

19. *Recensio* α does not have section 1a.

20. *Recensio* α has "For a single good person someone may perhaps dare to die or perhaps not dare to die, because the sentence is ambiguous. How can it come to pass that someone dares to die for the ungodly actions of many?"

21. *Recensio* α does not have section 2a.

22. *Recensio* α does not have sections 3a and 4a. The additional remarks may have been occasioned by a difficulty posed by the text: if a righteous person is better than a

the good. Even though the righteous should also be called good, the apostle nevertheless proposed these two classes to indicate that a righteous person is so through practice, but a good person is so by birth; the latter may be called "innocent" because of his guileless character.[23] Hence, although the righteous may have greater merit than the good as far as the above passage is concerned, the apostle nonetheless says, *For a good person perhaps one may dare to die*, to indicate that someone could perhaps be compelled to do this since the death of a good person is all the more wretched on account of his innocence. In short, parents choose to die for their good children.[24] (I will not talk about wives dying for their good husbands.[25]) (4a)[26] Now, if we wish to ponder the good and the righteous, sometimes we find the righteous to be better, sometimes we find that the good should be preferred. If according to the law of God a person who is righteous is better than a good person, this is true only for a good person who has not yet worked on himself to develop himself further in good works. For the righteous person has improved the good character of his nature.[27] If, however, a person is found to be righteous according to the world, one prefers a good person to him on account of the good person's innocence, since that sort of righteousness is not free of severity, nor is severity immune from corruption.[28] So, every nature is good. The righteousness of the law of God is the fruit that befits this nature. Therefore, righteousness is goodness. Consequently, the righteous are always also called good, but the good are not always called

---

good person, why would one not be even more ready to die for the righteous person? Ambrosiaster does not address this problem directly; instead, he explains the different senses of "righteous" and "good."

23. Ambrosiaster appears to have young children in mind; see the variant in *recensio* β at n. 24 below.

24. *Recensio* β has "young children" instead of "children."

25. The wife who dies with or for her husband is a common *topos* of Roman literature. See Holt Parker, "Loyal Slaves and Loyal Wives: The Crisis of the Outsider-Within and Roman *exemplum* Literature," in *Women and Slaves in Greco-Roman Culture: Differential Equations*, ed. Sheila Murnaghan and Sandra R. Joshel (London: Routledge, 1998), 163–69.

26. *Recensio* α does not have section 4a; see n. 22 above.

27. *Recensio* β has "For through practice the righteous person will improve the good character of his nature."

28. *Recensio* β has "since that sort of righteousness is not free of ungodliness" instead of "since that sort of righteousness is not free of severity, nor is severity immune from corruption."

righteous, since they are called good on account of not their works but their innocence. Righteousness is perfect goodness, when one has fulfilled the good character of one's nature through work.[29]

5:8 *But God demonstrates his love for us.*[30] He demonstrates his love when he is benevolent to those who are as yet enemies and sends the one who saves them although they in no way deserve it.

Because if Christ died for us while we were yet sinners, **5:9** *how much more shall we, who are now justified by his blood, be saved from wrath through him.* (1) The apostle says this because if God allowed his Son to be killed for sinners,[31] what will he do for the justified if not preserve them from wrath? That is, he will protect them from the deceit of the devil so that they may be safe on the day of judgment when vengeance will begin to devastate unbelievers. (2) In fact, because the goodness of God does not wish any to perish, he granted mercy to those who are worthy of death, so as to add eminence and glory to those who grasp the grace of God toward them.[32] The ungrateful are those who refuse God when he calls them and reject the grace of God, so that they remain in a state of error and evil disposition.

5:10 *For if we, although we were enemies, were reconciled to God through the death of his Son, how much more shall we, having been reconciled, be saved by his life.* It is obvious that if God handed his Son over to death in order to reconcile us to himself, how much more will he make us, now reconciled, to be saved by his life. Someone who shows favor to his enemies could hardly fail to love his friends. Indeed, if the Savior's death benefited us while we were still ungodly, how much more will his life, when he rises from the dead, benefit us, now that we have been justified. For just as his death rescued us from the devil, so too his life will set us free on the day of God's judgment.[33]

---

29. On Ambrosiaster's idea of the inherent natural goodness of all people and the concomitant responsibility to perfect that goodness through the cultivation of righteousness, see Emanuele Di Santo, *L'Apologetica dell'Ambrosiaster: Cristiani, pagani e giudei nella Roma tardoantica*, SEAug 112 (Rome: Institutum Patristicum Augustinianum, 2008), 379–80.

30. Ambrosiaster's biblical text places "God" before "for us" (*in nobis*), whereas the majority of biblical witnesses place "God" after "for us" (εἰς ἡμᾶς); see Jewett, *Romans*, 345.

31. *Recensio* α has "to die" instead of "to be killed."

32. *Recensio* α adds "while he heaps punishment on the ungrateful."

33. *Recensio* α has "the day of judgment."

5:11 *Not only this,*[34] *but we also glory in God through our Lord Jesus Christ,*[35] *through whom we have now received reconciliation.* The apostle teaches us not only to give thanks to God for the salvation and the safety that we have received,[36] but also to glory through Jesus Christ in God,[37] who saw fit that with his Son as arbitrator we who were ungodly and enemies should be called friends,[38] so that we rejoice in all the benefits that we have received through Christ. As a result, because we acknowledge God through him, when we glory in him we render to him honor equal to God the Father,[39] as he himself, a fitting witness to himself, foretold: *That they may honor the Son as they honor the Father* (John 5:23). After discussing, then, the providence of God the Father and the gift that he gave through Christ, so as to render the person of the Son someone for whom we are grateful (because we have been redeemed by the one God the Father through the one Christ), the apostle has added:

5:12 *Therefore, just as sin came into this world through one person and death through sin, and so it passed on to all people,*[40] *in whom all sinned.*[41] (1) Since[42] in what preceded he set out the grace of God that

---

34. The word "this" (*hoc*) in Ambrosiaster's biblical text and some other biblical witnesses is likely a secondary addition. See Jewett, *Romans*, 345.

35. Ambrosiaster's biblical text has the finite verb "we glory" (*gloriamur*), but among the biblical witnesses there is strong support for the participle "glorying" (καυχώμενοι). See Jewett, *Romans*, 345.

36. *Recensio* α adds "through our Lord Jesus Christ."

37. *Recensio* α adds "through our Lord Jesus Christ."

38. *Recensiones* α and β do not have "with his Son as arbitrator." Ambrosiaster also uses the term at In Rom. 5:2, where it appears in all three recensions.

39. *Recensio* α has "We hold the Son in the same honor as the Father, as he himself etc."

40. Among the biblical witnesses there is strong support for "death passed" (ὁ θάνατος διῆλθεν), but Ambrosiaster's biblical text omits "death." See Jewett, *Romans*, 369.

41. In Ambrosiaster's text of Rom 5:12 the phrase ἐφ' ᾧ was translated *in quo*. The phrase is capable of different interpretations. Ambrosiaster takes it to mean "in whom" (see n. 49 below), so I have translated it accordingly here. This reading is considered untenable today. For an overview of patristic interpretations of the phrase, see Karl H. Schelkle, *Paulus, Lehrer der Väter*, 2nd ed. (Düsseldorf: Patmos, 1959), 162–78. For a critical assessment of modern interpretations, drawing on ancient evidence, see Joseph A. Fitzmyer, "The Consecutive Meaning of ἐφ' ᾧ in Romans 5.12," *NTS* 39 (1993): 321–39.

42. *Recensio* α does not have "since."

was given in Christ according to the true providential arrangement,[43] Paul now explains this very arrangement devised by the one God, the Father, through the one Christ, his Son: namely, because the one Adam—that is, Eve, since woman is also "Adam"[44]—sinned in everyone, so too the one Christ, the Son of God, conquered sin in everyone. Since he set out the plan of God's grace toward humankind, the apostle, in order to reveal the very origin of sin, began with Adam, who was the first to sin, so that he might teach that God's providence restored through one person what through one person had fallen and been dragged into death. (2) Therefore, Christ, by whom we have been saved, is the one person to whom we owe the same reverence that we owe God the Father, as God himself wishes. Paul says the same thing[45] in another place: *One who serves Christ in these matters pleases God* (Rom 14:18), though it is written: *You shall worship the Lord your God and him alone shall you serve* (Deut 6:13; see Matt 4:10). If then the scripture says that God alone should be served and Paul commanded us to serve Christ, Christ clearly is in unity with God and is not an unequal or another god, since although the law warns that God alone should be served, one who serves Christ is said to please God.[46] Therefore, *just as sin came into this world through the one person*[47] *and death through sin*, so too through the one Christ came the condemnation of sin and the death of sin, granting eternal life,[48] as he explains below (see Rom 5:15–21). (2a) *In whom*—that is, in Adam[49]—*all sinned*. Although he is speak-

---

43. Ambrosiaster refers here to Paul's argument in Rom 5:1–11. On the reversal of substantives in the Latin construction *ordinem veritatis*, see Vinzenz Bulhart, "Gallimathias," *WSt* 66 (1953): 155–66.

44. *Recensio* α does not have this parenthetical remark. *Recensio* β has "that is, Eve, for she too is 'Adam.'" In specifying that it was Eve who sinned, Ambrosiaster is probably echoing 1 Tim 2:14; see In 1 Tim. 2:14 (§1) and In Col. 1:18 (§2).

45. *Recensio* α has "In another place Paul says."

46. Ambrosiaster also refers to Rom 14:18 at In Rom. 9:5 (§4) in order to demonstrate that the Father and the Son are one God and are equally owed worship and service.

47. *Recensio* α does not have "person."

48. *Recensio* α has "the condemnation of sin and eternal life" instead of "the condemnation of sin and the death of sin, granting eternal life."

49. *Recensio* α does not have this parenthetical remark. The relative pronoun in the Latin phrase *in quo*, as in the Greek phrase ἐφ' ᾧ, can be masculine or neuter. With this parenthetical remark Ambrosiaster explicitly reads the pronoun as masculine: "in whom." This is the first attestation of such a reading among extant Latin Christian interpreters of Romans; see Joseph Freundorfer, *Erbsünde und Erbtod beim Apostel Paulus: Eine religionsgeschichtliche und exegetische Untersuchung über Römerbrief 5,*

ing of the woman, he said *in whom* because he was referring to the race, not to a specific type.[50] (3) It is clear, consequently, that all sinned in Adam as in a lump.[51] Once he was corrupted by sin, those he begat were all born under sin. All sinners, therefore, derive from him, because we are all from him.[52] When he transgressed, he lost the gift of God, having become unworthy to eat of the tree of life, and as a result he died. This death is the separation of the soul from the body.[53] (4) There is another death—called the second death—in gehenna.[54] We do not undergo it on account of the sin of Adam; it is acquired by the opportunity one has for one's own sins.[55]

12-21, NTAbh 13 (Münster: Aschendorff, 1927), 130-33; Schelkle, *Paulus*, 174-75. The reading had a long life in the West largely because of Augustine's recourse to it in his writings on the effects of Adam's sin (see n. 51 below). On Ambrosiaster's understanding of the effects of Adam's sin, and the similarities and differences between his understanding and Augustine's, see Pier Franco Beatrice, *The Transmission of Sin: Augustine and the Pre-Augustinian Sources*, trans. Adam Kamesar, AARRT (Oxford: Oxford University Press, 2013), 128-41; Alessandra Pollastri, *Ambrosiaster, commento alla Lettera ai Romani: Aspetti cristologici*, CTSt (L'Aquila: Japadre, 1976), 106-45; Juan B. Valero, "Pecar en Adán según Ambrosiaster," *EE* 65 (1990): 147-91.

50. *Recensio* α does not have this sentence. Because Ambrosiaster understands the text to refer to Eve (see n. 44 above), he must explain why the masculine *quo* (see n. 49 above) is used rather than the feminine *qua*.

51. *Recensio* α does not have the phrase "as in a lump" (*quasi in massa*) or the particle "consequently." The word *massa* appears in Ambrosiaster's Pauline text at In Rom. 9:21; 11:16; In 1 Cor. 5:6; and In Gal. 5:9. Ambrosiaster himself uses the term to refer to the common substance shared by parts of a whole or instances of a kind, in this case, the flesh that is common to Adam and his descendants; see e.g., In Rom. 9:21 (§1) and In 1 Cor. 15:39. Ambrosiaster's comment here was later quoted by Augustine in *C. du. ep. Pelag*. 4.4.7 (CSEL 60:528) to refute the Pelagian view of the effects of Adam's sin; see A. C. de Veer, "Saint Augustin et l'Ambrosiaster," in *Premières polémiques contre Julien*, ed. F.-J. Thonnard, E. Bleuzen, and A. C. de Veer, BAug 23 (Paris: Desclée de Brouwer, 1974), 817. The wording of Augustine's quotation corresponds to the version of the comment in *recensio* β, not, as de Veer states, *recensio* γ.

52. See In Rom. 7:14 (§§2-3).

53. *Recensiones* α and β have "This death is the dissolution of the body, when the soul is separated from the body." As Ambrosiaster explains at In Rom. 7:24 (§5), the body was created mortal and avoided death only through its union with the soul. Physical death—the separation of the soul from the body—is a consequence of the sin of Adam, which deprived humankind of access to the tree of life.

54. For Ambrosiaster's understanding of the second death (see Rev 2:11; 20:6, 14; 21:8) in gehenna, a place of fiery torment to which the devil and all unrepentant sinners are condemned, see the introduction §5.4.

55. *Recensio* α has "for it is acquired by one's own sins."

The good are spared it, insofar as they are in the underworld,[56] but in the uppermost level as if under house arrest,[57] because it was not possible to be raised into the heavens.[58] They were held by the sentence given to Adam. This written bond with its decrees was erased by Christ's death.[59] The decreed sentence was this: that the body of an individual person would decay on earth, but the soul, held by the bonds of the underworld, would suffer torments.[60]

5:13 *Until the time of the law sin indeed was in the world. But sin was not reckoned as long as there was no law.* (1) The apostle says that in Adam all sinned, as I noted above,[61] and that until the law was given it was not reckoned to be sin. People thought that they sinned with impunity before God, though not before other people. For natural law had not become entirely imperceptible, since people were aware that they should not do to others what they did not wish to suffer themselves.[62] Indeed, sin was so far from being overlooked by people that when Laban, Jacob's father-in-law, searched for his idols among Jacob's entourage, Jacob pronounced the judgment that the person with whom the stolen objects would be found would be put to death (see Gen 31:17–32). Joseph, too, was imprisoned as a guilty person, even though this came about by means of false accusation (see Gen 39:6–23).[63] Likewise, both the baker and the butler of Pharaoh were sent to

---

56. The underworld is an interim state where the souls of the dead await final judgment. Ambrosiaster distinguishes between the "good" who were held there only by Adam's sin in a condition of refreshing coolness (*refrigerium*) until they were liberated by Christ when he descended to the underworld; "sinners" who, though saved because of their faith, must be purified of their sins by fire; and the "ungodly," who will suffer eternal punishment. See In Rom. 5:14 (§3a).

57. Alexander Souter, *A Study of Ambrosiaster*, TS 7.4 (Cambridge: Cambridge University Press, 1905), 155 n. 3, supplies the suggestion that Ambrosiaster understood the state of the good in the underworld to be a kind of "house arrest" (*libera custodia*).

58. *Recensiones* α and β and some manuscripts of *recensio* γ have "because they could not ascend to the heavens."

59. *Recensio* α has "This written bond with its decrees, which continued to be in effect, was canceled by Christ." See Ambrosiaster's comment at In Col. 2:13–15 regarding the written bond that, on account of Adam's sin, held the dead in the underworld until it was erased through Christ's unjust crucifixion.

60. *Recensio* α does not have this sentence. *Recensio* β does not have "this."

61. See In Rom. 5:12 (§2a).

62. See Ambrosiaster, *Quaest.* 4.1 (CSEL 50:24).

63. In *recensio* γ the sentence is attested only by MS Paris lat. 1759.

prison on account of transgressions (see Gen 40:1),[64] and Moses, terrified by the law after he had killed an Egyptian, fled (see Exod 2:11–15). (2) Why then *was sin not reckoned as long there was no law*? Or why is it said to be punished if the law was hidden?[65] In fact, natural law always exists and can never be unknown. But it was thought to have authority only for the time being, not rendering a person guilty also before God. It was not known that God would judge the human race,[66] and for this reason sin was not reckoned—as if it were not a sin before God—because people maintained that God was indifferent. However, when the law was given through Moses, it was plainly revealed that God cares about human affairs and that there will be punishment for those evildoers who for whatever reason escape at the present time.[67] (3) Now assuredly, if under the tutelage of justice or[68] nature people held that sins would not go unpunished[69] among them, they must have been aware that God, whom they knew to be the creator of the world, would call them to account for this,[70] particularly since Sodom and Gomorrah were condemned to perish by fire. This event had in fact sunk into oblivion, but Moses brought it to light by writing about it,[71] in order to confirm that God will be the judge. Nevertheless, when they neglected God and began to accept images with the honor due to God, their minds were corrupted and they suppressed part of natural law, the first part. (4) Natural law, in fact, has three parts. The first of these is that the creator is to be recognized and honored, and that his splendor and majesty are not to be accorded to anyone except the Son.[72] The second part is the moral part, that is, the part whereby one lives well under the guidance of moderation. It is fitting that a person who has knowledge of the creator govern his life according to the law, so that this knowledge not be rendered useless.[73] The

---

64. *Recensiones* α and β have "suffered in a similar way" instead of "were sent to prison."

65. *Recensiones* α and β have "unless the law was known" instead of "if the law was hidden."

66. *Recensio* α has "human activity" instead of "the human race."

67. *Recensiones* α and β do not have "for whatever reason."

68. *Recensiones* α and β do not have "justice or."

69. *Recensio* α has "would not be overlooked" instead of "would not go unpunished."

70. *Recensio* α does not have "for this."

71. See Ambrosiaster, *Quaest.* 4.1 (CSEL 50:25).

72. *Recensio* α has "to any of the creatures," and *recensio* β has "to anyone" instead of "to anyone except the Son."

73. *Recensio* α does not have "so that this knowledge not be rendered useless."

third part, finally, is the instructive part whereby one conveys knowledge of God the creator and an example of behavior to others, so that they learn how merit is laid up with the creator.[74] This is true Christian prudence.

5:14 *But death reigned from Adam to Moses.* (1) Because, as I have said, sin was not reckoned in the period before the law was given through Moses, death reigned with the impunity of a usurper,[75] knowing that these sinners had been consigned to it.[76] Death reigned, therefore, assured of its dominion as much over those who escaped for the time being as over those who even here suffered punishment for their evil deeds. Death viewed them all as belonging to it, since *one who commits sin is a slave of sin* (John 8:34). Indeed, since they thought that they were allowed to sin with impunity, they transgressed all the more, being especially inclined toward those sins that the world nourished as if they were permissible forms of behavior.[77] Consequently, Satan rejoiced, confident that he possessed the human being that had been surrendered by God on account of Adam. Death thus reigned[78] *over those who sinned after the manner of Adam's transgression,*[79] *who is a type of the one to come.* (2) We shall explain below who Adam *the type of the one to come* is.[80]

It is clear that death did not reign over everyone, because they did not all sin *after the manner of Adam's transgression*; that is, they did not all sin by disrespecting God. But who are those who sinned by disrespecting God, if not those who, having disregarded the creator,[81] served creatures, making gods for themselves whom they worshiped to the dishonor of God? The devil was overjoyed with such people because he saw that they had been turned into imitators of him.[82] Indeed, even Terah, the father of Abraham, and Nahor and Laban had their own gods (see Josh 24:2; Gen

---

74. *Recensio* α has "is kept safe" instead of "is laid up."
75. Literally, "of usurpation" (*usurpationis*).
76. *Recensio* α has "belonged to it" instead of "were consigned to it."
77. *Recensio* α does not have the clause "being especially inclined etc."
78. *Recensio* α does not have this introduction to the next portion of the lemma.
79. The majority of Greek witnesses state that death reigned "over those who did not [μή] sin after the manner of Adam's transgression." Ambrosiaster's biblical text omits "not." Ambrosiaster is aware of the alternative reading. He explains his text in sections 2–3a below and defends it against critics in sections 4–5a.
80. See section 7 below. *Recensio* α does not repeat the last clause of the lemma; *recensio* β does not have "Adam."
81. *Recensio* has α "having disrespected" instead of "having disregarded."
82. *Recensiones* α and β do not have this sentence.

31:30).[83] Adam's sin, too, was not far from idolatry, for he transgressed in believing that he, a human being, would be God. He judged that what the devil proposed would be more advantageous than what God commanded, putting the devil in the place of God, which is why Adam also was made subject to the devil. (3) So too, these people, by overlooking God when they serve creatures, sin in a similar way—not in the same way, because the expression "in a similar way" usually includes something that is different.[84] It cannot be said that these people also received the command[85] not to eat of the tree, as did Adam.

There were also people who sinned not by neglecting God, but against natural law. For if someone understood who God is, whether by inherited tradition or natural judgment,[86] and revered him, attributing to no one else the honor of his name and his majesty—if this person sinned (since it is impossible not to sin),[87] he sinned under God, not against God, whom he perceived to be judge. Therefore, death did not reign in such people; rather, as I have said, death reigned in those who served the devil under the appearance of idols.

(3a)[88] Since the law had not been promulgated in the form of a decree, people were unable to have a sense of God as judge; most of the world was not aware that God would be their judge. There were a few people in whom death did not reign. After the death called the first death, those in whom death reigned were received by the second death for future punishment and destruction. Those in whom death did not reign (because they did not sin after the manner of Adam's transgression) were set aside in house arrest in the hope of the Savior's coming,[89] as we read concerning Abraham; although he was in the underworld, he was set a great distance

---

83. *Recensiones* α and β have "claimed for themselves their own gods" instead of "had their own gods."

84. *Recensio* α has "in the manner" (*similitudo*), echoing the lemma (*in similitudinem*), instead of "in a similar way" (*simili modo*).

85. *Recenio* α adds "from God."

86. *Recensiones* α and β do not have "whether by inherited tradition or natural judgment."

87. Instead of "since it is impossible not to sin" and the remainder of this section, *recensio* α has "if this person sinned, he sinned against the law, because he denied it. Therefore, death did not reign in these people; rather, those in whom death reigned, they abused the Lord himself."

88. *Recensio* α does not have section 3a.

89. See nn. 56 and 57 above.

apart. Thus, just as the void between the righteous and the sinners was huge, it was even greater between the righteous and the ungodly, so that there was coolness for the righteous and heat for the sinners but burning flames for the ungodly. Accordingly, what each one deserved was disclosed before judgment came. In this way, then, death reigned in them, since it saw that its treacherous doings had brought them, like enemies, into punishment. For it did not escape death's notice that humankind had been created in the world to proclaim the rule of the one God, from which Satan had strayed.[90]

(4) Even if it is not stated so precisely in the Greek text—for it is said that it is written that death reigned even in those who did not sin after the manner of Adam's transgression[91]—the apostle seems here to have included the entire human race, so that because death, or destruction, was created through the jealousy of Satan (see Wis 2:24),[92] it reigned even in those who did not sin. For they die, which is Satan's desire. (4a)[93] But if this were true, there was no need to say *death reigned from Adam to Moses*, if, that is, death reigned in all people from beginning to end.[94] Or was the apostle perhaps establishing stages, namely, that death reigned from Adam to Moses, and from Moses to Christ, and finally from Christ until the end? But what would have been the advantage of this way of speaking, though it is not proven that the apostle in fact spoke in this manner. For the apostle said *death reigned from Adam to Moses* because the law had not been revealed; once the law was given, people lived under its authority and knew what to avoid so that death would not reign in them. (4b) If before the law

---

90. Ambrosiaster maintains that the derivation of all human beings from the man Adam reflects the derivation of all things from God. As a reflection of the single and original authority of God, Adam is a corrective to the devil, who, in disregarding the authority of God and in attempting to usurp that authority, introduced division and confusion into the created order. See In 1 Cor. 11:5–7 (§2) and *Quaest.* 2.3 (CSEL 50:18).

91. *Recensio* α has "If in the Greek text it reads that death reigned even in those etc." The version of the comment in *recensiones* β and γ indicates that Ambrosiaster had not consulted the Greek text himself: "it is said that it is written" (*sic enim dicitur scriptum*). See also Ambrosiaster's comment in *recensiones* β and γ at In Rom. 12:11c (§1b).

92. *Recensiones* α and β have "the devil" instead of "Satan."

93. *Recensio* α does not have sections 4a to 4d.

94. Ambrosiaster's argument is that if death reigned even in those who did not sin after the manner of Adam, it would not be necessary to specify that death reigned from Adam to Moses, since death would in fact reign in everyone.

was given someone kept, as a result of the tutelage of nature, what the law later commanded, how can it be said that death reigned in him? For look at what is written about him: *Sin was not reckoned*, the apostle says, *as long as there was no law*. And he added: *But death reigned from Adam to Moses*, at the very time when there was no law. Since death reigned before the law was given, it is in fact fitting that it should be said to have reigned in those who sinned after the manner of Adam's transgression, as was discussed above. (4c) Just as after the law was given death reigned in those who devoted themselves to fornication and idols and disrespected the lawgiver, so too before the law was given death in no way reigned in those who anticipated the meaning of the law and honored its author. The reason death is said to have reigned is that knowledge of the one God had disappeared on earth. When at last the law was given, it began as follows: *I am the Lord your God, who brought you out of Egypt, out of the house of slavery. You shall not have other gods besides me and you shall not make for yourself an idol or any likeness* (Exod 20:2–4). (4d) The law was given, therefore, so that death might not reign and so that once the preceding sins had been wiped out the human race might obey one God. For this reason the same apostle says in another passage: *Let not sin reign in your mortal body such that you obey it* (Rom 6:12). With this statement he shows that death reigns even now if the law is not respected. For what is the reign of death but the accomplishment of its will as it issues orders to the destruction of those who obey? The rule of its will is the source of idolatry.[95]

(4e) Still, they want to impose this reading on us on the basis of the Greek codices, as if these themselves did not disagree with each other![96] This is motivated by a love of controversy. When someone is not able to win his case by using the proper authority, he falsifies the wording of the law in order to assert his own interpretation as if it were in the wording of the law. Consequently, authority appears to decide the case rather than reasoning. However, there are certain Latin codices that were translated a long time ago from ancient Greek codices. (5) The simplicity of the times

---

95. On the inversion of nominative and genitive in the phrase *imperii voluntas*, see n. 43 above.

96. Ambrosiaster is reacting here to Jerome, who was correcting received Latin versions (the VL) of the gospels in light of the text found in Greek manuscripts. See the introduction, §§1 and 2.1, and Heinrich J. Vogels, "Ambrosiaster und Hieronymus," *RBén* 66 (1956): 14–19. See also In Rom. 12:11 (§1b).

preserved these codices uncorrupted and continues to commend them.[97] But after questions began to be tossed about by minds that diverged from consensus and by disruptive heretics, many things were changed to fit with human understanding, so that what seemed right to people was contained in the letter of the text. For this reason even the Greeks themselves have codices that vary. (5a)[98] But I deem a matter to be true when reasoning and history and authority are upheld. For indeed, the text in the Latin codices that is criticized today is found to be so cited by the ancients: Tertullian and Victorinus and Cyprian.[99]

The reign of death began to be destroyed first in Judea because *God was known in Judea* (Ps 75:2 LXX = Ps 76:1 ET). But now it is being destroyed daily among all the gentiles as people in large numbers leave the children of the devil to become children of God. So death did not reign in everyone, but only in those who sinned after the manner of Adam's transgression, as I discussed above.

---

97. Instead of this sentence and the following one, *recensio* α has "In response to this we cannot remain silent, since our codices derive from ancient Greek codices, which the simplicity of the times commends as being uncorrupted. But afterward many things were changed to fit with human understanding by disruptive heretics who tossed out questions, so that what seemed right to people was contained in the letter of the text."

98. *Recensio* α does not have section 5a. Instead it has section 6: "Now I do not think it is relevant to the argument [to say that] that the apostle says that death reigned because sin was not reckoned since the law had not been given. Almost everyone worshiped idols. Idolatry is, in fact, the worship of the devil, and this is why death reigned. Indeed, if death reigned even in those who did not sin after the manner of Adam's transgression, because they died, it also reigns now, because the saints also die. If death reigned solely because of idolatry, it also reigns now. But death does not reign; for death reigned not only because of idolatry but also in a reprehensible life, and today people leave the children of the devil to become children of God. Therefore, death does not reign. The law thus was given so that through the law those who were liable under God's judgment would be found guilty, subject to God, not to the devil. For this reason, once the law was given, the devil began not to reign. Everyone began to understand that God the creator would judge the human race, and they began little by little to withdraw from the devil's rule."

99. Ambrosiaster is referring to Victorinus, bishop of Pettau at the end of the third century, who wrote a number of commentaries in Latin. Little of his work has survived. See Stephen A. Cooper, *Marius Victorinus' Commentary on Galatians: Introduction, Translation, and Notes*, OECS (Oxford: Oxford University Press, 2005), 188–90.

(7) Moreover, Adam is a type of the one to come, because already at that time God in a hidden way determined to rectify through the one Christ the sin that had come about through the one Adam, as he says in the Apocalypse of the apostle John: *The lamb that was slain is from the foundation of the world* (Rev 13:8). Next the apostle has added:

5:15 *But the gift is not like the trespass.* (1a)[100] So that one does not think that the apostle meant that Adam's situation is the same sort as Christ's—because he said that the one Adam was in fact the type of the one Christ—he says: *But the gift is not like the trespass.* For Adam is the type of Christ in this regard alone: the sin that one person committed, one person rectified.

For if many died through one person's trespass, how much more have the grace of God and the gift in the grace of the one person Jesus Christ abounded in more people. (1) That is, *if many died through one person's trespass* when they imitated his transgression,[101] the grace of God and the gift abounded even further in more people when they took refuge in him.[102] For more people receive grace than died through Adam's trespass. From this it is clear that the apostle was not referring to the death that is common to all, since absolutely all people die and yet all people do not receive grace. It also is clear that death did not reign in all people,[103] but only in those who are denoted as having died as a result of Adam's trespass, that is, those whom the apostle says sinned after the manner of Adam's transgression.[104] (2) These are the people the apostle refers to when he says that many died as a result of the one person's trespass but the grace of God abounded in more people. For with the descent of the Savior, who granted forgiveness to all who were taken up with him in triumph into heaven,[105] the grace of God abounded both among those who are said to have died as a result of Adam's trespass, when they sinned like him, and among those who did not

---

100. *Recensio* α does not have section 1a.
101. *Recensio* α does not have "when they imitated his transgression."
102. *Recensio* α does not have "when they took refuge in him."
103. *Recensiones* α and β have "in them" instead of "in all people."
104. On the inversion of ablative and genitive in the phrase *in praevaricatione similitudinis*, see n. 43 above. *Recensiones* α and β retain the genitive found in the lemma at In Rom. 5:14: *in similitudine(m) praevaricationis*.
105. The beginning of this sentence in English appears at the end of the sentence in Latin. In place of it, *recensio* α has "For the grace of God abounded, granting forgiveness to all, both among etc."

sin after this manner of Adam's transgression but were in the underworld on account of ancestral sin as a result of God's judgment.[106]

5:16 *And the gift is not like what happened through one sinner. For the judgment following one sin led to condemnation, but the gift following many trespasses led to justification.* (1) It is clearly different, because as a result of Adam's one sin those who sinned after the manner of his transgression were condemned, whereas the grace of God through Christ justified people not from a single trespass but from many sins by granting them forgiveness of sins.[107] (2) This is spoken to glorify the kindness of God and of Christ, namely, that when many were held by the second death in the lower levels of the underworld as a result of Adam's trespass, the gift of God's grace not only forgives them but also justifies them, even though it was just that they were being punished.

5:17 *For if as a result of one trespass death reigned through one person, how much more will those who receive the abundance of grace and righteousness reign in life through the one person Jesus Christ.*[108] (1) It is important to recognize that the meaning is the same and does not differ in any way. The apostle says that death *reigned*, not reigns,[109] because those who understood through the law that the judgment of God would come were removed from death's rule. But death reigned because without the revelation of the law there was no fear of God on earth. (2) The meaning above, then, is that because death reigned from Adam to Moses in those who sinned after the manner of Adam's transgression, grace will reign all the more through the abundance of the gift of God that leads to life through the one person Jesus Christ. For if death reigned, will not grace reign even more—grace which justifies many more people than the number of those in whom death reigned? How much more should we believe that grace, which grants life through Christ, reigns!

---

106. *Recensio* α does not have "but were in the underworld on account of ancestral sin as a result of God's judgment." It concludes the section with a remark not found in *recensiones* β and γ: "Although some did not sin after the manner of Adam's transgression, there nevertheless can be no doubt that they sinned in some other way, since they were not without sin, all those who received the grace of God at the descent of the Savior."

107. *Recensio* α does not have "them."

108. Among biblical witnesses there is strong support for the presence of "the gift," omitted in Ambrosiaster's biblical text, before "of righteousness" (τῆς δωρεᾶς τῆς δικαιοσύνης). See Jewett, *Romans*, 370.

109. *Recensio* α does not have the remainder of this sentence.

5:18 *Thus, just as one person's trespass led to condemnation for all people, so too one person's righteousness leads to the justification of life for all people.* That is, just as through one person's trespass all who sinned in the same way deserved condemnation, so too in one person's righteousness will all who believe be justified. Now, if people think that this condemnation is universal, they will likewise take the justification to be universal as well. But this is not true, since all people do not believe.[110]

5:19 *For just as through the disobedience of one person many were made sinners, so too through the obedience of one person many will be made righteous.* (1) Those whom he spoke of above as *all*, he here refers to as *more* and *many*. For more people—not all—followed Adam's trespass by transgressing, and many people—not all—will be made righteous through faith in Christ.[111] (1a)[112] Death did not reign, therefore, in those who did not sin after the manner of Adam's transgression.

5:20 *Now, the law slipped in such that trespass abounded.*[113] (2a)[114] One can object: "Then it was not necessary to give the law to prevent sins

---

110. The idea that salvation would be universal and include the restoration of the devil became a flashpoint in the Origenist controversy in the last decade of the fourth century. Ambrosiaster's comment here does not anticipate that controversy or betray awareness of teachings attributed to Origen; his comment turns on the interpretation of 5:18. But it nevertheless offers another perspective on why the idea as construed in the controversy—not in Origen's own writings; see Henri Crouzel, *Origen*, trans. A. S. Worrall (Edinburgh: T&T Clark, 1989), 262–66—would not have been acceptable: Ambrosiaster takes it for granted that salvation is predicated on believing. On the principle of differentiated salvation in the Jovinianist and Origenist controversies, see Elizabeth A. Clark, *The Origenist Controversy: The Cultural Construction of an Early Christian Debate* (Princeton: Princeton University Press, 1992), 99–100; David G. Hunter, *Marriage, Celibacy, and Heresy in Ancient Christianity: The Jovinianist Controversy*, OECS (Oxford: Oxford University Press, 2007), 41–43.

111. *Recensio* α has "so that many—not all—may be made righteous through faith in Christ." *Recensio* β has "and many—not all—will be made righteous."

112. *Recensio* α does not have section 1a.

113. Ambrosiaster's comment suggests that the wording of the verse was problematic in two ways. First, the verb *subintrare* has connotations of stealth or subterfuge. Second, the *ut*-clause is ambiguous; it can mean that the law was introduced in order to increase sinning or that sin increased as a result of the introduction of the law. Ambrosiaster addresses the first problem in section 1 of the comment, preserved only in *recensio* α, and in section 2(d) of the comment, preserved in *recensiones* β and γ. He addresses the second problem in section 2(c) of the comment, preserved in *recensiones* β and γ.

114. *Recensio* α does not have sections 2a–2e. Instead it has "(1) That is: the law

from increasing. For if prior to the law people sinned less, there was no need for the law." Clearly, the law was necessary to show that sins which were believed to be committed with impunity were reckoned by God, so that from then on people would know what they ought to avoid. (2b) This is why the prophet Isaiah says: *The law was given as an aid* (Isa 8:20). That is, since the seeds of righteousness were somehow implanted in nature itself, the law was added so that by its authority and instruction the natural capacity might develop to produce the fruit of righteousness. Just as a newborn dies unless it has the nourishment by which, having been fostered, it matures, so too the natural capacity for righteousness does not readily develop, but becomes diseased and gives in to sins that overcome it, unless it has something to be mindful of and to revere. It is overwhelmed by the habit of transgressing so that it does not develop fruit, and in this way it is extinguished. (2c) The law, therefore, was given providentially, as the prophet testifies, but the people multiplied their sins by following their old habits. Through this tendency one began to sin more than one had previously. So it came about that after the law was given sins did not diminish but abounded. For the apostle has explained what came about after the law was given, not what the law did. Indeed, how could sins grow as a result of a weakness in the law that warned against sinning? But the law is said to have *slipped in such that* sin *abounded*. (2d) It is true that the law came in as something that would be beneficial and, in fact, with humility, but afterward it began to dominate those whom it commanded not to sin and who sinned nevertheless. For when people did what it prohibited more than they had done before, the law began to expose the growing amount of sins. In this way, then, the law was given *such that trespass abounded*. (2e) In commending the faith by which sins

---

was given in written form for the purpose of revelation. For the law that was indeed willingly accepted by the Jews when they said to Moses, *Whatever the Lord God has said, we will do* (Exod 24:7), had been implanted in nature. Nevertheless, the law *slipped in* because when it was willingly accepted it showed that those who had sinned prior to that time were guilty. For they recollected that God would require the fruit of the seed of righteousness that he implanted in nature. (2) To slip in, then, is to enter humbly and afterward to dominate. When the law slipped in, sin increased because the law showed that the older generations before the law as well as those after the law were sinners—and more so after the law, because the enemy burned all the more with envy when he saw that God was concerned about humankind. As a result, the enemy rendered humankind guilty through the law as well, so that God would not be considered worthy of regard."

are at last blotted out, the apostle said that the law brought it about that sins abounded, as I have said above, because the law was given not such that sins were abolished, but such that they abounded, as on the one hand it showed people to be sinners prior to the law and, on the other, found them all to be guilty after the law was given.

But where sin abounded, grace abounded all the more. (3) It is clear that when sin abounded, as I have said, *grace abounded all the more*, as the gift of God came as a result of the promise and covered the sins of all people, so that the envy of the devil was tormented by the fact that he had gained nothing.[115] (4a)[116] For although the law was given for the benefit of humankind, the devil acted to invert its effect by recommending unlawful behavior. As a result, what had been given to be beneficial came to have the opposite effect when the commandments were spurned. Consequently, the utility proceeding from the law was not commendation of the grace of God but rather judgment leading to punishment. At that point, in order to render futile the glory of the devil, which had sought to make a trophy of humankind, God, who is just as well as merciful, decreed that his Son would come. The Son forgave all sins; as a result, the rejoicing on account of the gift of grace was greater than the weeping had been on account of sin. For the joy of the gift of God benefits even those over whom Satan could not triumph. Therefore, grace abounded all the more over the sin that Satan promoted.

5:21 *So that, just as sin reigned in death, so too grace reigns through righteousness in eternal life through Jesus Christ our Lord.* (1) *Sin reigned* by seeing its work lead sinners to death—a death at which it rejoiced. Similarly, *grace, too, reigns* in those who are obedient to it, (1a) when those to whom it granted mercy conduct themselves rightly, becoming heirs of eternal life through Christ, just as they had been liable to perdition through Adam.[117]

---

115. *Recensio* α adds "and that God's providence toward humankind endures and that his astute plan cannot be waylaid." The reference to the envy of the devil continues a theme introduced in section 2, preserved only in *recensio* α; see n. 114 above.

116. *Recensio* α does not have section 4a.

117. Instead of sections 1 and 1a, *recensiones* α and β have "Sin reigned by seeing its work lead sinners to death—a death at which it rejoiced. Similarly, grace, too, reigns through righteousness in eternal life through Jesus Christ our Lord, so that just as sin reigned through Adam who first began to sin, so too grace reigns through Christ. (2) However, grace reigns through righteousness only if we follow the path of righteousness after we have received forgiveness of sins. Then grace, seeing that it bears fruit in the good people it has redeemed, reigns in eternal life, knowing that we shall be

eternal. Grace abounds all the more, because sin reigned for a time, but grace reigns forever. For the reign of God is when grace reigns, just as the reign of the devil was when sin reigned. Nevertheless, the entire passage refers to Christ, so that the entire grace of God is apprehended in [β: from] Christ. The apostle has responded to the above interpretation, then, by saying."

Romans 6

6:1 *What then shall we say? Are we to continue in sin that grace may abound? By no means!* (1) That is: Should not we sin all the time so that the gift of God may abound and cover our sins, and that as a result we promote the grace of Christ, since we are always hopeful of forgiveness of sins because God is faithful? Certainly not. For God had mercy on us through Christ so that by sinning no longer we may both create merit for ourselves and cause the grace of God to reign in us. (2) Someone who has gone back again to the old self—that is, to the routine of the previous life—withdraws from the reign of the grace of God and surrenders to sin. For we receive mercy for two reasons: so that the reign of the devil may be put to an end and so that the rule of God may be proclaimed to those who are unaware of it. In this way, in fact, we attain our status.

6:2 *How shall we who have died to sin still live in it?* The apostle says this because when we lived for sin we were dead in God's sight.[1] To sin is to live for sin, just as not to sin is to live for God.[2] Therefore, when the grace of God came upon us through Christ and the spiritual bath regenerated us through faith,[3] we began to live for God and to be dead to sin, who is the devil. This, however, is what it means to die to sin: to be freed from slavery to sin, but to become a slave of God. Therefore, let us who have now died to sin not return to the former evil ways, lest we live to sin once again and, dying to God and losing our status,[4] incur the punishment we escaped.

---

1. Instead of this sentence and the next one, *recensio* α has "For before, when we were living to sin, we were dead in God's sight."
2. Instead of this sentence, *recensio* β has "For one who sins lives for sin, just as one who does not sin lives for God."
3. The "spiritual bath" refers to baptism; see the comments that follow at In Rom. 6:3.
4. *Recensio* α does not have "and losing our status."

6:3 *Are you not aware that all of us who have been baptized into Christ Jesus, have been baptized into his death?* The apostle says this so that we may know that we who have been baptized should no longer sin,[5] because when we are baptized, we die together with Christ. This is what it means *to be baptized into his death*. At that point we die to all our sins, so that, having been renewed and having put off death, we may be seen to rise again to life,[6] reborn. Thus, just as Christ, who was dead to sin, has risen,[7] so too through baptism we have the hope of the resurrection. So baptism is the death of sin, leading to another birth. Although the structure of the body remains, this birth renews a person in the mind, now that the old existence with all its evil actions[8] has been buried.

6:4 *We therefore were buried with him through baptism into death so that, just as Christ has risen from the dead through the power of the Father,[9] so we too may walk in the newness of his life.* In saying these things, the apostle also indicates the essential thing that comes first: that Christ raised his body from the dead.[10] For he is the power of God the Father, as he says: *Destroy this temple, and in three days I will raise it up. But he said this*, it says, *about the temple of his body* (John 2:19, 21), and because he has risen to a new life[11] that can die no more. (2) It is called *new* because what constitutes the Christian way of life was given by Christ.[12] We who have been baptized were buried with Christ so that from now on we may follow this life into which Christ has risen. Accordingly, baptism is a pledge and figure of the resurrection, so that now by continuing in the commands of Christ we do not revert once again to our former way of life. For someone who dies sins no longer; death is the end of sin.[13] (3) This, in fact, is why baptism is celebrated with water, that just as water washes away dirt from the

---

5. *Recensio* α has "In saying this, the apostle shows that we are not unaware that we who have not been baptized should no longer sin etc."

6. *Recensio* β has "we may be able to" instead of "we may be seen to."

7. *Recensio* α has "just as Christ who was dead has risen from the dead." At In Rom. 6:4 (§1), Ambrosiaster describes how Christ raised his own body from the dead.

8. *Recensio* α has "the entire old existence with its actions."

9. Ambrosiaster's biblical text differs from the Greek text, which has "glory" (τῆς δόξης) instead of "power" (*virtutem*); see NA[28].

10. *Recensio* α has "The apostle said this to indicate that Christ raised his body from the dead."

11. *Recensio* α has "and because Christ has risen to a new life as well."

12. *Recensio* α has "Now it is new because it was given by Christ."

13. *Recensio* α does not have this sentence.

body,[14] so too we may believe that through baptism we have been spiritually cleansed from every sin and have been renewed.[15] For what is incorporeal is cleansed invisibly.[16]

6:5 *For if we have been planted with him in the likeness of his death, we shall also be planted with him in the likeness of his resurrection.* The apostle says that if we were *planted with him in the likeness of his death* we shall then happily be able to rise from the dead—that is, if, after having cast off all our faults in baptism and having been transplanted into a new life, we do not sin any longer. By this we shall at the same time resemble his resurrection as well, because likeness in death guarantees a like resurrection, as the apostle John reminds us when he says:[17] *We know that when he appears we shall be like him* (1 John 3:2). This means: to rise immortal and glorious from the dead. Moreover, this likeness will not be of the sort that eliminates all difference, because it will be similar in the glory of the body, not in the nature of the divinity.

6:6 *Knowing this, that our old self was crucified on the cross with him so that the body of sin might be destroyed [such that we do not serve sin any longer.* **6:7** *For one who has died is justified from sin].*[18] The apostle ties many points together and repeats them in order to teach the baptized that they should no longer sin—above all, that they should not revert to idolatry, which is a most serious offense and the source of every error[19]—so that they do not lose the grace they received from God through Christ. He therefore calls his previous actions *the old self*, because just as one is called

---

14. *Recensio* α does not have "from the body."
15. *Recensio* α does not have "and have been renewed."
16. *Recensio* α does not have this sentence, a clause in the Latin.
17. Up to this point in the comment *recensio* α has: "The apostle says that if we were planted with him in the likeness of his death we shall then happily be able to rise from the dead—that is, if in baptism we have cast off all our faults, rising renewed, and sin no longer, we shall at the same time resemble his resurrection as well, as the apostle John reminds us in his epistle when he says."
18. Rom 6:6c and 6:7—"such that ... from sin"—is found only in one group of manuscripts of *recensio* α and in MS Paris lat. 1759 of *recensio* γ. The absence of any discussion of this portion of the text in the comment confirms that it was in fact missing from Ambrosiaster's biblical text. On this lacuna, attested by other Latin writers, see Caroline P. Hammond Bammel, *Römerbrieftext des Rufin und seine Origenes Übersetzung*, vol. 10 of *AGLB* (Freiburg: Herder, 1985), 199–200.
19. *Recensio* α does not have "and the source of every error."

a *new self* through Christ and through faith in him, living a pure life,[20] so too one is called an *old self* through doubt and evil actions. The apostle says that these actions were crucified—that is, that they are dead—so that the *body of sin*—which is the entire lot of offenses—*might be destroyed*. For he calls all sins taken together *a body*[21]—a body that, he says, has been destroyed through a good life and a catholic faith.[22]

6:8 *But if we have died with Christ, we believe that we shall also live with him.* (1) It is clear that those who have crucified the flesh—that is, the world—along with its faults and desires die to the world and die together with Christ (see Gal 5:24),[23] and also that they conform to the image of eternal life and of salvation, so that they are worthy of being made to resemble the glory of Christ.[24] But the flesh—that is, the body[25]—is crucified only if its cravings are trampled underfoot. These cravings are produced by the sin that remains in the flesh on account of the initial transgression of the first human being. The devil is crucified in the flesh; it is he who deceives by means of the flesh. (1a)[26] Thus, the flesh is sometimes understood to mean the world—that is, the elements—and sometimes the body of a human being or, more precisely, the soul that pursues corporeal faults.

6:9 *Because we know that Christ in rising from the dead dies no more; death will no longer have dominion over him.* **6:10** *In that he died to sin, he died once for all; in that he lives, he lives to God.* The apostle discloses an assurance of eternity in the resurrection of the Savior.[27] One succeeds in arriving at this assurance[28] if there is an earnest desire for a better life. In

---

20. *Recensiones* α and β have "because just as one is called a *new self* through faith and a pure life." The change in *recensio* γ disrupts the parallelism between "faith and a pure life" and "doubt and evil actions" in *recensiones* α and β (*per fidem et puram vitam*; *per diffidentiam et malos actus*).

21. *Recensio* α does not have "taken together."

22. *Recensio* α has "a body that, he says, was destroyed by the cross of Christ. For on the cross the author of sin, who is the devil, was destroyed."

23. See In Gal. 5:24 (§§1–2).

24. *Recensio* α has "It is clear that those who have crucified their flesh along with its faults and desires conform to the image of eternal life and of salvation, so that they are worthy of being made to resemble the glory of Christ."

25. *Recensio* α does not have "that is, the body."

26. *Recensio* α does not have section 1a.

27. *Recensio* α does not have "of eternity."

28. The preposition *quam* admits of several possible antecedents. I take the antecedent to be *securitas*, which, like *quam*, is present in all three recensions.

fact, a person who lives to God by doing what is right truly does live, for he has eternal life.[29]

6:11 *So you also must consider yourselves to be dead to sin, but to live to God in Christ Jesus our Lord.*[30] The apostle says this to point out that the only way one can die to sin and live to God is to place all one's hope in Christ, whom he calls *our Lord*. Consequently nothing from the law[31] helps to attain salvation in the age to come, inasmuch as it is lived to God only through Christ.

6:12 *Therefore, do not let sin reign in your mortal body such that you obey it.*[32] (1) The body is mortal as a result of Adam's transgression, but as a result of faith in Christ one believes that it will be immortal. However, in order to arrive at this promise, the apostle says that one must not obey sin, so that sin may not reign in our mortal body.[33] Sin reigns when it commands.[34] If it does not reign, this body will not seem to be mortal, because it abides in the hope of eternal life. The apostle said that the body is mortal not because of its decomposition but because of the punishment of gehenna; one who is to be sent to gehenna is said to be mortal because those who obey sin do not escape the second death,[35] the death from which the Savior released those who believe in him.[36] (1a)[37] Thus, in saying that the body is mortal, the apostle meant the whole person, since those who obey sin are said to be mortal. *For the soul*, scripture says, *that sins shall die* (Ezek 18:4), that is, the whole person. For no one will be judged apart from the body.

---

29. *Recensio* α does not have this sentence.
30. The addition of "our Lord" is attested by many Greek and Latin witnesses, including Ambrosiaster, but the better witnesses omit it. See Bruce M. Metzger, *A Textual Commentary on the Greek New Testament*, 2nd ed. (Stuttgart: Deutsche Bibelgesellschaft, 1994), 453–54; and Robert Jewett with Roy D. Kotansky, *Romans: A Commentary*, Hermeneia (Minneapolis: Fortress, 2007), 391.
31. *Recensio* α has "no law" instead of "nothing from the law."
32. Among biblical witnesses there is stronger support for "its desires" (ταῖς ἐπιθυμίαις αὐτοῦ) instead of "it" (*illi*), as found in Ambrosiaster's biblical text. See Metzger, *Textual Commentary*, 454; and Jewett, *Romans*, 391.
33. *Recensio* α has "it may not reign," lacking the explicit subject "sin."
34. *Recensiones* α and β do not have this sentence.
35. Instead of "the second death," *recensio* α has "the death of sin," and *recensio* β has "the death of the underworld."
36. For Ambrosiaster's understanding of death, see the introduction §5.4.
37. *Recensio* α does not have section 1a.

6:13 *Also, do not present your members to sin as weapons of wickedness.* (1) The apostle explains that the devil attacks us with our own darts. For through our sins the occasion presents itself for him to sport with us and to put us to death, since God has forsaken us and the devil has assumed power. We should therefore restrain our members from every wicked deed, so that our enemy, found to be without weapons, may be subdued. Furthermore, the apostle did not say *do not present your body*, but *your members*. One is led astray by the subservient members, insofar as sins direct them,[38] not by the whole body.

But present yourselves to God as those who are alive from the dead. (2) The apostle indicates that death is ignorance and unfaithfulness along with an evil life, since life is to know God through Christ (see John 17:3). (2a)[39] Now, since no one enters life without a progenitor and all things have arisen from God into life through Christ, someone who does not acknowledge that God is the progenitor of all things through Christ is said not to have life;[40] that is, it is as if he does not exist. For he himself denies that he exists when he believes that he exists without God as progenitor. (3) Thus, ignorance and a shameful life are death. Such faults result in death, not the death that is common to all, but the death of gehenna, as I have discussed above.[41] Consequently, a knowledge of God as progenitor[42] and a holy way of life is life, not this life that is subject to death, but that life of the age to come, the life that is called eternal.[43] This is why the apostle says *present yourselves to God*, since in acknowledging him you have progressed toward salvation,[44] so that, having renounced a base life, you might be *those who are alive from the dead*.

And your members as weapons of righteousness for God. (4) The apostle wants us to conduct our lives with such decency that in performing our actions for the righteousness of God and not the righteousness of the world—because the righteousness of this world lacks faith in Christ, with-

---

38. *Recensiones* α and β do not have "insofar as sins direct them."

39. *Recensio* α does not have section 2a.

40. Ambrosiaster is referring to Christ's role in the work of creation. See, e.g., In Rom. 8:39 (§3); 14:9 (§1); and 16:16 (§2).

41. See In Rom. 6:12 (§1).

42. *Recensio* α does not have "as progenitor."

43. *Recensio* α has "but that eternal life of the age to come" instead of "but that life of the age to come, the life that is called eternal."

44. *Recensio* α has "whom you have acknowledged unto salvation" instead of "since in acknowledging him you have progressed toward salvation."

out which there is not life but death—we may supply him with the weapons to defend us. When we supply him with weapons through good works, we render ourselves worthy of his help, because the righteousness of God[45] shuns those who are unworthy. For where the righteousness of God is present, there dwells the Holy Spirit, to help our weakness. Just as we supply arms for sin when we behave in an evil way, so too we supply arms for righteousness when we occupy ourselves in the right way, preserving our members from all shameful behavior.

6:14 *Sin will no longer have dominion over you; you are not under the law, but under grace.* (1) If we walk in accordance with the commands he gives, the apostle says that sin cannot have dominion over us; it has dominion over those who sin.[46] When we do not walk as he commands, we are *under the law*. If, in fact, we do not sin, we are not under the law, but *under grace*. But if we sin, we place ourselves under the law, and sin begins to have dominion over us, because every sinner *is a slave to sin* (John 8:34).[47] (1a)[48] As long as a sinner does not receive a pardon, he must necessarily be under the law; sin renders the sinner guilty by the authority of the law. Thus, when someone is pardoned and takes care not to sin in future, sin will not have dominion over him, nor is he under the law; the authority of the law ceases to affect him because he has been set free from sin. For those whom the law detains as guilty are handed over to it by sin. Therefore, one who has been delivered from sin cannot be under the law.

6:15 *What then? Have we sinned because we are not under the law but under grace?*[49] *By no means!* (1) Because the law is from God, the apostle thus puts the question to himself (in case someone might object): "If the law is from God," he says,[50] "why should we not be under the law?" He removes[51] this objection and explains that we have been set free from the law by Christ in accordance with the will of God, who is the author of the law. (2) Although the law was given for good reason—it was given

---

45. *Recensio* α does not have "of God."
46. *Recensio* α does not have "it has dominion over those who sin."
47. *Recensiones* α and β have "because *one who commits sin is a slave to sin.*"
48. *Recensio* α does not have section 1a.
49. Ambrosiaster's biblical text has the perfect "have we sinned" (*peccavimus*), but among the biblical witnesses there is stronger support for the aorist subjunctive "are we to sin" (ἁμαρτήσωμεν). See Jewett, *Romans*, 413.
50. *Recensio* α has "If the law exists etc."
51. *Recensiones* α and β have "he acknowledges" instead of "he removes."

both to show that those who sinned prior to the law were guilty before God and so that one would be afraid to sin in future—the human race was nevertheless condemned to the death of the underworld because through its own frail weakness it could not keep itself from sinning. But God, being moved by the mercy of his kindness by which he always comes to the aid of the human race, provided through Christ the means whereby a remedy might now be given to those who were beyond hope. He did so in order that they, having received forgiveness of sins, having been rescued from the law which held them liable, and having been lifted up and restored with God's help,[52] might fight[53] against the faults by which they had previously been ruled. For this reason we have not sinned, scorning, so to speak, the law of God, but we have followed the providence of God himself through Christ.

6:16 *Do you not know that if you present yourselves to any one as obedient slaves, you are the slaves of the one whom you obey, either of sin[54] or of obedience, unto righteousness?* Now, so that we would not say one thing and do another, and be found to be slaves of the devil in our deeds although we are called slaves of God, the apostle warns and declares that we are slaves of the one whose will we fulfill in our works,[55] and that it does great harm to confess God to be Lord and to be among the slaves of the devil in one's actions. Indeed, long ago God pointed this out and made the accusation, when he said: *This people honors me with their lips, but their heart is far from me* (Isa 29:13). Likewise, in the gospel[56] the Lord says: *No one can serve two masters* (Matt 6:24). And in the law it is said: *God is not mocked* (Gal 6:7).[57]

6:17 *But thanks be to God, that although you were slaves of sin, you have obeyed from the heart the form of teaching to which you were entrusted,* **6:18** *because when you believed in Christ you were made slaves of righteous-*

---

52. *Recensio* α adds "through faith."
53. *Recensio* α has "renounce" instead of "fight."
54. The omission of "unto death" after "sin" in Ambrosiaster's biblical text appears to be accidental; among the biblical witnesses there is strong support for its inclusion (ἁμαρτίας εἰς θάνατον). See Metzger, *Textual Commentary*, 454; and Jewett, *Romans*, 413.
55. *Recensio* α has "follow" instead of "fulfill."
56. *Recensio* α does not have "in the gospel."
57. Ambrosiaster's ascription of this quotation from Galatians to "the law" is puzzling.

*ness.*⁵⁸ (1) We are called the slaves of the one we obey. Moreover, because it is right to obey Christ—for he is righteousness and the things he commands are right—the apostle says that we have become slaves of righteousness from the heart and not as a result of the law, of our own will and not out of fear, so that our profession is conveyed by the conviction of the soul.⁵⁹ For we were led to faith through nature, not through the law; we were made in this *form of teaching* by the command of God who fashioned nature.⁶⁰ (2) For by nature we have the ability to recognize from whom and by whom and in whom we have been created (see Rom 11:36). Therefore, *the form of teaching* is that which the creator conveyed to us naturally.⁶¹ This is what the apostle said above: *They are a law unto themselves* (Rom 2:14) when they see that it is part of their nature to believe. Consequently, what the law and the prophets prophesied to the Jews about Christ, the gentiles trust *from the heart.* Hence the apostle gives thanks to the Lord that although we were slaves of sin we obeyed from the heart when we believed in Christ, so that we might serve God not through the law of Moses but through the law of nature.

6:19 *I am speaking in human terms on account of the weakness of your flesh.* (1) When the apostle recalls the weakness of the flesh, he indicates that he requires less of a human being than is appropriate when honoring God. Consequently,⁶² he says:

Just as you presented your members to serve impurity and wickedness upon wickedness, so now present your members to serve righteousness unto

---

58. Ambrosiaster's text of verse 18a—"when you believed in Christ" (*credentes in Christum*), which recurs at the end of his comment—is not attested by other witnesses to the VL, which have "when you were freed from sin" (*liberati autem a peccato*), which corresponds to the Greek text (ἐλευθερωθέντες δὲ ἀπὸ τῆς ἁμαρτίας). Ambrosiaster appears to echo the latter, however, at In Rom. 4:16 (§2): *quia filii dei liberati sunt a peccato.*

59. In *recensio* α the sentence ends with "as a result of the law." The following phrase, "of our own will and not out of fear," is found only in *recensio* γ. The last clause, "so that our profession is conveyed by the conviction of the soul," is found in *recensiones* β and γ.

60. *Recensio* α has "Nature made us in this form of teaching."

61. *Recensio* α has "which the creator of nature conveyed to us" instead of "which the creator conveyed to us naturally."

62. *Recensio* α does not have "consequently."

sanctification.[63] (2a)[64] In order to deprive us of a pretext for fearing to approach the faith (since it might seem to us to be, as it were, unbearable and harsh), the apostle commands us to serve God to the same degree that we previously were slaves to the devil. (2) Although one should surely be more disposed to serve God than the devil—especially since in the one instance salvation is achieved, but in the other, condemnation—nevertheless, the spiritual physician has not required more of us, lest we, having weighed our weakness and fled the commands as being too heavy, might remain in death.[65] For this reason the Lord says: *Take my yoke upon you, for it is pleasant, and my burden is light* (Matt 11:29–30).[66]

6:20 *When you were slaves of sin, you were free from righteousness.* **6:21** *But then what fruit did you get from the things of which you are now ashamed? For the end of those things is death.* (1) It is obvious that someone who is free from God is a slave of sin. When one sins, one draws away from God and is placed under sin. What sorts of fruit, then, issue from sin? When we come to learn a good way of life, we are dismayed by these fruit, that formerly we lived so shamefully. (1a)[67] Not only this, because even the way of thinking of the pagans is shameful and disgusting, especially the way of thinking that is found in Phrygia, where unless a sordid character participates,[68] the mystery is mute and the ritual listless. (2) Here is a freedom covered with stains and given over to filth, whose work has a shameful recompense, whose culmination is death.[69] The apostle

---

63. Ambrosiaster's biblical text has the infinitive "to serve" (*servire*), but among the biblical witnesses there is stronger support for the adjective "enslaved to" (δοῦλα). See Jewett, *Romans*, 413.

64. *Recensio* α does not have section 2a.

65. *Recensio* α has "lest perhaps it might be too heavy for us and a pretext might be given us for fearing to come to the faith."

66. *Recensio* α does not have this sentence.

67. *Recensio* α does not have section 1a.

68. Ambrosiaster probably refers here to the *galli*, castrated devotees of the Great Mother or Cybele, who dressed in feminine garments and had long hair; see Robert Turcan, *The Cults of Roman Empire*, trans. Antonia Nevill (Oxford: Blackwell, 1996), 28–74, esp. 43–49. The cult was still active in Rome in the fourth century. Effeminate priests of pagan cults are a frequent object of Ambrosiaster's invective; see Ambrosiaster, *Quaest.* 114.7–8, 11 (SC 512:122–25, 128–31), 115.18 (SC 512:170–73); Emanuele Di Santo, *L'Apologetica dell'Ambrosiaster: Cristiani, pagani e giudei nella Roma tardoantica*, SEAug 112 (Rome: Institutum Patristicum Augustinianum, 2008), 135–37.

69. *Recensio* α has "Here is a freedom that is stained and bound up in shame, whose work has its recompense, whose end is death." *Recensio* β has "Here is a freedom

called the conclusion of life and of activity, which is followed by either death or life, *the end*. But in this instance death is twofold: one is conveyed from death to death.[70]

6:22 *But now that you have been set free from sin and have become slaves of God, you have your fruit in sanctification, and indeed eternal life as the end.* That is, if after having received forgiveness of sins you excel in good works, you acquire holiness, but the end—that is, the conclusion—that you will have is unending life. For by this death which the apostle called *the end* we pass into life which is without end.

6:23 *For the wages of sin is death.* (1) The apostle called what is gained from sin *death* because death comes through sin. Thus, those who refrain from sins in future will receive the recompense of eternal life; those who do not sin are strangers to the second death.

But the grace of God is eternal life in Christ Jesus our Lord. (2) Just as those who follow sin acquire death, so too those who follow the grace of God—that is, faith in Christ—which forgives sins will have eternal life. Consequently, they rejoice that they are released[71] for a certain time, since they know that they will arrive at that life that is free of all weariness and does not involve change. Longing for this life, the holy Simeon asks to be released here so that he may go forth in peace (see Luke 2:29),[72] that is, into the life that suffers no disturbance. Furthermore, the apostle bears witness that this gift is given to us by God through Christ our Lord, so that we may give thanks to God our Father through none else but his Son.

---

covered with stains and bound up in filth, whose work has its shameful recompense, whose end is death."

70. *Recensio* α has "But for him the end is death; he passes from death to death."

71. The word *dissolvi* also appears in Ambrosiaster's text of Phil 1:23, where it refers to physical death. According to Ambrosiaster, when the body dies, the soul is released; see In Rom. 5:12 (§3) and 7:5 (§2).

72. *Recensio* α has "which he calls peace" instead of "so that he may go forth in peace."

Romans 7

7:1 *Or do you not know, brothers—for I am speaking to those who know the law.* (1) To confirm their minds in divine teaching, the apostle uses the example of human law, so that once again he may convince them of heavenly things by means of earthly ones,[1] just as God, too, is known by the creation of the world (see Rom 1:20). Since everything belongs to a single whole, even though things are diverse, they still resemble each other in some respect. Because the Romans are not barbarians, they know about the law. But they grasped natural justice partly by themselves, partly from the Greeks, and partly from the Hebrews.[2] Although the law was not hidden prior to Moses, it was nevertheless without arrangement and authority.[3] For the arrangement of the law was conveyed to the Romans from Athens.[4] To those, therefore, who are knowledgeable about the law, the apostle says:

That the law governs a person as long as he is alive? (2) It is no secret that a person's entire life is under the law of nature, which was given to the world.[5] This law is general. In this passage, however, the apostle is referring to another, particular form of law—though it too is general, it is considered particular since it is not received by everyone[6]—by means of which

---

1. *Recensiones* α and β do not have "once again."
2. *Recensiones* α and β have "just as the Greeks grasped it from the Hebrews" instead of "partly from the Hebrews."
3. *Recensio* α does not have this sentence.
4. *Recensiones* α and β have "For the laws were brought [β: conveyed] to the Romans from Athens." Ambrosiaster accepts the tradition, recounted in Livy, *Ab. urbe cond.* 3.31.8, that the ten men (*decemviri*) commissioned to prepare the Law of the Twelve Tables sent an embassy to Athens to study the laws of Solon; see Ambrosiaster, *Quaest. app.* 75.2 (CSEL 50:468). See Othmar Heggelbacher, *Vom römischen zum christlichen Recht: Juristische Elemente in den Schriften des sogenannten Ambrosiaster*, AJSUFS 19 (Freiburg: Universitätsverlag, 1959), 47 n. 7.
5. *Recensio* α does not have "which was given to the world."
6. *Recensio* α does not have this parenthetical comment.

he wants to prove his point. He wants to convey the truth bit by bit. He therefore says:

7:2 *Now a woman who is under a man is bound by the law of her husband as long as he lives. But if her husband dies, she is released from the law of the husband.*[7] **7:3** *Accordingly, she will be called an adulteress if she is joined with another man while her husband is alive.* (1) This law is from the gospel, not from Moses, nor from earthly justice. Learning some things, therefore, from the guidance of nature and some things from the law of Moses, the Romans were made perfect through the gospel of Christ. With the example that follows,[8] then, the apostle explains more clearly that Christianity has been released from the law of deeds—not all law—and that from now on there is no advantage to being under the law. He does so lest one nullify the grace of God by having reverted to being under the law, since the grace of God has set humankind free from the law in order to serve God in spirit, that is, with the mind. (2) For just as a woman is freed from the law of her husband when he is dead, not from the law of nature, so too will they by the grace of God be freed from the law which held them guilty. It is therefore dead for them, and consequently they are not adulterers in being joined with Christianity. For if the law lives among them, they are adulterers, and it will profit them nothing to be called Christians, since they will be subject to punishment. Someone who was joined to the gospel once the law was dead and then afterward returns to the law will be an adulterer not of the law but of the gospel; the law is said to be dead when its authority expires.[9]

But if her husband dies, she is freed from the law, and is not an adulteress if she is joined with another man. (3) Those who have been released from the law when they received forgiveness of sins and have been joined with the gospel, are not adulterers of the law, because the law is dead for them. But if they think that they can enter upon the gospel while keeping the law,

---

7. The phrase "of the husband" (*viri*) is attested by only a few witnesses, the Vulgate among them; see NA[28] and Robert Jewett with Roy D. Kotansky, *Romans: A Commentary*, Hermeneia (Minneapolis: Fortress, 2007), 428. The variant is echoed in Ambrosiaster's comment in section 2 below but omitted when the lemma is repeated before section 3.

8. See section 2 of the comment.

9. *Recensio* α has "the law is said to be dead when the accused it detained is excused." *Recensio* β has "the law is said to be dead when the authority of the law expires."

they will be guilty of adultery, because they will join themselves to faith while the law is alive, and they will be adulterers against both.

7:4 *Likewise, my brothers, you too have become dead to the law through the body of Christ.* (1)[10] Because the Savior allowed the devil to crucify his body, knowing that it was for our benefit against him,[11] the apostle says that we were saved *through the body of Christ*. To die to the law is to live to God, because the law rules over sinners. Therefore, one whose sins are forgiven dies to the law; this is what it means to be freed from the law. So we receive this benefit through the body of Christ. By surrendering his body, the Savior conquered death and condemned sin. The devil sinned against him when he killed him—he who was innocent and who knew no sin whatsoever. (2) When the devil prosecuted the man on account of sin, he was found to be liable to the one he was accusing.[12] Thus it was accomplished that all who believe in Christ are released from the law by the condemnation of sin,[13] because once sin—that is, the devil—is vanquished through the body of Christ it does not have authority over those who belong to Christ, by whom the devil was vanquished.[14] (3) In not sinning and in being put to death as a guilty man, Christ conquered sin from sin; that is, he condemned the devil by the devil's own sin, which the devil perpetrated against him, and erased the written bond that had been decreed on account of Adam's sin.[15] Christ did this when he arose from the underworld, having granted a similar form of existence to those who believe in him so that they could not be held by the second death. This is how we are dead to the law *through the body of Christ*. For one who has not died to the law is guilty, and one who is guilty cannot escape the second death.

---

10. Ambrosiaster's comments in sections 1–3 draw on his understanding of Christ's conquest over the devil. See the introduction §5.4.

11. I.e., against the devil.

12. Under limited conditions in Roman law in the late imperial period, the plaintiff in a lawsuit could be required to make reparations to the defendant if the suit was not successful. See Cod. Justin. 7.45.14 (*Codex Iustinianus*, ed. Paul Krueger, vol. 2 of *Corpus juris civilis* [Berlin: Weidmann, 1892], 684), citing second-century jurist Papinianus; George Mousourakis, *Fundamentals of Roman Private Law* (Berlin: Springer, 2012), 339–40.

13. *Recensiones* α and β have "by the elimination of sin" instead of "by the condemnation of sin."

14. *Recensio* α has "because through the body of Christ sin, who is the devil, does not have authority over those who belong to Christ, by whom the devil was vanquished."

15. See In Rom. 5:12 (§4) and In Col. 2:13–15 (§§3–6).

So that you may belong to another, who has risen from the dead in order that we may bear fruit for God. (4) The apostle says this because we have died to the law so that from now on we may be slaves of Christ alone, and this is what it will mean to bear fruit for God. For one who remains in God's grace, worthy of the promised resurrection, is secured for God.

7:5 *While we were in the flesh.* (1) Although the apostle is in the flesh, he denies that he is in the flesh—he is, in fact, in a body[16]—because a person who pursues anything that is prohibited by the law is said to be *in the flesh*. The phrase *to be in the flesh* is, therefore, understood in several different ways.[17] For instance, every unbeliever is in the flesh, that is, fleshly, and a Christian who lives under the law is in the flesh, and someone who hopes for anything from humankind is in the flesh, and someone who misconstrues Christ is in the flesh,[18] and any Christian who lives a debauched life is in the flesh. (2) Nevertheless, in this passage we should understand *to be in the flesh* to mean that we were in the flesh before coming to faith;[19] we lived under the flesh,[20] that is, in following our fleshly senses we were subject to faults and sins. The sense of the flesh is not to believe spiritual realities, namely, that a virgin gave birth without relations with a man,[21] and that a person is born anew of water and the Spirit, and that a soul, having been released from its coupling with the flesh,[22] rises again in it. One who doubts these things is in the flesh. Hence he says:

The faults of sins, which were exposed through the law, were at work in our members to bear fruit for death. (3) It is clear that someone who does not believe operates under sin and, being captive, is drawn into committing faults, so that he bears the fruit of the second death. Indeed, when someone sins, death profits. Nevertheless, the apostle says that faults were at work *in the members*, not in the body, so that there might be no pretext for those who vilify the body, since in the event of slander the tongue is censured and in the event of theft the hand is blamed and in the event of dissembling

---

16. *Recensio* α has "One who is in the flesh denies that he is in the flesh, because etc."
17. *Recensio* α has "To say *in the flesh* is understood in several different ways."
18. *Recensio* α does not have "and someone who misconstrues Christ is in the flesh."
19. *Recensio* α has "to mean that we who before coming to faith were acting under the law were in the flesh" instead of "to mean that we were in the flesh before coming to faith."
20. *Recensio* α has "under sin" instead of "under the flesh."
21. *Recensio* α has "without union" instead of "without relations with a man."
22. *Recensio* α has "bond of the flesh" instead of "coupling with the flesh."

the ears may be reproached and so on for the other members. Although these things issue from the heart (see Matt 15:18–19), they nevertheless are carried out in actions through the service of the members.[23] (4) This argument has to do with the Jews and those who are called Christians and desire to live under the law,[24] so that those who are learning that they are fleshly might withdraw from the law. However, the apostle points out that *the faults of sins*, which he says rule in those who live according to the flesh, are *revealed through the law*, but do not come about through the law. When the law renders sinners guilty, it is the indicator of sin, not its source.[25]

7:6 *But now we have been released from the law of death, by which we were held captive.*[26] (1) We were released from the law when we received forgiveness of sins. It no longer has power over us;[27] it rules over unbelievers and sinners. It is called *the law of death* because it punishes the guilty, for it puts sinners to death. Therefore, it is not evil, but just. (1a)[28] However much what is inflicted by the law may be evil for those who suffer it, the law itself is not evil, since it justly inflicts wrath. Thus, the law is not evil for sinners, but just. (2) For the good, in fact, it is spiritual. Who doubts that it is spiritual to forbid sinning? But because the law was not able to save people by forgiving sins, the law of faith was given, which freed believers from the power of the law so that they, whom the law held unto death,[29] may be able to restore themselves unto life. The law was the law of death for those in whom it brought about wrath on account of sin.[30]

So that we serve in the newness of spirit and not in the oldness of the letter. (3) With these words[31] the apostle seems to allude to the law, which indeed he ranks lower compared to the law of faith, though he does not judge it to be opposed to the law of faith. The reason, in fact, that he says that we were rescued from the law of death to serve the law of faith, which

---

23. *Recensio* α has "they nevertheless come about through the service of the members."
24. *Recensio* α has "are Christians" instead of "are called Christians."
25. *Recensio* α does not have "not its source."
26. Ambrosiaster's biblical text differs from the majority of biblical witnesses, which have "law, dying to that by which we were held captive" (ἀποθανόντες ἐν ᾧ κατειχόμεθα). See Jewett, *Romans*, 428.
27. *Recensions* α and β have "does not have" instead of "no longer has."
28. *Recensio* α does not have section 1a.
29. *Recensiones* α and β have "guilty of death" instead of "into death."
30. *Recensio* α does not have "on account of sin."
31. I.e., "the oldness of the letter."

granted us the saving help that the old law was unable to grant,[32] is so that we do not appear to nullify the benefit of grace by keeping the old law. (4) The phrase *the old law* is certainly[33] not a term of reproach, but rather of time or age; it grew old because it came to an end (see Heb 8:13). Now, the law of the spirit is also the law of faith, because faith abides in the spirit and is not learned through actions but is believed with the heart. The mind, too, understands that it is in its nature to believe what is not seen by the eyes or felt by the hands, and that the gifts for which it hopes are not visible or earthly, but spiritual. Thus, the old law was composed in tablets of stone, whereas the law of the spirit was written spiritually on tablets of the heart, so that it may be eternal while the letters of the old law are destroyed by age. (5) There also is another interpretation of the law of the spirit: previously the law deterred from evil action, but since it says that one should not sin against it in the heart (see Matt 15:18–19), it is called the law of the spirit, so that it may make the entire person spiritual.

7:7 *What then shall we say? That the law is sin? By no means!* (1) In case one thought the apostle declared this law to be wicked—since he has called it *the law of death* (see Rom 7:6) and rejoices that we had been rescued from it and maintains that one does not serve God in it—he dispels this notion when he says: *By no means!*

But I did not recognize sin except through the law. (2) The apostle explains that the law is not sin, but is an indicator of sin. It pointed out sins that were concealed, and pointed out that they would not go unpunished before God.[34] Once this is detected, a person is found guilty and is therefore disinclined to give thanks for the law. For who readily welcomes someone who announces that punishment is soon to descend upon him?[35] But one gives thanks for the law of faith because a person who was found guilty through the law of Moses is reconciled to God through the law of faith. Even though the law of Moses is also just and good—for, indeed, it is good to point out imminent danger—one nevertheless gives greater thanks for the law of faith, through which, having been rescued from danger, one lives.

---

32. *Recensio* α does not have "saving."
33. *Recensio* α does not have "certainly."
34. *Recensiones* α and β have "Therefore, the law is not sin, but an indicator of sin. It shows that sins would not go unpunished before God."
35. *Recensio* α does not have this sentence.

For example, I should not have known covetousness if the law had not said: "You shall not covet" (Exod 20:17). (3) The apostle did not differentiate this covetousness from sin. This remark is, however, surprising, since although there was in fact no notion that such a thing was not permitted by God, he says, "I knew that it was sin."[36] By pretending to speak about himself,[37] the apostle is making a general point. So the law forbids covetousness, which was not considered sin because its object was pleasing. It seemed to be an innocent matter to desire something belonging to a neighbor.[38] This the law revealed to be sin. Truly, to worldly people nothing seems so harmless and soothing as pleasure.[39]

7:8 *Thus, once it gained opportunity through the commandment, sin worked in me every kind of covetousness.* (1) When the apostle says *every kind of covetousness*, he means all sins together. In the previous verse he is speaking about covetousness according to the law. Adding the rest of the faults to it now, he has said that *every kind of covetousness* worked in humankind at the devil's instigation,[40] to whom he refers with the word *sin*, so that the law, which had been given for beneficial ends, turned out to be against humankind. (2) When the devil saw the help that was provided to humankind through the law—whom the devil rejoiced to have in a state of subjection as much on account of Adam's sin as on account of its own sin[41]—he understood that it was directed against him. Once he saw humankind placed under the law, he knew for sure that it had been removed from his dominion; humankind had recognized how to escape the punishment of the underworld. This is why he burned with rage against humankind to the point that he turned the law against it, so that humankind, by committing things that were forbidden, offended God once again and fell anew into the power of the devil. The devil began not to command

---

36. *Recensio* α has "since although there was no notion that covetousness was not permitted by God, he knew that it was sin."

37. *Recensio* α has "by speaking about himself."

38. *Recensio* β has "when something belonging to a neighbor is desired" instead of "to desire something belonging to a neighbor."

39. *Recensio* α does not have "and soothing."

40. Since *homo* refers to people in general, not a specific person, I render it as "humankind."

41. *Recensio* α has "whom the devil rejoiced to have in his state of subjection on account of Adam's sin." On the additional mention of personal sin in *recensiones* β and γ, see In Rom. 5:12 (§§3–4), and Juan B. Valero, "Pecar en Adán según Ambrosiaster," *EE* 65 (1990): 164–74, esp. 173.

but skillfully to deceive, because once the law had been given the devil lost his dominion, for he knew that from then on humankind belonged to God's jurisdiction.[42]

Without the law sin was dead.[43] (3) This verse should be understood in two ways, so that you realize that the word *sin* means both the devil and the sin itself that is commonly called *sin*. The devil is said *to have died* because prior to the law he was not in such a fury to deceive humankind and was, as it were, quiet, confident in the fact that he held sway over it.[44] Sin *was dead* because people believed that it would not be reckoned in God's sight. Thus, it was dead among humankind; one sinned, as it were, with impunity. In fact, sin was not hidden, as I have said above, but one was unaware that God would come in judgment.[45] When the law was given, it is obvious that sin came back to life. Why has it come back to life, if not for the fact that previously it had been alive and afterward was thought to be dead because of the stupor of humankind, although it was alive? Sin was believed not to be reckoned even though it was reckoned. Therefore, while it was alive, it was held to be dead.

7:9 *I indeed once lived without the law.* (1) What does it mean to have lived *without the law*—since, as I have often explained, the law has always existed—if not that humankind lived without the fear of God,[46] confident that there was no God who would judge human acts.

But when the commandment came, sin revived. (1a)[47] The apostle has said *sin revived* to indicate that previously it had been alive but then was deemed to be dead through the stupor of humankind, even though it was alive, just as a false rumor is apt to be created about foreigners, rather than a

---

42. This sentence, found in *recensiones* α and β, is attested only by MS Paris lat. 1759 in *recensio* γ.

43. Ambrosiaster's biblical text differs from the majority of witnesses, which have the implicit present tense of the verb "to be" in the phrase "the law is dead" (ἁμαρτία νεκρά) instead of the explicit past tense "was" (*erat*). See Jewett, *Romans*, 440.

44. *Recensio* α has "The devil is said to have died because he ceased to deceive humankind, since he was confident of holding sway over it." *Recensio* β agrees with *recensio* γ, except it has "confident of holding sway over it" instead of "confident in the fact that he held sway over it."

45. *Recensio* α has "but it was hidden because one believed that God would not come in judgment."

46. *Recensio* α has "one lived" instead of "humankind lived."

47. *Recensio* α does not have section 1a.

true one.[48] This means, therefore, that in the beginning it was apparent that sin would be reckoned in God's sight; that is, sin lived. But when the habit of sinning had obliterated this awareness, sin was deemed to be dead, so that the offense was believed to expire with the person. (2) But when the law was given or reestablished, sin was revived among those who had deemed it to be dead; they began to understand that sin was reckoned.[49]

7:10 *But I died.* (1) Humankind died because it saw that it was guilty before God—humankind who previously believed that it would not be liable for the sins which it committed.

And I found that the commandment that had been given to bring life resulted in death. (2) It is true that the law *had been given to bring life*, but when it rendered guilty humankind who sinned not only before but also after the giving of the law, the law that had been given to bring life was made to result in death. However, as I have said, it did so only for the sinner, since it leads the obedient to life.[50]

7:11 *For once it gained opportunity through the commandment, sin led me astray and killed me by it.* (1) In this verse understand *sin* to mean the devil, who is the author of sin. He found an opportunity through the law,[51] how he might satiate his cruelty from the death of humankind.[52] Thus, when at his instigation humankind continually committed transgressions, to God's displeasure, it incurred the punishment of the law, since the law was a warning for sinners. As a result, humankind was condemned by the very law which had been given to benefit it. (1a)[53] Because the law was given against the will of the devil, he was consumed with jealousy against humankind and sought to defile it even more with corrupt pleasures so that it might not escape his grasp.

7:12 *So the law is indeed holy and the commandment is holy and just and good.* In order to remove any insinuation of wrong against the law, the apostle praises it to the point of declaring it to be not only just but also holy and good. In fact, the language of the gospel testifies that *commandment* is

---

48. *Recensio* β does not have "rather than a true one."
49. In section 2 *recensio* α has "Sin, which had been dead, was revived. This is what *revived* means: that it began to be understood that it was reckoned."
50. *Recensio* α has "However, it did so only for the sinner, since there were people to whom it had been given for life and led to life."
51. *Recensio* α has "humankind" instead of "an opportunity."
52. *Recensio* α has "craving" instead of "cruelty."
53. *Recensio* α does not have section 1a.

understood to mean *the law*. For it says, *If you desire to come into life, keep the commandments* (Matt 19:17).

7:13 *Did that which is good, then, become death for me? By no means!* (1) Absolutely not! For how is it possible that something judged to be good be understood to mean *death*?

But sin, in order that it might be shown to be sin, worked death for me through what is good. (2) The apostle says that the devil took the opportunity to work evil for humankind through what is good, when he led it astray into death. Before the law was given, people, lured by desire, did evil things. The law was set out clearly in writing so that such things might be shown to be sins and might be avoided in future.[54] So Satan was enraged *through what is* undoubtedly *good*. Since he saw that the law was made available to humankind, he suggested unlawful things to it so that death rather than life would come to it from the law.[55] This should, in fact, be attributed to human carelessness,[56] which so enfeebled the vigor of its nature by the craving for sinning that it was not able to suppress the devil's suggestions.[57] But the enemy—whom the apostle refers to as *sin* so that he may be shown to be the enemy—took the opportunity afforded by the law to work death for humankind.[58] When the devil entices humankind to do unlawful things, he is shown to be the enemy. (2a)[59] Even though he brought about death for humankind prior to the law as well, with the exception of the first instance of Adam, nevertheless after the law he devised greater penalties for humankind in the underworld, where the second death takes place. For it is less of a crime to have sinned before the law has been revealed than after it has been revealed.

So that sin itself became sinful beyond measure through the commandment. (3) What does *beyond measure* mean? It would seem to suggest that

---

54. *Recensio* α has "things that were done prior to the law might be shown" instead of "things that were done wrongly prior to the law as a result of the lure of desire."

55. *Recensio* α has "Then Satan was enraged *through what is good*, because he saw that the law was made available to humankind; he suggested unlawful things to humankind, so that death rather than life would come to it from the law." *Recensio* β has "Then Satan was enraged *through what is* undoubtedly *good*. He saw that it was made available to humankind and he suggested unlawful things to it, so that death rather than life would come to it from the law."

56. *Recensio* α has "Therefore, this should be attributed to human wickedness."

57. *Recensio* α has "by sinning" instead of "by the craving for sinning."

58. *Recensio* α has "the good law" instead of "the law."

59. *Recensio* α does not have section 2a.

there is a measure for transgressions even though it is not permissible to sin. (3a)[60] But the words are God's, who says, *The sins of the Amorites are not complete* (Gen 15:16). By this God shows that there is a certain measure for transgressions. Once sinners have filled it up, they are judged to be utterly unworthy of life, as, for example, Pharaoh was. Because he filled up this measure, the wonders and signs of God were displayed against him. On account of these wonders and signs, the rest of the people, terrified, applied themselves to gaining life, so that in death one came to know life. (4)[61] But there is another measure that the apostle is discussing. To show that there was more sin after the law than there had been before it, he indicates that a larger measure of sin over and above this earlier measure had arisen through the jealousy and craftiness of Satan. As a result, the providence of God turned against humankind, since it should not have sinned at all for fear of the law. (5) For this reason, in order to overcome the jealousy of the devil and secure his own providence for humankind, God changed the arrangement. God sent the savior Christ who overpowered the devil and set humankind free.[62]

7:14 *We know in fact that the law is spiritual. But I am fleshly.*[63] (1) Because he is speaking to people who know the law, he says: *We know that the law is spiritual.* They would not subject themselves to the law if they did not acknowledge it to be spiritual.[64] (1a)[65] He thus calls the law of Moses, which was given on tablets, *spiritual.* Since it forbids sinning, it is spiritual, particularly as it forbids worshiping visible and fleshly things. These statements serve to commend the law, lest perhaps the law should be considered blameworthy by anyone for having proceeded with severity against sinners. But the apostle calls humankind *fleshly* when it sins.

---

60. *Recensio* α does not have section 3a.

61. For section 4 *recensio* α has "But *beyond measure* means that the devil induced humankind to sin more after the law was given than it had avoided doing before, so that the providence [of God] turned against humankind, since it should not have sinned at all for fear of the law."

62. *Recensiones* α and β have "and establish God's resolution with regard to humankind" instead of "and set humankind free."

63. *Recensio* α places *but I am fleshly* here. *Recensiones* β and γ place *but I am fleshly, sold under sin* before section 1a. All three recensions precede section 2 with *sold under sin.* I have placed the sections of the verse where they make most sense.

64. Instead of this sentence, *recensio* α has "But he calls humankind fleshly when it sins or because it sinned before." See the end of section 1a.

65. *Recensio* α does not have section 1a.

Sold under sin. (2) This is what it means to be sold under sin:[66] to derive one's origin from Adam, who was the first to sin,[67] and to become subject to sin by one's own transgression. (2a)[68] As the prophet Isaiah says: *You were sold for your sins* (Isa 50:1). (3) Adam sold himself first, and as a result all his descendants are subject to sin. (3a)[69] For this reason one is not strong enough to keep the commandments of the law unless one is fortified by divine reinforcements. This is why the apostle says: *The law is spiritual, but I am fleshly, sold under sin.* That is: the law is strong and just and blameless, but humankind is weak and in subjection because of one's ancestor's and one's own transgression, such that one is unable to use one's ability in regard to obeying the law. Therefore, one should take refuge in God's mercy in order to escape the severity of the law and, once one has been freed from the burden of transgressions, to resist the enemy from then on with God's protection. (4) For what does it mean to be subject to sin, but to have a body that is corrupted through the weakness of the soul, by which sin insinuates itself and drives a person like a prisoner to transgressions, so that he does its will?[70] Hence, the Lord says, among other things:[71] *The devil comes and takes away what has been sown in their hearts, so that they may not be saved* (Luke 8:12). This is why the same apostle says in another letter: *Our struggle is not against flesh and blood but against princes and powers, against the spirits of wickedness in heavenly places* (Eph 6:12), whom he knows to be the attendants of Satan. Now, before the transgression of humankind—before humankind delivered itself into slavery to death—the enemy did not have the power to enter into the heart of a person and to introduce conflicting thoughts. (4a)[72] This is why the enemy's subterfuge came about, so that in conversation through the serpent he might deceive humankind (see Gen 3:1–7). (5) But once the enemy deceived humankind and subjugated it, the enemy took power over humankind so as to drive the inner person by uniting himself with a person's mind. As a result, one is unable to perceive what

---

66. *Recensio α* has "to be found" instead of "to be sold."
67. See In Rom. 5:12 (§3).
68. *Recensio α* does not have section 2a.
69. *Recensio α* does not have section 3a.
70. I.e., sin's will. *Recensio α* has "For what does it mean to be subject to sin, but to have a body that is corrupted, by which sin prevails."
71. *Recensio α* does not have "among other things."
72. *Recensio α* does not have section 4a.

are his own thoughts and what are the enemy's, unless one pays attention to the law.

7:15 *I do not understand what I do.* He does not understand what he does, because he sees that he knows one thing by means of the law[73] and does another.

For I do not do what I want, but I do the very thing I hate. Having been subjected to sin, he assuredly does what he does not want to do.[74]

7:16 *If then I do what I hate, I agree with the law.*[75] He shows that the law is right in its prohibitions when he professes that he unwillingly does what the law forbids, and he says that what the law commands conforms to his nature because he states that what he does outside of the law is hateful to him.

7:17 *So now it is no longer I that do it, but sin which dwells within me.*[76] Since he sees that what he does is prohibited by the law and agrees that it ought not to be done, he accordingly declares that it is at the instigation of some other thing that he does this, namely, sin. The apostle always says *sin*, though he should be understood to mean the devil,[77] because if the first human being had not sinned these things would not have come about. Consequently it is sin that does all these things.

7:18 *For I know that the good does not dwell within me, that is, in my flesh.* (1) He does not say—as it seems to some people[78]—that the flesh is evil, but rather that what dwells in the flesh is not *good* but is sin. How does sin dwell in the flesh, since it is not a substance but a transgression of the good?[79] Since the body of the first human being was corrupted through sin such that it became subject to decomposition, the corruption of sin remained in the body on account of the nature of the offense, maintaining

---

73. *Recensio* α does not have "by means of the law."

74. *Recensio* α does not have "assuredly."

75. Ambrosiaster's biblical text omits the phrase "that it is good" (ὅτι καλός), which concludes the verse in the Greek text. See the text and apparatus in NA[28].

76. Ambrosiaster's biblical text has literally "indwelling within me" (*inhabitat in me*), whereas the majority of biblical witnesses have "dwelling within me" (οἰκοῦσα ἐν ἐμοί).

77. *Recensiones* α and β have "though it should be understood to be the devil along with his angels."

78. *Recensio* α does not have "as it seems to some people." Ambrosiaster may be referring here to Christians who espoused radical forms of asceticism. See David G. Hunter, *Marriage, Celibacy, and Heresy in Ancient Christianity: The Jovinianist Controversy*, OECS (Oxford: Oxford University Press, 2007), 130–70, esp. 163–64.

79. *Recensio* α does not have "of the good."

the force of the divine sentence handed down to Adam.[80] This is the sign of the devil,[81] at whose instigation he sinned.[82] (2) Thus, by reason of the corruption that remains on account of the deed that was done,[83] sin is said to dwell in the flesh, to which[84] the devil has access as if to his own law—for it is now the flesh of sin and sin remains, as it were, in sin[85]—so as to deceive humankind with evil suggestions so that humankind does not do what the law ordains.

Now the will to act lies near me. (3) He affirms that what the law commands is so good that he says it naturally seems right to him and that he desires to fulfill it.

But I do not find it in myself to accomplish the good.[86] (4) Thus, what is commanded by the law seems right, and the will is there to do it, but the ability and the strength to fulfill it is missing because one is so overwhelmed by the domination of sin[87] that one cannot go where one wishes, and one neither can nor dare object,[88] because someone else is the master of its ability. Humankind is now weighed down with the habit of sinning and submits more readily[89] to sin than to the law, which it knows teaches what is good; even if one wishes to do good, habit, with the help of the enemy, overwhelms him.

7:19 *For I do not do the good I want, but the evil I do not want is what I do.* The apostle repeats himself often in order to be clear. Thus, his mean-

---

80. *Recensio* α does not have "handed down to Adam."

81. *Recensio* α has "of the law of the devil" instead of "of the devil."

82. *Recensio* α has "Adam sinned."

83. *Recensio* α does not have "on account of the deed that was done" (*facti causa*), i.e., the sin of the first human being.

84. *Recensio* α has *quod*, presumably referring to "sin," instead of *quam*, which refers to "the flesh."

85. *Recensio* α does not have this clause.

86. The final verb "I do not find" (*non invenio*) in Ambrosiaster's biblical text is considered to be a secondary addition to the original biblical text, which ends abruptly with the negative οὔ: "To wish it is within my reach, but to accomplish what is excellent is not" (τὸ γὰρ θέλειν παράκειταί μοι, τὸ δὲ κατεργάζεσθαι τὸ καλὸν οὔ). See Bruce M. Metzger, *A Textual Commentary on the Greek New Testament*, 2nd ed. (Stuttgart: Deutsche Bibelgesellschaft, 1994), 454–55; and Jewett, *Romans*, 454.

87. *Recensiones* α and β have "the power of sin" instead of "the domination of sin."

88. *Recensiones* α and β have "and one cannot object" instead of "and one neither can nor dare object."

89. *Recensio* α adds "by habit."

ing here, as has already been said, is that as a prisoner for the reasons given above, he is compelled to commit the sin that he does not want.[90]

7:20 *Now, if I do what I do not want,*[91] *it is no longer I that do it, but sin which dwells in me.* That is, the devil, whom the apostle discussed above.[92] For, having been overwhelmed and subjugated by sin, humankind performed the will of sin, not its own will. But then, given that the apostle says that humankind sins unwillingly, should humankind be regarded as free of offense because it has been overwhelmed by a powerful force and does what it does not want? Certainly not. These things arose through its own failing and indolence; since humankind subjected itself to sin by its own consent, it is ruled by the law of sin.[93] Sin persuaded humankind first, so that now it rules what it has conquered. However, the apostle explains all this—the extent of the evil from which God has freed humankind—to highlight the grace of God, to show what ruin humankind derives from Adam and what benefits humankind—to whom the law, in fact, could offer no assistance—has received through Christ.[94]

7:21 *I therefore find it to be a law for me, when I want to do good, that evil is there within me.* He states that the law of Moses agrees with his will against sin which dwells in the flesh and which forces him to do something different than what the self and the law wish.

7:22 *For I delight in the law of God according to the inner self.* He says that his soul delights in the things that are handed down by the law. This is the inner self, for sin dwells not in the soul but in the flesh, because the flesh originates from the sin of the flesh, and all flesh is sinful through transmission.[95] Sin is not allowed to dwell in the soul on account of the free choice of the will.[96] Therefore, sin dwells in the flesh as if at the doorway

---

90. *Recensio* α continues with "which rules over him" (*quod illius dominatur*).

91. Ambrosiaster's biblical text lacks the emphatic "I" (ἐγώ) found in many biblical witnesses, intensifying the subject in "I do not want." See Metzger, *Textual Commentary*, 455; and Jewett, *Romans*, 454–55.

92. *Recensiones* α and β have "This is what the apostle already discussed above."

93. *Recensio* α has "For unless humankind had subjected itself to sin by its own consent, it would not be ruled by it."

94. *Recensio* α does not have this sentence.

95. *Recensio* α has "but in the flesh, which originates from sin, and all flesh exists by transmission." Ambrosiaster held that one derives only one's body from the generative act of one's parents; the soul is given once the body is formed. See *Quaest.* 23 (CSEL 50:49–51).

96. This comment is found only in *recensio* γ (see n. 98 below). Ambrosiaster

of the soul,⁹⁷ so that it does not let the soul go where it wishes. If sin in fact did dwell in the soul, it would disturb the self to the point that it would not recognize itself at all.⁹⁸ But as it stands, the soul recognizes itself and delights in the law of God.

7:23 *But I see another law in my members fighting against the law of my mind and taking me prisoner for the law of sin, which is in my members.* (1) He mentions two laws. One of these, he alleges, he sees *in his members*, that is, in the outer self, which is the flesh or the body. This is the opposing law. It fights against the soul, taking it prisoner into a state of sin,⁹⁹ preventing it from finding an advocate¹⁰⁰ by venturing further afield. The other is the law *of the mind*, which is the law of Moses or natural law, which exists in the soul. This was overwhelmed by the violence of sin, and indeed by its own heedlessness, because when it delighted in faults it subjected itself to sin, so that it was held prisoner by its very habit. Habit, in fact, rules humankind.¹⁰¹ (2)¹⁰² Actually, the apostle refers to four laws. The first is the spiritual law, which is also the natural law that was restored by Moses and placed in a position of authority; this is the law of God. The second

---

here states explicitly what he implies elsewhere, that the soul retains its capacity to make moral choices after the fall. On the significance of this affirmation in relation to Ambrosiaster's comments on Rom 7:18–25, see Alessandra Pollastri, *Ambrosiaster, commento alla Lettera ai Romani: Aspetti cristologici*, CTSt (L'Aquila: Japadre, 1976), 132–38.

97. See In Rom. 7:24 (§5).

98. Instead of "Sin is not allowed … at all," *recensiones* α and β have "For if the soul existed by transmission as well as the flesh, sin would also dwell in the soul, because the soul of Adam sinned rather than the body. But the sin of the soul corrupted the body. Therefore, sin dwells in the flesh as if at the doorway of the soul, so that it does not let the soul go where it wishes. If sin in fact did dwell in the soul, the self would never recognize itself. But as it stands, it recognizes itself and delights in the law of God."

99. *Recensio* α has "to itself" instead of "into a state of sin."

100. The Latin word *adsertor* refers to "a free citizen who pleads in court the case, in particular the liberation, of a slave, who is incapable of being a party to a *lawsuit*" (Christoph Georg Paulus, "Adsertor," *BNP* A1:156).

101. *Recensio* α does not have this sentence.

102. In section 2 *recensio* α has "The apostle, thus, refers to four laws. The first of these is the law of sin which he says dwells in the members as a result of the transgression of the first human being; the second is the law seen in the members when it suggests evil and then retreats; the third is the law of God given through Moses; the fourth is the law of the mind which agrees with the law of God. If fact, these four laws are logically classified as two, the law of good and the law of evil."

is the law of the mind which agrees with the law of God. The third is the law of sin which the apostle says dwells in the members as a result of the transgression of the first human being. The fourth appears in the members when it suggests evil things and then retreats. Now, these laws appear to be four since they are mentioned repeatedly, although in fact they are two, namely, the law of good and the law of evil. For the law of the mind is in fact the spiritual law or the law of Moses, which is called the law of God. The law of sin is the same as the law which the apostle says is seen in the members, which opposes the law of our mind.

7:24 *What a wretched person I am! Who will set me free from the body of this death?* **7:25** *The grace of God through Jesus Christ our Lord.*[103] (1a) He says that he is *a wretched person* because he was born under sin.[104] Indeed, is not humankind wretched, which fell heir to this inheritance of transgression, harboring to itself the enemy sin, through which Satan may have access to it?[105] For Adam built a ladder by which the plunderer climbed up to his children, had not the merciful Lord, moved by compassion, granted his grace through Christ, so that the human race, having been restored by the forgiveness of sins which it had received, may thereafter behold sin overwhelmed and condemned. Once it has been relieved and purified of evil, it is able to resist the adversary through the power it has received against him when it is helped by God. (2) Here the apostle introduces, as it were, the third, more powerful law of faith, which he also calls *grace*. This law nevertheless derives from the spiritual law,[106] because humankind has been set free by it. Thus, because Moses gave this law and the Lord also gave it, they are called two laws but are understood as one, as befits their meaning or purpose.[107] (2a) The former was the initiator of salvation; the latter, the finisher.[108] (3) I am not speaking about that part of the law that consists in new moons and in circumcision and in foods, but rather about the part that relates to the mystery and teaching of God.[109]

---

103. Although Ambrosiaster's biblical text has "the grace of God" (*gratia dei*), among the biblical witnesses "Thanks be to God!" (χάρις δὲ τῷ θεῷ) is thought to be the original text. See Metzger, *Textual Commentary*, 455; and Jewett, *Romans*, 455.
104. *Recensio* α does not have this sentence.
105. *Recensio* β has "has" instead of "may have."
106. *Recensio* α does not have "spiritual."
107. *Recensio* α does not have "the meaning or."
108. *Recensio* α does not have this sentence.
109. *Recensio* α has "I spoke, however, of the law which was given on tablets."

Thus, it is by the grace of God through Christ that humankind has been set free *from the body of this death*. The apostle says *this death*, referring to the death that above he showed is located in the underworld at the demise of a person on account of sin;[110] it is called the second death.[111] The *body of death*, moreover, consists of a whole group of sins; many sins comprise a single body, individual members, as it were, devised by a single maker. When one has been delivered from these by the grace of God through baptism, one escapes the death mentioned above.[112] (3a)[113] Moreover, as someone who exists in a corporeal body, the apostle did not say that he was delivered from it itself; rather, he meant the body that he indicated above was destroyed through baptism and keeping the law.[114] In fact, when he says *from the body of death*, he shows that there is another body which is not of death.

So then, I myself serve the law of God with the mind. (4) When he says *the law of God*, he means both the law of Moses and the law of Christ.

But the law of sin with the flesh. (5) *I myself*, namely, I who have been set free from the body of death in the sense discussed above.[115] The apostle exists in a body: in what sense was he set free from the body of death, if not because he was set free from all evil? For the forgiveness of sin takes away all sins. Having, therefore, been set free from the body of death by the grace of God through Christ, *I serve the law of God with the mind* or the soul, *but the law of sin*—namely, the devil, who floods the soul with evil suggestions by way of the flesh which is subject to him—*with the flesh*. Since, then, a person is made up of two aspects, oriented by the flesh and the soul,[116] the apostle said that he serves the law of God with the mind, because the soul is dedicated to God and, once it has regained its power, is

---

110. See In Rom. 5:12 (§§3–4).

111. *Recensio* α does not have "it is called the second death."

112. *Recensio* α has "The *body of death*, moreover, consists of a whole group of sins; many sins comprise a single body of the second death, individual members, as it were, devised by a single maker. When one has been delivered from these by the grace of God, one escapes the second death."

113. *Recensio* α does not have section 3a.

114. See In Rom. 6:3.

115. *Recensiones* α and β do not have "according to the sense discussed above."

116. I agree with Alessandro Pollastri, trans., *Ambrosiaster, commento all Lettera ai Romani*, CTePa 43 (Rome: Città Nuova Editrice, 1984), 177 n. 15, in her reading of the phrase *carne conversus et animo*. Accordingly, I translate the text as found in the manuscripts and not the emendation proposed by R. Hanslik (CSEL 81.1:247).

able to fight against sin, which operates through the flesh. Since the flesh was corrupted and subjected to death—something that came about in such a way that it did not loose the association and connection with the soul—it received desires that it passes on as a kind of burden to the soul, so that the soul also degenerated. But having expelled this death by the grace of God,[117] *I serve the law of God with the mind* or the soul,[118] *but the law of sin with the flesh*, as stated above. The soul, now free and recalled to good habits, is able to reject evil suggestions with the help of the Holy Spirit.[119] The authority by which it dares to resist the enemy has been restored to it; one who is no longer submissive can in no way be entrapped against his will. But the flesh lacks the faculty of judgment and is incapable of discernment; it is, in fact, brute nature. Therefore, it is unable to block the entrance to the enemy so that when he approaches he may not come in and persuade the soul of the wrong things.[120] (5a)[121] This is why the apostle says, *I serve the law of sin with the flesh*. When a single person comprises flesh and soul, he serves God with the intelligent part, but the law of sin with the other, unintelligent part. If humankind had in fact continued in the state in which it was created, the enemy would have no power to gain access to the flesh and to whisper wrong things to the soul. But the sentence handed down to Adam made it impossible for the entire person to be restored by the grace of Christ to this pristine state; it was wrong to undo the sentence pronounced by law. (5b) For that reason, although the sentence remained in place, a solution was found by the providence of God, such that the wholeness that humankind had lost through its own fault could be given back to it. Humankind, now reborn, could believe that its adversary, having been subdued by the power

---

117. *Recensio* α has *sed qui respuit illam mors gratia dei*, and *recensiones* β and γ have *sed quid respuit illam mors gratia dei*. Either the text is corrupt or, following *recensio* α, there is a disjunction between the subject of the relative clause and the following quotation, which occurs frequently in this chapter when Ambrosiaster refers to the apostle in the third person while Paul himself is writing in the first person. I have translated the emendation proposed by R. Hanslik (CSEL 81.1:247): *sed qui respui illam mortem gratia dei*.

118. *Recensiones* α and β do not have "or the soul."

119. For the remainder of section 5, *recensio* α has "The soul, now free by the grace of God, recalled to good habits, and helped by the Spirit, is able to reject evil suggestions. The flesh is susceptible to faults because it is not able to discern and has been corrupted."

120. See In Rom. 7:22.

121. *Recensio* α does not have sections 5a and 5b.

of Christ, would not dare to claim humankind for itself when Adam's race was reunited, given that the sentence of the first death had been canceled; humankind, now entirely and enduringly immortal, would not be restored to the state of its original creation.[122]

---

122. Ambrosiaster refers here to the resurrection of the dead, when believers will be established in a new corporeal existence that will be permanently, not conditionally, immortal, unlike the original corporeal existence of Adam and Eve. See Pollastri, *Ambrosiaster, commento alla Lettera ai Romani: Aspetti cristologici*, 173–76.

Romans 8

8:1 *There is now no condemnation for those who are in Christ Jesus.* It is true that there will be no condemnation for those who are Christians, who keep the law of God with a devout soul.[1]

8:2 *For the law of the spirit of life in Christ Jesus has set you free from the law of sin and death.* (1) The apostle calls attention to the safe position of humankind through the grace of God, so that one need not be anxious about the suggestions of the devil as long as one rejects them. They will do humankind no harm with regard to the second death, because the law of faith—that is, *of the spirit*—has set humankind free from the second death, now that sin has been condemned. The apostle says that[2] it is no longer harmful[3] to humankind that sin exists in the flesh, provided that one fights against it, mindful of the help of God. In fact, one who overcomes the counsels of sin, which remains in the flesh, should be awarded a crown of victory; it requires great ingenuity to elude the snares of the enemy within one's household.[4] (2) The *law of the spirit of life*, then, is the same as the law of faith.[5] Now, even the law of Moses is a spiritual law

---

1. *Recensio* α has "It is true, there will be no condemnation for those who are in Christ Jesus, who keep the law of God from the heart [*animo*]." *Recensio* β has "It is true that there will be no condemnation for those who are in Christ Jesus, who keep the law of God conscientiously [*sollicite*]." For the expression "devout soul" (*devotio animi*) in *recensio* γ, see In Rom. 8:4 (§2).

2. I have supplied "the apostle says that" to complete the infinitive construction in the text; see n. 3 below.

3. This construction is in the future tense in *recensio* α, in the present tense in *recensio* β, and in the infinitive in *recensio* γ.

4. *Recensio* α has "In fact, the person whose resolve is not broken by the desires of the flesh should be awarded a crown of victory." *Recensio* β has the same text as *recensio* γ except for the words "in the flesh."

5. In section 2 *recensio* α has "The *law of the spirit of life*, then, is the same as the law of faith. Inasmuch as it forgives the sins of those guilty of death, it is the law of

because it prohibits sinning, but it is not a law of life, because it cannot forgive the sins of those guilty of death, so as to give life to those who are going to die. However, the law referred to here is called *the law of the spirit of life* because it both disallows sinning and recalls from death. It is established not by means of the letter but by means of the spirit, because it is believed with the heart and what is believed is of the spirit. (3) Thus, *in Christ Jesus*—that is, through faith in Christ[6]—this law sets the believer free *from the law of sin and death*. The law of sin is the law that the apostle says dwells in the members, the law that tries to persuade people of the wrong things; the law of Moses, however, is the law of death, because it puts sinners to death.[7] In fact, in another letter the apostle also speaks, among other things, about the authority of the law: *If the administration of death, carved in stones, was glorious* (2 Cor 3:7). It should not be surprising, therefore, that the spiritual law is called the law of death as well, since this is also the case with the gospel. For in another passage the apostle says, among other things: *To some it is a fragrance of life to life, to others a fragrance of death to death* (2 Cor 2:16).[8] (3a)[9] The gospel was the fragrance of life to those who were drawn to the faith by the report of miracles or the seeing or hearing of things that had happened. But to those whose mind was incited to denial by the event of a miracle, the proclamation of the faith was the fragrance of death. Thus, although there is one faith, it brings out the difference in people, just as also the sun, though it is one, melts wax and binds clay. Faith will benefit a person, therefore, in accordance with the mind with which one savors it. (3b) But perhaps someone will say: "If faith has the same effect as the law, why is it not in that respect also called the law of death? For it puts unbelievers to death." But this is it not so. Faith, which justifies those who take refuge in it, was given to forgive those whom the law found guilty, so that those who act under the auspices of faith are free from sin, whereas those who act under the auspices of the law

---

life. It is established not by means of the letter but by means of the spirit, because it is believed with the heart and what is believed is of the spirit."

6. *Recensio* α does not have "in Christ."

7. Instead of this sentence and the next one, *recensio* α has "The latter is the law of sin, because it instigated sin in order to render humankind guilty before the law, so that it would be condemned by the law. Consequently, it is the law of death for the guilty, but the spiritual law for the good. In fact, in another letter the apostle also says: *If etc.*"

8. *Recensio* α adds "For it grants believers life, but unbelievers death."

9. *Recensio* α does not have sections 3a–3c.

are liable.[10] Therefore, those who do not obey faith are killed not by faith but by the law, because in not coming to faith they are found guilty by the law. (3c) For this reason all who savor the words of faith with an evil mind remain in death. We now can see what the difference is when one speaks of *the spiritual law* and *the law of the spirit*. This is the difference: the one is called *the spiritual law* because it gives commands whereby one may avoid sinning,[11] since one who does not sin is called spiritual, emulating higher, heavenly beings; the other, however, is called *the law of the spirit* because God, in whom one believes, is spirit. Thus, in the former there are words, in the latter, reality; in the former, things which pertain to God, in the latter, God himself.

8:3 *For—what was impossible for the law inasmuch as it was weakened by the flesh—God, sending his Son in the likeness of the flesh of sin, for a sin condemned sin in the flesh.* (1) The apostle says this to reassure the baptized that they[12] have been set free from sin. *For what was impossible*, he says, *for the law*. For whom was it impossible? Clearly, it was impossible for us to fulfill the commandment of the law because we had been subjected to sin. For this reason God sent his Son *in the likeness of the flesh of sin*. The likeness of the flesh consists in this: although his flesh is the same as ours, it nevertheless was not formed in the womb and born in the same way our flesh is. It was sanctified in the womb and born without sin, and besides, he did not sin in it.[13] (2)[14] A virgin womb was chosen for the Lord's birth so that the Lord's flesh might be distinct from ours as regards sanctity. It is similar in condition, but not in the quality of sinful substance. The apostle therefore spoke of similarity, because from the same substance of the flesh the Lord did not have the same birth, since the body of the Lord was not subjected to sin. (3)[15] For the Lord's flesh was purified by the Holy Spirit so that it was

---

10. The comment also evokes the difference between free persons (*liberi*) and servile ones (*obnoxii*).

11. See In Rom. 7:14 (§1a) and 7:23 (§2).

12. *Recensio* α has "who" instead of "that they."

13. See In Rom. 7:18 (§§1–2) and 7:22.

14. In section 2 *recensio* α has "The apostle therefore spoke of likeness. He said *in the likeness of the flesh of sin* so that the likeness would consist in the fact that our flesh is the flesh of sin when it is subjected to sin."

15. In section 3 *recensio* α has "But the flesh of the Savior was purified from sin through the Holy Spirit. Therefore, when Christ had been sent, *for a sin he condemned sin*. The apostle says this because sin was condemned through its own sin. How? When Christ was crucified by sin, sin sinned in the flesh of the body of the Savior. Through

born in the kind of body that Adam had before sin, except that only the sentence handed down to Adam remained. Therefore, when Christ had been sent, God *for a sin condemned sin*, that is, condemned sin through its own sin. For when Christ was crucified by sin, who is Satan, sin sinned in the flesh of the body of the Savior.[16] Once this happened, God condemned sin in the flesh, where undoubtedly sin sinned, as the apostle also says in another letter: *triumphing over them in him* (Col 2:15), that is, in Christ. (3a)[17] Now, it is also customary to state the reason for which a condemned individual has been condemned; one replies, for example, "for murder." Accordingly, sin too was condemned in the flesh, that is, in the sin which it committed in the flesh. (4) So, having been found guilty through this sin, Satan lost the right to detain souls, so that he does not dare to hold in the second death those who have now been signed with the sign of the cross, by which[18] he was vanquished. The apostle discusses this, therefore, to reassure us.

8:4 *In order that the righteousness of the law might be fulfilled in us, who walk not according to the flesh but according to the Spirit.* (1) The apostle says that sin was condemned so that the righteousness of the law which was given by Moses might be fulfilled in us. (1a)[19] After having been discharged from the terms of the law, we have become friends of that same law. For the justified are friends of the law. (2) But how is righteousness fulfilled in us,[20] if not when forgiveness is granted for all sins,[21] so that, after sins have been removed, one may appear justified, serving the law of God with the mind? This is what it means to walk *not according to the flesh, but according to the Spirit*, so that the devout soul,[22] which is spirit, does not consent to the wish of sin,[23] because through the flesh sin generates the wrongful desires of the soul, since sin is present.[24] If sin has been condemned, why is it present? (3) Sin has been condemned by the Savior,

---

this sin he condemned sin in the flesh. It was condemned in the place where it sinned. As the apostle also says elsewhere: *triumphing over them in himself.*

16. On Christ's conquest of the devil, see the introduction §5.4.
17. *Recensio* α does not have section 3a.
18. *Recensio* α has *in quo*, referring to "sign," whereas *recensiones* β and γ have *in qua*, referring to "cross."
19. *Recensio* α does not have section 1a.
20. *Recensio* α has "But how is it fulfilled, if not etc."
21. *Recensio* α does not have "all."
22. See In Rom. 8:1.
23. *Recensio* α has "of the flesh."
24. *Recensio* α does not have "of the soul."

and has been condemned in three ways.[25] In the first place, the Savior condemned sin when, taking exception to sin,[26] he did not sin. Second, sin is said to have been condemned in the cross, because sin sinned.[27] (3a)[28] Hence, as a sinner its authority has been removed—the authority by which it detained humankind in the underworld on account of Adam's transgression—so that from now on it does not dare to detain those on whom the sign of the cross is found. Third, the Savior condemned sin when he rendered transgressions null and void through the forgiveness of sins that was granted. Although the sinner should have been condemned on account of the sin that had been committed, when the Savior forgave the sinner he condemned sin in the sinner. (4) Therefore, if we too, following the Savior's example,[29] do not sin, we condemn sin.

8:5 *For those who live according to the flesh think about things that are of the flesh.* (1)[30] The apostle says this because one who submits to suggestions that come through the flesh thinks about things that are of the flesh. It seems good to such a person to think about what he pursues,[31] (1a) craving against all that is right the practice and the thinking of the error of the flesh. In the flesh the error of the world is expressed in every respect.

But those who live according to the Spirit think about things that are of the Spirit. (2)[32] These are they who, now that error has been conquered, trample on the wrongful desires of the flesh. Even as they march in the flesh, they do not serve according to the flesh (see 2 Cor 10:3), having set the world behind them. Their glory is not from people, but is from God (see Rom 2:29). As, then, they continue in these spiritual works, they

---

25. *Recensiones* α and β have "It [β: sin] has been condemned, but by the Savior and in two [β: three] ways." *Recensio* α, mentioning only two ways, does not have section 3a below.

26. *Recensio* α does not have "taking exception to sin."

27. *Recensio* α adds "For everyone who sins deserves condemnation."

28. *Recensio* α does not have section 3a; see n. 25 above.

29. *Recensio* α has "this example."

30. Instead of sections 1 and 1a, *recensio* α has "The apostle says this because one who submits to the faults of the flesh thinks about the things that are of the flesh, because what he pursues seems delightful to him."

31. *Recensio* β has "What he pursues seems delightful to him, craving etc."

32. For section 2 *recensiones* α and β have "It is clear that one who keeps himself from the desires of the flesh lives according to the law of the mind; it seems good to him to think about what agrees with the law."

think about things that are of the Spirit of God, according to whose orders they march.

8:6 *Now the prudence of the flesh is death.* (1) The prudence of the flesh is death because it is a serious sin; through this sort of sin death comes.[33] Though it is foolish, it is called *prudence* because to worldly people errors conceived in thought or in deed against the law of God on the basis of visible reality appear to be prudent, especially since all their industry and intelligence is invested in sinning.[34] They seem wise to themselves if they attend to it with the utmost care, even though nothing is so foolish as sinning.[35] (2) There also is another prudence of the flesh that, puffed up with worldly reasoning, denies that something that lacks a this-worldly explanation can take place; thus, it scoffs at the virgin birth and the resurrection of the flesh.[36]

But the prudence of the Spirit is life and peace. (3) Indeed, this is the wisdom that obtains life and peace; pursuing spiritual things and scorning the allures of the present life, it will have life with peace,[37] that is, without trouble. For where there is unrest, there also is punishment.

8:7 *Since the wisdom of the flesh is hostile to God, it is not submissive to the law of God; nor can it be.* (1)[38] The apostle did not say that the flesh is hostile, but rather *the wisdom of the flesh*; that is, not the substance, but evil deeds or a thought or an assertion that is born of error.[39] The wisdom of the flesh, accordingly, is first of all the calculation of the stars as conjectured

---

33. *Recensiones* α and β have "The prudence of the flesh is sin that produces death."
34. *Recensio* α has "It is called *prudence* because all their industry and intelligence is invested in sinning."
35. *Recensio* α does not have the last clause. *Recensio* β has "although nothing is more foolish than sinning."
36. See In Rom. 8:7 (§§1–2).
37. *Recensio* α has "it will have this, life with peace"; *recensio* β has "it will have eternal life with peace."
38. For sections 1–3 *recensio* α has "(1) The apostle did not say that the flesh is hostile, but rather *the wisdom of the flesh*; that is, not the substance, but a deed or a thought or statement. The wisdom of the flesh, accordingly, is first of all the account of first principles, second, the delight in the visible world. These things are hostile to God, because those who focus on the mode of existence of the elements do not believe that God brought it about (2) that Sarah, pregnant when she was already old and when her natural cycle had ceased, bore a son, or that a dry branch could bear fruit and produce nuts, as well as other things that God did either then or later on account of the Savior. (3) This sort of assertion cannot be submissive to the law of God."
39. *Recensio* β does not have "evil."

by humankind, secondly, the delight in the visible world. These things are hostile to God because they equate the lord of the elements and the maker of the world with the things he made, asserting that nothing beyond what a this-worldly explanation supports can take place. (2) For this reason they deny that God brought it about that a virgin gave birth or that the bodies of the dead rise up, because, they say, it is foolish that God would have done something beyond what humankind understands; therefore, he did not do it.[40] O those deemed learned by the world, who suppose that God ought not to do anything other than what the creature made by him does, so that he is imagined to be like his creatures! They are so blind that they do not see what sort of insult[41] they bring against God. A work which deserves to lead to the proclamation of his praise these people disparagingly declare to be incredible and foolish. (3) Consequently, this sort of prudence of the flesh cannot be submissive to the law of God. They refine their pursuit of it to this end: to oppose the acts of God.[42]

8:8 *For those who are in the flesh cannot please God.* The wise of the world are *in the flesh* because they pursue a wisdom by which they oppose the law of God. Whatever is against the law of God is fleshly because it is derived from the world. The entire world is flesh. Everything that is visible is deemed to be of the flesh. Things that share the same origin are of the flesh. Indeed, the elements are of the flesh. So too, one who conforms to worldly matters and concerns is *in the flesh*.[43]

8:9 *You, however, are not in the flesh, but in the Spirit.* (1) Those who are in the flesh are said *not* to be *in the flesh* (1a)[44] if, concurring with the apostle John, they do not love the world (see 1 John 2:15–16). For a person's thinking essentially shapes that person's nature, so that one is named in accordance with what one thinks.

---

40. *Recensio* β does not have "therefore he did not do it."
41. *Recensio* β has "what insult."
42. *Recensio* β has "Consequently, this pursuit cannot be submissive to the law of God. By it one gains the skill to oppose the acts of God."
43. For the entire comment *recensio* α has "The entire world is flesh. Everything that is visible is deemed to be of the flesh. Things that share the same origin are of the flesh. So too, one who conforms to worldly matters is *in the flesh*." *Recensio* β has "The wise of the world are *in the flesh* because, in focusing on the world, they oppose spiritual wisdom, since the entire world is flesh. Everything that is visible is deemed to be of the flesh. Things that share the same origin are of the flesh. Indeed, the elements are of the flesh. So too, one who conforms to worldly matters is *in the flesh*."
44. *Recensio* α does not have section 1a.

Provided that the Spirit of God dwells in you. (2) The apostle says this in a qualified way because they did not yet have perfect faith, since they had been introduced to the law.[45] Nevertheless, he saw in them the hope of perfection. Hence, sometimes he addresses them as those who are perfect, at other times as those who are to be perfected; that is, sometimes he praises them, at other times he exhorts them. Accordingly, they are said to be *in the Spirit* if, as was discussed above, they live in keeping with the law of nature, because the Spirit of God cannot dwell in one who follows fleshly things.

If someone, however, does not have the Spirit of Christ, he does not belong to him. (3) The apostle now calls the Spirit of God *the Spirit of Christ*, because everything the Father has, the Son has. He says this because one who submits to the errors mentioned above does not belong to Christ. He does not have Christ's Spirit, the Spirit he had received in order to be a child of God. There are two reasons the Holy Spirit abandons a person: when one has either the thought or the actions of the flesh.[46] So by these warnings the apostle is urging a good way of life. For although people are restored[47] by God's goodness,[48] nevertheless once they are called children of God they will be accused unless they live in such a way as to not appear unworthy[49] of the name granted them.

---

45. Ambrosiaster refers here to the way, as he understands it, the Romans came to accept Christ, with a faith that entailed observance of the law. See Ambrosiaster's remarks at In Rom. synopsis (§§2–3) and 1:11 (§§1–2).

46. *Recensio* α does not have this sentence.

47. Literally "raised up" (*erigantur*).

48. *Recensio* α has "The apostle urges them on through a good way of life, because although people are restored by the goodness of God etc." *Recensio* β has "So through this the apostle urges them on to a good way of life. For although people are restored by the goodness of God etc." Vincent Bulhart suggested emendations to the text of both recensions; see CSEL 81.1:264.

49. *Recensio* α has "so unworthy."

8:10[50] *The body is indeed dead because of sin,*[51] *but the spirit is life because of justification.* (1)[52] The apostle declares that on account of sin the body of those whom the Holy Spirit abandons is dead, and that the experience of their death does not reach him, that is, the Spirit.[53] For the Spirit of God does not know how to sin; he was given for the purpose of justification, to justify by means of his assistance. Therefore, since he does not know how to sin, he is life. He cannot die, because death comes through sin. Consequently, the sinner will hurt himself, not the Spirit whom he received. (1a)[54] Nor will the Spirit, who seeks to justify, be responsible; he is the sign of justification in a person, so that by that which dwells in him the justified person may appear to be a child of God. For the Holy Spirit can dwell in neither a false person *nor in a body subjected to sins*, as Solomon says (Wis 1:4). (2) If someone again lives in a fleshly manner,[55] he will die in his unrighteousness,[56] abandoned by the Holy Spirit. Now,

---

50. In the Greek witnesses and many witnesses to the VL 8:10 begins, "But if Christ is in you" (*si autem Christus in vobis est*). Ambrosiaster omits this clause without comment, presumably because it was not present in his biblical text. The clause also is omitted by some early Latin manuscripts of Paul's letters; see John Wordsworth and Henry J. White, *Novum Testamentum domini nostri Iesu Christi latine* (Oxford: Clarendon, 1889–1954), 2:100. On these manuscripts, see Hugo S. Eymann, *Epistula ad Romanos*, VLB 21 (Freiburg: Herder, 1996), 20–21. In his defense of Latin versions at In Rom. 5:14 (§5a), Ambrosiaster notes that their readings are attested by earlier Latin Christian writers, including Tertullian, who also omits the opening clause of verse 10 (*Marc.* 5.14 [CCSL 1:623]; see *Res.* 46.4 [CCSL 2:983]). The clause that is missing in Tertullian and Ambrosiaster was known to Jerome (see *Did. Spir.* 39 [PL 23:136C]), who criticized Ambrosiaster for his adherence to Latin versions.

51. The linking verb "is" (*est*) in Ambrosiaster's biblical text is a secondary addition not found in most biblical witnesses. See Robert Jewett with Roy D. Kotansky, *Romans: A Commentary*, Hermeneia (Minneapolis: Fortress, 2007), 475.

52. For section 1 *recensio* α has "The apostle declares that on account of sin the body is dead, and that the experience of its death does not reach the Spirit of God, which is also the Spirit of Christ. For the Spirit of God does not know how to sin; he was given for the purpose of justification. Since he does not know how to sin, he is life, because he cannot die. For death comes through sin. Consequently, the sinner will hurt himself, not the Spirit whom he received."

53. *Recensio* β does not have "that is, the Spirit." In *recensio* γ "him, that is, the Spirit" is attested only by MSS Monte Cassino 150 and Paris lat. 1759. Because in Latin *spiritus* is masculine, I refer to the Holy Spirit as "he" and "him" in what follows.

54. *Recensio* α does not have section 1a.

55. *Recensio* α does not have "again."

56. *Recensio* α does not have "in his unrighteousness."

in referring to *the body*, the apostle means that the entire person dies on account of sin, just as the entire person is meant by the word *soul* by the prophet, as a part for the whole.[57] For the prophet says, *The soul that sins, it will die* (Ezek 18:4). How will it die without the body? The apostle took *the body* to refer to the entire person; the prophet, *the soul*. So too another prophet meant the entire person when speaking of *the flesh*, for he says: *All flesh will see the salvation of God* (Isa 40:5; Luke 3:6).[58] (3) Moreover, since the Holy Spirit is given to one who has been baptized—that is, purified—the Holy Spirit is now said to be the spirit of the baptized.[59] The apostle therefore called the rest of the person *the body* in comparison to the Spirit, and for this reason the soul may be called *the flesh* when it sins. One is named according to what one pursues, (3a)[60] as I have now often said. Likewise, when the Lord during his sufferings wanted it to be understood that his divinity was by no means afraid, but that the sorrow belonged to the human being, he says: *The spirit indeed is willing, but the flesh is weak* (Matt 26:41), thereby indicating God with *the spirit* and the human being with *the flesh*.[61]

8:11 *If the Spirit of him who raised Jesus from the dead dwells in you, he who raised Jesus*[62] *from the dead will give life to your mortal bodies as well because of his Spirit dwelling in you.*[63] The apostle makes his point using the same reasoning. He said *bodies*, by which he means people. Because he stated above that on account of sin the body dies a second death, here he

---

57. Ambrosiaster refers to the rhetorical figure of synecdoche, the use of the whole for the part or the part for the whole.

58. *Recensio* α has "of our God."

59. *Recensio* α has "Since the Spirit is given to one who has been baptized, the spirit of the baptized is said to be the Holy Spirit." *Recensio* β has "Since the Holy Spirit is given to one who has been baptized, the Holy Spirit is said to be the spirit of the baptized as well."

60. *Recensio* α does not have section 3a.

61. On this way of speaking about the divinity and humanity of Christ, see In Rom. 1:1 (§3) and Alessandra Pollastri, *Ambrosiaster, commento alla Lettera ai Romani: Aspetti cristologici*, CTSt (L'Aquila: Japadre, 1976), 76–78.

62. On the textual variants here, see Jewett, *Romans*, 475.

63. Among the biblical witnesses a formulation using the genitive, "through his Spirit dwelling in you" (διὰ τοῦ ἐνοικοῦντος αὐτοῦ πνεύματος ἐν ὑμῖν), is more widely attested than the formulation using the accusative, "because of his Spirit dwelling in you" (*propter inhabitantem spiritum eius in vobis*), found in Ambrosiaster's biblical text. See Jewett, *Romans*, 475.

again promised that on account of a good life *mortal bodies*—that is, the entire person—will be brought to life.

8:12 *So then, brothers, we are debtors, not to the flesh, to live according to the flesh.* (1) It is right and obvious that we should not follow the precedent of Adam, who behaved in a fleshly manner and, by sinning first, passed death on to us by title of inheritance. Rather, we should keep the law of Christ, who redeemed us from death by a spiritual means, as was said above. We are debtors of him who justified us, who were fouled by fleshly vices but then cleansed by the bath of the Spirit (see Titus 3:5), and made us children of God. For when we were first placed in the flesh, we lived according to the example of Adam and were subject to sins, but now that we have been set free we should render service to the redeemer.[64] (1a)[65] This service, in fact, does not in any way benefit him, since he needs nothing, but it obtains eternal life for us. For he loves us so much that he attributes to himself that which benefits us.

8:13 *For if you live according to the flesh, you will die.* (1) Nothing could be truer, that if we live according to Adam we will die. When Adam transgressed, he sold himself to sin and was deemed to be flesh; every sin is flesh. Because faults and transgressions are born from outside a person by way of the senses—namely, from hearing, sight, touch,[66] smell, or taste[67]— they are deemed to be flesh. Every thought,[68] when it turns its attention outside itself, leads to sin. Indeed, even in the case of the first human being sin was born from outside. Therefore, to live *according to the flesh* is death; every act of the flesh[69] is outside of the law.

But if by the Spirit you put to death the deeds of the flesh,[70] *you will live.* (2) The apostle wants the body to be ruled by the law of the soul. Therefore,

---

64. In Roman law the word *redemptor*, here rendered "redeemer," can refer to one who purchases another's freedom from slavery. See Franz-Stefan Meissel, "Redemptor," *BNP* A12:430.

65. *Recensio* α does not have section 1a.

66. *Recensio* β does not have "touch."

67. *Recensio* α has "Because faults and transgressions are born from outside a person, from the spectacle without and not from the soul within, they are deemed to be flesh."

68. *Recensiones* α and β have "Every thought [α: of sin], turning its attention outside itself, leads to transgression."

69. *Recensio* α has "the entire life of the flesh" instead of "every act of the flesh."

70. Ambrosiaster's biblical text has "of the flesh" (*carnis*), but the great majority of biblical witnesses have "of the body" (τοῦ σώματος). See Jewett, *Romans*, 475.

he explains that if, under the lead of the Holy Spirit, the actions and intentions of the flesh, which are devised[71] at the instigation of the powers of this world, have been suppressed so that they do not obtain the power to do what they intend, life will result. They are said to be put to death if they cease, especially because they do not exist if they are not done.[72]

8:14 *For all who are led by the Spirit of God are children of God.* The apostle says that people in whose actions the intentions of the principalities and powers of this world (see Eph 6:12) are not manifest are *led by the Spirit of God.* For those in whom they are manifest are not children of God, but children of the devil, because *one who is born of God does not sin* (1 John 3:9), says the apostle John. This is what distinguishes children of God and children of the devil. That is why the Lord says to the Jews, *You are of your father the devil* (John 8:44), because they were doing evil and planning murder.[73]

8:15 *For you did not receive once again the spirit of slavery in fear.* (1) The apostle says this so that in future we do not do anything for which we may once again feel afraid, because once the Holy Spirit has been received we are freed from every fear arising from evil deeds. Previously we lived in fear because all people were found guilty after the law had been given. The apostle called the law "the spirit of fear" because it put people in a position of fear on account of sin. However, the law of faith, which is signified by the expression *spirit of adoption*,[74] is the law of assurance because it rescues us from fear when it forgives sin. As a result, it makes us safe and is not called *the spirit of fear* (2 Tim 1:7) according to this world.

But you have received the spirit of adoption as children, through whom we cry, "Abba, Father." (2) Having been freed from fear by the grace of God, we have received *the spirit of adoption as children.* Therefore, when we consider what we were and what we have obtained by the gift of God, we should direct our life with great care so that the name of God the Father does not suffer any disrepute in us and so that we do not, like ungrateful wretches, fall into all those things we escaped. (2a)[75] We have received such grace that we dare to say to God, *Abba,* that is, *Father.* Therefore, the

---

71. *Recensiones* α and β have "brought about."
72. *Recensio* α has "They are said to die if they cease." *Recensio* β has "They are said to be put to death if they cease, for if they cease they do not exist, because sin does not exist if it is not done."
73. *Recensio* α does not have "because they were doing evil and planning murder."
74. *Recensio* α does not have "of adoption."
75. *Recensio* α does not have section 2a.

apostle warns that the trust we have received should not turn into audacity. For if we manifest a way of life contrary to this word we utter, *Abba, Father*, we insult God by calling him *Father*. Out of his goodness he has granted us something that is beyond our nature, so that we may merit by works what we in essence do not deserve.

8:16 *The Spirit himself testifies to our spirit that we are children of God.* (1) When we do what is right and as a result the Holy Spirit remains in us, the Spirit of God is witness to our soul through this utterance that we cry in prayer, *Abba*, that is, *Father*, that since he remains in us we do not say, *Abba, Father*, thoughtlessly.[76] For we present a life worthy of this utterance. (1a) Moreover, this is the proof that they are children: if through the Spirit a sign of belonging to the Father can be seen in them.

8:17 *And if children, also heirs. Heirs, in fact, of God, and co-heirs with Christ.* (1a)[77] Since God the Father can in no way be said to be dead, and Christ his Son may be said to be dead on account of the incarnation, why is one who is dead said to be the heir of one who is always living, since evidently only the dead have heirs? But this statement refers to the humanity, not the divinity.[78] Now, with God what is called an inheritance among us is a gift of the Father, transferred to obedient children, so that through one's own merit, not by virtue of a death, a person who is alive may be an heir to someone who is living. (1b) This is why the Lord, too, for divine reasons more than human ones, indicated in the gospel, albeit in a parable, that a living person divided his possessions among the living (see Luke 15:12–13); this parable was not composed for a nonsensical reason. Therefore, to make us eager to obey God the Father, the apostle encourages us with this hope, saying that we will be *heirs of God and co-heirs with Christ*, so that because the hope of reward is great, we may be all the more disposed toward the things of God, setting aside concern for worldly things. (2) What it means to be a co-heir with the Son of God, we learn from the apostle John. Among other things he says: *We know that when he appears we will be like him* (1 John 3:2).

---

76. *Recensio* α has "we rightly say" instead of "we do not say thoughtlessly."

77. *Recensio* α does not have sections 1a and 1b. It precedes section 2 with the following comment: "(1) This is a great encouragement, that as much as the apostle proclaims that we will receive very great benefits from God, even more so he warns us to render ourselves worthy of them, so that more and more we will live properly as future co-heirs with Christ."

78. *Recensio* β does not have "not the divinity."

Provided we suffer with him in order that we may also be glorified. (3) He states how we can become co-heirs with Christ: *provided we suffer with him in order that we may also be glorified.* Let us see, then, what it means to suffer with him. To suffer with him is to endure persecutions on account of the hope of things to come[79] and to crucify the flesh with its faults and desires, that is, to spurn the pleasures and pretentions of this age.[80] When all these things have died for a person, he crucifies the world, believing in the life of the age to come, in which he trusts he will be a co-heir with Christ.

8:18 *I consider that the sufferings of this present time are not worth comparing with the future glory which will be revealed in us.* (1) This encouraging remark relates to the preceding discussion, in which he shows that what can be inflicted here by unbelievers is small in comparison with the reward decreed for the age to come. For this reason he observes that we ought to be ready for every calamity, because the rewards promised for these things are enormous, so that in times of distress the spirit may encourage itself and grow stronger in hope. Indeed, we know what grueling and hard labors some people—or rather many people—endure for present gains, truly, for only a modest benefit, and that sometimes they cannot achieve their goals because this life is fragile and unpredictable.[81] (2) For such gains sailors consign themselves to so many storms and tempests, although they know that in them they are facing death rather than life! Soldiers, too, do not hesitate to rush into combat in hope of present reward, although victory is uncertain. How much more, therefore, should we suffer for Christ, from whom we enjoy benefits even if they are deferred.[82] He promises glorious rewards instead of paltry ones, heavenly rewards instead of earthly ones,[83] eternal rewards instead of temporal ones, accompanied by glory! We are said to suffer for Christ even though what we suffer benefits not him but us. But he ordains suffering because he is seeking an occasion to reward us. Like a kindly or generous benefactor he seeks occasions to bestow gifts on

---

79. *Recensio* α does not have "on account of the hope of things to come."

80. *Recensio* α has "When he says *the flesh*, he means the pleasures and pretentions of this age" instead of "that is, to spurn the pleasures and pretentions of this age."

81. *Recensio* α has "and that sometimes they do achieve them [*ad quos*]," referring either to "labors" (*labores*) or, incorrectly, to "gains" (*lucris*). *Recensio* β has "and that sometimes they cannot achieve them [*ad quae*]," referring to "gains."

82. *Recensio* α does not have this clause.

83. *Recensio* α does not have "heavenly rewards instead of earthly ones."

the undeserving or the shameful. (2a)[84] In the end, he himself supplies the strength whereby these calamities may be endured.

8:19 *In fact, the longing of creation awaits the revelation of the children of God.* Because he said that the sufferings of the present time do not merit the glory that is to come, the apostle added that the creation awaits the moment when the number of the children of God who are destined for life will be complete, so that then at last the creation itself can also be relieved of its bounden service and relax in ease.[85]

8:20 *For the creation was subjected to futility, not by choice.* (1) Having been established by the power of God the creator,[86] creation was certainly not subjected to futility of its own accord. Moreover, its being subjected will benefit not it but us. What, then, does it mean to be *subjected to futility*? Is it not that the things that creation brings forth are perishable? It operates in such a way that it produces corruptible fruit. This corruption, then, is futility. All things that come to life in the world are weak, perishable, and corruptible, and for this reason they are futile.[87] They are futile because they cannot maintain their state of being. All things, undone by the flow of change,[88] always return to themselves in a disordered state of nature. As Solomon, too, said about these things: *They are all futile* (Eccl 1:2).[89] (1a)[90] Nor does David disagree with such statements, when he says: *Surely futile is every living person* (Ps 38:6 LXX = Ps 39:5 ET). For is it not futile to eat and drink and be busy with the affairs of the world? Yet this futility has its uses. For it serves people well to have been born into the world in order that, as

---

84. *Recensio* α does not have section 2a.
85. *Recensio* α has "can also be freed from its bondage to corruption and cease from its labor in ease" (*ipsa creatura possit liberari a servitute corruptionis et cessaret in otio*). *Recensio* β has *in vitio* instead of *in otio*, which is clearly a scribal error. *Recensio* γ has *ipsa creatura possit discingi ab officio servitutis et pausare in otio*. Three MSS— Monte Cassino 150, Paris lat. 1759, and Oxford 756, which often agrees with MS Paris lat. 1759—have *in otio*. The reading *initio*, found instead of *in otio* in the manuscripts $FG^1MB^1Y^1$ (see CSEL 81.1:lvii) provides further evidence of a common archetype for these manuscripts (see CSEL 81.1:xxxv). This reading was corrected to *in vitio* by a second hand in MS St. Gall 101. MSS Vienna 743 and Amiens 87 end at *pausare*.
86. *Recensiones* α and β have "by the power of the Lord and creator."
87. *Recensio* α does not have this sentence.
88. *Recensio* α does not have "by the flow of change."
89. *Recensio* α adds "and the things that have been created in this way are not eternal but futile."
90. *Recensio* α does not have section 1a.

they thereby experience the rigors of bodily existence, they discover the mystery of the creator. These things are futile in comparison with things eternal. Nevertheless, they are good in their own sphere, especially because they are necessary.

But on account of him who subjected it in hope. (2) What this hope is, the apostle immediately adds, when he states:

8:21 *Because the creation itself will be set free from bondage to corruption into the freedom of the glory of the children of God.* Because the creation cannot oppose its creator, it is subjected on his account, but not without hope. While it is placed in this position of toil, it takes solace in the fact that it will have rest when all those whom God knows will come to faith believe, for whose sake in fact he subjected it.[91]

8:22 *We know that the whole creation has been groaning and is in labor until now.* (1) To be in labor is to suffer. The meaning of the verse is as follows: the whole creation groans and suffers in its daily toil until now. *Until now* means as long as the verse is read. Indeed, even the elements produce their works with difficulty, since both the sun and the moon fill the distance assigned to them not without exertion, and the spirit of the animals is compelled to perform its service with much groaning. In fact, we see from these groans[92] that they are forced against their will to toil. Therefore, they all await rest, so that they may be set free from servile labor.[93] (1a)[94] Now, if this were a servitude that made one progressively more worthy of God, the creation would rejoice, not suffer. But because it was subjected for our sake in servitude to corruption, it suffers. Every day its sees its works perish. Every day its work rises and falls. It is understandable, therefore, that it suffers, when its operation pertains not to eternity but to corruption. (2) Therefore, as much as one is given to understand, the elements are quite anxious for our salvation, knowing that the sooner we satisfy our maker,[95] the quicker it will lead to their release. Knowing this, then, let us with all care and diligence show ourselves to be worthy, so that we may be an example to others as well, moved not only by our own pitiful situation,

---

91. The last clause is found only in *recensio* β and one manuscript of *recensio* γ, MS Monte Cassino 150.

92. *Recensio* α has "We see from this refusal accompanied by groans that etc."

93. *Recensio* α has "so that they may be relieved of this duty"; see In Rom. 8:19.

94. *Recensio* α does not have section 1a.

95. *Recensiones* α and β have "acknowledge" (*agnoscamus*) instead of "satisfy" (*promereamur*).

but also for the sake of creation, which groans day and night as it endures loss.[96] For we are inclined to attend more readily to the situation of others.

8:23 *And not only the creation, but we too who have the receptacle of the Spirit, we ourselves groan within ourselves as we await*[97] *the redemption of our body.* (1) After the terrestrial creation he has added that we too await this and groan unto God that all we who are destined for life may be set free from this place, (1a)[98] because for Christians this world is a vast sea. Just as the sea when it is tossed to and fro by storms leaps up and creates a tempest for sailors, so too this age, agitated by the plots of unbelievers, disturbs the minds of the faithful. The enemy does this with such ingenuity that one does not know what one should avoid first of all; there is no shortage of occasions for trouble.[99] If the authorities cease to be against us, the enemy stirs up the minds of private individuals. If they too are held in check, he lights a fire by means of the household servants. If this has been doused, he sows dissension among the brothers and sisters themselves with his own cunning, so that, battered on four corners, the house may one way or another collapse in ruins. For this reason the only counsel for Christians is to flee this place; they should follow the example of the holy Simeon, who, knowing the war that was to be conducted here against unbelief, asked to be dismissed in peace (see Luke 2:29). (2)[100] This is why, when we individually pray for everyone, we pray that the kingdom of God may come (see Matt 6:10).[101] At that time the liberation of our body—that is, of all Christians—will occur. By *body* the apostle meant all Christians, because we are *members one of another* (Rom 12:5). (4)[102] Thus, through

---

96. *Recensio* α has "situation, but also creation's, which for our sake groans day and night as it endures loss."

97. Many biblical witnesses add "adoption" (υἱοθεσίαν), a variant omitted by Ambrosiaster's biblical text. Bruce M. Metzger, *A Textual Commentary on the Greek New Testament*, 2nd ed. (Stuttgart: Deutsche Bibelgesellschaft, 1994), 457; and Jewett, *Romans*, 505, differ on which reading should be preferred.

98. *Recensio* α does not have section 1a.

99. *Recensiones* α and β do not have the last clause.

100. In *recencio* γ section 2 is attested only by MSS Monte Cassino 150 and Paris lat. 1759.

101. Ambrosiaster's comment indicates that the Lord's Prayer was used in private prayer by Christians in Rome in the fourth century. The Lord's Prayer was one of the texts, but not the only text, used in private prayer. See Emmanuel von Severus, "Gebet I," *RAC* 8:1222–23.

102. *Recensio* α precedes section 4 with the following comment: "(3) Indeed, the

what has been said above, the apostle shows what violence the creation suffers for our sake, when we, for whom creation renders its service and who have the help of the Spirit of God, groan to be set free from this place, so that we may receive the promised reward. Even more, therefore, does the creation groan, which does not have the help of the Holy Spirit and does not toil for its own sake.[103] (4a)[104] On top of this, it sees that the things it produces through its own labor in order to provide food for the servants of God are sacrificed to idols, against all that is right! For this reason it suffers more and seeks to be set free sooner, knowing that this misuse contributes to the affront of the creator.

8:24 *For in hope we were saved.* (1) The apostle says this because by hoping for what God promised in Christ we have made ourselves worthy to be set free. Therefore, we were set free in hope, since what will come to pass is nothing other than what we believe.

But hope that is seen is not hope. (2) It is obvious that hope is not the hope that is seen, but what is not seen.[105] Consequently, believers[106] ought to be granted rewards, because they hope for things they do not see.

8:25[107] *Indeed, what someone sees, why does he hope for it?*[108] *But if we hope for what we do not see, we wait for it with patience.* (1a)[109] Without a doubt, things that are not seen are to be hoped for; they are awaited, in fact, as things to come. (1) This waiting is patience, which is highly meritorious before God, such that, waiting from day to day, it longs for the kingdom of God to come and does not doubt on account of its being delayed.

8:26 *In a similar way, then, the Spirit also helps the weakness of our prayer.*[110] (1) Because the apostle reminded us above to groan and to pray

---

apostle, as a divine man, thinks highly of us when he says that we groan to be set free from this place just as Simeon also groaned. I, however, see that we are held by the enjoyment of the world." It is a rare personal—and critical—observation from Ambrosiaster.

103. *Recensio* α has "in hope" instead of "for its own sake."

104. *Recensio* α does not have section 4a.

105. *Recensio* α has "It is obvious that hope is not the hope that is seen, but the hope that is not seen." In *recensio* γ the clause "but what is seen" is found only in MSS Oxford 756, Paris lat. 1759, and, in a second hand, St. Gall 101.

106. *Recensiones* α and β have "those who hope" instead of "believers."

107. In English translations of Romans, 8:25 begins with the next sentence, *But if we hope* etc.

108. On the textual variants for this sentence, see Jewett, *Romans*, 505.

109. *Recensio* α does not have section 1a.

110. Ambrosiaster's biblical text has "the weakness of our prayer" (*infirmitatem*

for freedom,[111] we, having been placed in this position of suffering, either want things which are said to occur far in the future to happen soon or things by which we achieve merit to be taken away quickly, and so we seem to pray a feeble prayer, as its request is denied. It is enfeebled because it asks for things which are contrary to reason. This weakness, the apostle therefore shows, is helped by the Holy Spirit who has been given to us. However, the Holy Spirit helps because he does not permit to happen things that are requested before they ought to be requested or that are harmful.

For we do not know how to pray as we ought. (2) The apostle has explained that the weakness of our prayer refers to ignorance. We are deceived in thinking that the things we request are beneficial, even though they are not. Indeed, the Lord said to the apostle himself, when he prayed for the third time that certain trials be taken away from him,[112] since they occurred frequently: *My grace is sufficient for you, for strength is made perfect in weakness* (2 Cor 12:9), that is: One acquires merit when one is found to be patient in tribulation. The Lord therefore taught him that what he was asking was contrary to his own interest. Sometimes a request is both arrogant and foolish, as was the case with the two apostles James and John, who, when they made an unrealistic and outlandish request, were told: *You do not know what you are asking* (Matt 20:22).

But the Spirit himself intercedes for us with sighs that are beyond words.[113] (3a)[114] The apostle says that the Spirit of the Lord intercedes for us not with human eloquence, but in keeping with his nature. When that which is of God speaks with God, it necessarily speaks in the same way that the one from whom he is speaks. No one speaks with his fellow citizen in a foreign tongue. (3) The Spirit which has been given to us pours himself out with our prayers in order to cover our clumsiness and imprudence with his action and to ask those things for us from God that are beneficial for us.

8:27 *And he who searches hearts knows what the Spirit desires, because it intercedes for the saints according to God.* (1) It is obvious that to God, for

---

nostrae orationis), but among the biblical witnesses the preferred text is simply "our weakness" (τῇ ἀσθενείᾳ ἡμῶν). See Jewett, *Romans*, 505.

111. *Recensio* α has "Because the passage reminded us to groan and to pray, we etc."

112. *Recensio* α does not have "for a third time."

113. The phrase "for us" (*pro nobis*) found in Ambrosiaster's biblical text is not found in the preferred biblical witnesses. See Jewett, *Romans*, 505.

114. *Recensio* α does not have section 3a; see n. 116 below.

whom nothing is unspoken or unseen, the prayer of every spirit is known,[115] and even more so the prayer of the Holy Spirit, (1a) who is without doubt of the same substance, and who speaks not by the movement of air nor as the angels nor as any other creatures, but as befits his divinity.[116] (2) The Spirit therefore speaks with God, though to us he seems to be silent, because he sees though he is not seen[117] and asks for those things that he knows are pleasing to God and good for us. This same Spirit rightly interposes himself for us[118] when he knows that we ask for things that are wrong out of ignorance, not out of arrogance.

8:28 *We know, in fact, that all things work for the good of those who love God, who are called according to his purpose.* The apostle says this because even if those who love God have prayed inappropriately, God will not hold it against them. Since God knows the intention and the ignorance of their heart,[119] he does not grant them the harmful things they ask for, but grants them things that ought to be given to those who love God. For this reason the Lord, too, says in the gospel: *Your father knows what you need before you ask him* (Matt 6:8). Those people, therefore, are called *according to his purpose* whom as believers God foreknew would be his own, so that before they believed they were known.

8:29 *Those whom he foreknew he also predestined.* (1) Those whom he foreknew[120] would remain faithful to him are the ones he chose[121] to strive for the promised reward. Thus, those who give the appearance of believing and do not persevere in the faith on which they embarked are deemed not to have been chosen by God, since those whom God has chosen in his own

---

115. *Recensio* α has "the prayer of the Holy Spirit is known" and ends the sentence here.

116. *Recensio* α does not have section 1a. In *recensio* γ the clause "and who speaks … divinity" is attested only by MSS Amiens 87 and Monte Cassino 150. The introduction of this section in *recensio* β is significant because, in explaining the nature of communication between the persons of the Trinity, Ambrosiaster extends divine consubstantiality to the Holy Spirit. See the introduction §5.2 and Theodore S. de Bruyn, "Ambrosiaster's Revisions of His *Commentary on Romans* and Roman Synodal Statements about the Holy Spirit," *REAug* 56 (2010): 61–65.

117. *Recensio* α does not have "because he sees though he is not seen."

118. *Recensio* α has "The Holy Spirit rightly interposes himself when etc."

119. *Recensio* α does not have "and the ignorance."

120. *Recensio* α has "knows."

121. *Recensio* β adds "in his own mind."

mind endure.[122] (1a)[123] In fact, there are people who are chosen temporarily, such as Saul and Judas, not on account of foreknowledge but on account of righteousness at the moment.

To be conformed to the image of his Son. (2) The apostle says this because they are predestined for a future age precisely so that they may become like the Son of God, as he noted above (see Rom 8:14–17).

In order that he might be the firstborn among many brothers. (3) *Firstborn* is the right word, because he[124] was born, not made, before all of creation. God has deigned to adopt human beings as his children in accordance with the model of the Son. He is the firstborn in the regeneration of the Spirit;[125] he is the firstborn of the dead, with which he is unacquainted by nature; and he is the firstborn to ascend into heaven once death was conquered.[126] So, our brother is said to be firstborn in all things because he deigned to be born a human being. Nevertheless, he is the Lord, because he is our God, as the prophet Jeremiah says: *He is our God* (Bar 3:36).[127]

8:30 *And those whom he predestined he also called.* (1) To call is to help a person be mindful of the faith or to prod the person one knows is listening.

And those whom he called he also justified, and those whom he justified he also glorified. (2) He repeats what he said above, that those whom God foreknew to be suited to him persevere as believers, since a thing cannot turn out differently than God has foreknown.[128] God also justified them and consequently also glorified them, so that they might become like the

---

122. *Recensio* α has "Thus, those who give the appearance of believing and do not behave in a way that is appropriate, are not said to have been chosen by God, since what God has chosen endures."

123. *Recensio* α does not have section 1a.

124. I.e., the Son.

125. *Recensiones* α and β have "Christ is also the firstborn in regeneration."

126. *Recensiones* α and β have "after the victory" instead of "once death was conquered."

127. *Recensio* α does not have "Jeremiah." Ambrosiaster also cites Bar 3:36 as a testimony that Christ is God at In 2 Cor. 6:16–18 (§1) and in a tract against the Arians, *Quaest.* 97.7 (CSEL 50.176–77). The verse is cited under the heading "Christ is God" by Cyprian, *Test.* 2.6 (CCSL 3:35), who, too, attributes the book to Jeremiah. The attribution was traditional.

128. *Recensio* β has "unless God has foreknown them" instead of "than God has foreknown." The text in *recensiones* α and γ makes better sense.

Son of God. (2a)[129] As for the rest, whom God did not foreknow, God does not attend to them in this grace because he did not foreknow that they would be pleasing to him.[130] Even if they are chosen temporarily as believers because they seem to be good (so that justice may not appear to have been disregarded), they do not persevere so as to be glorified. This was the case with Judas Iscariot (see John 6:70–71) and the seventy-two disciples who, although chosen (see Luke 10:1), withdrew from the Savior after they took offense (see John 6:60–66).[131]

8:31 *What then shall we say about this? If God is for us, who is against us?* Obviously, since God bears witness for us, who would dare to accuse us, when the one who is judge foreknew us beforehand and judged us to be pleasing to him?

8:32 *He who did not spare his own Son, but gave him up for us all.* (1) By explaining that God had, as it were, with foreknowledge given up his Son to death for us before we had turned from unbelievers into believers, the apostle encourages us to be confident with regard to the faith.

How will he not also give us all things with him? (2a)[132] The apostle says that long ago God decreed that those who believe in Christ would be rewarded. (2) Surely, if God undertook to do something great and extraordinary for us—to give up his true and beloved Son for us while we were still godless—why should he not be trusted to have done a lesser thing for us when we believe in him?[133] The reward has in fact already been prepared for believers.[134] It is indeed a lesser thing to give us all things with Christ than to give him up to death for our sake.

8:33 *Who will bring a charge against God's elect?* (1) It is evident that nobody either dares to or is able to call into question the judgment and foreknowledge of God concerning us. For who can disapprove what God approves, since no one is equal to God?

It is God who justifies. (2) The words that the apostle here writes as his own are found in the prophet Isaiah (Isa 50:8), that there is no other person

---

129. *Recensio* α does not have section 2a.
130. *Recensio* β does not have "that they would be pleasing to him."
131. See In Rom. 9:13 (§4a).
132. *Recensio* α does not have section 2a.
133. *Recensiones* α and β have "to do a lesser thing for us when [α: now that] we believe in him."
134. *Recensio* α does not have this sentence.

to censure something that does not displease God.[135] Or will God himself perhaps bring a charge against us? But he cannot bring a charge against those he justifies.

8:34 *Who will be there to condemn? Is it Christ who died, yes, who also arose and is at the right hand of God, who indeed intercedes for us?* (1) The apostle refutes the claim that God brings a charge against us, since God justifies us.[136] He adds, moreover, that Christ cannot condemn us, because he loves us with such feeling that he died for us and, rising from the dead, always acts on our behalf before the Father. His requests cannot be spurned because he is at the right hand of God, that is, in a place of honor because he is God. Thus, confident in God the Father and in Christ his Son who will come to judge, we rejoice in their surety. (2) This is why it is said to the apostle Peter: *Behold, Satan has demanded that he might sift you like wheat. But I have pleaded for you that your faith might not fail* (Luke 22:31–32). In this way, then, the Savior intercedes for us. For, knowing the might[137] and the profound malevolence of our enemy once he has mobilized against us, the Savior intercedes for us—provided that we do not consent to the enemy—so that he dare not do us any sort of violence and his arrogance is kept in check. Although the Son himself accomplishes everything and is equal to God the Father, the Son nevertheless is said *to intercede* so that, given that God is said to be one, the Father or the Son may not be thought to be singular or a union:[138] the

---

135. *Recensiones* α and β have "something God approves" instead of "something that does not displease God."

136. Instead of the next two sentences, *recensio* α has "At the same time he says that Christ cannot condemn us because he died for us."

137. *Recensiones* α and β have "arrogance" instead of "might."

138. The problem Ambrosiaster tackles here is the subordination implicit in the act of interceding. In the course of the fourth century it had become unacceptable among pro-Nicene theologians to speak of Father and Son as either singular entities (*singularis*) or a single entity (*unio*). In Hilary of Poitier's anti-Arian work *On the Trinity*—which Ambrosiaster knew; see Alexander Souter, *The Earliest Latin Commentaries on the Epistles of St. Paul* (Oxford: Clarendon, 1927), 66—the term *unio* refers to the notion of a personal identity of Father and Son, attributed to Sabellius (Hilary of Poitiers, *Trin*. 6.11, 7.5 [CCSL 62:207–8]), and the term *singularis* refers to the notion of a single, solitary God, articulated in different ways by both Sabellius and Arius (Hilary of Poitiers, *Trin*. 7.5, 7.8 [CCSL 62:264–65, 267–68], and continuing against Arius throughout book 7); see R. P. C. Hanson, *The Search for the Christian Doctrine of God: The Arian Controversy 318–381* (Edinburgh: T&T Clark, 1988), 479–80. In their own opposition to Sabellius, Arians in the West insisted that Father and Son were

scriptures speak in this manner to distinguish between the persons,[139] to present the Son as someone who is not different from the Father[140] and at the same time to give precedence to the Father because he is the Father and because all things are from him (see 1 Cor 8:6).[141]

8:35 *Who will separate us from the love of Christ?* (1) That is, who will be able to turn us away from the love of Christ, who has shown us such great and innumerable benefits?

Tribulation? (2) But tribulation does not, because no torments overcome the love[142] of the steadfast Christian. For the love of the lover is aroused all the more if he is forbidden to love him whose benefits he experiences. When he understands that he is cultivating ground in the latter's merits, he recalls the benefits.[143]

8:36 *Or distress? Or persecution? Or famine? Or nakedness? Or danger? Or the sword? As it is written: "For your sake we are being killed all the day long; we are reckoned as sheep for the slaughter"* (Ps 43:22 LXX = Ps 44:22 ET). **8:37** *But in all these things we overcome because of him who loved*

---

each singular (*singularis*) and incomparable (*incomparabilis*) at the level of nature; see Manlio Simonetti, "Arianesimo latino," StMed 8 (1967): 704–5. While the act of interceding would preclude thinking of Father and Son as a single entity, it implies that the Son is subordinate to the Father, as Arians in the West observed, citing Rom 8:34; see Simonetti, "Arianesimo latino," 722 n. 206. Ambrosiaster argues that the Scriptures speak in this way to distinguish the Father from the Son while at the same time maintaining their common substance; see n. 140 below. Thus, although the Son is equal to the Father and capable of accomplishing everything, he is nevertheless said to intercede for the believer. See In Rom. 8:39 (§3) and 16:25–27 (§1).

139. On the use of the term "person" (*persona*) to distinguish between the Father, Son, and Holy Spirit, see the introduction §5.2.

140. The word Ambrosiaster uses here, *dispar*, also appears in a tract he wrote against the Arians. To support his point that the Son's generation from the Father entails that they have one substance, Ambrosiaster twice observes "that what is born is not different [*dispar*] from what gives birth" (*Quaest.* 97.5 and 8 [CSEL 50:175, 178]). Because Christ as the Son is not different in nature from the Father, he is on par with and equal to the Father (*Quaest.* 97.11 [CSEL 50:179]).

141. *Recensio* α does not have "because he is the Father and."

142. *Recensio* α has "veneration" instead of "love."

143. This sentence is poorly transmitted in the manuscripts and thus difficult to translate. *Recensio* α has "When he understands that he is declining in the latter's merits, he recalls the benefits." *Recensio* β has "When he understands that he is cultivating ground in the latter's merits, he recalls the benefits." The manuscripts of *recensio* γ vary. I have translated the sentence as found in MSS Monte Cassino 150 and Paris lat. 1759, which have the same text as *recensio* β.

us.[144] (1a)[145] This is written in Psalm 43. (1) It is clear, therefore, that all the things the apostle enumerates—calamities, tribulations, afflictions, and death—cannot be compared to or equated with the love of Christ, which he has inculcated in us. The benefits we have from him are much greater than all those things which seem harmful. If we die for him—which seems to be the worst of these outcomes—he too died for us. (2) But he died in order to help us, while our death does not benefit him but us. For we place a temporal life in the balance in order to be repaid with an eternal one. What is there to wonder at if slaves die for a good master, when the master died for slaves and wrong-doers? Therefore, the benefits triumph and the spirit is encouraged to persevere for him who loved us.

8:38 *For I am sure that neither death.* This is the guarantee[146] of the pledge of Christ, by which he has undertaken to support in times of tribulation the faith that is committed to him.

Nor life, nor an angel, nor a miracle, **8:39** *nor height, nor depth, nor things present, nor things to come,*[147] *nor any other creature will be able to separate us from the love of God which is in Christ Jesus our Lord.* (1) All these are things which are inflicted by the devil in order to capture us. The apostle mentions them in order to protect us, so that if they arrive we may fight back against them, armed with faith and trusting in the hope and help of Christ. What then? If death should be inflicted, is it not the greatest gain to find an occasion to be taken more quickly into the promised kingdom? Even if we were to be promised a present life loaded with honor, it should not avert us from the hope and benefits of Christ, whom we know will benefit us not only in the future but also in the present. Indeed, even if an angel reveals himself to us in order to seduce us, fitted out with the stratagems of his father the devil, he ought not to prevail against us, since we know that nothing should take precedence over Christ, *the angel of great counsel* (see

---

144. Among the biblical witnesses the expression "through him who loved us" (διὰ τοῦ ἀγαπήσαντος ἡμᾶς) is more widely attested than the expression "because of him who loved us" (*propter eum qui nos dilexit*) in Ambrosiaster's biblical text. See Jewett, *Romans*, 532.

145. *Recensio* α does not have section 1a.

146. *Recensiones* α and β have "confidence" instead of "guarantee."

147. Ambrosiaster's biblical text differs from the accepted text at several points: the singular "angel" (*angelus*) instead of the plural "angels" (ἄγγελοι); the singular "miracle" (*virtus*) instead of the plural "powers" (δυνάμεις); the omission of "principalities" (ἀρχαί); and the placement of the elements in the list. See NA[28] and Jewett, *Romans*, 532.

Isa 9:5 LXX and Isa 9:6 VL).[148] (2) If a miracle were to be performed by someone, as is said to have been performed by Simon the magician, who is said to have flown up into the air,[149] so that he became a scandal to the people of Christ, it should not diminish our faith, since we know that the Savior, when he was taken up in an attendant cloud, ascended above all the heavens (see Acts 1:9). If the devil reveals himself to us in the heights—about which the same apostle says:[150] *Are you unaware of the heights of Satan?* (see Rev 2:24)—it should not draw us away from our devotion for the Lord Jesus, whom we know to have descended from heaven in order to unite things earthly with things spiritual. (3) If by means of a vision by which he intends to lead us astray, the devil shows us the depths—a wonder to be gazed upon with dread—so that we, terrified, perhaps may surrender to him, even so it would not be worth us breaking our trust in Christ, whom we know to have descended to the depths of the earth for our sake and, after he conquered death, to have set the human race free. If the devil promises us things to come, as he promised Eve (see Gen 3:4–5), we will not give him our approbation, since he has separated himself from Christ, whom we believe and know to be God in power and nature.[151] If by the skill and artifice of his cunning the devil creates another creature for a moment, as did Jannes and Jambres before Pharaoh (see 2 Tim 3:8;

---

148. *Recensio* α does not have "the angel of great counsel." The phrase comes from the VL of Isa 9:6 used in Rome and elsewhere in Italy and Europe. See Roger Gryson, ed., *Esaias*, VLB 12 (Freiburg: Herder, 1987–1993), 293.

149. The story is recounted in the apocryphal Acts Pet. 4 (*Acta apostolorum apocrypha post Constantinum Tischendorf*, ed. R. A. Lipsius and M. Bonnet, 2 vols. in 3 [1891–1903; repr., Hildesheim: Olms, 1990], 1:48–49) and referred to in Pseudo-Clementines, Rec. 3.47.2 (GCS 51^2:128).

150. The passage that follows was, in fact, not written by Paul. Ambrosiaster also attributes it to him—"the apostle"—at *Quaest.* 27.2 and 31.1 (CSEL 50:54, 58). Ambrosiaster appears to conflate Rev 2:24 with 2 Cor 2:11, which was written by Paul. In his reading of the passage, Ambrosiaster takes *altitudo* to mean "height" rather than "depth." The Latin word can take either of these meanings, but only the latter sense corresponds to the Greek τὰ βαθέα at Rev 2:24. This is further evidence of Ambrosiaster's unfamiliarity with the Greek text of the Scriptures.

151. The argument that Christ has both the nature and the power of God the Father, and that the latter implies the former, was advanced by pro-Nicene theologians such as Hilary of Poitiers in the mid-fourth century. See, e.g., Hilary of Poitiers, *Trin.* 5.4–5 (CCSL 62:154–55), and Michel R. Barnes, "One Nature, One Power: Consensus Doctrine in Pro-Nicene Polemic," StPatr 29:215–16. See Ambrosiaster's comment at In Phil. 2:9–11 (§9).

Exod 7:11–12), it makes no sense that he thereby draw us away from God the true creator,[152] whom we know to have fashioned the creation through Christ his Son, who has existed for ever. (4) To some interpreters it seems that *another creature* referred to the idols.[153] But this is not correct, since it ought to mean something that Satan appears to fashion in the form of an amazing but misleading ruse. Now, who among the faithful is misled toward things he abandoned once his mistake had been exposed? But the devil plans and fashions these things to mislead even the elect (see Matt 24:24). There is nothing, therefore, that can separate us from the love of God which is in Christ Jesus. God showed his love for us in Christ when he gave him up for us.

---

152. *Recensio* α does not have "true."
153. Who these interpreters were remains unknown. For explanations given by Greek and Latin commentators writing before and after Ambrosiaster of the list in 8:38–39, see Karl H. Schelkle, *Paulus, Lehrer der Väter*, 2nd ed. (Düsseldorf: Patmos, 1959), 324–26.

Romans 9

9:1 *I am speaking the truth in Christ, I am not lying. My conscience bears me witness in the Holy Spirit,* **9:2** *that I have great sorrow and unceasing anguish in my heart.* **9:3** *For I wished that I myself were cursed by Christ for the sake of my brothers, my kindred according to the flesh,* **9:4** *who are Israelites.* (1) Because above he seems to speak against the Jews, who think that they are justified on account of the law, now in order to show his desire and affection toward them, he says, with his conscience as witness, that he is speaking *in Christ* Jesus and *in the Holy Spirit*, so that faith cannot be thought to belong to someone who is, as it were, their enemy. He therefore presents Christ and the Holy Spirit as witnesses, from whom nothing is hidden[1] and whose testimony cannot be impugned; they bear witness to the apostle when they recommend him by the power of the signs that they performed through him.[2] (2) The apostle has presented the immense protection of Christ and his extraordinary love for the human race (see Rom 8:35–39), and the glorious stature of Christ and the unending promised reward (see Rom 8:29–30). This is why he grieves for his people according to the flesh, since through their unbelief they deprive themselves of this everlasting and salutary benefit. He says *I wished*, not I wish, because he knows that it cannot come about that so outstanding a member be cut off from the Christian body without any previous fault.[3] Nevertheless, he shows affection and love toward his people.

To them belong adoption as children. (3) When he offers praise for his people, he demonstrates that he is right to grieve, because, although they had been adopted as children long ago, they reduced the affection and the

---

1. *Recensio* α ends the sentence here.
2. See In Rom. 1:5 (§2).
3. *Recensio* α does not have "that so outstanding a member be cut off from the Christian body without any previous fault."

grace of God the Father to nothing. To make others grieve for them as well, the apostle has also added:

And the glory and the establishment of the law and the worship and the promises; **9:5** *to them belong the fathers and from them is Christ according to the flesh, who is God over all, blessed forever. Amen.*[4] (1) The apostle enumerates so many things commending the excellence and the greatness of the Jewish people, as well as the promises, in order to instill sorrow in everyone for them. By not accepting the Savior, they lost the prerogative of the fathers and the value of the promise; they became worse than the gentiles, whom previously they had abominated because they were without God. It is, indeed, a heavier misfortune to have lost standing than not to have had it.[5] (2) In the course of discussing this, the apostle says concerning the Savior: *who is God over all, blessed forever. Amen.* When no mention is made of the Father's name and the discussion is about Christ, one cannot claim that God is not the subject of discussion. If scripture is speaking about God the Father and adds a reference to the Son, it often calls the Father *God* and the Son *Lord* because of the confession of a single God. If someone, then, does not think that the statement *who is God* refers to Christ, let him propose the person to whom he believes it refers; there is no mention of God the Father in this passage.[6] (3) Moreover, what is so surprising about the fact that in this passage the apostle described Christ in plain language as God over all? In other letters he confirmed this under-

---

4. The ascription of the concluding doxology of this verse has been the subject of considerable discussion. It can be read as a dependent clause referring to Christ or an independent clause referring to God; see Bruce M. Metzger, *A Textual Commentary on the Greek New Testament*, 2nd ed. (Stuttgart: Deutsche Bibelgesellschaft, 1994), 459–62; and Robert Jewett with Roy D. Kotansky, *Romans: A Commentary*, Hermeneia (Minneapolis: Fortress, 2007), 567–69. Although Ambrosiaster takes it to refer to Christ, he still broaches but discounts the possibility that "God" may not refer to "Christ"; see section 2 below.

5. See Ambrosiaster, *Quaest.* 39 (CSEL 50:66).

6. In his tract against Photinus, who denied the preexistence of Christ, Ambrosiaster replies to an imaginary interlocutor who proposes that Rom 9:5 "perhaps refers to the person of the Father" (*Quaest.* 91.8 [CSEL 50:157]: *sed forte ad patris personam pertinere dicatur*). There, as well as here, it appears that Ambrosiaster is responding to an interpretation voiced in his own day. His own position is traditional; Rom 9:5 is cited by several writers known to Ambrosiaster as proof that Christ is God. See Cyprian, *Test.* 2.6 (CCSL 3.1:37); Novatian, *Trin.* 13.6, 30.18 (CCSL 4:33, 74); Marius Victorinus, *Ar.* 1.18 (CSEL 83.1:80).

standing of Christ in so many words, when he said: *so that at the name of Jesus every knee shall bow, in heaven, on earth, and under the earth* (Phil 2:10). These are all things over which Christ is God. Nothing is left out of this list to suggest that Christ is not God over everything. Moreover, the knee of all creation can bow only before God. Finally, because the apostle John unwittingly wanted to worship an angel,[7] he heard the angel say: *You must not do that! I am a fellow servant with you. Worship God* (Rev 19:10). (4) The Lord[8] would certainly not have allowed himself to be worshiped unless he was God. If not, one would have to say that Christ assumed the position of God unlawfully and sinned, which cannot be the case, since when he rebukes the devil, he himself indicates that one should worship the Lord, God of all things,[9] and serve him alone (see Matt 4:10). Therefore, it is not prejudicial to God the Father when Christ is worshiped as God, because, even though it is said that one should serve God alone, God is served in Christ as well. For elsewhere the apostle says: *One who serves Christ in these things, pleases God* (Rom 14:18). What, then, remains to be said, but that the Father is believed to be God and the Son is believed to be God and nevertheless both are believed to be one God?[10] For whether one worships the Father or the Son, one is said to worship one God, and to serve the Father or the Son is to exhibit the service of one God. There therefore is no distinction between them,[11] because one who worships the Son worships the Father as well,[12] and one who serves the Father serves the Son. (4a)[13] To point out that the profession of Christ's deity is not a matter of flattery, he ended with *Amen*, that is, truly, so that he might show that Christ is in truth God over all, blessed for ever.

9:6 *The word of God, however, did not fail.*[14] (1a)[15] *The word of God did not fail*, when he said: *Through Isaac shall your seed be named* (Gen

---

7. *Recensio* α adds "as God."
8. *Recensio* α has "Christ" instead of "Lord."
9. *Recensiones* α and β do not have "of all things."
10. *Recensio* α has "but that both God the Father and God the Son are believed to be God."
11. *Recensio* β does not have "between them."
12. *Recensio* α does not have "as well."
13. *Recensio* α does not have section 4a.
14. Ambrosiaster's biblical text differs from the great majority of witnesses, which have "It is not as though [ὅτι] the word of God had failed." See NA[28] and Jewett, *Romans*, 570.
15. *Recensio* α does not have section 1a.

21:12). In other words, what God said would happen, in fact happened: it was not those who were the children of Abraham according to the flesh who were not called his seed, but rather those who received the faith through which Isaac was born, the faith that was transformed at the time of Christ. This faith was not yet specific, but was general in nature, so that what Abraham believed concerning Isaac, his descendants believed concerning God and Christ: that the Son of God was born to restore the wholeness of the human race.

For not all who are descended from Israel are Israelites,[16] **9:7** *and not all are children of Abraham because they are his descendants. But "through Isaac shall your seed be named"* (Gen 21:12). (1) This is what the apostle wants to be understood: no longer are they all considered worthy[17] simply because they are children of Abraham; rather, those who are children of the promise are considered worthy, that is, those whom God foreknew would accept his promise, whether they are from the Jews or from the gentiles. They are worthy of being called *Israelites*, that is, those who, seeing God, believe.[18] For of course, all who come from Isaac are children of Abraham, because the entire line of the Jewish people is from Abraham through Isaac.[19] (2) This is why the rest of the children should not be called children of Abraham. When Abraham believed, he received Isaac on account of his faith, because he believed God. In Abraham the mystery of the faith that was to come was signified, namely, that Abraham would have brothers of Isaac who possessed the same faith as the faith through which Isaac was born. Isaac was born as a result of the promise as a type of the Savior, so that one who believes[20] that Christ Jesus was promised to Abraham is a child of Abraham, a brother, in fact, of Isaac.[21] (3) Moreover, it is said of Abraham that *through your seed shall all the nations be blessed* (Gen 22:18). This certainly did not happen through Isaac, but through him who was promised to Abraham through Isaac, namely, Christ, through whom all the

---

16. Ambrosiaster's biblical text differs from the better witnesses, which have "Israel" (Ἰσραήλ) instead of "Israelites" (*Is[t]ra[h]elitae*). See Jewett, *Romans*, 570.

17. *Recensio* α has "they cannot all be considered worthy etc."

18. *Recensio* α has "those who see God" instead of "those who, seeing God, believe."

19. *Recensio* α adds "But, as I have said, those who accept the promise that was made in Isaac are truly children of Abraham."

20. In *recensio* α the verb is in the present tense, whereas in *recensiones* β and γ it is in the future perfect tense, referring more precisely to someone who comes to believe after the time of Abraham.

21. See In Gal. 4:23 (§1).

nations who believe are blessed. The rest of the Jews, therefore, are children of the flesh, deprived as they are of the promise, and they cannot share in the merit of Abraham, since they do not follow the faith by which Abraham became worthy.

9:8 *That is, it is not the children of the flesh who are the children of God, but the children of the promise are reckoned as seed.* The apostle mentions both *the children of the flesh* and *the children of God*.[22] The former are born of the desire of the flesh, whereas the latter are born of faith, spiritually, as was promised to Abraham, that those who believed would be reckoned to be his seed.

9:9 *For this is the wording of the promise: "About this time I will come and Sarah will have a son"* (Gen 18:10, 14). This is found in Genesis.[23] What was prefigured now exists in Christ, so that the Christ who was to come was promised as the son of Abraham; in him the word of the promise was fulfilled, that in Christ[24] all the nations of the earth would be blessed. When the promise was made to Abraham and he heard that *through your seed shall all the nations be blessed* (Gen 22:18), it was of course Christ, in whom we see this promise fulfilled, who was promised to him by way of the line of Isaac.

9:10 *And not only she,* that is, Sarah, *but also when Rebecca bore children by Isaac our father as a result of a single conception.* (1) The apostle says, thus, that not only Sarah gave birth to Isaac as a type, but also Rebecca the wife of Isaac. But the case of Isaac is different than the case of Jacob and Esau, because Isaac was born as a prefiguration of the Savior, but Jacob and Esau bear the type of two peoples, namely, believers and unbelievers, so that although they derive from one person they are nevertheless different. In each of them is symbolized a race of people as well, so that those who are united either on account of the faith or on account of unbelief are said to belong to a single race of people. A single race is symbolized by many people, not through fleshly lineage but by a common cause, because some children of Esau should be called children of Jacob and some children of Jacob should be ascribed to Esau. (2) All who are born of Jacob cannot justifiably be said to be his children simply because Jacob is the subject of

---

22. *Recensio* α does not have a comment on Rom 9:8. Instead of this sentence, *recensio* β has "It is obvious that *the children of the flesh* cannot be called *the children of God*."

23. *Recensio* α does not have this comment.

24. *Recensio* α has "in him" instead of "in Christ."

praise, nor are all who derive from Esau condemned simply because Esau was displeasing, since we see both that people born of the line of Jacob have become unbelievers and that people born of the line of Esau have become believers and dear to God. In fact, there is no doubt that many who come from Jacob are unbelievers; all the Jews, believers and unbelievers, derive their origin from him. And Job is proof that good and faithful people come from Esau; Job comes from the children of Esau, the fifth generation from Abraham, in other words, a grandson of Esau.[25]

9:11 *Now though they had not yet been born or done anything good or bad, in order that the purpose of God according to his election might continue,* **9:12** *not because of works but because of the call was it said that the elder shall serve the younger* (Gen 25:23),[26] **9:13** *as it is written: "Jacob I loved, but Esau I hated"* (Mal 1:2–3). This is found in Malachi.[27] (1) The apostle invokes the foreknowledge of God in these cases, because nothing can come about in a way other than God knew it would. Because he knew what each of them was to become, God said: "The one who will be the younger will be worthy, and the one who will be the elder will be unworthy." Foreknowledge chose the one and rejected the other. In the one whom God has chosen, the purpose of God abides, because nothing can come about in a way other than God knew and planned for him, so that he might be worthy of salvation. In the one whom God rejects, the purpose that God planned for him similarly abides, because he will be unworthy. God does this foreknowingly, not out of partiality (see Acts 10:34),[28] for he condemns no one before that person sins, and he crowns no one before that person conquers. (2) This relates to the case of the Jews, who defend their prerogative, that they are children of Abraham. The apostle in fact consoles himself,

---

25. A note appended to the Septuagint version of Job, based on a Syriac version of the book, identifies him as the son of Zerah, "a son of the sons of Esau" (Job 42:17b LXX). In the list of Esau's descendants at 1 Chr 1:34–37, Zerah is listed among the sons of Reuel, who in turn is listed among the sons of Esau. Thus, according to this tradition Job is descended from Abraham as follows: Abraham, Isaac, Esau, Reuel, Zerah, Job. Among Ambrosiaster's contemporaries, Ambrose, *Enarrat. Ps.* 36.63.3 (CSEL 64:121) accepted the tradition, but Jerome, *Qu. hebr. Gen.* 22.20–22 (CCSL 72:27), rejected it because he did not find the appended note in the Hebrew manuscripts of Job.

26. Among the biblical witnesses the preferred reading is "said to her" (ἐρρέθη αὐτῇ); the omission in Ambrosiaster's biblical text is a secondary modification. See NA[28] and Jewett, *Romans*, 570.

27. *Recensio* α does not have this comment.

28. See section 5 below.

since he had said that he has unceasing anguish of heart on account of the unbelief of those to whom belonged adoption as children and the setting up of the law and from whom came Christ the Savior (see Rom 9:1–5)—just as Christ himself also says: *Salvation is from the Jews* (John 4:22). The apostle found it explained in the law that not all who are from Israel will be believers, and that not all should be called children of Abraham simply because they are called children of Abraham, as I noted above. (3) Therefore, when the apostle discovered that it was predicted long ago that they would not all be believers, he eased his anguish, so that he grieved only for those who did not believe[29] on account of jealousy. They can still believe, as he explains below (see Rom 11:1–24). For those who were predicted to be unbelievers, however, one should not grieve very much, because they were not predestined for life;[30] the foreknowledge of God decreed long ago that they should not be saved. Who weeps for someone who is believed to be long dead? (3a)[31] When the gentiles, who were previously without God, slipped in and accepted the salvation which the Jews have lost, anguish is roused. But then in turn it is calmed because the Jews themselves are the cause of their own ruin. (4) So God, who foreknows that they will be people of an evil will, did not include them among the number of the good, (4a)[32] even though the Savior says to those seventy-two disciples, the ones he had chosen as second class, who later fell away from him (see Luke 10:1; John 6:66–67): *Your names are written in heaven* (Luke 10:20). But he says this for the sake of justice, because it is just that each one be repaid on the basis of merit. In fact, because they were good, they were chosen to serve and their names had been written in heaven for the sake of justice, as I have said. From the point of view of foreknowledge, however, they were numbered among the evil.[33] (5) God judges on the basis of justice, not on the basis of foreknowledge. This is why he said to Moses as well: *If anyone has sinned before me, I will obliterate him from my book* (Exod 32:33), so that it is apparent that one is obliterated at the time one sins according to the justice of the judge, but has been never included in the book of life[34] according

---

29. *Recensiones* α and β have "who labor in unbelief" instead of "who do not believe."
30. *Recensio* α has "destined" instead of "predestined."
31. *Recensio* α does not have section 3a.
32. *Recensio* α does not have section 4a.
33. See In Rom. 8:30 (§2a).
34. *Recensio* α does not have "of life."

to foreknowledge. For this reason the apostle John also says of this type of disciple: *They went out from us, but they were not of us; for if they had been of us, they would surely have continued with us* (1 John 2:19). There is no partiality in the foreknowledge of God. The foreknowledge of God is the means by which it is determined what will be the will of each person in the future, the will in which one will abide, the will by which one will be either condemned or crowned.[35] In the end, those whom God knows to abide in good are often evil before, and those whom God knows to continue in evil are sometimes good before. This puts a stop to the complaint, because God shows no partiality (see Acts 10:34). Indeed, both Saul and Judas Iscariot were good before. As the scripture says about Saul: *He was a good man and there was none better than him among the children of Israel* (1 Sam 9:2), and the apostle Peter says about Judas Iscariot: *Who was allotted a share in this ministry* (Acts 1:17), in the performance of signs and wonders (see 2 Cor 12:12), in other words, in apostleship.[36] (6) Why would he have been allotted the ministry to save,[37] unless he was good? It was God's judgment that he was worthy to share for a while in the duty for which he was chosen, just as the seventy-two disciples I mentioned above.[38] This is why even Judas, moved by penitence after admitting to a crime of such wickedness, ended his life with the noose (Matt 27:3–4).[39] (7) In fact, it is not possible for every bit of good to be completely obliterated in a person, nor can the nature itself be changed,[40] although the will can—not, however, in every respect, because that which bears witness to the creator remains in the nature.[41]

9:14 *What shall we say then? Is there wickedness on God's part? By no means!* Because God loves one and hates another, the apostle asks whether God is wicked. Obviously not; rather, he is just. He knows what he does

---

35. *Recensio* α has simply "by which one will be condemned."

36. *Recensiones* α and β do not have "in other words, in apostleship."

37. *Recensio* α has "by the Savior" instead of "to save."

38. *Recensio* α does not have "just as the seventy-two disciples I mentioned above"; see section 4a above.

39. Instead of this sentence and the following section, *recensio* α has "But, moved by penitence after admitting to such wickedness, he ended his life with the noose. (7) What wonder is it that they are said to have been good, since every nature is good and no substance is an evil thing, but only transgression, which originates in the will. The will, moreover, is led astray by error."

40. *Recensio* β has "especially since the nature itself cannot be changed" instead of "nor can the nature itself be changed."

41. See In Rom. 5:7 (§§3a–4a) on the natural goodness of human beings.

and his judgment cannot be repealed. This is found in the prophet Malachi, as quoted above (see Rom 9:13):[42] *Jacob I loved, but Esau I hated* (Mal 1:2–3). Here God says this on the basis of judgment, but earlier he says on the basis of foreknowledge that *the elder shall serve the younger* (Gen 25:23; see Rom 9:12). So too, God ruled on the basis of foreknowledge that Pharaoh was to be condemned, knowing that he would not accept correction, whereas God chose the apostle Paul while he was persecuting (see Acts 8:3; 9:1–5),[43] foreknowing, of course, that he was going to be a believer.[44] God anticipated Paul before the event because he was indispensable, and he condemned Pharaoh before the judgment came about so that it might be believed that God would come to judge.

9:15 *For he says to Moses: "I will have mercy on whom I will have had mercy, and I will have compassion on whom I will have had compassion"* (Exod 33:19). (1) Therefore, he says, *I will have mercy* for the one *on whom I will have had mercy*. That is: I will have mercy on the person whom I foreknew I was going to show mercy, knowing that he would convert and abide with me. *And I will have compassion* for the one *on whom I will have had compassion*. That is: I will show mercy to the person whom I have foreknown is going to return to me with an upright heart after his error. (1a)[45] This means: to give to the one to whom it should be given; it does not mean: to refuse to give to the one to whom it should not be given. Thus, God calls the one whom he knows obeys, but does not call the one whom he knows does not obey at all. To call, in fact, is to spur one to accept the faith.

9:16 *So it depends not on the one who wills nor on the one who runs, but on the one who has mercy, God.* (1)[46] This is quite right, because the request that is made should depend not on the desire of the petitioner but on the decision of the benefactor. The judgment of the benefactor should, in fact, weigh whether the request ought to be granted. For example, although Saul requested forgiveness after sinning, he did not receive it (see 1 Sam 15:24–27), while on the other hand when David sinned and asked

---

42. *Recensiones* α and β do not have "as quoted above."
43. *Recensio* α has "persecuting the church."
44. *Recensiones* α and β have "good" instead of "a believer."
45. *Recensio* α does not have section 1a.
46. *Recensio* α has "This is quite right, because what is granted should depend not on the desire of the petitioner but on the decision of the benefactor, and the judgment of the benefactor should weigh what is requested, because he who desires that everyone be saved while justice is maintained judges justly."

to be forgiven, he received forgiveness (see 2 Sam 12:13).[47] On the basis of this we should certainly accept the judgment of God, who grants and who denies, because he who desires that everyone be saved (see 1 Tim 2:4) does not judge unjustly, even as justice is maintained. (2) He[48] who examines the heart knows the petitioner, whether he asks in a spirit that deserves to receive (see Prov 24:12).[49] (2a)[50] Although it is hazardous to discern the judgment of God, we will nevertheless examine it by way of actions rather than words, on account of doubters. We do this so that their mind may be assuaged, lest they think that God's judgment is unjust, saying, "He calls one and leaves the other" (see Luke 17:34), believing therefore that those who ought to be condemned can be excused. When the examples have to do with deeds, no one dares to complain or plead some excuse. There were two men: Saul and David. Let us examine their histories, what sort of person each of them is found to be after God passed judgment, whether God's judgment is unjust[51] if Saul is shown to have conducted himself well after he did not receive mercy, or if David is found to have shown contempt for God after he received mercy, or whether he continued in the state in which he received mercy. To be brief,[52] both of them endured the adversity of being a ruler. (2b)[53] What adversity David experienced, as his son sought to deprive him of his kingship! (see 2 Sam 15:1–12). In that adversity he made his way barefoot as he wept (see 2 Sam 16:30), the leader and king of the people a fugitive, humiliated to the point that he did not reply to his servant who cursed him even to his face (see 2 Sam 16:5–10). He did this so that by his patience he might make God merciful toward him, through whom he believed that the kingship was preserved for him. Saul did not meet up with such adversity, since a civil war is a greater evil than an external war. In addition, he was furious that time and again he

---

47. See *Quaest.* 18 (CSEL 50:44–45), where Ambrosiaster discusses the question "Why is it that Saul, when he sinned and asked for prayers so that he might be forgiven, could not obtain it, but David, when he sinned, asked for forgiveness and received it?"

48. *Recensio* α has "God."

49. *Recensio* α adds "For this reason it is rightly said: *It depends not on the one who wills nor on the one who runs* etc."

50. *Recensio* α does not have section 2a.

51. *Recensio* β has "whether we may deem God's judgment to be unjust—God forbid!" instead of "whether God's judgment is unjust."

52. *Recensio* β has *dispendio* instead of *conpendio*, perhaps meaning "to speak of danger" (*ut utatur dispendio*).

53. *Recensio* α does not have section 2b.

was not heard (see 1 Sam 28:6), because he was unworthy. Furthermore, he did not persist in prayer so as to acquire merit for himself by which he would become worthy, but instead, impatient and angry at the judgment of God, he sought help from idols (see 1 Sam 28:7–25), which previously he had condemned as useless (see 1 Sam 28:9). See, it is clear even to those who do not want to see it that the judgment of God's foreknowledge is just.

9:17 *For the scripture says to Pharaoh, "I have preserved you for this very purpose,*[54] *so that I may display my power against you and so that my name may be proclaimed in the whole earth"* (Exod 9:16). (1a)[55] Other codices have: *"I have raised you up so that I may display my power against you."* Whether one reads *I have preserved* or *I have raised up*, the meaning is the same.[56] (1) The scripture says this because Pharaoh—which was the name of the ruler among the Egyptians, just as among the Romans the rulers are called Augusti[57]—was never going to be reformed,[58] although he was guilty of so many evils to the point that he was unworthy of life.[59] So that he might not suppose either that he deserved to live or that God, whom he believed could be ignored again and again (see Exod 7:8–11:10),[60] was incapable of meting out punishment, he hears from God: *I have preserved you for this very purpose, so that I may display my power against you and so that my name may be proclaimed in the whole earth.* God says this so that through Pharaoh the rest of the nations might learn that that there is no

---

54. *Recensio* α adds "or 'I have raised you up'" (*sive excitavi*). This is probably a gloss introduced by a later scribe familiar with the Vulgate, since it refers to a reading Ambrosiaster does not mention in section 1a when he discusses variants known to him. See n. 56 below.

55. *Recensio* α does not have section 1a.

56. The reading Ambrosiaster had in his text, *servavi*, corresponds to the Septuagint of Exod 9:16, which has διετηρήθης. The reading he found in other codices, *suscitavi*, was also known to Ambrose and Rufinus; see Ambrose, *Exp. Ps. 118, serm.* 10.35 (CSEL 62:224); Origen-Rufinus, *Comm. Rom.* 7.14, lines 44–46, 81–82, 111 (*AGLB* 34:621, 622, 624). Manuscripts of the VL and other Latin writers have *excitavi*, as does the Vulgate, which corresponds to ἐξήγειρα in Paul's version of Exod 9:16.

57. *Recensio* α does not have "just as among the Romans the rulers are called Augusti."

58. *Recensiones* α and β have "was never going to be good" instead of "was never going to be reformed."

59. *Recensiones* α and β have "he did not deserve to live" instead of "he was unworthy of life."

60. *Recensio* α has "whom he ignored again and again" instead of "whom he believed could be ignored again and again."

other God than the one who was the God of the Jews and became the God of the Christians—although the Jews were Christians and we now are Jews on account of Judah from whom Christ descends according to the flesh (see Heb 7:14), because in hoping for the coming of Christ the redeemer the ancient Jews were Christians. (2) Now, Rahab the prostitute tells the Jewish spies, sent by Jesus Nave (Josh 2:1), who previously was called Auxes (see Num 13:17):[61] "The miracles and the plagues which were done in Egypt by your God are known here, and people are completely terrified; they are afraid of the sight of you" (see Josh 2:9–11). Therefore, Pharaoh was preserved so that many wonders and plagues might be displayed against him as one already dead. He is said to have been raised up because, although he was dead in God's eyes, he received a little time in which to appear to live, so that through his punishment and various torments, including death, all those who were without God might, terrified, confess with the utmost awe that the one from whom these punishments come is alone God. In the same way doctors in ancient times examined people[62] who deserved to die or who had received a sentence of death, to see how they might benefit the living,[63] so that from them, opened up,[64] they might know the causes of sickness that lie hidden in a person.[65] Thus, the punishment of the dead promotes the health of the living.[66]

---

61. See Ambrosiaster, *Quaest.* 80.1 (CSEL 50:136), where the name is spelled Auses, as in *recensio* α.

62. *Recensio* α has "those" instead of "people."

63. *Recensio* α has "the good" instead of "the living."

64. *Recensio* α has "cut to pieces" instead of "opened up."

65. Celsus, *Med.* proem. 23–26 (LCL 292:14), relates that vivisection was performed at Alexandria on criminals by Herophilus and Erasistratus. The report is known to Tertullian, *An.* 10.4 (CCSL 2:794), who could have been Ambrosiaster's source, given Ambrosiaster's familiarity with Tertullian's writings. According to Ambrosiaster the practice belongs to a bygone time: "doctors in ancient times" (*antiqui medici*). It appears to have been limited to Alexandria in the Ptolemaic era. See Ludwig Edelstein, "The History of Anatomy in Antiquity," in *Ancient Medicine: Selected Papers of Ludwig Edelstein*, ed. Oswei Temkin and C. Lilian Temkin, trans. C. Lilian Temkin (Baltimore: Johns Hopkins University Press, 1967), 250–51, 283–84, 297; James Longrigg, "Anatomy in Alexandria in the Third Century B.C.," *BJHS* 21 (1988): 459–62; Simon Byl, "Controverses antiques autour de la dissection et de la vivisection," *RBPH* 75 (1997): 114–17. See also John Scarborough, "Celsus on Human Vivisection at Ptolemaic Alexandria," *ClM* 11 (1976): 25–38, who argues that Celsus's report is unfounded.

66. *Recensio* α has "Thus, the punishment of the evil promoted the health of the good."

9:18 *Therefore God has mercy on whomever he wills,*[67] *and he hardens the heart of whomever he wills.* **9:19** *So you say to me.* (1) The apostle takes the part of someone who raises an objection, who believes, as it were, that God shows favor to a person while disregarding justice, so that of two people who are otherwise equal he accepts one and rejects the other. In other words, he spurs the one to believe and hardens the other so that he does not believe. To the objector the apostle replies categorically that justice nevertheless is preserved on account of the foreknowledge that was discussed above, as follows:[68]

"What is he still looking for? Who can resist his will?" (2) The apostle teaches, first of all, that God cannot be resisted; he is the most powerful of all. Secondly, that he is the God and author of everything, and therefore does not wish ill of anything; he wants the things he made to remain whole. It does not befit him to be unjust—he whose goodness is so evident, as he not only brought things into being that did not exist, but also gave them eternal life and glory, so that his handiwork might likewise share somewhat in his splendor. There should be no uncertainty, therefore, that one who is so provident and good is just.

9:20 *Who are you, a human being, to answer back to God?* (1) It is a huge affront and presumption, the apostle says, for a human being to answer back to God, the wicked to the just, the evil to the good, the novice to the master, the weak to the mighty, the corruptible to the incorruptible, the mortal to the immortal, the slave to the lord, the creature to the creator.

Does what is molded say to its molder, "Why have you made me thus?" (Isa 45:9). (2) This is from the prophet Isaiah (Isa 45:9), which the apostle here writes as his own words. By this he shows that a work cannot find fault with its maker; it is in the power of the maker to fashion the thing being created as he wishes.

9:21 *Does not the potter have the right to make out of the same lump one vessel for beauty, the other for menial use?* (1) It is obvious that some

---

67. Ambrosiaster's text differs from the better witnesses, which have "he" (implied in the verb ἐλεεῖ) instead of "God" (*deus*).

68. Ambrosiaster reads Rom 9:18 as the objection of an imaginary interlocutor and Rom 9:19 as the reply of the apostle. Other patristic interpreters assign Rom 9:14/15–18 to the interlocutor; see Karl H. Schelkle, *Paulus, Lehrer der Väter*, 2nd ed. (Düsseldorf: Patmos, 1959), 339–41. For a current analysis of Rom 9:14–29 that explains Paul's rhetoric in light of the genres of midrash and diatribe and assigns only 9:19 to the interlocutor, see Jewett, *Romans*, 571–73, 588–90.

vessels are made for beauty, such as those which are needed for the purpose of adornment, while others are made for ignoble use, such as those used for cooking; they are made of the same substance, but they differ in status on account of the will of the maker. So too, since we are all from one and the same lump in terms of substance and are all sinners,[69] God (1a)[70] not unjustly has mercy on some and spurns others. In a potter there is only will, but in God there is will accompanied by justice. (2) For he knows on whom he should have mercy, as I have discussed above.

9:22 *What if God, desiring to show his wrath and to make known his power with much patience in vessels of wrath prepared for destruction.*[71] This is the meaning of the verse: by the will and forbearance of God, which is patience, unbelievers are prepared for punishment. Although God waited a long time for them, they were unwilling to convert. God waited for them, therefore, so that they would perish without excuse, for God knew that they were not going to believe.

9:23 *And in order to show the riches of his glory in vessels of mercy which he has prepared for glory.* (1) This is the patience and forbearance of God, which prepares the good for the crown, just as it prepares the bad for destruction. The good are those in whom the hope of faith exists. God

---

69. Ambrosiaster uses *massa* in the sense of a common substance that all human beings share; see In Rom. 5:12 (§3). On the difference between Ambrosiaster's usage and Augustine's, see Juan B. Valero, "Pecar en Adán según Ambrosiaster," *EE* 65 (1990): 189–91. As Ambrosiaster states at In Rom. 5:12 (§4), human beings are ultimately condemned for their own sins. Ambrosiaster offers a more complete explanation of the consequences of Adam's sin for human beings at In Rom. 7:18 (§§1–2), 7:20, and 7:22.

70. Recensio α does not have section 1a. Its comment, running from section 1 to section 2, reads: "So too, since we are all from one and the same lump in terms of substance and are all sinners, God knows on whom he should have mercy, as I have discussed above."

71. The Greek text of 9:22 has "bore with much patience vessels of wrath prepared for destruction" (ἤνεγκεν ἐν πολλῇ μακροθυμίᾳ σκεύη ὀργῆς κατηρτισμένα εἰς ἀπώλειαν), which corresponds to *sustinuit in multa patientia vasa irae aptata in interitum* in the Vulgate. The VL lacks the verb *sustinuit* and alters the syntax of the remainder of the clause; the resulting sentence, found here in the lemma, is incomplete: *quod si volens deus ostendere iram et manifestare potentiam suam in multa patientia in vasis irae praeparatis in interitum*. Ambrosiaster's handling of the problem at In Rom. 9:23 (§§1–2) is interesting. On the one hand, he quotes the lemma without the verb: *hoc est autem manifestare potentiam suam in multa patientia* (CSEL 81.1:329, lines 23–24). On the other hand, he supplies the verb *sustinere* in his explanation: *omnes enim sustinet* (CSEL 81.1:329, line 18); *diu sustinuit* (CSEL 81.1:331, line 2).

bears with them all because he knows the end of each of them. For that reason God's patience is what prepares[72] those who are converted from evil or who persevere in good for glory. The *riches of glory* are the manifold honors that have been prepared for believers. But God's patience prepares for destruction those who, originally among the good, became bad and continued in the evil they had taken up. (2) This, then, is *to make known his power with much patience*, because, although it was believed that God was not going to punish because he hid his judgment for a long time, when he begins to punish his power will be revealed. Although he could punish immediately, he forbore for a long time so that when the wicked are condemned they may not be able to complain.[73] To prepare is to foreknow each and every one who will be worthy.[74]

9:24 *Even us whom he also called, not only from the Jews but also from the gentiles.* He prepared for glory those whom he called, those who were near or those who were far (see Eph 2:17),[75] knowing that they were going to continue in the faith.

9:25 *As he also says in Hosea: "I will call 'not my people' 'my people', and 'not beloved' 'beloved'"* (Hos 2:23). **9:26** *"And in the place where they were called 'not my people', there they will be called 'children of the living God'"* (Hos 1:10). It is clear that this was foretold about the gentiles, since in the past they were not the people of God. But later, when they received mercy, they were called the people of God as a reproach to the Jews, and, once the Jews were disowned, those who previously were not beloved were adopted as children and are beloved. As a result, in the place where they were not called the people of God, there they were called *children of the living God*. In the past people were called children of God only in Judea, that is, in Jerusalem, where the house of God was, as it says in Ps 75: *God is known in Judea* (Ps 75:2 LXX = Ps 76:1 ET). Later, in the prophet Zechariah:[76] *I will place Jerusalem among all the nations* (Zech 12:2), because the children of God were going to be everywhere and the house of God, which is the church, was going to be in every place. For this reason the Lord says to the

---

72. *Recensio* α has "God's patience prepares those etc."
73. *Recensio* α has "Although he could punish, he forbore for a long time."
74. *Recensiones* α and β have "To prepare is to know what each and every one will be."
75. *Recensio* α does not have "those who were near or those who were far."
76. *Recensio* α does not have "in the prophet Zechariah."

Jews: *The kingdom of God will be taken away from you and will be given to a nation producing the fruit of it* (Matt 21:43).[77]

9:27 *And Isaiah cries out for Israel.* (1) He says that *Isaiah cries out for* those who believe in Christ. They indeed are Israelites, as the Lord says about the holy Nathaniel: *Behold, an Israelite indeed, in whom there is no deceit* (John 1:47).

"If the number of the children of Israel is as the sand of the sea, a remnant will be saved." (2) While the Jews withdraw from the merit and the promise of the fathers as long as they do not accept the promise, the remnant is those who by believing remain steadfast in the faith of the promise made to the fathers. Those who do not believe in him whom the law promised would alone fulfill the requirements of salvation in fact withdraw from the law. As long as they do not accept Christ, they[78] are guilty of breaking the law[79] and must therefore be considered apostates. So the prophet says that out of a huge multitude only believers, whom God foreknew, are saved.

9:28 *"(The Lord is) executing his word and shortening it in equity, for the Lord will dispatch a shortened word upon the earth"* (Isa 10:22–23).[80] The prophet promises that those he calls the remnant are saved through the word that the Lord shortened upon the earth, when he rightly defined its meaning. It is fitting, in fact, that creation obtains salvation only in the name of the Lord and creator,[81] that is, through faith, because, once the new moons and the sabbath and circumcision and the law concerning foods and the sacrifice of animals had all been set aside, faith alone was given as the basis for salvation. Faith is an abridged form of the law, because the content of faith is found in the law, essentially as its central element, as the Savior says:[82] *About me Moses wrote* (John 5:46). With the law having been

---

77. *Recensio* α does not have "of God."

78. *Recensio* α specifies "the remnant."

79. *Recensio* α has "are under the law" instead of "are guilty of breaking the law."

80. Ambrosiaster's biblical text supplies words found in Isa 10:23 LXX (ἐν δικαιοσύνῃ ὅτι λόγον συντετμημένον) but absent in the better-attested text of Rom 9:28, which reads "for the Lord will execute his word with rigor and dispatch upon the earth" (λόγον γὰρ συντελῶν καὶ συντέμνων ποιήσει κύριος ἐπὶ τῆς γῆς). See Metzger, *Textual Commentary*, 462; and Jewett, *Romans*, 588.

81. In *recensio* α the comment begins "The prophet promises that those he calls the remnant are saved through the word that the Lord shortened upon the earth, that is, through faith, etc."

82. *Recensio* α has "because the contents of faith are found in the law, as the Savior says."

abbreviated, therefore, a remnant of the Jews are saved; the rest, however, cannot be saved, because they rejected God's prior resolution, by which he determined the human race would be saved.[83]

9:29 *And as Isaiah predicted, "If the Lord Sabaoth had not left us a seed, we would have been just as Sodom and we would have been like Gomorrah"* (Isa 1:9). (1) This seed, which the apostle says was alone left and set aside from among all the people for the renewal of the human race, is Christ and his teaching, as he himself says: *The seed is the word of God* (Luke 8:11). This seed, then, promised to us long ago, he left for the purpose of redemption after the things which pertained to the burden of the law were removed, so that when we received forgiveness of sins[84] we would not be punished by the law in the way that Sodom perished. (1a)[85] The apostle says, therefore, that a savior was left for us in order to sustain life, which the law was not able to provide. From the outset God decreed that a savior would be born who, since he alone was found to be without sin, blotted out the sins of all people after the enemy of the human race had been conquered. (2) One also reads about this in the Revelation of John: *For no one was found to be worthy in heaven or on earth to open the book and its seals* (see Rev 5:1–4), except the Savior, who has conquered death. This, then, is the seed which, promised long ago, God set aside so that it would bear fruit at the time when the sins of all the Jews as well as all the gentiles had reached their quota. Its fruit, in fact, is the forgiveness of sinners. (2a)[86] If Christ had not been set aside—whom he calls *the seed* because through him the human race was restored—the descendants of Abraham would have perished because they had been overwhelmed with sins and the law was not able to help them. For this reason the apostle teaches that the one who brought help in the form of life should be followed.

9:30 *What then shall we say? That the gentiles, who did not pursue righteousness, have obtained it, the righteousness, that is, which is by faith.* (1) Since there is a righteousness that comes from the law, which was given credence by the world and which prohibits sin,[87] the apostle says that the gentiles obtained not the righteousness that is discerned through nature

---

83. *Recensio* α does not have "because they rejected God's prior resolution, by which he determined the human race would be saved."
84. *Recensiones* α and β have "were given" instead of "received."
85. *Recensio* α does not have section 1a.
86. *Recensio* α does not have section 2a.
87. This clause could refer either to "righteousness" or "law." I take it to refer to "law."

the instructress, but the righteousness that comes from faith in Christ. From God's point of view, true and enduring righteousness occurs when he is acknowledged. For what[88] can be more right than to recognize God the Father, from whom are all things, and Christ his Son, through whom are all things (see 1 Cor 8:6)? Righteousness therefore consists first of all in acknowledging the creator, then in keeping what he has commanded. (1a)[89] Thus, the gentiles, who previously did not seek after righteousness (that is, the law that bore witness to the creator), found a righteousness exceeding that of the scribes and the Pharisees by following Christ when he came (see Matt 5:20).[90] They who in an earlier time did not pursue what was less important, later understood what was more important; but the Jews, who were endowed with the law and ought to have progressed even more, went downhill.

9:31 *But Israel by pursuing the law of righteousness did not arrive at the law?* Faith is the fulfillment of the law. In grasping faith, the gentiles are considered to have fulfilled the entire law. But since the Jews out of jealousy do not believe the Savior and champion instead the righteousness that is stipulated by the law (namely, the sabbath, circumcision, and the rest),[91] they have not arrived at the law.[92] That is to say, they have not fulfilled the law, and those who do not fulfill the law are deemed guilty according to the law. A person who arrives at faith in Christ from the law of Moses in fact fulfills the law.[93]

9:32 *Why? Because they did not pursue it by faith, but as if it were by works.* (1) Rejecting faith (which, as I have said, is the fulfillment of the law), they declared that they were justified by works of the law (that is, by the sabbath, the new moons, circumcision, and other observances), forgetting the scripture which says that *the righteous lives by faith* (Hab 2:4).

---

88. I translate *quid*, which is attested by *recensiones* α and β, rather than *quis*, which is attested by *recensio* γ but does not agree with *iustum*, which is attested by all three recensions.

89. *Recensio* α does not have section 1a.

90. *Recensio* β has "when Christ came" instead of "by following Christ when he came."

91. *Recensio* α does not have this parenthetical explanation.

92. *Recensio* α has "at the law of righteousness" instead of "at the law."

93. *Recensio* α does not have this sentence. In *recensio* γ it is attested only by MS Monte Cassino 150. But Ambrosiaster refers back to his argument here at In Rom. 9:32 (§2a), which is attested by all the manuscripts of *recensio* γ. Thus, in this instance the witness of the Monte Cassino manuscript is corroborated.

One speaks, nevertheless, of *the righteousness of the law* because by God's just judgment these observances were given to the Jews on account of the hardness of their heart. Consequently, if someone by chance had stepped on a dead weasel or touched the carcass of some other animal (see Lev 11:29–31),[94] or if a mouse had fallen into a jar (see Lev 11:33), it was said to be unclean. Although the Jews observed such regulations with great care, it nevertheless happened that they became unclean for some reason or other. Moreover, if the blood of a weasel had stained the floor, the spot had to be removed with considerable effort (1a) in order, as well, to keep it from contact with better food.[95] The sabbath and circumcision, on the other hand, possessed their own righteousness in their day, because they were given as a type of things to come.[96] (2) The Lord reveals this through the prophet Ezekiel when he says, among other things:[97] *Therefore I gave them commandments that were not good* (Ezek 20:25), for they were ungodly and unfaithful. (2a)[98] But since Christ is the gift that was to be given to save people, God foretells of his coming through the prophet Jeremiah when he states: *I will give them a new covenant, not like the covenant which I gave to their fathers* (Jer 31:31). He calls this latter covenant the law, at which they did not arrive, as I have discussed above.[99] (3) Now, when believing Jews wished to lay this burden of observance upon gentiles who believed, the apostle Peter says: *Why are you placing on the neck of the brothers a yoke that neither we nor our fathers have been able to bear* (Acts 15:10).[100] For from the time of Christ the pardon that was promised in the law was granted. The prophet Isaiah says: *One will come from Zion who will root out and turn away godlessness from Jacob* (Isa 59:20). *And this will be a covenant from me to them, when I will take away their sins* (Isa 27:9). This is the new covenant that was promised by God in Christ.

9:33 *They have stumbled over the stone of stumbling* (Isa 8:14), *as it is written: "Behold, I am laying in Zion a stone of stumbling and a rock of*

---

94. *Recensio* α has "if someone had by chance stepped on or touched a dead weasel."
95. *Recensio* α has "Moreover, if blood of a weasel was spilled in the house, it was not said to be a minor stain." Ambrosiaster also refers to the need to purify the blood of a weasel at In Titus 3:9 (§2).
96. *Recensio* α does not have this sentence.
97. *Recensio* α does not have "among other things."
98. *Recensio* α does not have section 2a.
99. See In Rom. 9:31 and n. 93 above.
100. Ambrosiaster also quotes Acts 15:10, and alludes to Ezek 20:25, at In Titus 1:14 (§§2–3).

offense, and one who believes in him will not be put to shame" (Isa 28:16). (1) This is found in Isaiah. From the language of many writers one can ascertain that Christ is meant by references to a rock or a stone. The prophet Daniel calls him a stone that, cut from a mountain without human hands, struck and crushed every dominion and filled the whole earth (see Dan 2:34–36). This obviously was said about Christ. (2) In the law Christ is called the rock from which water flowed, as the apostle himself testifies:[101] *They will drink from the spiritual rock which followed them.*[102] *The rock, he says, was Christ* (1 Cor 10:4). Among other things, the apostle Peter says to the Jews: *This is the stone that was rejected by you builders* (Acts 4:11). The cause of stumbling laid in Zion, therefore, is Christ, but Zion is the heights or rather the city of Jerusalem itself, which quite rightly was said to be exalted on account of its knowledge of God. When the Savior was placed by God his Father as a preacher in Jerusalem, he became a cause of stumbling for the Jews, when he, who was born from the Holy Spirit of a woman,[103] declared that he was the Son of God.[104] On account of his body they took offense and kept on saying: *Are not his mother and his brothers among us? Why then does he say that he has come down from heaven?* (see Matt 13:53–57; John 6:42). (3) For they were unwilling to interpret his words in light of his deeds. Then they might have realized that it was not absurd for him to say that he had come down from heaven, as if a body were bringing this about and not God, who was hidden but nevertheless making himself known in a body through actions. This *rock* is, thus, an offense and a cause of stumbling for the Jews. It undoubtedly refers to the flesh of the Savior.[105] It was cut out without human hands,

---

101. *Recensiones* α and β do not have "as the apostle himself testifies."

102. *Recensio* α does not have this quotation.

103. The statement that Christ was "born from the Holy Spirit of (or and) the virgin Mary"—the exact wording varied—had long been an element of baptismal questions and declaratory formulae in Rome and was probably incorporated into the Roman creed in the third century. See Liuwe H. Westra, *The Apostles' Creed: Origin, History, and Some Early Commentaries*, Instrumenta Patristica et Mediaevalia 43 (Turnhout: Brepols, 2002), 21–72, 230–33. The statement is evidently echoed here and in the final sentence of section 3.

104. *Recensio* α has "The cause of stumbling laid in Zion, therefore, is Christ, but Zion is understood to mean Jerusalem or the temple of God. When they saw a body, they did not believe in him and stumbled."

105. *Recensiones* α and β have "body" instead of "flesh."

because without the intervention of a man it was made from the Holy Spirit of the virgin.¹⁰⁶

---

106. See n. 103 above.

Romans 10

10:1 *Brothers, my heart's desire and prayer to God for them is for salvation.* **10:2** *I bear witness for them, that they have a zeal for God, but it is not in accordance with knowledge.* (1) The apostle wishes to draw them away from the law, since for the Jews it is a veil (see 2 Cor 3:15). But in order not to seem to do so out of hatred for Judaism, he displays his feelings toward them and gives the law a lot of credit. Nevertheless, he explains that it is no longer the time to observe the law and avows that in so doing he has their best interests at heart, if only they will listen to him and trust that he is not their enemy, given that he also bears witness to them about the nobility and the tradition of their ancestors.

10:3 *For, being ignorant of God's righteousness and seeking to establish their own,*[1] *they did not submit to God's righteousness.* The apostle says that out of ignorance they did not believe in Christ, for they indeed had a zeal for God. But because they were unaware of God's will and plan, they acted against the one they professed to defend. The apostle is speaking about those who out of error rather than spiteful ill will did not accept Christ. The apostle Peter also speaks of them: *I know, brothers, that you acted in ignorance, as did also your rulers* (Acts 3:17). Not realizing that Christ was the one whom God had promised, they said that another was to be expected, valuing their own forms of righteousness, which they based on the law, over him who is the righteousness of God in faith. He is righteousness because in him God fulfilled what he had promised.[2]

---

1. Although Ambrosiaster's biblical text has simply "their own" (*suam*), there is strong support among the biblical witnesses for "their own righteousness" (τὴν ἰδίαν δικαιοσύνην). See Robert Jewett with Roy D. Kotansky, *Romans: A Commentary*, Hermeneia (Minneapolis: Fortress, 2007), 606.

2. In *recensio* γ this sentence it attested only by MSS Amiens 87, Oxford 756, and Paris lat. 1759. The other manuscripts have "who is the righteousness of God in faith, because in him he [i.e., God] fulfilled what he had promised."

10:4 *For Christ is the end of the law for the righteousness of all who believe.* The apostle says this because one who believes in Christ has achieved the fulfillment of the law. Since no one was justified by the law because no one fulfilled it except the person who hoped in Christ as the promised one,[3] faith was given instead, reckoned as the fulfillment of the law. As a result, all else was disregarded and faith sufficed for the entire law and the prophets.[4]

10:5 *Moses in fact wrote of the righteousness which is based on the law, that the person who does these things will live by them.* The apostle says this because the righteousness of the law of Moses did not render them guilty for the time being, as long as it was kept.[5] In other words, they lived by keeping the law; they were in its debt. This is stated in Numbers and Leviticus (see Lev 18:5).

10:6 *But the righteousness which is based on faith speaks thus: Do not say in your heart, "Who will ascend into heaven?"* (Deut 30:12–13). This is stated in Deuteronomy. It is here understood to refer to Christ, as the apostle says:[6]

(That is, to bring Christ down) **10:7** *or "Who will descend into the abyss?" (that is, to bring Christ up from the dead).* (1) These are the apostle's words.[7] He thus is saying that this is the righteousness of faith: not to doubt the hope of God[8] which is in Christ, so as not to say in disbelief: "Who is able to ascend into heaven?"[9] In fact, Christ died so that, once the underworld had been pillaged through the power of the Father[10] and death had been conquered, he might ascend into heaven, rising with the souls who had been released. For when the Savior was seen in the underworld, absolutely everyone who hoped for salvation from him was set free.[11] The apostle Peter bears witness to this, for he says that *the gospel was preached*

---

3. *Recensio* α does not have "except the person who hoped in Christ as the promised one."
4. *Recensio* α does not have "and the prophets."
5. See In Rom. 3:20 (§§1–1a).
6. *Recensio* α does not have this comment.
7. *Recensio* α does not have this sentence.
8. *Recensio* α does not have "of God."
9. *Recensio* α does not have "so as not to say in disbelief: 'Who is able to ascend into heaven?'"
10. *Recensio* α does not have "through the power of the Father."
11. On Christ's conquest of death and descent to the underworld, see the introduction §5.4.

even to the dead (1 Pet 4:6). (2) Therefore, the person who does not doubt these things in his heart is justified by faith. Fear motivates one to be justified by the law. One fears the law because one sees the punishment that it inflicts on sinners. For this reason the righteousness of the law is of no great importance and does not acquire merit before God; it is meritorious only at the time.[12] Since faith, in contrast, is folly to the unbeliever, it is rewarded by God, from whom one hopes for that which is not seen (see Rom 8:24–25).

10:8 *But what does the scripture say?*[13] *"The word is near, in your mouth and in your heart"* (Deut 30:14). (1) This is written in Deuteronomy, that what is said to us so that we might believe is not far removed from our soul or nature.[14] Although it is not seen with the eyes, what we believe is not out of keeping with the nature of souls and the character of speech.[15] In nature itself are planted, as it were, seeds which, when tended by listening and agreeing, bear fruit in witnessing to the creator.

That is, the word of faith which is preached. (2) The apostle says that no work of the law[16] but faith alone is acceptable with regard to Christ.

10:9 *Because if you confess the Lord Jesus with your mouth and believe in your heart that God raised him from the dead, you will be saved.* **10:10** *For one believes with the heart unto righteousness, but confession is made with the mouth unto salvation.* Everything the apostle discussed above he has stated clearly here, namely, that this is the rule of faith: to believe that Jesus is Lord and not to be ashamed to profess that God raised him from the dead and led him in bodily form[17] into heaven, from which he had come to be in an incarnate form.[18] With this rule of faith one is preserved from the censure of the gospel: *Many of the rulers believed in Jesus, but they did not profess this openly on account of the Jews; for they preferred the praise of people to the praise of God* (John 12:42–43).

---

12. See In Rom. 3:20 (§§1–1a).
13. The specification of "the scripture" as the subject of "say" in Ambrosiaster's biblical text (*sed quid dicit scriptura?*) and some other witnesses is likely a secondary addition. See Jewett, *Romans*, 622.
14. *Recensiones* α and β have "mouth" instead of "nature."
15. *Recensio* α has "the law of nature" instead of "the character of speech."
16. *Recensio* α does not have "of the law."
17. Literally, "with a body" (*cum corpore*). See In Rom. 9:33 (§§2–3).
18. After the colon *recensio* α has "to believe and not be ashamed to confess."

10:11 *For the scripture says* through Isaiah:[19] *"Everyone who believes in him will not be put to shame"* (Isa 28:16). When the examination of all matters starts to take place on the day of judgment and all false inventions or doctrines begin to be led away in disgrace, then those who believe in Christ will jump for joy. They will see it plainly revealed to everyone that what they believed is true and that what was thought to be stupid is reasonable.[20] They will observe that they alone among the rest of the people are glorious and wise—they who were deemed to be contemptible and irrational.[21] For a true test occurs where there is reward and condemnation.

10:12 *There is no distinction between Jew and Greek.* (1) The apostle says that, across the board, everyone will be either disgraced on account of their unbelief or exalted on account of their faith, since without Christ there is no salvation with God, only punishment or death.[22] It will not be possible on the basis of ancestral prerogatives or the giving of the law to commend Jews who did not accept the merit and promise of their fathers. Moreover, gentiles have no grounds by which they might be commended even in terms of lineage,[23] unless they believe in Christ.

For the same Lord is Lord of all, generous toward all who call upon him. (2) It is obvious that this applies to all people, whether Jews or Greeks, because without calling upon Christ the Lord no one lives with God.[24] Thus, although he is the *Lord of all*—as the apostle Peter also holds, when he says, *"He is the Lord of all"* (Acts 10:36)—he nevertheless is generous only toward those *who call upon him*, because they will receive a reward. Toward unbelievers he is certainly not generous, since they do not share in his benefits; they will not receive what they did not believe he would give. (3) The apostle did not say, however, that God is generous toward those who believe, but toward those who call upon him, so that after the soul believes it may not cease to ask for what it has been taught by the Lord always to ask for (see Matt 6:13). For in the Gospel of Luke the Lord says

---

19. *Recensio* α does not have "through Isaiah." In *recensio* γ the phrase is attested only by MSS Amiens 87 and Monte Cassino 150.

20. *Recensio* α does not have "and that what was thought to be stupid is reasonable."

21. *Recensiones* α and β have "stupid" instead of "irrational."

22. *Recensio* α does not have "or death."

23. Literally, "according to the flesh" (*secundum carnem*). In *recensio* γ the phrase is attested only by MSS Amiens 87 and Paris lat. 1759.

24. *Recensio* α does not have "because without calling upon Christ the Lord no one lives with God."

that one should always pray (see Luke 18:1) on account of the enemy, since he is cunning and crafty. Forgiveness of sins alone is given to those who believe. But then what happens is that one who is devoted to prayers is delivered from evil (see Matt 6:13) and is able to receive what God promised to those who await him with all their heart.

10:13 For *"everyone who calls upon the name of the Lord will be saved"* (Joel 2:32). This is stated in Micah.[25] God himself, who was beheld by Moses, says: *My name is the Lord* (see Exod 6:2-3). He is the Son of God, said to be both *an angel* and *God* so that he is not taken to be him from who are all things, but rather to be him through whom are all things (see 1 Cor 8:6). Thus, he is said to be *God* because the Father and the Son are one, while he is said to be *an angel* because he was sent by the Father as a messenger of the promised salvation.[26] Furthermore, he is said to be *sent* so that he is not believed to be the Father himself, but the one who is begotten of the Father. So it is that *everyone who calls upon the name of the Lord will be saved*. Moses also spoke with this understanding: *Everyone who will not heed the prophet will be cut off from the people* (see Deut 18:19). If he is the *Lord of all* (see Rom 10:12), he is the one who is called upon by his servants, and since this is the case, the apostle has added:

10:14 *How then are they to call upon one in whom they have not believed?*[27] (1) Evidently the Jews do not believe that he whom the apostle

---

25. *Recensio* α does not have this remark. Paul is in fact quoting Joel 2:32. It has been suggested that Ambrosiaster may have been thinking of Mic 6:9. Alessandra Pollastri, *Commento all Lettera ai Romani*, CTePa 43 (Rome: Città Nuova Editrice, 1984), 237 n. 13, observes that Cyprian's version of Mic 6:9 in *Test.* 3.20 (CSEL 3.1:137) comes close to the sense of Rom 10:13: "The voice of the Lord will be called upon in the city, and he will save those who fear his name" (*vox domini in civitate invocabitur, et timentes nomen eius salvabit*).

26. Ambrosiaster identifies the angel of the Lord in the theophanies in the Old Testament, including God's appearance to Moses, with the second person of the Trinity; see Ambrosiaster's comment on 1 Thess 4:18 (§§2-3). The identification was traditional; see, e.g., Cyprian, *Test.* 2.5 (CSEL 3.1:33-34). Its significance for a pro-Nicene understanding of the Trinity was explicated in the fourth century by, among others, Hilary of Poitiers, *Trin.* 4.23-24 (CCSL 62:125-27). For more complete discussion, see Joseph Barbel, *Christos Angelos: Die Anschauung von Christus als Bote und Engel in der gelehrten und volkstümlichen Literatur des christlichen Altertums, zugleich ein Beitrag zur Geschichte des Ursprungs und der Fortdauer des Arianismus*, Theophaneia 3 (Bonn: Hanstein, 1941), 145-62.

27. Among the biblical witnesses there is stronger support for the middle aorist subjunctive "might they call upon" (ἐπικαλέσωνται) than for the future indicative

called *the Lord* is the Christ. It thus follows, as the apostle said above, that it is necessary to believe first, so that the one may have confidence in making a request.

Or how will they believe him whom they have not heard? (2) It is obvious that it is not possible to believe in someone to whom one does not pay attention.

And how will they hear without a preacher?[28] (3) This, too, is not hard to see, because one who refuses to accept a preacher does not accept the one who authorizes him to preach.

10:15 *Or how will they preach unless they are sent?*[29] This also is beyond doubt, since apostles are not true apostles unless they are sent by Christ, nor can they preach without authorization. No powerful signs bear witness to such apostles.

As it is written: "How beautiful are the feet of those who preach peace,[30] *who preach good news!"* (Isa 52:7; see Nah 1:15). The prophet Nahum says this.[31] In saying *feet* Paul means the arrival of the apostles who go around the world and preach that the kingdom of God is coming. Their arrival gave light to people by showing the way to travel in peace to God, the way that first of all John the Baptist had come to prepare. This is the peace to which those who believe in Christ hasten. Then, since the world is a place of conflict,[32] the holy Simeon, rejoicing at the birth of the Savior, says: *Lord, now let your servant depart in peace* (Luke 2:29), because the kingdom of God is peace (see Rom 14:17); all conflict is eliminated and everyone bends

---

"are they to call upon" (*invocabunt*) found in Ambrosiaster's biblical text. See Jewett, *Romans*, 634.

28. Among the biblical witnesses there is stronger support for the aorist subjunctive "might they hear" (ἀκούσωσιν) than for the future indicative "will they hear" (*audient*) found in Ambrosiaster's biblical text. See Jewett, *Romans*, 634.

29. The Greek text has the aorist subjunctive "might they preach" (κηρύξωσιν) instead of the future indicative "will they preach" (*praedicabunt*) found in Ambrosiaster's biblical text.

30. The phrase "who preach peace" (*evangelizantium pacem*) is judged to be a secondary addition meant to harmonize Paul's quotation of Isa 52:7 with the Septuagint. See Bruce M. Metzger, *A Textual Commentary on the Greek New Testament*, 2nd ed. (Stuttgart: Deutsche Bibelgesellschaft, 1994), 463; and Jewett, *Romans*, 634.

31. *Recensio* α does not have this remark. Paul's quotation is in fact closer to Isa 52:7 than to Nah 1:15.

32. *Recensio* α has "was" instead of "is."

the knee to one single God. In fact, Jerusalem above refers to the city of peace, the city *which is our mother* (Gal 4:26).

10:16 *But they do not all heed the gospel.* (1) It is true that although the world is illumined by the brilliance of the Lord's teaching[33] there still are people who resist, who call the light *darkness*. The sharpness of their minds has been dulled[34] to the point that they do not admit the brilliance of true light. The gospel denounces such people when it says: *The light shines in the darkness and the darkness has not comprehended it* (John 1:5).

For Isaiah says: "Lord, who has believed our hearing?" (Isa 53:1). (2) That is: who has believed[35] what we have heard from you and have said? By quoting the prophet, the apostle has shown the Jews to be opponents of the gospel of truth—the law in fact reproves the Jews—since the situation now is just the same as it was with their ancestors. This refers to the group that does not accept the faith.

10:17 *So faith comes from hearing, and hearing through the word.*[36] It is obvious that unless something is said it cannot be heard or believed.

10:18 *But I say, have they not heard?*[37] (1) That is: they have heard and were unwilling to believe. Although faith comes from hearing, there are nevertheless those who do not believe when they hear. They hear and do not understand, because their heart has been darkened by ill will.

For "their sound has gone out to all the earth and their words to the ends of the world" (Ps 18:5 LXX = Ps 19:4 ET). (2) The apostle bears witness that God's proclamation was heard by the Jews[38] to such an extent that the apostle reports that the world was in fact filled with the divine news. Just as, in the words of the prophet David, the construction of the world proclaims the creator, so too the word of the gospel has reached every corner.[39] The

---

33. In *recensio* γ "Lord's" is attested only by MSS Amiens 87 and Monte Cassino 150.
34. *Recensiones* α and β add "by error."
35. *Recensiones* α and β have "who believes" (*credit*) instead of "who has believed" (*credidit*). This would appear to derive from *recensio* α, which has *credit* in the lemma. *Recensio* β has *credidit* in the lemma.
36. In Ambrosiaster's biblical text the verse ends with "the word" (*verbum*). Among the biblical witnesses the reading "the word of Christ" ($\dot{\rho}\dot{\eta}\mu\alpha\tau\text{o}\varsigma$ Χριστοῦ) is preferred. See Metzger, *Textual Commentary*, 463–64; and Jewett, *Romans*, 635.
37. Ambrosiaster's biblical text omits the emphatic particle "Indeed!" (μενοῦνγε).
38. *Recensio* α has "by them" instead of "by the Jews."
39. Instead of this sentence and the remainder of section 2, *recensio* α has "For the sound and the news has even reached places where perhaps no one was physically present, just as word of the mighty deeds in Egypt had reached all nations, as Rahab

sound and the news has even reached places where there was no one to preach, just as word of the mighty deeds in Egypt had reached all nations, as Rahab the prostitute reported (see Josh 2:9). If then the word of the gospel has reached every corner, it was impossible for the Jews not to hear the preaching of the apostles. Thus, none of them can be absolved of the crime of unbelief.

10:19 *But I say, did Israel not understand?* (1) That is: Israel understood. Although the apostle has denounced, by way of the testimony quoted above, the people of Israel on account of their unbelief, he nevertheless does not wish to appear to bewail, gloomily, the state of all Israelites. He does not deny, therefore, that Israel has understood and received what had been promised it in the law. However, he means the Israel that is Israel in spirit rather than in the flesh, the Israel God, too, had foreknown was going to believe. For everyone heard and not everyone believed. Therefore:

First Moses says in the song of Deuteronomy:[40] *"I will make you jealous of those who are not a people; with a foolish people I will make you angry"* (Deut 32:21). (2) These are the words of one who is angry because the Jews were always found to be doubting;[41] for all forms of evil he assigns a single origin and cause. When he berates the present generation, he simultaneously fingers future generations to whom this applies. For all these people there is a single condemnation if they persist in doubting. A jealous envy arises among the Jews, therefore, when they see a people that previously lived in beastly ignorance because they were without God call the God who had been the God of the Jews *their God* and receive the gift that had been promised to the Jews. On account of this people they became jealous and were swollen with rage, thereby paying the price of their malice and unbelief.[42] Nothing, in fact, so consumes a person as envy; God made it the avenger of unbelief because unbelief is a grave sin. Indeed, they are always

---

the prostitute reported. Thus, none of them can be absolved of the crime of unbelief." Instead of the same sentence, *recensio* β has "The very construction of the world proclaims the creator. What the psalmist said about the creation, the apostle says about the evangelists, that the preaching of the name of Christ was heard everywhere and has reached every corner." The remainder of section 2 in *recensio* β is the same as in *recensio* γ.

40. *Recensio* α does not have this remark.
41. *Recensio* α does not have "always."
42. *Recensio* α does not have "and unbelief."

thrown into a rage and tormented when they hear that the law and the prophets belong to us who believe in Christ.[43]

10:20 *Isaiah is so bold as to say: "I have been revealed to those who did not seek me, and I have been found by those who did not ask for me"* (Isa 65:1). Because he cited the words of Moses above about the exclusion of the Jews, he has added a quotation from the prophet Isaiah as well, so that by means of Isaiah's accusation he may explain more clearly that once the Jews had been expelled God offered grace to the gentiles instead, to the disgrace and condemnation of the Jews. Isaiah in fact declares this in the person of Christ.[44]

10:21 *But what does he say to Israel? "The whole day I have held out my hands to an unbelieving people"* (Isa 65:2).[45] (1) This is the Israel of the flesh, that is, the children of Abraham,[46] but not according to faith. Now, the true and spiritual Israel is the Israel that by believing sees God.[47] *The whole day* means *always*, for they have always stood corrected. The reason, therefore, they are reproached for not believing is so that they may know that they themselves are the cause of their own perdition. This passage can also be understood as coming from the Savior,[48] who, with his hands stretched out on the cross, denounced the sin of those who were executing him. The proceedings scream out the Jews' heinous deed.[49] (1a) What

---

43. See *Quaest.* 44.11–13 (CSEL 50:78–79), where Ambrosiaster also defends the Christian claim to being included among the people of God as foretold by the prophets. Although elsewhere in this tract Ambrosiaster rehearses themes and passages found in the Letter to the Romans, he does not quote the passages cited here (Deut 32:21; Isa 65:1–2).

44. *Recensio* α does not have this sentence.

45. Ambrosiaster's biblical text differs from that found in most biblical witnesses, which have "a disobedient and disputatious people" (λαὸν ἀπειθοῦντα καὶ ἀντιλέγοντα). See Jewett, *Romans*, 635.

46. *Recensio* α has "child" or, literally, "son" (*filius*) instead of "children."

47. In his reading of the story of Jacob and the angel (Gen 32:22–32) at *Quaest.* 37.1 (CSEL 50:64), Ambrosiaster takes "Israel," the name given to Jacob, to mean "one who sees God."

48. See In Rom. 10:20.

49. See In Rom. 15:3 (§§1–3), as well as *Quaest.* 65.1–2 (CSEL 50:114–15), where Ambrosiaster maintains that Jesus was executed not by Pontius Pilate but by "the Jews." The charge that "the Jews" killed Jesus was a long-standing Christian claim; see, e.g., Stephen G. Wilson, *Related Strangers: Jews and Christians 70–170 C.E.* (Minneapolis: Fortress, 1995), 295; Paula Fredriksen, *Augustine and the Jews: A Christian Defence of Jews and Judaism* (New Haven: Yale University Press, 2010), 82–84. On its origins in

Isaiah was so bold to say above about those who had been enemies of God shows that they would become friends of God and that those who were called Israelites would have to be given up as enemies because they were disobedient.[50]

---

the gospels, and the purposes served by the narratives of Jesus's trial and execution in the gospels, see John Dominic Crossan, *Who Killed Jesus? Exposing the Roots of Anti-Semitisim in the Gospel Story of the Death of Jesus* (San Francisco: HarperSanFrancisco, 1995), 82–117, 147–59.

50. *Recensio* α does not have section 1a.

Romans 11

11:1 *I say, then, has God rejected his inheritance?[1] Not at all.* (1) Having shown that the people of Israel were unbelieving, the apostle now shows that God has not rejected his inheritance, the inheritance he promised to the descendants of Abraham.[2] The apostle does this lest one should suppose him to have said that all of Israel did not believe. For God would not have promised the kingdom to them[3] if he knew that none of them would believe. Therefore, the inheritance of the Lord belongs by law to the children of Abraham, to the children, however, who believe.[4]

In fact, I too am an Israelite of the seed of Abraham, of the tribe of Benjamin. (2) Using himself as an example, the apostle shows that part of Israel has been saved, the part that God foreknew would be saved, and that even the part of Israel that has been assigned to perdition on account of persistent unbelief could still be saved.

11:2 *God has not rejected his people, whom he foreknew.* This is what the Savior says: *Father, I have guarded those whom you have given me, and none of them has been lost except the son of perdition* (John 17:12). So too with those whom God foreknew would believe; none of them has been

---

1. Ambrosiaster's biblical text differs from that found in most biblical witnesses, which have "people" (τὸν λαόν) instead of "inheritance" (*hereditatem*). See Bruce M. Metzger, *A Textual Commentary on the Greek New Testament*, 2nd ed. (Stuttgart: Deutsche Bibelgesellschaft, 1994), 464; and Robert Jewett with Roy D. Kotansky, *Romans: A Commentary*, Hermeneia (Minneapolis: Fortress, 2007), 650.

2. The text in *recensio* α is complicated by a textual difficulty (see the apparatus) but otherwise resembles the comment in *recensio* γ. Instead of the last clause, *recensio* β and MS Monte Cassino 150 of *recensio* γ have "the inheritance he foreknew, namely, the children of Abraham whom he knew would remain faithful to him."

3. *Recensio* α does not have "the kingdom to them."

4. *Recensio* α does not have this sentence. In *recensio* γ it is attested only by MS Amiens 87.

barred from the promise, because events unfolded as God foreknew they would.[5]

Do you not know what the scripture says of Elijah? How he pleads with God against Israel? **11:3** *"Lord, they have killed your prophets, they have demolished your alters, and I alone am left, and they seek my life."* (1 Kgs 19:10). **11:4** *But what does the divine answer tell him? "I have kept for myself seven thousand men who have not bowed the knee before Baal."* These things are obvious. The apostle shows that there remained not only Elijah, who out of devotion to God did not worship idols, but also many people who persevered in their faith in God, just as quite a few from the Jews have also believed.[6] History also corroborates this account, since many people hid themselves in caves on account of Ahab, king of Samaria, and Jezebel, his wife (see 1 Kgs 18:3–4), who, believing false prophets, persecuted the prophets of God and called on the people to practice idolatry (see 1 Kgs 18:18).[7]

11:5 *So too at the present time a remnant has been saved according to the election of grace.* That is: So too now, the apostle says, those whom God foreknew beforehand have continued in the promise of the law while many withdrew from it. Those who have accepted Christ as the one promised in the law have stood firm in the law, while those who have not accepted him have withdrawn from the law. For this reason believers are called *a remnant*, that is, those who remain in the law.

11:6 *But if it is by grace, it is no longer on the basis of works.* (1) It is obvious that since grace is a gift from God it is not owed as wages for work, but is granted at no cost through the intervention of mercy. *Otherwise grace is no longer grace.* (2) It is true that if it is wages, it is not grace. But since it is not wages, it undoubtedly is grace, because to grant pardon to sinners is nothing other than grace. Moreover, it is offered to those who do not seek it, so that they may believe. Grace therefore has a twofold character, in that it is in the nature of God, who overflows in mercy, also to seek out those whom he takes care of without charge.

---

5. *Recensio* α has "knew" instead of "foreknew."

6. *Recensio* α does not have this clause. In *recensio* γ it is attested only by MS Monte Cassino 150.

7. *Recensio* α has "forced" instead of "called on."

11:7 *What then? Israel has not obtained what it was seeking.*[8] *The election has obtained it.* These Israelites are fleshly Israelites;[9] though they thought that they were justified by works of the law, they did not succeed in being righteous before God through faith,[10] especially since all are guilty through the law. For *cursed is everyone who does not abide by everything that is written in the book of the law, to do it* (Deut 27:26).[11] Nevertheless, even if they abided by everything that was written down—which is hardly possible—they would not be justified before God, since *the righteous lives by faith* (Hab 2:4). The former is righteous for the moment, the latter before God.[12]

But the rest were blinded, **11:8** *as it is written:* What follows can be read in Isaiah.[13] *"God gave them a spirit of stupor, eyes that do not see and ears that do not hear, down to this very day"* (see Deut 29:4; Isa 6:9–10). **11:9** *And David says: "Let their table become a snare and a trap and a stumbling-stone and a retribution for them.* **11:10** *Let their eyes be darkened so that they cannot see, and let their backs be bent forever"* (Ps 68:23–24 LXX = Ps 69:22–23 ET). David curses[14] the table of the wicked because the innocent often are snared at it; they are invited by a deceitful subterfuge to a banquet in order to be murdered. Amnon, the son of David,[15] was tricked by his brother Absalom in this way (see 2 Sam 13:28),[16] and the nefarious Holofernes thought that he could take advantage of the holy Judith through a feast (see Jdt 12:1, 10–12), and evildoers were consumed with fury for the head of the prophet John at

---

8. Among the biblical witnesses there is stronger support for the present "is seeking" (ἐπιζητεῖ) than for the imperfect "were seeking" (*quaerebat*) found in Ambrosiaster's biblical text. See Jewett, *Romans*, 651.

9. On Ambrosiaster's understanding of the meaning of "fleshly," see In Rom. 3:1–2 (§1) and 7:5 (§§1, 4).

10. *Recensio* α has "through the law" instead of "through faith."

11. For the remainder of the comment *recensiones* α and β have "However, those who believed that they were justified through faith obtained the election, so that, having been justified as children of God, they might recall the scripture which says that *the righteous lives by faith,* [β: that is,] not by the law."

12. See In Rom. 3:20 (§1a) and 10:7 (§2).

13. *Recensio* α does not have this remark.

14. *Recensiones* α and β have *devotat* instead of *maledicit*, which perhaps conveys the sense of inveighing a curse more strongly.

15. *Recensio* α does not have "the son of David."

16. *Recensiones* α and β do not have "by his brother Absalom."

the table of the vicious Herod (see Mark 6:21–28).[17] The two prophets[18] are of one mind about such people, who from the outset are found to be untrustworthy and hostile, enemies of good people.[19] Some of these were corrected and set right, albeit late in the day. Some, however, persisted in their obstinacy and have not escaped the heavy sentence of being bent forever. (1a)[20] In other words, they have been blinded to the point of being unable to see the way of truth—the way they had rejected out of ill will and from which they had turned aside—and arrive at the grace of salvation. For someone who does not want to believe, though he has understood, should get what he wants, so that thereafter he will be unable to accept the faith, which he knowingly and deliberately rejected,[21] and be saved. (2) Thus, the quotations from the prophets, cited above, have a double meaning; they were proclaimed and written in two ways. Two types of people, in fact, are implicated here. There is one type that because of their own ill will is blinded forever in order that they may not be saved. They are possessed of such ill will to the point that they say that they do not understand what they hear even though they do understand. For instance, regarding the Savior they would say: *What is he saying? We do not understand what he says* (John 16:18). *Why do you listen to him? He has a demon and he is mad* (John 10:20). But the other group, which is the true Israel, spoke out against them: *These are not the words of one who has a demon. How can a demon open the eyes of the blind?* (John 10:21). (3) Since, then, the former group was jealous of the Savior, they were unwilling to give the impression that they understand what they were hearing. Their goal was to make others think that, inasmuch as he did not seem to be understood by the teachers of the law and the Pharisees, what he said was nonsense and beyond the pale of the law; that what he said could in fact turn others away from the faith. About these people the Savior says:[22] *You have the key of knowledge, and you neither enter yourselves nor let others enter* (Luke 11:52). For who would not follow the counsel and the wisdom of the teachers of the law and Pharisees, who are not to be taken lightly but quite seriously and who are regarded as

---

17. *Recensio* α does not have the last example involving John the Baptist.
18. I.e., Isaiah and David.
19. *Recensio* α does not have "enemies of good people."
20. *Recensio* α does not have section 1a.
21. *Recensio* β does not have "which he knowingly and deliberately rejected."
22. *Recensiones* α and β have "Therefore, they hear from the Savior."

defenders of the law? In fact, to those who are the true Israel they said: *Have any of the authorities believed in him?* (John 7:48). Consequently, if the teachers of the law and the Pharisees had gotten many people to share their position, they would appear to be justified in not having believed, since what is defended only by a few people is not usually considered credible. (4) They were blinded so that thereafter they would be unable to believe and be saved. Thus, they were supported in their wish, so that because they declared what they knew was true to be false, they thereafter did not understand what is true. As a result, the falsehood they desired, they held to be true. (5) There is another type of people that in following the righteousness of the law do not accept Christ. Because they do so not out of a jealous ill will, but out of a mistaken zeal for the tradition of their fathers, they are blinded temporarily. Although they ought to realize from the mighty deeds of Christ that he cannot be wrong—since his power, which is so astounding, was revealed through his deeds—and though they ought to compare his preaching with the new covenant that was promised through the prophets and on that basis profess that he is the one who was promised, they were found to disregard God and agree with other people. For that reason they are blinded, so that once the gentiles have been admitted to their promise, they may return to the faith of God out of their own zeal, when they become jealous of the gentiles. (5a)[23] Because some of the Jews resisted the Savior out of zeal for the law, not out of ill will but rather out of ignorance, they were not blinded forever. For this reason the apostle has added:

11:11 *So I say, have they stumbled so as to fall? By no means!* (1) As I have discussed above, he says that they did not disbelieve to the extent that they could never believe.[24] In other words, they were not blinded by their unbelief to the point that they could not be healed, in the way that we read that the devil too had fallen, as the prophet Isaiah says: *How Lucifer has fallen from heaven!* (Isa 14:12). By *fall* he meant *apostasy*. Thus, the apostle has said that they have not stumbled *so as to fall*, but have been dulled temporarily because of their offense.

But their trespass has been the salvation of the gentiles, so that they may become jealous of them. (2)[25] This is what the apostle has said, that

---

23. *Recensiones* α and β do not have section 5a.
24. *Recensiones* α and β have "they would now never believe" instead of "they could never believe."
25. For section 2 *recensio* α has "Because of their sin salvation was given to the

on account of their sin, salvation was given to the gentiles. Since the Jews declined the gift of God, it was transferred to the gentiles, so that the Jews, fired up with a jealous zeal, might be converted to Christ who was promised to Abraham.²⁶

11:12 *Now if their trespass is riches for the world and their loss is riches for the gentiles, how much more their fullness!* It is obvious that if *their trespass* benefited the world, given that the loss of them results in a greater number of good people (since the gentiles are far more numerous than the Jews), and if *their loss*, which is the forfeiture of the promise, is riches for the gentiles in that they have gained eternal life, *how much more their fullness!* It is clear that the world will be all the richer in good people if they too, who were blinded, convert. Then the world will in large part be saved. *The world* means *people*, as is said of the Savior: *See, the whole world has gone after him* (John 12:19).

11:13 *I am speaking to you gentiles. Inasmuch, then, as I am an apostle to the gentiles, I magnify my ministry,* **11:14** *if somehow I may make my flesh jealous so that I may save some of them.* The apostle shows the gentiles how much he loves the Jews. In fact, he magnifies his ministry, by which he is an apostle to the gentiles, to see if out of love for his people he may by means of the work he has been given bring the Jews to faith as well. For it would be even more praiseworthy if he also gained them, to whom he was not sent, for life. His standing with his fathers will be especially high if he finds the brothers who had gotten lost.

11:15 *For if the losing of them is the reconciliation of the world, what is the gaining of them if not life from the dead?* The apostle says this since, if by means of unbelieving Jews gentiles have been reconciled to God, thereby increasing the amount of faith in Christ in the world, what will happen in this regard and how great will be the fullness of salvation when the Jews too are gained for faith in Christ? It will be as if the world of humankind were brought to life *from the dead*. Since, therefore, there is a benefit to be had, the apostle says that the work must be undertaken for them to believe, because the moment the trespass has been paid for, the

---

gentiles, so that since the Jews declined the gift of God, they would be converted by this wrong itself, becoming jealous of the promise of their fathers." I assume that the siglum β preceding the text in the left-hand column at CSEL 81.1:370 is a typographical error.

26. After "Christ" *recensio* β has "becoming jealous of the promise of their fathers" instead of "who was promised to Abraham."

dullness of blindness will be removed so that they recover the free choice of their will.

11:16 *If the dough offered as first fruits is holy, so is the whole lump.* (1) It is obvious that whatever is of a single substance comprises a single reality. For this reason it is impossible for the first fruits to be holy and the lump unclean; the first fruits come from the lump. Thus, he demonstrates that they, whose fathers already possessed the faith,[27] cannot be said to be unworthy of the faith. For if part of the Jews believed, why should it not be said that the other part can believe as well?

And if the root is holy, so are the branches. (2) He has repeated the same thing in different words to reinforce the point with two examples.

11:17 *But if some of the branches were broken off.* (1) That is, if some of them have not believed, they have been cut off from the promise.

And you, though you were a wild olive shoot, were grafted into them and made to share in the root of the olive tree.[28] (2) This means that while many Jews do not believe, the gentiles have been grafted through faith into the hope of the promise so that the Jews might be chagrined. This, however, does not follow the agricultural practice whereby one grafts a good shoot into a root that is not good, since although they were from a bad root they were grafted into a good tree. The reason the apostle says that a wild olive shoot was grafted on is this: so that the shoot would bear the fruit of the root and share in its yield.

11:18 *Do not boast over against the branches.* (1) That is: do not rejoice in their unbelief. It displeases God if someone gloats over the transgressions of another, as Solomon says (see Prov 24:17–18).[29] Indeed, the Jews have not been rejected for the sake of the gentiles; rather, because they have not believed, they have provided an opportunity for the gospel to be preached to the gentiles.[30]

---

27. *Recensiones* α and β have "ancestors" (*parentes*) instead of "fathers" (*patres*). One could translate *patres* as "ancestors." However, I have rendered it "fathers" to distinguish the terms that Ambrosiaster uses.

28. Ambrosiaster's biblical text omits the phrase "of the fatness" (τῆς πιότητος), which is the preferred reading among the biblical witnesses. See Metzger, *Textual Commentary*, 464; and Jewett, *Romans*, 666–67.

29. *Recensio* α does not have "as Solomon says."

30. *Recensio* α has "Indeed, the Jews have not been rejected for the sake of the gentiles, so that the latter may rejoice, but because they have not believed."

If you do boast, you do not support the root, but the root supports you. (2) That is: if you exalt yourselves over those into whose root you have been grafted, you insult the people that has received you in order that you, originally bad, might become good. You will not remain standing if you cut down that by which you stand.

11:19 *So you say: "Branches were broken off so that I might be grafted in."* The apostle is speaking in the character of a gentile believer[31] who thinks it is right to gloat over the fall of unbelieving Jews and says: "Their rejection has made room for the gentiles." But they were not rejected by God in order that the gentiles might come in;[32] rather, they have alienated themselves by rejecting the gift of God,[33] and they thereby have offered an opportunity for the gentiles to be saved. The apostle wants this gloating to be stopped, so that instead of reviling sickness one rejoices in health. It is in fact easy for someone who reviles a sinner to be ensnared in turn.[34]

11:20 *True.* That is: you are right in saying that you were grafted in after branches were broken off.[35]

But they were broken off through unbelief. (1) That is:[36] they were broken off not on your account, but by their own fault,[37] for when they did not believe, you were called to salvation in order to make them jealous. Therefore, you should give thanks for the gift of God through Christ, rather than revile them, and you should also ask that if their sin has brought you salvation,[38] they too may return to the original plant. Then you will please God, who was merciful to you; in fact, that is the reason he has summoned you, to lead them also back to grace out of jealousy for you.[39]

While you stand fast through faith. (2) Since the Jews have been cast down through unbelief, the apostle says that the gentiles *stand fast through*

---

31. *Recensio* α does not have "believer." In *recensio* γ it is attested only by MS Monte Cassino 150.
32. *Recensio* α does not have "in order that the gentiles might come in."
33. *Recensio* α does not have "by rejecting the gift of God."
34. *Recensio* α has "who rejoices at another person's wrongs" instead of "who reviles a sinner."
35. *Recensio* α does not have this comment.
36. *Recensio* α does not have "that is."
37. *Recensio* α does not have "by their own fault" (*sed suo vitio*).
38. *Recensio* α does not have "if their sin has brought you salvation."
39. *Recensio* α has "to lead them, out of jealousy for you, to that which they had lost."

faith, for although previously the gentiles were prostrate on account of unbelief,[40] they have begun to stand by believing.

Do not be high-minded, but be afraid. (3) That is: do not be arrogant, but take care that you too do not stumble.

11:21 *For if God has not spared the natural branches, perhaps he will not spare you as well.*[41] It is true that if God has blinded Jews on account of unbelief—people who had been vested with the prerogatives of their fathers, people in fact to whom the promise was made that they would be adopted by God as children—what would he do to gentiles if they doubted or exalted themselves—people who have been raised up in the absence of anything to commend them, people who have been honored though they possessed no rank whatsoever?

11:22 *Note then the kindness and the severity of God: severity to those, indeed, who have fallen, but kindness toward you,*[42] *provided that you continue in his kindness.*[43] *Otherwise you too will be cut off.* (1) The apostle attests to the fact that God is good to the gentiles, since although they followed idols and surely were deserving of death, he waited for them patiently and, when they still did not seek him of their own accord, called them and forgave them their sins. But to the Jews God is severe; he blinded them because they rejected the gift of God. (1a)[44] Here, however, the apostle is referring to those Jews who on account of their ill will have been blinded forever. This is why he says that they have fallen—the others he mentioned above had stumbled but not fallen, since he explained that they had been blinded temporarily—and that therefore God has been severe to them, so that as apostates they would be blinded forever.

---

40. *Recensio* α does not have "on account of unbelief."

41. Scholars are divided as to whether "perhaps" (μή πως), present in Ambrosiaster's biblical text (*ne forte*), should be considered original to Paul's text. See Metzger, *Textual Commentary*, 464–65; and Jewett, *Romans*, 667.

42. Ambrosiaster's biblical text omits "of God" after "kindness" in this phrase, but its inclusion has strong support among the biblical witnesses. Although the second instances of "severity" and "kindness" in 11:22 are in the accusative case (*severitatem, bonitatem*) in Ambrosiaster's biblical text, there is stronger support for their being in the nominative case (ἀποτομία, χρηστότης). See Jewett, *Romans*, 667.

43. In Ambrosiaster's biblical text the verb "continue" in this clause is a perfect subjunctive (*permanseris*), but there is stronger support among the biblical witnesses for the present subjunctive (ἐπιμένῃς). See Jewett, *Romans*, 667, and n. 45 below.

44. *Recensio* α does not have section 1a.

11:23 *And they too will be grafted in if they do not continue in unbelief,*[45] *for God has the power to graft them in again.* The apostle explains that the justice of God does not remain severe toward those whom he has blinded temporarily, nor in fact toward those who are unwilling to believe, if they believe,[46] because God has not cut off the Jews in such a way that he would not be able to graft them in again if they turn back.[47] Indeed, he has said through the prophet, *When they return to me, I will replant them* (see Jer 24:6), so that, knowing this, gentile Christians would not revile the Jews, certain that the mercy of God would be kept in reserve for them as those who had slipped.[48]

11:24 *For if you were cut from what is by nature a wild olive tree, and were grafted, contrary to nature, into a cultivated olive tree, how much more will they in accordance with their nature be grafted into their own olive tree!* We should take the *olive tree* to mean the faith by which Abraham was justified, and the *wild olive tree,* on the other hand, to mean unbelief, because it is by nature wild and unfruitful. Therefore, if those who have always been enemies of God were grafted into the faith of Abraham when they converted, though they are not originally descended from him, how much more should the Jews be restored to their ancestral nature, grafted again into their own promise, if after their unbelief they believe.

11:25 *For I do not want you to be ignorant, brothers, of this mystery, so that you are not wise in your own eyes: a dullness has come over part of Israel, until the full number of gentiles come in,* **11:26** *and so all Israel will be*

---

45. In Ambrosiaster's biblical text the verb "continue" in this clause is a perfect subjunctive (*permanserint*), but there is stronger support among the biblical witnesses for the present subjunctive (ἐπιμένωσιν). See Jewett, *Romans,* 667, and n. 43 above.

46. Ambrosiaster seems to qualify what he says at In Rom. 11:8–10 (§§1a–4) about the fate of those Jews who were "unwilling to believe." Whereas in those comments he states that they were blinded such that they would be unable to believe and be saved, here he still allows for the possibility of their being saved, provided they believe. However, the clause in question—"nor in fact toward those who are unwilling to believe, if they believe"—is found only in *recensio* γ; see n. 47 below.

47. *Recensio* α has "The apostle explains that the justice of God does not remain severe, because he has not cut them off in such a way that he would not be able to graft them in again if they turn back." *Recensio* β and MS Monte Cassino 150 of *recensio* γ have "The apostle explains that the justice of God does not remain severe toward those whom he has blinded temporarily, because he has not cut them off in such a way that he would not be able to graft them in again if they turn back."

48. *Recensio* α does not have "as those who had slipped."

saved. (1) This is not difficult to understand, since *a dullness* of blindness has temporarily come upon those Jews who, being zealous for the law, did not see that the gift promised by God had come,[49] the gift that was being proclaimed by Christ. They were blinded by their zeal in thinking that the law of deeds should never come to an end, which is why they were zealous for the sabbath. (2) Because of this mistake their understanding was partly dulled, so that on account of their unbelief they were tormented when they saw the gentiles joyfully announce that they had obtained the promise of Abraham.[50] When, however, a multitude of gentiles had been admitted, the fog was lifted from the eyes of their mind,[51] so that they could believe. Thus, by removing *the spirit of stupor* (Rom 11:8) from their hearts, the one who imposes blindness on them restores free choice of will to them, so that, since their unbelief was a result not of ill will but of error, they might be corrected and then be saved.[52]

As it is written. (3) In order to prove that a gift has been kept in reserve for them by God, the apostle in what follows supplies a quotation from the prophet Isaiah. He does so to explain that they too can be set free by the grace by which Jews who believed were set free,[53] since grace is not exhausted but is always plentiful.[54]

"There will come from Zion one who takes away and drives away godlessness from Jacob" (Isa 59:20). **11:27**[55]*"And this will be the covenant from me with them, when I take away their sins"* (Isa 27:9). The basis for this quotation remains in effect as long as there are people who believe. Even now, the Lord Jesus, who was promised to come from heaven to free the human race, himself daily forgives the sins of those who turn back to God. He does not immediately condemn those who do not believe, but waits for them in the knowledge that they can progress toward an awareness of God.

---

49. *Recensio* α does not have "by God."

50. *Recensio* α has "Because of this mistake their understanding was partly dulled, so that since they did not believe, gentiles were admitted to the faith whereas the Jews were temporarily hardened so that they should not see the way that leads to life."

51. *Recensiones* α and β have "from their eyes" instead of "from the eyes of their mind."

52. *Recensio* α has "Thus, since their unbelief was a result not of ill will but of error, they were corrected so that they might then be saved."

53. *Recensio* α has "the people who preceded them" instead of "Jews who believed."

54. *Recensio* α adds "Therefore, he says."

55. The beginning of 11:27 is placed here, as in modern texts of Romans, rather than at the beginning of the lemma, as in the CSEL edition.

11:28 *As regards the gospel they are indeed enemies for your sake.* (1) On account of unbelief they are enemies of the gospel, so that their mistake and transgression opened the way for the gentiles to enter the faith prematurely, as I have discussed above. The gospel was to be preached first to all Jews everywhere; not till then was it fitting for the word of God to be believed by gentiles as well.[56] But because the Jews did not believe, the kingdom was taken from them and given to the gentiles. So the apostle warns that the people whose transgression has benefited the gentiles should not be reviled; only someone whose sin has hurt other people should be reviled. If the Jews are slow to convert, their unbelief should be a cause not for celebration but for lament, so that, just as the gentiles experienced joy in the sin of the Jews because they themselves were saved, they likewise may rejoice in the conversion of the Jews. For on account of the Jews, the gentiles received the grace of God more quickly.

As regards election, however, they are beloved for the sake of their fathers. (2) Although the Jews have sinned gravely in rejecting the gift of God and are worthy of death, nevertheless because they are the children of exemplary people, whose privileged position and meritorious conduct garnered many blessings from God, they will be received with joy when they return to the faith, since God's love for them is kindled by the memory of their fathers.

11:29 *For the gifts and the call of God are without repentance.* This is true, because the grace of God in baptism does not require wailing or lament or any act except a confession from the heart. Because the gentiles saw that the Jews were not very sorrowful, the apostle explains that such behavior is not required in the early stages of faith,[57] so that the gentiles might not think that, since the Jews sinned gravely by not accepting the promise of God and since those who sin gravely do not obtain forgiveness without wailing and weeping, the Jews therefore could not receive mercy now. For the gift of God forgives sins freely in baptism.[58]

11:30 *Just as you too once did not believe God but now have received mercy because of their unbelief,*[59] **11:31** *so too they now have not believed*

---

56. *Recensio* α does not have this sentence and the next one.

57. *Recensio* α has "the apostle explains that this step, which is guaranteed to lead to faith, does not require such behavior."

58. *Recensio* α has "grace" instead of "gift."

59. Among the biblical witnesses there is stronger support for the absence of "too" (*et*). See Jewett, *Romans*, 694.

in the compassion shown to you so that they might also receive mercy.[60] The apostle recalls the unbelief of the gentiles so that they, blushing at the recollection, do not become arrogant and revile Jews who do not believe, but rather treat them graciously so that they accept the promise of God. For, he says, since you gentiles were hostile at the time when the oracles of God were entrusted to them, but now have received mercy—this not of your deserving but to their shame—why indeed should not they who previously were conversant in the law of God and to whom the promise was made receive mercy when they have converted?[61]

11:32 *For God confined all things in unbelief so that he may have mercy upon all.*[62] (1) From ancient times, then, the nations[63] lived in ungodliness and ignorance—in other words, without God. For this reason the law was revealed in writing, so that those who were rushing headlong to destruction could be restrained. Then through the adversary's cunning sins began to pile up, so that by means of the prohibition of the law humankind was instead found guilty. Therefore, out of his merciful goodness God rescued humankind forever, so that both what was considered sin outside the law and what was considered sin under the law could be wiped out. He decreed that he would establish faith alone as the means by which the sins of all people might be obliterated. He did this so that everyone might be saved by the mercy of God, since there was no hope for anyone through the law. (2) This is what it means to have *confined all things in unbelief,* so that then the gift decreed by God might come, when everyone labored in unbelief, and the liberality of the gift might be especially generous. Therefore, no one should think highly of themselves; it is pathetic when someone who has been pardoned puts on airs.

11:33 *O the depths of the riches of the wisdom and the knowledge of God!*[64] *How inscrutable are his judgments and how unsearchable his ways!* (1) Offering every sort of praise in thanksgiving, the apostle testifies that

---

60. Among the biblical witnesses there is slightly stronger support for the presence of "now" (νῦν) in the clause "so that they might now also receive mercy" than for its absence. See Metzger, *Textual Commentary,* 465; and Jewett, *Romans,* 694.

61. *Recensio α* does not have "when they have converted."

62. Although Ambrosiaster's biblical text has "all things" (*omnia*), there is stronger support among the biblical witnesses for "all people" (τοὺς πάντας). See Metzger, *Textual Commentary,* 465; and Jewett, *Romans,* 694.

63. Although *gentes* usually means "gentiles" in Ambrosiaster's comments, here it seems to refer to all people.

64. Although Ambrosiaster's biblical text has "the depths of the riches of the

God is exalted and boundless in the riches of his wisdom and knowledge; his thinking and judgment are, in fact, incomprehensible. For since he understood from the very beginning the conduct and works of humankind—that the human race could neither be saved by the severity of justice alone nor attain complete worthiness by mercy alone[65]—at a certain time he decreed what was to be proclaimed, but before that time he left everyone to their own judgment, since justice can be recognized through the guidance of nature itself. (2) Then, since the authority of natural justice has been deadened by the habit of sinning, the law was given so that the human race might be kept in check through fear of the law that had been revealed. But because people did not restrain themselves and were found guilty by the law, the mercy that saves those who flee to it for refuge was proclaimed. Those who rejected this mercy, God blinded temporarily, and into the promise that belonged to them God welcomed gentiles who previously were unwilling to follow the righteousness of God given through Moses. This was done so that when the Jews became jealous of the salvation of the gentiles, by this very jealousy they might restore themselves to the original root of the Savior.[66] Such is *the depths of the riches of the wisdom and the knowledge of God*, which through diverse providential means gained Jews as well as gentiles for life.

11:34 *"For who has known the mind of the Lord? Or who has been his counselor?"* (Isa 40:13). **11:35** *"Or who has given him a gift first and will be repaid?"* (see Job 41:3). (1) One finds this written in Isaiah.[67] It is obvious that only God knows every thought and that he alone needs nothing, since everything comes from him. Therefore, his thinking is not grasped or weighed by anyone, since subordinates cannot know the mind of a superior. (2) Consequently, to believing Jews it seemed impossible that God's thinking and intention was to redeem the gentiles. Likewise, to the gentiles it seemed dubious[68] and incredible that Jews who had not believed could be converted

---

wisdom" (*altitudo divitiarum sapientiae*), the Greek text (NA[28]) has "the depths of the riches and the wisdom" (βάθος πλούτου καὶ σοφίας). See Jewett, *Romans*, 713.

65. See n. 78 at In Rom. 3:21.

66. Literally, "to the origin of the root of the Savior" (*ad radicis salvatoris originem*). Recensiones α and β add "the root promised in the law," probably an allusion to Isa 11:1–10.

67. *Recensio* α does not have this remark. Ambrosiaster does not discuss the text Paul quotes in 11:35. It does not correspond exactly to either the Hebrew or LXX texts of Job 41:3; see Jewett, *Romans*, 719–20.

68. Recensiones α and β have "difficult" instead of "dubious."

or accepted as believers, and thus be saved. This, among other examples, is the thinking of God, which was hidden and could not be grasped.

11:36 *For from him and through him and in him are all things. To him be the glory.*[69] (1) The apostle has stated why the mind and thinking of God cannot be searched. For, he says, *from him and through him and in him are all things. To him be the glory.*[70] With this comment the apostle has uncovered the mind that was concealed to the world. For since God is the creator of all things, *from him are all things.*[71] Because they are from him, they began to exist through his Son,[72] who is in truth of the same substance and whose work is the Father's work.[73] (2) Since, then, God worked through the Son, *through him are all things.* Because the things that are from God and through God were later reborn in the Holy Spirit, *in him are all things,* since the Holy Spirit, too,[74] is from God the Father. This is why he also knows the things that are in God. The Father is, therefore, also in the Holy Spirit, for what is from God the Father cannot be anything other than God the Father.[75] (3) Therefore, *to him be the glory,* since *from him and through*

---

69. Although the verse ends here in Ambrosiaster's biblical text, in the Greek text (NA[28]) it continues with "forever, amen" (εἰς τοὺς αἰῶνας, ἀμήν).

70. *Recensio* α does not have this sentence, "For, he says ... the glory."

71. *Recensio* α has "For since God is the creator of all things—for he made the things that did not exist to exist—therefore *from him are all things*."

72. *Recensio* α adds "as well."

73. The phrases *unius substantiae* and *eiusdem substantiae* were commonly used in the West to refer to the common divine substance of the Father and the Son. This language echoes the Latin version of the Nicene Creed, which confessed that the Son is "of one substance with the Father, what the Greeks call *homoousion*" (*unius substantiae cum patre quod Graeci dicunt homoousion*). Ambrosiaster uses various expressions in the Commentary to express the same idea; see In 2 Cor. 5:18–21 (§2) (CSEL 81.2:237): *pater enim per id intellegitur esse in filio, quod una eorum sit substantia*; In Eph. 2:3 (§2) (CSEL 81.3:79): *ut in virtute et substantia et nomine nihil distet filius a patre*; In Phil. 2:9–11 (§9) (CSEL 81.3:145): *ut una gloria sit patris et filii per communem substantiam et virtutem*; In 2 Thess. 2:16 (CSEL 81.3:243): *quoniam pater et filius una virtus unaque divinitas et substantia est.* See the introduction §5.2 and Theodore S. de Bruyn, "Ambrosiaster's Revisions of His *Commentary on Romans* and Roman Synodal Statements about the Holy Spirit," REAug 56 (2010): 61–62.

74. *Recensio* α does not have "too." With this addition to *recensio* β, Ambrosiaster emphasizes the consubstantiality of the Holy Spirit with the Father; see In Rom. 8:27 (§1a) with n. 116.

75. In *recensio* γ "for what is from God the Father cannot be anything other than God the Father" is attested only by MSS St. Gall 101, in a second hand, and Troyes 128.

him and in him are all things. Accordingly, whatever came into being *from him and through him and in him,* so as to exist, cannot know his mind and thinking, whereas he knows all things, since absolutely all things are in him. The apostle has brought to light the mystery of God—the mystery, he said above, of which they should not be unaware (see Rom 11:25).

Romans 12

12:1 *I therefore appeal to you, brothers, by the mercy of God, to present your bodies as a living sacrifice, holy, pleasing to God, your reasonable service.* **12:2** *Do not be conformed to this world, but be renewed in the newness of your mind,*[1] *so that you may prove what is the will of God, what is good and pleasing and perfect.* (1) The apostle prays for these things *by the mercy of God*, by which the human race is saved. After having discussed the law and faith and people who by birth were Jewish and gentile, he urges them to live a good life, for by this means one attains the hope of faith.[2] This, then, is his warning: that they remember that they have received mercy and that they be attentive to the service of the one from whom they received it[3]—the mercy by which they have been freely justified from among the wicked.[4] For they should know that a *living sacrifice, holy* and acceptable to God,[5] is this: if we keep our bodies undefiled, unlike worldly folk, who pursue pleasures. (1a)[6] *For this is the will of God,*

---

1. Among the biblical witnesses the preferred reading is "in newness of mind" (τῇ ἀνακαινώσει τοῦ νοός), omitting "your" (*vestrum*). See Robert Jewett with Roy D. Kotansky, *Romans: A Commentary*, Hermeneia (Minneapolis: Fortress, 2007), 724.

2. Instead of the first two sentences in section 1, *recensio* α has "The appeal is not made to them on the basis of their salvation nor through Christ, even though God's mercy is in Christ. Rather, he prays these things through the mercy by which they were brought to life from among the dead, so that, bearing this mercy in mind, they take care that it endures unchanged toward them."

3. In *recensio* γ the phrase "from whom they received it" is attested only by MS Paris lat. 1759.

4. *Recensio* α has "the one by whom" instead of "the mercy by which."

5. *Recensio* α does not have "holy."

6. *Recensio* α does not have sections 1a and 1b. Instead it ends the comment on Rom 12:1-2 as follows: "(2) To serve God spiritually—this occurs when justice intervenes and we are conformed to spiritual things, demonstrating through the patience of the spirit we have received, what pleases God, and following it, since what pleases God is the perfect good."

our sanctification (1 Thess 4:3). Now, bodies that are subjected to sins are not considered to be alive, but dead, for they are deprived of the hope of the promised life. We were cleansed from sins by the gift of God so that in future we might draw out God's love toward us by living a pure life, by not invalidating the work of his grace. In fact, this was the reason a sacrificial victim was killed among the ancients, to represent people who were subject to death because of sin. (1b)[7] But now, because people have been purified by God's gift and set free from the second death, they should offer a living sacrifice, as a sign of eternal life. For now bodies are not sacrificed in place of bodies, as happened then; instead, the vices of the bodies, not the bodies themselves, ought to be destroyed. Moreover, to obtain the effect of our service, let us preserve our modesty after having upheld justice; for if justice is disregarded, modesty is useless and cannot seem reasonable.[8] This is what it will mean to be conformed to spiritual things, renewed in spirit and faith: to know that what pleases God, and nothing else, is *good* and *perfect*.

12:3 *For by the grace that was given to me I say to all who are among you, not to think more highly than one ought to think, but to think prudently and according to the measure of faith which God has apportioned to each one.* He clearly shows that we ought to think in a way that does not exceed just limits,[9] so that our thinking may be helpful not just to us, but also may not injure anyone else.[10] This, in fact, is prudence: to benefit others rather than injure them, to be content with the lot which God has measured out with regard to the merit and faith of each person,[11] and not to claim for oneself what one sees has not been allotted to oneself. This is what it means *not to think more highly*, because everything cannot

---

7. See n. 6 above.

8. In Ambrosiaster's comments on Rom 12 I have translated *iustitia* with "justice" because at several points Ambrosiaster's usage has the connotations of meting out justice; see In Rom. 12:16 (§4), 12:17 (§§1–1a), and 12:21. However, one should bear in mind that the word can also be rendered "righteousness"; see In Rom. 3:21 n. 78.

9. Literally, "the limits of justice" (*iustitiae terminos*).

10. Recensio α does not have "but also not injure anyone else."

11. *Recensio* α has "on account of the faith of each person" (*merito fidei uniuscuiusque*), whereas *recensio* β and some manuscripts of *recensio* γ have "with regard to the merit and faith of each person" (*merito et fidei uniuscuiusque*). The latter may be the result of an error in transmission. The phrase as found in *recensio* α is consistent with what Ambrosiaster states in all recensions at In Rom. 12:6 (§1): "those functions that are assigned to members on account of faith" (*ipsa officia deputata membris merito fidei*).

be allotted to one person. If someone leads a good life, he should not for that reason assert for himself an understanding of teaching as well, nor should someone who is an expert in the law claim for himself the Levitical service.[12] The apostle therefore exhorts and instructs *by the grace given to him*. This grace refers to expertise in the teaching of the Lord, through which the apostle passes on what should be pursued with regard to humility and justice.[13]

12:4 *For as in one body we have many members, but all members do not have the same function,* **12:5** *so too we, though many, are one body in Christ, and individually members one of another.* Through the example of a body the apostle teaches that we are not individually capable of everything, since we are members of one another, meaning that each one needs the other. We therefore should take care of each other and not oppose each other, for we have need of one another's functions. This is what it will mean to love Christ: if the members urge one another to fulfill the role through which the body will be complete in Christ.

12:6 *Having the gifts of God that differ according to the grace that was given to us.*[14] (1) The apostle now lists those functions that are assigned to members on account of faith, so that when a member sees the function that is assigned to him he does not complain loudly about another member to whom he sees another function given, but rejoices with him, so that the body of the church may be complete.

If prophecy, according to the proportion of faith. (2) The apostle begins with prophecy, which is the principal evidence that our faith is reasonable: finally, having received the Spirit, the believers prophesied (see Acts 2:4). Prophecy, then, is given in accordance with the capacity of the receiver, insofar, that is, as it requires a basis for being given.

---

12. Ambrosiaster held to clearly delineated ecclesiastical functions; see the introduction §7.1 and Sophie Lunn-Rockliffe, *Ambrosiaster's Political Theology*, OECS (Oxford: Oxford University Press, 2007), 113–15. In *Quaest.* 101 (CSEL 50:193–98) he castigates deacons in Rome who presumed to perform functions reserved for presbyters, equating the difference between them to that between Levites (*levitae*) and priests (*sacerdotes*). In the present comment he may be alluding to teachers who took on tasks reserved for deacons.

13. *Recensio* α does not have "and justice."

14. The Greek text of the verse (NA^{28}) omits "of God" (*dei*).

12:7 *If in a ministry, in ministering.* (1) One who ministers is confirmed[15] in the service of the church[16] to the extent that he believes that he ought to serve, so that he may not grow weary in vain by performing a service that is beyond his faith, since each one is doing something undertaken from the heart.

One who teaches, in teaching. (2) Similarly, the apostle says that a teacher is to be supported in teaching, so that, insofar as the purpose of his faith is to teach, he may be inspired to hand on the heavenly instruction.

12:8 *One who exhorts, in exhortation.* (1) In the same way, one who exhorts should have his way primed, in the matter in which he exerts himself, through the help of the Spirit, so that he may possess grace when he challenges others. For he rouses brothers to what is good and unbelievers to faith.

One who gives, out of sincerity. (2) The apostle says that one who gives out of the goodness of his heart will, through the care of the Spirit, have help always to be richly supplied,[17] so that he may not lack the means to give liberally and sincerely, as Solomon says: *One who gives to the poor will not be in want* (Prov 28:27).[18] A person gives sincerely, therefore, when he does so not as a pretense to garner praise from people, but rather in order to obtain merit from God for the act itself.[19]

One who is in charge, out of concern. (3) The apostle says that he who takes on the responsibility to be in charge of the community assumes vigilance and authority in accordance with his faith, (4) so that he may prosper in the matter about which he is concerned, bearing fruit in the people of whom he is in charge.[20]

---

15. *Recensio* α has "one is confirmed" instead of "one who ministers is confirmed." Ambrosiaster is probably thinking of deacons here. In other contexts he uses *minister*, the word used here, to refer to deacons; see In 1 Tim. 5:21–22 (§1) and *Quaest.* 101.5 (CSEL 50:196).

16. *Recensiones* α and β have "of the community" instead of "of the church."

17. *Recensio* α has "Such a person will have help always etc."

18. *Recensio* α does not have "as Solomon says: *One who gives to the poor will not be in want.*"

19. Instead of this sentence, *recensio* α has "A person who gives sincerely is one who does not do so as a pretense, nor in order to garner the praise of people."

20. For section 4 *recensio* α has "so that unwavering respect for the people of whom he is in charge may develop in him."

One who shows mercy, cheerfully. (5) The apostle says that one who acts mercifully with a glad heart,[21] not like someone who is forced to do so grudgingly, will be enriched and invigorated by God in accordance with his intentions[22] so that he will suffer no wavering in this matter, recognizing what was said by Solomon: *When you have the opportunity, do good* (Prov 3:27). But this should be understood in various ways; in a single word there are multiple meanings.[23] In fact, since above the apostle said, *One who gives,*[24] *sincerely*, why was it necessary to repeat himself unless he meant many good works by the single term *mercy*? (6) Indeed, it is mercy to forgive sinners, and it is mercy to offer help to someone who is in any sort of need or overwhelmed,[25] and it is mercy to clothe the naked and to break bread with the hungry and to gather up an abandoned child and to attend to a corpse and to do similar works. Accordingly, if one does these things readily and tirelessly, one will enjoy the reward of this work both in the present and in the future. (6a)[26] Therefore, all mercy should be performed sincerely and with joy, so that sincerity may rule out hypocrisy, while joy may demonstrate trust in the hope to come.

12:9 *Let love be without pretense.* When someone is of a mind to love a brother because he knows that this pleases God the creator, and not to receive praise in this present life, the Spirit comes to his aid so that, because he seeks to love with a devout mind, he may be able to fulfill his service.[27] For such people hear what was said by the Lord: *A new commandment I give you, that you love one another* (John 13:34).

---

21. "The apostle says" must be supplied to complete the Latin construction.

22. For the remainder of the comment in section 5, *recensio* α has "so that he may have the resources with which to be merciful and so that a reward may be kept for him in future. *To show mercy cheerfully* is close in meaning to *giving sincerely*. Nevertheless, to show mercy is a more important activity. In fact, there are many works which are subsumed under this term."

23. Instead of this clause, *recensio* β has "there are multiple forms of mercy in a single word."

24. *Recensio* β has *largitur*, as in the lemma above, while *recensio* γ has *tribuit*, as in the Vulgate.

25. For the remainder of the comment in section 6, *recensio* α has "and it is mercy to intervene before someone with prayers on his behalf, and it is mercy to give to one who is in need. Accordingly, if one does these things readily and ungrudgingly, such a person will enjoy help now and a reward in future."

26. *Recensio* α does not have section 6a.

27. *Recensio* α does not have "his service."

12:10 *Shrinking from evil, holding fast to what is good, being kind to one another with brotherly love, outdoing one another in showing honor.* The apostle says that it is no great achievement to avoid evil if one does not hold fast to what is good—the former issues from fear, the latter from love[28]—or to be kind or show brotherly love[29] if the members do not outdo themselves in service to one another.

12:11 *Not sluggish in showing concern.* (1) This is what the prophet Jeremiah says: *Cursed is the one who does the work of the Lord in a slack way* (Jer 48:10).[30] For one who is sluggish in a godly way of life is without hope.[31] Therefore, the apostle has added:

Glowing with the Spirit. (1a)[32] In other words, so that one is not lukewarm in performing godly work or the law, as it says in the Apocalypse of John: *Because you are lukewarm, I will spit you out of my mouth* (Rev 3:16). Daily meditation, in fact, does away with lethargy and makes one alert. However, works of the Lord are those which he commands to be done for the benefit of the church, that is, the brothers.[33]

Serving the time.[34] (1b)[35] It is said that in the Greek one reads:[36] *Serving the Lord*, which does not fit the context here.[37] What was the point of

---

28. *Recensio* α does not have this parenthetical remark.

29. *Recensio* α has "and that brotherly love is not kind." *Recensio* β and MS Monte Cassino 150 of *recensio* γ have "and that brotherly honor [*honorem*] is not kind"; *honorem* would appear to be a scribal error.

30. For the quotation *recensio* α has "*Cursed by God is the one who does the work of God in a slack way.*"

31. *Recensio* α does not have this sentence and the next one.

32. *Recensio* α does not have section 1a.

33. In *recensio* γ this sentence is attested by only by MS Monte Cassino 150.

34. See n. 37 below.

35. *Recensio* α does not have section 1b. The addition of this section in *recensio* β is likely a response to Jerome's *Ep.* 27, which he wrote to Marcella in 384 to defend his practice of correcting received Latin versions of the New Testament (the VL) in light of the text found in Greek manuscripts. Jerome cited three VL readings from the Pauline letters that his opponents preferred to the Greek readings, including the reading that Ambrosiaster supports here, *tempori servientes* (*Ep.* 27.3 [CSEL 54²:225–26]). See the introduction §1.

36. The phrasing of this remark, like that at In Rom. 5:14 (§4), suggests that Ambrosiaster did not himself consult the Greek text but relied on the observation of others.

37. The preferred reading, found in a majority of witnesses, including several VL manuscripts, is in fact "serving the Lord" (τῷ κυρίῳ δουλεύοντες/*domino servientes*);

placing this at the top of one's entire devotion, especially given that the apostle is calling to mind the individual elements that pertain to the worship and service of God? For in all the things he lists, the complete service of God is exhibited. (2) Elsewhere, in fact,[38] the apostle has explained what it means *to serve the time*, when he says: *Making the most of the time, because the days are evil* (Eph 5:16), *so that you may know how you ought to answer everyone* (Col 4:6). But because he had said: *Glowing in the spirit*, he does not want them to take this to mean that they should talk incessantly and intrusively about religious matters, when the time is not favorable,[39] so as to risk causing offense. He therefore immediately added: *Serving the time*, so that they would speak about the faith of the religion with dignity and credibility, when the place and the people and the time are right. For even at this time, when there is peace,[40] there are some who detest the words of God so much that when they hear them they profane the way of Christ in a huge rage. (2a)[41] Indeed, the apostle himself also

---

see Jewett, *Romans*, 755. A few Latin manuscripts of Paul's letters have "serving the time" (*tempori servientes*), based on the variant τῷ καιρῷ δουλεύοντες; see John Wordsworth and Henry J. White, eds., *Novum Testamentum domini nostri Iesu Christi latine* (Oxford: Clarendon, 1889–1954), 2:128. On these manuscripts, see Hugo S. Eymann, *Epistula ad Romanos*, VLB 21 (Freiburg: Herder, 1996), 19–21. Cyprian, one of the Latin authorities to whom Ambrosiaster appealed at In Rom. 5:14 (§5a) when defending his preference for older Latin translations of the Greek codices of the New Testament, alludes to the reading at *Ep.* 5.2.2 (CCSL 3B:28). It was also known to Rufinus, who, however, rejected it when translating Origen's *Commentary on Romans*; see Origen-Rufinus, *Comm. Rom.* 9.10 (*AGLB* 34:738), and Caroline P. Hammond Bammel, *Der Römerbrieftext des Rufin und seine Origenes Übersetzung*, vol. 10 of *AGLB* (Freiburg: Herder, 1985), 227.

38. *Recensio* α does not have "in fact," which bridges the added section 1b with the existing section 2.

39. *Recensio* α does not have "when the time is not favorable."

40. *Recensio* α does not have "even in this time, when there is peace." The absence of this remark suggests that the earliest version of the commentary on Romans was written toward the end of or, more likely, shortly after the reign of Julian (355–363), when Christians would have been less certain of their position within the empire. Other evidence suggests that the version was completed before 375 and possibly before 371; see Theodore S. de Bruyn, "Ambrosiaster's Revisions of His *Commentary on Romans* and Roman Synodal Statements about the Holy Spirit," *REAug* 56 (2010): 65; Alexander Souter, *A Study of Ambrosiaster*, TS 7.4 (Cambridge: Cambridge University Press, 1905), 167–68.

41. *Recensio* α does not have section 2a. In *recensio* γ it is attested only by MSS Monte Cassino 150 and Paris lat. 1759.

served the time when he did something he did not want to do. He reluctantly circumcised Timothy (see Acts 16:3) and went up to the temple after he had purified himself by shaving his head in accordance with the law (see Acts 21:24), in order to mollify the indignation of the Jews.

12:12 *Rejoicing in hope.* (1) After the apostle said: *Serving the time*, he added: *Rejoicing in hope*, so that if because of the evilness of the time it was perhaps not possible to speak about the faith publicly, but only to live in fear, one may rejoice that this distress brings forth gladness.

Patient in tribulation. (2) This is what *to rejoice in hope* means: to be patient in tribulation. In fact, because of the joy of hope one endures tribulation, knowing that the things that have been promised to compensate for these tribulations are much greater.

Persistent in prayer. (3) Prayer is exceedingly important because one must be persistent in prayers in order to be able to endure tribulation.

12:13 *Sharing in the remembrances of the saints.*[42] (1) It is obvious that someone who wants his prayers to be heard ought to emulate the life of the saints. When one imitates, one *shares in*,[43] so that this is what it means to remember and share in: to imitate their action. (1a)[44] Furthermore, if they need financial support, one should share with them, as the apostle says elsewhere: *Concerning the contributions which are for the saints* (1 Cor 16:1), and to the Galatians: *So that we remember the poor* (Gal 2:10).

Ready to offer hospitality. (2) One who imitates and loves[45] the saints is *ready to offer hospitality* according to the example of holy Abraham (see Gen 18:1–8) and Lot (see Gen 19:1–3), who were righteous men.[46]

---

42. The preferred reading, supported by the great majority of witnesses, is "sharing in the needs (ταῖς χρείαις/*necessitatibus*) of the saints." See Jewett, *Romans*, 755.

43. *Recensio* α does not have "When one imitates, one *shares in*."

44. *Recensio* α does not have section 1a. The section seems to refer to the version of 12:13 that reads "sharing in the needs of the saints" (see n. 42 above), though it lacks a clear allusion to the word *necessitatibus*. It would be unusual for Ambrosiaster to acknowledge the alternate reading, since he prefers—and defends—the VL when it varies from the Greek; see n. 37 above. Several decades later both Pelagius and Rufinus are aware of "remembrances" (*memoriis*), though they prefer "needs" (*necessitatibus*); see Pelagius, In Rom. 12:13 (TS 9.2:98) and Origen-Rufinus, *Comm. Rom.* 9.12 (*AGLB* 34:738–39).

45. *Recensio* α does not have "and loves."

46. In early Christian literature, both Abraham and Lot were held up as paradigms of hospitality. See Andrew Cain, *The Greek Historia monachorum in Aegypto:*

12:14 *Bless, and do not curse.*[47] In order to make Christians new in every respect,[48] the apostle wishes to distance them even from this habit, which is common to all people. Thus, when they are provoked into an angry state of mind they should not be quick to curse,[49] as before, but should rather bless, having mastered their temper, so that the way of life taught by the Lord may be commended.[50]

12:15 *Rejoice with those who rejoice, weep with those who weep.* (1) In other words, as the apostle says elsewhere: *If one member suffers, all the members suffer together, and when one member rejoices, all the members rejoice together* (1 Cor 12:26). When someone helps a brother in need, he cheers him up and lays up merit for himself with God because he is attentive to a member of the body of Christ. (1a)[51] If he should console an unbeliever, he may motivate him to adopt instead the way of life taught by the Lord.

12:16 *Having the same opinion, one of another.* (1) This is what was just said, that one ought to commiserate in the tribulation of the brothers, as the apostle has also said in another letter:[52] *Looking to yourself lest you too be tempted, bear one another's burdens* (Gal 6:1-2).

Do not think highly of yourself. (2) *To think highly of oneself* is pride; indeed, even the devil, when he thought highly of himself, apostatized. One should not feel superior and, possibly taking the rightness of one's actions for granted, accuse a brother as a sinner rather than comfort him.[53] This is

---

Monastic Hagiography in the Late Fourth Century, OECS (Oxford: Oxford University Press, 2016), 239 n. 209.

47. The Greek text of the verse reads (NA[28]): "Bless those who persecute [you], bless and do not curse" (εὐλογεῖτε τοὺς διώκοντας [ὑμᾶς], εὐλογεῖτε καὶ μὴ καταρᾶσθε). The omission of the first clause in a few witnesses, including Ambrosiaster's biblical text, may have been due to the repetition of εὐλογεῖτε in the Greek, which could have lead a scribe to jump from the first instance to the second when completing the clause; see Jewett, *Romans*, 755.

48. *Recensio* α has "the servants of Christ" instead of "Christians."

49. *Recensio* α has does not have the adverb here rendered "quick."

50. *Recensio* α does not have the last clause.

51. *Recensio* α does not have section 1a.

52. *Recensio* α has "That is, to commiserate in the tribulation of the brothers, as the apostle has said elsewhere."

53. Instead of the first two sentences of section 2, *recensio* α has "*To think highly of oneself* is to think too much of oneself, so that one feels superior and, possibly taking the rightness of one's actions for granted, accuses a brother as a sinner or as

pride, which gives offense when it sets itself over another.[54] The Lord also observed this when he said: *First take the beam out of your eye and then you will see clearly to take the speck out of your brother's eye* (Matt 7:5). In fact, a sense of superiority is itself a sin; even if one is not a sinner—which is impossible—one becomes a sinner when one is proud. Finally, Solomon says: *God opposes the proud* (Prov 3:34).

But associate with the lowly. (3) That is, after getting rid of pride, one should make another's concern one's own, and one's own concern, so to speak, another's,[55] (3a)[56] so that one may have grace with God, for *everyone who exalts himself will be humbled* (Luke 4:11).

Do not be wise in your own eyes. (4) This sentence is written in the prophet Isaiah (see Isa 5:21). The apostle places it here as if it were his own words to make the point that justice should be applied universally, rather than that someone is just to himself but unjust to others.

12:17 *Repaying no one evil for evil.* (1) This is what the Lord says: *Unless your righteousness is greater than that of the scribes and the Pharisees, you will not enter into the kingdom of God* (Matt 5:20). For in the law it had been commanded: *Love your neighbor and hate your enemy* (Matt 5:43). This, it seems, is justice. But in order that the justice of Christians may be greater, one is instructed not to repay one another for evil,[57] so that Christians may become perfect and may be rewarded at God's judgment for this. In fact, one appears to have surpassed justice itself when, in order to be better, one who imitates heavenly justice does not do what the law permits.[58] (1a)[59] Thus, the justice of the world, conceded to it by God, renders one innocent for the time being,[60] but heavenly justice renders one perfect so that one has merit with God.

---

someone who through negligence failed to anticipate what would happen, rather than comfort him."

54. *Recensio* α has "This too is pride, which can hurt."

55. *Recensio* α does not have "so to speak" (*quasi*). Ambrosiaster's meaning is that one's own concerns should be as irrelevant as a stranger's might be.

56. *Recensio* α does not have section 3a.

57. *Recensiones* α and β have "evil for evil," echoing the lemma, instead of "one another for evil."

58. *Recensio* α has "when, in order to be better, one does not do what is permissible."

59. *Recensio* α does not have section 1a.

60. *Recensio* β does not have "for the time being." See In Rom. 3:20 (§§1–1a).

Bearing in mind good things not only before God, but also before people.[61] (2) *To bear in mind* is to keep future good things in view, such that one does things which cannot be subjected to criticism after they have been done, but rather can be praised by God or people. The apostle warns that one ought to do both what does not displease God and what does not give offense to a brother. The apostle says this lest one should think that, since things that are lawful never displease God, one therefore need not be concerned if they give offense to a brother. Even if it is lawful, if it also offends a brother, it does not please God, because God admonishes one to be concerned about salvation. (2a)[62] Good things, therefore, are kept in mind before God and people if things that are lawful are done in such a way that they may not give offense.

12:18 *If possible, as far as it depends upon you, living in peace with everyone.* (1) The apostle wants the person who upholds divine justice to be at peace with everyone.[63] It can happen that if someone else rejects this peace, he is not peaceable with such a man,[64] because the former perhaps does not want to be admonished by latter or is envious of his possessions. Nevertheless, inasmuch as it depends upon the just person, he is not at odds with those who behave well.[65] The person who has transgressed the will of the law and pursues his own justice is not peaceable,[66] as David says: *With those who hated peace I was peaceable* (Ps 119:7 LXX = Ps 120:7 ET). (1a)[67] But this occurred out of necessity, on account of the powerful

---

61. Among the biblical witnesses the preferred reading is "taking into consideration what is excellent in the sight of all people" (προνοούμενοι καλὰ ἐνώπιον πάντων ἀνθρώπων). The addition of "not only before God, but also" (*non solum coram deo, set etiam*) in Ambrosiaster's biblical text is a secondary addition. See Bruce M. Metzger, *A Textual Commentary on the Greek New Testament*, 2nd ed. (Stuttgart: Deutsche Bibelgesellschaft, 1994), 466; and Jewett, *Romans*, 756.

62. *Recensio* α does not have section 2a.

63. *Recensio* α has "He wants all who uphold divine justice to be at peace." *Recensio* β alters *servant* to *servat*, which results in an ungrammatical construction.

64. I.e., it can happen that another person is not peaceable with the person who upholds divine justice; *tali viro* refers back to *qui divinam servat iustitiam*. *Recensiones* α and β have "be an enemy of" instead of "not be peaceable with."

65. I.e., the person who upholds divine justice is not at odds with those who behave well.

66. Ambrosiaster uses *ius* rather than *iustitia* to refer to what someone deems to be his own justice or right.

67. *Recensio* α does not have section 1a.

status of certain people, such that, for instance, one wins over through humble service a person whom pride puffs up to the point that he rejects the commandments of the law. It also can happen that out of fear of God[68] one renders oneself peaceable with someone who hates peace. For when one does not wish to repay the evil deeds of another, one is peaceable. (2) This is what it means to overcome evil with good, such that, for example, one wins over through service a person whom the commandments of the law do not win over. Therefore, *if it is possible*, the apostle says, *as far as it depends upon you*, we should be seen to love peace by behaving well. Even if someone is not a lover of peace, you still seek to be peaceable to the extent that it pertains to you. But if someone is irreverent and blasphemous, and you cannot be at peace with him, it certainly will not be attributed to you, because the apostle John does not permit a person who denies that Christ has come in the flesh to be saved (see 2 John 7). We should be ready, therefore, to be at peace with everyone, if possible. But when others are antagonistic, it will not be possible, though not on account of us, if the dispute about us is nonetheless not set aside.[69] (2a)[70] Someone who offends nobody appears to be peaceable.

12:19 *Not defending yourselves, beloved, but giving place to anger.* (1) In order that they may be able to preserve the bonds of peace, the apostle warns them to refrain from anger,[71] especially because one often sins through anger, as, for example, when someone has been roused by fury and demands more than is necessary on account of an offense,[72] or is detrimental to himself if he wants to avenge a fairly serious sin with an inappropriate punishment. Such a person damages the very one he could have kept faultless and pure.[73] For this reason Solomon, too, says: *Do not be excessively righteous; for*, he says, *a person can perish in their righteousness* (Eccl 7:16). (2) By seeking to address every single sin, one can by way of the punishment arrive at death, as much for oneself as for the person one assails with blows; people often transgress in meting out punishment. The

---

68. *Recensio* β does not have "of God."
69. I.e., if the other party continues to pursue the dispute.
70. *Recensio* α does not have section 2a.
71. *Recensio* α does not have "In order that they may be able to preserve the bonds of peace, the apostle warns them to refrain from anger, especially etc."
72. In *recensio* γ the remainder of section 1, as well as sections 2 and 3, is attested only in MS Paris lat. 1759.
73. I.e., the person with just cause damages himself by giving way to anger.

apostle prohibits proper punishment not only for one's inferiors, but also for one's equals and superiors. In other words, we should not seek to be avenged against a brother who perhaps sins against us, but we should forgive, deferring to God's judgment, lest when we are consumed with anger the adversary should find occasion to propose and recommend something that is bad for us.

For it is written. (3) In order to be even more persuasive, the apostle supports this with a quotation from the law, citing what is written in Proverbs:[74]

"Vengeance is mine, and I will repay," says the Lord (Deut 32:35). (4) The apostle indicates that we show contempt for God if we disregard what he teaches. (4a)[75] Therefore, if vengeance is entrusted to God, it is advantageous in two ways, since one becomes perfect when one conquers wrath and one will be avenged by God's judgment.

12:20 *"If your enemy is hungry, give him food;*[76] *if he is thirsty, give him drink. For by doing this you will heap coals on his head"* (Prov 25:21–22). (1) The apostle indicates not only that vengeance should be left to God, but also that kindness should be shown to enemies. In this way we demonstrate convincingly that it is not our fault that we have enemies. We try to win them over by our attentions so that they cease from wrong.[77] If they persist in hostilities on account of the wickedness of their mind,[78] our attentions contribute to their punishment;[79] alternatively, no doubt chagrined by the assiduousness of our attentions, they come to life like dead coals.[80] (2) Therefore, to make us so perfect that we gain not only ourselves but also others for life, the Lord through Solomon not only forbids us from

---

74. The quotation that follows is not from Proverbs but from Deuteronomy. Ambrosiaster may be referring here to 12:20, which is from Proverbs.

75. *Recensio* α does not have section 4a.

76. There is strong support among the biblical witnesses for the reading "but if" (ἀλλὰ ἐάν) instead of the softer "if" (*si*) found in Ambrosiaster's biblical text. See Jewett, *Romans*, 756.

77. *Recensiones* α and β have "from hostilities" instead of "from wrong."

78. *Recensio* α does not have "on account of the wickedness of their mind."

79. In *recensio* γ the remainder of section 1 is attested only by MSS Paris lat. 1759 and Troyes 128.

80. Ambrosiaster does not often resort to figurative interpretation. That he does so here suggests that he is disinclined to accept the literal meaning of the verse from Proverbs, which he has just explained in the first part of this sentence, since it undermines the idea that one should show kindness in the hope of saving one's enemy, not in the hope of adding to his punishment.

repaying enemies in turn but even requires us to incite them to friendship through kindness.[81]

12:21 *Do not be overcome by evil, but overcome evil with good.* This is the interpretation of the apostle as he exhorts us not to repay enemies in turn,[82] as was said.[83] It will benefit us a lot if we give way in the face of ill will.[84] One who appears temporarily to be conquered by evil in fact conquers evil; indeed, even the Savior conquered evil in this way, when he did not resist. For ill will works against itself and thinks that it conquers when it is conquered. An enemy works to distract us from our purpose, seeking an opportunity for us to sin. Therefore, if when we are provoked by him, we do not repay him in turn, we overcome him with good. The reason we do not resist is to preserve what is good by overlooking the justice that should be avenged,[85] because justice insists on being avenged.[86]

---

81. *Recensio* α has only "the Lord through Solomon forbids us from repaying enemies."

82. I.e., 12:21 is the apostle's interpretation of the quotation from Proverbs in 12:20 and is in line with the apostle's advice about showing kindness to one's enemies.

83. *Recensio* α does not have "as was said."

84. *Recensio* α does not have "a lot."

85. *Recensiones* α and β do not have "that should be avenged."

86. In *recensio* γ the last clause is attested only by MS Paris lat. 1759.

Romans 13

13:1 *Be subject to all the higher authorities,*[1] *for there is no authority except from God.* (1a)[2] Since the apostle directed them to follow the law of heavenly justice,[3] he commends the law of current justice so as not to appear to disregard it, especially since the former cannot be kept if the latter is not observed.[4] The current law is a sort of pedagogue who instructs children so that they may be able to enter upon the path of greater justice.[5] In fact, mercy cannot be accorded someone who does not possess justice.[6] (1) Thus, to affirm the rule and fear of natural law,[7] the apostle states that God is its author and that those who administer it derive their appoint-

---

1. Although Ambrosiaster's biblical text has "Be subject to all the higher authorities" (*omnibus potestatibus sublimioribus subditi estote*), among the biblical witnesses there is strong support for "Let every soul be subject to the higher authorities" (πᾶσα ψυχὴ ἐξουσίαις ὑπερεχούσαις ὑποτασσέσθω). See Bruce M. Metzger, *A Textual Commentary on the Greek New Testament*, 2nd ed. (Stuttgart: Deutsche Bibelgesellschaft, 1994), 467; and Robert Jewett with Roy D. Kotansky, *Romans: A Commentary*, Hermeneia (Minneapolis: Fortress, 2007), 780. The Latin word rendered "authority" or "authorities" in the text and the comments in Rom 13 is *postestas*.

2. *Recensio* α does not have section 1a.

3. See In Rom. 13:10 (§§2–2a).

4. Here, as in Rom 12, I have rendered *iustitia* as "justice"; see n. 8 at In Rom. 12:1–2 (§1b).

5. In the Greco-Roman world the *paedagogus* was a slave who, in upper-class families, took the child to and from school, minded him at home, and made him learn his lessons. He could be responsible for some elementary instruction, as well as training in good behavior, using discipline if necessary. See Stanley F. Bonner, *Education in Ancient Rome from the Younger Cato to the Elder Pliny* (Berkeley: University of California Press, 1977), 38–39, 42. On Ambrosiaster's use of the image here and at In Rom. 13:4 (§2), see Sophie Lunn-Rockliffe, *Ambrosiaster's Political Theology*, OECS (Oxford: Oxford University Press, 2007), 142–43.

6. See In Rom. 3:21 (§2).

7. *Recensio* α has "to affirm the fear of natural law."

ment from God.[8] The apostle has then added, *and those that exist have been appointed by God*, (2) so that no one should suppose that authorities can be defied as human contrivances; he discerns, in fact, that divine rule has been delegated to human authorities.[9] Thus, a person subject to an authority[10] is one who out of dread for God refrains from things the authority prohibits.[11]

13:2 *Therefore, one who resists the authority resists what God has appointed.* (1) This contradicts those who perhaps because of political power or some other reason do not believe they can be caught, and therefore think that they can laugh off the law. The apostle shows them that the law is from God and that those who escape judgment at the time through some kind of deal will not escape the judgment of God.

And those who resist bring condemnation upon themselves. (2) It is obvious that everyone will be justified or condemned by his works. Those who hear the law and sin are without excuse.

13:3 *For those who rule are not a terror to good conduct, but to bad.* (1) The apostle calls *rulers* those kings who are put in place to correct people's way of life and prohibit wrongs; they bear the image of God so that the rest of the people should be subject to one person.[12]

Do you wish to have no fear of the authority? Do what is good, and you will win praise from him. (2) Praise issues from the authority when one is found to be blameless.

13:4 *For he is God's servant for your good.* [13] (1a) It is obvious that rulers have been established to prevent people from doing wrong.

---

8. *Recensio* α adds "so that no one should suppose that authorities can be defied as human contrivances." It does not have the sentence that follows, "The apostle … human authorities."

9. See n. 8 above.

10. *Recensio* α does not have "to an authority."

11. For the idea that the authority of the ruler is an extension and expression of the authority of God, see Ambrosiaster, *Quaest.* 110.6 (CSEL 50:272), and Lunn-Rockliffe, *Ambrosiaster's Political Theology*, 140.

12. For the idea that the ruler bears the image of God, see Ambrosiaster, *Quaest.* 35 and 106.17 (CSEL 50:63, 243), and Lunn-Rockliffe, *Ambrosiaster's Political Theology*, 127, 130–34, and 178. For earlier literature, see Alessandra Pollastri, *Ambrosiaster, commento alla Lettera ai Romani: Aspetti cristologici*, CTSt (L'Aquila: Japadre, 1976), 277 n. 2.

13. *Recensio* α does not have the lemma and the comment in section 1a.

But if you do wrong, be afraid, for not without reason does he bear the sword. (1) That is: The apostle warns that if the authority is defied, it will punish.

For he is God's servant, an avenger of wrath upon the person who does wrong. (2) Because God has ordained that there will be a future judgment and does not want anyone to perish, he has appointed rulers for this age to act as pedagogues for the people by instilling fear, teaching them what to observe so that they may not incur the penalty of future judgment.[14]

13:5 *Therefore, be subject not only out of regard for anger, but also out of regard for conscience.* The apostle rightly states that they should be subject *not only out of regard for anger*,[15] that is, present retribution—for anger gives rise to vengeance—, but also out of regard for future judgment, because if they escape here, punishment awaits them there,[16] where, accused by their own conscience (see Rom 2:15–16), they will be punished.

13:6 *Indeed, for this reason you also pay tribute, for the authorities are servants of God, attending to this very thing.* The apostle says that tribute,[17] or what are called *fiscalia*,[18] are to be handed over for this reason: to demonstrate submission. By this people may know that they are not free, but live under an authority which is from God. To their ruler, who acts in the place of God,[19] as the prophet Daniel says: *For the kingdom belongs to God,*

---

14. On Ambrosiaster's belief that fear of the ruler, an extension of the fear of God (see In Rom. 13:1 [§2]), serves to check sin, see Lunn-Rockliffe, *Ambrosiaster's Political Theology*, 138–42.

15. *Recensio* α does not have "that they should be subject."

16. *Recensio* α does not have "because if they escape here, punishment awaits them there."

17. The word *tributa* refers to tribute levied on the provinces of the Roman Empire as an expression of their subjugation to Rome. It was the major tax of the Roman Empire, among a myriad of taxes levied on goods and services. For an overview, see Brent Shaw, "Roman Taxation," in *Civilization of the Ancient Mediterranean: Greece and Rome*, ed. Michael Grant and Rachel Kitzinger (New York: Scribner's Sons, 1988), 809–27.

18. The Latin term *fiscalia* refers to funds exacted by and owed to Roman authorities; see, e.g., Rufinus's translation of the Rule of Saint Basil, *Basil. reg.* 196 (CSEL 86:214–15). Lunn-Rockliffe, *Ambrosiaster's Political Theology*, 137, paraphrases the term with "exactions for the treasury."

19. *Recensiones* α and β have "To their ruler, who acts in the place of God, they are subject as if to God." On the idea that the ruler acts in the place of God on earth, see Ambrosiaster, *Quaest.* 91.8 (CSEL 50:157), and Lunn-Rockliffe, *Ambrosiaster's Political Theology*, 136–38.

and he will give it to whom he wishes (Dan 4:14)—which is why the Lord also says: *Render to Caesar the things that are Caesar's* (Matt 22:21)[20]—to him they should therefore be subject as if to God. The proof of their submission is that they pay him tribute.

13:7 *Therefore, render all of them their dues.* (1) The apostle wants dues to be rendered to one another,[21] because even the powerful are debtors to lesser people in repayment for what they accomplish.

Tribute to whom tribute is due, revenue to whom revenue is due. (2) The apostle commands that what is owed to the imperial authority be discharged first, since the purpose or obligation of these payments is more important.[22]

Fear to whom fear is due. (3) The apostle says that one should show fear for the authority because fear prevents sin. Likewise for a parent or an earthly master, so that the parent or master may give thanks for his son or his Christian slave.

Honor to whom honor is due. (4) Honor can be shown here even to those who are considered grand in the world, so that when they see the humility of Christ's slaves they may praise rather than disparage the teaching of the gospel.

13:8 *Owe no one anything, except to love one another.* (1) The apostle wants us to be at peace,[23] if possible, with everyone, but truly to love the brothers. (1a)[24] This is what it will mean to owe no one anything: to show each person the regard that befits his position. (2) But all the while, honor is preserved. The apostle speaks of debtors[25] because it is proper and due to show deference to a person who is worthy of honor, whether present or future. One shows deference to the person from whom one receives an honor; therefore, one is called a *debtor*. If you do not do this to your ruler, you are arrogant. A person should be honored either for their achievement or for their age.

---

20. *Recensio* α does not have this sentence.
21. *Recensio* α has "by all" and *recensio* β has "by people" instead of "to one another."
22. *Recensio* α does not have "purpose or."
23. *Recensio* α has "The apostle desires peace etc."
24. *Recensiones* α and β do not have section 1a.
25. Ambrosiaster's word *debitores*, translated as "debtors," echoes the lemma, which has *debeatis*, translated as "owe." The echoes continue in the remainder of the comment but are not easily conveyed in English.

For one who loves a neighbor has fulfilled the law. (3) One who loves a neighbor fulfills the law of Moses. The commandment of the new law, in fact, is to love even enemies.

13:9 *Now "you shall not commit adultery, you shall not kill, you shall not steal, you shall not covet"* (Exod 20:13–17). (1) Moses received this in writing from God in order to reestablish natural law.

And any other commandment is summed up in this sentence: "You shall love your neighbor as yourself" (Lev 19:18; see Matt 22:39). (2) This is written in Leviticus. While the commandments mentioned above are still valid, the apostle indicates that the law is also fulfilled by love, as I have said.[26] Even if there are other laws which he has not mentioned at this time,[27] love nevertheless satisfies all the commandments.[28] Indeed, if the human race had loved itself from the beginning, there would be no iniquity on earth. For the origin of injustice is discord. Therefore, from the point of view of iniquity, love is iniquity, because what is good to a good person is evil to an evil person.

13:10 *Love does no wrong to a neighbor; love, in fact, is the fulfillment of the law.* (1)[29] Love does no wrong because it is good, and it is impossible to sin by means of that which is the completion of the law. The apostle wants to arrive at the gospel's meaning through the words of the law. Therefore, he calls to mind the summary of the law in order to connect the gospel with it, demonstrating that their meaning derives from a single author. But because something had to be added in the time of Christ, Christ commanded that not only neighbors but also enemies be loved (see Matt 5:44). This is why the apostle adds:[30] *love is the fulfillment of the law*, meaning that

---

26. *Recensio* α does not have "as I have said."
27. *Recensio* α does not have "which he has not mentioned at this time."
28. For the remainder of section 2 *recensio* α has "For someone who loves his neighbor—that is, his brother—cannot not love God. Such a person is not proud, because love tempers him."
29. For section 1 *recensio* α has "He says that love does what is good and therefore is the fulfillment of the law, because by not doing evil through love one fulfills the law. Now, someone who loves his enemies fulfills the law in such a way that it is not only full but even overflowing. For to overflow is more than to fulfill. The fullness of the law consists in the commandments of the gospel, which, as we know, are heavenly, so as to make people resemble God the Father."
30. *Recensio* β and most manuscripts of *recensio* γ have "This is why *love* etc."; "the apostle adds" (*subditur*) is attested only by MSS Paris lat. 1759 and, in a second hand, St. Gall 101.

righteousness consists in loving a neighbor, but overflowing and perfect righteousness consists in loving even enemies. (2)[31] Moreover, what else does it mean to love an enemy than to desire that he stop hating and not to seek any harsh recourse against him? To love him is this: to desire for him the behavior whereby he may find God to be merciful. (2a)[32] This is heavenly justice.[33] It makes us resemble God the Father, who bestows the gifts of the seasons also on those who do not worship him (see Matt 5:45). Indeed, the Lord too, when he was on the cross, prayed for his enemies (see Luke 23:34), in order to demonstrate the fullness of righteousness that he had taught.

13:11 *As well, we know that it is time, that now is the hour for us to arise from sleep*.[34] (1) The apostles says that it is time for us to advance toward our reward. This is what it means *to arise from sleep*: to do what is good as if in daylight, that is openly, for unlawful things are done at night, that is secretly. Since we have already been brought into the clear light—that is, into the knowledge of God—and since we know what we ought to do, we should act accordingly, so that by living purely we may arrive at the promised reward, having shaken off sleep, that is, ignorance or carelessness.[35]

For our salvation is nearer now than when we believed. (2) It is obvious that they are not far from the reward of the promised resurrection, because after the washing of baptism they lived in the right way and made every effort to love.[36] The good life of a Christian is a sign of the salvation to come. (2a)[37] Therefore, when anyone is baptized, it pertains to forgiveness, not to the crown; afterward, when one walks in newness of life (see Rom 6:4), one already is close to eternal life.

13:12 *The night has gone by, and the day has drawn near*. (1)[38] By *night* the apostle meant the old self who has been renewed through bap-

---

31. In *recensio* γ section 2 is attested only by MS Paris lat. 1759.
32. *Recensio* α does not have section 2a.
33. See In Rom. 13:1 (§1a).
34. Among the biblical witnesses, although "for you" (ὑμᾶς) is the reading preferred by many scholars and adopted by NA[28], "for us" (ἡμᾶς; *nos* in Ambrosiaster's biblical text) has strong manuscript support and is rhetorically apt. See Metzger, *Textual Commentary*, 467; and Jewett, *Romans*, 816.
35. *Recensio* α does not have "or carelessness."
36. *Recensio* α does not have "and made every effort to love."
37. *Recensio* α does not have section 2a.
38. Instead of section 1, *recensio* α has "By *night* he means every age of the world, because the world is already in its sunset, and the kingdom of God—that is, the day

tism. He says that this old self has gone by like the night, and that the day has drawn near, that is, the sun of righteousness (see Mal 4:2),[39] by whose light the truth has been revealed to us so that we know what we ought to do. Before, when we did not know Christ, we were in darkness. But when we were instructed, the light dawned on us; we passed over from the false to the true.

Let us therefore cast off the works of darkness and put on the armor of light.[40] (2) *Darkness* refers to fleshly vices that are stirred up by worldly delights.[41] (2a)[42] These things are worthy of darkness, as the Lord says: *Take him and bind him hand and foot and cast him into the outer darkness* (Matt 22:13). (3) But *to put on the armor of light* means to do good things, because just as wicked actions are equated with darkness since those who behave wickedly do so secretly,[43] so too those who behave rightly do so openly, because they are not afraid but are glad.[44] Therefore, good actions are the armor of light; they attack darkness, which consists of the vices of the flesh.

13:13 *Let us conduct ourselves becomingly as in the day.* (1) It is true that,[45] since one does not sin publicly, we should behave as one does publicly. Nothing, in fact, is as public as the truth.[46]

Not in revels and drunkenness. (2) *Revels* are extravagant banquets which are thrown with a contribution from all the participants or are put on by each of the comrades in turn.[47] Consequently, no one there is ashamed

---

of judgment—is near. In comparison to this day of the Lord, when he will lighten the world by his coming, the present day is night."

39. *Recensio* β does not have "that is, the sun of righteousness."

40. Among the biblical witnesses there is strong support for "let us put off" (ἀποθώμεθα), but some biblical scholars prefer the reading found in Ambrosiaster's biblical text, "let us cast off" (*abiciamus*). As well, "but" (δέ) is preferred to "and" (*et*). See Metzger, *Textual Commentary*, 467; and Jewett, *Romans*, 816.

41. *Recensiones* α and β have "The *works of darkness* is a fleshly life, which is [β: are] stirred up by worldly delights." For Ambrosiaster's notion of "fleshly vices," see In Rom. 7:5 (§§1–2) and 8:13 (§1).

42. *Recensio* α does not have section 2a.

43. *Recensiones* α and β have "since they occur secretly" instead of "since those who act wickedly do so secretly."

44. In *recensio* γ "but are glad" is attested only by MS Paris lat. 1759.

45. *Recensio* α does not have "It is true that."

46. *Recensio* α does not have this sentence.

47. *Recensio* α does not have "or are put on by each of the comrades in turn."

to say or do anything indecent, since everyone assumes that it is his own banquet; at someone else's table they usually are restrained by a sense of propriety.[48] (2a)[49] But in this instance[50] one gathers for the purpose of behaving disgustingly, thanks to an abundance of wine, and of arousing various sensual pleasures. (3) The apostle therefore has commanded that such banquets be avoided.

Not in sex and shamelessness. (4) The apostle has added what ensues after a pleasure-filled banquet and drunkenness, namely, shameless sex. It is in fact the fruit of this excess.

Not in quarreling and jealousy. (5) The apostle quite rightly warns them to refrain from these, because all quarreling and jealousy give rise to enmity. He calls these things *darkness* because they cannot attain the reward of the light.[51]

13:14 *But put on the Lord Jesus Christ, and do not pay attention to the flesh, to its desires.* (1) The apostle forbids *paying attention to the flesh*—that is, pleasure—so that everything that is forbidden by the law is not desired, or if it is desired, the desire at least is overcome. The things mentioned above are in fact the works of the flesh. Consequently, having stripped them off, people should *put on the Lord Jesus Christ*;[52] in other words, having been renewed by Christ, they should keep themselves from these evils.[53] (1a)[54] Now, one who disassociates himself from all error and baseness for fear that he may be cast off and thrown into darkness because he was found in disgrace without a new garment at the wedding banquet (see Matt 22:13), has put on Christ. (2)[55] If they have not done so, they have not put on Jesus Christ, but have put on old clothes over his new garment. After having stripped off the old self, one must remain in newness of life.

---

48. *Recensio* α adds "so that they are not immoderate."
49. *Recensio* α does not have section 2a.
50. In *recensio* γ "everyone assumes … in this instance" is attested only by MS Paris lat. 1759.
51. *Recensio* α has "He calls all these *darkness* because they cannot arrive at the presence of the light."
52. *Recensio* α has "Consequently, having *put on the Lord Jesus Christ*, etc."
53. *Recensio* α has "from these things" instead of "from these evils."
54. *Recensio* α does not have section 1a.
55. In *recensio* γ section 2 is attested only by MS Paris lat. 1759.

Romans 14

14:1 *Welcome one who is weak in faith, but not for disputes over opinions.* (1a) Because the people who had welcomed Romans to faith in Christ with the law mixed in[1] were from a Jewish background (as I have discussed at the beginning of the letter),[2] some Roman Christians thought that they should not eat meat which had been prohibited.[3] But others who followed Christ without observing the law thought, on the contrary, that it was permissible to eat.[4] As a result there were disputes between them, which the apostle, in pursuit of concord and well-being, averts by means of an inspired discussion, showing that in the sight of God there is no advantage for one who eats and no disadvantage for one who does not eat. The apostle says that someone who is afraid to eat foods because they are forbidden for the Jews is *weak*. He prefers to leave such a person to his own judgment so as to avoid a situation in which that person, having been affronted, may withdraw from love (which is, so to speak, the mother of souls) in a state of mental distress.[5] For Christians ought to be peaceful and calm.[6]

14:2 *One person believes he may eat everything.* (1) This person, confident in his reading of scripture, does not doubt that everything that has been given for the use of humankind should be eaten. He reads in Genesis

---

1. *Recensio* α has "who had welcomed Romans to the name of Christ in a mixture." *Recensio* β has "who had welcomed Romans to the name of Christ, with the law mixed in."

2. See In Rom. synopsis §2.

3. In *recensio* γ "which had been prohibited" is attested only by MSS St. Gall 101 in a second hand and Troyes 128.

4. *Recensio* β has "thought that, contrary to the law, it was permissible to eat." *Recensio* γ agrees with *recensio* α at this point, though the phrasing is different; in other respects *recensio* γ is the same as *recensio* β.

5. In *recensio* γ "in a state of mental distress" is attested only by MS Paris lat. 1759.

6. In *recensio* γ this sentence is attested only by MS Paris lat. 1759.

that everything that God created was very good (see Gen 1:31). Therefore, nothing should be rejected, since neither Enoch, who was the first to please God (see Gen 5:24), nor Noah, who during the flood was the only righteous person to be found (see Gen 6:8), nor Abraham, the friend of God (see Isa 41:8; Jas 2:23), or Isaac and Jacob, righteous men and friends of God, among whom Lot too was included,[7] or the rest of the righteous are read to have abstained from these things.[8]

But let the person who is weak eat vegetables.[9] (2) Given that he eats vegetables because he judges this to be appropriate,[10] he should not be urged to eat meat,[11] lest he should eat in an uneasy state of mind and believe himself to be sinning since he does not keep to his purpose.

14:3 *And so let not the one who eats despise the one who does not eat, and let not the one who does not eat judge the one who eats.* (1a) Since it is a matter of choice to eat or not to eat,[12] (1) there should be no dispute on this point. In fact, all things have been made to be subject to the will,[13] because they have been subjected to human dominion (see Gen 1:28–29).

For God has welcomed him. (2) He was welcomed by God when he was called to grace.

14:4 *Who are you to pass judgment on someone else's slave? Before his own master he stands or falls.* It is obvious that a slave should not be judged by the choice of a fellow slave to whom the law concerning this matter has not been conveyed. Indeed, as to the reason one eats or does not eat, God, whose slave one is, is the judge.

---

7. In *recensio* γ "or Isaac … was included" is attested only by MS Paris lat. 1759.

8. *Recensio* α has "since neither Enoch, who pleased God, nor Noah, nor Abraham or Isaac and Jacob, righteous men and friends of God, among whom Lot too was included, are read to have abstained."

9. Ambrosiaster's biblical text has the hortatory subjunctive "let him eat" (*manducet*), but among the biblical witnesses there is stronger support for the indicative "he eats" (ἐσθίει). See NA[28] and Robert Jewett with Roy D. Kotansky, *Romans: A Commentary*, Hermeneia (Minneapolis: Fortress, 2007), 829.

10. *Recensio* α does not have "Given that he eats vegetables because he judges this to be appropriate."

11. *Recensio* α does not have "meat."

12. *Recensio* α does not have section 1a.

13. For ease of understanding I have used "choice" and "will" to translate *voluntas* in this comment and at In Rom. 14:4 (§1).

And he will stand; for God is able to make him stand.[14] (2)[15] The apostles says, *before his own master he will stand*, because he is neither guilty if he eats nor blameworthy if he does not eat, so long as he does so out of devotion, not avoiding meat[16] as if it were pernicious.

14:5 *Indeed, one person distinguishes one day from another.* (1) That is: some think it is right to eat meat on certain days.[17] (1a)[18] Indeed, there are some who have held that one should not eat meat on the third day of the week; some, that one should not eat meat on the sabbath; some, yet again, who eat meat from Easter to Pentecost.[19]

But another distinguishes every day. (2) The person who never eats meat *distinguishes every day.*

Let everyone be convinced in his own mind. (3) That is: let everyone yield to his own resolve.

14:6 *One who observes a day, observes it for the Lord.* (1) This is true, since one who always abstains thinks that he is pleasing God.[20]

---

14. Ambrosiaster's biblical text has "God" (*deus*), but among the biblical witnesses there is stronger support for "Lord" (ὁ κύριος). See Bruce M. Metzger, *A Textual Commentary on the Greek New Testament*, 2nd ed. (Stuttgart: Deutsche Bibelgesellschaft, 1994); and Jewett, *Romans*, 829.

15. For section 2 *recensio* α has "One who neither will be guilty if he eats nor is blameworthy if he does not eat stands before his master." *Recensio* β is the same as *recensio* γ except that, like *recensio* α, it has "will be guilty."

16. I have supplied "meat" (*carnem*) as the implied antecedent of *hanc*. I interpret Ambrosiaster's remark as allowing for abstemiousness provided that one does not believe that meat is somehow bad. Ambrosiaster is explicit on this point at In Rom. 14:6 (§2).

17. I have supplied "meat" (*carnem*) in sections 1 and 2; it is present in the Latin in section 1a.

18. *Recensio* α does not have section 1a.

19. Ambrosiaster's comment alludes to variability in the practice of fasting in Rome in his day. Although among Christians fasting could comprise a range of dietary restrictions, at a minimum it entailed refraining from meat. Wednesday and Friday were traditionally fast days in the West, but in Rome Christians fasted on Saturday as well. The fast before Easter, which by the fourth century had extended to a period of forty days, typically ended on Easter morning; there was no fast from Easter to Pentecost. Ambrosiaster implies that the practice of fasting on Wednesday and Saturday was not universal. He also implies that some Christians refrained from meat after Easter. For an overview of the practice, see Rudolf Arbesmann, "Fastenspeisen" and "Fasttage," *RAC* 7:493–524.

20. *Recensio* α does not have "always."

And one who eats, eats for the Lord.[21] He eats for the Lord, since he gives thanks to the creator.[22]

And one who does not eat, does not eat for the Lord and gives thanks to God.[23] (2) He *gives thanks*[24] when he professes that the creation is from God and that created things are good,[25] but that he refrains from them and does not condemn them.

14:7 *None of us lives for himself and none of us dies for himself.* A person would be living *for himself* if he did not behave according to the law. But one who is governed by the constraint of the law certainly does not live for himself, but for God, who has given the law so that one might live according to his will. Likewise, one who dies, dies for God; he will be either crowned or condemned by him as judge.

14:8 *If we live, we live for the Lord; if we die, we die for the Lord.* The meaning is the same.

Therefore, whether we live or whether we die, we are the Lord's. (2) It is true that we all are the Lord's, like slaves in servitude and under the authority of the redeemer, and that each person will be treated according to his merit.

---

21. Ambrosiaster's biblical text lacks the concluding clause of this sentence of the verse, "for he gives thanks to God" (εὐχαριστεῖ γὰρ τῷ θεῷ), which parallels the concluding clause in the next sentence of the verse; see NA[28]. However, the comment that follows, found only in *recensiones* β and γ (see n. 22), echoes the missing clause. In other witnesses to the VL the clause is present; see, e.g., Jerome, *Jov.* 2.16 (PL 23:310C): *gratias enim agit deo*.

22. *Recensio* α does not have this comment.

23. *Recensio* α does not have *and one who does not eat, does not eat for the Lord.* The absence of this portion of the lemma, along with the prior comment (see n. 22), appears to be the result of a scribal error at some point in the manuscript transmission of *recensio* α.

24. *Recensio* α adds "*to God*" (*deo*).

25. In calling attention to the goodness of creation, Ambrosiaster may be countering obliquely the negative view that Manichaeans had of the material world and food. The Manichaean Elect, whose responsibility in eating was to release light from matter, fasted regularly, ate only grains, vegetables, and fruits that were thought to contain more light, and abstained from meat altogether. See Samuel N. C. Lieu, *Manichaeism in the Later Roman Empire and Medieval China: A Historical Survey* (Manchester: Manchester University Press, 1985), 19–21; J. Kevin Coyle, "Mani, Manichaeism," in *Augustine through the Ages*, ed. Allan D. Fitzgerald (Grand Rapids: Eerdmans, 1999), 523. See also In Rom. 14:16 and 14:20 (§§1, 4).

14:9 *For to this end Christ lived and died and was raised,*[26] *so that he might be lord of both the living and the dead.* (1) The creation was made by Christ the Lord, but when it was estranged from its author through sin, it was taken captive. So that he would not lose his handiwork, God the Father showed the creation what to do to escape the grasp of the pirates by sending his Son from heaven to earth. For this reason the Son allowed himself even to be killed by enemies, so that when he descended to the underworld he might render sin culpable, since he had been killed even though he was innocent. He did this to release those who were held in the underworld.[27] (2) Therefore, because he showed the way of salvation to the living and gave himself up for them, and also freed the dead from the underworld, he is *lord of the living* as well as *the dead*. He has recreated them again from people who were lost into slaves for himself.

14:10 *So why do you pass judgment on your brother for not eating?*[28] *Or why do you despise your brother for eating? For we all will stand before the judgment seat of Christ.*[29] The apostle teaches that there is no need to pass judgment on this point,[30] since it is not discussed in the law, especially while we await God the judge.

14:11 *For it is written, "As I live, says the Lord, every knee shall bow and every tongue confess God"* (Isa 45:23). This is written in Isaiah, that every tongue will confess God in the faith of Christ. Now, since he was killed, has risen, and will be judge, he rightly says, *As I live, says the Lord*. Not only *I live*, but also I will come to judge, and the enemies will

---

26. Ambrosiaster's biblical text has "lived and died and was raised" (*et vixit et mortuus est et resurrexit*), but among the biblical witnesses there is stronger support for "died and lived" (ἀπέθανεν καὶ ἔζησεν). See Metzger, *Textual Commentary*, 468; and Jewett, *Romans*, 830.

27. On Christ's death and descent to the underworld, see the introduction §5.4.

28. The phrase "for not eating" (*in non edendo*) in Ambrosiaster's biblical text is also attested by several early Latin manuscripts of Paul's letters; see John Wordsworth and Henry J. White, eds., *Novum Testamentum domini nostri Iesu Christi latine* (Oxford: Clarendon, 1889–1954), 2:136, v. 10 apparatus: *in non manducando*. On these manuscripts, see Hugo S. Eymann, ed., *Epistula ad Romanos*, VLB 21 (Freiburg: Herder, 1996), 19–21. The phrase is not found in the Greek text (NA²⁸).

29. Ambrosiaster's biblical text has "Christ" (*Christi*), but among the biblical witnesses there is stronger support for "God" (τοῦ θεοῦ). See Metzger, *Textual Commentary*, 468–69; and Jewett, *Romans*, 830–31.

30. *Recensio* α does not have "on this point."

acknowledge me and will bend the knee, acknowledging me to be *God from God*.³¹

14:12 *So each of us shall give account for himself to God*.³² Because, the apostle says, we are not going to give account for one another, we should not be condemning one another on the point that was discussed above.

14:13 *Therefore, let us no longer pass judgment on one another*. (1) That is: knowing this, we should stop arguing.

But decide instead not to put an obstacle or a cause for stumbling in a brother's way. (2) The apostle advises them to consider what is best in this matter, and also what can be defended on the authority of the law, and to cause none of the brothers to stumble either by eating meat or by not eating it.

14:14 *I know and am convinced in the Lord that nothing is unclean in itself*.³³ (1) It is obvious that everything is pure, thanks to the Savior. By freeing people from the yoke of the law and by justifying them, he has restored the original state of freedom, such that people have the right to make use of the entire creation, as did the saints of old. But those who are still under the law are not permitted to make use of³⁴ things the law disallows because they reject the forgiveness that was granted. (1a)³⁵ Things are impure not because of their nature but when they are eaten contrary to a prohibition.³⁶ Certainly it says so in the law: *They are impure to you* (Lev 11:4).

But obviously, for someone who thinks that it is unclean, it is unclean. (2) Whether he is a Christian of Jewish origin or a gentile believer, the person who thinks that something like this should be avoided is an example of what the apostle described above as *weak* (see Rom 14:1–2); by hesitating, he is, in effect, not confident. For him, what he thinks should not be eaten

---

31. In *recensio* γ this sentence is attested only by MS Paris lat. 1759. The concluding phrase echoes the second article of the Nicene Creed, which declares that the Son is *God from God*.

32. Ambrosiaster's biblical text has "to God" (*deo*), contrary to what Jewett says, but among biblical witnesses there is stronger support for its omission. See Metzger, *Textual Commentary*, 469; and Jewett, *Romans*, 831.

33. Ambrosiaster's biblical text has "the Lord" (*domino*), but the Greek text (NA²⁸) has "the Lord Jesus" (κυρίῳ Ἰησοῦ).

34. *Recensiones* α and β have "make use of or eat."

35. *Recensio* α does not have section 1a.

36. *Recensio* β has "precept" instead of "prohibition."

is impure, and because he does so not out of superstition but out of fear, he should be left to his own judgment.

14:15 *Now if your brother is distressed because of food, you are no longer walking in love.* (1) In another letter the apostle says: *Food is for the belly and the belly is for food; and God will destroy both the one and the other* (1 Cor 6:13). Since with regard to food one neither pleases nor displeases God, the apostle advises them that they should practice love, on account of which God thought it right to set us free. As the apostle says: *But God out of great love had mercy on us* (see Eph 2:4).[37] Therefore, one who is mindful of this kindness cultivates this love and does not value anything above it, but overlooks a great number of things that he knows do not lead to what is promised by God.

Do not let what you eat cause the ruin of one for whom Christ died. (2) The value of the salvation of a brother is measured by the death of Christ. So, one who knows what that value is ought to strengthen a brother, not create difficulties for him such that he who perhaps used to eat easily, secure in his own conscience, becomes apprehensive because of something trivial and begins to wonder whether or not he should eat meat. Moreover, once the dispute has begun, he will begin, distraught, to sin against God's creation and the result will be a wrong toward the creator, which will lead to the ruin of the doubter.[38]

14:16 *So do not let our good be slandered.*[39] That is: since the teaching of the Lord is good and saving, it should not be slandered through a trivial matter. It is slandered, however, when one harbors doubts about God's creation.[40] The phrase *our good to be slandered* can also be understood as follows: if someone who does good things is criticized on some minor point,[41]

---

37. Ambrosiaster's text of Eph 2:4 in *recensio* γ agrees with a quotation at In 1 Cor. 13:4–8 (§1) and the lemma at In Eph. 2:4; for the latter, see Heinrich J. Vogels, *Das Corpus Paulinum des Ambrosiaster*, BBB 13 (Bonn: Hanstein, 1957), 122, not CSEL 81.3:80. The biblical text in *recensiones* α and β, which both have *nimiam caritatem*, appears to be influenced by the Vulgate; see Hermann J. Frede, ed., *Epistula ad Ephesios*, VLB 24.1 (Freiburg: Herder, 1962–1964), 58.

38. In *recensio* γ the latter half of section 2 is attested only by MS Paris lat. 1759. The other manuscripts conclude: "not create difficulties for him such that he becomes apprehensive because of something trivial."

39. Ambrosiaster's biblical text has "our" (*nostrum*), but among the biblical witnesses there is stronger support for "your" (ὑμῶν). See Jewett, *Romans*, 853.

40. See n. 25 above.

41. *Recensio* α does not have "on some minor point."

it obscures what is good about him[42] and the good attributed to him will begin to be the object of slander because of the evil attributed to him, as is written in Ezekiel: *Righteousness will not benefit the just if he makes a mistake* (Ezek 33:12). An example of this is when a handsome person happens to have some flaw in his features whereby his appearance is disfigured.[43] This is why the apostle advises that one should emphasize things that do not detract from other good characteristics.

14:17 *For the kingdom of God is not food and drink.* (1) It is obvious that no one pleases or displeases God by means of food.

But justice and peace and joy in the Holy Spirit. (2) The apostle says that those who pursue justice enter the kingdom of God. Moreover, they possess the Christian peace that the Lord gave when he said: *My peace I give you, my peace I leave you* (John 14:27). From it issues *joy in the Holy Spirit*. A dispute, however, is characterized not by joy, but anger. Therefore, the Holy Spirit does not look upon such situations with favor, because it rejoices only in those who are peaceful. Just as it is saddened by us, so too it rejoices in us.

14:18 *One who serves Christ in this pleases God and is approved by people.* Since Christ has redeemed us, the apostle says: *One who serves Christ in this*—that is, so as not to offend anyone—submits as is fitting to the redeemer and pleases God. Why? Because God sent Christ to redeem the human race,[44] as the Lord himself says: *One who does not honor the Son does not honor the Father who sent him* (John 5:23). Therefore, one who *pleases God is approved by people*. In what way? Because he has received a gift by which he may appear worthy before God.

14:19 *Let us therefore pursue what makes for peace and let us observe what makes for mutual edification.*[45] Because dispute leads to conflict, the

---

42. In *recensio* γ the remainder of the sentence and the quotation from Ezekiel are attested only by MS Paris lat. 1759.

43. *Recensio* α has "An example of this is when a handsome person happens to have a flaw in his face or a broken nose. Is not this a disfigurement of his appearance?" *Recensio* β has "An example of this is when a handsome person happens to have a flaw in his face or a broken nose, whereby his appearance is disfigured."

44. *Recensio* α has "Since it is Christ who has redeemed us, the apostle says: *One who serves Christ in this, pleases God.* One who serves him whom God sent certainly pleases God, as the Lord himself says etc." *Recensio* β has "Since Christ has redeemed us, the apostle says: *One who serves Christ in this*, as a redeemer, *pleases God.* Why? Because God sent Christ to redeem the human race, as the Lord himself says etc."

45. Ambrosiaster's biblical text has the hortatory subjunctive "let us pursue" (*sectemur*), but among the biblical witnesses there is stronger support for the indicative

apostle teaches us to relinquish the intention of eating or not eating, so that we may be able to be peaceable. He urges us instead to pursue the path of edification, so that in peace we talk about matters by which we edify each other, steering clear of matters that are unfruitful and especially matters that are conflictual. A debate can be beneficial—in fact, it stimulates the mind—provided that one eschews the desire to win. It is this desire that leads to strife.

14:20 *Do not destroy the work of God for the sake of food.* (1) Humankind is the work of God through creation and is again the work of God when it is restored through regeneration.[46] Food, too, is the work of God.[47] However, humankind was not made *for the sake of food*, but food was made for the sake of humankind. The difference between them, therefore, is great. For this reason, the apostle says, do not destroy the *work of God* which is exceptional for the sake of a thing which is so commonplace. (2) To seek the salvation of a brother is this: not to make a big deal about food and thereby distress the brother. One who through an argument incites a brother who had been freed from sin to sin once again in fact nullifies the gift of God, undoing in the brother the work of Christ which Christ undertook to free humankind from sin.

All things, indeed, are pure. (3) It is true and obvious that *all things are pure*, especially since in Genesis one reads that all the things that God made were very good (see Gen 1:31).

But it is wrong for the person who eats while stumbling. (4) Although, then, all things are good and pure by nature,[48] they nevertheless become impure for those who have reservations. It will become a cause of stumbling for one who eats although he has reservations, doing so without a clear conscience because he does something he thinks is harmful to himself. Therefore, no one should be challenged about what he observes on this point.

14:21 *It is good not to eat meat and not to drink wine.* (1) Since the discussion was about meat alone, the apostle has added drink as well, to

---

"we pursue" (διώκομεν). See Metzger, *Textual Commentary*, 468; and Jewett, *Romans*, 853–54. The second verb in Ambrosiaster's biblical text, "let us observe" (*custodiamus*), is not found in the majority of biblical witnesses. See Jewett, *Romans*, 854.

46. *Recensio* α has "Humankind is the work of God when it is restored through regeneration."

47. See n. 25 above.

48. *Recensio* α does not have "good and." On this particular addition, see n. 25 above.

reassure those who abstain from these things. Thus, in order that they not be distressed by those who use them—given that it is permissible both to eat meat and to drink wine—he has given them some room to breathe, so that they might rest easy in their choice and that dispute, which gives rise to conflict, might stop. For since he acknowledges that it is good both to eat meat and to drink wine, and since they, on the contrary, learn that it is good not to eat meat and not to drink wine, no one has cause for complaint. The creation has been given to be used by those who wish it, but not to be imposed as a necessity, whether one wishes it or not.[49]

Nor anything that causes your brother to fall or to stumble or to be weakened.[50] (2) The apostle repeats himself: it should not become an issue for a brother who has made up his mind that to eat is a sign of a weak spirit, lest he become upset and fall, not knowing what to believe.

14:22 *You have faith.*[51] *Keep it to yourself before God.* (1) That is: are you someone who eats with confidence because God's creation is good? There is no need for you to pass judgment on another, since it is more important that you be at peace with a brother. In fact, it is right in God's eyes.[52] With respect to food there is, to be sure, a use for flesh, but with respect to peace, a use for both flesh and soul.[53] Therefore, one should desist from this sort of dispute, so that each person may abide in the conviction of his own heart.[54]

Blessed is the one who does not judge himself for what he approves. (2) The apostle is of the view that anyone who does what he says he should not do should be condemned by his own judgment, and that the person who does only what he thinks is right for himself is *blessed*.

---

49. In *recensio* γ "whether one wishes it or not" is attested only by MS St. Gall 101 in a second hand.

50. The words "or to stumble or to be weakened" (*vel scandalizatur aut infirmatur*) in Ambrosiaster's biblical text are not included in the Greek text (NA[28]) on the strength of a number of important witnesses. See Metzger, *Textual Commentary*, 469; and Jewett, *Romans*, 854.

51. A number of important biblical witnesses include the relative pronoun ἥν, such that the verse reads: "Keep the faith which you have etc." (σὺ πίστιν ἥν ἔχεις ... ἔχε). See Metzger, *Textual Commentary*, 469–70; and Jewett, *Romans*, 854.

52. *Recensio* α does not have "in God's eyes."

53. Ambrosiaster plays on the double meaning of "flesh" (*caro*): "meat" and "body."

54. *Recensio* α does not have "so that each person may abide in the conviction of his own heart."

14:23 *But one who makes distinctions is condemned if he eats.* (1) It is true that someone who judges that something should not be eaten and who nevertheless eats it *is condemned*. Such a person renders himself guilty[55] when he does what he believes is not right for himself.[56]

Because it is not of faith. (2) Someone who says that something should not be eaten and nevertheless eats it certainly eats contrary to faith.[57]

And all that is not of faith is sin. (3) Anything other than what has been approved rightly is called *sin*. As I noted at the beginning of the letter,[58] the Romans had been introduced to the law, but with the arrival of those whose belief was more correct, questions were raised about whether or not meat should be eaten. The group which said that it should be eaten and that it was not wrong to do so, seemed better, because all things actually are quite pure.[59] The apostle therefore says that those who say that meat should not be eaten are weak (whether they come from the Jews or the gentiles), and that they should be left to the conviction of their own heart—for in God's sight not to eat does no harm and to eat brings no advantage—to avoid the possibility that they might transgress, having been pressured by some argument to eat, but with qualms. (3a)[60] Thus, in everything which relates to the conscience, if one does something other than what one knows ought to be done, the apostle says it is a sin.

---

55. *Recensiones* α and β have "condemns himself" instead of "renders himself guilty."
56. I have translated *inutile* (*recensiones* α and β) rather than *utile* (*recensio* γ). The latter makes no sense in the context; it is either a medieval scribal or a modern editorial error.
57. *Recensiones* α and β have "does not eat out of faith" instead of "eats contrary to faith."
58. See In Rom. synopsis §§2–3.
59. *Recensio* α has "good" instead of "pure."
60. *Recensiones* α and β do not have section 3a.

Romans 15

15:1 *We who are stronger ought to bear with the infirmities of the weak.* (1) The apostle rightly says *we ought*, because it behooves teachers to strengthen the weak and instruct beginners with mildness. Otherwise, when they have been challenged, they may become worse, as they seek to argue back so as not to appear to be people of no account.

And not please ourselves. (2) That is: we should not defend what benefits and pleases us,[1] but what benefits and pleases the brothers as well, because we should take care of one another.

15:2 *Let each one*[2] *please his neighbor for his good, to build him up.* At this point the apostle has set aside his own persona. He reminds them to practice love and please their neighbors with regard to what is right.[3] This is *to build up*. As he says elsewhere: *I please all people in everything* (1 Cor 10:33).[4]

15:3 *For Christ too did not please himself, but as it is written: "The accusations of those who denounced you fell upon me"* (Ps 68:10 LXX = Ps 69:9 ET). (1) In Ps 68 it says that the Savior did not please himself but God the Father,[5] because he says: *For I have not come down from heaven to do my will, but the will of him, the Father, who sent me* (John 6:38). Because he was killed as a sinner after he said these things to the Jews who were arguing against him (see John 6:41), the psalmist in the persona of the Savior directs the words to God the Father, saying: *The accusations of those who*

---

1. *Recensio* α has "not only defend" instead of "not defend."
2. Ambrosiaster's biblical text lacks the pronoun "of us" (ἡμῶν) found in the earlier and more reliable biblical witnesses. See Robert Jewett with Roy D. Kotansky, *Romans: A Commentary*, Hermeneia (Minneapolis: Fortress, 2007), 874.
3. Instead of this sentence and the next one, *recensio* α has "He reminds them to practice love and please their neighbors *to build* them *up*."
4. In *recensio* γ this sentence is attested only by MS Paris lat. 1759.
5. *Recensio* α does not have "In Ps 68."

denounced you fell upon me. (2) That is: "When I do your will, they say that I sin against you, denouncing you by not accepting the one you have sent." For when the Jews sinned against God by not accepting Christ whom he sent, they also killed him as someone who sinned against God.⁶ Thus, the sins of those who sinned against God fell upon Christ. (3) Although he was innocent, he was killed by sinners as a blasphemer, as is written in the gospel (see Matt 26:65).⁷

15:4 *For whatever was written, was written to strengthen us, so that through patience and the exhortation of the scriptures we may have hope.* It is obvious that whatever was written, was written for our instruction,⁸ so that as a result of its exhortation we may advance in hope, not doubting the promises if so far they are delayed.⁹

15:5 *And may the God of patience and encouragement grant you to be of one mind with one another in accordance with Christ Jesus,* **15:6** *so that together you may with one voice glorify the God and Father of our Lord Jesus Christ.* (1) Inasmuch as he was sent to save, the apostle with good intent follows up with the people, desiring that God grant them a single sense of understanding *in accordance with Christ Jesus,* so that they understand things according to the teaching of Christ. Then indeed will they be able to sustain love in keeping with the example of the Lord, who says: *Greater love has no one than this, that he lay down his life for his friends and brothers* (John 15:13), and thereby *with one voice*, with one confession, glorify God the Father in Christ.¹⁰ (2)¹¹ They will be able to do this, provided that they have exhorted one another according to the mind of Christ, so that they praise God without ceasing for all the things he has created through Christ and for seeing fit to raise up and restore them by the same way after

---

6. *Recensio* α does not have "in addition also." On the accusation that the Jews killed Jesus, see In Rom. 10:21 (§1) with n. 49.

7. Instead of this sentence, *recensio* α has, continuing on from the last sentence in section 2, "when they say that he must die because he sins against God."

8. *Recensio* α has "teaching" (*doctrinam*) instead of "instruction" (*disciplinam*).

9. *Recensio* α has "not doubting the promises that so far are delayed."

10. *Recensiones* α and β have "and thereby *with one voice* they praise [β has the infinitive: praise] God the Father of our Lord Jesus Christ." In *recensio* γ the sentence as translated is attested only by MS Paris lat. 1759. The other manuscripts have "Then indeed will they be able with one confession to glorify God the Father in Christ."

11. Instead of section 2, *recensio* α has "Those who understand things *in accordance with Christ* also praise God *with one voice*."

they had fallen by going astray, bestowing a double benefit, both mercy and knowledge.

15:7 *Therefore, welcome one another as also Christ has welcomed you into the honor of God*, just as we have been welcomed by Christ when he took on our weaknesses and bore our sorrows (see Isa 53:4; Matt 8:17), so that in keeping with this example we too might through patience strengthen one another with regard to our weaknesses in order that the name of the honor of God received by us may not be invalidated. For we are called children of God through the grace of Christ.

15:8 *For I declare that Christ became a minister to the circumcision for the sake of the truth of God, in order to confirm the promises of the fathers.* (1a)[12] The apostle speaks highly of the origin of the Jews. By *the circumcision* he means the children of Abraham, to whom Christ, when he was sent, administered the grace that had been promised to the fathers.[13] This is why Savior says: *I came among you not to be served but to serve* (Luke 22:27), so that the truth contained in the promise made to the fathers may be confirmed. (1) The circumcision of the flesh was given to Abraham as a figure of the circumcision of the heart which the prophets indicated would come later, saying: *Circumcise the hardness of your heart* (Jer 4:4). Of this promised circumcision, then, the minister—that is, the preacher—is Christ, and after him the apostles, sent to administer the circumcision of the heart to those who are circumcised in the flesh.[14] As he says: *As you sent me into this world, so too have I sent them into this world* (John 17:18). (2) Circumcision of the heart is when the error that has beset the heart like a festering wound is cut away so that, after the truth has been revealed, the heart may be able to acknowledge that God the creator is the Father of Christ Jesus,[15] through whom he has created all things. In this way God's truth could be fulfilled. For he had promised that he would grant mercy, and he had promised this to the fathers of the Jews. Indeed, he had said to Abraham: *In your descendants will all nations be blessed* (Gen 22:18), and to David he said: *From the fruit of your loins I will set someone on your*

---

12. *Recensio* α does not have section 1a.

13. In *recensio* γ "to the fathers" is attested only by MS Monte Cassino 150.

14. *Recensio* α has "The minister of the circumcision—that is, the preacher—is Christ, and after him the apostles."

15. *Recensiones* α and β have "The circumcision of the heart is, once the cloud of error has been lifted, to acknowledge God the creator as Father and Christ his Son, through etc."

throne (Ps 131:11 LXX = Ps 132:11 ET), and: *A star will arise out of Jacob* (Num 24:17).

15:9 *And that the gentiles honor God for his mercy.* (1) Since no promise was given to them, as they were unworthy,[16] they were welcomed into salvation by mercy alone, so that they might honor God through their confession. For unbelievers dishonor God.[17]

As it is written: "Therefore I will confess you among the gentiles and sing praises to your name" (Ps 17:50 LXX = Ps 18:49 ET). (2) He proves the point by a quotation from the prophet, for it is written in Ps 17[18] that the gentiles are to be admitted to the grace of God in order to receive salvation. This voice is the voice of Christ, which declared that it would come about that among the gentiles his preaching would bear fruit in the confession of the mystery of God.[19] Therefore, the Son gives thanks to God for this, in that the gentiles have obeyed.[20] This is why he says in the gospels: *I confess to you, Father, Lord of heaven and earth, that you have hidden these things from the wise and understanding, and have revealed them to children,*[21] *because it was well-pleasing to you* (Matt 11:25). This confession thus is of one God in the Trinity. It gives rise to joy, such that after confessing the truth one sings, rejoicing, of the mercy and gift of God.

15:10 *And again it says: "Rejoice, O gentiles, with his people"* (Deut 32:43). This is in the song of Deuteronomy.[22]

15:11 *And again it says:*[23] *"Praise the Lord, all gentiles, and glorify him, all peoples"* (Ps 116:1 LXX = Ps 117:1 ET). In Ps 116[24] God is shown to have decided long ago to make peace between Jews and gentiles by means of his mercy, so that the gentiles, having received grace, might be

---

16. *Recensio* α does not have "as they were unworthy."

17. *Recensio* α has "dishonor God"; in *recensiones* β and γ "God" is implied, not stated.

18. *Recensio* α has "for it is written, proclaimed long ago, in Ps 107." See n. 24 below for another instance of confusion over the number of the psalm.

19. *Recensio* α has "that among the gentiles his preaching would be confessed to God, giving him glory for the gift that had been received."

20. *Recensio* α does not have this sentence.

21. *Recensio* α adds *"yes, Father."*

22. *Recensio* α does not have this comment.

23. The biblical witnesses are divided on the presence or absence of "it says" (λέγει/ *dicit*). See NA[28] and Jewett, *Romans*, 886.

24. *Recensio* α does not have this clause. *Recensio* γ has "Ps 106," but *recensio* β has, correctly, "Ps 116."

associated with the Jews who, too, had been named the people of God long ago through his gift. Whereas the Jews were already exalted,[25] the lowly gentiles have been exalted by the mercy of God, so that together all may rejoice in the awareness of the truth. With the gentiles praising God,[26] *all peoples*—the twelve tribes—may glorify the one God, since he has increased the number of his people by adding the gentiles. Indeed, when the Jews criticized the apostle Peter about Cornelius, they were silenced by the explanation he gave them, glorified God, and said: *It would seem that to the gentiles also God has granted repentance leading to life* (Acts 11:18).[27]

15:12 And Isaiah says: *"The root of Jesse will come, even the one who rises to rule the gentiles; in him will the gentiles hope"* (Isa 11:10). (1) In order to give the gentiles greater assurance and unwavering hope, the apostle confirms with many quotations that it was God's decision that all peoples would be blessed in Christ. He does this so that the arrogance of unbelieving Jews would not distress and introduce doubts into the minds of believing gentiles[28]—suggesting, as it were, that in vain they hold out for themselves the hope that their faith comes from the God beloved of Abraham—so that they might grow in this joy and confidence. (2) Why, then, did Christ come from the root of Jesse and not from the root of Boaz, a righteous man, or the root of Obed? Because he is called the son of David on account of his reign (so that just as he was born of God to be king, so too he might have his beginning according to the flesh from David the king),

---

25. *Recensio* α does not have "already."
26. *Recensio* α does not have "God."
27. The patristic reception of the story of Cornelius in Acts 10:1–11:18 has been exhaustively studied by François Bovon, *De vocatione gentium: Histoire de l'interprétation d'Act. 10, 1–11, 18 dans les six premiers siècles*, BGBE 8 (Tübingen: Mohr Siebeck, 1967). The inclusion of the gentiles in the plan of salvation—Ambrosiaster's reason for mentioning the story here—is only one of many issues that led later interpreters to draw on the story. Luke refers to Peter's critics as "those of the circumcision" (Acts 11:2). Many patristic interpreters repeat this expression, taking it to refer to believers of Jewish origin who are not to be identified with the apostles mentioned at Acts 11:1 (an ambiguous point in Luke's narrative). Ambrosiaster, however, identifies Peter's critics simply as "the Jews," who, by his reading, join the gentiles in praising God for receiving all peoples. See Bovon, *De vocatione gentium*, 295–303.
28. In *recensio* γ "believing" is attested only by MSS Monte Cassino 150 and Paris lat. 1759.

the root of Jesse is the tree of David, which bore fruit through the branch that is the virgin Mary,[29] who bore Christ.[30]

15:13 *Now may the God of hope fill you with all joy and peace in believing, so that you may abound in hope and in the power of the Holy Spirit.* **15:14** *For I myself am sure of you, brothers,*[31] *that you yourselves also are full of goodness, filled with all knowledge, so that you are able to remind one another.* These verses have to do with exhortation. Through praise the apostle rouses them to both a better understanding and a better life, for someone who finds himself to be the object of praise takes pains with what he was doing[32] so that what is said of him may in fact be true. Therefore, the apostle did not say that they would teach one another, but rather that they would remind one another; one usually needs to be reminded of something that, although it is known, sometimes eludes the mind or is held inattentively.[33] The rest of text is not so unclear that it requires explanation.

15:15 *I have, however, written to you quite boldly, brothers,*[34]*—partly so as to remind you—on account of the grace which was given me by God* **15:16** *to be a servant of Christ Jesus among the gentiles, sanctifying the gospel of God, so that the offering of the gentiles might be accepted, sanctified in the Holy Spirit.* The apostle means that he has not written by chance. He says that authority was given him by the grace of God so that he has the boldness to write to all the gentiles, reminding them and assuring them of their purpose in Christ. He does this to show his attentiveness in the service of the gospel as *the teacher of the gentiles* (see 1 Tim 2:7) and so that their sacrifice may be rendered acceptable on account of its sanctification in the Holy Spirit. For whatever is offered with complete faith and sober mind is purified by the Holy Spirit.

---

29. In *recensio* γ "virgin" is attested only by MS Monte Cassino 150 and Paris lat. 1759.

30. See In Rom. 1:3 (§3).

31. Ambrosiaster's biblical text has "brothers" (*fratres*), but among the biblical witnesses there is stronger support for "my brothers" (ἀδελφοί μου). See Jewett, *Romans*, 900.

32. *Recensio* α has "does what he does" instead of "takes pains with what he was doing."

33. *Recensiones* α and β do not have "or is held inattentively."

34. Although Ambrosiaster's biblical text has "brothers" (*fratres*), among the biblical witnesses there is stronger support for its absence. See Jewett, *Romans*, 900.

15:17 *Therefore I have glory in Christ before God,*[35] **15:18** *for I do not venture to say anything about things which Christ does not accomplish through me for the obedience of the gentiles, by word and deed,* **15:19** *by the ability to work signs and wonders in the power of the Holy Spirit.* (1) The apostle says that he has glory before God through Christ Jesus. By believing Christ Jesus and serving him with a pure conscience, he creates merit for himself before God the Father, to the point that he says that there was nothing that Christ did not do through him to call the gentiles, in giving signs and wonders by his hand (see Acts 14:3) so that power might corroborate his preaching. (1a)[36] This is the reason he explains that he has *glory in Christ before God*. By serving Christ, he has glory before God to the point that nothing of the divine power he had was not provided him by God; he acknowledges that, because he was deemed to be a capable steward (see 1 Cor 4:1), he obtained everything that might advance the conversion of the gentiles through the power of signs. (2) This serves to show that he was no less powerful than the rest of the apostles, who were with the Lord, and that God worked no fewer wonders among the gentiles, so that by this very fact they may grow, seeing that they received the same grace that the Jews, who claim for themselves the prerogative of their fathers, had received.

So that from Jerusalem and as far around as Illyricum I have thoroughly dispensed the gospel of God and of his Son Jesus Christ.[37] **15:20** *Moreover I have preached this gospel not where Christ was named,*[38] *so as not to build on another's foundation.* (1) Not without reason does the apostle say that he was compelled to preach[39] *where Christ was not named.*[40] He knew, in fact, that false apostles delivered another Christ than they should have;[41] they were traveling around to subject people to another teaching in the name of

---

35. Among the biblical witnesses there is stronger support for "Christ Jesus" (Χριστῷ Ἰησοῦ) than for "Christ" (*Christo*) as found in Ambrosiaster's biblical text. See Jewett, *Romans*, 901.

36. *Recensio* α does not have section 1a.

37. Ambrosiaster's biblical text has "the gospel of God and his son Jesus Christ" (*evangelium dei et filii eius Iesu Christi*), but the Greek text (NA[28]) has "the gospel of Christ" (τὸ εὐαγγέλιον τοῦ Χριστοῦ).

38. Ambrosiaster's biblical text has "I have preached" (*praedicavi*), but the Greek text (NA[28]) has "making it an ambition to preach" (φιλοτιμούμενον εὐαγγελίζεσθαι). See Jewett, *Romans*, 902.

39. *Recensio* α has "that he preached" instead of "that he was compelled to preach."

40. *Recensio* α adds "that is, proclaimed."

41. *Recensio* α has "many false apostles" instead of "false apostles."

Christ,[42] which required a lot of work afterward to correct. Therefore, he wanted to prevent this, to deliver words of unadulterated preaching to his audience, (2) so that the building, constructed along sound lines, would have the sturdiness of a solid foundation.[43] Because he was appointed teacher to the gentiles, it was important for him diligently to make sure that he taught in places where Christ had not yet been proclaimed, both so that he might establish his authority and so that he might enjoy abundant fruit from his labors in the fields that he had planted. This is why a church resided in every locale. But afterward heresies attempted with malicious cunning to corrupt in the name of Christ the meaning of the law and of faith. (3) The apostle supports this with a quotation from the law, saying:

15:21 *As it is written: "They will see who have never been told of him, and they will understand who have never heard of him"* (Isa 52:15). This is found in Isaiah.[44] Therefore, so that this understanding of the true Son of God would be true and unadulterated,[45] the apostle says that he always made haste to instruct the gentiles with the gospel truth.

15:22 *This is the reason why I have so often been hindered in coming to you.* **15:23** *But now, since I do not have any more room for work in these regions and since I have longed for many of the past years to come to you,* **15:24** *I will see you as I begin to make my way to Spain,*[46] *to be sent on there by you, once I have first enjoyed your company for a while.* (1) The apostle has now cleared up what he mentioned at the beginning of the letter, when he said: *I often intended to come to you and have thus far been prevented* (Rom 1:13). He explains the reason he was prevented: although he wanted to come, he attended to other more urgent matters in order to block the nefarious plans of the false apostles. At last, after he preached to everyone in the area, he says that he is free to come to Rome,[47] as he had long wanted to do. (2) In the meantime, since the Romans had been introduced to the

---

42. Instead of this clause, *recensio* α has "they were traveling around to teach in a misleading manner."

43. *Recensio* α has "Therefore, he wanted to prevent this, in order to lay a foundation according to the right specification in the name of Christ. (2) For someone who is initially taught differently is slower to be persuaded of a thing." *Recensio* α does not have the remainder of section 2.

44. *Recensio* α does not have this comment.

45. *Recensio* α does not have "and unadulterated."

46. Ambrosiaster's biblical text has "I will see you" (*videbo vos*), but the Greek text (NA[28]) has "I hope to see you" (ἐλπίζω ... θεάσασθαι ὑμᾶς).

47. *Recensio* α has "the city" instead of "Rome." See In Rom. 1:9–10 (§4) with n. 59.

law, he corrects them by way of a letter.[48] It was better, however, that those who had not yet heard the proclamation be taught by him in person, so that, after having been established in the correct faith,[49] it would be difficult for them to accept something else. Nevertheless, he promised that he would come while he was on his way to Spain—for Christ had not been proclaimed there—to engage their minds. Because it was difficult for the false apostles to reach them, there was no harm if the apostle came later.

15:25 *At present, however, I am going to Jerusalem to minister to the saints.*[50] **15:26** *For the Macedonians and the Achaians thought it right to make some contribution for the poor among the saints who are in Jerusalem.*[51] The apostle says, however, that first he will go *to minister to the saints in Jerusalem*. He wants the Romans to learn from this that they should practice such works,[52] for those who are alive as a result of mercy and have been justified before God should show themselves to be attentive to the brothers.[53]

15:27 *For they are debtors to them,*[54] *because if the gentiles have come to share in their spiritual things, they should also minister to them in material things.* (1a)[55] The apostle says that since they obviously are debtors to the believing Jews, they should contribute to their material needs just as they have come to share in their spiritual things, so that believers of Jewish origin may rejoice and praise God's providence for their deliver-

---

48. See Ambrosiaster's explanation of the purpose of the letter in his synopsis at the beginning of the commentary.

49. *Recensio* α does not have "in the correct faith." It also has a number of variations in vocabulary in section 2.

50. Among biblical witnesses there is stronger support for the participle "ministering" (διακονῶν) than for the infinitive "to minister" (*ministrare*) as found in Ambrosiaster's biblical text. See Jewett, *Romans*, 918–19.

51. Among the biblical witnesses there is stronger support for "Macedonia and Achaia" (Μακεδονία καὶ Ἀχαΐα) than for "the Macedonians and the Achaians" (*Macedones et Achaii*) as found in Ambrosiaster's biblical text. See Jewett, *Romans*, 919.

52. *Recensio* α has "they should devote effort to good works" instead of "they should practice works."

53. Instead of "should show themselves to be attentive to the brothers," *recensio* α has "should undertake these things, mindful of the blessings of God," and *recensio* β has "should be devoted to this."

54. Ambrosiaster's biblical text has "for they are debtors" (*debitores enim sunt*), but among the biblical witnesses there is stronger support for "for they were well pleased and are debtors" (εὐδόκησαν γὰρ καὶ ὀφειλέται εἰσίν). See Jewett, *Romans*, 919.

55. *Recensio* α does not have section 1a.

ance through the ministry of the gentiles. Indeed, by devoting themselves entirely to godly service and giving no thought to worldly matters, the gentiles were providing an example of good conduct to the believers. **(1)** Consequently, the apostle wants us to be humane and merciful so that he may say that we too are debtors with regard to bestowing alms and practicing good works without a second thought,[56] because a person who hopes for mercy from God should be merciful, to show that he is right to hope for it. For if a human being is merciful, how much more so is God! It is, in fact, a recompense or reward, that those who receive mercy show mercy. This is why the Lord says: *Blessed are the merciful, for God will be merciful to them* (Matt 5:7).

15:28 *When therefore I have completed this and consigned this fruit,*[57] *I will go by way of you to Spain.* **15:29** *For I know*[58] *that when I come to you I will come in the fullness of the blessing of Christ.* Being certain of the plan and grace of God, the apostle promises that he will come in the fullness of the blessing of Christ whom he proclaims. This blessing consists in the power of signs,[59] by which they have been strengthened.

15:30 *Therefore I appeal to you, brothers, through our Lord Jesus Christ and through the love of the Holy Spirit,*[60] *to think of me in prayers to the Lord on my behalf,*[61] **15:31** *that I may be delivered from the unbelievers who are in Judea.* Accordingly, the apostle prays that he may be helped with prayers and elude the hands of the unbelieving Jews, not because he deserves less, but because he follows the arrangement whereby prayer is offered by a church for its leader.[62] When many otherwise insignificant people gather together

---

56. *Recensio* α has "as concerns this work" instead of "with regard to bestowing alms and practicing good works without a second thought."

57. Ambrosiaster's biblical text omits "to them" (αὐτοῖς) after "consigned." On the merits of this omission, see Jewett, *Romans*, 919.

58. Ambrosiaster's biblical text has "for I know" (*scio enim*), but among the biblical witnesses there is stronger support for "but I know" (οἶδα δέ). See Jewett, *Romans*, 919.

59. *Recensio* α does not have "of signs."

60. Ambrosiaster's biblical text has "the Holy Spirit" (*spiritus sancti*), but the Greek text (NA[28]) has "the Spirit" (τοῦ πνεύματος).

61. Ambrosiaster's biblical text has "to the Lord" (*ad dominum*), but the Greek text (NA[28]) has "to God" (πρὸς τὸν θεόν).

62. Ambrosiaster may be alluding here to prayers offered for the bishop during the Eucharist. While the reconstruction of the prayers of the faithful in Rome in the third and fourth century is complex, the bishop is consistently listed in early sources that allude to or preserve the invitation to pray for the orders of the clergy. At In 1 Tim.

with one mind,⁶³ they become great, and it is impossible for the petitions of many people to be disregarded.⁶⁴ So if they themselves are also longing to see the apostle, they should pray all the more zealously, so that they may be able to welcome him in the joy of love, once he is free to leave there.

15:32⁶⁵ *And that the offering of my gifts may be accepted by the saints in Jerusalem,*⁶⁶ *so that I may come to you with joy through the will of Christ Jesus and be refreshed with you.*⁶⁷ (1) The apostle says that they also should pray for the provision of his gifts to be accepted by the saints in Jerusalem, so that he may demonstrate that he does all these things in accordance with God's will. Since his soul is intent on bringing gifts, he also wants their soul to respond to him in accordance with God's judgment, so that when they perceive his love for them they may with one mind give thanks to God because of him.⁶⁸ Great indeed is his success when many, made joyful by his ministry, honor God with praise.⁶⁹

15:33 *May the God of peace be with you all. Amen.*⁷⁰ The God of peace is Christ, who says: *My peace I give to you, my peace I leave you* (John

---

2:1–4 (§1) Ambrosiaster alludes to other petitions from the prayers of the faithful, though not the petition for the clergy. See Paul de Clerck, *La "prière universelle" dans les liturgies latines anciennes: Témoignages patristiques et textes liturgiques*, LWQF 62 (Münster: Aschendorff, 1977), 63–65, 127, 136–39.

63. *Recensio* α does not have "with one mind."
64. *Recensiones* α and β have "not to succeed" instead of "to be disregarded."
65. In English translations of Romans, 15:32 begins at *so that I may come to you*.
66. Ambrosiaster's biblical text has "and that the offering of my gifts may be accepted by the saints in Jerusalem" (*ut et munerum meorum oblatio accepta fiat in Hierosolima sanctis*), but among the biblical witnesses there is stronger support for "and that my service for Jerusalem may be acceptable to the saints" (καὶ ἡ διακονία μου ἡ εἰς Ἰερουσαλὴμ εὐπρόσδεκτος τοῖς ἁγίοις γένηται). See Jewett, *Romans*, 920.
67. Ambrosiaster's biblical text has "I may come to you with joy through the will of Christ Jesus" (*veniam ad vos cum gaudio per voluntatem Christi Iesu*), but among the biblical witnesses there is stronger support for "coming to you with joy through the will of God" (ἐν χαρᾷ ἐλθὼν πρὸς ὑμᾶς διὰ θελήματος θεοῦ). See Bruce M. Metzger, *A Textual Commentary on the Greek New Testament*, 2nd ed. (Stuttgart: Deutsche Bibelgesellschaft, 1994), 474; and Jewett, *Romans*, 920. In his comment Ambrosiaster speaks of "God's will" (*dei voluntate*).
68. *Recensiones* α and β have "they may together with him with one mind give thanks to God" instead of "they may with one mind give thanks to God because of him."
69. Instead of this sentence, *recensio* α has "Great indeed is the success (2) if many brothers are in agreement, especially since the Lord says: *If two of you agree, everything they ask of my Father will be done for them* (Matt 18:19)."
70. There is a contradiction between Heinrich J. Vogels, *Das Corpus Paulinum des*

14:27). The apostle desires that Christ be with them, knowing that the Lord has said: *And behold, I am with you all the days until the end of the age* (Matt 28:20). Therefore, he wants them to behave in such a way that the Lord Jesus Christ would be with them. Having cut off all human strife arising from error, Christ has shown and provided what is true, so that they may remain at peace in that truth.

Ambrosiaster, BBB 13 (Bonn: Hanstein, 1957), 59, which notes the omission of "Amen" in only some of the manuscripts of *recensio* γ, and CSEL 81.1:476–78, which records "Amen" as present in *recensio* α but absent from *recensiones* β and γ. For the biblical witnesses that support its presence, see Jewett, *Romans*, 920, who includes Ambrosiaster among these witnesses.

Romans 16

16:1 *I commend to you our sister Phoebe, who is a minister of the church at Cenchreae,* **16:2** *that you may receive her in the Lord as befits the saints and help her in whatever she may require of you. In fact, she herself has also helped many, myself as well.* The apostle commends Phoebe, who is on her way, as a mutual sister, that is, as a sister from the law. To show that he has good reason to recommend her, he says that she is a servant of the church of Cenchreae. Because she was helpful to many, he says that she deserves to be assisted in her journey. Moreover, to persuade them that she is to be received without fail and helped in whatever she requires, should she come, he attests that she was helpful even to himself, to show that just as he is a person of greater importance than the others, the service due to her should all the more be rendered in love.

16:3 *Greet Aquila and Priscilla, my co-workers in Christ Jesus,* **16:4** *who have risked their necks for my life, to whom not only I but also all the churches of the gentiles give thanks,* **16:5** *and their household church.* (1) They came from the Jews, and as believers they were made co-workers with the apostle because they had believed correctly, so that they too might exhort others to a faith like theirs.[1] Indeed, Apollo was quite thoroughly instructed by them in the way of the Lord even though he was already knowledgeable in the scriptures (see Acts 18:24–28). The apostle therefore calls them his co-workers *in Christ Jesus*, for they have been his collaborators in the gospel of God. Aquila is the husband of Priscilla, and it is clear that they have come to Rome for a reason; they were quite similar in dedication to God.[2] Now, in order to strengthen the Romans, it is understood that all the people whom the apostle greets were living here, that is, in Rome.[3] (2) This is why

---

1. *Recensiones* α and β have "the correct faith" instead of "a faith like theirs."
2. *Recensio* α does not have "they were quite similar in dedication to God."
3. *Recensio* α has simply "here," without referring to Rome; *recensio* β has "here at Rome." See In Rom. 1:9–10 (§4) with n. 59.

he says that not only he but also all the churches of the gentiles give thanks to them, and he refers to people in Rome as well, so that they heed those whom they hear labor for the advancement of the gentiles by promoting faith in Christ.[4] The apostle praises them[5] so that they may not hesitate to endure danger for Christ.[6] Indeed, they did not disdain to endure the animosity of both Jews and false brothers while they were assisting the apostle in service and love. (3) The false brothers were those who, although they believed in Christ, were saying that the law still had to be kept; they taught that Christ was not enough to achieve complete salvation.[7] The apostle was demolishing this view, which is why he too was enduring persecutions at their hand. The apostle greets even Aquila and Priscilla's household members and slaves, whom he calls *the church*, because as regards the faith they were disciples of holy men.

Greet my beloved Efenitus, who is the first fruit of Asia in Christ. The apostle is not silent about the honor that this Efenitus currently possesses in order to show that even eminent people believe and are brought to the faith, so as to encourage leading Romans, or at least so that the lowly might grow in honor.[8]

16:6 *Greet Mary, who has worked hard among you.*[9] He reminds them of Mary by name, whom we understand to have labored at great cost in order to encourage them.[10]

---

4. *Recensio* α has "the true faith" instead of "faith in Christ." Ambrosiaster's point is that Paul greets leading Christians in Rome so that believers in Rome, seeing that these leading Christians are acknowledged by churches everywhere, will pay attention to them.

5. I.e., Aquila and Priscilla.

6. *Recensio* α has "for the apostle" (*pro se*) instead of "for Christ" (*pro eo*). I take this to be an erroneous use of the reflexive pronoun, subsequently corrected in *recensio* β.

7. *Recensio* α does not have "they taught that Christ was not enough to achieve complete salvation."

8. *Recensio* α has "in order to show that even eminent people believe and to invite leading Romans to the faith, or at least so that the lowly may grow in honor." *Recensio* β has the same text as *recensio* γ but omits "and are brought to the faith."

9. The biblical witnesses are divided between the spelling of "Mary" (Μαρίαν) and "Miriam" (Μαριάμ); see NA[28] and Robert Jewett with Roy D. Kotansky, *Romans: A Commentary*, Hermeneia (Minneapolis: Fortress, 2007), 949. The Latin *Mariam* in Ambrosiaster's biblical text can refer to either name. Ambrosiaster in his comments takes it to mean "Mary."

10. *Recensio* α does not have "at great cost" and adds "so that they thank her" at the end of the sentence.

16:7 *Greet Andronicus and Julia,*[11] *my relatives and fellow prisoners, who are eminent among the apostles, who were in Christ Jesus before me.*[12] They are relatives according to both the flesh and the spirit, just as the angel said to Mary: *And, behold, Elizabeth, your relative,* etc. (Luke 1:36). With his testimony the apostle declares that they in fact followed the first apostles and that they endured imprisonment with him for the sake of the faith.[13] Therefore, they should be honored all the more.

16:8 *Greet Ampliatus, my dearly beloved in the Lord.* The apostle greets him like a friend—a friend, though, *in the Lord,* not one who shared in his work or was imprisoned.

16:9 *Greet Urbanus, a partner in our work in Christ.* (1) The apostle says that Urbanus has been not only his own partner,[14] but also a co-worker of others in encouraging belief.

And my beloved Stachys. (2) Although the apostle calls this Stachys *beloved,* he nevertheless subordinates him to Urbanus, a partner in the work of the gospel.

16:10 *Greet Apelles, who is approved in Christ.* (1) The apostle greets this Apelles not as his friend or a partner in the work, but because he was put to the test with temptations and found to be faithful in Christ.

Greet those who belong to Aristobulus. (2) This Aristobulus is understood to have brought together brothers in Christ. The apostle approves of this activity so much that he deems those whom Aristobulus was bringing together to be deserving of his greeting.

---

11. Among the biblical and patristic witnesses there is strong support for the feminine name "Junia" (Ἰουνίαν) rather than the feminine name "Julia" (*Iuliam*) in Ambrosiaster's biblical text. See NA[28] and Jewett, *Romans,* 950.

12. Ambrosiaster's biblical text, "who were in Christ Jesus before me" (*qui ante me fuerunt in Christo Iesu*), varies from that found in other biblical witnesses (οἳ καὶ πρὸ ἐμοῦ γέγοναν ἐν Χριστῷ). On the relative merits of the two variants, see Jewett, *Romans,* 950.

13. *Recensio* α adds "For the Jews were inciting the gentiles to persecute or imprison them."

14. *Recensio* β has "helper" (*adiutorem*) instead of "partner" (*participem*). This variant, attested by Pelagius (see Theodore S. de Bruyn, *Pelagius's Commentary on St Paul's Epistle to the Romans,* OECS [Oxford: Oxford University Press, 1993], 191), and Rufinus (see Caroline P. Hammond Bammel, *Der Römerbrieftext des Rufin und seine Origenes Übersetzung,* vol. 10 of *AGLB* [Freiburg: Herder, 1985], 536), made its way into the Vulgate. That probably accounts for its presence here.

16:11 *Greet Herodion, my relative.* (1) The apostle indicates that this person, whom he calls simply a *relative*, was consecrated in the love of rebirth,[15] but does not attest to his attentiveness.[16]

Greet those who belong to the house of Narcissus, who are in the Lord. At that time this Narcissus is said to have been a presbyter,[17] (2a)[18] as we read in other codices.[19] Given that he was absent, you will understand why the apostle greets those who belonged to his house as saints in the Lord. This Narcissus evidently performed the duties of presbyter in an itinerant capacity, strengthening the believers with his encouragement. (3) Because the apostle did not know the worthiness of those who had been with him, he has expressed himself in this way: *Greet those who belong to the house of Narcissus, who are in the Lord*; that is, those whom you know to be worthy of my greeting in the household, who have placed their hope in the Lord, greet them in my name.

16:12 *Greet Trifena and Trifosa, who work in the Lord.* (1) The apostle declares them to be worthy of a common honor in Christ. *Greet the beloved Persida, who has worked hard in the Lord.* (2) She seems to be ranked above those who are named above, because she *has worked hard in the Lord*. This work consists in encouragement and in service to the saints[20] in times of both distress and need on account of Christ, because the saints, having been forced to flee, abandoned their homes and were scorned by unbelievers.

---

15. I.e., he had been baptized; see Ambrosiaster, *Quaest.* 115.5 (SC 512:156, with the accompanying note at p. 237).

16. *Recensio* α adds "and worthiness."

17. Narcissus is identified as a presbyter in the apocryphal Acts Pet. 3, 4, 6, 13, 14 (Lipsius, 1:48, 49, 53, 61), a work that was known to Ambrosiaster; see In Rom. 8:39 (§2), and Alexander Souter, *The Earliest Latin Commentaries on the Epistles of St. Paul* (Oxford: Clarendon, 1927), 65–66.

18. *Recensio* α does not have section 2a.

19. The variant "Narcissus the presbyter" (*Narcissi presbyteri*) is found in the manuscript Budapest 1 (ca. 800) of an anonymous commentary on the Pauline Epistles (see Hermann J. Frede, *Ein neuer Paulustext und Kommentar*, vols. 7–8 of *AGLB* [Freiburg: Herder, 1973–1974], 2:91), and in the manuscript Oxford 157 of Pelagius's *Commentary on Romans* (see Alexander Souter, ed., *Pelagius's Expositions of Thirteen Epistles of St Paul*, TS 9.2 [Cambridge: Cambridge University Press, 1922; repr., Eugene, OR: Wipf & Stock, 2004], 2:123 apparatus, and de Bruyn, *Pelagius's Commentary*, 192 apparatus). On the basis of Ambrosiaster's remark, Frede, *Ein neuer Paulustext*, 1:122, suggests that the Budapest manuscript may preserve a version of the epistle that antedated Ambrosiaster.

20. *Recensio* α does not have "and in service to the saints."

16:13 *Greet Rufus, chosen in the Lord, and also his mother and mine.* The apostle placed this Rufus ahead of his mother on account of his being chosen to administer the grace of God, a function in which a woman has no place.[21] He was chosen—that is, promoted—by the Lord to administer the Lord's affairs. Nevertheless, the apostle esteemed the mother to be so holy that he calls her his own mother as well.

16:14 *Also, greet Asincretus, Flegonta, Herma, Patroba, Herme and the brothers who are with them.* The apostle greets them all together because he knew that they were at peace in Christ and had not fallen out of friendship.[22] At the same time he also greets the brothers who were with them, whose names he has forgotten.[23]

16:15 *Greet Filologus and Julia and Nereus and his sister and Olympas and all the saints who are with them.* They are understood to all have been of one mind, and for this reason the apostle greets them all together. Their worthiness is discerned from those who were united with them. The apostle calls them *saints* so that he may be seen to greet them deservedly.

16:16 *Greet one another with a holy kiss.* (1) The apostle commands everyone to whom he has written and whom he names to greet one another *with a holy kiss*, that is, a kiss in the peace of Christ, not in carnal desire but in the Holy Spirit, so that the kisses are religious, not physical.[24]

All the churches of Christ greet you. (2a)[25] From this one is given to understand that one can speak of a church which is not of Christ; this is why David also calls the plotting of the wicked *the church of the malicious* (Ps 25:5 LXX = Ps 26:5 ET).[26] So that they increase in faith, the apostle says that the churches in all those places greet them. (2) The reference to Christ thus relates back to a prior point, to show that Christ is the one in whom there is salvation and that he is the one to whom faithful people[27] belong and by whose pleasure the whole creation lives, because he is *the author of*

---

21. On Ambrosiaster's views on official roles in the church, see the introduction §7.1.
22. *Recensiones* α and β have "Christ, that is, joined in Christian friendship."
23. *Recensio* α has "whose names he did not know."
24. *Recensio* α does not have "so that the kisses are religious, not physical." See *In 1 Thess.* 5:26.
25. *Recensio* α does not have section 2a.
26. The word from the psalm that Ambrosiaster translates as "church" (*ecclesiam*) in its context means "company."
27. *Recensio* α has "Christian people" instead of "faithful people."

life, as the apostle Peter says (see Acts 3:15), and not the law, in which some of them thought one ought to hope.[28]

16:17 *I appeal to you,*[29] *brothers, to take note of those who create disagreements and difficulties, in opposition to the instruction which you have been taught, and to avoid them.* **16:18** *For such persons do not serve Christ the Lord, but their own belly, and by enticements and flattering words they seduce the hearts of the innocent.* **16:19** *Your obedience, however, is publicly known everywhere.* (1) At this point the apostle burst out vehemently about the false apostles whom throughout the letter he warns should be avoided, here as well.[30] But he censored their teaching without going into details. These false apostles were compelling believers to judaize,[31] so as to nullify God's blessing toward them, as he has discussed above.[32] With well-chosen words about genealogy they assembled writings for themselves to advance their teaching (see 1 Tim 1:4; Titus 3:9),[33] by which they deceived the hearts of the simple. *Your obedience, however, is publicly known everywhere.* This is what he says at the beginning of the letter: *because your faith is proclaimed throughout the whole world* (Rom 1:8). (2)[34] This means that he may be confident of their obedience. For it was unlikely that they, being wise, would not submit after becoming aware of the truth about this foolish matter.

---

28. *Recensio* α has "and by whose pleasure one lives, not, as some of them thought, to keep the law."

29. Ambrosiaster's biblical text has "I appeal to" (*oro*), but among the biblical witnesses there is stronger support for "I exhort" (παρακαλῶ). See Jewett, *Romans*, 985.

30. The change in rhetoric and tone at 16:17 did not escape Ambrosiaster. It likewise has confronted modern interpreters. For the case for regarding 16:17–20a as a later interpolation, see Jewett, *Romans*, 986–88.

31. *Recensio* α has "Christians" instead of "believers."

32. *Recensiones* α and β have "I have discussed" instead of "he has discussed."

33. *Recensio* α has "With well-chosen and pleasing words they prepared writings for themselves, by which etc."

34. For section 2 *recensio* α has "He says that the teaching they had followed is not the same as the one he has explained throughout the letter, but is the one they followed after they had been converted. He wants them to advance by means of those whom he greets." The commentary on Romans in *recensio* α ends with this comment. This is one of the distinguishing features of the manuscripts of this recension; see the introduction §2.1 and CSEL 81.1:488 apparatus.

Therefore I rejoice in you. (3)[35] This too is the point of the first part of the letter. He rejoices that the Romans, who are seen as exercising dominion, submit to the Christian faith.[36]

I want you to advance so that you are adept in what is good, but inept in what is evil. (4) A person who does good things is *adept in what is good*, whereas people who are unaware of unjust actions—in other words, who are unacquainted with malevolent conduct—are *inept in what is evil*.

16:20 *The God of peace will crush Satan under your feet quickly.* (1) That is, shortly. The apostle is speaking of his own arrival, because his arrival quashed the devil on account of the fact that the Romans accepted spiritual grace. Satan tries to prevent this from happening; he wants people to remain in error so that they quarrel, even though they belong to a single profession of faith.[37]

The grace of our Lord Jesus Christ be with you.[38] (2) The apostle wants the grace that he has promised them upon his arrival to be with them now. If they are worthy to receive it, it is already with them in anticipation.

16:21 *Timothy, a companion in my work, greets you, and so do Lucius and Jason and Sosipater, my relatives.* Timothy is *a companion in* his *work*, like a co-bishop, and governed the church with great care. He was opposed by the Jews to the point that at the outset he was circumcised to avoid offending the Jews; because his mother was Jewish, he could not be a teacher as long as he was uncircumcised (see Acts 16:1–3). The others, however, the apostle calls *relatives* partly on account of ancestry, partly on account of faith.

16:22 *I Tertius, who wrote this letter, greet you in the Lord.* Tertius in name, not in number.[39] He is the scribe of the letter, and he is permitted in his own name to greet the Roman people, to whom he writes so that they

---

35. The remainder of the commentary is attested only by *recensiones* β and γ; see n. 34 above.

36. See In Rom. 1:8 (§§1–3, 4).

37. In *recensio* γ "so that they quarrel, even though they belong to a single profession of faith" is attested only by MS Monte Cassino 150.

38. The form of the benediction with "Christ" (Ἰησοῦ) instead of "Jesus Christ" (*Iesu Christi*) is likely older; see Bruce M. Metzger, *A Textual Commentary on the Greek New Testament*, 2nd ed. (Stuttgart: Deutsche Bibelgesellschaft, 1994), 476. In the original text of the letter to the Romans, this benediction probably came after 16:23, concluding the letter as 16:24; see Jewett, *Romans*, 4–8. Ambrosiaster's biblical text omits 16:24 and repeats the benediction at 16:28.

39. In Latin *tertius* can mean "third."

greet the others whom he names.[40] At this time churches had leaders in only a few places.

16:23 *Gaius, who is host to me, greets you, as do all the churches.*[41] This, I think, is the Gaius to whom the apostle John writes, rejoicing in the love that he showed for the brothers when he covered the cost of what they needed (see 1 John 1:1, 5–8). Although the apostle says above: *All the churches of Christ greet you* (Rom 16:16), he repeats himself here when he says: *All the churches greet you.*[42] I do not consider this repetition to be pointless, for a man as important and accommodating as the apostle wrote nothing that is superfluous. Rather, because he says: *All the churches of Christ greet you* (Rom 16:16)—that is, all the saints, as he says in another passage: *And those who belong to Christ have crucified their flesh* (Gal 5:24)—he has now added that the following people greet the Romans as well so as to denote the entire population of the church by mentioning it twice, since in every church there are two groups of people. It is also possible that he was referring to churches in two provinces, having spoken first of all the churches in one place, then of all the churches in another place. Alternatively, it certainly is possible that he was referring to the churches of the Jews and the gentiles.

Erastus, the city treasurer, and our brother Quartus, greet you. (2) The city treasurer is like a manager who governed the city according to the dictates of justice, especially in regulating prices. The apostle mentions all these people by name as greeting the Romans so that the Romans might know how many and what sort of people rejoice with them in their good start.

---

40. It was common practice in the ancient world for writers of letters to make use of the services of a secretary, whose role might range from merely transcribing the text to editing it or even composing it. Paul also employed secretaries, since in several letters he adds a postscript in his own hand (1 Cor 16:21; Gal 6:11; Col 4:18; 2 Thess 3:17; Phlm 19); for an overview, see E. Randolph Richards, *Paul and First-Century Letter Writing: Secretaries, Composition and Collection* (Downers Grove, IL: InterVarsity Press, 2004), 81–93. Tertius is the only secretary mentioned by name in Paul's letters. It would appear that he came from Rome and therefore was in a position to greet believers there by name (see Rom 16:3–15); see E. Randolph Richards, *The Secretary in the Letters of Paul*, WUNT 2/42 (Tübingen: Mohr Siebeck, 1991), 170–71.

41. This translation of the verse, and of the phrase "all the churches" (*universae ecclesiae*), corresponds to Ambrosiaster's comment; see n. 42 below. A more likely translation would be: *Gaius, who is host to me and to the whole church, greets you.*

42. The Latin word for "all" in the first quotation is *omnes*, and *universae* in the second.

16:25[43] *Now to him who is able to establish you according to my gospel and the preaching of Christ Jesus, according to the revelation of the mystery which was kept secret from time eternal,* **16:26** *but now is disclosed through the prophetic writings by the command of the eternal God for the obedience of faith among all the gentiles,* **16:27** *known to the only wise God through Jesus Christ, to whom be glory forever.*[44] *Amen.* (1) The apostle glorifies God the Father *from whom are all things* (1 Cor 8:6) so that he may deign to complete what was begun with the Romans—since he is able to do so—by confirming their souls in the faith for the advancement of the gospel and the revelation of the secret hidden for ages (see Eph 3:9), but revealed through Christ or in Christ. The mystery that always was hidden in God was proclaimed in the time of Christ, since God is not solitary,[45] but both the Word and the Paraclete are with him from eternity. (2) God has decreed that in this truth all creation would be saved by way of knowledge. The truth of this mystery, known *to the only wise God*, had in fact been indicated by the prophets in certain manner of speaking; he wanted the gentiles to share in this grace, something that the human race was unaware of. He alone is wise because all wisdom comes from him, as Solomon says: *All wisdom comes from the Lord God and with him has it always been* (Sir 1:1). (3) This wisdom is Christ, because Christ is from him and was always with him; through Christ be glory to him forever and ever. Amen. Nothing, therefore, is complete without Christ, because *through him are all things* (1 Cor 8:6); because when he is acknowledged, praise is given to God the Father through him; because God the Father is known through Christ, in whom he caused believers to be saved, as though through his wisdom. Therefore, glory be to the Father through the Son—that is, glory be to both of them in the Holy Spirit, because each dwells in one single glory.

16:28 *The grace of the Lord Jesus Christ be with you all. Amen.*[46] The apostle puts Christ at the end, through whom we were made and by whose grace we have been remade once more, so that he may be firmly impressed

---

43. Some biblical witnesses have as 16:24 the benediction that Ambrosiaster's biblical text has as 16:20b; see n. 38 above.
44. The biblical witnesses are divided on the variants "forever" (εἰς τοὺς αἰῶνας) and "forever and ever" (εἰς τοὺς αἰῶνας τῶν αἰώνων). On the merits of the two variants, see Metzger, *Textual Commentary*, 477; and Jewett, *Romans*, 997.
45. The Latin term is *singularis*. See In Rom. 8:34 (§2) with n. 138.
46. This verse is not included in the Greek text of Romans (NA^{28}). On its placement in the various families of texts of Romans, see Jewett, *Romans*, 4–8.

on our minds. For if we remember his benefits, he will always watch over us, as he said: *Behold, I am with you all the days until the end of the age. Amen* (Matt 28:20).

Bibliography

The bibliography of sources (editions and translations) gives bibliographical details for Ambrosiaster's works alone; bibliographical details of other sources are given at point of reference. The bibliography of literature aims to be fairly comprehensive for studies of or relating to Ambrosiaster. It also includes bibliographical details for any study cited more than once in this volume.

1. Editions

Bussières, Marie-Pierre, ed. *Ambrosiaster: Contre les païens (Question sur l'Ancien et le Nouveau Testament 114) et Sur le destin (Question sur l'Ancien et le Nouveau Testament 115)*. SC 512. Paris: Cerf, 2007.

Mercati, Giovanni. "Anonymi chiliastae in Matthaeum c. XXIV fragmenta." Pages 3–49 in *Varia Sacra* I. StT 11. Rome: Tipografia Vaticana, 1903.

Queis, Dietrich von, ed. "Ambrosiaster, Quaestiones Veteris et Novi Testamenti: Quaestio 115: De fato. Einleitung, Text, Übersetzung, Kommentar." PhD diss., University of Basel, 1972.

Souter, Alexander, ed. *Pseudo-Augustini Quaestiones Veteris et Novi Testamenti CXXVII*. CSEL 50. Vienna: Tempsky; Leipzig: Freytag, 1908.

Vogels, Heinrich J., ed. *Ambrosiastri qui dicitur commentaries in epistulas paulinas*. CSEL 81.1–3. Vienna: Hoelder-Pichler-Tempsky, 1966–1969.

2. Translations

Bray, Gerald L., trans. *Ambrosiaster: Commentaries on Galatians–Philemon*. AChrT. Downers Grove, IL: InterVarsity Press, 2009.

———, trans. *Ambrosiaster: Commentaries on Romans and 1–2 Corinthians*. AChrT. Downers Grove, IL: InterVarsity Press, 2009.

Fatica, Luigi, trans. *Ambrosiaster: Commento alla Lettera ai Galati; Traduzione, introduzione e note*. CTePa 61. Rome: Città Nuova Editrice, 1986.

———. *Ambrosiaster: Commento alla Prima Lettera ai Corinzi; Traduzione, introduzione e note.* CTePa 78. Rome: Città Nuova Editrice, 1989.

———. *Ambrosiaster: Commento alla Seconda Lettera ai Corinzi; Traduzione, introduzione e note.* CTePa 79. Rome: Città Nuova Editrice, 1989.

Pollastri, Alessandra, trans. *Ambrosiaster: Commento all Lettera ai Romani.* CTePa 43. Rome: Città Nuova Editrice, 1984.

3. Literature

Adkin, Neil. "Tertullian in Jerome: (Epist. 22, 37, 1 f.)." *SO* 68 (1993): 129–43.

———. "An Unidentified Latin Quotation of Scripture Related to Is. 31,9." *RBén* 93 (1983): 123–25.

Alcamesi, Filippa. "Il commento dell'Ambrosiaster e la traduzione gotica delle Epistole Paoline." *FG* 1 (2009): 1–28.

Anderson, R. Dean. *Ancient Rhetorical Theory and Paul.* Rev. ed. CBET 18. Leuven: Peeters, 1999.

Araud, R. "'Quidquid non est ex fide peccatum est' (Rom 14:23): Quelques interprétations patristiques (Orig., JChrys., Ambrosiaster, Pelag.)." Pages 129–35 in *Exégèse et patristique.* Vol. 1 of *L'homme devant Dieu: Mélanges offerts au Père Henri de Lubac.* Edited by J. Guillet. Théologie 56. Paris: Aubier, 1963.

Ayres, Lewis. *Nicaea and Its Legacy: An Approach to Fourth-Century Trinitarian Theology.* Oxford: Oxford University Press, 2004.

Babiarz, Grzegorz. "Wiara jako akt poznawczy: Analiza *Quaestiones* Ambrozjastra" ["The Faith—Act of Cognition: Analysis of Ambrosiaster's *Quaestiones*"]. *VoxPat* 34 (2014): 387–97.

Bankert, Dabney Anderson, Jessica M. Wegmann, and Charles D. Wright. *Ambrose in Anglo-Saxon England with Pseudo-Ambrose and Ambrosiaster.* Old English Newsletter Subsidia 25. Kalamazoo, MI: The Medieval Institute, Western Michigan University, 1997.

Bardy, Gustave. "Formules liturgiques grecques à Rome au IVe siècle." *RSR* (1940): 109–12.

Barnard, Leslie W. "L'intolleranza negli apologisti cristiani con speciale riguardo a Firmico Materno." *CNS* 11 (1990): 505–21.

Bastiaensen, Antoon A. R. "Augustin commentateur de saint Paul et l'Ambrosiaster." *SacEr* 36 (1996): 37–65.

———. "Augustine's Pauline Exegesis and Ambrosiaster." Pages 33–54 in *Augustine: Biblical Exegete.* Edited by Frederick Van Fleteren and Joseph C. Schnaubelt. New York: Lang, 2001.

Baxter, James Houston. "Ambrosiaster Cited as 'Ambrose' in 405." *JTS* 24 (1922–1923): 187.

Beatrice, Pier Franco. *The Transmission of Sin: Augustine and the Pre-Augustinian Sources*. Translated by Adam Kamesar. AARRT. Oxford: Oxford University Press, 2013.

Bévenot, Maurice. "Ambrosiaster's Thoughts on Christian Priesthood." *HeyJ* 18 (1977): 152–64.

Bielawski, Maciej. "Simpliciano e Ambrosiaster: Potrebbero essere la stessa persona?" Pages 533–39 in *Le "Confessioni" di Agostino: Bilancio e prospettive, 402–2002*. SEAug 85. Rome: Institutum Patristicum Augustinianum, 2003.

Bonino, Serge-Thomas. "Toute vérité, quel que soit celui qui la dit, vient de l'Esprit-Saint: Autour d'une citation de l'Ambrosiaster dans le corpus thomasien." *RThom* 106 (2006): 101–47.

Boodts, Shari. "The Reception of Augustine in a Ninth-Century Commentary on Romans (Paris, BnF, lat. 11574), with an Analysis of Its Position in Relation to the Carolingian Debate on Predestination." Pages 437–57 in *"Felici curiositate": Studies in Latin Literature and Textual Criticism from Antiquity to the Twentieth Century; In Honour of Rita Beyers*. Edited by G. Guldentops, C. Laes, and G. Partoens. IPM 72. Brepols: Turnhout, 2017.

Børresen, Kari Elisabeth. "Gender and Exegesis in the Latin Fathers." *Aug* 40 (2000): 65–76.

Bracht, Katharina. "Can Women Be Called 'Man'? On the Background of a Discussion Held at the Second Council of Mâcon (585 AD)." *APB* 17 (2006): 144–53.

Brewer, Heinrich. "War Ambrosiaster der bekehrte Jude Isaak?" *ZKT* 37 (1913): 214–16.

Brown, Peter. *The Body and Society: Men, Women, and Sexual Renunciation in Early Christianity*. New York: Columbia University Press, 1988.

Bruyn, Theodore S. de. "Ambrosiaster: *Commentarius in xiii epistulas Paulinas*." In *Traditio Patrum: The Transmission of the Latin Fathers in the Middle Ages*. Edited by Emanuela Colombi et al. Turnhout: Brepols, forthcoming.

———. "Ambrosiaster's Interpretations of Romans 1:26–27." *VC* 65 (2011): 463–83.

———. "Ambrosiaster's Revisions of His *Commentary on Romans* and Roman Synodal Statements about the Holy Spirit." *REAug* 56 (2010): 45–68.

———. "Constantius the Tractator: Author of an Anonymous Commentary on the Pauline Epistles?" *JTS* NS 43 (1992): 38–54.
———. *Pelagius's Commentary on St Paul's Epistle to the Romans*. OECS. Oxford: Oxford University Press, 1993.
Bruyne, Donatien de. "Prologues biblique d'origine marcionite." *RBén* 24 (1907): 1–16.
Buonaiuti, Ernesto. "The Genesis of St. Augustine's Idea of Original Sin." *HTR* 10 (1917): 159–75.
———. "Pelagio e l'Ambrosiastro." *RicRel* 4 (1928): 1–17.
Burn, A. E. "The Ambrosiaster and the Converted Jew Isaac." *The Expositor* 10 (1899): 368–75.
Bussières, Marie-Pierre. "Ambrosiaster's Method of Interpretation in the *Questions on the Old and New Testament*." Pages 49–65 in *Interpreting the Bible and Aristotle in Late Antiquity: The Alexandrian Commentary Tradition between Rome and Baghdad*. Edited by Josef Lössl and John W. Watt. Farnham, Surrey, UK: Ashgate, 2011.
———. "Ambrosiaster's Second Thoughts about Eve." *JECS* 23 (2015): 55–70.
———. "Le commentaire au 4e siècle ou, pour reformuler le dicton, ancienneté a-t-elle toujours autorité?" Pages 83–99 in *The Reception and Interpretation of the Bible in Late Antiquity: Proceedings of the Montréal Colloquium in Honour of Charles Kannengiesser, 11–13 October 2006*. Edited by Lorenzo DiTommaso and Lucian Turcescu. BibleAncChr 6. Leiden: Brill, 2008.
———. "La doctrine indigeste des hérétiques: Le message de l'Apocalypse chez l'Ambrosiaster." Pages 111–26 in *Les visions de l'Apocalypse: Héritage d'un genre littéraire et interprétations théologiques d'Irénée à Augustin*. Edited by F. Vinel. CBiPa 14. Turnhout: Brepols, 2014.
———. "L'esprit de Dieu et l'Esprit Saint dans les 'Questions sur l'Ancien et le Nouveau Testament' de l'Ambrosiaster." *REAug* 56 (2010): 25–44.
———. "Le genre des questions et réponses encourageait-il à l'autocorrection? L'exemple des récritures dans les Questions de l'Ambrosiaster." Pages 105–20 in *La littérature des questions et réponses dans l'Antiquité profane et chrétienne: De l'enseignement à l'éxegese*. Edited by Marie-Pierre Bussières. IPM 64. Turnhout: Brepols, 2013.
———. "L'influence du synode tenu à Rome en 382 sur l'éxègese de l'Ambrosiaster." *SacEr* 45 (2006): 107–24.
———. "Le public des 'Questions sur l'Ancien et le Nouveau Testament' de l'Ambrosiaster." *ASEs* 24 (2007): 161–80.

———. "Les *quaestiones* 114 et 115 de l'Ambrosiaster ont-elles été influencées par l'apologétique de Tertullian?" *REAug* 48 (2002): 101–30.

Cain, Andrew. "In Ambrosiaster's Shadow: A Critical Re-evaluation of the Last Surviving Letter Exchange between Pope Damasus and Jerome." *REAug* 51 (2005): 257–77.

———. *The Letters of Jerome: Asceticism, Biblical Exegesis, and the Construction of Christian Authority in Late Antiquity*. OECS. Oxford: Oxford University Press, 2009.

———. *St. Jerome: Commentary on Galatians*. FC 121. Washington, DC: Catholic University Press of America, 2010.

Cantalamessa, Raniero. "'Ratio paschae': La controversia sul significato della Pasqua nell'Ambrosiaster, in Girolamo e in Agostino." *Aevum* 44 (1970): 219–41.

Casamassa, Antonio. "Il pensiero di Sant'Agostino e l'Ambrosiastro." Pages 43–66 in vol. 1 of *Scritti Patristici*. Rome: Facultas theologica Pontificii Athenaei lateranensis, 1955.

Chadwick, Henry. *The Church in Ancient Society: From Galilee to Gregory the Great*. Oxford History of the Early Church. Oxford: Oxford University Press, 2001.

Chapa Prado, Juan. "El comentario de Ambrosiaster a las epistolas de San Pablo." *EDST* 10 (1986): 11–93.

Cipriani, Nello. "Un'altra traccia dell'Ambrosiaster in Agostino (*De pecc. mer. remiss*. II, 36, 58–59)." *Aug* 24 (1984): 515–24.

Cho, Dongsun. "Ambrosiaster on Justification by Faith Alone in His Commentaries on the Pauline Epistles." *WTJ* 74 (2012): 277–90.

Clauss, Manfred. *The Roman Cult of Mithras: The God and His Mysteries*. Translated by R. Gordon. New York: Routledge, 2001.

Cohen, Jeremy. "The Mystery of Israel's Salvation: Romans 11:25–26 in Patristic and Medieval Exegesis." *HTR* 98 (2005): 247–81.

Cohen, Shaye J. D. *The Beginnings of Jewishness: Boundaries, Varieties, Uncertainties*. HCS 31. Berkeley: University of California Press, 1999.

———. "Was Timothy Jewish (Acts 16:1–3)? Patristic Exegesis, Rabbinic Law, and Matrilineal Descent." *JBL* 105 (1986): 251–68.

Compton, Michael. "From Saul to Paul: Patristic Interpretation of the Names of the Apostle." Pages 50–68 in *In dominico eloquio/In Lordly Eloquence: Essays on Patristic Exegesis in Honor of Robert Louis Wilken*. Edited by Paul M. Blowers, Angela Russell Christman, David G. Hunter, and Robin Darling Young. Grand Rapids: Eerdmans, 2002.

Consolino, Franca Ela. *Pagani e cristiani da Giuliano l'Apostata al sacco di Roma*. SFAM 1. Soveria Mannelli, Italy: Rubbettino, 1995.

Cooper, Stephen A. "*Communis magister Paulus:* Altercation over the Gospel in Tertullian's *Against Marcion.*" Pages 224–46 in *Tertullian and Paul*. Edited by Todd D. Still and David Wilhite. PPSD. London: T&T Clark, 2013.

———. *Marius Victorinus' Commentary on Galatians: Introduction, Translation, and Notes.* OECS. Oxford: Oxford University Press, 2005.

———. *Metaphysics and Morals in Marius Victorinus' Commentary on the Letter to the Ephesians: A Contribution to the History of Neoplatonism and Christianity.* AUS 5.155. New York: Lang, 1995.

———. "*Narratio* and *Exhortatio* in Galatians according to Marius Victorinus Rhetor." *ZNW* 91 (2000): 107–35.

———. "Philosophical Exegesis in Marius Victorinus' Commentaries on Paul." Pages 67–89 in *Interpreting the Bible and Aristotle in Late Antiquity: The Alexandrian Commentary Tradition between Rome and Baghdad*. Edited by Josef Lössl and John W. Watt. Farnham, Surrey, UK: Ashgate, 2011.

———. "Scripture at Cassiciacum: I Corinthians 13:13 in the *Soliloquies.*" *AugStud* 27 (1996): 21–47.

Cooper, Stephen A., and David G. Hunter. "Ambrosiaster *redactor sui*: The Commentaries on the Pauline Epistles (Excluding Romans)." *REAug* 56 (2010): 69–91.

Corssen, Peter. "Zur Überlieferungsgeschichte des Römerbriefs." *ZNW* 10 (1909): 1–45, 97–102.

Coşkun, Altay. "Der Praefect Maximinus, der Jude Isaak und der Strafprozeß gegen Bischof Damasus von Rom." *JAC* 46 (2003): 17–44.

Courcelle, Pierre. "Critiques exégétiques et arguments antichrétiens rapportés par Ambrosiaster." *VC* 13 (1959): 133–69.

Cracco Ruggini, Lellia. "Un cinquantennio di polemico antipagana a Roma." Pages 119–44 in *Paradoxos politeia: Studi patristici in onore di Guiseppe Lazzati*. Edited by Raniero Cantalamessa and Luigi F. Pizzolato. Milan: Vita e Pensiero, 1979.

———. "'Fame laborasse Italiam': Una nuova testimonianza sulla carestia del 383 d. C." Pages 83–98 in *L'Italia settentrionale nell'età antica: Convegno in memoria di Plinio Fraccaro*. Athenaeum fasc. special. Pavia: Tipogr. del Libro, 1976.

Crouzel, Henri. "Divorce et remariage dans l'Église primitive: Quelques réflexions de méthodologie historique." *NRTh* 98 (1976): 891–917.

———. "Les Pères de l'Église ont-ils permis le remarriage après separation?" *BLE* 70 (1969): 3–43.
Cumont, Franz. "La polémique de l'Ambrosiaster contre les païens." *RHLR* 8 (1903): 417–40.
Da Ripabottoni, Alessandro. "La dottrina dell'Ambrosiaster sul privilegio paolino." *Laur* 5 (1964): 429–47.
D'Alès, Adhémar. "L'Ambrosiastre et Zénon de Vérone." *Greg* 10 (1929): 404–9.
Dels Sants Gros, Miguel. "L'Ambrosiàster, autor d'un text litúrgic: Una nova hipòtesi de treball." *RCT* 26 (2001): 267–73.
Den Boeft, J. "Ambrosiaster." *DNP* 1:582.
Denecker, Tim. "Heber or Habraham? Ambrosiaster and Augustine on Language History." *REAug* 60 (2014): 1–32.
Di Berardino, Angelo, ed. *The Golden Age of Latin Patristic Literature from the Council of Nicea to the Council of Chalcedon.* Vol. 4 of *Patrology*. Westminster, MD: Christian Classics, 1992.
Di Santo, Emanuele. *L'Apologetica dell'Ambrosiaster: Cristiani, pagani e giudei nella Roma tardoantica.* SEAug 112. Rome: Institutum Patristicum Augustinianum, 2008.
———. "La critica dell'Ambrosiaster e di Girolamo all'arroganza dei diaconi romani." Pages 387–98 in *Diakonia, diaconiae, diaconato: Semantica e storia nei padri della chiesa*. Rome: Institutum Patristicum Augustinianum, 2010.
Doignon, Jean. "L'esprit souffle où il veut (Jean III,8) dans la plus ancienne tradition patristique latine." *RSPT* 62 (1978): 345–59.
———. "'J'acquisce à la loi' (Rom. 7,16) dans l'exégese latine ancienne." *FZPhTh* 29 (1982): 131–39.
Dulaey, Martine. "L'apprentissage de l'exégèse biblique par Augustin: Première partie; Dans les années 386–389." *REAug* 48 (2002): 267–95.
———. "L'apprentissage de l'exégèse biblique par Augustin (3): Années 393–394." *REAug* 51 (2005): 21–65.
———. "Recherches sur les *LXXXIII Diverses Questions* d'Augustin (1): Questions 44 et 58–60." *REAug* 52 (2006): 113–42.
———. "Rm 9–11: Le mystère du plan divin selon l'Ambrosiaster." Pages 29–46 in *L'exégèse patristique de Romains 9–11: Grâce et liberté, Israël et nations, Le mystère du Christ*. Edited by Isabelle Bochet and Michel Fédou. Paris: Centre Sèvres, Facultés jésuites de Paris, 2007.
Eno, Robert B. "Some Patristic Views on the Relationship of Faith and Works in Justification." *RechAug* 19 (1984): 3–27.

Eymann, Hugo S., ed. *Epistula ad Romanos*. VLB 21. Freiburg: Herder, 1996.

Faber, Riemer. "The Function of Ambrosiaster in Erasmus's Annotations on the Epistle to the Galatians." Pages 70–85 in *The Unfolding of Words. Commentary in the Age of Erasmus*. Edited by Judith Rice Henderson. ErasSt. Toronto: University of Toronto Press, 2012.

Fairweather, Janet. "Ambrosiaster: A Fourth-Century Commentator on Paul." Unpublished seminar paper, 1998.

Fatica, Luigi. "L'Ambrosiaster: L'esegesi nei commentari alle Epistole ai Corinzi." *VetChr* 24 (1987): 269–92.

Field, Lester J., ed. *On the Communion of Damasus and Meletius: Fourth-Century Synodal Formulae in the Codex Veronensis LX*. STPIMS 145 Toronto: Pontifical Institute of Medieval Studies, 2004.

Fisch, Thomas, and David G. Hunter. "Echoes of the Early Roman Nuptial Blessing: Ambrosiaster, *De peccato Adae et Evae*." *EO* 11 (1994): 225–44.

Foley, Desmond. "The Christology of Ambrosiaster—I." *MilS* 39 (1997): 27–47.

———. "The Christology of Ambrosiaster—II." *MilS* 40 (1997): 31–52.

Frakes, Robert M. *Compiling the "Collatio Legum Mosaicarum et Romanarum" in Late Antiquity*. Oxford: Oxford University Press, 2011.

Frede, Hermann J., ed. *Altlateinische Paulus-Handschriften*. Vol. 4 of *AGLB*. Freiburg: Herder, 1964.

———. *Ein neuer Paulustext und Kommentar*. 2 vols. Vols. 7–8 of *AGLB*. Freiburg: Herder, 1973–1974.

———, ed. *Epistula ad Ephesios*. VLB 24.1. Freiburg: Herder, 1962–1964.

———, ed. *Epistulae ad Thessalonicenses, Timotheum, Titum, Philemonem, Hebraeos*. VLB 25. Freiburg: Herder, 1975–1982.

Fröhlich, Uwe, ed. *Epistula ad Corinthios I*. VLB 22. Freiburg: Herder, 1995–1998.

Geerlings, Wilhelm. "Die Lateinisch-Patristischen Kommentare." Pages 1–14 in *Der Kommentar in Antike und Mittelalter: Beiträge zu seiner Erforschung*. Edited by Wilhelm Geerlings and Christian Schulze. CCAM 2. Leiden: Brill, 2002.

———. "Römisches Recht und Gnadentheologie: Eine typologische Skizze." Pages 357–77 in *Homo Spiritalis: Festgabe für Luc Verheijen*. Edited by Cornelius Mayer. Cassiciacum 38. Würzburg: Augustinus Verlag, 1987.

———. "Das Verständnis von Gesetz im Galaterbriefkommentar des Ambrosiaster." Pages 101–13 in *Die Weltlichkeit des Glaubens in der alten Kirche: Festschrift für Ulrich Wickert*. Edited by Dietmar Wyrwa. Berlin: de Gruyter, 1997.

———. "Zur exegetischen Methode des Ambrosiaster." Pages 444–49 in *Stimuli: Exegese und ihre Hermeneutik in Antike und Christentum; Festschrift für Ernst Dassmann*. Edited by George Schöllgen and Clemens Scholten. Münster: Aschendorff, 1996.

Geerlings, Wilhelm, and Christian Schulze, eds. *Der Kommentar in Antike und Mittelalter: Beiträge zu seiner Erforschung*. CCAM 2. Leiden: Brill, 2002.

Greer, Rowan. *Theodore of Mopsuestia: The Commentaries on the Minor Epistles of Paul*. WGRW 26. Atlanta: Society of Biblical Literature, 2010.

Gregory, Casper René. "The Essay *Contra Novatianum*." *AmJT* 3 (1899): 566–70.

Grelot, Pierre. "La traduction et l'interprétation de Ph 2, 6–7: Quelques éléments d'enquête patristique." *NRTh* 93 (1971): 897–922, 1009–26.

Gryson, Roger, ed. *Esaias*. VLB 12. Freiburg: Herder, 1987–1993.

Hadot, Ilsetraut. "Der fortlaufende philosophische Kommentare." Pages 183–99 in *Der Kommentar in Antike und Mittelalter: Beiträge zu seiner Erforschung*. Edited by Wilhelm Geerlings and Christian Schulze. CCAM 2. Leiden: Brill, 2002.

Hammond Bammel, Caroline P. *Der Römerbrieftext des Rufin und seine Origenes Übersetzung*. Vol. 10 of *AGLB*. Freiburg: Herder, 1985.

Harnack, Adolf von. "Ius ecclesiasticum: Eine Untersuchung über den Ursprung des Begriffes." *SPAW.PH* (1903): 212–26.

———. "Der pseudoaugustinische Traktat *Contra Novatianum*." Pages 54–93 in *Abhandlungen Alexander von Oetiingen zum siebzigsten Geburtstag gewidmet von Freuden und Schülern*. Munich: Beck, 1898.

Hauschild, Wolf-Dieter. "Geist/Heiliger Geist/Geistesgaben: IV Dogmengeschichtlich." *TRE* 12:196–217.

Hauser, Alan J., and Duane Watson, eds. *The Ancient Period*. Vol. 1 of *A History of Biblical Interpretation*. Grand Rapids: Eerdmans, 2003.

Heggelbacher, Othmar. "Beziehungen zwischen Ambrosiaster und Maximus von Turin? Eine Gegenüberstellung." *FZPhTh* 41 (1994): 5–44.

———. *Vom römischen zum christlichen Recht: Juristische Elemente in den Schriften des sogenannten Ambrosiaster*. AJSUFS 19. Freiburg: Universitätsverlag, 1959.

Heil, Johannes. *Kompilation oder Konstruktion? Die Juden in den Pauluskommentaren des 9: Jahrhunderts*. FGJ, Abteilung A: Abhandlungen 6. Hannover: Hahn, 1998.

Henry, Paul. "Kénose." *DBSup* 5:7–161.
Houghton, H. A. G. *The Latin New Testament: A Guide to Its Early History, Texts, and Manuscripts*. Oxford: Oxford University Press, 2016.
———. "The Layout of Early Latin Commentaries on the Pauline Epistles and Their Oldest Manuscripts." StPatr, forthcoming.
Hoven, René. "Notes sur Érasme et les auteurs anciens." *AnCl* 38 (1969): 169–74.
Hughes, Kevin L. *Constructing Antichrist: Paul, Biblical Commentary, and the Development of Doctrine in the Early Middle Ages*. Washington, DC: Catholic University Press of America, 2005.
Hunter, David G. "Ambrosiaster." Pages 19–20 in *Augustine through the Ages: An Encyclopedia*. Edited by Alan D. Fitzgerald. Grand Rapids: Eerdmans, 1999.
———. "Clerical Celibacy and the Veiling of Virgins: New Boundaries in Late Ancient Christianity." Pages 139–52 in *The Limits of Ancient Christianity: Essays on Late Antique Thought and Culture in Honor of R. A. Markus*. Edited by William E. Klingshirn and Mark Vessey. Rec. LLTC. Ann Arbor: University of Michigan Press, 1999.
———. "Fourth-Century Latin Writers: Hilary, Victorinus, Ambrosiaster, Ambrose." Pages 302–17 in *The Cambridge History of Early Christian Literature*. Edited by Frances Young, Lewis Ayres, and Andrew Louth. Cambridge: Cambridge University Press, 2004.
———. *Marriage, Celibacy, and Heresy in Ancient Christianity: The Jovinianist Controversy*. OECS. Oxford: Oxford University Press, 2007.
———. "*On the Sin of Adam and Eve*: A Little-Known Defense of Marriage and Childbearing by Ambrosiaster." *HTR* 82 (1989): 283–99.
———. "The Paradise of Patriarchy: Ambrosiaster on Woman as (Not) God's Image." *JTS* NS 43 (1992): 447–69.
———. "The Significance of Ambrosiaster." *JECS* 17 (2009): 1–26.
———. "Rivalry between Presbyters and Deacons in the Roman Church: Three Notes on Ambrosiaster, Jerome, and *The Boasting of the Roman Deacons*." *VC* 71 (2017): 495–510.
Hušek, Vít. "*Duplex gratia*: Ambrosiaster and the Two Aspects of His Soteriology." Pages 151–59 in *Für uns und für unser Heil: Soteriologie in Ost und West*. Edited by Th. Hainthaler et al. ProOr 37. Innsbruck-Vienna: Tyrolia Verlag, 2014.
———. "Human Freedom according to the Earliest Latin Commentaries on Paul's Letters." *StPatr* 44 (2010): 385–90.

---. "Inpossibile est non peccare: Kategorie hříchů u Ambrosiastera" ["Categories of Sins in Ambrosiaster"]. *ST* 16 (2014): 119–29.

---. "Ježíšovo příbuzenstvo u Ambrosiastera" ["Ambrosiaster on the Relatives of Jesus"]. *ST* 15 (2013): 226–37.

---. "Koho zachrání Kristův sestup do pekel? Ambrosiastrův výklad Ř 5,14–15" ["Who Will Be Saved by Christ's Descent to Hell? Ambrosiaster's Commentary on Romans 5:14–15"]. Pages 73–86 in *Miscellanea patristica*. Edited by V. Hušek, L. Chvátal, and J. Plátová. Brno: CDK, 2007.

---. "Models of Faith: Women in Mark's Gospel Interpreted by Jerome, Ambrose and Ambrosiaster." *ETJ* 2 (2016): 9–18.

---. "Přirozenost u Ambrosiastra" ["Nature in Ambrosiaster"]. Pages 81–90 in *"Přirozenost" ve filosofii minulosti i současnosti* [Nature in Philosophy Past and Present]. Edited by L. Chvátal and V. Hušek. Brno: CDK, 2008.

---. "Pojetí svobody v komentářích Maria Victorina k pavlovským epištolám" ["The Concept of Freedom in the Pauline Commentaries of Ambrosiaster"]. *ST* 8 (2006): 19–31.

---. "Svoboda a milost v nejstarších latinských komentářích k pavlovským epištolám: Marius Victorinus, Ambrosiaster, Jeroným" ["Human Freedom according to the Earliest Latin Commentaries on Paul's Letters: Marius Victorinus, Ambrosiaster, Jerome"]. *Teologický časopis* 5 (2007): 35–44.

---. "The True Text: Ambrose, Jerome and Ambrosiaster on the Variety of Biblical Versions." Pages 319–36 in *Process of Authority: The Dynamics in Transmission and Reception of Canonical Texts*. Edited by Jan Dušek and Jan Roskovec. Berlin: de Gruyter, 2016.

Jacobs, Andrew S. "A Jew's Jew: Paul and the Early Christian Problem of Jewish Origins." *JR* 86 (2006): 258–86.

---. "'Papinian Commands One Thing, Our Paul Another': Roman Christians and Jewish Law in the *Collatio legum Mosaicarum et Romanarum*." Pages 85–99 in *Religion and Law in Classical and Christian Rome*. Edited by Clifford Ando and Jörg Rüpke. PAB 15. Stuttgart: Steiner, 2006.

Jäntsch, Josef. "Führt der Ambrosiaster zu Augustinus oder Pelagius?" *Schol* 15 (1939): 92–99.

Jewett, Robert, with Roy D. Kotansky. *Romans: A Commentary*. Hermeneia. Minneapolis: Fortress, 2007.

Jones, A. H. M. *The Later Roman Empire 284–602: A Social, Economic, and Administrative Survey*. 2 vols. Oxford: Blackwell, 1964. Reprint, Baltimore: Johns Hopkins University Press, 1992.

Jülicher, Adolf. "Ambrosiaster." PW 1.2:1811–12.

Kannengiesser, Charles. *Handbook of Patristic Exegesis*. BAC 1. Leiden: Brill, 2006.

Kelly, J. N. D. *Early Christian Doctrines*. Rev. ed. San Francisco: Harper & Row, 1978.

Kennedy, George, ed. *Classical Criticism*. Vol. 1 of *The Cambridge History of Literary Criticism*. Cambridge: Cambridge University Press, 1989.

Klijn, A. F. J., and G. J Reinink. *Patristic Evidence for Jewish-Christian Sects*. NovTSup 36. Leiden: Brill, 1973.

Koch, Hugo. "Der Ambrosiaster und zeitgenössiche Schriftsteller." *ZKG* 47 (1928): 1–10.

———. "Cyprian in den *Quaestiones Veteris et Novi Testamenti* und beim Ambrosiaster." *ZKG* 45 (1927): 516–54.

Krans, Jan. "Who Coined the Name 'Ambrosiaster'?" Pages 274–81 in *Paul, John, and Apocalyptic Eschatology: Studies in Honour of Martinus C. de Boer*. Edited by Jan Krans, Bert Jan Lietaert Peerbolte, Peter-Ben Smit, and Arie Zwiep. NovTSup 149. Leiden: Brill, 2013.

Kugel, James L. *The Bible as It Was*. Cambridge, MA: Harvard University Press, 1997.

Laistner, Max L. W. "The Western Church and Astrology during the Early Middle Ages." *HTR* 34 (1941): 251–75.

Langen, Joseph. "De commentariorum in epistulas Paulinas qui Ambrosii et quaestionum biblicarum quae Augustini nomine feruntur scriptore dissertatio." PhD diss., Bonn, 1880.

Leeming, Bernard. "Augustine, Ambrosiaster and the *massa perditionis*." *Greg* 11 (1930): 58–91.

Lössl, Josef, and John W. Watt, eds. *Interpreting the Bible and Aristotle in Late Antiquity: The Alexandrian Commentary Tradition between Rome and Baghdad*. Farnham, Surrey, UK: Ashgate, 2011.

Lunn-Rockliffe, Sophie. "Ambrosiaster Revising Ambrosiaster: Introduction." *REAug* 56 (2010): 21–24.

———. "Ambrosiaster's Political Diabology." StPatr 43 (2006): 423–28.

———. *Ambrosiaster's Political Theology*. OECS. Oxford: Oxford University Press, 2007.

———. "Bishops on the Chair of Pestilence: Ambrosiaster's Polemical Exegesis of Psalm 1:1." *JECS* 19 (2011): 79–99.

———. "A Pragmatic Approach to Poverty and Riches: Ambrosiaster's *quaestio* 124." Pages 115–29 in *Poverty in the Roman World*. Edited by Margaret Atkins and Robin Osborne. Cambridge: Cambridge University Press, 2009.

———. "Prologue Topics and Translation Problems in Latin Commentaries on Paul." Pages 33–47 in *Interpreting the Bible and Aristotle in Late Antiquity: The Alexandrian Commentary Tradition between Rome and Baghdad*. Edited by Josef Lössl and John W. Watt. Farnham, Surrey, UK: Ashgate, 2011.

Mansfeld, Jaap. *Prolegomena. Questions to Be Settled before the Study of an Author, or a Text*. PhA 61. Leiden: Brill, 1995.

Manthe, Ulrich. "Wurde die Collatio vom Ambrosiaster Isaak geschrieben?" Pages 737–54 in *Festschrift für Rolf Knütel zum 70: Geburtstag*. Edited by Holger Altmeppen. Heidelberg: Müller, 2009.

Mara, Maria Grazia. *Paolo di Tarso e il suo epistolario*. CTSt 16. L'Aquila: Japadre, 1983.

Marold, C. "Der Ambrosiaster nach Inhalt und Ursprung." *ZWT* 26 (1883): 415–70.

Martini, Coelestinus. *Ambrosiaster: De auctore, operibus, theologia*. SPAA 4. Rome: Pontificium Athenaeum Antonianum, 1944.

———. "Le recensione delle 'Quaestiones veteris et novi testamenti' dell'Ambrosiaster." *RicSRel* 1 (1954): 40–62.

Mercati, Giovanni. "Il commentario latino d'un ignoto chiliasta su s. Matteo." Pages 3–22 in *Varia Sacra I*. StT 11. Rome: Tipografia Vaticana, 1903.

Merkt, Andreas. "Wer war der Ambrosiaster? Zum Autor einer Quelle des Augustinus—Fragen auf eine neue Antwort." *WiWei* 59 (1996): 19–33.

Metzger, Bruce M. *The Canon of the New Testament: Its Origin, Development, and Significance*. Oxford: Clarendon, 1987.

———. *A Textual Commentary on the Greek New Testament*. 2nd ed. Stuttgart: Deutsche Bibelgesellschaft, 1994.

Meyer zu Uptrup, Klaus. "Die anthropologischen Begriffe im exegetischen Werk des Ambrosiaster." PhD diss., University of Heidelberg, 1960.

Michael, Robert. *Holy Hatred: Christianity, Antisemitism, and the Holocaust*. New York: Palgrave Macmillan, 2006.

Miranda, Americo. "*Homo spiritalis* nell'Ambrosiaster: La prima esegesi latina di un passo controverso della Prima ai Corinti." Pages 501–14 in *L'esegesi dei padri latini dalle origini a Gregorio Magno*. SEAug 68. Rome: Institutum Patristicum Augustinianum, 2000.

Morin, Germain. "L'Ambrosiaster et le Juif converti Isaac, contemporain du pape Damase." *RHR* 4 (1899): 97–121.

———. "La critique dans une impasse: À propos du cas de l'Ambrosiaster." *RBén* 40 (1928): 251–59.

———. "Hilarius l'Ambrosiaster." *RBén* 20 (1903): 113–31.

———. "Qui est l'Ambrosiaster? Solution nouvelle." *RBén* 31 (1914–1919): 1–34.

———. "Una nuova possibilità a proposito dell'Ambrosiastro." *Athenaeum* 6 (1918): 62–71.

Motherway, Thomas J. "The Creation of Eve in Catholic Tradition." *TS* 1 (1940): 97–116.

Mundle, Wilhelm. *Die Exegese der paulinischen Briefe im Kommentar des Ambrosiaster*. Marburg: Schaaf, 1919.

———. "Die Herkunft der 'marcionitischen' Prologe zu den paulinischen Briefe." *ZNW* 24 (1925): 56–77.

Norelli, Enrico. "La tradizione ecclesiastica negli antichi prologhi latini alle epistole paoline." Pages 301–24 in *La tradizione: Forme e modi*. SEAug 31. Rome: Institutum Patristicum Augustianum, 1990.

Palma, Marco. "Die patristischen Glossen des neapolitanischen Geistlichen Donatus in einigen Handschriften des 6. Jahrhunderts." *S&C* 24 (2000): 5–16.

———. "Per lo studio della glossa tardoantica: Il caso di Donato, prete napoletano." *S&C* 22 (1998): 5–12.

Pautler, André, ed. *Hilaire de Poitiers, Ambroise de Milan, Ambrosiaster*. Vol. 6 of *Biblia patristica: Index des citations et allusions bibliques dans la littérature patristique*. Paris: Centre national de la recherche scientifique, 1995.

Pépin, Jean. "Réactions du christianisme latin à la sotériologie métroaque: Firmicus Maternus, Ambrosiaster, Saint Augustin." Pages 256–75 in *La soteriologia dei culti orientali nell'impero romano*. Edited by Ugo Bianchi and Maarten J. Vermaseren. EPRO 92. Leiden: Brill, 1982.

Pereira Lamelas, Isidro. "Ambrosiaster e o *Commentarius in Epistulam ad Romanos*." *Itinerarium* 58 (2012): 117–41.

Perrone, Lorenzo. "Echi della polemica pagana sulla Bibbia negli scritti esegetici fra IV e V secolo: Le *Quaestiones Veteris et Novi Testamenti* dell'Ambrosiaster." *ASEs* 11 (1994): 161–85.

Pesce, Mauro. "Il commento dell'Ambrosiaster alla Prima Lettera ai Corinzi." *ASEs* 7 (1990): 593–629.

Pollastri, Alessandra. *Ambrosiaster, commento alla Lettera ai Romani: Aspetti cristologici*. CTSt. L'Aquila: Japadre, 1976.

———. "Dal *De Petro apostolo* possibili luci su conflitti ecclesiali." Pages 215–41 in *Scritti in onore di Gilberto Mazzoleni*. Edited by A. Santiemma. Rome: Bulzoni, 2010.

———. "Escatologia e Scrittura nell'Ambrosiaster." *ASEs* 17 (2000): 109–32.

———. *Frammenti esegetici su Matteo: il Vangelo di Matteo (Mt 24,20–42), le Tre Misure (Mt 13,33), l'apostolo Pietro (Mt 26,51–53.72–75)*. BPat 50. Bologna: Dehoniane, 2014.

———. "Nota all'interpretazione di Matteo 13,33 / Luca 13,21 nel frammento *Incipit de tribus mensuris*." *SSRel* 3 (1979): 61–78.

———. "Il prologo del commento alla Lettera ai Romani dell'Ambrosiaster." *SSRel* 2 (1978): 93–127.

———. "Il sangue testimone del beneficio divino nel commento dell'Ambrosiaster a 1 Cor 11, 26, II." Pages 199–215 in vol. 1 of *Atti della Settimana Sangue e antropologia biblica nella patristica*. Edited by Francesco Vattioni. Rome: Pia unione Preziosissimo Sangue, 1982.

———. "Sul rapporto tra cristiani e giudei secondo il commento dell'Ambrosiaster ad alcuni passi paolini." *SSRel* 4 (1980): 313–27.

Porro, Mario. "Circostanze e significato teologico della colletta paolina nell'esegesi dell'Ambrosiaster." Pages 149–56 in *"Chi semina in benedizioni, in benedizioni raccoglie": Teologia della solidarietà cristiana nei commenti patristici a 1 Cor 16, 1–4; 2 Cor 8–9*. Edited by Rosario Scognamiglio and Carlo dell'Osso. AnNic 1. Bari: Ecumenica, 2007.

Prat, Ferdinand. "Les prétensions des diacres romaines au quatrième siècle." *RSR* 3 (1912): 463–75.

Raspanti, Giacomo. "Aspetti formali dell'esegesi paolina dell'Ambrosiaster." *ASEs* 16 (1999): 507–36.

———. "L'esegesi della lettera ai Galati nel IV secolo d. C. Dal commentario dottrinale di Mario Vittorino ed Ambrosiaster a quello filologico di Girolamo." *HTh* 25 (2007): 109–28.

———. "Il peccato di Adamo e la grazia di Cristo nella storia dell'umanità: Rilettura del Commento di Ambrosiaster a Rom. 5,12–21." *Aug* 48 (2008): 435–80.

———. "San Girolamo e l'interpretazione di Gal. 2, 11–14." *REAug* 49 (2003): 297–321.

Reemts, C. *Samuel: Biblische Gestalten bei den Kirchenvätern, mit Texten und deutscher Übersetzung von Origenes, 1. und 5. Samuelhomelie und Ambrosiaster, Quaestio 27 und 46*. Münster: Aschendorff, 2009.

Rivière, Jean. "Le 'droit' du démon sur les pécheurs avant saint Augustin." *RTAM* 3 (1931): 113–39.

Rutgers, Leonard Victor. *The Jews in Late Ancient Rome: Evidence of Cultural Interaction in the Roman Diaspora.* RGRW 126. Leiden: Brill, 1995.

Salzman, Michele Renee. "Elite Realities and Mentalités: The Making of a Western Christian Aristocracy." *Arethusa* 33 (2000): 347–62.

Sancti Ambrosii Mediolanensis episcopi opera, ad manuscriptos codices Vaticanos, Gallicanos, Belgicos, &c. necnon ad editiones veteres emendata, studio et labore monachorum Ordinis S. Benedicti, è Congregatione S. Mauri. 2 vols. Paris: Coignard, 1686–1690.

Savon, Hervé. "Les recherches sur saint Ambroise en Allemagne et en France de 1870 à 1930." Pages 111–28 in *Patristique et antiquité tardive en Allemagne et en France de 1870 à 1930: Influences et échanges.* Edited by Jacques Fontaine, Reinhart Herzog, and Karla Pollmann. Paris: Institut d'études augustiniennes, 1993.

Schäfer, Karl. "Marcion und die ältesten Prologe zu den Paulusbriefen." Pages 135–50 in vol. 1 of *Kyriakon: Festschrift Johannes Quasten.* Edited by Patrick Granfield and Josef Jungmann. Münster Westfalen: Aschendorff, 1971.

———. "Marius Victorinus und die marcionitischen Prologe zu den Paulusbriefen." *RBén* 24 (1970): 7–16.

Schäublin, Christoph. "Homerum ex Homero." *MH* 34 (1977): 221–27.

———. "Zur paganen Prägung der christlichen Exegese." Pages 148–73 in *Christliche Exegese zwischen Nicaea und Chalcedon.* Edited by Jan van Oort and Ulrich Wickert. Kampen: Kok Pharos, 1992.

Schelkle, Karl H. *Paulus, Lehrer der Väter.* 2nd ed. Düsseldorf: Patmos, 1959.

Schepens, Prosper. "L'Ambrosiastre et saint Eusèbe de Verceil." *RSR* 37 (1950): 295–99.

Scherbenske, Eric W. *Canonizing Paul: Ancient Editorial Practice and the Corpus Paulinum.* Oxford: Oxford University Press, 2013.

Schreckenberg, Heinz. *Die christlichen Adversus-Judaeos-Texte und ihr literarisches und historisches Umfeld (I.–XI. Jh.).* Rev. ed. EHS, Ser. 23 Theologie, 497. Bern: Lang, 1990.

Schulz-Flügel, Eva. "Paulusexegese: Victorinus, Ambrosiaster." Pages 115–18 in *Augustin Handbuch.* Edited by Volker Drecoll. Tübingen: Mohr Siebeck, 2007.

Simon, Richard. *Histoire critique des principaux commentateurs du Nouveau Testament, depuis le commencement du Christianisme jusques à nôtre tems: Avec une dissertation critique sur les principaux actes manuscrits qui ont été citez dans les trois parties de cet ouvrage*. Rotterdam: Leers, 1693.

Simonetti, Manlio. *Lettera e/o allegoria: Un contributo alla storia dell'esegesi patristica*. SEAug 23. Rome: Institutum Patristicum Augustinianum, 1985.

Sirna, Francesco G. "Arnobio e l'eresia marcionita di Patrizio." *VC* 18 (1964): 37–50.

Skarsaune, Oskar, and Reidar Hvalvik, eds. *Jewish Believers in Jesus*. Peabody, MA: Hendrickson, 2007.

Smelik, K. A. D., and E. M. Hemelrijk. "'Who Knows Not What Monsters Demented Egypt Worships?' Opinions on Egyptian Animal Worship in Antiquity as Part of the Ancient Conception of Egypt." *ANRW* 17.4:1852–2000.

Souter, Alexander. *The Earliest Latin Commentaries on the Epistles of St. Paul*. Oxford: Clarendon, 1927.

———. "The Genuine Prologue to Ambrosiaster on 2 Corinthians." *JTS* 4 (1903): 89–92.

———. "Reasons for Regarding Hilarius (Ambrosiaster) as the Author of the Mercati-Turner Anecdoton." *JTS* 5 (1904): 608–21.

———. *A Study of Ambrosiaster*. TS 7.4. Cambridge: Cambridge University Press, 1905.

Speller, Lydia. "Ambrosiaster and the Jews." *StPatr* 17 (1982): 72–78.

———. "A Note on Eusebius of Vercelli and the Council of Milan." *RSR* 37 (1950): 295–99.

———. "New Light on the Photinians: The Evidence of Ambrosiaster." *JTS* NS 34 (1983): 99–113.

Staniek, Edward. "Spór o Melchizedecha: Ambrozjaster–Hieronim" ["Discussion of Melchizedek: Ambrosiaster–Jerome"]. *VoxPat* 7 (1987): 345–53.

Stanula, Emil. "Nauka Ambrozjastra o stanie pierwotnym człowieka: Studium z zakresu antropologii teologicznej" ["Ambrosiaster's Understanding of the Primitive State of Human Beings: A Study in the Field of Theological Anthropology"]. *SAChr* 1–2 (1977): 3–130.

Stüben, Joachim. "Erasmus von Rotterdam und der Ambrosiaster: Zur Identifikationsgeschichte einer wichtigen Quelle Augustins." *WiWei* 60 (1997): 3–22.

———. "Das Heidentum im Spiegel von Heilsgeschichte und Gesetz: Ein Versuch über das Bild der Paganitas im Werk des Ambrosiaster." ThD diss., Universität Hamburg, 1990.
Stuiber, Alfred. "Ambrosiaster." *JAC* 13 (1970): 119–23.
———. "Ambrosiaster." *RAC* Suppl. 1:301–10.
———. "Ambrosiaster." *TRE* 2:356–62.
Tolmie, D. François. "Ambrosiaster se uitleg van die Filemonbrief en die retoriese analise van hierdie brief." *IDS* 49.2 (2015). doi:10.4102/ids.v49i2
———. "Paul's Exercise of Authority in the Letter to Philemon: A Perspective from the Fourth and Fifth Centuries CE." *IDS* 50.2 (2016). doi:10.4102/ids.v50i2
Torti, Giovanni. "'Non debet imputari matrimonium': Nota sull'Ambrosiastro." *GIF* 36 (1984): 267–82.
———. "Vicende di un testo dell'Ambrosiaster." *CClCr* 3 (1982): 235–46.
Turner, Cuthbert H. "Ambrosiaster and Damasus." *JTS* 7 (1906): 281–84.
———. "Niceta and Ambrosiaster." *JTS* 7 (1906): 203–19, 355–72.
Turner, Cuthbert H., and Eduard Schwartz, eds. *Ecclesiae occidentalis monumenta iuris antiquissima: canonum et conciliorum Graecorum interpretationes Latinae.* 2 vols. Oxford: Clarendon, 1899–1939.
Valero, Juan B. "Pecar en Adán según Ambrosiaster." *EE* 65 (1990): 147–91.
Veer, A. C. de. "Saint Augustin et l'Ambrosiaster." Pages 817–24 in *Premières polémiques contre Julien.* Edited by F.-J. Thonnard, E. Bleuzen, and A. C. de Veer. BAug 23. Paris: Desclée de Brouwer, 1974.
Voelkl, L. "Vom römischen zum christlichen Recht: Stellungnahme zu Heggelbachers gleichnamigem Werk im Sinn eines Beitrages zur Ambrosiaster-Forschung." *RQ* 60 (1965): 120–30.
Vogels, Heinrich J. "Ambrosiaster und Hieronymus." *RBén* 66 (1956): 14–19.
———. *Das Corpus Paulinum des Ambrosiaster.* BBB 13. Bonn: Hanstein, 1957.
———. "Librarii Domitantes: Aus der Überlieferung des Ambrosiaster-Kommentars zu den Paulinischen Briefen." *SacEr* 8 (1956): 5–13.
———. "Die Überlieferung des Ambrosiasterkommentars zu den Paulinischen Briefen." *NAWG* 7 (1959): 107–42.
———. *Untersuchungen zum Text paulinischer Briefe bei Rufin und Ambrosiaster.* Bonn: Hanstein, 1955.
Volgers, Annelie. "Damasus' Request: Why Jerome Needed to (Re-)Answer Ambrosiaster's *Questions.*" *StPatr* 43 (2006): 531–36.

Volgers, Annelie, and Claudio Zamagni, eds. *Erotapokriseis: Early Christian Question-and-Answer Literature in Context.* CBET 37. Leuven: Peeters, 2004.

Wallach, Luitpold. "Ambrosiaster und die Libri Carolini." *DA* 29 (1973): 197–205.

Watson, E. W. Review of Alexander Souter, *Pseudo-Augustini Quaestiones Veteris et Novi Testamenti. ClR* 23 (1909): 236–37.

Williams, Daniel H. "Justification by Faith: A Patristic Doctrine." *JEH* 56 (2006): 649–67.

——. "Monarchianism and Photinus of Sirmium as the Persistent Heretical Face of the Fourth Century." *HTR* 99 (2006): 187–206.

Wipszycka, Ewa. "The Institutional Church." Pages 331–49 in *Egypt in the Byzantine World 300–700.* Edited by Roger S. Bagnall. Cambridge: Cambridge University Press, 2007.

Wittig, Joseph. "Der Ambrosiaster 'Hilarius': Ein Beitrag zur Geschichte des Papstes Damasus I." Pages 3–66 in vol. 4 of *Kirchengeschichtliche Abhandlungen.* Edited by Max Sdralek. Breslau: Aderholz, 1906.

——. "Filastrius, Gaudentius und Ambrosiaster." Pages 3–56 in vol. 8 of *Kirchengeschichtliche Abhandlungen.* Edited by Max Sdralek. Breslau: Aderholz, 1909.

Young, Frances. "Alexandrian and Antiochene Exegesis." Pages 334–54 in *The Ancient Period.* Edited by Alan J. Hauser and Duane Watson. Vol. 1 of *A History of Biblical Interpretation.* Grand Rapids: Eerdmans, 2003.

Zappala, M. "A proposito dell'Ambrosiastro." *RTSFR* 3 (1922): 460–67.

Zelzer, Michaela. "Zur Sprache des Ambrosiaster." *WS* 83 (1970): 196–213.

Index of Biblical Citations

Old Testament

Genesis
1:26	cxxiii
1:28–29	242
1:31	249
2:21–22	cxxiv
3:1–7	134
3:4–5	168
5:24	242
6:8	242
9:4	82 n. 41
15:5	84
15:16	133
17:4	48, 83–84
18	50
18:1–8	226
18:10	175
18:14	175
19:1–3	226
19:24–25	36
21:12	174
22:18	174–75, 255
25:23	176, 179
31:17–32	98
31:30	100
32:22–32	201 n. 47
32:28	48
39:6–23	98
39:7–20	66
40:1	99
40:1–3	66
49:8	48

Exodus
2:11–15	99
6:2–3	197
7:8–11:10	181
7:8–13:16	55
7:11–12	169
9:16	181, 181 n. 56
12:48–49	71
16:4	55
19:3–6	55 n. 2
20:2–4	103
20:13–17	237
20:17	129
24:7	108 n. 114
32:7–14	55 n. 2
32:33	177
33:19	179
34:1–35	55 n. 2

Leviticus
3:17	82 n. 41
7:26–27	82 n. 41
11:4	246
11:29–30	82 n. 41
11:29–31	189
11:33	189
15:31	5
17:10–14	82 n. 41
18:5	75 n. 4, 194
19:18	237

Numbers
3:6	cxx
9:14	71
13:17	182

Numbers (cont.)

24:17	256

Deuteronomy

6:5	24
6:13	xlviii, 96
10:16	54
12:16	82 n. 41
12:23	82 n. 41
18:19	197
27:26	205
29:4	205
30:12–13	194
30:14	194
32:21	200, 201 n. 43
32:35	231
32:43	256

Joshua

2:1	182
2:9	55, 200
2:9–11	182
5:13–15	50
9:27	cxx
24:2	100

Judges

20:18	48

1 Samuel

9:2	178
15:24–27	179
28:6	181
28:7–25	181
28:9	181

2 Samuel

11:1–12:25	58
12:13	180
13:28	205
15:1–12	180
16:5–10	180
16:30	180

1 Kings

12:25–33	28
18:3–4	204
18:18	204
19:10	204

1 Chronicles

1:34–37	176 n. 25
6:31–53	cxxii
23:26	cxx

2 Chronicles

16:7–10	62
16:12	62

Job

2:6	34
41:3	216, 216 n. 67
42:17	176 n. 25

Psalms ET

1:1	cxii
1:5	47
2:7	51
2:8	80, 80 n. 34
5:9	62
10:7	62
14:1	61
14:2	62
14:3	62
18:49	256
19:1	24
19:4	199
26:5	269
32:1–2	77, 78 n. 16
32:9	lxviii, lxviii n. 31
36:1	63
39:5	157
44:22	166
51:4	xlix, 57, 59
69:9	253
69:22–23	205
76:1	104, 185
85:11	11
100:3	8

Index of Biblical Citations

117:1	256	Ecclesiastes	
120:7	229	1:2	157
132:11	256	7:16	230
140:3	62		
		Isaiah	
Psalms LXX		1:4	64
1:1	cxii	1:9	187
1:5	47	5:21	228
2:7	51	6:9–10	205
2:8	80, 80 n. 34	7:14	11
5:11	62	8:14	189
9:28	62	8:20	108
13:1	61	9:5	168
13:2	62	10:22–23	186
13:3	62	10:23	186 n. 80
17:50	256	11:1–10	216 n. 66
18:2	24	11:10	257
18:5	199	14:12	207
25:5	269	27:9	9 n. 13, 189, 213
31:1–2	77, 78 n. 16	28:16	189–90, 196
31:9	lxviii, lxviii n. 31	29:13	118
35:2	63	40:5	65, 152
38:6	157	40:13	216
43:22	166	41:8	242
50:6	xlix, 57, 59	42:14	xlvii, 39
68:10	253	45:9	183
68:23–24	205	45:14–15	50
75:2	104, 185	45:23	245
84:12	11	50:1	134
99:3	8	50:8	164
116:1	256	52:5	51
119:7	229	52:7	198, 198 nn. 30–31
131:11	256	52:15	260
139:4	62	53:1	199
		53:4	255
Proverbs		56:7	70
1:7	63	59:7	63
1:16	63	59:8	63
3:27	223	59:20	9 n. 13, 189, 213
3:34	228	65:1	201
24:12	180	65:1–2	201 n. 43
24:17–18	209	65:2	201
25:21–22	231		
28:27	222	Jeremiah	
		4:4	52 n. 84, 54

Jeremiah (cont.)
24:6	212
26:8	63, 63 n. 55
26:16	63, 63 n. 55
31:31	189
31:31–32	72
31:34	70
48:10	224

Ezekiel
18:4	115, 152
20:25	cvi, cvi n. 41, 189, 189 n. 100
33:12	248

Daniel
2:18	lxxx
2:34–36	190
4:14	236
9:21–23	72
9:26	72
9:27	72
14:22–30	28

Hosea
1:10	185
2:23	185

Joel
2:32	197, 197 n. 25

Micah
6:9	197 n. 25

Nahum
1:15	198, 198 n. 31

Habakkuk
2:4	xcvi n. 68, 23, 70, 188, 205

Zechariah
3:1	34
12:2	185
12:3	73

Malachi
1:2–3	176, 179
3:6	56
4:2	239

Apocryphal/Deuterocanonical Books

Baruch
3:36	163, 163 n. 127

1 Maccabees
1:41–64	23 n. 86
3–6	22 n. 85

Sirach
1:1	273
1:16	45

Wisdom of Solomon
1:4	151
2:24	102
15:17	27

New Testament

Matthew
3:7	64
3:17	51
4:10	xlviii, 96, 173
5:7	262
5:11–12	90
5:17	72
5:20	188, 228
5:43	228
5:44	237
5:45	39, 238
6:8	162
6:10	159
6:13	196, 197
6:24	118
7:5	228
8:17	255
11:25	256
11:29–30	120
12:8	8

Index of Biblical Citations 299

12:27	46	16:16	5, 72
12:39	64	17:34	180
13:17	77	18:1	197
13:33	xxiv	22:27	255
13:53–57	190	22:31–32	165
15:18–19	127	23:34	238
18:19	263 n. 69	24:13	12 n. 29
19:17	132	24:21	12
20:22	161		
21:43	186	John	
22:13	239, 240	1:5	199
22:21	236	1:14	lxxxviii, 10
22:39	237	1:29	80
23:37	64	1:45	45
24:24	169	1:47	186
26:41	152	2:19	112
26:65	254	2:21	112
27:3–4	178	3:18	47
27:21–54	11	4:22	177
28:7	48	4:23–24	16
28:19	87	4:24	lxxxviii, 10
28:20	87, 264, 274	5:23	95, 248
		5:46	186
Mark		6:38	253
3:14–15	12	6:41	253
6:21–28	206	6:42	190
16:7	48	6:66–67	164, 177
		6:70–71	164
Luke		7:48	207
1:8–23	84	8:28	12
1:36	267	8:34	100, 117
2:29	121, 159, 198	8:44	154
2:52	8	10:20	206
3:6	152	10:21	206
4:6	33	12:19	208
4:11	228	12:32	12
8:11	187	12:42–43	195
8:12	13	13:34	223
9:48	51	14:9	lxxxiv
10:1	164, 177	14:26	lxxxvi
10:5	14	14:27	248, 263
10:20	177	15:13	254
11:52	206	16:14	lxxxvi
13:21	xxiv	16:15	lxxxvi
15:12–13	155	16:18	206

John (cont.)

17:3	xlvii, 9, 116		
17:12	203		
17:18	255		
19:12	cv		

Acts of the Apostles

1:9	168
1:17	178
2:4	221
2:4–11	91
3:15	53, 270
3:17	193
4:11	190
4:12	9, 80
8:3	179
9:1–5	179
9:15	lxxxi
10	71
10:1–11:18	256 n. 27
10:2	cxvii
10:34	176, 178
10:36	8, 196
11:1	257 n. 27
11:2	257 n. 27
11:18	257
13:9	7 n. 1
14:3	259
14:22	90
15:10	189, 189 n. 100
16:1–3	cii n. 18, 271
16:3	civ, 226
16:7	20
18:1–4	19 n. 69
18:9	20
18:10	20
18:18–19	19 n. 69
18:24–28	265
21:7–23:11	17 n. 64
21:24	226
23:11	17
23:12–24:25	17 n. 64
24:26–27	17 n. 64
25:10–12	17 n. 64
27:1–28:10	17 n. 64

Romans

1:1	lxxxvi, lxxxviii, xciii
1:1–17	5
1:3	lxxxviii
1:4	11 n. 28
1:7	19
1:8	270
1:13	260
1:17	23 n. 90, 67 n. 78
1:20	123
1:22–23	xcviii
1:24	30 n. 142, 31
1:25	30 nn. 140-41
1:26	30 n. 142
1:26–27	31 n. 142
1:27	31 n. 145
1:29–32	33 n. 158
1:31	34 n. 159, 35 n. 164
1:32	34 n. 159, 35 n. 164, 37
2:12–13	46
2:14	119
2:15	47
2:15–16	235
2:16	41 n. 22
2:17–24	52 n. 86
2:17–29	55
2:21-23	49 n. 65
2:29	147
3:4	56 n. 8
3:4–6	56 n. 8
3:10–18	61 n. 44
3:12	63
3:13–18	61 n. 44
3:21–22	66 n. 78
3:24	xciii, xcv
3:27	cvi
4:3	86
4:7–8	78 n. 16
4:10	lxviii n. 30
5:1–11	96 n. 43
5:12	xxxi, xxxix, 95 n. 41
5:12–21	xci
5:14	xl, xci
5:15–21	96
6:4	238

6:6	113 n. 18	16:3–15	272 n. 40
6:7	113 n. 18	16:16	272
6:12	103	16:19	xxxv
6:13	67 n. 78		
7:6	128	1 Corinthians	
7:18–25	138 n. 96	1:14–16	cxii
8:3	xci	1:24	lxxxiv n. 31
8:14–17	163	4:1	259
8:24-25	195	5:6	xcii
8:29–30	171	5:7	lxviii n. 30
8:32	lxxiv	5:12	47
8:34	166 n. 138	6:13	247
8:35–39	171	7:5	cxvi
9:1–5	177	7:34–35	cxxvi
9:5	30, 30 nn. 140-41, 172 n. 6	8:5	xcix
9:8	175 n. 22	8:6	8, 8 n. 10, 16, 20, 45, 50, 166, 188, 197, 273
9:12	179		
9:13	179	10:4	190
9:14	183 n. 68	10:33	253
9:14–29	183 n. 68	11:3–16	cxxiv
9:15–18	183 n. 68	11:7	cxxiv
9:17–10:11	xxxvi	11:10	cxxv
9:18	183 n. 68	11:26	lxvii n. 30
9:19	183 n. 68	12:26	227
9:21	xcii	13:2	cviii
9:28	186 n. 80	14:22	ciii
10:3	67 n. 78	14:34	cxxv
10:4	53	16:1	226
10:5	75 n. 4	16:21	272 n. 40
10:12	197		
10:13	197 n. 25	2 Corinthians	
11:1–24	177	1:3	lxxxiii
11:8	213	2:11	168 n. 150
11:13	45	2:16	144
11:16	xcii	2:17	50
11:25	218	3:7	144
11:36	lxxxiii, 119	3:15	193
12:5	159	3:16	54
12:11	lxvii n. 28	5:4	lxxxvi
12:20	lxviii n. 30	5:18–21	lxxxiv
13:2	76	5:19	xcv
14:1–2	246	5:20	13
14:17	198	6:16–18	
14:18	96, 96 n. 46, 173	10:3	147
16:3	19 n. 69	12:9	161

2 Corinthians (cont.)		3:9	23 n. 90
12:12	178	3:19	54
Galatians		Colossians	
2:5	lxv n. 17	1	lxxxiv
2:10	226	1:15–16	lxxxiv
2:18	52	2:8	c
3:11	cv	2:8–9	ci
3:12	75 n. 4	2:13–15	xciv
3:13	xciv, 69, 69 n. 96	2:15	146
3:20	4 n. 4	2:16	45
4:9	c	2:20	c
4:9–10	ci	3:11	lxxiv
4:23–24	lxix	4:6	225
4:26	199	4:18	272
5:4	83		
5:9	xcii	1 Thessalonians	
5:24	lxviii n. 68, 114, 272	2:19	17
6:1–2	227	3:9–10	lxxx
6:7	118	4:3	220
6:11	272		
		2 Thessalonians	
Ephesians		2:4	33
1:4	lxxxi n. 21	3:17	272 n. 40
1:7	xciii		
2:3	lxxxv, 64, 64 n. 59	1 Timothy	
2:4	247, 247 n. 37	1:4	270
2:17	185	1:9	43
3:9	9, 273	2	lxxxiii
3:15	15	2:4	180
3:17	lxxxvi	2:5	89
3:19	xcvi	2:7	lxxvii, 258
5:2	lxxiv	2:11–14	cxxv
5:16	225	2:12	cxxiv
6:12	134, 154	2:14	96 n. 44
6:13	xcv n. 66	3:11	cxii
6:13–17	lxx n. 35	3:12–13	cxxii
		4:2	cix
Philippians		4:14	cxix
1:23	121 n. 71	5	cxxvii
2:5–11	lxxxix		
2:6	lxxxix	2 Timothy	
2:7	lxxix	1:7	154
2:10	25, 173	2:20	cxiii
3:5	civ	3:8	168

4:4	cx
Titus	
1:13	cvi
2:11	lxxxii
3:5	153
3:9	270
Philemon	
19	272 n. 40
Hebrews	
7:14	182
8:13	128
James	
2:23	242
1 Peter	
4:6	195
1 John	
1:1	272
1:5–8	272
2:15–16	149
2:19	178
3:2	113, 155
3:8	22, 33
3:9	154
2 John	
7	230
Revelation	
2:11	9, 97 n. 54
2:24	168, 168 n. 150
3:16	224
5:1–4	187
13:8	105
19:10	173
20:6	9, 97 n. 54
20:14	9, 97 n. 54
21:8	9, 97 n. 54

Index of Ancient Works

Greco-Roman Literature

Celsus, *De medicina*
   proem. 23–26 — 182 n. 65

Cicero, *De inventione rhetorica*
   2.40 — lxvii n. 25

Cicero, *In Catalinam*
   1.21 — 91 n. 15

Codex justinianus
   7.45.14 — 125 n. 12

Livy, *Ab urbe condita*
   3.31.8 — 123 n. 4

Porphyry, *Quaestionum homericarum ad Odysseam pertinentium reliquae*
   12–14 — lxvi

Quintilian, *Institutio oratoria*
   8.6.44 — lxix n. 32
   9.3.23–27 — lxvi n. 21
   9.4.44–53 — lxvi n. 22

Rhetorica ad Herennium
   4.1 — lxvi n. 21

Tacitus, *Historiae*
   1.4 — lxxii n. 46

Rabbinic Literature

Mekilta of Rabbi Ishmael, Bahodesh
   5 — 43 n. 31

Mishnah Qiddushin
   3:12 — civ n. 28

Mishnah Yebamot
   7:5 — civ n. 28

Sifre Deuteronomy
   343 — 43 n. 31

Christian Literature

Acts of Peter
   3 — 268 n. 17
   4 — 168 n. 149, 268 n. 17
   6 — 268 n. 17
   13 — 268 n. 17
   14 — 268 n. 17

Ad Gallos episcopos
   1.2 — cxxi n. 15
   2.5 — cxxi n. 15

Ambrose, *De officiis ministrorum* — cxxi
   249 — cxxi n. 15

Ambrose, *Enarrationes in XII Psalmos Davidicos*
   36.63.3 — 176 n. 25

Index of Ancient Works 305

Ambrose, *Epistulae*
   7.1   lxiv n. 15

Ambrose, *Expositio Psalmi CXVIII*
   serm.10.35   181 n. 56

Ambrosiaster, Commentarius in Epistulam ad Colossenses
   1:15 (§3)   lxxxiv
   1:18 (§2)   96 n. 44
   1:25–26   54 n. 100
   2:1–3 (§2)   xc
   2:1–3 (§3)   ci
   2:8   c
   2:8–9 (§§1–3)   26 n. 114
   2:8–9 (§2)   ci
   2:8–9 (§3)   ci
   2:11–12 (§2)   c n. 13
   2:13–15   98 n. 59
   2:13–15 (§§3–6)   125 n. 15
   2:13–15 (§6)   xciv–xcv
   2:13–15 (§7)   cii
   2:18–19 (§2)   c
   2:20   c
   2:20 (§2)   c n.15
   3:5 (§2)   xcix, c
   3:5 (§§2–3)   c, c n. 12

Ambrosiaster, Commentarius in Epistulam ad Corinthios primam
   argumentum (§2)   cviii
   1:2 (§2)   cix
   1:13 (§1)   xl
   1:14–16 (§2)   cxii
   2:1–2 (§§1–2)   lxxxviii
   2:10 (§1)   lxxx n. 19, lxxxi
   2:11 (§2)   lxxxvi n. 35
   4:8 (§1)   lxvi n. 22
   5:6   97 n. 51
   5:7   lxviii n. 30
   6:18 (§§1–5)   cxiii
   7:5 (§§1–2)   xxviii n. 25
   7:33–34   xl
   7:35 (§2)   cxxvii
   7:40   xxviii n. 24, cxv
   8:5   xcix
   8:6   8 n. 10
   10:14   xci
   10:19–20   c
   11:5–7 (§2)   cxxiv, 102 n. 90
   11:8–10   cxxv
   11:23–25   lxxx
   11:26   lxviii n. 30
   12:6 (§1)   lxxxvi n. 35
   12:28   civ
   13:2 (§3)   cviii
   13:4–8 (§1)   247 n. 37
   14:14   xxviii n. 24, cxvi
   14:19   cxvi
   14:31   ciii
   14:34   cxxv, cxxv n. 19
   15:24–26   xlvii n. 78
   15:39   97 n. 51
   16:21–24   xxxvii n. 42

Ambrosiaster, Commentarius in Epistulam ad Corinthios secundam
   1:21 (§2)   lxxxvi n. 36
   2:17   50 n. 69
   5:4   lxxxvi, lxxxvi n. 35
   5:17   lxxxii
   5:18–21 (§1)   xcv
   5:18–21 (§§1–2)   lxxxvi n. 39
   5:18–21 (§2)   lxxxiv, 217 n. 73
   6:16–18 (§1)   163 n. 127
   10:4   lxxxi
   10:7   lxxvii n. 1
   11:1   lxvi n. 23
   11:19 (§2)   lxvi
   11:26 (§1)   lxxxviii
   13:3   xxxv–xxxvi

Ambrosiaster, Commentarius in Epistulam ad Ephesios
   1:7   xciii
   1:9 (§1)   xciii
   1:17 (§2)   lxxxiii
   2:1–2   c n. 13
   2:3   lxxxv
   2:3 (§1)   ci

Ambrosiaster, In Eph. (cont.)
2:3 (§2)	217 n. 73
2:4	247 n. 37
2:17–18	cvii n. 42
2:19	cvii n. 42
3:9–11	lxxxii n. 25
3:10 (§1)	lxxxii
3:10 (§2)	c n. 13
3:17 (§§2–3)	lxxxvi
3:19 (§2)	xcvi
4:11–12 (§2)	civ
4:11–12 (§§2–5)	xxviii n. 23
4:11–12 (§4)	cxviii
4:11–12 (§5)	cxviii
4:26	lxxiv n. 55
5:5 (§1)	xcix, c
5:5 (§§1–2)	c
6:20	xxxviii

Ambrosiaster, Commentarius in Epistulam ad Galatas
argumentum	lxxiv n. 52
1:6	lxxiii n. 50
1:13–14 (§2)	cvi
1:19	xl
1:23	xxxviii
2:4–5 (§§4–5)	civ
2:5 (§8)	lxv n. 17
2:8	lxxvii n. 1
3:1	lxvi
3:13 (§2)	cv
3:13 (§4)	cv
3:14	cv n. 36
4:6	lxxxvi n. 36
4:9	c
4:10 (§§1–2)	ci
4:23 (§1)	174 n. 21
5:2	lxxvii n. 1
5:4	lxvi, lxviii n. 28
5:9	97 n. 51
5:12	lviii n. 8
5:24 (§§1–2)	lxviii n. 27, 114 n. 28

Ambrosiaster, Commentarius in Epistulam ad Philippenses
1:1	cxviii n. 9
1:8	lxxxviii n. 46
1:18–21	lxvi
2:6–7 (§6)	xc
2:7–8 (§2)	xc
2:7–8 (§§4–5)	lxxxix, lxxxix n. 48
2:9–11	lxxiii n. 50
2:9–11 (§9)	168 n. 15, 217 n. 73
2:10	lxxxvii
2:13–14	lxxiv n. 55
3:5–6 (§1)	cviii n. 46
3:19	54 n. 101

Ambrosiaster, Commentarius in Epistulam ad Philemonem
1:22	xxxvi n. 34

Ambrosiaster, Commentarius in Epistulam ad Romanos
1:1	lxxxvii–lxxxviii
1:1 (§1)	xlviii
1:1 (§§2–3)	lxxxviii
1:1 (§3)	51 n. 81, 152 n. 61
1:1 (§5)	liii, liii n. 93
1:1 (§5a)	xlvii, xlvii n. 77, lxxxii, xciii
1:2 (§3)	lxxx n. 19, lxxxi, lxxxii n. 24
1:3	lxxxvii
1:3 (§2)	lxxxviii
1:3 (§3)	258 n. 30
1:3–4	lxxiv n. 52
1:4 (§1)	lxxxii
1:5 (§2)	171 n. 2
1:7 (§1)	liii
1:8 (§§1–3, 4)	271 n. 36
1:9–10 (§4)	xlviii n. 81, 17 n. 63, 260 n. 47, 265 n. 3
1:9–10 (§7)	16 n. 59
1:10 (§2a)	8 n. 10
1:11 (§2)	41 n. 19, 82 n. 45
1:13 (§1)	16 n. 59, 17 n. 63
1:13 (§§1–2)	13 n. 40
1:14	lxxxvii n. 1
1:16 (§2)	liii, xci n. 54

1:17 (§1a)	liv	3:23 (§1)	68 n. 88
1:17 (§2)	41 n. 19, 67 n. 83	3:24	xciii–xciv, xcv
1:18–19	lxxxii n. 24	3:26 (§1a)	cv
1:19	xci	3:26 (§3)	xcvi n. 68
1:20	xci	4:4	xcv n. 66
1:20 (§2)	xliv–xlv	4:10	lxviii n. 30
1:22 (§1)	c	4:16 (§2)	119 n. 58
1:22 (§§1–1a)	c	4:25 (§2)	xcii
1:23 (§1)	xcviii	5:2	95 n. 38
1:23 (§2)	lxxiv n. 55	5:7 (§§3a–4a)	178 n. 41
1:23 (§§3–5)	xcix	5:12	xxxi, xxxix
1:25 (§§1–2)	xcix	5:12 (§1)	xcii
1:27 (§2)	35 n. 166	5:12 (§2a)	98 n. 61
1:29–32	liv–lv	5:12 (§§2a–3)	xxxix n. 57
1:29–32 (§1a)	xci n. 53	5:12 (§3)	xcii, 121 n. 71, 134 n. 67, 184 n. 69
1:30–32 (§§1a–2a)	c		
1:30–32 (§2a)	c	5:12 (§§3–4)	129 n. 41, 140 n. 110
2:3 (§3)	c n. 15, cii	5:12 (§4)	xcii, 125 n. 15, 184 n. 69
2:4 (§1)	xlvii, xlvii n. 79	5:13 (§3)	36 n. 167
2:4 (§2)	39 n. 10, 40 n. 16	5:13 (§4)	lxxxii n. 24
2:12 (§1)	79 n. 25	5:14	xci n. 52, 105 n. 104
2:12 (§2)	43 n. 29	5:14 (§2)	xci n. 53
2:14	8 n. 10	5:14 (§3a)	xcii, 98 n. 56
2:28 (§2)	lxxxii	5:14 (§4)	224 n. 36
2:28–29 (§1)	52 n. 84	5:14 (§4a)	xcii
3:1–2 (§1)	205 n. 9	5:14 (§4d)	xci n. 53
3:4	liii, liv	5:14 (§4e)	xl, lix n. 11
3:4 (§3)	xlix	5:14 (§5)	xl, lix n. 11
3:4 (§5a)	69 n. 97	5:14 (§5a)	xl, lix n. 11, 151 n. 50, 225 n. 37
3:4–9	liii–liv		
3:5	xlix	5:17 (§1)	xcii
3:6	liii	6:3	111 n. 3, 140 n. 114
3:7	liii, liii n. 97	6:4 (§1)	112 n. 7
3:8	xlix	6:6	xci n. 53
3:8 (§1)	xlix, liii	6:12 (§1)	116 n. 41
3:8 (§2)	liii, liii n. 99	6:20–21 (§1a)	xcix
3:8 (§2a)	liv, liv n. 100	7:5 (§1)	205 n. 9
3:9	liv, liv n. 102	7:5 (§§1–2)	239 n. 41
3:20 (§§1–1a)	75 n. 3, 194 n. 5, 195 n. 12, 228 n. 60	7:5 (§2)	121 n. 71
		7:5 (§4)	205 n. 9
3:20 (§1a)	205 n. 12	7:14 (§1a)	145 n. 11
3:20 (§4)	cvi	7:14 (§§2–3)	97 n. 52
3:21	216 n. 65, 220 n. 8	7:18 (§§1–2)	145 n. 13, 184 n. 69
3:21 (§2)	66 n. 78, 69 n. 100, 233 n. 6	7:20	184 n. 69
3:22 (§2)	9 n. 13		

Ambrosiaster, In Rom. (cont.)
7:22 xciii n. 60, 141 n. 120, 145 n. 13, 184 n. 69
7:23 (§2) 145 n. 11
7:24 (§1a) xcii
7:24 (§5) 97 n. 53, 138 n. 97
8:1 146 n. 22
8:3 (§1) xcii
8:4 (§2) 143 n. 1
8:7 (§§1–2) ci, 148 n. 36
8:12 xcvi
8:12 (§1) xci–xcii
8:13 (§1) 239 n. 41
8:13 (§2) xcvi
8:19 158 n. 93
8:20 (§1a) lxxxi
8:22 (§1) c
8:27 (§1a) 217 n. 74
8:29 (§3) lxxxii
8:30 (§2a) 177 n. 33
8:34 (§2) 273 n. 45
8:39 (§2) 268 n. 17
8:39 (§3) 25 n. 106, 116 n. 40, 166 n. 138
9:1–4 (§2) cv
9:5 (§4) xlviii n. 84, 96 n. 46
9:11–13 (§3) cv
9:13 (§4a) 164 n. 131
9:17–10:11 xxxvi
9:21 (§1) 97 n. 51
9:23 (§§1–2) 184 n. 71
9:30 (§1) 8 n. 10
9:31 189 n. 99
9:32 (§1a) cvi
9:32 (§2a) 188 n. 93
9:32 (§3) 9 n. 13
9:33 (§§2–3) 195 n. 17
10:7 (§2) 205 n. 12
10:19 (§2) cvi
10:20 201 n. 48
10:21 (§1) 254 n. 6
11:8–10 (§§1a–4) 212 n. 46
11:16 97 n. 51
11:33 (§§1–2) 66 n. 78
11:36 (§1) lxxxiii
11:36 (§2) lxxxvi
12:1–2 (§1b) 233 n. 4
12:6 (§1) 220 n. 11
12:11 (§1b) xl, lix n. 11, 102 n. 91, 103 n. 96
12:11 (§2) xl n. 59
12:13 (§1a) lv
12:16 (§4) 220 n. 8
12:17 (§§1–1a) 220 n. 8
12:20 lxviii n. 30
12:21 220 n. 8
13:1 (§1a) 238 n. 33
13:1 (§2) 235 n. 14
13:2 76 n. 7
13:4 (§2) 233 n. 5
13:10 (§§2–2a) 233 n. 3
14:4 (§1) 242 n. 13
14:6 (§2) 243 n. 16
14:9 (§1) 116 n. 40
14:11 lxxxiii
14:16 244 n. 25
14:20 (§§1, 4) 244 n. 25
15:3 (§§1–3) 201 n. 49
15:15 lxxxvii n. 1
15:22–24 (§1) 16 n. 59
16:3–5 (§1) 16 n. 59, 19 n. 69
16:3–5 xxvi, xxvi n. 14
16:16 (§2) 116 n. 40
16:19 xxxv
16:25–27 (§1) lxxxvi, 54 n. 100, 166 n. 138

Ambrosiaster, Commentarius in Epistulam ad Thessalonicenses primam
2:7 c n. 13
2:15–16 cv n. 36
3:9–10 lxxx
3:9–10 (§2) xl, lxxxiv–lxxxv, lxxxv n. 32
4:18 (§§2–3) 197 n. 26
5:22 (§3) cxii
5:26 269 n. 24

Index of Ancient Works

Ambrosiaster, Commentarius in Epistulam ad Thessalonicenses secundam
- 2:7 — xl, ci n. 17
- 2:16 — 217 n. 73
- 2:16–17 — lxxxiii

Ambrosiaster, Commentarius in Epistulam ad Timotheum primam
- *argumentum* — civ
- 2:1–4 — xlvii n. 78
- 2:1–4 (§1) — 262 n. 62
- 2:5 — 89 n. 4
- 2:5 (§1) — lxxxiv
- 2:13–14 — cxxv n. 19
- 2:14 (§1) — 96 n. 44
- 3:3–4 — cxxvi
- 3:8–10 (§1) — cxix
- 3:8–10 (§2) — cxviii
- 3:11 — cxii
- 3:12 (§1) — xxviii n. 24, cxv
- 3:12–13 (§§2–3) — cxxii
- 3:12–13 (§3) — cxviii
- 3:12–13 (§§3–4) — cxxiii
- 3:12–13 (§4) — cxv
- 3:14–15 (§1) — xl
- 3:15 — xxvi, xxvi n. 13
- 4:2 (§5) — cix
- 4:13–14 (§2) — cxx
- 5:1–2 (§1) — ciii
- 5:14–15 — cxxvii
- 5:21–22 (§1) — 222 n. 15

Ambrosiaster, Commentarius in Epistulam ad Timotheum secundam
- 2:20 (§1) — cxiii
- 3:6–7 (§2) — cx
- 4:4 (§3) — cx
- 4:22 — lxxxviii

Ambrosiaster, Commentarius in Epistulam ad Titum
- 1:13 (§2) — cvi
- 1:13 (§4) — cvi n. 40
- 1:14 (§2) — 81 n. 41
- 1:14 (§§2–3) — 189 n. 100
- 2:11 (§1) — lxxxii
- 3:9 (§2) — 81 n. 41, 189 n. 95

Ambrosiaster, *Quaestiones veteris et novi testamenti*
- 2.3 — 102 n. 90
- 3.1 — cix
- 3.4 — xlvii n. 78
- 4.1 — 98 n. 62, 99 n. 71
- 4.4 — cv n. 32
- 21 — cxxiv
- 23 — 137 n. 95
- 27.2 — 168 n. 150
- 31.1 — 168 n. 150
- 33.2 — 9 n. 16
- 36 — 234 n. 12
- 37.1 — 201 n. 47
- 38 — lxviii n. 31
- 39 — 172 n. 5
- 44 — ciii n. 21
- 44.3 — 9 n. 13
- 44.9 — cvi n. 41
- 44.11–13 — 201 n. 43
- 44.12 — ciii n. 21
- 45 — cxxiv
- 45.3 — cxxiv
- 47.4 — 9 n. 16
- 65.1–2 — 201 n. 49
- 77.2 — 12 n. 29
- 80.1 — 182 n. 61
- 81.1 — civ n. 28, 52 n. 85
- 84.3 — lxxx
- 91 — cvii n. 44
- 91.6 — xlviii n. 84
- 91.8 — 172 n. 6, 235 n. 19
- 92 — ciii n. 21
- 97 — lxxvii n. 2, lxxix n. 15, cvii n. 44
- 97.5 — 166 n. 140
- 97.7 — 163 n. 127
- 97.8 — 166 n. 140
- 97.11 — 166 n. 140
- 101 — xxvi n. 15, xxviii, cxix n. 11, cxx, 221 n. 12
- 101.2 — cxx
- 101.3 — cxx n. 13

Ambrosiaster, Quaestiones (cont.)

101.4	cxviii n. 8
101.5	222 n. 15
102	xxvi n. 15, cvii n. 44, cxii, cxiii
102.22	cxiii n. 61
102.28–32	cxiii
102.31	cxvii n. 7
106.17	cxxiv, 234 n. 12
108	civ
108.1	c
110.2	32 n. 152
110.6	234 n. 11
110.7	cviii n. 46
112.8	xcii n. 58
113.1	xlvii n. 78
113.5–7	c n.13
114	xxvii, xcviii
114.7–8	xcix n. 8, 120 n. 68
114.11	28 n. 127, 120 n. 68
115	xxvi, xxvii, xcviii, cii
115.5	268 n. 15
115.16	xxvi n. 14
115.18	xcix n. 8, 120 n. 68
115.82	45 n. 43
116	cxvi n. 5
117.3–5	86 n. 64
120	xxviii n. 24, xxviii n. 26
120.3	cxvi–cxvii
120.5	cxvii
121	cxvi n. 5
122	lxxxiv n. 31
122.12	lxxxvi n. 39
123.16	9 n. 15
124	cxxvii
124.1	cxxvii
124.2	cxxvii
124.7	cxxvii
125.5	lxxxvi n. 38
125.12	lxxx
125.16	lxxx
127	cxxi–cxxii, cxxvi
127.3	xxviii n. 24, cxv n. 1
127.17	cvii n. 45
127.17–18	cix
127.18	cvii n. 45, cix, cx
127.29–30	cxxv n. 19
127.34	cviii
127.35	cxvi
127.35–36	xxviii n. 25, cxvi n. 4
127.36	cxxii
app. 18	87 n. 70
app. 51	cvi n. 41
app. 60.2	civ n. 27
app. 75.2	cvi n. 41, 123 n. 4
app. 78.1	xlvii n. 78

Apocyrphon of John

11.15–20	cix n. 48

Augustine, *Confessionum libri XIII*

5.10.19	cix n. 49
7.19.25	cxi

Augustine, *Contra duas epistulas Pelagianorum ad Bonifatium*

4.4.7	xxxix n. 57, 97 n. 51

Augustine, *Contra Faustum Manichaeum*

30.4	cix n. 47

Augustine, *De diversis quaestionibus ad Simplicianum*

	xxv n. 11

Augustine, *De haeresibus*

46.1	cvii n. 45

Augustine, *Enarrationes in Psalmos*

72.4	7 n. 2

Augustine, *Epistulae*

37	xxv n. 11

Augustine, *In epistulam Johannis ad Parthos tractatus*

8.2	7 n. 2

Augustine, *Retractionum libri II*

1.6(7)	cx n. 51

Index of Ancient Works

Augustine, *Sermones*
130   xciv n. 63
295.7   7 n. 2

Cassiodorus, *Institutiones divinarum et saecularium litterarum*
1.8.10   xxxii n. 5

Cyprian, *Ad Quirinium testimonia adversus Judaeos*
2.5   197 n. 26
2.6   163 n. 127, 172 n. 6
3.20   197 n. 25

Cyprian, *Epistulae*
5.2.2   225 n. 37

Epiphanius, *Panarion (Adversus haereses)*
49.2.5   cxii n. 57

Eusebius, *Historia ecclesiastica*
6.43.11–12   cxviii n. 8

Filastrius of Brescia, *Diversarum hereseon liber*   cvii

Gospel of Judas
13.1–7   cix n. 48

Gregory of Nazianzus, *Oratio panegyrica in Origenem*
29   lxxxv n. 34

Hilary of Poitiers, *De Trinitate*
4.23–24   197 n. 26
5.4–5   168 n. 151
6.11   165 n. 138
7.5   165 n. 138
7.8   165 n. 138
10.22   xc n. 49

Jerome, *Adversus Jovinianum libri II*
2.16   244 n. 21

Jerome, *Commentariorum in Epistulam ad Titum liber*
1:5b   cxix n. 11

Jerome, *Commentariorum in Osee libri III*
1.2.16–17   28 n. 125

Jerome, *Epistulae*
27   xxvi, xl, 224 n. 35
146   cxix, cxix n. 11

Jerome, *Liber Didymi de Spiritu Sancto*
39   151 n. 50

Jerome, *Quaestionum hebraicum liber in Genesim*
22.20–22   176 n. 25

Innocent I, *Epistulae*
2.8.11   cxiii n. 60
6.2.6   cxiii n. 60
17.5.10   cxiii n. 60
25.5.8   cxix

Lactantius, *Divinarum institutionem libri VII*
1.23.2   28 n. 125

Leo I, *Epistulae*
12.6   cxiii n. 60

Marius Victorinus, *Adversus Arium*
1.18   172 n. 6
4.14   lxxxiii n. 28

Mosaicarum et Romanarum legum collatio   xxiv, xxiv n. 8
15.3   cx n. 50

Novatian, *De Trinitate*
13.6   172 n. 6
30.18   172 n. 6

Origen, *Fragmentum ex homiliis in Deuteronomium*   43 n. 31

Origen-Rufinus, *Commentarii in Romanos*
2.1   77 n. 16

Origen-Rufinus, *In Rom.* (*cont.*)
7.14   181 n. 56
9.10   225 n. 37
9.12   226 n. 44

Pelagius, Commentarius in Epistulam ad Philippenses
2:5–8   xc

Pelagius, Commentarius in Epistulam ad Romanos
4:8   78 n. 16
12:13   226 n. 44

Pseudo-Clementines, Recognitions
3.47.2   168 n. 149

Pseudo-Jerome, Indiculus de haeresibus
                                               cvii

Pseudo-Tertullian, Adversus omnes haereses   cvii

Rufinus, *Regula Basilii*
196   235 n. 18

Siricius, *Epistulae*
1.7   cxxi n. 15
5.3   cxxi n. 15

Tertullian, *Adversus Marcionem*   lxii n. 4
5.14   151 n. 50

Tertullian, *Adversus Praxean*
8   lxxxv n. 33

Tertullian, *De anima*
10.4   182 n. 65

Tertullian, *De idolatria*
1.1   c n. 12

Tertullian, *De resurrectione carnis*
46.4   151 n. 50

Theodoret, *Historia ecclesiastica*
5.10   lxxviii n. 8

Index of Manuscripts

Amiens 87 xxxvii, xxxviii, xxxix, lii, lii nn. 88–91, liii, liii nn. 95–96, liv, 4 n. 9, 5 n. 12, 5 n. 14, 9 n. 13, 14 n. 41, 14 n. 45, 15 n. 53, 16 n. 55, 17 n. 60, 17 n. 63, 21 nn. 77–79, 22 n. 80, 22 n. 83, 23 n. 88, 23 n. 90, 24 n. 94, 29 n. 131, 30 n. 141, 31 n. 144, 32 n. 150, 38 n. 4, 46 n. 49, 49 nn. 65–66, 50 n. 67, 53 n. 89, 57 n. 14, 60 n. 30, 60 n. 32, 60 n. 35, 61 n. 37, 61 n. 39, 157 n. 85, 162 n. 116, 193 n. 2, 196 n. 19, 196 n. 23, 199 n. 33, 203 n. 4

Ashburnham 60 xxxvii
Augiensis 108 xxxviii, xxxix
Brussels 971 xxxvii
Brussels 972 xxxvii
Budapest 1 lxiii, 268 n. 19
Clm 6265 xxxii, xxxiii, xxxv, xxxvi, xxxvii
Cologne 34 xxxv, xxxvii, liv
Cologne 39 xxxvi, xxxviii, liv
Dublin 52 xxxvi
Fulda Aa 18 xxxvii
Göttweig 42 xxxv, xxxvi
Graz 369 xxxvi
Guelf. 64 Weiss xxxii, xxxix, xxxix n. 56
Laon 107 xxxviii
Laud. Misc. 106 xxxvi, xxxvi n. 36
Lyell 9 xxxviii, xxxix
Monte Cassino 150 xxxii, xxxvii, xxxvii n. 43, xxxix, xxxix n. 56, xl n. 57, lii, liii, liv, 66 n. 76, 71 n. 118, 76 nn. 8–9, 81 n. 36, 85 n. 60, 151 n. 53, 157 n. 85, 158 n. 91, 159 n. 100, 162 n. 116, 166 n. 143, 188 n. 93, 196 n. 19, 199 n. 33, 203 n. 2, 204 n. 6, 210 n. 31, 212 n. 47, 224 n. 29, 224 n. 33, 225 n. 41, 255 n. 13, 257 n. 28, 258 n. 29, 271 n. 37

Monza C 2 xxxvii, xxxviii
Oxford 157 268 n. 19
Oxford 756 xxxvii, lii n. 91, 60 n. 35, 157 n. 85, 160 n. 105, 193 n. 2
Padua 94 xxxvii
Paris lat. 1759 xxxviii, lii, lii nn. 88–89, lii n. 91, liii, lv, 14 n. 45, 17 n. 60, 21 nn. 77–79, 22 n. 83, 23 n. 88, 24 n. 94, 31 n. 144, 32 n. 154, 33 n. 158, 34 n. 159, 35 n. 165, 39 n. 10, 41 n. 21, 42 n. 27, 46 n. 49, 46 n. 51, 48 n. 59, 49 nn. 65–66, 50 n. 67, 53 n. 89, 57 n. 14, 59 n. 28, 60 n. 30, 60 n. 32, 60 n. 35, 61 n. 37, 61 n. 39, 72 n. 121, 76 nn. 8–9, 81 nn. 36–37, 83 n. 49, 86 n. 62, 98 n. 63, 113 n. 18, 130 n. 42, 151 n. 53, 157 n. 85, 159 n. 100, 160 n. 105, 166 n. 143, 193 n. 2, 196 n. 23, 219 n. 3, 225 n. 41, 230 n. 72, 231 n. 79, 232 n. 86, 237 n. 30, 238 n. 31, 239 n. 44, 240 n. 50, 240 n. 55, 241 nn. 5–6, 242 n. 7, 246 n. 31, 247 n. 38, 248 n. 42, 253 n. 4, 254 n. 10, 257 n. 28, 258 n. 29

Paris lat. 1761 xxxvii
Paris lat. 1763 xxxvii
Paris lat. 13339 xxxviii
Salzburg a IX 25 xxxii–xxxiii, xxxv, xxxvi
St. Gall 100 xxxvii
St. Gall 101 xxxvii, lii, lii n. 91, liv, 21 n. 77, 23 n. 88, 30 n. 141, 31 n. 143, 32 n. 150, 42 nn. 26–27, 60 n. 35, 71 n. 118, 157 n. 85, 160 n. 105, 217 n. 75, 237 n. 30, 241 n. 3, 250 n. 49

St. Gall 330	xxxviii
St. Mihiel 16	xxxviii
Trier 122	xxxviii
Troyes 128	xxxvii, 217 n. 75, 231 n. 79, 241 n. 3
Troyes 432	xxxix
Vat. lat. 4919	xxxvi
Verona 75	xxxvi, xxxviii
Vienna 743	xxxviii, liv, 157 n. 85
Vienna 4600	xxxvii
Zwettl 33	xxxv, xxxvi

Index of Modern Authors

Ballerini, Paulo Angelo xxxiv
Bévenot, Maurice cxix n. 10
Bray, Gerald L. xlii
Brewer, H. xxxiv–xxxv
Brown, Peter cxxvi
Bruyn, Theodore S. de xxvii, xlii
Bussières, Marie-Pierre xxv n. 9, n. 12, xxvii, lxxix
Cohen, Jeremy civ
Cohen, Shaye J. D. civ
Cooper, Stephen A. xxvii
Denecker, Tim civ
Di Santo, Emanuele xcvii, civ
Duval, Yves-Marie cxxi n. 14
Fairweather, Janet xli–xlii
Foley, Desmond lxxxvii, xc
Greer, Rowan lxv
Gy, Pierre-Marie cxix n. 10
Hanslik, Rudolf liii, 140 n. 116, 141 n. 117
Hornung, Christian cxxi n. 14
Hunter, David G. xxvii, cxxi n. 16, cxxiii n. 17, cxxvi n. 23
Hušek, Vít xciii, xcv
Jacobs, Andrew xcvii, civ
Krans, Jan xxiii
Langen, Joseph lxxxvi
Lohse, Bernhard lxi
Lunn-Rockliffe, Sophie xxvii, xxviii–xxix, xlviii, cxix n. 11, cxxvii–cxxviii
Martini, Coelestinus lxxx, lxxxvii
Migne, Jacques-Paul xxxiv
Morin, Germain xxv, cii–ciii
Pollastri, Alessandra xcii
Prat, Ferdinand cxix n. 11
Raspanti, Giacomo lxxiv–lxxv
Schäublin, Christoph lxvi n. 24
Simon, Richard lxviii
Simonetti, Manlio lxix n. 31
Souter, Alexander xxiii, xxvii–xxviii, lxiv, ciii, cxix n. 11
Stüben, Joachim lxi, lxxii
Tolmie, François lxxiii
Vogels, Heinrich Josef xxvi, xxxiii, xxxiv, xxxv–xli, xlviii, lviii

Index of Subjects

Abraham, cv, 22, 42, 48, 52–53, 55–56, 70, 75–86, 100, 101–2, 174–77, 187, 201, 203, 208, 212, 213, 226, 242, 255, 257
Alexandria, synod of, lxxviii
allegory, lxix
Amalarius of Metz, xxxii
Ambrose of Milan, xxxii–xxxiii, lxviii–lxix, cxi, cxvi n. 3, cxxi n. 15, cxxvi, 68 n. 94
Ambrosiaster
  apologetics, xcvii
  anonymity, xxiv–xxv
  date of writings, xxv–xxvii
  knowledge of Greek, lvii, lxvii, 102 n. 91, 224 n. 26
  as presbyter, xxviii–xxix, cxv
Ambrosiaster's biblical text, xlvii, lvii–lix, 102–4, 224–25, 268. *See also* Vetus Latina
  variance from the Greek text, 13 n. 38, 14 n. 43, 19 n. 67, 24 n. 95, 32 n. 155, 33 n. 157, 41 n. 20, 46 n. 47, 51 n. 82, 69 n. 101, 70 nn. 110–11, 75 n. 1, 79 n. 22, 79 n. 26, 79 n. 28, 81 n. 40, 85 n. 57, 89 n. 1, 89 n. 3, 94 n. 30, 95 nn. 34–35, 95 n. 40, 100 n. 79, 106 n. 108, 112 n. 9, 113 n. 18, 115 n. 32, 117 n. 49, 118 n. 54, 120 n. 63, 127 n. 26, 130 n. 43, 135 nn. 75–76, 136 n. 86, 137 n. 91, 139 n. 103, 151 nn. 50–51, 152 n. 63, 153 n. 70, 159 n. 97, 160 n. 110, 161 n. 113, 167 n. 144, 173 n. 14, 174 n. 16, 176 n. 26, 186 n. 80, 193 n. 1, 195 n.13, 197 n. 27, 198 nn. 28–29,

Ambrosiaster's biblical text: variance from the Greek text (cont.)
  199 nn. 36–37, 201 n. 45, 203 n. 1, 205 n. 8, 209 n. 28, 211 nn. 41–43, 212 n. 45, 215 n. 62, 215 n. 64, 217 n. 69, 227 n. 47, 229 n. 61, 231 n. 76, 233 n. 1, 238 n. 24, 239 n. 40, 242 n. 9, 243 n. 14, 244 n. 21, 245 n. 26, 245 nn. 28–29, 246 nn. 32–33, 247 n. 39, 248 n. 45, 250 n. 50, 253 n. 2, 258 n. 31, 258 n. 34, 259 n. 35, 259 nn. 37–38, 260 n. 46, 261 nn. 50–51, 261 n. 54, 262 nn. 57–58, 262 nn. 60–61, 263 nn. 66–67, 267 nn. 11–12, 270 n. 29, 271 n. 38, 273 nn. 43–44, 273 n. 46
Ambrosiaster's Commentary on the Pauline Epistles
  argumenta, lxxi–lxxiii, xcviii
  authorship, xxxv–xli
  didacticism, lxxiv–lxxv
  editions of, xxxiii–xxxiv
  exegetical methodology, lxv, lxix–lxxv
  genre, lxix
  lemmata, lvii–lviii
  recensions of, xxxv–lv
  scriptural citations in, lxxiii–lxxiv
  transmission of, xxxi–xxxiii, lviii
Ambrosiaster's Commentary on Romans
  argumentum, 3–5
  interpolations in, xlii, liv–lv
  written in Rome, xlviii, 16 n. 59, 17 n. 63, 19 n. 68, 260 n. 47, 265 n. 3
Ambrosiaster's *Quaestiones*, lxxix, xcvii
  authorship, xxiii–xxiv

Index of Subjects

Amerbach, Johann, xxxiii
ancient literary criticism, lxvi, lxix n. 33
Antiochene exegesis, lxvii–lxviii
Apollinaris, lxxvii, lxxxviii, 11 n. 24
apostles; apostleship, 12–13, 22, 259–60, 270
    false, 259–61, 270
Aquila, 4, 19, 265–66
Arius, cvii, cviii, cx
astrology, c–cii, 26–27, 148–49
atonement xciv–xcv
Augustine of Hippo, xxxi, xxxix, lxiii, cvii, cxi
baptism, xcvi, cxiii, cxv, 22, 59 n. 27, 77–78, 87, 111 n. 3, 112–13, 126, 140, 145, 152, 190 n. 103, 214, 238
bishops, cxxv, 262 n. 62, 271. See also clergy
Cassiodorus, xxxi–xxxii, lxiv
Cataphrygians. See Montanists
Chalcedon, council of, lxxxvii
Christology, lxxxvii–xc, 10–11, 155, 165–66, 168–69, 172–73, 197, 273
Cicero, lxvii, 91 n. 15
Claudius of Turin, xxxii, xxxvi
clergy, xxviii, cxvii–cxxiii
Constantinople, council of, xxvii, xl, lxxviii, lxxxvii, cx
Cyprian of Carthage, cxiii, cxix, 104
Damasus, bishop of Rome, xxv, xxvi, xl, lxiii, lxxviii, lxxxiii cii, cxvii, cxxi
David, king of Israel, 179–80, 257
deacons, cxii, 222 n. 15 See also clergy
    conflict with presbyters, xxvi, xxviii, cxx, 221 n. 12
death
    Christ's victory over, 12, 87, 92, 115, 141–42, 168, 194
    physical, 97, 115, 116
    reign of, 100–103, 105
    second, xci, xcii, 9, 22, 32, 63, 87, 97–98, 101, 106, 115–16, 118, 121, 125–26, 132, 140, 143, 146, 152, 220
devil, xciv–xcv, c, 29, 32, 100–101, 102 n. 90, 107 n. 110, 109, 111, 114, 116, 118,

devil (*cont.*)
    120, 129–32, 134, 135–37, 140, 143, 146, 154, 167–69, 207, 215, 227, 271
    children of, 104, 154
    Christ's victory over, xciv–xcv, 57, 58, 69, 94, 125, 133, 141–42, 146, 187, 245
Diocletian, emperor
    edict against the Manichaeans, xxiv n. 8, cx
doctrinal controversies, lxxvii
Donatists, xl, cxi, cxii, 47
elements, c–ci, 25, 26, 34, 39, 114, 149, 158
Epiphanius of Salamis, cvii
Erasmus, xxiii, xxxiii
Esau, 175–76
eternal life, 56, 63, 96, 109, 114, 115, 116, 121, 148 n. 37, 153, 156–57, 183, 208, 220, 238
Eucharist, cxv
    intercessions during, 262 n. 62
Eusebius of Caesarea, cxviii n. 8
Eve, 96, 97 n. 50, 168
faith, lxxxii, lxxxvi, xciv–xcvi, cvi, 79–80, 82–83, 85–86, 89, 144–45, 195, 215
    and the law, 52–53, 72, 89, 144–45, 194, 195, 204–5
    rule of, 195
fasting, xxviii, cxvi–cxvii, 243 n. 19
Felice di Montalto, cardinal, xxxiii
figures of speech, lxvi
Filastrius of Brescia, cvii
filioque, lxxxvi
flesh, 114, 126, 134–38, 140–41, 143, 146–50, 153–54, 239–40, 250
    of Christ, 10–11, 48, 145–46, 190, 230. See also Christology
foreknowledge, God's, cv, 19, 163–64, 176–79, 183, 185, 203–4
gehenna, 47, 63 n. 51, 97, 115–116. See also underworld
gentiles, lxxiii, lxxxii, xcviii, 5, 20, 21, 22, 43–47, 51, 61, 64, 70, 71, 79–80, 83–86, 104, 119, 173, 174, 177, 185, 187–88,

gentiles (*cont.*)
 196, 201, 207–16, 251, 256–62, 266, 272, 273
grace, xcii–xcvi
Gratian, emperor, xl
Great Mother, xcix, 120
Greek, as liturgical language, cxv–cxvi
Haymo of Halberstadt, xxxii
heresy, heretics, cvii–cxiii, 48
 distinct from schism, cviii
Hilary of Poitiers, xxxi, lxviii, lxxi, cxi, 165 n. 138, 168 n. 151, 197 n. 26
Hincmar of Reims, xxxii
Holy Spirit, xxvii, xl, lxxvii–lxxix, lxxxiv–lxxxvi, xcvi, 10, 11, 20, 86, 87, 90–91, 117, 141, 145–46, 150–52, 154, 155, 160, 161–62, 171, 190–91, 217, 258, 269, 273
Hrabanus Maurus, xxxii, xxxvi
idolatry, xci, xcix–c, 26–30, 32, 33, 36, 49, 51, 54, 60, 98, 100–101, 103, 113, 160, 169, 181, 204, 211
incarnation, lxxxviii, xci, 10, 126, 145–46, 148, 163, 190–91, 195
Innocent I, bishop of Rome, cxix
Isaac, 80, 84, 174–75, 242
Jacob, 48, 98, 175–76, 201 n. 47, 242
Jerome, xxvi, xxvii, xl, lix, lxii–lxiii, lxiv, lxix n. 69, lxxi, ciii n. 23, cvii, cxvii, cxix, cxxi, cxxv, cxxvi, 103 n. 96, 151 n. 50, 176 n. 25, 224 n. 35
Jerusalem, 19, 64, 73, 185, 190, 199, 263
Jews lxxxviii, cii–cvii, 171–72, 174–75, 189, 193, 196, 199–202, 203, 206–16, 253–54, 255, 261–62
John the Baptist, 80, 84, 87 n. 70, 198, 205
Judas Iscariot, 164, 178
judgment, 46, 66, 184–85, 231, 234, 235
 day of, 39–41, 46, 47–48, 94, 196
Julian, emperor, xl, ci, 225 n. 40
justice, xciv, 53, 59, 66 n. 78, 99, 124, 132, 164, 177, 180, 183, 184, 212, 216, 220, 228, 230–31, 232, 233, 238
justification, xcv–xcvi, 23–24, 43, 44, 65–67, 68 n. 94, 71, 76, 77, 81

law
 of faith, cvi, 127–28, 139, 143, 154
 of Moses, 25, 43, 61, 64, 66, 76, 81, 99, 124, 128, 133, 138, 143–44, 188–89, 194, 212–13, 216, 236–37
 of nature, lxxxii, 18, 24, 25, 43, 44, 61, 66, 76, 98, 99–101, 123–24, 138, 150, 216, 233, 237
 of the Romans, 123
 spiritual, 138–39, 143–45
Manichaeus; Manichaeans, xxiv n. 8, cvii, cviii, cix–cx, cxxi, cxxvi, 244 n. 25
Marcellus of Ancyra, cx
Marcion, lxii n. 4, lxxxvii, cvii, cviii, cix, cxxi, 8
Marcionites, cix, cxxvi
Marius Victorinus, lxii, lxxi, lxxx, lxxxiii, cxi
marriage, cxxv–cxxvii. *See also* nuptial blessing
Mary, mother of Jesus, lxxxviii, 10–11, 190, 258, 267. *See also* virgin birth
Maurists, xxiii, xxxiii–xxxiv
Maximilla, cxi–cxii
Mithraism, xcviii–xcix, 28 n. 127
Montanists, cxi, 47
Montanus, cxi–cxii
Moses, 64, 99, 197. *See also* law, of Moses
mysterium; lxxx–lxxxi, 4, 9, 10, 11, 22, 54, 65, 139, 158, 174, 218, 256, 273
Nicene Creed, lxxvii, lxxix, lxxxii–lxxxiii, cx, 217 n. 73, 246 n. 31
Novatian; Novatianists, xxvi n. 15, cvii, cviii, cxi, cxii–cxiii, cxvii, 47
nuptial blessing, cxv
ordination, cxviii
Origen, lxi, lxviii, lxxi, 107 n. 110
original sin, xci–xciii, xcvi. *See also* sin.
pagans, lxxx, xcviii–cii
Paul, the apostle
 name of, xlviii–xlix, 7–8
Pauline commentaries, Latin lxi–lxiv, lxviii, 77 n. 16, 226 n. 44

Pelagius xxxi, xxxiv, xxxvii, lxiii, lxxxix–xc, xcvi n. 69, 68 n. 88, 77 n. 16, 226 n. 44, 227 n. 14
penance, cxii–cxiii
Pharaoh, 133, 168, 179, 181–82
Photinus, lxxxviii, cvii, cviii, cx–cxi, 8, 51, 172 n. 6
    teaching on *mia hypostasis*, cx
Porphyry, lxvi
predestination. *See* foreknowledge, God's
presbyters, 268. *See also* clergy
    relation to bishops, xxviii, cxvii–cxx
Priscilla, associate of Aquila, 4, 19, 265–66
Priscilla, associate of Montanus, cxi–cxii
Prudentius of Troyes, xxxii
Pseudo-Jerome, xxxiv, cvii
Pseudo-Tertullian, cvii
Rahab, 55, 182, 200
rebaptism, cvii, cxii–cxiii
resurrection, 11–12, 50, 57, 58, 87, 112–14, 126, 142, 148–49, 152–53, 195, 238
Romans, Epistle to the
    reason for, 3–4, 15, 18–19, 21, 241, 251, 260–61, 271
Rufinus of Aquileia, xxxviii
rulers, authority of, 234–36
Saclas, cix
sacraments, lxxx
Satan, 21, 32, 87, 100, 102, 109, 146, 165, 168, 169, 271. *See also* devil
Saul, king of Israel, 163, 178, 179–81
Sedulius Scottus, xxxii
sexual continence
    of clergy, cxx–cxxiii
    of laity, cxvi
Simeon, 121, 159, 198
Simon Magus, 168
sin, 111–17, 125, 126–27, 130–32, 135–37, 146–47, 215, 245, 251. See also original sin
    Adam's, 96–97, 101, 134, 153
    after the manner of Adam's, 97–98, 100–103, 105–6, 134, 153
Siricius, bishop of Rome, cxix n. 12, cxxvi

slaves; slavery, xciii, xcix, cxx, 15, 45, 86, 100, 111, 117–20, 134, 153 n. 64, 167,
slaves; slavery (*cont.*)
    183, 233 n. 5, 236, 242, 244–45, 266
Sodom and Gomorrah, 35–36, 99, 187
soul, lxxxviii, xcii, xciii, cix, cxvi–cxvii, 11, 29, 92, 97, 98, 114, 115, 119, 121 n. 71, 126, 134, 137–38, 140–41, 143, 146, 152, 153, 155, 194, 195, 196, 241, 250, 263, 273
synagogue, ciii
ten commandments, cvi
Tertullian, lxii n. 4, lxxxv, xciv n. 7, cviii, 104, 151 n. 50, 182 n. 65
Timothy, lxv n. 17, civ, cviii, 226, 271
Trinity, xl, lxxviii, lxxxi–lxxxvi, 11, 54, 86, 87, 162 n. 116, 197 n. 26, 217–18, 256, 273
underworld, xcii, xciv–xcv, 58, 68, 69, 87, 92, 98, 101–2, 106, 115 n. 35, 118, 125, 129, 132, 147, 194, 245. *See also* death, second; gehenna
Valentinian, emperor, xl
Vetus Latina, xxvi, xlvii, lvii–lviii, lxxx, 9 n. 13, 11 n. 28, 34 nn. 159–60, 46 n. 47, 68 n. 88, 70 n. 110, 82 n. 46, 103 n. 96, 119 n. 58, 151 n. 50, 168 n. 148, 181 n. 56, 184 n. 71, 224 n. 35, 224 n. 37, 226 n. 44, 244 n. 21
Victorinus of Pettau, 104
virgin birth, xci, cxi, 11, 126, 145, 148–49, 190–91, 258
Vulgate, xlvii, xlviii, lv, lvii–lviii, lxxx, 34 nn. 159–60, 61 n. 44, 68 n. 88, 82 n. 46, 124 n. 7, 181 n. 54, 181 n. 56, 184 n. 71, 223 n. 24, 247 n. 37, 267 n. 14
women 96–97, 124
    excluded from the clergy, cxii, 269
    not in God's image, cxxiii–cxxv

CPSIA information can be obtained
at www.ICGtesting.com
Printed in the USA
BVOW03*2354041117
499305BV00007B/3/P